NICK TOCZEK'S
WOOL CITY ROCKER

LS ARTS BOOKS

Published in the United Kingdom in 2025 by
LS Arts Publishing
West Yorkshire

Leeds Streets Ltd

www.leeds-streets.uk

nicktoczek.com

© 2025 by Nick Toczek

The Author hereby asserts his moral right to be identified as the Author of the Work.

Book design and artwork digital restoration by Matt Webster.

New cartoons © 2025 by Stan Engels.

All images in this book are copyright of the original creators.

All rights reserved. No part of this publication may be reproduced, stored in a retrieval system, or transmitted, in any form or by any means, electronic, mechanical, photocopying, recording or otherwise, without the prior permission of the publisher and copyright holders.

British Library Cataloguing in Publication Data
A catalogue record for this book is available from the British Library

ISBN 978-1-7391481-6-4

Printed in the UK by Lightning Source

FOREWORD
by Aki Nawaz

Bradford was buzzing during the punk era, the young weirdos all out to play, express, pogo, and resist. It was vibrant and anarchic. The Wool City Rocker fanzine came out and captured the alternative reality of Bradford. Nick was in juggernaut mode, and of the extremely healthy mental state of madness to be everywhere and anywhere, a requirement of healthy journalism, and more so, a lover of music. He was fully present in every dingy, exciting place hosting punk bands, and we awaited his words in print. It could have been on stone!

We needed it so that we, in bands, could use it to get more gigs and justify our existence and ego. The review of Violation supporting The Clash was sent outside the borders of Bradford, to promoters, John Peel, and the media. We rinsed it, cos we had to!!!

Wool City Rocker was packed and anarchic in every way. It influenced others to start fanzines or, like me, pretend I could also write! WCR is part of Bradford history. It was the 'go-to mag' for all. And, alongside the many other creative minds in the city, it wrote with wit, style, and - more importantly - with passion.

Nick was there as Southern Death Cult broke. He was part of our history too, and we were part of his.

VIVA WOOL CITY ROCKER!

Bradfordian Aki Nawaz, who was successively the prime mover in Violation, Southern Death Cult, Getting The Fear, and Fun-Da-Mental, now runs Nation Records and makes documentary films.

INTRODUCTION
by Simon Nolan

Wool City Rocker was an admirable publication which actively facilitated the DIY ethic throughout its 14 issue run from Winter 1979 to Summer 1981. The initial impetus for WCR was to champion the music scene in Bradford, however its remit quickly expanded to incorporate West Yorkshire, and latterly the entire North of England.

There was an undoubted practical application for WCR during its lifespan. It proved an invaluable gig guide for local punters whom had hitherto been reliant upon the thin gruel partiality of local press and the big weeklies: NME, Sounds and the like. Punters at this time might have been forgiven for believing that the only place to see gigs was at civic halls, and Working Men's Clubs. This writer first bought a copy whilst queuing to see The Clash at St George's Hall in Bradford. Ever the grafter, WCR editor Nick Toczek himself was flogging them down the line. Scoring a copy of WCR issue 5 was truly revelatory, opening up as it did an hitherto unknown realm of smaller local venues where youth of this writer's ilk were doing their thing. Furthermore, via its Band Aid feature, WCR provided aspiring bands and performers with an ever-expanding directory of venues, P.A. and lighting hire, rehearsal and studio spaces - addresses, phone numbers, names...the lot!

It ought to be acknowledged that the publication retrospectively offers an unwitting social document of the West Yorkshire music scene of the period. Considering its relatively short lifespan it is astonishing to note that WCR offered exposure to some 157 bands, many of whom were seeing their name in print for the first time, with a goodly number counting WCR coverage as their sole mention in any publication. Assiduously tight editing rendered each band profile as wonderful potted histories of the band in focus, including detailed information about influences, direction of travel, and the minutae of line-up changes - I mean, where else but in WCR could you discover that the band Trampus once included in its personnel the extremely gifted guitarist Gary Taylor, whose departure from that band in late 1979 would see him exit the music scene forever - - further, in which other publication could you find a photograph of the fleeting seminal Bradford punk band, Total Confusion? WCR is absolutely crammed with trivia of this type - there are rich pickings for enthusiasts and music historians alike. WCR fairly appraised no fewer than 185 tapes and records, and offered reviews of over 150 gigs. Remember, whilst WCR's signature trait was its unremitting encouragement, it always endeavoured to swerve any kind of sycophancy and never balked at giving an honest opinion.

But by far the most telling metric is seen in the astounding number of gigs that were promoted within its pages: approximately 2776 live events were clarioned by WCR - averaging out at roughly 200 gigs per issue! Impressive as these promotional activities are, it is sobering to note that they are but the tip of the iceberg when considered alongside Nick's Herculean efforts with his later ventures such as Gory Details at Keighley Funhouse and Bradford's Palm Cove, Fatal Shocks at Bradford's Bibi's, and Natural Disasters at Leeds' Brannigans. Crucially, as a finding during his endeavours with WCR, Nick had discerned an issue expressly confronting punk, skinhead, and post-punk bands, that is, there was a distinct lack of gigging opportunities for outfits in those genre. True, other notable promoters were at large, but Nick's tireless efforts saw an earsplitting explosion of gig opportunities for performers and punters alike. At this point, Nick had moved way beyond the Wool City and its environs and was routinely scheduling events featuring a worldwide roster of artists. Amazingly, all of this got off the ground within a 3 year period!

Upon its launch WCR was jointly edited by Nick, and Kay Russell, however Kay's commitments elsewhere saw her withdrawal from editorial duties and hence, from issue 3 onwards, Nick was the helmsman. Throughout the entire run of WCR Nick was accompanied by Stan Engels, whose cartoons and illustrations went some way towards lending WCR its charming aesthetic. WCR also enjoyed input from a host of contributors. Certainly the role call of WCR co-conspirators is impressive: Geoffrey Ballpoint, Chris Boojum, Steve Brown, Bill Byford, Steve Cairns, Paul Clark, Geoff Crumack, Andy Darlington, Barry Dawson, F I Denning, Phil Foster, Dave Green, Kev Hopgood, Lindsay Ineson, Duncan McCarrol, Mo Maklouf, Harry Marsden, Mick Martin, Mick Mitchell, Pip Nana, Mark Nicholls, Ocky, Tino Palmer, Dave Parkinson, Andy Proctor, Stuart Rhodes, Keith E Rice. Corn Robinson, John Roseveare, John Row, Brian Rushgrove, Albert Rutherford, Nick Ryle, Julz Sale, Mary Samuel, Nigel Schofield, Ron Shirt, Andy Steele, John Tempest, Ian Tilliard, Gaynor Toczek, Ken Turner, Wilko, and Winston (Roots). It is with the assistance of this discerning squad of roving reporters that WCR achieved a reputation for honest and insightful coverage of the northern live music scene.

Bear it in mind that all of the above was achieved on the tightest of shoestring budgets. It's fair to say that funding for WCR was the main barrier to its continuance beyond issue 14 - issue 15 was compiled, but the funds to see it printed were wanting. Still, in the midst of such travails Nick kept good humour, such as jokingly renaming the December and January gig listings in issue 11 as, 'Dismember' and 'Penury'!

Despite the fact that WCR rapidly expanded beyond the Bradford border, it is as Bradford's first fanzine that this fabulous publication will chiefly be remembered and cherished. It is rather exciting that the full run of WCR are collected in book form, and delightful to see it joining other august publications such as Ablaze, Adventures in Reality, Grim Humour, In The City, Jamming, Ripped and Torn, Sniffing Glue, and Vague in been given such respectful compendium treatment. It is a fitting testament indeed to Nick, whom in his determined and characteristically declamatory manner ever championed, jostled for and boasted about Bradford.

As the lad said, 'Y' Gotta Shout'!

Bradfordian Simon 'Nogsy' Nolan was the singer for Bradford anarcho-punk bands Anti-System and Morbid Humour in the early 1980s. He was also guitarist for Bradford rockers Zed and numerous other bands. In recent years, he has appeared on the albums *Walking The Tightrope* and *The Columbus Memoirs* by Nick Toczek and Signia Alpha. His website Essential Ephemera - UK Punk Literature and Images discusses a whole host of early publications and is well worth a visit.

si-site-nogsy.blogspot.com

PREFACE
by Nick Toczek

In 1968, I moved from my hometown of Bradford to Birmingham, where I spent the next three years as a student of Industrial Metallurgy at the University of Birmingham. While there, I began preparing to become a full-time writer and performer, my chosen career, and one which I've pursued ever since.

In 1969, using the University as my launchpad, I began performing my poetry. That same year, I also co-founded and co-edited *Black Columbus* as the Student Union's poetry magazine. This was my first experience of editing and producing a magazine. It lasted nine issues — 1 per term for 3 years — and was the start of a steep learning curve for me.

In 1972, very shortly after graduating, I launched my own poetry magazine, *The Little Word Machine*, which was well-produced and featured previously unpublished work by a mix of new, up-and-coming, and established writers. Over eleven issues, it established itself as one of Britain's leading poetry journals, ceasing abruptly in 1979 when my distributor went bankrupt, leaving me with no funds to continue publishing. A 1977 spin-off from the magazine was *Melanthika*, a 192-page anthology of pan-Caribbean writing, which I published and co-edited with Philip Nanton and Yann Lovelock. Featuring work from twenty islands by many respected black writers, it was the first comprehensive collection of Caribbean literature to be published in Britain.

Stereo Graffiti (l-r): Francis Mallon, Kay Russell, Alec Angel, Pete The Feet (honorary member), John Row, Nick Toczek

Also in 1972, Aquila Publishing Company produced my first poetry pamphlet. I've since published more than sixty books and released over twenty albums of music and/or spoken word.

While still a student, I'd moved into a flat in Moseley, a suburb of Birmingham, which was, at that time, the centre of a very active 'underground' music, literary, and artistic scene. In 1974, I co-founded the Moseley Community Arts Festival, serving as its director for several years. This, and its spin-off, the Moseley Folk Festival, continue as annual events in Birmingham.

That year, I met the Birmingham guitarist, singer, and songwriter, Kay Russell. We moved in together and began touring as a music-and-poetry duo under the name Cut-Glass Cabaret. The following year, we added more musicians and the poet John Row, and became Stereo Graffiti (stereo = music, graffiti = words). As such, with a few line-up changes, we spent the next four years touring the UK, clocking up around 250 gigs.

In the early summer of 1976, on a train returning from a gig, I read an interview (either in NME or Sounds) with a guy named Joe Strummer who fronted a new London band called The Clash. His views and lyrics (quoted in the article) so impressed me that I began writing my first punk lyric on that train journey. Weeks later, on 31 July, Kay & I went to see The Clash perform live at Barbarellas, a long-gone Birmingham venue. Supported by local proto-punks, Model Mania, The Clash were utterly amazing. Just the best band I'd ever seen. There were only a few dozen people in the audience. We were there again when they returned to Barbarellas three months later on 27 October. This time, the venue was packed and the band was even better. They were supported by another local punk outfit, Suburban Studs, and a solo Brummie called Spizz, who'd later front Spizzenergi and release the classic single *Where's Captain Kirk?*. We saw The Clash for a third time a year later, on 7 November 1977, at Birmingham's Top Rank. Here, they performed to a

Ulterior Motives (l-r): Nick Toczek, John Nelson, Kay Russell, Rick Green

couple of thousand fans, with the brilliant American combo, Richard Hell And The Voidoids, as their stellar opening band. Once more, The Clash were mindblowingly good.

In the meantime, I'd begun buying punk and indie singles, beginning with The Jam's *In The City*. I was also buying fanzines—some local to Birmingham, others from London (notably *Sniffing Glue*). And, during '77, Kay and I saw some more truly amazing punk gigs, including The Ramones and Talking Heads as a double bill (24 May at Barbarellas), The Slits and The Prefects (14 September at the Bull's Head pub), and The Adverts and Steel Pulse (20 September, my 27th birthday, back at Barbarellas).

On 22 June 1978, Kay and I moved out of our flat at 39 Queenswood in Moseley and headed north. Next day, we moved into 5 Beech Terrace, the terraced house in Undercliffe in Bradford on which we'd taken out a mortgage. In July '78, we began working on punk songs—my lyrics, Kay's tunes. As a duo, we did our first punk set supporting Bradford's first and best punk band, The Negatives, at Chicago Express (a Bradford pizza restaurant that briefly served as a music venue).

On 9 March 1979, Kay and I did our first rehearsal with bassist Rick Green for what would become our punk band, Ulterior Motives. On 25 May, following a stint of heavy rehearsing, Ulterior Motives did their debut gig, 5th on the bill at one of Geoff Robinson's Rock Against Racism gigs at Queens Hall (then Bradford College Students' Union). The next night, the band began a 6-day series of late-night pub gigs in Ilkley (as part of Ilkley Literature Festival) during which we had a full-on pub brawl, the only proper fight I've ever had, an all-out punch-up that lasted for about fifteen minutes. From August 20-23, Ulterior Motives recorded tracks at Yorkshire Arts Studios on Chapel Street in Little Germany (which was where we and New Model Army both had rehearsal space). On 30 September, we re-recorded and re-mixed both sides of our forthcoming double A-side single, *Another Lover* c/w *Y'Gotta Shout*. On 2 November, Rivelin Press published my poetry collection *Lies* (my fourth book that year - busy times!). On 22 November, I travelled to London to collect 2,500 copies of our debut single on our own label, Motive Music Records. On 26 November, Kay and I agreed to end our relationship. On 30 November, the pilot issue of *Wool City Rocker* was published.

The final issue of *The Little Word Machine* had been published earlier in 1979, and I was ready to start a new and very different journal. Jointly with Kay, I had begun planning this. We'd decided that what we wanted to co-produce was a monthly Bradford-based music magazine that was midway between a fanzine and a mainstream rock mag.

PILOT ISSUE
December 1979, 1,500 copies printed, 20 pages, A4, black & white

We called issue #1 'The Pilot Issue' because, although we felt the magazine was needed and timely, we weren't certain that it would be successful. We needn't have worried on that score. From the outset, it was extraordinarily well received. When we sold it in venues and then outside as they were closing, people bought it. Music shops, venues, recording studios, and other outlets stocked copies. Several people who'd bought it offered to help us, either by selling copies or by contributing to future issues. Additionally, many music-related businesses were eager to pay to place advertisements in the magazine. Everything began falling into place. The mag really filled a gap. This was a time before the internet, mobile phones, and social media. Bands were delighted to be interviewed, reviewed, or merely mentioned in our pages; our local gig guide really helped to bring people to gigs, and the whole WCR project fitted perfectly into the rapidly expanding local music scene.

This first issue was planned, prepared, co-edited, produced, distributed, and sold at various venues by Kay and me. She compiled the gig guide, wrote the live reviews, and created the feminist poster on page 12. All the rest—interviews, record and cassette reviews, etc.— were mine. Because we couldn't afford typesetting, Kay hand-wrote her contributions, and I hand-wrote all the rest. The fantastic cartoonist, Stan Engel, was a good friend of mine who also lived in Undercliffe. His cartoons feature in every issue of WCR. Stan was also a talented and sharply witty political writer. The two of us briefly gigged together as Two Blokes Who Like Curries, memorably as the opening act for Alan Bennett at Lancaster Literature Festival.

Nick in 1980

We knew that the monthly gig guide would be a strong selling point, as would the interviews with Bradford bands active on a burgeoning local music scene. Having scraped together the funds to print the first issue, we knew that attracting advertising was the only way we'd be able to keep it going. If it continued, the mag would greatly benefit local venues, recording studios, instrument shops, and other music-related businesses. We therefore focused hard on attracting their adverts.

Content-wise, we simply wanted to promote local gigs and bands. We were both active solo performers. Ulterior Motives, our band, had just released a single. We had a vested interest in this local scene. WCR was also provided a platform for our own opinions and political views.

Much of what's contained in this first issue became the template for future issues. However, changes were already afoot. Having worked together and been a couple for the past eight years, Kay and I split up entirely during that final month of the seventies, both finding female partners. By the time of our breakup, issue two was going to print. By issue three, Kay had moved on, and I'd become the sole editor of WCR.

Kay and I spoke intermittently by phone for a few years. With the Susan Fassbender Band, she had brief pop success with *Twilight Cafe*, which charted, earning them two TV appearances on Top Of The Pops. Their two follow-up singles, *Stay* and *Merry-Go-Round*, were less successful despite more TV appearances, notably on Cheggers Goes Pop and Multi-Coloured Swap Shop. Soon after that, she contacted me, needing money. I bought out her share of 5 Beech Terrace. Shortly after that, we lost touch.

Kay died on 29 September 2024. An album of her later songs, *Walking In Space*, was released one year after her death.

Notes on bands profiled in this issue.

Barry and Aky from Violation later formed Southern Death Cult and then Getting The Fear, with Aky going on to form Fun-Da-Mental and to found Nation Records. (N.B. There's a second feature on Violation in issue 8).

Steve 'Syd' Sidelnyk, the drummer in Vex, has to be the most successful musician ever to emerge on the Bradford rock scene. He once stood in on drums in Ulterior Motives, but went on to better things. At the first Live Aid, he was The Style Council's drummer. At the second Live Aid, he was the drummer in Madonna's band, a post he retained for many years. As a session drummer and percussionist, his other credits include appearances on tracks by The Rolling Stones, Annie Lennox, Geri Halliwell, Toyah, S Club 7, Robbie Williams, Tina Turner, M People, Primal Scream, Jimmy SomerWWWville, Dido, Kylie Minogue, Seal, Moby, Lisa Stansfield, P.J. Harvey, David Gray, and dozens more.

On a more personal note, Tricia Kusack, who fronted Press Release, a band that had played support to Ulterior Motives at The Vaults Bar, invited me and Rick to a party at her house on Christmas Day 1979. There, she introduced me to her best friend, Gaynor Doherty. Gaynor's in the next room as I type this. We've just celebrated our 41st wedding anniversary.

THE WOOL CITY ROCKER

THIRTY PENCE

PILOT EDITION... — DECEMBER '79

BRADFORD ROCK SCENE MAGAZINE

ME AND YOUR PENELOPE'S GITTIN' SPLICED, VICAR...

9 BRADFORD BANDS IN PROFILE:
- Vex
- Violation
- The Scene
- Deadringer
- Remainz
- Press Release
- Ulterior Motives
- Negatives
- Shaftdrive

plus:—
PULL-OUT GIG GUIDE
+
REVIEWS & INFO.
+
INTERVIEWS & RECORD REVIEWS
+
ARTICLES, CARTOONS, etc.

PALM COVE CLUB

Hollings Road, Bradford 8
Tel: 499895

Live Entertainment Fri. & Sat (8pm - 1am)
Club also open throughout the week
(9pm - midnight)

Late Bar Nightly

Car Park at Rear

New Wave/Mod/Reggae Jukebox

Good West Indian Food

Pool Tables

Bradford College Students Union invites you to

THE VAULTS BAR

- Live Entertainment 4 Nights a Week
- William Youngers Traditional Hand-Pulled Ales

Bar Snacks Always Available

CODA MUSIC

28 Church Bank, Bradford 1.

Tel: Bradford 307433
VAT No: 181-2254-83

Musical Instruments Sales Hire Tuition Repairs Rehearsal Rooms Bands Groups Artists Recording and Video Studios

P.A. Hire (100W - 3000W) + Crew and Transport

<u>Agents For</u>:- Marshall, Ludwig, Carlsboro, Ovation, Premier, Olympic, Tama, Ibanez, Pearl, Beyer, AKG, Korg, Peavey, Gretsch, Slingerland.

This page should have been professionally typeset. However, because several potential advertisers kept us waiting beyond the copydate before deciding against taking space, we've had to hand-set it.

We'd like therefore to give special thanks to CODA, JSG, THE PALM COVE and THE VAULTS BAR, whose support has made this pilot issue possible.

W.C.R.

JSG MUSIC

108B Main Street, Bingley.
Phone 68843

ACCESS + BARCLAYCARD WELCOME
Part exchange welcome ~ Amazing Discounts

<u>MAIN AGENTS FOR</u>
Moog, Gibson, Lab Series, Korg, Fender, Rickenbacker, Music Man, H/H, Marshal, Park, M.M., Custom Sound, Ampeg, Ovation, Yamaha, Laney, Crumar, Peavey, Roland, Carlsbro and lots more.

Custom P.A.'s up to 2KW
Full H/H Concert P.A. in stock

ADVERTISING RATES

Standard size = 3½" x 3½"

First advert. costs £20-00 thereafter, they are half price.

Current print run = 1,500 (estimated readership = 3,000+).

Colour, special layout or positioning, different size, etc. by arrangement.

Ring Nick or Kay on B'ford 21867.

EDITORIAL

Here's the first edition of the city's own rock monthly. Hope that you like the thing. Putting it together - collecting material & the hand-setting each page - has been quite a task.

We had hoped for more contributors - but they, like the majority of people who promised to support the mag. by placing adverts, seemed to evaporate as our copy date approached. Apologies then that most of the text is our own work. Please get in touch if you'd like to join our gang of fanatical pen-pushers. Likewise, if you've anything to say that'd maybe grace a posh letters page, then we'd be glad to hear from you.

Entries in the gig guide (see centre pages) are free, so are the classified ads (at least for the next couple of issues) - so if you've any wants/for sales/etc. please ring or write.

If you'd like to sell copies - then we give ⅓ discount on 15 or more copies - i.e. you'd make 10p per copy sold. We want to hear from/about local bands. And we welcome ideas &/or criticism. No more space. That's it till next issue (January '80). Happy Xmas & New Year - that's the wonder of Wool City... yrs, Nick + Kay.

THE WOOL CITY ROCKER

PILOT EDITION

DECEMBER '79

EDITORS: - NICK TOCZEK
KAY RUSSELL

with contributions from:-
STAN ENGEL on electric cartoons (cover + p.8, 9 & 15). JULES on mini-poster (p.12).

Terms of sale:-
30p sold direct to public or 45p by mail order from address given below. Bulk sales (to shops or to individuals willing to sell the magazine): ⅓ discount on 15 or more copies.

Copyright Wool City Rocker Publications © 1979

All correspondence to:-

THE EDITORS
5 BEECH TERRACE
UNDERCLIFFE
BRADFORD
BD3 0PY
WEST YORKSHIRE
ENGLAND
tel. (0274) 21867.

CONTENTS

BANDS IN PROFILE:	Violation	4
	Deadringer	4
	The Scene	4,5
	Press Release	5
	Shaftdrive	5,6
	Ulterior Motives	6
	Negatives	6,7
	Vex	7
	Remainz	7,8
BLOOZE n ROCK: an interview with Jed Turner		8
MINI-POSTER 1: Wool City Rocker fake freebie		9
GIG GUIDE: for December		10,11
MINI-POSTER 2: "Don't be fooled..."		12
VENUES: some recent changes		13,14
JOHN FARQUHAR interviewed		14
CHRIS GROVES interviewed		14,15
CLASSIFIED ADS.		15
RECORD REVIEWS: singles by local bands		15,16
LIVE REVIEWS: Samson at The Princeville		16
	Mod night at Palm Cove	17,18
NEXT ISSUE: some of our plans laid bare		18
MAP: Where the venues are in Bradford		20

BANDS
Compiled & Written by Nick Toczek...

VIOLATION

Voc. = Oxfam Harry
Gtr. = Mick
Bass = Barry
Dms. = Aky

A punk band, they've been together - rehearsing and writing songs - for the past six months. They've been using a church hall in Lidget Green and it was here on Wed. 7th Nov. that they did a demo gig to get some idea of how their material would work. Apparently the small invited audience of about two dozen (small because the church management weren't keen to play host to a larger publicised punk gig) enjoyed the set of nine original numbers.

Aky: "We're all from Bradford except the singer who lives in Leeds. We're an original punk band - in the style of the '76-'77 punk bands, but not just bam-bam-bam - we can all play our instruments well. It's just that we are punk, not 'new wave' or anything like that."

Barry writes most of the songs - sometimes with Mick. Most of the lyrics are by Harry. Their songs include: "Hymn 20" (with lyrics taken out of a hymn book!), "Boys in Blue" and "Chaos".

They hope to be gigging round Bradford during the next few months - maybe as support to The Negatives. One gig they're keen to organise is a large all-punk event with several local punk bands plus a punk disco: "We'd want it to be a charity gig. That way it'd serve a useful purpose as well as being a good fun gig for punks and anyone else who'd want to come."

Contact Aky on B'ford 71793 (& he'd like to hear from Press Release who owe him £10).

DEADRINGER

Lead Voc. = Jonny Hoyle
Dms. = Kenny Jones (not that one)
Bass = Lee Flaxington
Lead Gtr. = Neil Hudson } both double
Lead Gtr. = Al Scott } on rhythm & lead gtrs.

The stage is blacked-out except for a single ultra-violet spotlight focused on the drum kit. The opening music from 2001 comes over the p.a. Then suddenly the vocalist's voice opens with "FIRE!", three smoke bombs go off, the whole band comes in & the light come on - all in the space of a couple of seconds.

Deadringer, a heavy rock band in the mould of U.F.O. or AC/DC, put a lot into their stage act. In addition to the band and their manager, the full entourage includes a sound engineer, a lighting engineer and two roadies. Their dedication to the future of the group is such that the musicians put most of their earnings back into group funds, and though 2 of them still hold down day-jobs, the band always comes first. The current gigging schedule of at least three gigs a week - as far north as Newcastle and south to The Midlands and Wales - has them away for several days at a time. They hope soon to make the move to becoming a full-time road band - probably via a long-term recording deal. They want to work up a heavy touring schedule, feeling that live appearances are the main way in which the band'll build its reputation. Already they have a core of fans who follow them from gig to gig around the country. They don't want one-off recording deals - seeing the sustained financial and recording backing of a major company as an important factor in their future plans. Surprisingly, perhaps, the company currently expressing an interest is Stiff Records (formerly strongly linked with new wave acts). They are recording one of the band's gigs in the near future.

Deadringer appeared at The Princeville on Nov. 22nd. They don't plan to appear in Bradford during December, but will be at The Staging Post (Leeds) on 2nd, at The Good Mood (Halifax) on 7th and 31st & at The Fforde Green (Leeds) on 26th. Fans will find Deadringer badges and t-shirts on sale at these venues.

Contact Des Frazer (manager) on (0274) 875268.

The SCENE

Voc. + Rhythm Gtr. = Ian Harding
Bass Gtr. = Ian James
Lead Gtr. = Dave Green
Dms + Backing Voc. = George Mazur

The group first formed in October '78 as 'The Upbeats' - a name under which they rehearsed but never actually did any gigs. Phil Harding (Ian's brother) was the group's 5th member, playing rhythm guitar - but after a couple of months he left to rejoin his former band 'Eaten Alive By Insects' – "He wasn't into the music – we were aiming at a 60's beat sound but it didn't work – we sounded weedy & horrible." When his brother left, Ian took up rhythm guitar, teaching himself to play. Their first gig was at The Royal Standard in January '79. A week before the gig they decided to change their name to 'The Scene' – it sounded better (The name was, in fact, the idea of Kris – a friend who was the lead singer with 'The Drive', Bradford's first new mod band – a group that split up that January).

Soon after this they got a manager who wanted them to change completely, get a black vocalist, become a soul group. Once again, it wasn't working. "We can't just reel off other people's songs like he wanted us to do." They disbanded.

A month later, Ian got a phone call offering them a gig at Huddersfield Polytechnic on a bill with 3 other mod bands, The Killermeters, The Chords and The Fixations. With time for only one proper rehearsal, they reformed. "Everything just fell into place during that rehearsal. We got that 60's sound that we'd been after from the start. It was great. That month off must have been what we needed."

Now, with more successful gigs behind them, they feel that they're a good danceband and – as such – will appeal to a wider audience than just mods, though they're keen to keep that following as well.

Over the coming months they've got two or three bookings a week at venues throughout the country, topping the bill in most cases. This set of gigs has been lined up to coincide with the release of their first single "Hey Girl (won't you be mine)" c/w "Reach The Top" which will be out in December on Manouvre Records (a new label based in York). They're two supporting spots lined up at The Palm Cove during December.

Contact Ian James on B'ford 687975 or Ian Harding on 499245 (a communal phone, so ask for Flat 6).

# PRESS RELEASE
Voc. = Tricia Kusack
Lead Gtr. = Niall McDonough
Kbds. + Gtr. = Paul Everett
Bass Gtr. = Mick Rennard
Dms. = Chris Parker

———+———

As 'Dark Horse' (same line-up as above except that they'd a different lead guitarist – a guy called Phil Crowther) they worked around Bradford during summer '79. They played their last gig at Jolly's in Shipley on 4th Sept. Exit Phil, enter Niall and a name-change for the group. Press Release did their first performance at St. George's Youth Club on 28th Sept. (supporting them – & also on their first live appearance – was another Bradford band, Vex).

The band will soon go into Tab End Studio, a small 4-track set-up in Heaton that's owned by J.S.G. The resulting demo tape will then be used to get the group booking &, they hope, some interest from record companies.

They are currently lining up a tour during early '80 that'll take them down south. Their idea is for the band to take bookings on Fridays, Saturdays & Sundays – thus allowing the members to keep their jobs.

Contact Eric Smith (management) on B'ford 497092.

SHAFTDRIVE
Lead Voc. + Bass = Rick Ironmonger
Gtr. + Voc. = Keith Graham
Lead Gtr. + Back-up Voc. = Steve Davis
Dms. + Perc. = Pete Emmonds

———+———

The band's been going for two years – though Steve Davis is the only original member. The most recent new-comer is Pete Emmonds who used to be the drummer with 'Trampus'. Steve writes most of the lyrics of their own songs – with the whole group working jointly on the music. They do almost exclusively original numbers.

The group feel confident about this newest line-up, but need more gigs to tighten up the sound which is driving heavy metal. They tend to draw mostly a heavy rock audience, though Rick's punky appearance means that there's often a handful of punks in their audience.

The new songs that they're currently writing are more melodic and sophisticated than much of the material that they've produced to date, which should keep the band's sound progressive.

"Bradford's got a lot of good new bands around at the moment. It should really develop into a good exciting scene over the coming months."

Shaftdrive's current plans are to do as many gigs as possible. For the future, they want to get a demo done for sending

out to record labels.
Contact Rick or Pete on B'ford 834460.

ULTERIOR MOTIVES

Voc.+ Gtr. = Kay Russell
Voc. + Perc.= Nick Toczek
Bass + Voc. = Rick Green
Dms. = a Roland 77 Rhythm Unit

A case of self-writeousness (!) with both Kay and myself in this group. The two of us have been in various mixed-media groups (notably our 'Stereo Graffiti Show' with which we did about 250 performances between '75 & '77). We moved from Birmingham (Kay's hometown) to Bradford (my hometown) in summer '78. Kay did solo gigs around the area for about 8 months & we then ask Rick (a friend of my brother) to join us in a new band. We wanted to try using the drum machine from the start.

The Motives' first set was 5th on the bill to The Negatives at The Queen's Hall on 25th May '79 – a Rock Against Racism benefit.

In August we set up Motive Music as a recording co. jointly owned by the 3 of us and went into The Communication Centre on Chapel Street, using their 4-track studio to record 11 titles – from which we selected 2 numbers to go on our first single. "Another Lover" c/w "y' Gotta Shout" was released in mid-November on Motive Music Records. As we had set up a distribution deal with Red Rhino of York (&, through them, other small label distributors) we were able to increase the number of copies pressed from 1,000 to 2,500. We're now lining up gigs round Yorkshire to promote the record. We're also auditioning drummers – though not to completely replace the drum machine which we'll still use on some numbers. If this single goes well, we've already got a follow-up in mind.

Contact Nick or Kay on B'ford 21867.

THE NEGATIVES

Lead Voc. = Dave Wilcox
Gtr. = Pete Stobbs
Bass = Bob Robinson
Dms. = Tino Palmer

The name and line-up of the band have remained unchanged since they first formed in summer '78. Their two debut appearances were unpublicised try-outs, the first at The Royal Standard, the second at Metro '78 (in a marquee on Horsforth Playing Fields). The first publicised gig was at Chicago Express (now called Panache) in Darley St. when support was Kay Russell – now with this magazine + Ulterior Motives.

The first Bradford punk/new wave band (did '76 really take 2 years to travel from London to Bradford?), they've since done a large number of local dates – "a lot of them were for R.A.R. which is good as an idea, but is so often badly organised in our experience." They were booked (with 'The (Layton) Buzzards' + 'Sheeny & The Goys') for an R.A.R. tour a couple of months ago. Originally offered a large number of dates, they ended up only doing one in Bradford and a second in Leeds. "I don't think any of us are keen to do more R.A.R. gigs unless we're surer of the way they're organised."

The original idea with the single was to record it at The Yorkshire Arts Association's Communication Centre, pay Pye to do the pressing and then release it on their own label. They booked into the studio, turned up on the day, waited outside for 1½ hr. without the engineer turning up. (She overslept). Plan two was to us the 8-track Box Studio in Heckmondwyke but there was a 6-week wait. Finally, trying Look Studios (a 16-track in Huddersfield), they got a booking 14 days ahead. After 5/6 hours they came out with 3 tracks – "Stakeout", "Love is not real" & "We're from Bradford". The total cost (including master tape, a copy tape and 5 cassettes) was £89-74p. A friend "with contacts" offered to take a tape to Polydor. They waited – didn't even get an acknowledgement. The record's now being pressed at Look Studio & will come out on Look Records. The money's being put up by Guy Watson who's also handling distribution (via Guy Watson shops round Yorkshire, through some record stores, at gigs, etc.). The first pressing will be of 1,000 copies.

They get fed up with critics who say they've got to change. "We're a good fast dance band. We're not political but we sing about what we feel. The oppression that punk started out to fight hasn't just vanished in the past 3 years – it's still there."

The band have a very loyal Bradford following – one that they've worked hard for and one of which they're rightly proud. Few local bands have such fans. They also do a lot to encourage other punk/new wave bands – giving them support spots at their gigs and even standing in on some of the instruments. The single - "Love is not real" c/w "Stakeout" - will be out before Xmas. Anyone unable to get it can order it direct by ringing the number given below ⓐ

Contact George Thackray (Manager) on B'ford 33531.

VEX

Voc. + Gtr. + Synth. = Andy Tyson
Gtr. + Voc. = Dave Pickard
Bass Gtr. = Clare Jowett
Electronic Perc. + Synth = Steve Peyton
Dms. = Steve Sidenyk

---+---

Andy & Dave formed the band 'Icon Leadz', Andy later joining 'Counterdance'. Clare, a founding member of the band 'Eaten Alive By Insects', was already in 'Counterdance' when Andy joined. In early summer '79 their band split up. So did 'Icon Leadz': "It was all getting political. Andy & I (Dave) don't think that politics should come into rock. We formed 'Vex' as a non-political band."

The band formed in June, doing their first gig in Sept. as support to 'Press Release' (q.v.): "It was just a try-out to see if we could do it. We did 6 numbers & put most of the sound through a small 100-watt p.a. system with no foldback. Our first real gig was at The Vaults Bar (Oct. 7th). It was really good - & ended with a 15-minute jam session, guesting Janet & Barry of the band 'Remainz'."

This was the first of several mentions of this other Bradford band. It transpired that the two groups work very closely together, finding such co-operation works to their mutual advantage.

Vex's drummer is a new addition & their next gig (in Bolton on Dec. 1st) will be his debut. His brother, incidentally, also rocks - as voc./gtr. in 'The Invaders'.

Mike Morris (reporting in The Keighley News & Bingley Guardian) - "Vex take the better parts of Joy Division & Wire and mould them into a sound that is still original & exciting."

The outfit use all their own material - written by Andy & Dave. "We don't believe in doing cover versions."

Together with 'Remainz' & 'Beezer Bob & The Brainwaves' (the latter being a poet who use a drum machine etc. for backing) they're going out as a package tour round college venues. "Beezer was going to do the Bolton gig with us but he's waiting for his new dentures to come through" (joke!). The tour'll take them through into spring '80, with 2/3 bookings per week if things go according to plan. The limiting factors are that all of Vex have jobs and that a tour involving 11+ people plus gear etc. takes a lot of organising & the travel expenses become prohibitive over 100 miles from home.

They want to do a tape in the early new year - "it's a shame there's not a good studio in Bradford". If things go well, they'd hope to be able to look towards full-time gigging later in '80.

Contact Dave on 27845 or Clare on 44289.

REMAINZ

Dms. = Ellis D.
Gtr. + Voc. = Janet Cook
Gtr. + Voc. = Graham Cook
Bass + Voc. = Chairman Bao

---+---

'Dawnweaver' - with the above line-up (except a different bass player - with C.B. on kbds.) - was a longhair hippy band that lasted 2 years up till Xmas '78. "Graham & the bassist left, so I (C.B.) moved onto bass & 'Remainz' started gigging as a 3-piece. As 'Dawnweaver' had been out of date, we just cut our hair & played all the material faster!" After 4 months & about a dozen gigs, Graham rejoined the group. They supported 'Gang of Four' at Queens Hall, 'The Only Ones' at a hall in Cheltenham, 'Fingerprintz' at The Fan Club, Leeds, etc. "We've played most Bradford venues, but haven't had much luck. Not many people round here are interested in seeing local bands - they seem to go for name acts & northern soul. It's much easier outside Bradford."

"This package tour with Vex & Beezer Bob looks like it'll work well. Dave (a.k.a. Ellis D) does the phoning cos there aren't any good rock agents in Bradford. He finds that the offer of the package (for £150 + expenses) is much more interesting to social secretaries than if we were just offering ourselves as one of maybe half a dozen bands that phone him every day."

"As 'Dawnweaver' we did a lot of studio sessions. In July '79, we (Remainz) went into Cargo (a 16-track studio in Rochdale) for one day at a total cost of £190 which we'd collected together ourselves. The plan was to release a single, but - having sold some of our equipment to get this far - we ran out of cash. We weren't too happy with the tape - one track was a write-off, the other 3 were O.K. but they all needed more work doing on them. I think it was just that we tried to do too many numbers in too short a time. Anyway, we took the tape to Virgin, but they didn't even want to hear it. Mayo Thompson at Rough Trade did listen & he was great. It wasn't their sort of thing, but he gave us a lot of advice & constructive criticism. We're still trying elsewhere. There's now also a chance that we may bring out our own E.P. featuring all three groups from the package tour."
Contact

BLOOZE n ROCK - an interview with Jed Turner.
by Nick Toczek.

N:- "How did you start up as a musician based here in B'ford?"
J:- "I was born here - just off Otley Rd. near Barkerend (in '53) - & now live a bit further up the hill above Pollard Park. My brother was - & still is - a drummer & harmonica player. I started learning on his instruments when I was about 12. I've actually been playing in bands for the past 11 yrs. The first - a school band - was 'The Delta Blues Band' in which I played dms."
N:- "And since then...?"
J:- "Well, I've been in dozen or so bands - some just as an occasional member, others as a long-term member. They've all been just for the music - semi-pro, never more than that. And it's only over the past couple of years that I've been putting together my own groups."
N:- "You do a lunchtime blues jam at The Royal Standard on Sundays, don't you?"
J:- "Used to, but that ended last summer when, if we'd been in our right minds we'd have been out there in the sun with everyone else instead of hassling over making more money for him" (ie Malcolm Fairplay). "It ran from Feb-July, with about 15 musicians and a fairly big audience there each week. The other regulars were Chris Groves - see p.14, Colin Hingston - now bassist with 'Boogie Chillun' & Biddie Baxter - on accordion or trombone, he now gone out to Holland."
N:- "So, what're your current

& future plans? Is 'Dirty Jed's Blues Band' still in action?"
J:- "No, that group had been going for 18 months when it split up in June but, since then I've been doing gigs with 'Jammerwocky', a line-up that came together out of the jam-sessions at The Standard. And I've been doing a few gigs with various friends - members of bands like 'Radio 5', 'Boogie Chillun' & 'Oral Sax'. I'm now putting together a new full-time band that'll do blues/blues-rock." (see classified ads. on p.15).

KAY RUSSELL'S MUSIC CLUB
at
Bradford College
VAULTS BAR

8.15pm   40p

Contemporary folk & blues
Guests:
TUE 11 DEC ~ Chris & Lynn Metcalfe
WED 2 JAN ~ T.B.A.
WED 16 JAN ~ Roger Sutcliffe

FINAL COPYDATE FOR NEXT ISSUE : SUNDAY 16 DECEMBER : PHONE KAY RUSSELL BRADFORD 21867

SAT. 1 DEC.	BRADFORD UNIVERSITY GREAT HALL	NEIL INNES
	COMMUNAL BUILDING	FOLK NIGHT Kay Russell & others
	PALM COVE CLUB	QUAKER CITY HI-FI
	ROYAL STANDARD	MOTIVATOR
SUN. 2 DEC.	PRINCEVILLE	RHINO
	VAULTS BAR	ULTERIOR MOTIVES
MON. 3 DEC.	VAULTS BAR	ORAL SAX
TUE. 4 DEC.	ROSE + CROWN (ILKLEY)	ZANATHUS
	VAULTS BAR	CHARITY CONCERT (SHOWBAND)
WED. 5 DEC.	ST. GEORGES HALL	THE DAMNED + VICTIMS
	QUEENS HALL	STILETTOS
	BRADFORD UNIVERSITY	DR. FEELGOOD
	VAULTS BAR	SHADOWFAX
THU. 6 DEC.	PALM COVE	SALFORD JETS
	PRINCEVILLE	WHITE FIRE
FRI. 7 DEC.	QUEENS HALL	TAROT
	PALM COVE	VEX + REMAINZ + BEEZER BOB
	ILKLEY	ANDREW SNELL
SUN. 9 DEC.	PRINCEVILLE (LUNCHTIME)	STALLION
	ILKLEY COLLEGE	CARTER & JONES BAND
	VAULTS BAR	RHINO
MON. 10 DEC.	VAULTS BAR	ORAL SAX
TUE. 11 DEC.	VAULTS BAR	KAY RUSSELL'S MUSIC CLUB with Chris & Lynn Metcalfe
	ROSE + CROWN (ILKLEY)	ROCKETS
WED. 12 DEC.	VAULTS BAR	OMEN
THU. 13 DEC.	PRINCEVILLE	WHITE SPIRIT
FRI. 14 DEC.	PALM COVE	SMALL HOURS + THE ACT
SAT. 15 DEC.	ST. GEORGES HALL	U.F.O + SHADOWFAX
	PALM COVE	THE MOLESTERS + RADIO 5
SUN. 16 DEC.	PRINCEVILLE (LUNCHTIME)	RED EYE
	VAULTS BAR	THE NEGATIVES

MON. 17 DEC.	VAULTS BAR	:	ORAL SAX
TUE. 18 DEC.	ROSE + CROWN (ILKLEY)	:	VYE
WED. 19 DEC.	QUEENS HALL	:	RADIATION
THU. 20 DEC.	VAULTS BAR	:	SORE POINT
	PALM COVE	:	Revving-up-to-Christmas Party with RADIO 5, DIRTY JEDS BLUES BAND + OTHERS
FRI. 21 DEC.	PRINCEVILLE	:	LIMELIGHT
SAT. 22 DEC.	PALM COVE	:	THE NEGATIVES Christmas Fun Party
SUN. 23 DEC.	PALM COVE	:	JAB-JAB'S Reggae Party
	PALM COVE	:	THE MODS
MON. 24 DEC.	PRINCEVILLE (LUNCHTIME)	:	SPIDER
	VAULTS BAR	:	ORAL SAX
WED. 26 DEC.	PALM COVE	:	JAB JAB
THU. 27 DEC.	PALM COVE	:	LONG TALL SHORTY + BEGGARS
FRI. 28 DEC.	VAULTS BAR	:	ONE ADULT
SAT. 29 DEC.	PALM COVE	:	THE LAMBRETTAS
SUN. 30 DEC.	PALM COVE	:	ONE ADULT + OTHERS
	PRINCEVILLE (LUNCHTIME)	:	ONE ADULT
MON. 31 DEC.	VAULTS BAR	:	REMAINZ
	VAULTS BAR	:	ORAL SAX
1980			
WED. 2 JAN.	VAULTS BAR	:	KAY RUSSELL'S MUSIC CLUB
THU. 3 JAN.	PRINCEVILLE	:	LUIGI ANA DA BOYS
SUN. 6 JAN.	PRINCEVILLE (LUNCHTIME)	:	KYRO
WED. 9 JAN.	VAULTS BAR	:	JAPANESE SOLDIERS
THU. 10 JAN.	VAULTS BAR	:	HUSTLER STREET BAND
	PRINCEVILLE	:	QUAD
WED. 16 JAN.	VAULTS BAR	:	KAY RUSSELL'S MUSIC CLUB with Roger Sutcliffe

WOOL CITY ROCKER GIG GUIDE

Don't be fooled – the government intends to IMPRISON ALL WOMEN

IN THE HOME

- no nurseries
- no school meals
- no afternoon school
- no abortions
- no pregnancy leave
- hospitals closing
- longer queues
- cuts in welfare services for young, old and sick

VENUES (written by Nick Toczek)

Malcolm Day (a.k.a. Malcolm Fairplay) manager of The Royal Standard on Bradford audiences: "They're just a load of fucking wankers. I've been putting on the best punk bands in the country & no fuckers are turning up to see them. I wish you the best of luck with the magazine but you're wasting your time doing it for Bradford. Anyway, I'm getting out at the end of the month."

Apparently Malc Day put in for the transfer before the recent court case in which he was accused of racial discrimination against Pakistanis. Always outspoken & uncompromising, he had - to say the least - a very mixed reputation amongst the musicians who worked for him. The fact that he actually asked for payment from some local bands for "allowing" them to play The Standard did little to make him popular. It reached the point where few local bands were prepared to work the venue while it was under his management. The other side of the coin is that he certainly has continued to promote an extremely ambitious series of gigs in which recent guests included Generation X, U.K. Subs, Adam & The Ants, Angelic Upstarts & many others that would otherwise have been unlikely to play this city. We'll have to see what the new manager (who starts there in early December) plans to do with the venue.

The Metro (downstairs bar of The Golden Cockerel) on the corner of Kirkgate & Westgate, which has operated as an irregular rock venue over the past couple of years, has closed. Apparently the bar failed to draw enough custom to cover the expense of extra staff. Press Release played there (to a small audience) in October. Since then it's been sold off & converted into a men's clothier. The upstairs area still has occasional bands but the landlord only pays expenses. Talisman (a Leeds-based rock group) played there in mid-November. It appears, though, that the pub is to be sold off in early 1980 for conversion into offices.

The Palm Cove's bid to move from being a predominantly black music venue to becoming a major general rock venue began in earnest in the first week of November with a run of 3 gigs.

Thurs. 1st Nov. featured The Fall, an experimental/avant garde rock band who've put out a couple of singles, one E.P. & (recently) a well-received album. They are an acquired taste & so met with a mixed reception from the large audience.

Friday night featured Ginger Baker's new outfit Energy, ably supported by Jedrell Bank (featuring local bluesboy Jed Turner). Baker - who's kept a low profile for the past few years - was the drummer in Britain's first super-group Cream (the other 2 members of which were Jack Bruce & Eric Clapton). He later worked in several of his own bands including Baker-Gurvitz Army & Airforce. A capacity audience wasn't slow to show its mounting enthusiasm throughout the evening.

Finally, the Saturday guests were The Squire - one of the new mod bands whose excellent first single "Walking down the Kings Road" originally appeared as one of the tracks on the 'Mods Mayday Album' - live recordings from The Bridge House, London (the founding venue of the current mod revival). They put in two excellent sets & provided a good finish to a most varied weekend of music. It's unfortunate that a few fights broke out between the mods & a handful of punks. Most reports suggest that the clashes were initiated by a couple of the punks who'd had a few too many drinks. Outside, there were more fights & several parked cars had their paintwork scratched. The result was a complete ban on punks at the next few gigs plus cancelling of all events that billed punk & mod bands together. It was an unpleasant note on which to end an otherwise highly promising start.

During Oct./Nov. The Vaults Bar has been repainted with suitably ghoulish murals. A stage (carpeted!) has been installed & so has coloured lighting. Using a line-out from the p.a., this lighting can be rigged to operate as a sound-to-light system — i.e. the lights flash from colour to colour in time with the music, the intensity increasing with the volume.

JOHN FARQUHAR
interviewed by Nick Toczek...

The tail-end of a long day. That evening I'd already interviewed The Scene & The Negatives. It was near closing-time when I tracked down the man in a small bar room at the back of Queens Hall. We're both on the wrong side of a good quantity of alcohol, so this'll be a short interview.

John came to Bradford 6 months ago to take up his current job as "licencee of The Vaults Bar & bars manager of Bradford College Students' Union" (Queens Hall, to you).

Originally from Peebles in Scotland, he came here via pub management jobs in Leicester & Derby. He won a CAMRA pub-of-the-month award in Leicester & then took on a brand-new pub in Derby. It was here that he had his first experience of running a live-music venue with a jazz-rock band who played there once a week.

The facilities offered by The Vaults Bar gave him a chance — with assistant bars manageress June holding the fort over the road — to expand on this experience. "I wanted to put on a series of live events throughout the week to entertain anyone who was interested in local musical talent." The result is that the venue offers local rock bands twice a week, a resident progressive jazz group (Oral Sax) every Monday, American Folk & Blues fortnightly (Kay Russell + guests) and there may soon be regular country & western music too.

"I'd like it to continue to be a venue that features new & up-&-coming local bands. The city's full of real talent that's still largely undiscovered. It might even be possible for The Vaults to earn something of the kind of reputation that Liverpool's Cavern Club had in the early 60's. I'd like that."

CHRIS GROVES
interviewed by Nick Toczek

Another end-of-the-night interview. Kay & I spent the first half of the evening at The Princeville where she wrote up Samson's gig (q.v.). We then cut across to The Palm Cove — Thursday & the women's bop. Kay goes through for a dance while I interview Jed.

Palm Cove's owned by Robbie & Diane Lawrence but the programme of events is worked out by Chris Groves. After learning about life on this planet as seen through the eyes of Jed Turner, I thought I'd interrogate Chris. I began by asking him how he came to be running events here.

"I used to have a lot to do with The Royal Standard. My band rehearsed there three nights a week." (Chris is drummer with Radio 5 — by all accounts an excellent band, though I've yet to hear them myself). "In addition, I used to do the Sunday lunchtime blues jams with Jed & co. We'd fill up an otherwise empty pub, but there were a lot of hassles which culminated in us being thrown out of there for no apparent reason. Then I was introduced to Robbie & Di through a mutual friend. We soon started rehearsing here. The difference was really surprising. Instead of the hassles, there was a lot of trust. They even let us use the rehearsal space for nothing — Malcolm at The Standard had charged us £12 for the 3 nights a week.

At that time Robbie was booking the bands & having problems with some of them — they weren't turning up on the night, that sort of thing. Having access to some London agencies, I offered to help out with some of the work on bookings. I anyway wanted to repay the favours he'd given us. The result was a programme of regular weekend bookings from the beginning of November.

It now looks like things are really taking off — with Palm Cove developing as a major Northern venue for up-&-coming bands of all kinds. It's been a deliberate policy to keep it a really open choice of bands — the most popular bookings at the moment being of mod, new wave, punk & reggae. Mod bands in particular seem to be working well — this being virtually the only Bradford venue open to them (with the exception of the token university gig). We've now got mod gigs at least once a week till the end of the year."

That was it. I had intended to interview Dave & Clare of Vex after that, but didn't have the energy. When Kay came through, the 4 of us went for a curry instead. (Did the Vex interview a couple of days later - q.v.).

N.B. The Shah (top of Carlisle Rd.) does excellent curries - amongst the best in Bradford. If you're in the centre of town, try The Taj (Morley St., just above the old Chester St. bus station). Towards Undercliffe (home for us) is The Koh-i-noor on Barkerend Rd. or The Amber on Leeds Rd.

CLASSIFIED ADS.

(this section's free - at least for this & for the next couple of issues).

BLUES MUSICIANS WANTED - Lead Gtr. + Bass Gtr. + Brass (Sax., Tromb., Trumpet) + Kbds. to work with well-known Bradford Vocalist/Harmonica Player.
phone Jed Turner on B'ford 634638

2 VANS + DRIVERS Available to transport groups/equipment etc. Both have 35 c.w.t. walk-through Bedford vans. They work for reasonable rates. Day or evening/night. Short notice jobs. Ring for estimate or terms. One is Malc Douglas on B'ford 44428, the other is Ken Drake on B'ford 683195.

RECORD REVIEW

Band: Excel. E.P: 'If it rains' + 'Rolling Home' c/w 'She's One of The Boys' + 'Rock Show'. Label: A.R.S.S. Records. Pressing No: Not known. Released: Early '79.

A band firmly rooted in 60's revival - if they'd gone for mod, they'd have hit gold by now. Shame then that they went for early R&B (Pretty Things & their ilk). As such, they're O.K. The songs are nothing special & it looks like the R&B revival won't be with us for a few days yet. The main problem with reviving a sound is that people only remember the best bands/songs, so that's what the new bands have to compete with if they want to achieve any popular success.

Band: The Scene. Single: 'Hey Girl (won't you be mine)' c/w 'Reach The Top'. Label: Manouvre Records. Pressing: 1,000. Released: Dec '79 (on review here is a pre-release cassette).

《 more reviews p.16, col.3

THE PRINCEVILLE

ON THURSDAY 15th NOVEMBER
Reviewed and Written by
Kay Russell.

".....And the band tonight is......SAMSON." By 9.30 the Princeville concert room is packed tight with an assortment of rock fans of all ages, all eagerly waiting to hear Samson, who play the club fairly regularly. The performance begins with smoke bombs and a long, ear-splitting instrumental passage, played by the lead guitarist (silk shirt), drummer (black-stockinged head, leopard-skin jumpsuit) and bass-player (royal-blue tracksuit, tri-color hairdo).

It is immediately obvious that the band comprises three very accomplished players in the heavy-metal tradition. As the engineer at the back of the room fights with the sound balance, on struts the lead vocalist, complete with red leather trousers. We are straining to hear what sort of a voice he has; during the second song, "6 feet under", it becomes apparent that he has an excellent voice. There follows a new song "from the album" called "Hard Times", which is a thumping good number with powerful vocal harmonies. The glass-collector, a little chap with a hearing-aid, says, "Tell me, are they any good?" I nod enthusiastically.

Next number is "Mr. Rock & Roll", leading into "Inside Out", a sort of heavy boogie played fast and slow by turns, and including audience participation in the form of rhythmic handclaps. During the next song, "Vice Versa" ("about the sort of woman who goes through people like a dose of salts") [!] the audience has decided that it likes the band, a few dedicated headbangers move to the front, and the Princeville comes into its own as "the North's last outpost of heavy metal."

Samson are an exciting band ~ I would like to have seen how they work on a larger stage. Good stuff - even the glass collector is bopping up and down, but I have to leave to visit another venue. Pity.

———·—·—·—·———

SAMSON are currently on tour supporting MOTORHEAD. Apparently they were unable to set up a laser-rig which, I was told, normally adds much to their visual impact.

RECORD REVIEWS
continued from previous page

A double A-side, these are two very good copies of 60's pop from a Bradford mod band. The first sounds like a cross between early Beatles & Herman's Hermits. It includes some great bubble-gum lyric lines like: 'I know that you know cos I told you so'. The second track has even more of an authentic Merseybeat sound to it. Both will seem a bit weak on first hearing - but play them again a couple of times. Fab! Oi! give it foive! (Where are you now Janice Nicolls?).

<u>Band</u>: **Agony Column**. <u>Single</u>: '(I had it) All Worked Out' c/w 'Good Grief'. <u>Label</u>: Tyger Records. <u>Pressing</u>: 2,000. <u>Released</u>: Early '79.
An interesting first single from the band that, nationally, is probably the best-known of those under review here. Excellent mix. Good clean sound. Both numbers are fresh & snappy, though maybe not the best choice for a single. Now that the band are signed to a major label, they should soon deliver the goods. Having seen them live, I'd suggest they'd be likely to come up with an excellent L.P.

<u>Band</u>: **Shadowfax**. <u>Single</u>: 'Really into you' c/w 'Spare Wheel Driver'. <u>Label</u>: Bradford Records. <u>Pressing</u>: 1,000. <u>Released</u>: August '79.
Clever & catchy lyric on the A-side which is a tight rock-pop song. Very distinctive & appealing vocal sound. This is an attractively commercial number that should have sold out by now. As it is, only about 500 have gone. Get yourself a copy from Pearsons in Rawson Market. You'll also get the B-side, a mainstream heavy rock number that's made above-average by some impressive fast guitar work. I imagine the latter's a popular stage number - though, on record, I've heard better.

<u>Band</u>: **The Negatives**. <u>Single</u>: 'Stakeout' c/w 'Love is not real'. <u>Label</u>: Look Records. <u>Pressing</u>: 1,000. <u>Released</u>: Dec. '79 (on review here is a pre-release cassette).
Two fast 77-ish punk songs. The second title (it's a double A-side) is lifted by 'Clash' harmonies on the chorus. Two years ago this would has sold 1,000's - now, they'll have problems getting the airplay essential for good sales. Even Pennine, with its present policy, may not playlist it. Shame. It is a very good single of its kind.

<u>Band</u>: **Ulterior Motives**. <u>Single</u>: 'Another Lover' c/w 'Y Gotta Shout'. <u>Label</u>: Motive Music. <u>Pressing</u>: 2,500. <u>Released</u>: Nov. '79.
You'll have to decide for yourself on this one, Brian. We're keen on it!

NICK TOCZEK

MOD NIGHT AT THE PALM COVE   SAT. 17th NOVEMBER
THE FIXATIONS and THE KILLERMETERS
Reviewed and written by Kay Russell.

Walking into the Palm Cove on Saturday night was like walking straight back into my past. The boys and girls moving around to the Ska and Beat disco were wearing trilby hats, short hair, sludge-green parkas festooned with badges and 'Who' stickers, mohair Italian-cut suits with single back-vents, and pointed shoes. I even saw a couple of mini-skirts. All very authentic, and I should know — I was one of the original Mods ya see, back in the old days when one thought nothing of waiting for 4 hours in the pouring rain in the hope of getting a ticket to see the Who. Ah, it fair takes you back.

We waited quite a while for the Fixations, but eventually on they bounced, a young 4-piece band: bass, rhythm guitar and vocals, lead guitar and vocals, drums. During the first song a few people moved to the front; some to lip-read the lyrics, some to stand and stare, some to stand and sneer. Undaunted, the group carried on cheerfully into their second song which I think was called "Congratulations." One thing must be said about the Palm Cove Club. The club is great, but the acoustics are appalling, and until the ceiling is lowered there is little a band can do except turn down the guitar amps so that the singing can come through. Unfortunately, bad acoustics mean that the audience blames the group for the rotten sound, and the audience on Saturday was no exception. The Fixations worked hard, played well, and deserved a better reception than they got.

Their style was hard to define, usually a good sign, but there was something about them which reminded me of Talking Heads (from the States). The guitar playing in the riffs and especially in the intros was particularly good, and one or two of the songs were outstanding. Two which moved me, and a kid in a Union Jack waistcoat, were "Clever Remarks", a potential single, and "Contact" (?) which although slightly slower had a really haunting melody. I liked the build-up into "Follow the Crowd" (sorry if I've got these titles wrong boys, but it was so difficult to hear what was said) and there was some exciting drumming during this; also in "Everywhere I Look" the rhythm guitar riff added a lot to the sparkle of the song. The Fixations' songs are catchy and fairly short, with memorable choruses. They are a good band, and it is to their credit that the quality of their material shone through a muddy sound mix.

When the Fixations had finished, the disco came back on, this time with some old Stax favourites, and dancing resumed. I wish I'd taken a camera. There were several girls carefully dressed in styles from the early '60's doing dances that must have taken hours of painstaking practice at home. You think The Twist is dead, yeah? Well, some of these kids were doing a close approximation and it was a fascinating sight to see them, half of them scooter-kids and the other half gangsters, including a Bonnie and Clyde look-alike couple who turned up complete with violin case. When the disco had treated us to "In with the in-crowd," "Midnight Hour", "Sweet Soul Music", and some Tamla-Motown type records, it was time for the KILLERMETERS..............

"We're from Yorkshire and we sound a bit like this." Hundreds of people materialized and frenzied dancing began from the first note played by the Killermeters. The sound-quality was much improved by this time, due partly to a little jiggery-pokery by the sound engineer during the interval. And he had his work cut out, as I understand that the entire mid-range section of his mixer had blown (technicalities, sorry!).

Line-up of the Killermeters ~ bass and lead vocals, drums, lead guitarist and 2 rhythm/lead guitarists who also sang back-up vocals. They appeared on stage looking very smart and very confident, and their stage prescence reminded me of the Jam. I can remember thinking, in the excitement of the moment, that they were potentially (dare I say it?) better than the Jam. They're certainly a knockout dance band.

The audience loved them, especially when they went into their second number, an accurate copy of the Who's "Legal Matter." The harmonies and playing were very tight, they'd done a lot of rehearsing and a lot of gigs and it showed.

The third excellent song was "Cardiac Arrest" (recorded a while back) and soon they were into their last single, "Why should it happen to me." Magic. By now the audience had lost its self-consciousness and had become a solid mass of bopping appreciation. Someone good-naturedly poured a bottle of beer over someone-elses head, and the band began "Look but don't touch", a newly-written song, and a good-'un. ".............. Is anyone in love in here? Are you sure! This is for you, it's called 'Love on the Rebound'." A slightly slower piece, this, with some beautiful guitar work during the verse and nice full harmonies.

Well, we had to leave early (the story of my life). This is what I have to say about the Killermeters. I tried to be critical but I couldn't fault 'em. If they've not an important charting band in the future I'll want to know the reason why. GO AND SEE THEM.

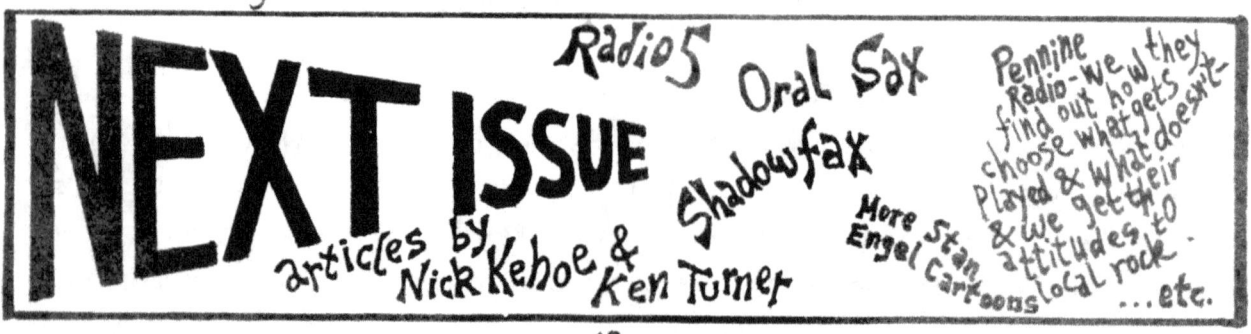

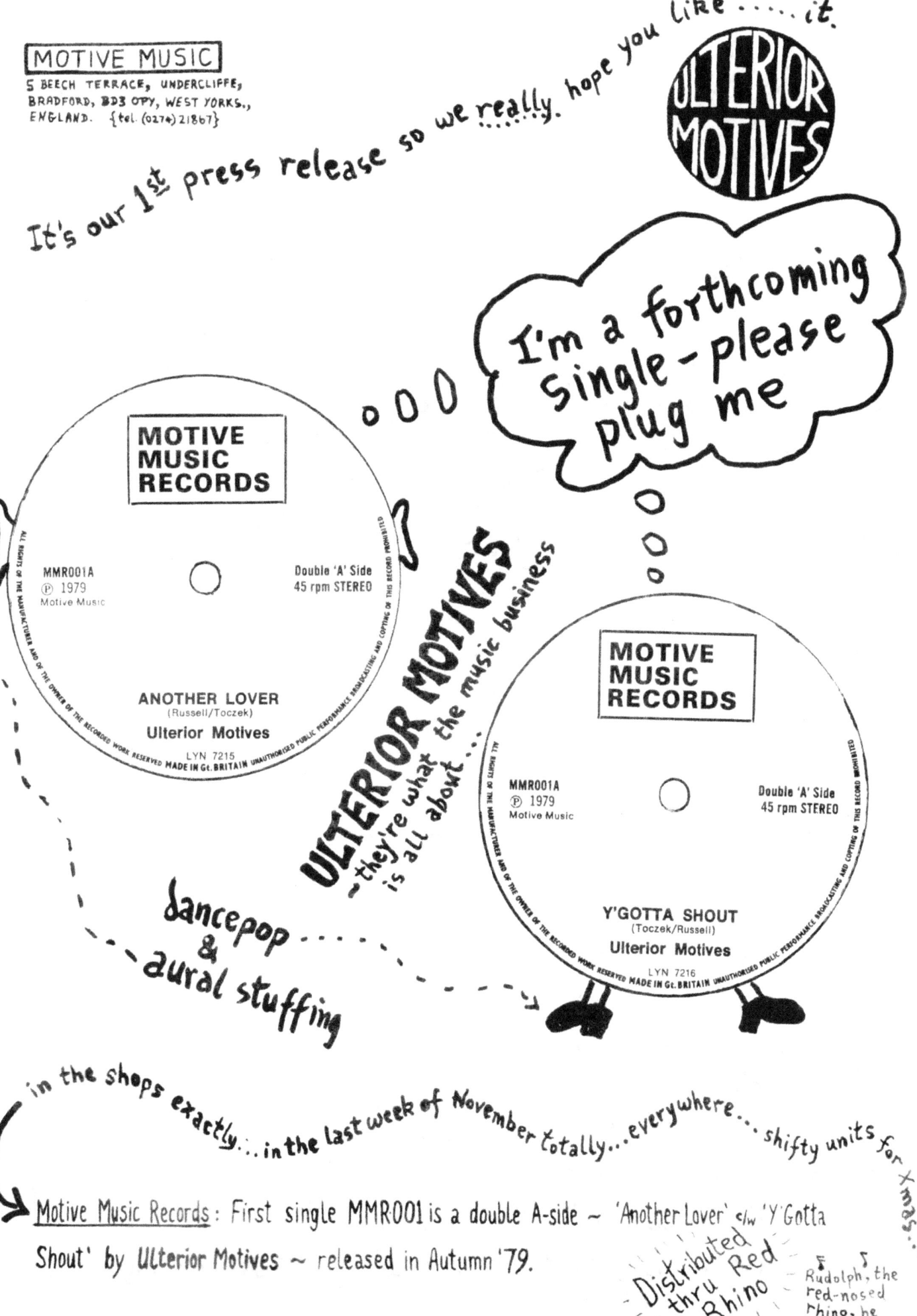

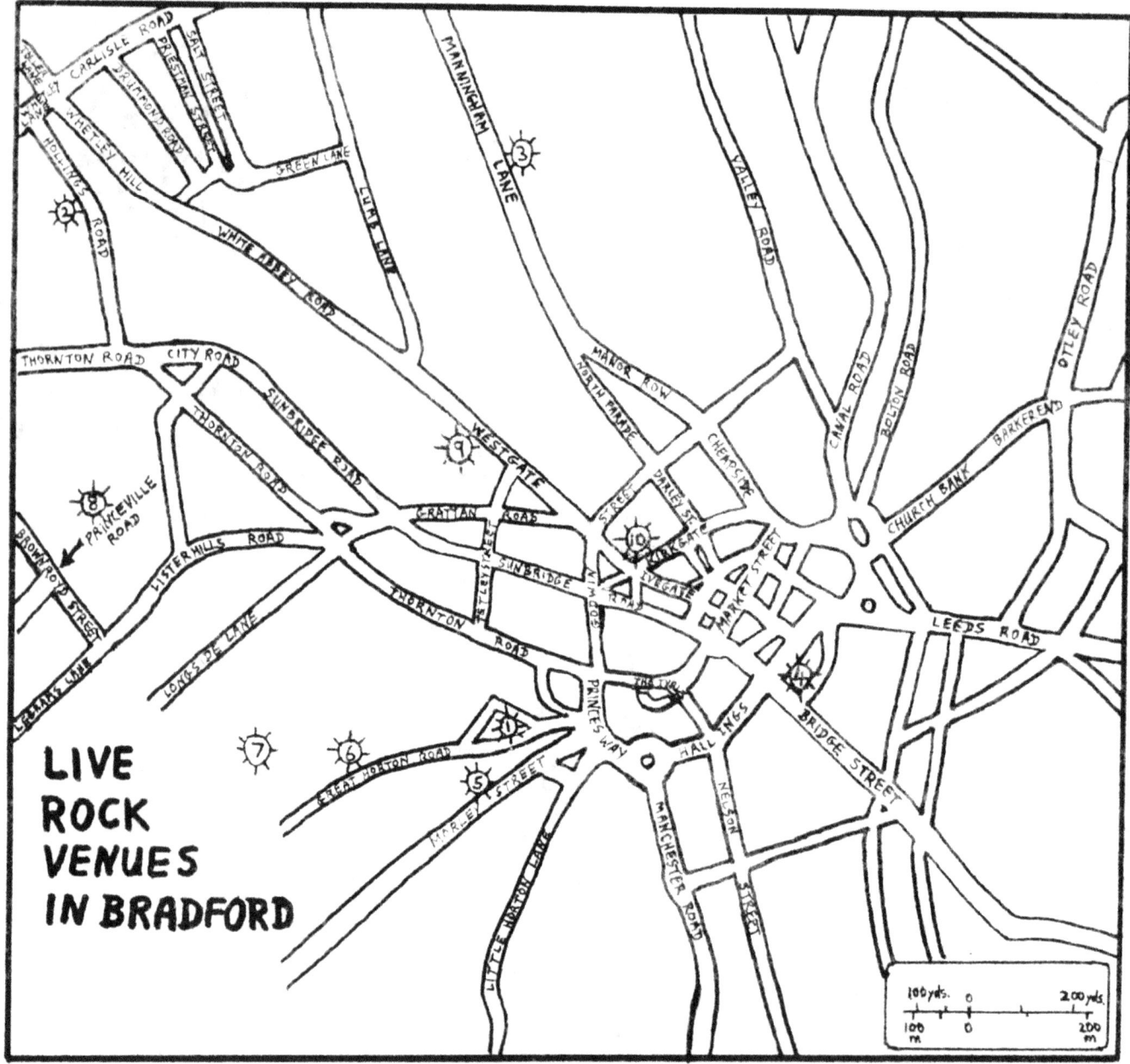

ISSUE #2

January 1980, 1,500 copies printed, 20 pages, A4, coloured paper, coloured ink

This is a slightly slicker issue. I painstakingly typed out much of the text in long, narrow columns. There are five guest contributors and several new features, including Brian Rushgrove's Rock'n'Roll Page and Ken Turner's Wool City Rockword... and the mag even secures its own monthly slot on local radio station Pennine Radio. Also, the pages have gone from black and white to coloured paper and printing (not apparent in this book, but the pages of the original mag were yellow with blue print, and the cover was orange with red print). Our gig guide is more extensive, we've more paid adverts, and there's even a photograph of a band.

Notes on bands profiled and reviewed in this issue.

It's worth pointing out that, from the outset, I wanted WCR to serve as a platform for interesting gigging bands and solo artists who weren't receiving much coverage elsewhere. As a result, many of those featured in the mag had never previously had proper press coverage.

A few of the demo cassettes. Some of these were sent to me after 1981, but all feature northern musicians I knew or worked with while producing Wool City Rocker.

Mr Twang HAS ARRIVED AT KITCHENS

To bring you all the big names in music at low, low PRICES!!!

FENDER		GIBSON	
Strat LTRN	£250	Les Paul Custom	£475
Strat WTRN	£275	Les Paul De Luxe	£415
Strat LTMN	£275	Les Paul Standard	£450
Strat WTMN	£299	The Paul	£299
Tele Std	£249	R.D. Standard	£375
Prec. Bass RN	£245	Les Paul "55"	£399
Prec. Bass MN	£260	S.G. Standard left-hand	£390

Aria – Full range of todays best value for money electric guitars carry a very special 10% Cash or H.P. discount until Christmas

KORG Synths		HOHNER Keyboards		YAMAHA Synths	
MS10	£199	Planet T	£198	CS 5	£205
MS20	£325	Clavinet D6	£299	CS10	£280
SQ10	£235	Hohner Duo	£499	CS15	£350
Vacorder	£575	K2 Piano & Strings	£555	CS30	£575
Sigma					

RODGERS 5 Drum Kits – Very special at an incredible £750 Save £251

MOOG Polymoog (1 only) £2225

Plus
ACOUSTIC AMPLIFICATION (Sole to Kitchens in Yorkshire, North East)
BIAMP (Exclusive to Kitchens)
ODYSSEY (Coming Soon – A brand new world beating range of guitars – watch out for these incredible guitars and basses)

Now to CHRISTMAS SPECIAL Except the Pollymoog – every one of the above items will be sold at these prices even if we are temporarily out of stock.

Mr Twang ONLY AT **Kitchens** EST.1875 THE MUSIC PEOPLE

26 North Parade, Bradford.
Telephone: 23577

also at Leeds, Barnsley, Newcastle, Huddersfield
"The Everything in Music Stores"

CALLING... ALL YOU PUNKS & ALL YOU TEDS, BRADFORD MODS & NATTY DREADS

the HMV shop (OPPOSITE Y.E.B.)

5 CHEAPSIDE   BRADFORD   TEL. 28882

LARGEST SELECTION OF RECORDS & TAPES IN TOWN INCLUDING U.S. & EUROPEAN IMPORTS.
   OUR TOP 50 ALBUMS at up to £2.00. off.
EXTENSIVE RANGE OF NEW WAVE & REGGAE INCLUDING INDEPENDENT LABELS & IMPORTS. HUNDREDS OF BADGES, PATCHES & POSTERS & A FAST AND EFFICIENT ORDERING SERVICE...... LOOK HERE.

ADVERTISING RATES

Standard size = 3½" x 3½"

First advert. costs £20-00 thereafter, they are half price.

Current print run = 1,500 (estimated readership = 3,000+).

Colour, special layout or positioning, different size, etc. by arrangement.

Ring Nick or Kay on B'ford 21867.

BRADFORD COLLEGE STUDENTS UNION

Presents the ultimate in live entertainment every Friday Night

AT

QUEENS HALL

ADMISSION RIGHTS KEPT!!!

 **PALM COVE CLUB**

HOLLINGS ROAD, BRADFORD 8.
TEL. 499895.

LIVE ENTERTAINMENT FRI. & SAT.
              (8pm – 1am)
Club also open throughout the week
              (9pm – midnight)

LATE BAR NIGHTLY
                    CAR PARK AT REAR
NEW WAVE / MOD / REGGAE JUKEBOX
GOOD WEST INDIAN FOOD
                    POOL TABLES

THE WOOL CITY ROCKER

From:- 5 Beech Terrace, Undercliffe, Bradford, BD3 OPY, West Yorkshire, England. (tel. 0274-21867)

A Northern rock magazine from the home of the band 'Ulterior Motives' & the record label 'Motive Music'

EDITORIAL

Been a bit of a crazy, overworked & underslept month for us both - but here we are, bouncing back with a second issue. Hope you like the coloured inks & paper on this one. We were very relieved at the generally enthusiastic reaction to our first issue. You spend so much time working the thing that, by the time it's actually printed, you're past being able to assess it yourself.

We're still after more writers + ideas + (sober & constructive) criticism. Also, get in touch if you're in a band or running any events. Letters for a letters page or entries for the classified ads. section (free!) are welcomed.

At time of going to press, we've shifted about 1,000 of the 1,500 copies of No 1. With shop discounts & other expenses, we're still about £30 down - but there is a bunch of days to go before this 2nd issue's printed up, so we've still some hopes of breaking even. We're off to the printer now. Xmas rears it's ugly head.

Over & out, Nick & Kay (20/12/79)

EDITION No 2 JANUARY '80

Editors:-
Nick Toczek
Kay Russell

Contributors:-
Brian Rushgrove
Stan Engel
Ken Turner
Keith E. Rice
F. I. Denning

Terms of sale:
30p direct to public or 45p by mail order from address below. 20p ea. on orders of 15 or more copies.

COPYRIGHT © 1980 WOOL CITY ROCKER PUBS.

Editorial Address:-
5 Beech Terr.,
Undercliffe,
Bradford,
BD3 OPY,
West Yorkshire,
England.
tel. (0274) 21867.

CONTENTS

COVER CARTOON by Stan Engel		1
GIRAFFES OVER BRADFORD		4
BANDS IN PROFILE	Silver Screen Girls	5
	Shadowfax	5/6
	Radio 5 + CARTOON - Stan Engel	6
	Planet	7
	Total Confusion	7
ROCK 'N' ROLL PAGE		8
LIVE REVIEW - 'Upanatom' (Vex + Remainz) at The Palm Cove		9-11
LIVE REVIEW - White Spirit at The Princeville		11/12
RECORD & TAPE REVIEWS		12
CARTOON - Stan Engel		12
LIVE REVIEW - Ulterior Motives at The Vaults Bar		13/14
CARTOON - Stan Engel		13
CLASSIFIED ADS. + NEXT ISSUE		14
TOTAL CONFUSION - a psychotic blend in chaos		15
LIVE REVIEW - The Salford Jets at The Palm Cove		16/17
WOOL CITY ROCKWORD No 1		18
NOWTZ		13
GIG GUIDE for January		20

Cloth cap noise & mill town pop... Edible words... We're dancing the Right away... I am who you are... It's only one night

Keeping it out of London... Not a fanzine... Circulation on a shoestring... Never trust a rocker...

3

Giraffes over Bradford

Palm Cove on 18th Jan. promises to be an evening of musics with a difference – I spoke to a couple of the bands involved....

EATEN ALIVE BY INSECTS

Line-up for this gig is Phil Insect (Tenor Sax, Gtr., B.Gtr., Tapes, Dm. Machine, Violin) + Peter Lindup (Perc., B.Gtr., Tapes) + Alistair MacDonald (B.Gtr., Gtr., Tapes) + Andy ? (Sine Wave Generator, Tapes, Dm.Machine, Gtr.).
E.A.B.I. started life in summer '78 with a fixed line-up of Pete Insect, Phil Insect & Clare Insect (now Jowett – B. Gtr. with Vex). They did no gigs, but a lot of tapes. Phil: "We planned a couple of gigs which involved a lot of theatre (Pete was mainly theatre) but our show was too gory for Chicago Express (now Panache) & we used too much tape echo (Musicians' Union ruling) for The F Club – so both gigs fell thru. There followed several different line-ups, ending up as a 5-piece but "there were too many conflicting ideas so it just split up completely."
"Since then, I've carried it on with a flexible line-up. I've found that the only way to function as a successfully creative group is to have one person in charge of the unit's output – no matter how many people are contributing. That person is more of an editor than a censor." - Phil Insect.
This will be the 3rd E.A.B.I. gig – the 2 previous ones having been at Queens Hall in early '79.

"Now I write a series of numbers – partly composed, partly improvised. I write the basics but leave room for improvised sections. That way, the overall result is what I've written, but with other people's ideas prominent." - Phil Insect.

"Our pieces are improvised in rehearsal – but are fairly structured by the time we go on stage. However, if the gig's going well, we might introduce an element of live improvisation." - Mephisto Waltz.

E.A.B.I. releases:– 1) A cassette called 'Insect Comics' which came out in summer '78 "about a month after we formed. We did just 10 copies of which 5 were sold & 5 went to the band." 2) A new cassette is due out in a couple of weeks (see review elsewhere). It'll consist of 3 tracks – 'Dead Sparrows Can't Boogie' c/w 'Do The Cedric' & 'The Outskirts'. "It will be in an initial run of about 25 cassettes – though I hope to follow it up with a single containing the same tracks."

MEPHISTO WALTZ

Line-up: John Jankowitz (L.Gtr, L.Voc., Kbds.) + Mirko Jovanovic (Gtr. treatments) + Luby Jovanovic (no relation – on Bass) + Ivor Jones (Kbds. + Voc.) + Tim Charge (Dms.).
They formed in Aug.'79 & this'll be their first gig. They describe their work as being structured & experimental music. Some song titles: 'Blood & Roses'+'Picnic on a Battlefield'+'Old Soldiers Never Die'+ 'March of the Insects' (inst.)+'Words of War'. "They're something outside of punk/new wave & work to tribal rhythms though some of the tunes are quite catchy. The lyrics are anti-violence." The group originates from a band called Section 4 – a 3-piece comprising John Jankowitz + Ian James (now with The Scene) + Aky (now with Violation).
"We're planning to incorporate a slide show into The Palm Cove gig – though we're still working on the overall stage show."
"Any money we make'll go towards a film that Phil Insect is making. Simon Vincenzi is producing it & John Jankowitz has written a script that might be used."
No influences, but some interesting groups include Scritti Politi, The Pop Group, The Slits, Human League, Eno & Fripp, P.I.L.

Contact: John on 676851 (evenings only).

Also on the bill on 18th will be Mesopotamears + another band being formed by Pete Insect (of orig. E.A.B.I.) + guest artists.

If this package is a success then there will be further Giraffes over Bradford gigs. In addition, this gig'll be recorded with a view to releasing a compilation tape of the bands.

1980:- The Year of The Giraffe

BANDS.
written up by Nick Toczek

SILVER SCREEN GIRLS

Voc. = Tonie Whitaker
Gtr. = Paul Duff
Gtr. = Mick Potter
B. Gtr. = Steve Holton
Dms. = Kendall
Kbds. = Alan Bailey

Accosted in The Vaults Bar by Silver Screen Girls (all male) wanting a write-up...
The band formed in Spring '79 - basing the group's image on New York Dolls as they all felt that the fem/glam rock front still had a lot of mileage in it. They've been into Cargo Studio (Rochdale) & were pleased with the results - though they hadn't booked enough time for what they wanted to do & so will go back there or else into Eel Pie Studio (London) to record again - using the results to bring out a first single (probably on their own label) to be released in Spring.
"The name has a strange effect on audiences - with many of them coming along expecting us to be girls or gays or some sort of piss-take or even strippers!"
Their stage set consists of their own numbers & they rely heavily on stage energy + visual impact to put them over. "The songs are fast, short & melodic - we're modern music in a rock & roll idiom."
Motives:- 1) We all get a kick out of being up there on stage - a mix of ego & fun. 2) To entertain - ie our music is fun, not political. 3) We're after fame & fortune - ie the whole rock star bit appeals to us & we're ready to do whatever it takes to really make it - go to London, crawl for a record contract, act in blue movies, sleep with anyone...
"Obviously we're rooted in the early 70's glam rock, but our music is more dadaist/nihilist & modern. If you imagine T-Rex, Sweet & Garry Glitter + rough edges, anger & repulsion then that's us - pretty & ugly at the same time. We're taking 70's destruction/glam/power into the 80's. We're not influenced by any of the 60's pop/rock". It was long past closing time & John Farquhar (the manager of The Vaults) came over to chuck us out "...& you can end with a quote from me - that I've never seen a band work so hard on publicising themselves!"

Contact: Tonie on B'ford 675040 or Paul on B'ford 574295.

SHADOWFAX

Voc. = Matti Unnuk
Gtr./Voc. = Allan Unnuk
Dms. = Roy Klymenko
Bass = David Fairfax

The 2 Unnuk brothers have been playing music since they were kids - starting out with piano & singing lessons. Later they played in old time dance bands with their father, Helmuth Unnuk.
In '71 the two of them formed a rock band with a drummer & went through bands with different names & line-ups, though always with the 2 of them involved. With Roy & a couple of other musicians they had some success on the northern club circuit as Midnight Blues (doing covers of Beatles, Stones & other 60's commercial pop songs).
Shadowfax came into being in early '73 with them doing their own songs. They played throughout Yorks., Lancs., N.E. & The Midlands, but in '76 Roy left (pissed off after they'd had all the gear nicked - they never got it back). Their last gig was at St. Luke's nurse's home.
The Unnuks returned to the club circuit for 2 years. Then, in '78, Dave (an old friend) joined up with them - at first on guitar, later on bass. They wrote to Roy (in Bournemouth) urging him to return, which he did. By late Feb. Shadowfax was together again in its current line-up.
After a lot of rehearsals & about 3 club gigs, Sil (who they'd known for years) offered to put up the money for a single. With the previous experience of having done an L.P. (of Latvian folk music!), Sil formed Bradford Records & the single - "Really Into You" c/w "Spare Wheel Driver" eventually came out in August '79. It's sold slowly but steadily though a few hundred still remain. One of the problems was that Pennine Radio playlisted it for 2 weeks. There was also a misunderstanding over responsibility for distribution, with Sil & the group each assuming that the other would deal

with it.

"We've grown up through all the trends - rocker, orig. mod, hippy, progressive, new wave, new mod, etc. - but to us rock is rock & we just aim at doing good entertaining music. We don't want to go on stage with the sort of processed sound that's straight out of a studio with a load of special electronic effects - in fact we deliberately steer clear of being influenced by fashions or gadgetry. We're all good musicians who just want to come across as such. We've always been into direct basic pop music ever since the early 60's & still feel that that's what it's all about."

Matti: "The 70's have been really shit & we've only survived by playing what the audiences have wanted to hear - rock music. In the 60's I felt that the songs were that good that I couldn't write anything, but in the 70's it was all so crap that I just felt I could write better music than most of what was going on. Music died in '69 & we waited a couple of years but nothing happened, so we thought that we'd do it. We're still going today."

Bill (manager): "The Beatles formed in '58, brought out "Love Me Do" in '62. Matti & Allan played it & every single since in front of people from '64 (when they were only kids) to date. The Beatles split in '69. Shadowfax are still going in '79/'80. Musically, this group has been going for 17 years."

Contact: Bill Chapman (eve) on Pudsey 576991 or Matti/Allan on B'ford 27636.

RADIO 5

Voc./Gtr. = Jock Cotton
Bass = Don Hayes
L.Gtr./Voc. = Geoff Haran
Dms. = Chris Groves
Rhythm Machine = Roland77

The full band's been together for 9 months, having formed from a bunch of friends - all of whom wanted to play something that was more adventurous than punk - though their starting point was from fast punk music. They've gradually worked towards a minimal sound, stripping down each number. "The ultimate would be a song with just one note - only we've not found that note ... yet!"

They went into Cargo in Sept. & would consider a record deal if the right company came along - but in the meantime they're bringing out their own single in the early new year.

"It's hard getting gigs outside Bradford at the moment without a single out or a recording contract or a string of gigs behind us - so it's something of a vicious circle. Anyway, we got tired of lying about ourselves..."

"Did we tell you that we've got this agreement between us that none of us can touch alcohol before we go on stage? I got a pint earlier tonight & got 15ft. from the bar before they made me give it away."

Their prime aim is to build up a good musical reputation for the band - though they'd like it to eventually pay them a wage.

"The road crew (Andy & Terry) are great. They are sure to be there ½ hr. after the gear's in & ¾hr. after it's packed away. They insist on having the front seat in the van, leaving us to rough it in the back. But they give us verbal support & keep us sane!"

Contact: 496272 (Jock) & 639142 (Don) - both B'fd

PLANET

A letter arrives from an F.I. Denning of Thornton, B'ford & I'll just quote from it:-

"There was one heavy rock band from Bradford which wasn't mentioned in your 'Bands in Profile' (issue one) section, but it is a band that has quite a large following in B'ford as they have played at The Princeville, The Metro Inn, The Royal Standard & various places in Leeds & throughout Yorkshire.

The name of the band is Planet. The last time they gigged in B'ford they were a 3-piece comprising Pat Dee (Ld. Gtr./Voc.), Charles Neal (Bass) & Tony 'Rocker' Riley (Dms.). However, since then they've added another guitarist - Andy Dunucan - & are now in the process of rehearsing with him with a view to getting back on the road as soon as possible. So in the very near future the band will be on stage again in B'ford, supplying their audience with their own brand of heavy-heavy metal."

There you are, F.I.D., it's in print - o.k.?

TOTAL CONFUSION

Voc. = Boredom
Gtr. = Splodge
Bass = Big John
Dms. = Talib

They've only been in existence since the end of September (1st bash in the practice room on 27th). Two weeks later (Oct. 12th) they played support to The Negatives at the (now closed down) Downtown Club in Keighley when they did just 9 numbers, of which 4 were their own. A week later they again supported The Negatives (+ Vex & Remainz) at The Palm Cove & felt that they went down well with the audience despite a bad sound mix. 3rd gig was same venue on 16th Nov., yet again supporting The Negatives - a bad sound mix then too.

Hassles:- 1) With no p.a. system of their own, it's a matter of playing in support to other bands at the moment - though they feel that's o.k., at least until they've done a few more gigs. 2) They've no regular rehearsal space - only Coda, at £8 a time. 3) With Big John working nights & Talib sometimes on evening shifts (both are male nurses) their jobs interfere with band work.

The band is basic punk, but without the politics. Their songs include 'S.L.R.' (Self-loading Rifle) & 'War' - both of which are anti-war songs + 'Total Confusion' - the band's anthem & the most popular stage song. They're now injecting more variety into their numbers - a new one, 'Just Another Punk' has a reggae intro.

The group's sound is influenced by early Sex Pistols, Stiff Little Fingers & The Damned - the latter for their lack of pretention.

The drummer & bassist are both very keen on 40's/50's jazz & big band music:- "We'd like to work in jazz bands some time in the future. Talib's idol is Buddy Rich."

The latest number - one specially worked out for The Negatives' Xmas Party (Palm Cove 21st Dec) is a version of 'Auld Lang Syne'.

"We've been in existence for 10 weeks & already have 9 of our own songs."

"The band hopes to maintain the early punk ideals, standards & image, & although there is not a great demand for basic punk music today, we feel we are making a small contribution towards Bradford punk music in 1980."

"And anyway there's still a hard core of punks in the town who are good dependable fans of the music."

"We like playing small clubs - ones like The Vaults Bar or how The Downtown Club was - close-packed crowds generate the best sort of atmosphere."

"Yeah - The Palm Cove is a good place for local groups but with sound problems & the place being so large & hard to fill, it tends to lack any real atmosphere."

"On Feb 3rd we're doing a gig with Violation & Chronic (a new Heaton band) but we're not sure of the venue yet."

"We don't want management because we prefer to sort out our own gigs - that way we know what to expect - what the deal & the set-up are."

"We hate soul & disco."

Contact: Boredom on B'ford 570750.

BACK ISSUE...

Copies of Wool City Rocker No.1 available by post (address in frontpiece). Just send us 45p (cheque or P.O.) - includes 15p p.&p. Or 30p from us when we're out & about selling this issue...

ROCK'N'ROLL PAGE

DRAINPIPES & PARAFFIN LAMPS
~ by Brian Rushgrove

*"Some folk don't understand it
That's why they don't demand it
They're always trying to ruin
Forgive them for they know not what they're doing"*

Time and time again groups have proved the above phrase to be true - e.g. *The Who* recording 'Summertime Blues' or *The Sex Pistols* doing 'Something Else' & 'C'mon Everybody' - all of which were, incidentally, written and recorded by the late Eddie Cochran. "Forgive them for they knew not what they were doing."

The above groups, leaders in their respective fields of mod and punk, recording Rock'n'Roll is a laugh in itself (the equivalent of Elvis Presley recording a punk number). Now *Queen* have released a pure Rock'n'Roll record, letting their fans down. This again is the equivalent of Gene Vincent singing 'Over The Rainbow' and it being accepted by the mass Rock'n'Roll fans of the time; another example of letting the fans down.

COR BLIMEY!
WISH I 'ADN'T CALLED YA ELVIS

If you are wondering what all this is leading up to, the point is that the fans of *The Who*, *The Sex Pistols* and *Queen* all accepted that their beloved group changed their attitude and style of music for greener pastures, leaving the fans holding the baby and remembering that their music would never die and now listening to them doing someone else's - in this particular case - Rock'n'Roll influenced.

But what of the Bradford fans? In January 1960, Eddie Cochran and Gene Vincent played the old Gaumont (Odeon 1 & 2). Gene Vincent sang on stage 'Over The Rainbow'. After the local Teddy Boys had thrown everything at him except the kitchen sink because he was singing somebody else's music and not their own (Rock'n'Roll), Vincent stormed off stage, vowing never to play Bradford again (he did, twice). It's a typical example of the fans knowing exactly what they wanted, their own music and nobody else's, and demanding it.

And now, 20 years later, the system has brainwashed the kids so much that they don't know the difference between 1950s Rock'n'Roll and Mary Poppins. They dress like 'Paraffin Lamps' to create an image and use somebody from the 50s as their idol (James Dean). "Some folk don't understand it" is an understatement, is it not?

Brian Rushgrove produced several issues of the now-defunct, Bradford-based magazine 'Yorkshire Rock'n'Roll Scene' around '75/'76. He now owns and runs Bradford Rock'n'Roll Exhibition - putting on displays during '79 in The Arndale Centre, at The Odeon (during the showing of *The Buddy Holly Story*) and at The Central Library.

GAUMONT, Bradford TEL.: 26716
Manager: J. S. G. PHILCOX

SATURDAY, JANUARY 30th, 6 & 8.15 p.m.

LARRY PARNES PRESENTS — **ONE NIGHT ONLY**

The Two Sensational American Stars!
In person — First time ever in England.

GENE VINCENT | **EDDIE COCHRAN**
BACKED BY THE FABULOUS WILDCATS | HIT RECORDER of "C'mon Everybody" & "Summertime Blues."

VINCE EAGER
STAR OF TV, RADIO, STAGE & RECORDS. Plus
ALL STAR SUPPORTING COMPANY

TICKETS: 7/6, 6/6, 5/6, 5/-, 4/6 & 3/6.

"UPANATOM"
7TH DECEMBER
VEX and THE REMAINZ at the PALM COVE
~ Written and Reviewed by Kay Russell.

First thing to say about this gig is that the publicity was excellent. There were "Upanatom" posters all over Bradford and the size of the audience clearly showed that the publicity reached people. They were as mixed a bunch as you've ever likely to see: age range from weenies to pensioners, mods, punks, hippies, straights, gays, drop-outs, drop-ins, ordinary members of the public, and general wierdos.

The Remainz came on at about 11.30, a four-piece comprising female guitarist (hooray) and vocalist, bass guitarist/vocalist, lead/rhythm guitarist, and drummer. From the first number it was obvious that we were not going to be able to hear the lyrics; I couldn't even make out the spoken introductions, so there's no point trying to list the song-titles for you.

Now to describe the music. I would say that the Remainz are a progressive new-wave group. They're not particularly commercial, and they can sound samey at times, but I found them very powerful to listen to and fascinating to watch. The drummer is fast and accurate, if rather loud, and he puts a lot of energy in. The bassist obviously knows his instrument well and barely needs to look down to play. This leaves him free to share the lead vocals and to move around a lot on stage; it's refreshing to see a bass player who doesn't stand immobile, plugging away, looking as if he'd really rather be elsewhere! The lead/rhythm guitarist plays an interesting-looking semi-acoustic guitar, from which he squeezes a sizeable range of sounds and tone colour. Most of the Remainz' stage prescence is created by the girl singer/guitarist, who moves with the grace of Kate Bush and performs with the power of Patti Smith; but that's not to say that her own striking personality doesn't come through strongly, because it does. She's pretty good on that guitar, too ~ a lot of the band's inventiveness seems to be due to her instrumental work.

Most of the Remainz' pieces are quite complex. Listening to them, I got the impression that they'd put together elements of several songs in each one, changing pace, rhythm and atmosphere to suit. Some stop dead at the end, and some come to a screaming conclusion. They rely on rhythms to create excitement, rather than a lot of singing. Musically and politically, the material includes punk and reggae influences. Incidentally, when you go to see the Remainz, listen out for a song about the Ayatollah (spelt?), which shows how a band can absorb eastern musical patterns and present them in a way that is very palatable to a western audience. Overall, the Remainz have a nice balance of tightness and improvisation, liquidity and structure, whilst still being a band you can dance to. It works well live, but it'd frighten me silly if I had the job of arranging their music in the studio!

"We want Vex, we want Vex!" This lone chanter yelling into my left ear rouses me from my alcoholic stupor, giving me a painful reminder that I am at the Palm Cove to <u>work</u>. Okay. Walks over to stage, where Vex are organising themselves. Line-up appears to be, from left to right, drum-machine and synthesiser/keyboards, rhythm guitar and vocals, lead/rhythm guitar and vocals, bass (a girl - hooray again), with drummer at rear.

The first number begins on synthesiser and rhythm machine, and it's a clear and exciting sound. A young lad looking a little like Gary Newman moves to take the role of lead singer. I can't hear the words, again a disappointment, but I really like the music. Real electronic space-age rock, this.

As the performance continues, I realise that what I'm seeing and hearing is teamwork, faintly surprising because from listening to Vex in interview I'd have thought more ego would've come into play onstage. However, the absence of rock-star behaviour fits very well with their music which is a satisfying wash of sound, meshed, deep and complex, with no particular instrument coming to the fore.

For my money, this throws them well into the 1980's. There <u>are</u> comparisons to be made; two bands who do similar work are Joy Division and Simple Minds, but Vex are more "commercial", so if they keep going they're going to be a success. It's just a question of timing and testing the market. At this point some IDIOT (who shall remain nameless) comes up and says, "Ya can't dance to 'em, can ya?" Well, that's wrong. Vex do several good dance numbers, but who the hell wants to dance ~ this is head music, my friend; some of the most interesting I've heard in a long time.

Visually, they are nice to look at, and the only thing which detracts is the bright light over the synth. box, which keeps dragging your eyes to the left. If they could invest in some stage-lighting it would help a lot, especially in a place like the Palm Cove which can be rather dim and dismal. The Remainz certainly would also have had much more impact if there'd been sympathetic stage-lighting.

I shall tell people, especially musicians, to go and see Vex. Their music is capable of pulling things out of you you never knew were there. As for the 'Upanatom' Package, it gives good value for money, is enter-

-taining, and provides an evening of contrasts. All the musicians concerned sing and play well, and the music is right at the forefront of modern tastes. But let's be able to hear the lyrics next time!

SUPPORT THE PALM COVE. IT'S ONE OF THE FEW BRADFORD CLUBS WHICH PUTS ON A WHOLE RANGE OF MODERN LIVE BANDS. YOU CAN PARK THE CAR, DRINK, DANCE, SIT DOWN + TALK, EAT FOOD PREPARED BY ONE OF THE BEST COOKS AROUND, PLAY POOL, AND LISTEN TO THE JUKE BOX. But just one other thing ~ take your own loo roll when you go!

WHITE SPIRIT at THE PRINCEVILLE
THURSDAY 13TH DECEMBER. Reviewed & written by Kay Russell.

WHITE SPIRIT are a top-class group. They have a very clear and distinctive sound, and all the instruments cut through well, especially the bass which is as clear as a bell. At the Princeville it seemed as though they'd been playing together all their lives. I learned afterwards that they'd been on the road for 6 months, living in the van, gigging every night. This being the case, it's hardly surprising they were so tight musically, but credit must also go to them for putting in a fresh and energetic performance ~ not easy when you've been hanging around Bradford in appalling weather conditions since 5.30 in the morning!

Their music has heavy rock influences, but is so melodic I'd hesitate to call it heavy metal. They do a few cover versions, notably by Deep Purple and Ian Gillan, but their own material is of a very high standard and would sound just as good (if not better) on record as on stage. But have they got a record contract? No. Which just goes to show that the record executives in the metropolis STILL don't know what they're doing.

The lead/rhythm guitarist has to be one of the best in the country, not only because of his skill and sensitivity but also because of his faultless ear for melody. None of this sticking-to-the-blues all-the-time which can make bands (like AC/DC/) boring after the first few numbers. He gives just enough rhythm guitar to create the excitement, then hands over to the bass and drums who take over the chugging and smashing (much appreciated by the heavy-metal fans in the Princeville). Then he and the keyboards man lay the melody lines over the top. What comes out is a sound which could easily be used for film soundtracks.

The lead singer has a vocal range and strength that belies his mild manners and soft features. He adds to the depth of the overall sound by singing high and clear (like Roger Daltrey) but he can also pull out a powerful gravelly sound when necessary. I felt though that in places he could do with a little more support on vocals, perhaps from the bassist, who also has a good strong voice.

As for the songs, listen out for "No Reprieve" ~ this drew cheers and whistles from the Princeville audience. "Red Skies" is a well-constructed piece beginning with heartbeat drumming and going on to reveal whole symphonies' worth of theme tunes which would be found moving to even the most tone-deaf ears.

Congratulations to the drummer for his excellent playing throughout (I didn't miss those double rolls!) and to the bassist and keyboardist who didn't play a note out of place all night. The lighting engineer also deserves a mention, because his hard work added tremendously to the theatrical impact of the stage show and to the atmosphere of the music.

At the Princeville, White Spirit endeared themselves to a lot of people. We'll be there when they return.

RECORDS + TAPES RECEIVED

Sixties pop: suddenly they're all doing it. I love the waggon but begin to wonder how many bands it'll hold before the axle breaks.

The **Salford Jets** E.P. (on R.C.A) is of love songs in old-60s pop style. Side One: 'Gina' is a straightforward love song with a good bouncy melody & some classically simple lead gtr. chords in the break. "Gina I gotta new Cortina...". 'Steady with you' is another good pop song - like a light-weight Ramones number. Side two: 'I want you' - harmonica intro. + harmonised "Oh Yeah"s on the chorus could be straight out of early Beatles. 'Hey (Can I fall in love with you) - a fine drum intro. with echo & into another Beatles-like song. This E.P. is already getting airplay & the band deserve some success from it.

The Odds 'Saturday Night' c/w 'Not Another Love Song' (on Double R Records). A-side is another love song - with a good sax break in the middle. A cross between 60's pop (again!) & Elvis Costello. B-side opens with phased gtr. & almost immediately comes in with lazy jazzy sax + effective drums & bass. Echo on vocals. A beautiful sax solo takes over mid-way through track. This should be the A-side - it's one of best pop songs I've ever heard - the arrangement & mix are superb. A great first single from Red Rhino (who're also a York record shop + a major distributor for independent labels).

Akrylykz come on a pre-release cassette from Red Rhino. The single - 'Smartboy' c/w 'Spiderman' will be out this month. They're in the Specials/2-Tone mould - which is a pretty safe horse to back at the moment. Brass to the fore + bouncing ska rhythm section. Radio One is bound to pick it up. This cassette has 4 of their songs on it &, apart from an inevitable sameness, I can't fault them - they're fun, infectious & irresistably danceable.

A total change now for **Eaten Alive By Insects** (see also page 4). 'Do The Cedric' is a fragmented rhythmic instrumental with gtr./bass/dm. machine/wierd recorder/etc. Nearest I can site is a track on the first P.I.L. album. 'The Outskirts' - about a girl assulted in a late-night street is an intensely atmospheric piece. I suppose it comes down to what you want from your music. This track is a nightmarish blend of processed noises/sounds. I think it's excellent &
cont'd p.14

AT THE VAULTS BAR
2nd December

Reviewed by Keith E. Rice.

It's been said of Ulterior Motives that you either love them or loathe them. Me, I love them; but I can understand why a lot of people don't.

Quite simply, the band make no compromises. Even in appearance they look odd: Nick Toczek (lead vocals/percussion) plays the sophisticated new-waver, while Kay Russell (lead vocals/

rhythm guitar) is the demure female, looking like she'd be more at home in a folk club than with a rock band [EDITOR'S NOTE - I DO BOTH - K], and Rick Green (bass/vocals) looks like a refugee from the 1969 Woodstock Festival! (They'll look even odder when they start gigging with the Neutrals' former drummer, a non-freaky black guy!)

Neither do the Motives make any compromises in their music, playing lightweight pop-rock with just a touch of that new-wave hard edge. More often than not, it's delivered at sprint pace, with Nick and Kay creating full and strident vocal harmonies ~ all too rare among Bradford bands ~ above the clatter of their infernal drum machine and Rick's amazing basswork (which is very much responsible for holding the whole thing together). Their material consists mainly of well-crafted pop songs – "Another Lover", "Attack! Attack! Attack!" and "I Wanna be a Commodity" are certainly the most commercial songs I've heard in this area – although Kay's newie "What about the Money", seemed a little weak on first hearing.

The Motives' sound is fun (humour and panache combined) and has great potential, yet there are deficiencies. One is the aforementioned robot drummer, but thankfully that is being replaced by a human. Another is their lack of a lead instrument – for example, their bouncing version of "They Call it 'Rock'" just begged for either a blistering guitar solo or some boogie piano – something to break up the verse/chorus patterns of the songs and add a little more colour. Also, you can't help wishing for the occasional slower number; such might provide Rick with the opportunity to experiment with some counterpoint bass ideas, perhaps using a fuzz-box or a flanger.

Considering the Motives' sound, it was quite a challenge for them to play the Vaults – a predominantly heavy-metal audience – and once or twice, it looked as if the band might lose. (In addition, Nick seemed a little tired and careworn, though he still made an excellent front man). Yet by the end of the evening, the sheer quality of the Motives' set had won grudging approval even from those members of the audience who disliked their musical stance.

In conclusion, it can be said that Ulterior Motives most certainly do have that elusive IT that separates the real talent from the copyists and the rip-offs; but their IT still needs a lot of developing.

RECORDS + TAPES RECEIVED (cont. from page 12).
highly original. 'Dead Sparrows Can't Boogie' is a longer & more demanding piece. Sax + processed sounds. It reminds me of those underwater recordings of whales. This'll be released as a limited edition cassette in a few weeks – probably selling at Cat's Pyjamas in Morley Street.

CLASSIFIED ADS. (still free!)
35 c.w.t. van hire - light removals, groups, etc. 2 vans. Either Ken Drake on 683195 or Malc Douglas on 44428 - ring for estimate - cheap & reliable.

Alan Joy - Mobile Disco - all tastes catered for - ring Janet on 34291 (9a.m. - 5p.m.).

Pub pianist wanted for Westgate Hill Hotel, Tong, Bradford - ring Geoff on b81215.

NEXT ISSUE

Already in the bag:-
Pennine Radio - plans & policies
Mod Page
'Trampus' -reformed
'Shaftdrive' - management deal
'Radios' -gig review
'U.F.O' + 'Shadowfax' - gig review

Others planned for inclusion:-

Bands:-
'Chaos'
'Oral Sax'
'Scum'

Interviews:-
Maxim's new manager on future plans for live bands.
Malcolm Fairplay on running gigs at The Royal Standard.

& more & more & more & more & more & more & ....

toTal conFusion

A PSYchotic BLEND IN CHAOS

WHERE WERE YOU?
THE SALFORD JETS at the PALM COVE 6.12.79
WRITTEN AND REVIEWED BY KAY RUSSELL.

The Palm Cove Club is almost empty; the small turnout for the Salford Jets is probably because The Damned are on at St. Georges' Hall and the Killermeters are on at Maxim's. I have arrived just in time to grab a drink and wander through the blue corridor into the concert room. The first impression of the Salford Jets is of a group of smallish guys dressed neatly enough to get a good response from even a cabaret audience. The sound is nice and clear (good quality equipment) and the coloured stage lights help make you feel you're in for a visually interesting evening. And off they go..........

A tribal beat introduces the first song and the lead singer jumps around as though he has enough energy for all of us. During the next number he uses a harp (mouth-organ) very deftly, still jumping around and still managing to sing clear and strong. It's a commercial '60's-type song remeniscent of early Beatles complete with head-shaking "Oh Yeah's" and I think it's called "I Want You". After politely thanking the support band "Beats Working" (more about this band in the next issue), the Jets go into a slightly slower one called "I gotta new suit"; beautiful back-up harmonies and good keyboard playing, and nice visually with two lads on the left singing into the same microphone. Do I hear hints of the Who's old song "Pictures of Lily" in the music here?

I'm glad I came. They play well, move well, have a remarkable variety of well-paced songs, and they all sing, which makes for a full rich sound. My compliments to the sound and lighting blokes an'all, who do an excellent job. The material appears to be Merseybeat with modern and reggae influences, and it looks as though this band could appeal to a wide variety of people.

Where the hell are you, Bradford? Can't you get your asses away from the goggle-box or have you all gone to see the Killermeters? As for those who stay in the back room, they must be deaf or dead.

In the concert room, the small audience seems pinned to the bar - but there is definitely some foot-tapping going on. "better than a kick in the knackers" chuckles the lead singer, and after a fast short song there is a reggae called "Say it ain't so". It's a lovely one this, could be chart material. It has two-part harmonies throughout the verse, and the chorus goes "Oh no, oh no, say it ain't so". Wish I'd written it myself. The drummer joins in the singing, and does some skilful tapping of sticks on the edge of the snare drum, which together with the blue-beat rhythms on the keyboard adds a Caribbean flavour. The lighting engineer never rests, dimming and switching, and we can't take our eyes off the stage.

"The next one is a track from our E.P., and it's called "I don't wanna go steady with you". A good dance song. A neat little band. An entertainment. I look around me, then I begin to think about how the band has put this act together. Everything seems well organised, and I notice at least one spare guitar at the back of the stage. It's a very good idea this, if you can afford it. At the last 'Ulterior Motives' gig at the Palm Cove my guitar conked out on me and I had to use someone else's. It can be a terrifying experience!

The Salford Jets break into their next piece, "I don't mind", which is slow and very moving. Mind you, anything with the word "baby" in it melts me immediately - just a personal weakness, you understand. There's a good build-up during this number, and it's interesting the way the lead singer delivers the lyric. He has the sort of tragi-comic features that make it easy for him to slip into comedy, even during a sad song. Often he plays an imaginary guitar - maybe someone should give him a real one! Next comes a tribute to the Pretty Things, called "Short Skirts" (self-explanatory title). A neat guitar intro - sounds more like old Yardbirds stuff to me, actually. It's great to hear a fast rhythm & blues in the middle of a set like this, it really gives a lift to the performance and shows the group's versatility as musicians. And this little guy dances around so much I don't know where he finds time to get to the mike!

The introduction to the next song is really very funny indeed, a long thing about people who fart in churches, people who are out of fashion, and rude remarks about those unfortunates who have "snot coming out of their noses without being aware of it".... social misfits, you might say. Everyone laughs and joins in the chorus which goes "Walking round the town town, looking at the squares". An irresistible reggae, "Bright city lights", follows Excuse me, but I have to dance to this. The song seems fairly long, mainly because at the end the phrase "Bright city lights" is sung many times, whilst there is a talk-over describing the evils of the big city.

Now a song à la Del Shannon, called "I want my girlfriend back". Again a pleasant break in rhythm, and I collapse into a red armchair to meditate upon how soothing rock music is to a broken heart. But there, you don't want to know about my personal problems, do you. The Indian alcoholic who always turns up at the Palm Cove is swaying on the dance floor, waving his beer glass at the band.

The last song, "Who you looking at" is so fast we can all pogo to it - (remember punk rock, anyone?). Even a few stragglers from the back room are wandering in. Too late, folks! You should've come in earlier.

The Salford Jets' enthusiasm never faltered despite what it must have looked like (lonely) from onstage. I suppose it's difficult for an audience to realise that if you give something to a live band, they'll give it all back and more - it's an ongoing thing.

WOOL CITY ROCKWORD N° 1.
by Ken Turner.

Partially filled grid entries visible: TRAILFLY (down), LITIGATED (down).

Clues Across.

1. This gnome bothered... in the way she moves. (9)
6. What Brittania does to the waves, and others O.K. (5)
9. First man insect becomes stubborn new waver. (7)
10. After 50 I'm tied, erratic, thus restrained. (7)
11. Loads mix up Manchester Road. (5)
12. As Steely Dan were doing with the years. (7,2)
13. I lie, fans combine to complete arrangements. (8)
15. Arts form brightens sky. (4)
19. Spex used at Infirmary? (1-3)
20. As fans at a concert or sardines in a can. (6,2)
23. Local band photographs? (8)
24. Raised on every pub at opening time. (5)
26. Root rep used for soldier. (7)
27. Elect democratically oft over argument. (4,3)
28. Kind of 15 most bands would like to be. (5)
29. Tunes rode around style of good musician. (4,5)

Clues Down.

1. Local band sounds like info after dark. (9)
2. As men make ways to an end. (5)
4. Site rent spread concern. (8)
5. Bradford's musical cockrel that was. (6)
6. Stay for local band in the singular. (6)
8. Edna's crumpled car. (5)
14. Well-dressed band for wedding photo? (4,5)
16. Might some Bradford cowboys have been this? (5,4)
17. Fly above religious festival. (8)
18. Seen playing bones in the Vaults Bar, perhaps? (8)
21. U.S. Port confused in alcoholic state!! (6)
22. We are below above (4,2)
23. Stone ground makes music? (5)
25. Good denims shrink this way. (2,3)

Solution next issue!!! But if you can finish it, by all means send it to me (or a copy) at the Ed's address. I might think of a prize for the first correct entry! Ken.

NOWTZ
written up by Nick Toczek

Maxim's (formerly Sadie's) had The Killermeters on last month & were happy with the large turnout. As a result, they're going to put on other mod bands. The deal (no fee, just a bunch of tickets to the value of about £75 - which the band can sell to fans to get their money) is one that won't suit all comers - but a new Bradford venue is a nice step into the 80's.

Guitarists should take a look at the neat new combo amps from Roland. They're cheap, light, _very_ compact & pack a real punch + good clean sound. They come in 20, 40 & 60 watt versions, with a bass amp also available at 60 watts. Coda have a 20-watt demo model in at the moment - try it.

Wool City Rocker now has a monthly 6-8 minute spot on Pennine Radio. It'll be at the start of each month, when we can talk about the highlights of the coming month's events on the local rock scene. It'll go out on the community programme at around 6.30pm (peak time) - so let us know if you're involved in anything special that might benefit from a mention.

Bob Preedy, who does Pennine Radio's Wed. rock show, will mention all gigs. All he needs is the info. _in writing_.

CODA music

28 CHURCH BANK, BRADFORD 1.
TEL. 307433. V.A.T. NO: 181-2254-83

MUSICAL INSTRUMENTS SALES HIRE
TUITION. REPAIRS REHEARSAL ROOMS
BANDS GROUPS ARTISTS RECORDING
& VIDEO STUDIOS

P.A. HIRE (100W-3000W)
    Plus crew and transport.

AGENTS FOR: marshall, ludwig, carlsbro,
ovation, premier, olympic, tama,
ibanez, pearl, beyer, AKG, korg,
peavey, gretsch, slingerland.

JSG music

108B Main Street, Bingley.
Tel. 68843.

ACCESS & BARCLAYCARD WELCOME

Part exchange welcome –
amazing discounts.

MAIN AGENTS FOR
MOOG, GIBSON, LAB SERIES, KORG,
FENDER, RICKENBACKER, MUSIC MAN,
H/H, MARSHALL, PARK, M.M.,
CUSTOM SOUND, AMPEG, OVATION,
YAMAHA, LANEY, CRUMAR, PEAVEY,
ROLAND, CARLSBRO & lots more.
Custom P.A.'s up to 2KW
FULL H/H CONCERT P.A. IN STOCK.

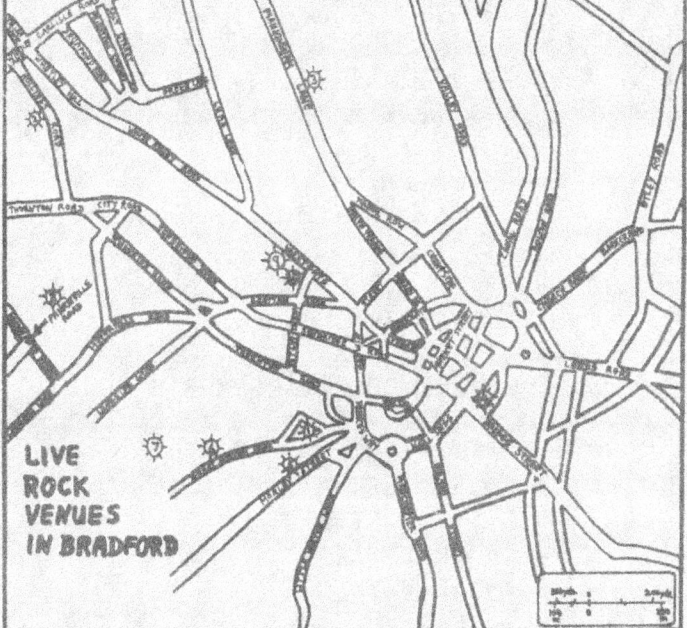

LIVE ROCK VENUES IN BRADFORD

VAULTS BAR Bradford

LIVE ENTERTAINMENT 4 nights a week

JAZZ * ROCK * FOLK * POP

Admission still only 30p

TRADITIONAL HAND - PULLED ALES

* BAR SNACKS *

1. VAULTS BAR (ring Queens Hall on 392712 & ask for Vaults Bar extension – or, evenings only, ring direct on 392713)
2. PALM COVE (499895)
3. ROYAL STANDARD (27898)
4. ST. GEORGE'S HALL (32514)
5. QUEENS HALL (392712)
6. UNIVERSITY (MAIN HALL) } (Students' Union № 34135)
7. UNIVERSITY (COMMUNAL BUILDING)
8. PRINCEVILLE (78845)
9. TEXTILE HALL (WEST INDIAN COMMUNITY CENTRE TOP FLOOR - SIDE ENTRANCE)
10. MAXIM'S (20206)

Stop Press: Ulterior Motives' debut with new drummer (John Nelson) will be on a Tuesday in January at Vaults Bar – read the posters!

WOOL CITY ROCKER — GIGS

T.B.A = To be announced.

BRADFORD UNIVERSITY
Jan. 9 GINGER BAKER (Comm. Blg)
16 PURPLE HEARTS " "
19 CHARITY CONCERT
    LOCAL BANDS   (Great Hall)
23 BRUCE WOOLEY'S
    CAMERA CLUB   (Comm. Blg.)
30 DEF LEPPARD (Comm. Blg.)
Feb. 2 GANG OF 4 (Great Hall)
6 PRETENDERS (Comm. Blg.)
7 SPECIAL CONCERT T.B.A.

THE PRINCEVILLE (Bradford)
Dec. 27 VARDIS
30 ONE ADULT (lunch)
Jan. 3 LUIGI ANA DA BOYS
6 KYRO (lunch)
10 QUAD
13 T.B.A (lunch)
17 SLENDER THREAD
20 Al (lunch)
24 LEARGO
27 PRESS RELEASE (lunch)
31 ONE ADULT

THE VAULTS BAR (Bradford)
Dec. 31 ORAL SAX
Jan. 2 KAY RUSSELL'S MUSIC CLUB
3 OMEN
6 JAPANESE SOLDIERS
9 HUSTLER ST. BAND
13 EASY RIDER
14 ORAL SAX
15 RED EYE
16 KAY RUSSELL'S MUSIC CLUB
20 ONE ADULT
21 ORAL SAX
22 SAWAKA
27 PROPOSITION 31
28 ORAL SAX
29 REALTO REVIEW
31 TALISMAN
Feb. 3 SHAKE APPEAL
5 PRESS RELEASE
10 STRESS

ROSE & CROWN (Ilkley)
Jan. 8 OMEN
15 FROG BORIS
31 PRESS RELEASE

HADDON HALL HOTEL (Leeds)
Jan. 6 SANOES & PRESS RELEASE

FOLK
TOPIC FOLK CLUB (Bradford)
Dec. 28 TONY CAPSTICK
Jan. 4 SOMERVILLE GENTLEMEN'S BAND
11 SEAN CANNON
18 SINGERS' NIGHT hosted by
Frank Cahill & Roger Sutcliffe
- proceds to cancer research.
25 CAULDRON

VAULTS BAR (Bradford)
Jan. 2 KAY RUSSELL & DAVE ROBSON
       plus IAN.
16 KAY RUSSELL & ROGER SUTCLIFFE.

STAGING POST (Leeds)
Jan. 5 DEVOTION
6 DEADRINGER
12 DODGY TACTICS
15 GOODNIGHT VIENNA
19 SIDE EFFECT
20 CITY LIMITS
26 SHAKE APPEAL
27 WINKER
Feb. 2 2 T.V.
3 2 T.V.
9 FODO
10 BREAKER

ST. GEORGES (Bradford)
Jan. 29 THE CLASH
31 WISHBONE ASH
Feb. 7 T.B.A.

PALM COVE CLUB (Bradford)
Bands every Fri. & Sat.,
hopefully to include
THE BEAT & DEXY'S
MIDNIGHT RUNNERS both
of which have been linked
with the 'Two-Tone' Label.
Women's Disco Thurs. nights.

BRADFORD COLLEGE QUEENS HALL
Jan. 11 JEDEDIAH STRUT
18 JABBERWOCKY & SHADOWFAX
25 SPINOES & PRESS RELEASE
Feb. 1 RUFARO
8 THE CLIENTS & LOCAL BAND
    T.B.A.
14 VALENTINES' DAY CONCERT
* LOCAL BANDS T.B.A

ISSUE #3

February 1980, 1,500 copies printed, 20 pages, A4, coloured paper, coloured ink

This issue sees me as the sole editor. There are other changes. Readership and distribution are both broadening. While issues one and two were subtitled 'Bradford Rockscene Magazine', this one is subtitled 'West Yorkshire's Rock Mag'. Knackered trying to run the mag alone, I reverted to handwritten script because it proved quicker. I wasn't entirely alone, there were now ten contributors.

Notes on bands profiled and reviewed in this issue.

Two bands featured in this issue would find success after changing their name. Japanese Soldiers would morph into Zodiac Mindwarp and the Love Reaction, and The Hustler Street Band would find fame as New Model Army.

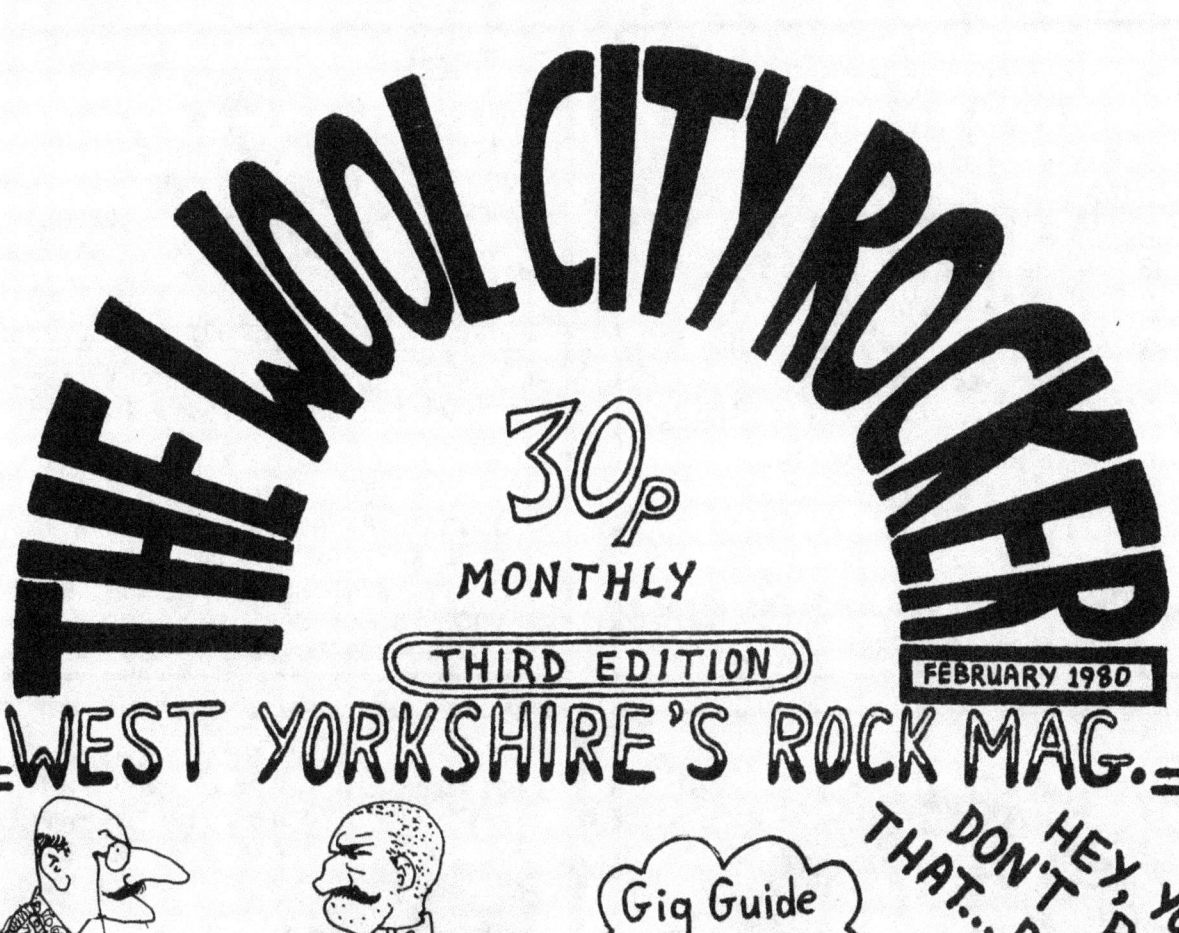

J.S.G.
8-TRACK STUDIO
BRADFORD
NOW OPEN
Alan & Heath 16 x 8 mod. III
Tascam 80/8
Revox B77   Space Echo
MXR Stereo Graphics
A.K.G., Shure, Electrovoice, Calrec Mikes
Resident Producer
RECORD PRESSING

Rates: £7 per hr. + tape, £50 per 8 hr. day + tape
tel. Bingley 68843 or B'ford 832187/491231

CALLING... ALL YOU PUNKS & ALL YOU TEDS, BRADFORD MODS & NATTY DREADS
the HMV shop (OPPOSITE Y.E.&B.)
5 CHEAPSIDE BRADFORD TEL. 28882

LARGEST SELECTION OF RECORDS & TAPES IN TOWN INCLUDING U.S. & EUROPEAN IMPORTS. OUR TOP 50 ALBUMS at up to £2.00. off.
EXTENSIVE RANGE OF NEW WAVE & REGGAE INCLUDING INDEPENDENT LABELS & IMPORTS. HUNDREDS OF BADGES, PATCHES & POSTERS & A FAST AND EFFICIENT ORDERING SERVICE...... LOOK HERE.

The Vaults — Live Entertainment 3 or 4 nights a week. Jazz + Pop, Rock + Folk. Traditional hand-pulled ales + bar snacks. Admission still only 30p. Bradford Students Union.

BRADFORD UNIV-ENTS
GARY GLITTER
PRETENDERS
MEKONS
The Jags
The Quads
SQUEEZE
Gang of Four
SKIDS
DAVE EDMUNDS

Bradford University Concert enquiries, Phone Bfd 34135. Tickets from Union Shop, H.M.V. and Pearsons.

CODA MUSIC
28 Church Bank, Bradford 1. (tel. 307433).

MUSICAL INSTRUMENTS — SALES + HIRE + EXPERT TUITION ON GUITAR, BASS, DRUMS, KEYBOARDS + REPAIRS

REHEARSAL ROOMS + RECORDING & VIDEO STUDIOS + LIVE RECORDINGS FOR BANDS, GROUPS, ARTISTS.

P.A. HIRE (100 - 3,000 watts) + CREW and TRANSPORT.

<u>Agents for</u>:- Marshall, Ludwig, Carlsboro, Ovation, Premier, Olympic, Tama, Ibanez, Pearl, Beyer, A.K.G., Korg, Peavey, Gretsch, Slingerland.

JUST IN !! LARGE STOCKS OF IBANEZ GUITARS FROM £150 - £700.

QUEENS HALL
Live Ents Every Friday

BRADFORD COLLEGE S.U.

WOOL CITY ROCKER No 3
FEB 1980

Several big changes this time around. ① The mag's now claiming to be a West Yorks. monthly - though there's still more on B'ford area than elsewhere - however, this'll be less marked over the next couple of issues. We need to hear from bands/reviewers/etc. elsewhere in W. Yorks. Likewise with entries for the gig guide (they're free). ② Kay Russell - who co-edited the first 2 issues - has left the mag. (too many other commitments). She'll still write occasional reviews, though. ③ There are a lot more contributors to this edition - which helps me & also makes for a broader coverage of the scene. Let us know what you think of the mag. - we're open to ideas, criticisms, etc. Send us letters & we'll start a letters page - though try to keep it brief as we're short of space. If we get more advertising, I promise to put more pages together... meanwhile, I hope this bunch of twenty suits you. Finally, if you can help out by selling the mag. then please ring me. Anyone taking 15 or more copies gets them for 20p each... should pay for a couple of drinks. Don't stay home, go to a gig tonight. *Nick Toczek*

Contents:-
Pages 4→8 are band profiles: THE PLATES, AGONY COLUMN, HUSTLER ST. BAND, EXCEL, SCUM, ANOTHER WRIST ACTION, BEATS WORKING. Page 9's all about SHAFTDRIVE & Heavy Metal revival. The West Yorks. Gig Guide is on pages 10 & 11. Rock'n'roll + classified ads. = p.12. TRAMPUS & Mods fight it out on the next page (unlucky for some). 14→17 have live reviews: JAPANESE SOLDIERS, SHADOWFAX, HUSTLER ST. BAND (again), LIMELIGHT ending with a bit more Mod + info. on some of the gigs coming this way. 18's the rockword. 19's all about Pennine Radio & a bit of folk + record reviews + nowtz takes us though 20. Thereafter is next issue. All of the cartoons are by Stan Engel except for Wilko's on page 12. All of the photos are by cameras & the whole of this issue took me over 50 hours to write out & about as long again to research & collect together... & I'm still losing money on the whole adventure. Tough!

Editor: Nick Toczek

Contributors:-
Stan Engel
Brian Rushgrove
Ken Turner
Keith E. Rice
Steve Brown
F.I. Denning
Dave Green
John Roseveare
Nigel Schofield
Wilko

Terms of sale:-
30p direct to the public or 45p by mail order from the address below. Discount terms on orders of 15 or more copies = 20p each.

Advertising rates:-
Standard 3½"x 3½" box is £20 first ad., going down to £10 for subsequent ads. Colour, special lay-out, different size, etc. by arrangement. Ring or write to address/phone no. given below.

COPYRIGHT © 1980
WOOL CITY ROCKER PUBLICATIONS

Editorial Address:-
5 Beech Terrace,
Undercliffe,
Bradford BD3 0PY,
West Yorkshire,
England.
tel. (0274) 21867

BANDS...

Researched & written up by Nick Toczek

N.B. If you're in a band, let me know about it - ring B'ford 21867.

THE PLATES
(formerly *Idle Rich*)

Gtr. = Chris Scurrah
Gtr.+Voc. = Brendan Staunton
Bass = Dez Staunton
Dms. = "Sid" Sidelnyk

The above line-up formed in mid-Dec. '79. A year before, Brendan, Chris & Chris Elley wrote a bunch of songs that now form the core of the new band's set. The three of them, with a succession of temporary drummers, had a band called 'Teenage Romance'.

Chris S. - "That was a frustrating twelve months when we had the set all written, but no permanent band to perform it."

Meanwhile, Brendan's brother, Dez, & Sid had been working in various local bands. They came together as a rhythm section & spent some time looking for others to form a band. The two brothers therefore decided to join forces & form the one band.

They've so far done just two gigs, both at The Palm Cove, Bradford. The first (21st Dec) was 5th on the bill at The Negatives' Xmas Party which was just done as a try-out. "We wanted a trial-by-fire. We gatecrashed it, really. The sound was great on stage, but apparently a jumbled mess off stage. We'd not used p.a. equipment like that before & had no idea how loud to set everything." The second was the Jab-Jab Xmas Party (3 days later). "Their p.a. guy was very helpful. We got a much better sound."

They're making a demo-tape in Feb. & are hopeful of some success as they already have some contacts with record companies.

Disappointingly, they've had to turn down a chance to play support to Ginger Baker's Energy at Fforde Grene in Leeds - their guitarist, Chris, having to be down south on the day of the gig. However, they're currently lining up a set of several local gigs for the coming months.

Contact: Brendan or Dez on B'ford 21361 or Chris on B'ford 575777.

AGONY COLUMN

Voc.+Lyrics = Malcolm Raeburn
Gtr.+Tunes = Ian Heywood
Dms. = Jon Rust
Bass = Brian Rawson

Malcolm, Ian & Jon first met up years ago at Leeds University. All 3 went on to work in fringe theatre.

By early '78, Malcolm had started writing lyrics & mailing them to Ian for him to work on music for them. They were both getting pissed off with theatre & so decided to form a band. Some of those early numbers still crop up in their current stage set. These include: *Mister Sister*, *Losing My Lust*, *Urban Refugee*, *Glasgow* & *Home Movies*.

Brian, their third bassist, has just accepted a job as sound engineer for The Roy Sundholm Band (in which his brother is bassist). This means that he's leaving the band. ("It's money, really. We still have real problems earning money from Agony Column & the Sundholm job'll pay well - that band's doing a lot of work, including a big U.S. tour"). They'll be auditioning for bassists from mid-January onwards, but may still be without one by the time this comes out. Interested locals might try ringing one of the contact nos. at the end of this profile.

The band's first single came out on Tyger Records in Spring '79 (see reviews section of W.C.R. 3). "There were 2,000 copies pressed & it sold out in about 3 months - mainly due to the John Peel session that we did."

The band has recently signed to Phonogram & have a single out any time now on the independent

~page four~

"Ah Mr. and Mrs. Pokett, how nice to see you again... and this must be the issue your union was blessed with...."

HUSTLER ST. BAND

B'ford 664885 or Leeds 460679.

R.Gtr./L.Voc./Harmonica = Justin Sullivan
B.Gtr./Voc. = Stuart Morrow
Dms. = Phil Tompkins
L.Gtr. = Sean Sullivan (bro)
Elec. Pno/Voc. = Martin Wilkes.

The band takes its name from Hustler Street - just up the road from Wool City Rocker's Undercliffe H.Q.

Justin & Stuart formed the nucleus of the band about 2 years ago. Since then, they've only done about ½-doz. gigs under a variety of names (Misfits, New Misfits, Fitmis, etc.) with different line-ups each time - though they've had the same drummer on all the gigs. Past members have included Stuart's brother-in-law, Mick Rennard, & Tricia Kusack (both now with Press Release).

The present line-up was put together in the weeks before their gig at The Vaults Bar on Jan. 9th. & it's now a permanent one - i.e the band's name & line-up will be constant, at least for forthcoming gigs. They're booked back into The Vaults, & are planning gigs at other local venues including Queens Hall

subsidiary label - *Back Door*. The A-side will be a number called *Love In The Head*.

"We did our 4th demo tape at Smile Studio in Manchester (a 16-track that's cheap & very good - we'd highly recommend it to any other band). There were just 2 numbers on this demo - of which one was a version of the new single. That's what persuaded Phonogram to sign us. Stuart Coxhead, who's in charge of Phonogram in Leeds, was the one who pushed us in London & got us the deal. We've rerecorded the title-track of the single at Parkgate Studio (a 24-track in Battle, near Hastings). We had Chris Hughes & Hugh Jones on production - they are members of a bunch of session men & producers known collectively as *The Blitz Brothers*."

The deal with Phonogram is good in itself, but not great as deals go. They only got £300 in cash & commitment to the one single only, with an option on a second single & an album - though these depend on the success of the forthcoming single.

"So if you want to hear an album, buy the single is the message."

"A lot depends on this single. We feel it's good, better by far than the first single - but we'll need to get playlisted on radio - airplay's *the* most important factor."

"This single's much more commercial & classy than the first."

"We're no longer a new wave band (which is how we started out). We've now got a style that's very much our own."

The band are still without an agency deal & so don't find it that easy getting work - a problem that's compounded at the moment by the current absence of a bass-player.

Contact: Ring either

~ page five ~

& The Palm Cove.

The band bring together a whole spectrum of influences, with all the members coming from very different musical roots. "The basic ground-rule is that we write songs - i.e. verse/chorus/middle-8 with a strong melody-line, & with a good deal of instrumental interplay."

All the band's songs are their own - except for a reggae version of the Pink Panther Theme (!) which they might include in their stage set one of these days.

"Our lyrics tend to be based on themes of dramatised city life - from an emotional rather than political standpoint."

Jools Denby is the band's manager & occasional co-lyricist.

<u>Contact</u>: Jools on B'ford 583972 or Stuart on B'ford 601504.

EXCEL

R.Gtr.+Voc. = Alan Walsh
L.Gtr.+Kbds.+Voc.= Richard Taylor
B.Gtr.+Voc. = Stephen Smith
Dms.+Perc.+Voc. = Stephen Gawtry

A kbd-player, the two Stephens plus a guitarist formed Excel in Sept.'76 as a Cleckheaton school group (they were all in the same class). The played mainly in clubs & w.m.c.'s. In March '78, Alan replaced the original guitarist. In Nov. '78, Richard replaced the original keyboards player. They've been together since then - recording their first E.P. the following Jan. (see review in W.C.R. No1). "We released it on our own label, having raised the money through gigs. We were travelling as far south as The Midlands, as far north as Tyneside - though most of the time it was around Yorkshire."

Steven G.: "It started off as a hobby - it was fun in those days & still is... most of the time." Richard: "Yes, when we don't see each other, then it's fun".

In Aug.'79 they signed to Polydor (both C.B.S. & Polydor wanted to sign the band, so they put the two offers into the hands of a solicitor who handled the negotiations for them) The following month they moved down to London which is where they are now based.

On Feb. 8th their first single on Polydor will be released (see pre-release review elsewhere in this issue). When I interviewed the band a couple of days before Xmas, they'd just finished recording it. "We did the final mix last Wednesday. Alan Sizer, the A. & R. boss at Polydor, is very keen on it. We're particularly pleased with the job done on production by Dave Moore who is really good."

They've recently been playing London venues like The Music Machine, The Hope & Anchor, Dingwalls & The Greyhound. They've done a lot of photo sessions & some demo gigs for T.V. & radio programmers that's got them several slots on kids' T.V. shows, etc. Around late Jan./early Feb., they've live tapes going out on both Pennine Radio & Radio Leeds.

A recent 'tour' of Scotland turned out to be a disaster - one disco, two small village halls & a small w.m.c. They lost money & went down badly. "They were the wrong venues for us. It's a new agency deal for us - but we'll sort that out. We want to play colleges, universities & London rock venues. We can't afford to lose money - especially when it's on bad gigs."

"People think we've got it made, but there are still a whole lot of problems for us to sort out."

The band is still very young (2 Stephens are 19, the other two are 17 & 16) which still gives them hassles. "I have to carry my passport round with me to prove I'm 19."

"Looking young means that some audiences think that we'll be rubbish before they've even given us a chance to play."

"Last March/April, we had a residency at the American Legion Club in Frankfurt, Germany. We had trouble getting there because of our ages. Alan had to get special leave from school, but once we got there, it was the best time we've ever had. Hard work. We had to do 4 sets of 45 minutes each every night (!!) - but, once we got to know the regulars, it was just great. We'd gig all evening & then there'd be party's right through the night. We'd perform a lot of cover versions - songs by Lynard Skynard, Elvis Costello, The Beatles, The Jam, The Kinks, Dylan, We could do anything that we wanted. The audience was made up of Germans & Americans - some of them really weird - drunks, transvestites, crazies, etc. The more we played up to them, the more they liked us. We'd wear drag, smash thing, do anything that occurred to us. We'd go back, but commitments here in U.K. & an argument with the agents who got us the residency have combined to rule it out."

Contact: Ring the band on 01-985-9192.

SCUM

Dms.+ Voc. = Stan
Voice+Kazoo+ other noises = Scum Lennon
Pno.+ Elec.organ + Voc. = Ned Lud

They got together in Oct.'78 with no intention of doing gigs. They just wanted to make music for their own amusement. They've done about 20 home cassettes (one reviewed elsewhere in this issue). "There are no rehearsals (we only get worse if we rehearse the songs!), we just do a cassette when we feel like it - with the minimum of pre-planning. That's why almost all our songs are short & rather rough. We write the basics & just let the song work itself out from there."

They're all still at school. Scum's in the 6th at Belle Vue, the other two are 5th formers at Fulneck.

"The music's sparse, but it's quite fast & could be danceable."

"We sound a bit like Joy Division - at least with our kbd./ drum rhythms."

Since this interview, the band have added a fourth member on guitar & have done their first real gig - a 10-minute spot supporting Cameras In Cars at Queens Hall, B'ford in early Jan.

"It started just for fun - an alternative to homework or going to the football - but now we're getting interested in the idea of doing some gigs."

Contact: Milan on B'ford 44462.

ANOTHER WRIST ACTION

Gtr./Voc. = Mark Sullivan
Voc./Gtr. = Nick Patterson
+ Drummer & Bassist.

The band began life in Nov.'77 as *Grammar School Puffs*. Nick was co-songwriter at first, but became lead vocalist in March '79.

Dave Hoyle, the original drummer, left in Feb'79 "due to mutual lack of interest" & was soon replaced by John Dickinson. Till then, the band had been rehearsing & only playing the odd gig at Youth Clubs &

"Hello, to the Scum baby."

such venues, but they now began to work on a more serious level. The name change (to A.W.A.) came in the Feb. — "most people just know us as Wrist Action, I don't know why the 'Another' keeps getting missed out."

"It was around then — about a year ago — that we began writing the songs that are in our current set." The lyrics are Nick's, with music by Mark (+ contributions from the rest of the group).

Arguments over gig commitments versus work lead to drummer John's departure in Aug. '79. There followed a succession of stand-in drummers (including the ubiquitous Chris Groves of Radio 5). Most recent drummer has been Martin Hickey, a school friend.

Nick & Mark are currently the only permanent group members (though they always have been the nucleus of the group) & both are now living in Manchester, though they regularly return to Bradford.

With Dave Wilcox now departed as The Negatives' vocalist (he's forming his own band at the moment), there were plans for Nick & Mark to join up with the 3 remaining Negatives to form a new band. These plans have fallen through, so you can expect to see further incarnations of A.W.A. in the future.

They didn't give me a contact number, but I'll try to get hold of one — if so it'll go in the next issue.

BEATS WORKING

Pno./Organ/Voc.= Richard Hall
Bass = Graham Hooper
Dms.= Chris Lumb
Gtr./Voc.= Gareth Harwood

Richard & Gareth, together with a bassist & drummer former the original Beats Working in Oct. '78 as a new wave band — "playing a mixture of punk & rock". They played 10 gigs around The North before splitting up in April '79. The week after that, they played as a duo supporting Agony Column at Queens Hall, B'ford (a R.A.R. gig).

The current line-up came together in June/July '79, playing their debut gig (as support to The Scene) at The Downtown Club in Keighley. "That was our first 'new mod' gig. After that, we did several others with The Scene. It was o.k., but we're not a mod band. We were going down well enough with the majority of them but the violence & narrow attitudes of a few of them really depressed us. The fights at the gig at The Palm Cove (23rd Dec. — with The Scene & The Mods) showed up that minority for us. That sort of thing is a shame for everyone involved in that movement.

At the moment, they're rehearsing — sharpening up their set & adding half a dozen new numbers with which they're pleased. And they're lining up a few local gigs (they're on at The Royal Standard just before this issue's out — on Sat. 26th Jan.).

All the band's songs are written by Richard & Gareth & then arranged by the group as a whole. "We want to perform new rock songs with good melodies — something that's just beginning to work out for us, though we've still got a lot to do. We'd hope to come up eventually with the sort of fresh, commercial sound on the lines of Joe Jackson & his ilk".

I asked them what they felt were the main problems facing local bands. They came up with four:— ① Rehearsal space & the price of it when they do get it (eg. £8 a night at Coda — which quickly mounts up for a struggling group. ② Gigs are hard to get. ③ It's difficult to build up a strong reliable following — "It's a vicious circle in that you can't get the gigs without a following but you only get the fans through gigs." ④ They need money to get better equipment. "What would really help would be a few pub landlords who were more willing to risk booking local bands on a regular basis."
Contact: Gareth on B'ford 390085 or Richard on B'ford 638141.

SHAFTDRIVE SCORE MANAGEMENT DEAL

Heavy-metal rockers Shaftdrive (profiled in W.C.R. No.1) have signed a 5-year management deal with Leeds businessman Alan Brown. The former manager of Jeddediah Strutt, Brown was apparently on the lookout for a new band to run & had Shaftdrive recommended to him by Bradford College Students Union President Paul Moyhan. The contract was then inked without the manager having heard the band play or sing a note!

Brown told Shaftdrive:- "I don't care what you play as long as it's marketable & I can make money from it." - & then invested £200 in studio time at September Sound, Hudds., where they cut four tracks (Trees, Solitary, No Return, When I've Got You). Brown intends using the demo for bookings & sending round record companies - though he has said he will only deal with major labels. He is also lining up a publicity agency for the band & has secured late January gigs in Halifax, Middlesborough & Huddersfield, which will be their first gigs outside Bradford.

For a band as much in the doldrums as Shaftdrive were - internal friction & no gigs - the deal with Brown is a miracle of mammoth proportions. He is obviously a high-risk gambler & will use any & every means to ensure success. (Already he has forbidden the band to drugs or alcohol while on stage, to ensure that they are 'together'!). Shaftdrive have the potential that might just fulfill Brown's expectations, but whether their set of bumptious egos can cope with such a pressured route may be another matter. The band are currently writing new material & auditioning for a new vocalist.

~ Keith E. Rice

HEAVY METAL - GETTING BIGGER BY THE DECIBEL

At the present time heavy metal music is proving very popular & fans are flocking to gigs all over the country as, once again, new heavy metal bands appear on the scene.

When punk rock (a.k.a. New Wave) came along, record companies seemed to favour signing up safety-pins instead of guitarists & heavy metal music went into a slump. Sure, all the old favourites were still around (somewhere!) but new heavy metal bands appearing on the circuit seemed to be few & far between. But when punk died, or at least became terminally ill, heavy metal made a comeback. Personally, I thank (although some of you may blame) Motorhead for this. They have taken music back to its roots - goodtime very loud rock music. No self-indulgent boring solos from the musicians, but a rocking, driving powerhouse of a show, during which the band & the audience become as one, & the excitement that is generated is unbelievably powerful & frenzied. If Motorhead started the revival, then Def Leppard, Saxon, Samson, U.F.O., etc. have carried it on, taking their shows on the road & filling theatres, halls & clubs once again.

So it is then that long-trying bands are being given contracts whilst new ones such as Def Leppard are also being given the chance. Waiting in the wings we have Angelwitch, Praying Mantis, Iron Maiden, etc. So all you heavy metal musicians who are struggling for recognition & may be thinking of changing to mod or something, stick to playing the music your heart's in, & remember that heavy metal has been going longer than mod or new wave, which proves that the people who buy heavy metal albums & go to the gigs don't suddenly don a suit & narrow tie when 'Quadrophenia' has a showing at the local cinema. Heavy metal lives on. Rock on.

~ F.I. Denning

WEST YORKS. GIG GUIDE...

FEBRUARY 1980 FEBRUARY

-incomplete first half of gigs, etc. All gigs are correct but it's pleased now gigs, at time of going to press - venues are bound to change - some attempt has been made to check the venue to doubt, if in any doubt, if in....

KEEP IT MUSIC LIVE!

Special thanks to Linda Lane for her telephone and specialist knowledge of venues

Compiled and Written Up by Nick Toczek.

N.B. T.B.A. = to be arranged - i.e. there will be bands but they weren't booked when we went to press.

28	FFORDE GRENE, LEEDS = The Flying Saucers (50's R&R)
	VAULTS BAR, B'FORD = Oral Sax
29	VAULTS BAR, B'FORD = Hustler St. Band
	ST. GEORGE'S HALL, B'FORD = The Clash + Violation
30	WHITE LION, HUDDERSFIELD = The Limit
	PEACOCK, YEADON = Dave Lee Sound (50's R&R)
31	LEEDS UNIVERSITY = The Clash (in conjunction with The Fan Club)
	FFORDE GRENE, LEEDS = 2TV
	ST. GEORGE'S HALL, B'FORD = Wishbone Ash
1	QUEEN'S HALL, B'FORD = Rufaro (raw Afro-rock/Reggae) PRINCEVILLE, B'FORD = One Adult
	HUDDERSFIELD POLYTECH = Exkel + Aftrkraft + Treatment (all local bands) ROYAL STANDARD, B'FORD = Mirror Boys
	FFORDE GRENE, LEEDS = Cliches + The Numbers PALM COVE, B'FORD = T.B.A.
2	LEEDS UNIVERSITY = Robin Trower FFORDE GRENE, LEEDS = Downwatcher + Shy Tots
	B'FORD UNIVERSITY = Gang of Four + Mekons DEVONSHIRE HOTEL, SKIPTON = The Rockets
	WHITE LION, HUDDERSFIELD = Geneva HADDON HALL, LEEDS = Side Effect PALM COVE B'FORD = TBA
3	VAULTS BAR, B'FORD = Shake Appeal FAN CLUB, LEEDS = The Revillos (4.30 & eve. shows)
	PRINCEVILLE, B'FORD (lunch) = Shake Appeal FFORDE GRENE, LEEDS = Bruce Woolly & The Camera Club
	WHITE LION, HUDDS. = The Dots COACHHOUSE, HUDDERSFIELD = The Chords
4	VAULTS BAR, B'FORD = Oral Sax
	FFORDE GRENE, LEEDS = Ronnie Lane's Band
5	VAULTS BAR, B'FORD = Press Release
	ROSE & CROWN, ILKLEY = Shake Appeal
6	LEEDS UNIVERSITY = Spiro Gyra + The Pretenders (Rock Goes To College gig)
	B'FORD UNIVERSITY = Heritage PEACOCK, YEADON = Rockin' Rebels (50's R&R)
	WHITE LION, HUDDS. = Heritage
7	PRINCEVILLE, B'FORD = Slender Thread FAN CLUB, LEEDS = Doll by Doll + Dance Chapter
	B'FORD UNIVERSITY = Dave Edmunds, Rockpile (with Nick Lowe)
	FFORDE GRENE, LEEDS = Splodgenessabounds + The Sex Beatles + The Lone Groover's Band
8	HUDDERSFIELD POLYTECH = Iron Maiden + Praying Mantis ROYAL STANDARD = T.B.A. (3 yo Sun) B'FORD
	FFORDE GRENE, LEEDS = Japanese Toy CLEOPATRA'S, HUDDS = Regulars
	PALM COVE, B'FORD = T.B.A. WHITE LION, HUDDS. = Glossy Mags
9	HUDDERSFIELD POLYTECH = Dexy's Midnight Runners HADDON HALL, LEEDS = Red Eye
	FFORDE GRENE, LEEDS = Dave Taylor & The Roccos (50's R&R) PALM COVE, B'FORD = T.B.A.
	ST. GEORGE'S, B'FORD = Uriah Heep
10	VAULTS BAR, B'FORD = Stress FFORDE GRENE, LEEDS = The Heat (from USA) + Micky Dorre
	PRINCEVILLE, B'FORD = J.G. Spoils (lunch) COACHHOUSE, HUDDS = The Switch FAN CLUB, LEEDS = Wreckless Eric (4.30 + eve)
	WHITE LION, HUDDS. = Forst HADDON HALL, LEEDS = The Switch FAN CLUB, LEEDS = Wreckless Eric (4.30 + eve)
11	VAULTS BAR, B'FORD = Oral Sax
	FFORDE GRENE, LEEDS = Tonny Storm & Memphis (50's R&R)
12	VAULTS BAR, B'FORD = Jedediah Strutt
	ROSE & CROWN, ILKLEY = Press Release
13	WHITE LION, HUDDS. = Evasive Action
	PEACOCK, YEADON = 6.5 Special (50's R&R)
14	QUEENS HALL, B'FORD = Radiation (St. Valentines Rag Week Fancy Dress Ball!!)
	PRINCEVILLE, B'FORD = Shadowfax LEEDS POLYTECH = reggae band
	FAN CLUB, LEEDS = Knox (ex-Vibrators) + Defectors

Vaults Bar, Vaults Horton (St. Horton, Wash for Vaults) B'ford (tel. 392713) (day: 392713) (eve: Fan Club at Brannigan's, 174 Briggate, Leeds. (tel. 446985).

Peacock Hotel, Harrogate Rd., Yeadon, Leeds. (tel. Rawdon 502416).

Fforde Grene, Roundhay Rd., Leeds 8. (tel. 490984).

Coachhouse, King St., Huddersfield, 78-81 Hudders.

Haddon Hall Hotel, Bankfield Rd., Leeds 4. (tel. 751115).

Royal Standard, Manningham Lane, Bradford. (tel. 27892).

Leeds University, Students Union, University Rd., Leeds 2. (tel. 39071).

White Lion, Cross Church St., Huddersfield. (tel. 22407).

Palm Cove Rd., Holdings, Bradford. (tel. 499845).

Leeds Polytechnic, Students Union, Calverley St., Leeds 1. (tel. 30171).

Devonshire Hotel, Newmarket St., Skipton. (tel. 2078).

Princeville W.M.C., Princeville, Bradford 7. (tel. 78845).

Bradford Uni. Students Hall, Queens Rd. Bradford 7. (tel. 392112).

Huddersfield Polytechnic. Students Union, Gt Hall, Queensgate, Huddersfield. (tel. 38156).

Bradford University, Students' Union, Bradford 7. (tel. 34135).

Rose & Crown, Church St., Ilkley. (tel. 607260).

That's it. No future issues. That is my last one. Thanks for staying all. Thanks to all. He also the phone, but they aren't here, but the phone.

Rogues' Gallery

Boredom & Telib of B'ford's Total Confusion photo'd at Downtown Club, Keighley in Oct. '79 (club's now closed).

EXCEL

Gang of Four (Leeds) defending Pink Floyd's latest waxing.

...so send us your band's photo.

Handwritten note (top left):
...has gig time (+ex-direction) but them next time. Leeds are ex-directory get them and Hell, Leeds are not contact Heaven & Hell, Leeds help me contact — can anyone help? This double page has them? This hard work & tough been really hard work — so hope on my phone bill — so hope it's useful to you. If you're in Keighley, Pudsey, etc. in know what's going on in your town! Nick Toczek 4 p.m. sat 26th Jan '80

Speech bubble: PALM COVE, B'FORD = Ulterior Motives + The Scene + Japanese Soldiers

SAT	16	LEEDS UNIVERSITY = In The 80s Festival with The Beat + The Selecter + The Ruts / HUDDERSFIELD POLYTECH. = T.B.A. WHITE LION, HUDDS. = The Dots PALM COVE, B'FORD = T.B.A. / FFORDE GRENE, LEEDS = Buffalo HADDON HALL, LEEDS = Shake Appeal
SUN	17	FFORDE GRENE, LEEDS = Charlie Dore's Back Pocket COACHHOUSE, HUDDS. = Beggar / PRINCEVILLE, B'FORD (lunch) = Rocker VAULTS BAR, B'FORD = The Negatives / WHITE LION, HUDDS. = The Dots FAN CLUB, LEEDS = T.B.A. HADDON HALL, LEEDS = T.B.A.
MON	18	VAULTS BAR, B'FORD = Oral Sax / FFORDE GRENE, LEEDS = Sunsets
TUE	19	VAULTS BAR, B'FORD = Barnsley Bulldozers / ROSE & CROWN, ILKLEY = The Vye
WED	20	B'FORD UNIVERSITY = Gary Glitter / WHITE LION, HUDDS. = Torpedoes / PEACOCK, YEADON = Hotfoot Gale ('50s R&R)
THU	21	PRINCEVILLE, B'FORD = Alex Johnson Band / FFORDE GRENE, LEEDS = T.B.A. / FAN CLUB, LEEDS = Orchestral Manouevres In The Dark + The Xpelaires
FRI	22	QUEENS HALL, B'FORD = The Cliënts PALM COVE, B'FORD = T.B.A. / HUDDERSFIELD POLYTECH. = The Vapours (promoted by Hudds. Tech. S.U.) / LEEDS UNIVERSITY = Tom Petty & The Heartbreakers FFORDE GRENE, LEEDS = T.B.A.
SAT	23	BRADFORD UNIVERSITY = Brum Beat Tour featuring The Quads + Gangsters + Thrillers / WHITE LION, HUDDS. = Guest PALM COVE, B'FORD = T.B.A. / HADDON HALL, LEEDS = Luigi And Da Boys FFORDE GRENE, LEEDS = T.B.A.
SUN	24	FAN CLUB, LEEDS = Throbbing Gristle + Monty Cazzaza + Clockdva HADDON HALL, LEEDS = The Vye / GOOD MOOD, HALIFAX = Electrofumes VAULTS BAR, B'FORD = Rhino COACHHOUSE, HUDDS. = T.B.A. (mods) / FFORDE GRENE, LEEDS = Def Leppard WHITE LION, HUDDS. = Talisman PRINCEVILLE, B'FORD (lunch) = Mask
MON	25	VAULTS BAR, B'FORD = Oral Sax / FFORDE GRENE, LEEDS = Bop Street Gang BINGLEY ARTS CENTRE = Dawnwatcher + 633 Squadron
TUE	26	VAULTS BAR, B'FORD = Dirty But Nite / ROSE & CROWN, ILKLEY = Chainsaw
WED	27	VAULTS BAR, B'FORD = Aires Enterprises promote a performance poetry event (see p.17) / B'FORD UNIVERSITY = Squeeze PEACOCK, YEADON = Let The Good Times Roll ('50s R&R) / WHITE LION, HUDDS. = Treatment
THU	28	PRINCEVILLE, B'FORD = White Spirit / FAN CLUB, LEEDS = Cockney Rejects + support band(s) / FFORDE GRENE, LEEDS = T.B.A.
FRI	29	HUDDERSFIELD POLYTECH. = Charlie Dore's Back Pocket / FFORDE GRENE, LEEDS = T.B.A. PALM COVE, B'FORD = T.B.A.
SAT	1	PALM COVE, B'FORD = T.B.A. / B'FORD UNIVERSITY = The Jags HADDON HALL, LEEDS = T.B.A. / WHITE LION, HUDDS. = Stallion
SUN	2	LEEDS UNIVERSITY = The Pretenders WHITE LION, HUDDS. = The Dots / VAULTS BAR, B'FORD = Ulterior Motives COACHHOUSE, HUDDS. = T.B.A. (mods) / PRINCEVILLE, B'FORD (lunch) = Spinoes HADDON HALL, LEEDS = Side Effect
MON	3	VAULTS BAR, B'FORD = Oral Sax
TUE	4	VAULTS BAR, B'FORD = Airkraft / ROSE & CROWN, ILKLEY = Metal Fatigue
WED	5	B'FORD UNIVERSITY = Ian Gomm Band / WHITE LION, HUDDS. = House of Om / LEEDS POLYTECH. = City Limits
THU	6	PRINCEVILLE, B'FORD = Anniversary
FRI	7	PALM COVE, B'FORD = T.B.A.
SAT	8	PALM COVE, B'FORD = T.B.A. / WHITE LION, HUDDS. = Dawnwatcher
SUN	9	VAULTS BAR, B'FORD = Shadowfax ROYAL STANDARD, B'FORD = Psychedelic Furs / PRINCEVILLE, B'FORD (lunch) = Dawnwatcher T.B.A. = Side Effect / FAN CLUB, LEEDS = The Cramps + The Fall

Excel (B'ford)

Deadringer (Leeds/B'ford)

Ulterior Motives (B'ford) minus drums at The Vaults Bar.

...photo taken by Steve Ripley...

~ page eleven ~

Rockborough Records doing album of Northern bands - will include some from Leeds/B'ford/Huddersfield...

Brian Rushgrove's Rock'n'Roll Column
BE AN EXHIBITIONIST...

Captain's Log: star date 1990. Place: The Arndale Centre, Bradford. A massive exhibition on the music scene 1950s-1980s, ranging from Presley to punk and beyond, and covering the fashion scene - teddy boy to teeny bopper. Who knows? This might happen.

Meanwhile, back to reality. Those who are into the 1950s music will - in August - be able to enjoy their third annual display in the Arndale Centre.

Who gave a second thought, some three years ago, to the fact that a few teddy boys and rock fans alike from the Bradford area had foreseen a trend towards preserving this lost era and had set out to recreate the atmosphere by way of an exhibition?

Once you have the necessary material (juke-boxes, records, press cuttings, books, etc.) and a way of presenting them (e.g easels), not to mention transport (too much), then you're half way there. Then, of course, there is the small problem of venues. Did you know that the Arndale Centre, the Odeon & Central Library foyers, the Cartwright Hall and the window of H.M.V. Record Shop all cost nowt (subject to management approval)?

By the end of 1980, we will be into our twelfth display and, with a little help from the press, well into realising the above prediction. So remember, your music needs you! With the aid of myself, Steve Cairns, Teresa Khan, Egghead, Andy and Tony ours will be o.k. - what about yours?

"YOUR MUSIC NEEDS YOU!"

CLASSIFIED ADS.

EKO 12-string gtr. Excellent condition. £45 o.n.o. J. Holt, flat 1, 16 Blenheim Rd., Manningham, B'ford. (Or phone Wakefield 60341 weekdays 9/5 p.m.).

Agony Column P.A. HIRE: 400w. rig = £25 + petrol. 800w. rig = £30 + petrol. Ring B'ford 664885 or Leeds 460679.

Charismatic lead vocalist wanted for up-&-coming Bradford-based rock band with new management deal. Ring Alan on Halifax 53479

Experienced female vocalist seeks band or else musicians to form band. Post-punk in style own songs. Leave message for Anne on Brighouse 714 47.

Transport. Bands or light removals. Very reasonable rates. Reliable. Ring Malc. Douglas on B'ford 44428.

ROLAND 77 drum machine/rhythm unit for sale. Extremely versatile. As new. With foot-switch, leads etc. £250.00 o.n.o. Ring Nick on B'ford 21867.

Driver/roadie. Bands + removals 35 cwt van. Low rates. Ring Ken Drake on B'ford 683195.

Simms-Watt echo unit + tapes + assorted leads. £50 o.n.o. Ring Nick on B'ford 21867.

BACK ISSUES of Wool City Rocker Nos. 1 & 2 still available - 45p each (inc. 15p post & packing) from address in front of magazine, or 30p each direct from Nick Toczek if you see him when he's out & about selling this issue.

These ads are free & will be free in issue 4 (except to business concerns). After that, there'll be a nominal charge.

The Bradford Rock'n'Roll Exhibition was formed in December 1977 during the 'David Oxtoby's Rockers' exhibition of paintings at The Cartwright Hall. This was done with the help of two of the hall's administrating officers, namely Tony Rae and Howard Smith.

TRAMPUS REBORN!

Trampus, Bradford's purveyors of skilled & melodic hard rock, will be gigging again in late Jan. after a 4½ month gap during which they've been presumed dead & buried. However, with Chris Bartlett (bass gtr.) now in One Adult, Pete Emmons (dms.) in Shaftdrive & Gary Taylor (ld. gtr.) simply a.w.o.l., it'll be a very different band. Only Dereck Moulson (voc./gtr.) remains from the old line-up. He's recruited Phil Mitchell (bass) & Mick Wake (dms.) - both ex-Smokestack - plus Dave Lyons (ld. gtr.). Dereck has insisted on the old name because it was established with a good reputation & because the sound is much the same - although a lot of the material will be new, they're retaining a heavy smattering of old favourites like 'Just Leaving On The Tide'.

An all-too-brief sit-in on them rehearsing at Queen's Hall revealed that the new Trampus may turn out to be a lot 'heavier' than the old band - though there is still that intelligence & melodic flare to their music. Dereck's vocals are just the same, of course, but he's using the flanger more in his rhythm playing & is backed by a sheer wall of sound. Phil may not be as spectacular in his basswork as his predecessor, but he provides a driving foundation & combines perfectly with his longtime drummer. And then there is Dave Lyons!

Jimi Hendrix was the master of overstatement & young Dave has his guitar hero off to a tee. While the rest of the band are setting up their gear & tuning up, Dave plays snatches of 'Hey Joe' & succeeds in all the Hendrix distortions wonderfully; then he throws his guitar on the floor & strums it with his boot! He restrains himself a little when the band gets down to serious practice, but his frequent use of feedback gets a little out of control at time. How he'll handle Trampus' more subtle moments remains to be seen. Certainly, as Mick says: "It's more adventurous than the old band."

The return of Trampus will be *interesting* - & almost certainly very good & enjoyable. Watch out for them!

~ Keith E. Rice

THE KIDS ARE ALRIGHT...

New mod music isn't just '60s music. It stems from a *part* of the '60s - possibly one part that will stand up & SHOUT OUT more, but still only a part of a decade of free love, high living & death.

In '65, mods follow The Who & The Small Faces, but later many moved on to what was to become the 'Northern Soul' of the late '60s & the '70s. Otis Redding & Wilson Pickett led Motown & Tamla stars to the kids on scooters.

The mods of the '60s went to all-night parties. This in itself is no big thing, but to keep the pace, they popped pills - blues, dex & vallium & many paid the price for it.

In '78, after 3 years of new & exciting music from the punks & the new wave bands, a new scene arrived from London. Mods were back. By '79 they were firmly rooted as a new movement for the '80s.

Locally, mods really began around '77-'78 with people following The Jam & their ilk, but soon local bands started forming. The first Bradford mod band was The Drive who led the field until they split up early in '79. Others followed :- The Scene (Bradford), The Killermeters (Huddersfield), Handsome Jack & The Casualties (Huddersfield), Beats Working (Bradford/Leeds), Moving Targets (Leeds), Yorkshire Mods (Wakefield), etc. The Killermeters have a single out that's sold quite well since its release in August '79 & The Scene have a single out this month.

Mods - very neat dressers - wear Fred Berry t-shirts, button-down collars, suits with small-collared jackets & the obligatory Parka. Since Quadraphenia came out, a new & more casual style of dress has been seen, with macs similar to that worn in the film by Sting.

The Who now deny being the mods or fashion-setters of '65, but there's no way Pete Townsend can deny cultivating mods now.

During '64 & '65, most local mods, like their London counterparts, had a favourite spot in which to hang out. In Bradford,
....continued on page 17.

Bill Chapman (Shadowfax's manager) + others are forming Bradford-based label: plans to do L.P. of local bands

LIVE REVIEWS

JAPANESE SOLDIERS
at The Vaults Bar, B'ford. Jan 6.

The long-awaited debut of the bizarrely-named Japanese Soldiers was a joy; a sheer joy that meant two encores & a packed audience demanding still more of their light, bright sound.

Yet the Japs were shambollic (never mind the bollics - ed.), somehow seeming to just about stagger through their songs without falling apart. This stems mainly from Mark Manning (vocals/rhythm guitar) whose thick chording predominates in the mix (rather like recent Blondie output), thus partially masking - but not concealing - the tight & powerful rhythm section. Alex McGregor (bass) & John Binns (drums) might not be that obvious in the final sound, but their solid playing provides the necessary support on which Manning can - & does! - lean rather like a drunk on a lamp-post.

Manning is the band's genius, although he may also turn out to be their problem. He writes all their material, & his songs are brilliant. 'Let's Go To The Paki Shop' (complete with its 'Rule Britannia' opening), 'Louise', 'Cholie' & 'Charlie's Girl' are wry, witty pieces of light-weight pop with irresistible hook-lines that just beg to be heard again & again. But, for me, the song of sheer inspiration is 'No Love Songs In Space', a eulogy for astronauts' suppressed sexual urges - "I've got to remember the mission comes first" - that has the same timeless sound of deep-space loneliness as Bowie's 'Space Oddity'. Manning sings all this with a curious kind of passionate unfeeling, which is reflected in his stage act - or total lack of it. He looks & sounds like a man who has just been awoken from deep sleep & hasn't a clue what's going on. So untogether it's charming!

Yet this 'unprofessionalism' is self-destructive when Mark simply doesn't care that his singing is sometimes flat or that his guitar is out of tune on the encore version of 'Cholie', thus ruining a beautiful song.

All bands need some kind of image, & it may be that Manning can extract considerable mileage from his anti-presence; but if it's going to work for him, then he's going to have to work at it. Appearing untogether is one thing; actually being untogether is another. It would also be nice to hear more of Barry Greenwood's fluid lead guitar & to have other endings to songs than the abrupt halt!

Yet, at this stage, no criticisms are too serious because, like any other infant, the band should develop progressively. After giving as good a show as they did for their debut, the light has got to be green-for-go for Japanese Soldiers. They really are a piece of heady delight.

~ Keith E. Rice

SHADOWFAX
at St. George's Hall, B'ford. Dec. 15th

As support to U.F.O., this was to be the largest audience to which any of the band had previously played &, as the time rapidly approached for the band to go on stage, there was definitely a sense of false joviality with the band trying not to show their nervousness. At about 8 o'clock the band trooped on stage & were greeted by rapturous applause from the local crowd. However, it was obvious that the band had overcome their nerves as they went straight into their opener 'More Likely To Motor'. The larger frames of the two Unnuk brothers dominated the stage, with Matti showing himself to be a clear, distinctive singer & a competent guitarist & Alan - who for the most part played lead guitar - established himself as a very

The Scene's 1st single - 'Hey Girl' c/w 'Reach The Top' (reviewed W.C.R. No.1) due out this month...

good musician indeed. The rest of the band - Dave on bass guitar & Ray on drums - showed themselves to have unquestionable musical ability. Deserved applause, & into their second number - 'Spare Wheel Driver' (the B-side of their single) - which is a faster song & well-constructed, showing Shadowfax to be a tight band good enough to play anywhere. This was followed by 'Every Schoolgirl's Dream' which incorporated a nice guitar solo from Alan, although by now it had become evident that the sound would have been immensely improved by a significant increase in volume.

The slower tempo of 'Snowblind' worked well on an audience who'd come to see one of the world's top heavy rock bands. Then the bass-line of Dave Fairfax indicated another well-wrought song in 'Maybe I'm a Fool' which preceded without doubt the best song in the set - 'Really Into You' - the A-side of the single, an excellent & strongly commercial song. And it was greeted, quite rightly, by the best response of the set.

Shadowfax closed their set with 'Close in the Year', the announcement of it being the last song of their set bringing a loud sarcastic cheer from sections of the audience. The song itself became a bit 'hazardous' in the middle but was overshadowed by a nice dual guitar line, though perhaps the song on the whole was too intricate. However, it deserved the applause it received, as did Shadowfax.

The overall impression I got of the group was that, despite the lack of stage presence (there was very little space due to all the gear on stage), they were good musicians. The songs were all well crafted, though one or two tended to drag on a little without any significant (& necessary) changes in style or tempo. The fact that the songs lacked any great weight or depth was due entirely to the lack of volume. However, they produced a highly enjoyable & commendable set, & that's without taking into consideration the fact that they had to adapt to totally foreign conditions, which they did extremely well.

Shadowfax, while grateful for the chance to support U.F.O., had a lot of complaints about the lack of time & trouble from U.F.O's road crew on their behalf. In particular, they'd have liked to have had more than a 3-minute sound-check.

~ Steve Brown

(Steve & W.C.R. would like to thank the manager & staff of St. George's & the promoter for their help & co-operation).

HUSTLER ST. BAND
at The Vaults Bar, B'ford.   Jan. 9th

Considering it was their first ever appearance, The Hustler St. Band are entitled to feel elated, & quietly confident of the future after their performance at The Vaults on Wed. None of the members are new to the game, but there is always a feeling of apprehension when a new band presents itself to the public. Yet they quickly dispersed doubts by launching into a raunchy set, which grabbed you immediately for its originality & intensity.

Their music is impossible to categorise - which is probably a good thing at a time when too many bands limit themselves by adopting a rigid style. There were many different influences; reggae, Springsteen & New Wave shows the diversity.

In songs like 'Teasing Time' (which opened the set), 'Anaesthetic' & 'Beltoine' they demonstrated their ability to rock fast & hard. But in the quieter songs like 'The Cat' -

The Negatives' single - 'Love is not Real' c/w 'Stakeout' - in Guy Watson shops now (reviewed W.C.R. No 1)

You may find this hard to believe but I too was a rebel in my youth. We have resisted the temptation to be influenced by this, however, and we have decided to castrate you and send you to Ulan Bator in a crate......

Ulan Bator is capital of Outer Mongolia or somewhere else...

built around a brilliant bass riff - they were equally entertaining. To play a song with just keyboards & vocals takes courage. This lot did it, & did it well.

There were, of course, a few teething problems. Lack of confidence caused slight hesitancy at times & a loss of direction. The band themselves would admit that the overall sound from an audience point of view could be improved upon. These adjustments can be made in time, with experience & practice.

The lead singer, Justin Sullivan, can let his voice do the work. It's good enough. Around him, he's got a tight band with a high standard of musicianship - but they don't show off, which is important. In 'Morrison's Blues' they sounded impressive, and combined this with amusing lyrics. At other times, though, the lyrics were deadly serious. This contrast of mood within a set is an asset which I hope they keep. T

The band finished their set with 'Animals' which overflowed with a passion which you felt you could almost reach out & touch. I was entertained & I wanted to hear more of it. Judging by their reaction, so did the audience.

~ John Roseveare

LIMELIGHT
at The Princeville, B'ford.   Dec. 20th

They describe themselves as 'an incredible rock outfit from Mansfield'. How true those words ring as they leave an audience virtually awestruck at the end of their set.

Limelight - Glenn Scrimshaw (ld. gtrs, 12-string ld., kbds.), Mike Scrimshaw (double neck 6/4, gtr., kbds., voc.) & Pat Coleman (dms, voc) - are 3 energetic individuals who have become a major attraction on the rock circuit, gaining well-deserved public acclaim.

They appeared on stage at about 9pm to the sort of welcome they've become accustomed to on their visits to The Princeville, starting their set with Rainbow's 'Kill The King', one of several cover versions in their set. Their rendition of this number immediately justified their reputation & it was easy to see why Princeville had been full since 7.30.

They followed this with the first of their own compositions, a marvellous number called 'Don't Look Back' which showed the band to have a strong identity of their own despite the number of cover versions they do - an identity which incorporates the best of bands like 'Led Zeppelin', 'Yes' & especially 'Taste', Glenn's guitar style & sound being very reminiscent of Rory Gallagher's.

Their next item, Led Zeppelin's 'No Quarter,' saw Glenn take to electric piano, leaving Mike to play an inspired guitar line throughout the song whilst playing the basic bass notes on a console with his foot. Once again, the audience showed their approval as Limelight captured the unique sound of Led Zeppelin.

Then came the band's showstopper - their own 'Man of Colours'. With Glenn producing a quite amazing sound from the melotron, the hypnotic vocals of Mike & the outstanding technical ability of Pat on drums, the song received a standing ovation from the knowledgable & appreciative audience.

Two more cover versions were delivered note-perfect - Thin Lizzie's 'Roisin Dubh (Black Rose) a Rock Legend' & Bob Dylan's 'All Along The Watchtower' done along the lines of Jimi Hendrix's version.

They ended - as always - with their own arrangement of 'Sabre Dance', a version delivered with such venom that I have long considered it one of the

Radio 5 (profiled in W.C.R. No 2) are recording 1st single this month - due out March/April....

best numbers to be performed live by any band at any venue. A fitting end to a fine set.

Limelight left the stage to ecstatic applause but soon returned to perform 'Stairway to Heaven' faultlessly. The houselights came up, but the audience refused to leave until, after a few minutes, the lights went down & the band again returned to perform a stunning version of Thin Lizzie's 'Emerald'.

Limelight are, without doubt, the most professional band that comes to Princeville & their undoubted ability & class raise several questions concerning the lack of coverage by the music media & their lack of work on the recording scene. Personally, I think they'll only gain the success they deserve if they phase out some of the cover versions & replace them with their own songs, but however long they continue to perform as they are doing now, they will always prove to be great crowd-pullers.

For the regulars at Princeville, the periodic attendance of Limelight is nothing short of a blessing & these apparently nice guys of the rock circuit enhance greatly the reputation of Princeville as one of the best venues in the North of England.

~ Steve Brown

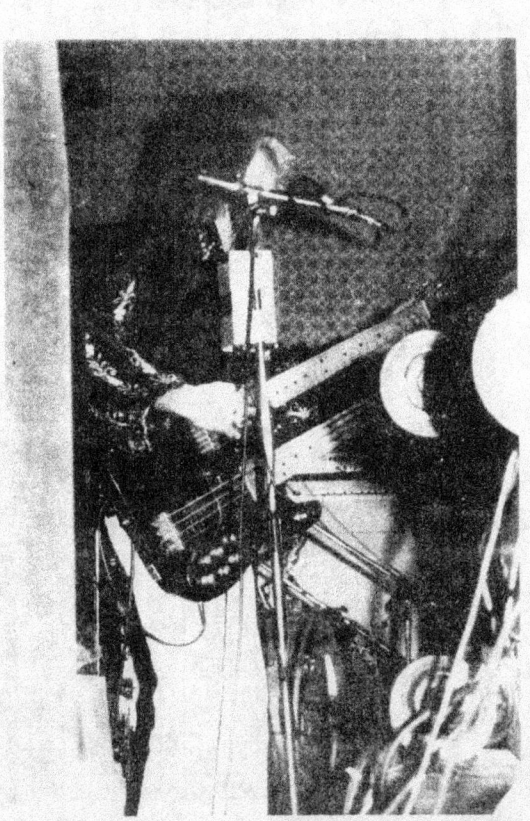

LIMELIGHT'S MIKE SCRIMSHAW PHOTO'D AT PRINCEVILLE

THE KIDS ARE ALRIGHT... continued from page 13.

The Hole in The Wall café (Godwin St.) was a big meeting place. Today, pubs more than cafés provide the liaison points for new mods. The Turf & The Queens are the places to go. Another notable difference between '60s mods & new mods is that they now begin much younger.

Local mod Mick Smith "When I first became a mod in '78, the only places to get the right gear to wear were shops like Oxfam." But now the commercial boys are in, turning what used to be plastic punks into plastic mods - but you can't blame the kids for this, because they naturally want to wear similar gear to that worn by the bands they follow.

~ Dave Green

GIGS

On Wed. 27th Feb at The Vaults Bar, B'ford Aries Enterprises will be presenting an evening of 'Poetry in Motion'. Featured performers (all of whom are locals) are: Wild Willy Beckett - described as 'a performer in the grand style', this'll be his first public poetry gig, for which his plans include costume changes & musical help from members of The Hustler Street Band; Geoffrey Colin Thornton - a surrealist poet & theatrical performer who may be using light/projection show; Barry Jepson, Violation's bassist; Ian Alexander, Bradford character & (it says here) 'an experienced poet' (experienced by whom? - ed.); with other guest appearances expected on the night. Something different at the Vaults - give it a try.

On Feb 14th at Queens Hall, B'ford Radiation are playing for a St. Valentine's gig that kicks off B'ford students' rag week. Entry is only 30p for union card holders, 40p for their guests, but they must be in fancy dress. Plainclothes & you pay double (60p & 80p, respectively). You have been warned!

On Sat. Feb 23rd, B'ford Uni. plays host to an interesting package of Birmingham bands: The Quads, The Gangsters & The Thrillers. Quads had an excellent single out late last year on Big Bear Records that was picked up & much played by someone called John Peel (still a good show).

Afternoon matinees at The Fan Club for those who are too young to sing the booze: Sun 10th = Wreckless Eric, Sun 3rd = Revillos. All shows start 4.30. Nice idea. Park your trikes & prams round the back.

WOOL CITY ROCKWORD No 2
by Ken Turner

Clues Across.
1/ Fine, our bad VAT returns for most loved group. (9,4)
10/ Prime tart hardly like almost every Bradford band member. (4,5)
11/ London borough sounds useful as stage. (5)
12/ Palindrome detector? (5)
13/ Second-hand sight employed intelligence. (4,5)
14/ Briton, surrounded by water with Royal connection. (8)
16/ Miss opportunity by choice. (4,2)
19/ Paralyzed again - or is that a mask? (6)
20/ See 24.
22/ Poison cures sound like relative worships. (9)
24 and 20. "— —'s a — —'s gonna fall." Dylan. (3,2) and (4,4)
25/ What a band used to be. (5)
26/ More wrath moves soil dweller. (9)
27/ What else is fifty nine seconds? (4,2,1,6)

Clues Down.
2/ Is a red ale confusing dogs? (9)
3/ Space, but not inside. (5)
4/ Graham Parkered? Could be true. (8)
5/ Goes round doing crosswords, perhaps! (6)
6/ Local music maker with colour, sauce, etc.. (5,4)
7/ Lack of container out. (3,2)
8/ Arrange to string champ for even contest. (8,5)
9/ Now how do I start?.... (4,4,1,4)
15/ Indent too rashly - becomes bottomless! (2,3,2,2)
17/ Sad nuts to blend. Obvious! (6,3)
18/ Charrington percussion, perhaps. (4,4)
21/ Fit Les out - that's the object. (6)
23/ Toe M.P. stubbed beating rythmically. (5)

Clued in!

All you stalwarts of the crossword came up with three completely correct answers to Rockword 1. The solution is below for your perusal, but a prize goes to SUE PRINCE who was the first out of the hat. Congratulations to you, and commiserations to — M. ROBB of Frizinghall, Bradford 9 — and also to STEPHEN BROWN from Clayton, Bradford 14. Hope you'll keep trying! You'll probably be pleased to hear that we've even received some crosswords from other folks who are interested in filling this spot when yours truly is not contributing. Thanks for your interest — keep them coming in. Just for the record, it was my mother (bless her!) who spotted my not-so-deliberate mistake in Rockword 1. Apparently I spelled Britannia incorrectly, so my thanks to mother, and what were the rest of you looking at? Anyway, there's no prize for the spotting of any mistakes this time! Cheers. Ken

Last Month's Solution.

Booked into J.S.G. Studio this month :- Cheap'N'Nasty (Keighley) + Another Cinema (B'f'd) + Harsh Words (B'f'd)

Researched & written up by Nick Toczek.

PENNINE RADIO

There are 2 breeds of local radio — BBC & ILR. In this region, Radio Leeds is the former, Pennine the latter. The main difference is financing. BBC stations are funded from licence revenue &, as such, have a fairly stable & assured income. But Independent Local Radio revenue is all via advertising.

In charge at Pennine is Geoff Winston. Music Programmer is Nigel Schofield. The Wednesday rock programme (7-9pm, following on from Radio Leeds' excellent 'Metronome' rock programme) is run by Bob Preedy. One of the news team — Tim Waite — also takes a personal interest in local rock (& has recently been doing a documentary series on local bands that bring out singles).

<u>The playlist.</u> This is the rota of records that D.J.'s have to play during general airtime. It's compiled weekly by Nigel Schofield from the 80 (summer) to 160 (winter) singles + tracks from the 60 albums that are sent to the station weekly.

N.S.:- "The choice <u>is</u> highly subjective. However, several factors influence my choice. ① We're an alternative to Radio 1... really, we're Radio 1½. ② As we rely entirely on advertising revenue, we can't play records that'll make listeners switch off. By day, the typical listener is a housewife in her early to mid twenties. In the evening, it's less so & we can play a wider range of music. ③ A survey 6 months back asked our listeners what they did & didn't want to hear on Pennine. They most wanted (a) oldies, (b) chart records, (c) new releases. They didn't want (a) punk, (b) reggae, (c) new wave, (d) heavy rock. Rock 'n' roll had ½ the voters for it, ½ against it."

I.R.L. is dependent on its image, reputation & listenership to earn advertisers — a point on which both Nigel Schofield & Geoff Winston are maybe too emphatic. The result is <u>very</u> 'safe' programming.

N.S.:- "We'd <u>like</u> to give more than the present 2 hours per week over to rock (say up to 6 or 7 hrs. or more) but when we did that a few years ago, it proved to be just not viable." However, we are putting out more rock in our general daytime programming — recent examples: The Police, The Lurkers, Sham 69... & the last release by Orchestral Manouvres in the Dark was a Pennine featured single."

On the other hand, The Jam's recent big hit — 'Eton Rifles' — got no airplay because Nigel felt it sounded too harsh for them to broadcast!

N.S.:- "Local bands we'd tend to judge less severely. If they send us their singles, saying in a covering letter that they're local, then I'll certainly give them special attention over the bulk of incoming records. We playlisted the singles by Shadowfax & Ulterior Motives."

G.W.:- "We're still in the area of experimenting & defining our markets. We've around 850,000 adults (over a million, counting kids) who could be listening. It's hard to please each of them & we have just the one station, where the BBC have 5 (Radios 1-4 + local radio). ILR is still new & still needs to win over listeners. We're certainly far from perfect, but we are genuinely open to ideas — if you've suggestions, try us; though you'll have to appreciate our problems: ① We've all the community to cater for, ② we're always very short of money, ③ we have to be aware of public sensitivity to anything out of the ordinary — & watering down ideas is often the only way to get new things across, at least initially."

> IN NEXT ISSUE — HOW MUSICIANS, ORGANISERS & OTHERS CAN GET ACCESS TO LOCAL RADIO.

FOLK / FOLK-ROCK

Every Saturday, at eight, Pennine Radio brings you two solid hours of folk music.

The show covers the full range of folk... from archive field recordings to the best in folk-rock.

The show has been running for over a year now, & I thought it was time we extended our horizons. As a regular weekly feature in the show, I include a folk gig guide, covering all events that lie within easy reach of Pennine listeners. If you are organising, taking part in, or simply know of any such gigs, then please drop me a line & let me know about it. As an extension of the guide, I'd also like to include reviews of good, or bad gigs: & to prevent myself sounding like a self-opinionated d.j. (ha!), I need <u>your</u> opinions of any appealing or appalling folk acts you've encountered.

Of special interest to any of you who actually perform folk music will be a new feature which began this year. Each week, around a quarter of the music in the show is made up of sessions recorded at Pennine Radio. So far, listeners have heard from Dave O'Flaherty, Swift Nicks, Kathy Sykes, & Pint Pot. More sessions are planned, so if you're a folk performer, get in touch with me, & I'll try to arrange a session.

I look forward to hearing from you & hope you'll listen to me every Saturday.

~ Nigel Schofield
Pennine Radio,
P.O. Box 235, Pennine House,
Forster Sq., B'ford, BD1 5NP.

Stop Press:- GIG:- MEANWOOD ARMS, LEEDS (Fri. Feb. 2nd) = THIS IS IT

JSG music

108B Main Street, Bingley.
Tel. 68843.

ACCESS & BARCLAYCARD WELCOME

Part exchange welcome —
amazing discounts.

<u>MAIN AGENTS FOR</u>
MOOG, GIBSON, LAB SERIES, KORG,
FENDER, RICKENBACKER, MUSIC MAN,
H/H, MARSHALL, PARK, M.M.,
CUSTOM SOUND, AMPEG, OVATION,
YAMAHA, LANEY, CRUMAR, PEAVEY,
ROLAND, CARLSBRO & lots more.
Custom P.A.'s up to 2KW
FULL H/H CONCERT P.A. IN STOCK.

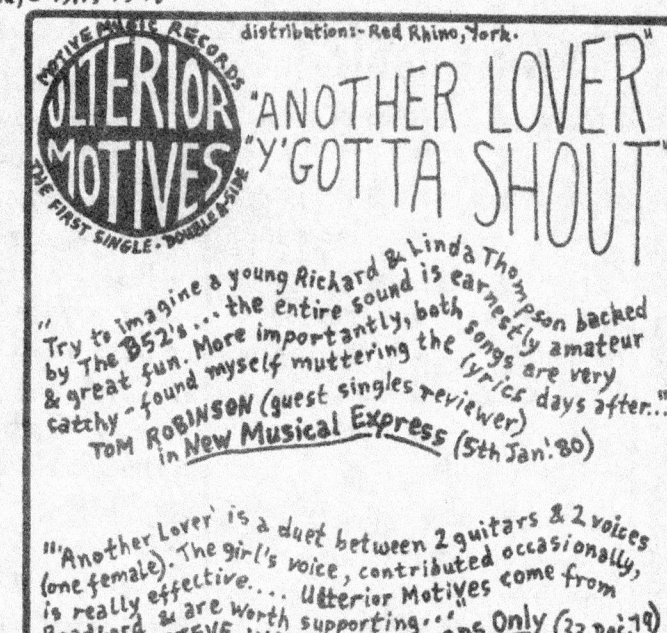

ULTERIOR MOTIVES — "ANOTHER LOVER" "Y' GOTTA SHOUT"
MOTIVE MUSIC RECORDS — distribution:- Red Rhino, York.
THE FIRST SINGLE · DOUBLE A-SIDE

"Try to imagine a young Richard & Linda Thompson backed by The B52's... the entire sound is earnestly amateur & great fun. More importantly, both songs are very catchy — found myself muttering the lyrics days after..."
TOM ROBINSON (guest singles reviewer) in <u>New Musical Express</u> (5th Jan. '80)

"'Another Lover' is a duet between 2 guitars & 2 voices (one female). The girl's voice, contributed occasionally, is really effective.... Ulterior Motives come from Bradford & are worth supporting..."
STEVE WALL in <u>Musicians Only</u> (22 Dec. '79)

Ulterior Motives want a drummer urgently! Ring Nick on B'ford 21867.

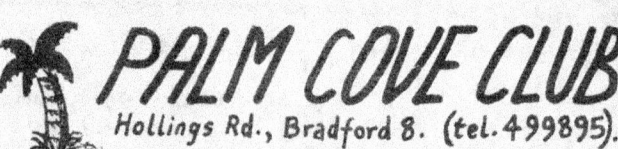

🌴 **PALM COVE CLUB**
Hollings Rd., Bradford 8. (tel. 499895).

Live Entertainment every Fri. & Sat.
(9pm - 1am). February bookings to include:-
Barry Brown (Reggae), One Adult, The Cling-ons, Les Johnson's Hair Restorers, Idle Rich, Shake Appeal, Mirror Boys, Seventeen, Ulterior Motives, Radio 5, Japanese Scene, Dirty Jed's Band, The Soldiers, Cheap 'n' Nasty, Mephisto Waltz

dates being fixed — see guide to week's gigs in Tues. T. & A.

Club also open throughout the week (9pm - midnight).

Late bar nightly * car park at rear * pool tables * Good West Indian food * New wave, mod, reggae jukebox.

RECORD & TAPE REVIEWS

<u>EXCEL</u> (pre-release cassette of single due on Feb. 8th from Polydor) - 'What Went Wrong' c/w 'Junita'. Both songs are credited to Smith/Taylor - in fact, the A-side is by Smith, the B-side by Taylor. Stephen Gawtry (dms):- "It was hard getting the sound we wanted. First time it was very wooden. We mixed down again with overdubs & eventually it came out right, close to a live sound." It's a good commercial A-side, pop-rock & with Steve Smith's vocals sounding very like John Lennon's. The B-side has Richard Taylor on vocals & the song sounds more of a studio-produced number. It will appeal less to the kids who buy the 'A', but is musically more accomplished.

<u>PRESS RELEASE</u> (demo tape done at J.S.G. Studio, B'ford). 'Off The Job' is a good, if a little uninspired, medium-paced rocker. 'This', a slow number with effective use of keyboards & of Tricia Kusack's mature & distinctive voice. This number could take a full studio production - with orchestra & all - to really beef it out. 'Violent Times' is a great song. One of the band's really commercial numbers, it has a fast gtr./dms. background over which Tricia's voice packs a punch. 'Who Killed The Music' is another good raunchy song with effective back-up vocals from the multi-talented Paul Everett (gtr. & kbds.) Niall McDonough's ld. gtr. is also good. 'Reggae Ship' has a nice solid bass-line from Mick Rennard that sets the reggae. Paul's kbd. work here is really inventive - reggae into rock into 50's rock'n'roll, all to the steady reggae backing. Tricia's voice is at it's most stunningly powerful. Overall, this is a good demo. With Chris Parker's clean drumming throughout, it shows off the whole band to good effect.

<u>MUGGINS BLIGHT</u> (single, self-financed, on Look. Released late '79) - 'Mr. Somebody' c/w 'They go up! They go down!' + 'Malcolm Where's The Talcum!' A-side opens with ringing guitars & moves into a fairly appealing, slightly folky rock song that's reminiscent of the late 60's/early 70's. Good of it's kind, but not really likely to cut a dash in 1980. 2nd side is about big tits & body odour. Different lyrics & the first song could make a better A-side. The guitar sound is great. 3rd number's straight folk - like 5penny Piece - & about as contrivedly unfunny.

<u>SCUM</u> (home-made cassette entitled 'Renaissance of the Scum babies). 3 pieces : 'Ants Across The Road', 'In The Vortex' & 'This is My Life. I played this to Kay Russell (she left the mag. just after!) & she said: "Well... it does have a certain abysmal charm!" There is no guitar, just percussion (not dms.) + rough piano + verbals. Minimal. Spontaneous. Anti-melody. Or accompanied performance poems. In early '77 I saw bands like Slits, Prefects & Spizz 77 & they were similar to this... I pass no judgement.

NOWTZ No room left. The ad. at the top of this column is for Diane R. Fairfax + Ian Copley with my love. Column 88 send their best wishes to B'ford: "a great town full of great people." More about this + gig violence + Asian music + Centrepoint co-op, Leeds, etc. in a longer 'Nowtz' in March W.C.R. That's all......

~ page twenty ~

ISSUE #4

March 1980, 1,500 copies printed, 20 pages, A4, glossy cover, improved printing

The cover of this issue says 'Bradford Rock Scene Magazine', an error corrected in the editorial. There are improvements. The front cover, designed by Mo Maklouf, is more stylish, and the whole cover is printed on glossy paper. I found the time to go back to the more professional-looking typed text. Also, the photos, mostly by Lindsay Ineson, and the more sophisticated printing gave the whole mag a more professional feel.

Notes on those profiled and reviewed in this issue.

My interview with Little Brother, the first he'd ever done, details the very start of his career. When Bradford's first and best punk band - The Negatives - split with their remarkable frontman, Dave Wilcox, the other three formed the brilliant but sadly underrated white reggae trio Mysterious Footsteps. Both bands released excellent debut singles.

For my account of interviewing Gary Glitter and my story about meeting Joe Elliott of Def Leppard, you'll have to wait for the publication of a forthcoming book of mine, *My Life Sentences*.

CODA MUSIC
28 Church Bank, Bradford 1. (tel. 307433)

MUSICAL INSTRUMENTS — SALES + HIRE + EXPERT TUITION ON GUITAR, BASS, DRUMS, KEYBOARDS + REPAIRS

REHEARSAL ROOMS + RECORDING & VIDEO STUDIOS + LIVE RECORDINGS FOR BANDS, GROUPS, ARTISTS.

P.A. HIRE (100 – 3,000 watts) + CREW and TRANSPORT.

<u>Agents for</u> :- Marshall, Ludwig, Carlsboro, Ovation, Premier, Olympic, Tama, Ibanez, Pearl, Beyer, A.K.G., Korg, Peavey, Gretsch, Slingerland.

JUST IN !! LARGE STOCKS OF IBANEZ GUITARS FROM £150 – £700.

QUEENS HALL
Live Ents Every Friday

BRADFORD COLLEGE S.U.

The Vaults
JAZZ + POP — ROCK + FOLK
LIVE ENTERTAINMENT 3 or 4 NIGHTS A WEEK
TRADITIONAL HAND-PULLED ALES + BAR SNACKS
ADMISSION STILL ONLY 30p

BRADFORD UNIV-ENTS

5th March
DEXY'S MIDNIGHT RUNNERS
£1.25 Advance
£1.50 Door

NEXT TERM: GIRL | BRAND X | IRON MAIDEN | GEORGE MELLY + MANY MORE

J.S.G. 8-TRACK STUDIO
Bradford

Allan & Heath 16 x 8 mod. III
Tascam 80/8
Revox B77   Space Echo
MXR Stereo Graphics
AKG Shure Electrovoice Calrec Mikes
Resident Producer

RECORD PRESSING

Rates: £7 per hr. + tape
£50 per 8 hr. day + tape

<u>Tel.</u> Bingley 68843 or B'f'd 832187
also B'f'd 491231

the HMV shop

CALLING ALL YOU PUNKS & ALL YOU TEDS
BRADFORD MODS & NATTY DREADS

5 CHEAPSIDE BRADFORD TEL. 28882

LARGEST SELECTION OF RECORDS & TAPES IN TOWN INCLUDING U.S. & EUROPEAN IMPORTS.
OUR TOP 50 ALBUMS at up to £2.00 off.
EXTENSIVE RANGE OF NEW WAVE & REGGAE INCLUDING INDEPENDENT LABELS & IMPORTS. HUNDREDS OF BADGES, PATCHES & POSTERS & A FAST AND EFFICIENT ORDERING SERVICE..... LOOK HERE.

BRADFORD ROCK SCENE MAGAZINE

EDITORIAL

Bouncing back with issue 4 - & getting to look more like a rock mag & less like a fanzine. Big error on the cover that I didn't spot till it'd been printed up - this is now a <u>West Yorkshire Rock Mag</u>, not just Bradford - oops! It'll be put right next time.

Mo's done a lot to make the cover look less formal than my efforts to date. I've tried to make the contents more varied & am gradually getting a feel for the mag's overall identity. The photos - most of which are by Lindsay Ineson - should come out better than last issue as I've gone for a better printing process & her original photos are all very good quality. Hope you like the new typed layout.

Keep the letters, ideas, criticisms, review tapes & records, phone calls from bands, info for the gig guide, etc. coming in.

Ho hum - April next - so who's fooling who...?
Here I go at 45rpm...zoom zoom zoom,
Nick Toczek

EDITION No.4   MARCH '80

EDITOR: NICK TOCZEK

CONTRIBUTORS:-
  Stan Engel
  Mo Maklouf
  Lindsay Ineson
  Ken Turner
  Brian Rushgrove
  Steve Brown
  Keith E Rice
  Nick Ryle

CONTENTS

Cover design by Mo Maklouf of Witch Design	1
Profiles:- Dance Chapter (from Leeds)	4
Dawnwatcher (from Keighley)	4
Coast to Coast (from Bradford)	5
Cameras in Cars (from Bradford)	6
The Quick (from Keighley)	7
Silent Movie (from Bradford)	7
The Oscillators (from Harrogate)	8
The Distributors (from Wakefield)	8
Little Brother (from Bradford)	8
The Motivators (from Leeds)	9
Mini Poster = Rasta Posta by Mo Maklouf	10
Mysterious Footsteps interviewed + Reggae Choice	11
Gary Glitter speaks & gets photo'd	12
The Clash: reviewed in Leeds/photo'd in B'ford	13
Live reviews:- Elvis Costello in Bradford	14
Side Effect in Ilkley	14
Witchfynde/Def Leppard in B'f'd	15
Reviews of tapes & records received	16
Gig round-up (cancelled due to lack of space)	16
Brian Rushgrove's Rock'n'Roll Page	17
Classified ads	17
Ken Turner's Rockword	18
West Yorkshire gig guide	20
+ Lindsay's photos, Stan's cartoons, etc.	

<u>Terms of sale</u>: 30p each direct to the public or 45p each by mail order from the address given below. Bulk orders of 15 or more copies can be placed at discount rate of 20p each.

<u>Advertising rates</u>: Standard 3½" x 3½" box is £20 for first advert. & 10 for subsequent placings. Colour, diff. size, special lay-out, etc. by arrangement. Ring or write to editorial address given below.

COPYRIGHT © 1980 W.C.R. Publications.

5 BEECH TERRACE, UNDERCLIFFE, BRADFORD, BD3 0PY, W. YORKS. (B'f'd 21867)

dance chapter
(from Leeds)

Voice – Cyrus
Gtr/Voc – Steve Hadfield
Bass/Voc – Stu
Dms – Jonnie

The group formed in Sept '78 with one A.P. Jagger on gtr & the ½-dozen gigs that they did before he left in the following March included a support to Gang of 4 at Leeds Poly + gigs at The Fan Club etc.

Stuart Green came in on gtr from May-Nov '79 & they supported The Selecter at The Fan Club & appeared at The Sci-Fi Festival at Queens Hall, Leeds (where P.I.L. were bill-toppers). There were other local gigs & one treck out to Hull – "then we threw him out".

Steve Hadfield joined in Nov '79 to complete the current line-up. And since then they've been rehearsing/talking/phoning/recording. This month will see their 1st live appearance.

They've recently been in Ram Studios – a new 8-track in Leeds. "We got a really good sound – nothing tinny & amateurish like so many new bands seem to get, but a full one. The dms & bass came out well." They recorded just one track – 'Anonymity' – which they've submitted for possible inclusion on a compilation album of northern bands. "The guy putting the LP together likes the track but wants us to shorten it from 6 mins down to 4 or 5 & we're reluctant to do that because we feel that it'll destroy the song's atmosphere."

They describe their music as being strong on rhythm, without any lead breaks or solos & with the emphasis on a whole-band sound throughout. "The starting-point for most of the songs is the emotional feel generated by Cyrus's words. That is, the overall atmosphere of each song tends to hinge on the lyrics." Other instrumentation is then added to this as & where it fits. The final product isn't complex, rather it tends towards the simple & rhythmically repetative, with the lyrics often tending to merge with the music in the final mix. Similarly, they try to avoid letting the gtr adopt a lead role – though the whole thing is very fluid: "We continually question & experiment with what we're doing, & try to avoid writing to any specific formula."

"We'd like to think that people would have an emotional reaction to the songs as well as simply enjoying the music itself." They're experimenting with other instruments & re-working some of their existing songs as well as writing new ones. "Most of all, we want to keep our music minimal & our approach to it flexible."

Contact: Luke or Cyrus on Leeds 659518.

****
****

Dawnwatcher
(from Keighley)

Kbds – Peter Darley
Bass – Ges Smith
Gtr – Craig Richardson
Dms – Peter Kaberry
Voc – Billy Barton

They started gigging in early '77 with the above line-up except for a different kbd-player. After a few gigs, he left & they continued to gig as a 4-piece until mid-'79 when Pete joined them. "That'd been a real headache – we'd wanted a good kbd-player but, until he came along, we'd just not been able to find one – loads of gtrists, but no-one who could play good kbds & who had good enough gear."

As a heavy rock band, they find that the main problem is getting gigs in venues that are big enough to take their 1,000-watt p.a. rig & allow them to get a good sound out of it. "It often involves us in the added expense of going round checking out possible venues ourselves."

Locally, there are really only two regular venues for them – The Princeville in B'ford & Fforde Greene in Leeds. "But we've always gone in for promoting a lot of our own gigs round here. This year, we've done Brighouse Civic Hall (organised jointly with Stallion who're from Brighouse), Bingley Arts Centre (with 633 Squadron) & Hope Bank Grammar School in Keighley."

"We used to play Keighley Leisure Centre which is the biggest & best hall in Keighley but in early '79 the council put a ban on bands going over 85db which is crazy – a good drumkit, unmiked, will register about 130 & even normal crowd applause hits about 120!"

FORTHCOMING SINGLES ON RAM RECORDS (Leeds) include singles by 'The Beans' & 'You' (both from Leeds) & 'The Forst' (Wakefield)

Want to do your own posters, t-shirts, etc. or have them done for you? Cheap! Ring B'f'd Printshop on 22518.

They do a lot of gigs in the N.E. - probably more than they do here in Yorks. "It's really good up there. You get huge crowds turning out - even doing Sun. lunch spots. They're hard to please, but if they like you then they really let you know. If there's a rock club open, then it's always full - & they'll give any band a listen, even if they've never heard of them before. And that's so different from attitudes round here."

They aim at a loud & powerful sound with a lot of bass, with the kbds. serving to fill it out & broaden the scope for the gtrist. However, until recently the kbds had only been fitting into material that they already had before he joined. New material that they're writing takes much fuller advantage of his skills. "The two tracks going onto our forthcoming single are more representative of how the band's now developing."

The single (see reviews) will be out in early March & will be on sale at gigs & in some local musical instrument shops It's a double A-side of 'Spellbound' c/w 'Hall of Mirrors' on their own Dawnwatcher Records label.

"We're hoping to bring out more heavy rock singles on the label. It'd be on the basis of bands paying for the production of it, but we'd aim to be cheap & would give a lot of help with recording, promotion & other aspects. If any bands are interested in the idea they can get in touch with us."

Contact: Billy on Keighley 69131.

DAWNWATCHER
****
****

coast to coast (from Bradford)

Gtr/Voc - Gerry Clark
Bass/Voc - Tony Creed
Kbd/Voc - David Fahy
Dms - Ray Horton

Gerry, the founder-member, originates from Southend - traditionally a hotbed of r-&-b (Feelgoods, etc). As a member of John Potter's Clay, he played all the major London rock venues & the band released an EP on Nighthawk (a subsid. of Faulty Records which is run by Miles Copeland). "The band split up around June last year - just as the EP came out. I don't even have a copy myself, but I've been told that it sold about 5,000 copies. The band was all r-&-b/r-&-r which wasn't the sort of stuff that I was writing so I felt very frustrated & was glad to be out of it. The bass-player & I moved up to Leeds with the aim of forming a new group. He (John Raymond) & I recruited Dave within the first week."

Dave takes up the narrative: "I'm from Cleckheaton & was the original kbd-player with Excel - in fact I formed that band & gave it its name (then spelt X-L). Until I joined this band, I'd been working in a group called Snoots, playing round Leeds/B'ford.

Ray Horton joined in July: "I'm from Warley in The West Midlands & played all round there with a B'ham-based band called Killer."

With John still on bass, & under the name Breakdown, they went to Germany for a month of nightly gigs at The American Legion Club, Frankfurt - "It was shit, but it served to tighten up the band".

Back in England, they had £700-worth of gear nicked & lined up some gigs to recoup the money. (Lesson one:- always insure gear against loss or theft). "John was involved with a woman & didn't want to tour - so we had to sack him."

After a month of auditions, they got John (who's from B'ford & was formerly in the band Al): "Al looked like getting a deal with EMI on the strength of our demos, but egos within the band messed it up & we disbanded. I joined this band early in Feb."

Current plans include

a tour in Germany & an EP which they're going to record in April. For the immediate future, the band's based in B'ford but are lining up gigs wherever possible (including a short weekly residency in B'ham - driving down for each gig). "We'll eventually base the band in whatever area gigs seem to be working out best.

Currently, they're rehearsing 6hrs a day for 4 nights a week - with the gear set up in a disused school.

Gerry & Tony each write songs & the new set consists entirely of their numbers. They describe it as being mostly commercial heavy rock - but not heavy metal.

Contact: Tony on B'ford 832843 or Dave on Cleckheaton 879197.

(There you are, Gerry, your street credibility's intact - good thing I didn't mention that you were also in pop-pap band Love Affair!)
****
****

Cameras in Cars (from Bradford)

Ld Voo - Martin Sadofski
Gtr/Voo - Tim Beckenham
Kbds - Robin Hoyle
Bass - Anthony Sowden
Dms - Phil Hawksworth
Bkg Vocs - The Axles
(Jennie, Susan & Debbie)

C-in-C had their start some 2 yrs ago in domestic taping sessions by Martin & Robin on gtrs & Anthony on 'Tupperware tubs'.

Martin & Robin began to think seriously about forming their own group after seeing heavy rockers Elf at their school (Belle Vue); subsequently, they somehow bamboozled Elf bassist Tim into joining them. (Tim was once a member of Shaft Drive & still keeps his hand in at hippie music by moonlighting with an ad-hoc conglomeration called Angel Dust).

Recruiting another friend - Phil - to play dms, they began rehearsing at Coda with borrowed & hired equipment. Tim switched to gtr & Robin took up bass - only he didn't work out, so they put him on kbds: "We didn't have the heart to throw him out!" A gent called Victor briefly played bass for them before Anthony was drafted back in & taught how to play it by Tim.

Under the name Various Artist, they debuted at Belle Vue & then played 10 youth clubs for free "to get experience", playing "primitive punk" to unreceptive audiences. In summer '78, Tony Ingham started managing the band & got them a gig at The Royal Standard supporting Dirty Max. They went down well & played there twice as billtoppers later in the year under the new name of Cameras in Cars - the name change being purely on a whim of Martin's.

Now the band are moving into a more sophisticated & eclectic new wave music & are planning to work with a girlie backing trio, The Axles (!). Martin, who writes all the band's material & is very much the leader, cites Wire, Ultravox & Gary Glitter (!) as the band's major influences but adds: "People in our band like different kinds of music. Our image is not having an image."

The band hope to be recording their first single at JSG Studio (B'ford) in March - to be released on their own INCINC label (geddit?) - & then'll be gigging all over Yorkshire to promote it. (No contact no. given - what is it, C-in-C?) ←

Keith E. Rice did this profile interview.

Recording at JSG Studio this month: HARSH WORDS + ORAL SAX (B'd), THE MESS (Leeds), CHEAP 'N' NASTY + THE QUICK (Keighley)

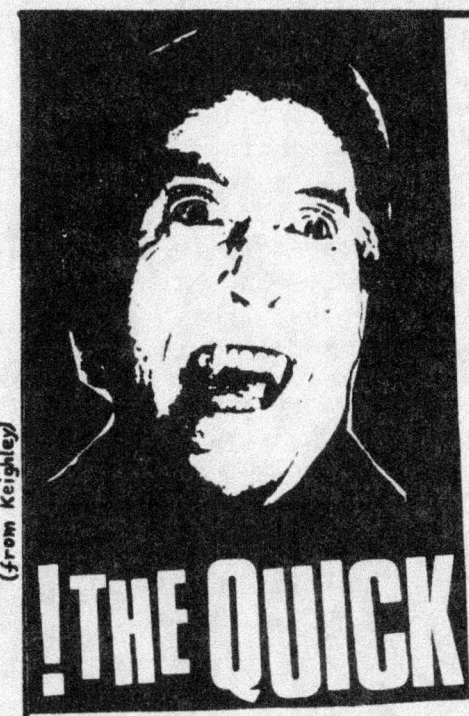

(from Keighley)

!THE QUICK

Gtr/Voc - Dale Kitson
Gtr/Voc - Ian Spencer
Bass/Voc - Steve Wilson
Dms/Voc - Rob (comfortable) Waddington

They're a new band who came together last year, though all are experienced musicians.

Dave, Steve & Ian have been together in various line-ups for about 6 yrs playing in pubs & youth clubs around Skipton. Rob has played in all kinds of bands in L'pool, London & Leeds. He once even jammed with Gary Moore (of Thin Lizzy fame) when he was in a London band called Slick Mick & The Dirty Chicks. After forming a punk band in Shipley called New Threat which split up, Rob joined the other 3 & they became The Quick in summer '79.

Their set consists of original numbers - with the exception of their own version of Gary Glitter's (he's getting a lot of mentions in this issue! - Ed) 'Never thought I loved you till I saw you rock-n-roll'. Their prime aim is to get across to the audience. They play loud with speed & energy. "Live gigs are what we really want to do. Recording would be a bonus. We play so fast that I don't think we could go on for more than the 40 mins. There are no intros, we just go straight through the numbers." - Rob.

The lead voc is taken by Dale, but they'd like to get in a good lead singer - probably male. "We've tried out a few girls, but they weren't what we wanted."

Though they're not amateurs, they're not after pushing musicianship for its own sake. Their music's not as fast as The Dickies' - more like (say) Stiff Little Fingers. "It's a very solid sound, not heavy metal, but nor is it as bitty & empty as a lot of punk."

At the moment, their plans are to get more local gigs. "We want more experience & a chance to sound out audience reaction. If it's what we expect, then we'll take it from there - though turning pro is something we'd have to consider carefully."

Contact: Rob on Keighley 605675.
****

Silent Movie

(from Bradford)

Kbd/Synth/Voc - Zenko Zdolyny
Ld Gtr/Voc - Paul Hudson
Rm Gtr/Voc - Ian Hinitt
Bass/Voc - Chris Firth
Dms - Ade Lee

In April '79 Zenko, Paul & Chris together with a rhythm gtrist & dmer formed a band called Stress Factor, changed the name to Ad Astra, then to Active Skies & finally, in Nov '79, when Ian & Ade joined, to Silent Movie.

"Every one of our songs is different, but it's basically melodic hard rock, though not heavy metal. It's all our own material & it's good."

All are from Belle Vue school where they did their first two gigs in Dec '79 as part of the school revue. Their 1st public gig was at Queens Hall, B'ford on Jan 12th. "We went down quite well - especially considering that nearly all the audience was punk." That gig was as support to school-mates Cameras in Cars (q.v.). For March/April they're lining up more local gigs including The Princeville, Vaults Bar & Palm Cove.

Their plan is to work locally-based for about 18 months to build up a professionally experienced attitude & to get the band really tight. "And it's not a matter of individual commitment, but a total group commitment. Do or die - if we get a chance, we take it, whatever happens. In 18 months we're shoving off down to London to make it."

Contact: Zenko on B'f'd 491463 or Paul on B'f'd 41710 or else Derek on B'ford 496529 (OK, that's enough - what do you think this is - a bloody telephone directory?! - Ed.).
****
HOPE YR ALL ENJOYING THIS ISSUE...BAMALAMALOO

Recording at Ram (Leeds) this month: BEANS + YOU + THE FOREST + TOM EGAN'S BAND + DANCE CHAPTER + GOODNIGHT VIENNA

The Vye (Leeds) have a single out (at last!) on Dead Good Records called "5 Hours 'Til Tonight".

THE OSCILLATORS
(from Harrogate)

Voc - Mervin Treedisease
Bass/Voc - Dave Proton
Gtr/Voc - Gregory Peckory
Dms/Swearing/Voc - Vee Dee

A new wave band - "We try fantastically hard to be funny, but only succeed in being silly. We believe fun's the most important thing about music. We love The Mekons."

Vee, Dave & Neil Down (gtr/voc) went into Cargo Studios, Rochdale on 20th July '79. The result was The Oscillators' 1st single - 'Leonard Cheshire' c/w 'Fast Breeder Reactor' which they brought out on The Warren Records label (that being the pressing plant which they used). Both songs are credited to the 3 of them. (See reviews section).

On 1st March they'll be in Cargo again to record their 2nd single - the titles being 'Marylin Brown' c/w 'E-boat'.

"The band's sound has changed immensely since we recorded 'Leonard'. We're now much more of pop/new wave/punk sound. This change was precipitated by a new gtrist (Gregory) who can play proper chords! Neil left the band after we got thumped by a bunch of bikers."

Contact: Mark (early evening) on Harrogate 879408.
****
****

IF WE'VE NOT YET COVERED YOUR FAVE W. YORKS BAND THEN TELL THEM TO CONTACT US!

THE Distributors
(from Wakefield)

Dms - David Holmes
Gtr/Synth/Voc - Keith James
Bass/Voc - Enzo Raphael
Gtr/Synth/Tapes/Voc - Mick Switzerland

They formed in Oct '78 as a drummerless trio doing experimental music, using taped percussion/rhythm. "It gave the band a very electronic sound."

David Holmes joined up in Jan '79. He uses only two drums & 3 cymbals to effect a unique drumming style.

During '79 they gigged successfully around London - getting some media attention which resulted in a session for the John Peel Show in June.

Their first single - 'TV Me' c/w 'Wireless' was released in Feb '80. They had 2,000 copies pressed & it's already selling very well - with most of the copies out in the shops or taken by distributors (sic). As a direct result, they're lining up a follow-up release - probably an EP that will be out in May.

"The first track 'TV Me' has a solid repetitive bass line & a continuous single note guitar sound with a bizarre guitar solo in the middle. The other side has a heavy dub sound to it."

Immediately prior to the planned release date of the EP, they're lining up a series of London dates.

Contact: Tony Stephens on 01-748-8141/Enzo on W'field 259595/Mick on W'field 251313.
****
****

I woke up this morning feeling very badly drawn.....

****
****

little brother
(from Bradford)

Suddenly Bradford seems to be sprouting poets who're taking to the stage at rock venues (with Aries Enterprises having taken over the Vaults Bar at the end of last month for the first of a projected series of poetry events. Probably most active amongst these is Little Brother (a.k.a. David Stockwell).

He's read his work out in public a few times, but has only recently started working the local rock circuit. In fact, his first gig was The Mods' Xmas Party at Palm Cove. He went on last - after The Mods had done their

Once upon a time, young men went down on their bended knees; now, thank God, they'll go down on anything...

Bradford bands Shaft Drive, The Scene, Radio 5 all have singles out this month.

set. "I did a short set - about 10 mins - with a lot of heckling from mods at the front who wanted music on, not me. It was a couple of mins after I'd come off that there was that fight that got The Palm Cove closed to groups for the next few weeks."

He supported The Mekons at Manchester Polytech. - a small venue (200 cap.) but it was about full & they liked him - "the best since John Cooper Clarke" - which is fair praise from a Manchester audience.

At the beginning of this year, he supported The Clash at Leeds Univ. - by far his biggest audience to date. The bill in order of appearance was Expelaires + Mikey Dread + Little Brother + The Clash. "It was o.k., but I only did about 5 mins. before the DJ stopped me - I was reading from his console & a couple of cans got thrown so he was worried for his gear."

His next gig was an unannounced spot at B'ford Univ. between The Mekons & Gang of 4 - about half of the audience had gone to the bar, but he reckons he went down o.k. with the ones who were still there.

"I'm not really a poet, more of a lyric-talker. I've been trying to put a band together for a while now, but've not had much success in finding the right musicians... ones that play well, have the right spirit & also look good."

He's thinking of doing a collection of his performance poems - if so, then it'll be on sale at his gigs.

Contact: 171 Broadstone Lane, Holmewood, B'f'd 4 (no phone).

****

the MOTIVATORS (from Leeds)

Gtr/Voc - Paul McKendrick
Gtr/Voc - Leon Phillips
Bass/Spoons - Iain Denby
Dms/Piles - Dave Robinson

Paul & Leon originally got together with Paul's brother, Martin, on dms. With various bassists, they formed the original Motivators, gigging around the area between Oct '78 & July '79. At that point, they drafted in Iain & Dave - a duo who'd been working together in various youth club bands for about 3 yrs.

The current line-up began gigging life with a Monday night residency as support band at The Cosmo Club - as the weekly opening band, they supported Shake Appeal, 2TV, Stranger Than Fiction, Butterflies & Teardrop Explodes. Since then, they've done few gigs but have been working hard on their material - which they've rewritten & designated 'Newbeat'.

Musically, they believe that they've come up with a new & original approach to the two guitar format, though they give a nod in the direction of recent XTC material. Rhythms are of prime importance in their music, but they still retain the standard pop song format of verse, chorus & middle 8.

They are very confident keen to do more local gigging.

As for recording, they have a home demo out with small record labels at the moment & are going into Ram Studios (in Leeds) towards the end of this month to spend 2 days recording 4 tracks to what they hope will be recording standard. They'll then look for a label to sign them. "We're already all in debt for equipment we've bought etc. & so don't have the money to release a disc on a label of our own."

They'll do demo gigs or supports cheaply at any venue that'll consider rebooking them if they go down well.

Contact: Iain on Leeds 585044/Dave on Leeds 585102/Paul on Leeds 650974 - leaving a message if he's not there.

****

This youth has beaten his face flat with a frying pan, as a protest against opera. His girlfriend is hoping to become a single vertical stripe.

POSTER BY MO MAKLOUF OF WITCH DESIGN

Excel (from Cleckheaton) have single out now on Polydor: 'What Went Wrong' c/w 'Junita' (reviewed WCR3)

Negatives develop to reveal
MYSTERIOUS FOOTSTEPS!

interviewed by Nick Toczek... ...photos by Rob are of 'Gunrunners' at Vaults Bar

Mysterious Footsteps is the new band formed from ¾ of The Negatives. The new band's line-up is Pete Stobbs (gtr/voc), Bob Robinson (bass/voc) & Tino Palmer (dms).

On 19th Jan '80, The Negatives did their final gig - The Lord Mayor's Benefit at B'ford Univ. (with The Squids & Shadowfax). After that, their vocalist - Dave Wilcox - left to form his own band.

Apart from the line-up change, the band had two reasons for the name-change - a single's just been released by a Sheffield band called The Negatives &

PETE STOBBS

also, Dave's departure has resulted in a very different musical style: "Our music's not punk any more - it's white-dread rock-beat." "Yeah, we were the first B'ford punk band. Now we're the first white-dread band."

The threesome did two try-out gigs last month under the name of The Gunrunners - one at B'ford's Vaults Bar, the other at Batley's Club 70.

"Our aim is to widen our audience whilst hopefully retaining some of The Negs fans." They feel that the new set'll go down well

at gigs - some of the new numbers they're sure of include: 'Requiem For Youth' + 'Like They Do In The Movies' + 'Tomorrow's World' + 'Last Tango In Watford'.

I asked them what'd been happening with The Negs' single that came out a few months ago. It appears that, of the 1,000 pressed, over 600 have been sold. Two small label distributors - Pinnacle (London) & Red Rhino (York) have just ordered a further 300 after the record got played by John Peel. "The rest should sell out within a couple of months or so. We'd not intended to repress it, but if it takes off in London, then Pinnacle will take a lot more, so we may go for a second pressing after all."

Future plans for the band include more local gigs, a projected M.F. single on their own label, & a short tour with an Irish band called The Tearjerkers (who've a single out on Back Door called 'Murder Mystery'.

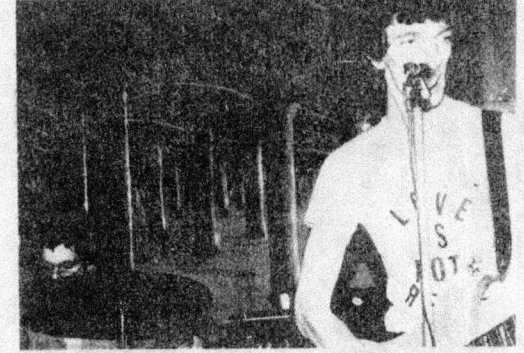

TINO PALMER   BOB ROBINSON
(both photos taken at Vaults Bar)

Finally, I asked the band what they felt like suddenly reduced to a 3-piece. Rehearsals, it seemed, were much tighter & they feel there's already a much better general sound. However, they've still got to see what it's like on stage without Dave there to front the band.

"We noticed at the last few Negs gigs that everyone knew the songs & jumped about, but we got none of the old applause. We really got to feel that we' played ourselves out."

"We now feel a lot freer to extend the music - beyond power chords & 1-2-3-4 bashes."

Contact: B'ford 33531.

REGGAE CHOICE — Roots Records, 16 Lumb Lane | Rob at H.M.V., Cheapside.

① STRUGGLE - Bunny Wailer (Solomonic)
② CHILDREN CRYING IN THE GHETTO - Jimmy London (Roots Man)
③ BLACK ROOTS - Sugar Minott (Mango)
④ BURNING SPEAR - Burning Spear (Studio One)
⑤ BOAT TO ZION - The Mighty Maytones (Burning Sounds)
⑥ MYSTIC MAN - Peter Tosh (Rolling Stones Records)

① ALL BURNING SPEAR
② ROCKING UNIVERSALLY - Willy Williams + Jackie Mittoo (12")
③ BOB MARLEY & THE WAILERS - a re-release on Hammer.
④ AFRICAN ANTHEM - Mikey 'Dread' Campbell (LP)
⑤ EQUAL RIGHTS - Peter Tosh (LP)
⑥ GENERAL PENITENTIARY - Black Uhuru (from LP 'Showcase')

I went into these 2 Bradford record shops & asked them to select 6 personal favourites from the reggae stock.

GLITTER SPEAKS

BRADFORD UNIVERSITY - 20 FEB.1980.
INTERVIEW by NICK TOCZEK.
PHOTOS by LINDSAY INESON.

"I've been living in Paris for the past 4 years. Last year I toured for 3 months in 'The Rocky Horror Show' round New Zealand & Australia. You see, the author based it on me & Bowie so he was keen for one of us to do it - which is why he approached me. That was great... actually learning lines & playing another character - quite thrilling in fact."

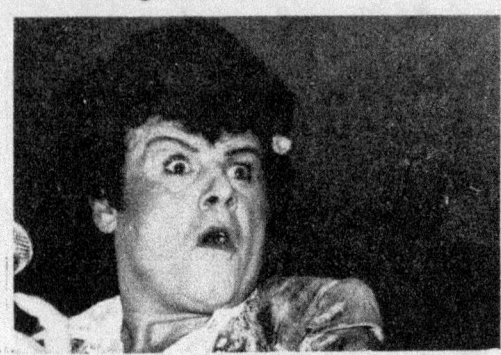

"There are 2 ways of touring - either you bring out the record first & then tour or else the tour comes first. Most of my song-writing ideas come from gigs - so I decided to do them first before the whole recording machinery moved in. So I'm now getting back into shape - it's rather like training for the Olympics. And the audience are very much part of the whole thing. It's always down to them & me."

"This tour really began in October & was only going to last about 8 weeks - but it's still going strong. When I had that run of hits, we were touring halls - the university & college circuit's a new venture & it's amazing, but I'm pulling a whole new audience - like at Essex University the whole place was full of punks & they'd all come to see me do the old hits. It's really very exciting!"

"Everything's running late tonight so I'm a bit edgy"(he grins)"...We were recording last week. The single - probably 'I'm Not Just A Pretty Face' - should be out towards the end of March. It'll most likely be on our own label, Glitter Records. I'd like to start recording other bands too. Do some producing. I love a lot of the music that's happening now."

"For the future, Mike Leander & I are writing more material - so there'll be an album later in the year. As I said, I want to do some producing for other bands. I'd also like to do more acting - theatre, movies, whatever - to expand. I always put a lot of energy & enthusiasm into whatever I do, it's how I work. Now I want to diversify. At my age you want to try other fields. I'll be 25 next birthday, you know!"

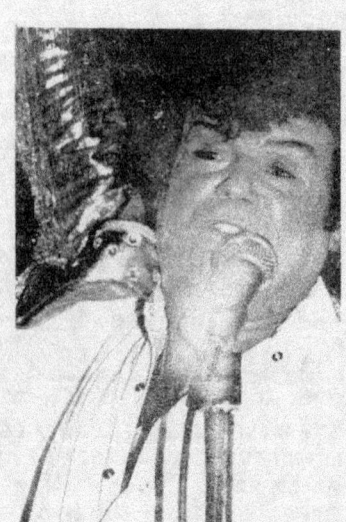

CLASH!

The hall had been sold out for weeks, & expectations were running as high as the temperature inside the Union building when The Clash played the university. 2000 people crammed themselves inside, & during the evening it became hotter & hotter - in every possible way.

Local band The Expelaires opened, & showed a lot of promise, with a sharp, edgy set that augered well for the future, although, as is now the fashion, the crowd hardly acknowledged their presence. It's a sad & destructive attitude; new talent needs all the encouragement it can get. Mikey Dread followed, & proceeded to bore everyone half to death with his monotonous brand of reggae. Odd; I always thought light & shade were integral parts of Jamaican music. Then a brief appearance from punk poet Little Brother who came & went to a thoroughly deserved chorus of boos & insults, & it was time for The Clash.

So much has been written, so much said, & now it's time for the legend to stand up & be counted. Frankly, I was prepared for an anti-climactic evening. All I had to go on were the records, & they didn't seem enough to build the edifice on. As a result I was caught entirely unawares. Urged on by the continuous frenzy of the delerious crowd, the band charged through a set of old favourites & new songs, bringing that special edge to rock'n'roll that singles out the great bands; the commitment The Clash bring to their music is awesome in its intensity; the whole 80 minute set was one non-stop dose of adrenalin.

Aided by some highly effective lighting, they looked sharp, & played sharper. Mick Jones has become a superb guitarist; totally in tune, yet constantly probing, exploring round the edges. Strummer backs him up perfectly, doing the simple things well, while Topper Headon & Paul Simenon thrashed & thumped in best demented fashion. Add to this a sense of on-stage dynamics that I have rarely seen equalled & the result is a rock band on peak form with the pedal pushed right to the floor.

Just one drawback. There was a problem in the vocal department. Joe Strummer's voice has been shot to pieces as a result of the exhausting schedule the band have set themselves, & there were times when the normal snarl was replaced by a sort of hit-or-miss gurgle. The others took their turns at the mike, but none of them have strong voices, & I can see this remaining the weakest aspect of the band. Thoroughly encouraging though was the way in which new stuff from 'London Calling' has been brought into the set, & it's songs like the title track & 'Jimmy Jazz' that provide much-needed contrast, as well as pointing the way for The Clash; a way that leads away from the limiting confines of punk, & into an era when they pluck ideas from every quarter & mould them into something truly special. The legend did not, & does not lie.

Reviewed at Leeds University by Nick Ryle
Photo'd at St George's Hall, B'f'd by Lindsay Ineson.

COSTELLO (Bradford Univ. 7th Feb.'80)

The Horace Barlow Band - a late 3rd act on a sold-out bill headlined by Rockpile (with Dave Edmunds & Nick Lowe) & supported by US bluesband The Fabulous Thunderbirds - turned out to be, as rumoured, Elvis Costello & The Attractions.

This was a try-out of the set they'd lined up for their forthcoming tour & it featured most of the numbers from their new album 'Get Happy'.

They took the stage amid loud cheers & immediately launched into their 1st number. A good clean sound with the band really tight & sharp. Costello, not always the most cheerful of guys, was obviously in fine mood.: "Hello, how are you?"(cheers)"This is Horace Barlow..." (nods towards guitarist) "... & this is a number called 'The Beat'. He gives brief thanks to Rockpile for this guest spot, plugs the album & they go into 'Possession' which earns loud approval. They go straight on into another typical E.C. number with a powerful dms/kbds intro. & a slow build-up into a pounding rocker. Again, no announcement - it's 'Less Than Zero' - a good punchy version, but I always feel it's just a bit slow. "Thank you. Like to do a new song for you now. It's called '5 Gears In Reverse'. This could make a fine single. It's got some good gtr/kbds work that's reminiscent of their earlier hit 'Pump It Up'. Good rhythm changes too. "This is a great town!" And he jokes about Top of The Pops which he's just been watching "... dancing away to The Nolan Sister in my hotel room... & The Buggles... & Gary Numan... c'mon, let's hear it for Lena Martell!" (Loud cheers) "Anyway, this is for my great (!) friends The Jags - it's called 'The Imposter'!" Next up is his own version of a song he wrote for Edmunds - 'Girls Talk'. It's followed by the final number - their recent hit 'Oliver's Army'. This has been a great set with the excellent Attractions providing subtle back-up vocals as well as the immaculate instrumentation. The audience goes crazy for an encore & they're back for one number - their new single - 'I Can't Stand Up For Fallin' Down'. "Thank you. That's it... Good night!"

A great rock-song writer, E.C.'s rapidly becoming a star-quality singer & performer - if he can hold the pace, he'll be up there for a good few years. If you missed this one, make sure you catch him next time around.

Nick Toczek

****

Side Effect (Rose & Crown, Ikley 22nd Jan.'80)

The competence level of the average rock band continues to rise & rise. Take Side Effect; a modest, semi-pro group with no earth-shattering aspirations, playing an uninspiring venue, yet managing to turn in a thoroughly well-played set of considerable promise.

Basing most of their songs around the gtr/kbd interchange, the band manage to whip plenty of life from that much-exploited rock warhorse, the solo, with John Bedford (kbd) & Bruce Wilson (gtr) meshing nicely, & occasionally soaring to unexpected heights. Standout numbers? Well, 'No Chance' totally belies its title, & convinces, & later in the set 'This Time' & 'Contra-indications' wind themselves up into balls of energy & bounce around the room. Otherwise, nothing too spectacular; a couple of songs nosedived to the level of a filler on an early Steppenwolf album, but mostly it was adequate, enjoyable rock, with plenty of bite.

Vocalist Tony Hall makes an engaging frontman in the Roger Chapman mould although The Rose & Crown crowd showed few signs of life, & the rhythm section (Dave Maude - dms, Steve Pearson - bass) play their parts with enthusiasm.

Although they played for over an hour, I got the impression that the main problem was lack of material. Padding out the set with old Stranglers favourites simply doesn't wash, especially when the band's original songs are stretched out way beyond their natural length, only to be found wanting. It's an exceptional song that will stand an 8-10 minute live version, & SE don't have many of those. This is the instant age &, if New Wave has taught us anything, it's the lesson of the 3 minute song; snappy, punchy & taut. The closing song, 'Ball Games', came closest to this ideal, & a few more like it, & they'll have cracked it, because there's plenty of promise & guts in this band, & they're worth an hour of anyone's time.

A final P.S. to The Rose & Crown; full marks for your policy of Tuesday night rock, but let's get something done about the lighting. Nick Ryle

WITCHFYNDE/DEF LEPPARD (BRADFORD UNIV. 30th JAN. '80)

Arriving about ½-way through the Witchfynde set, I was hit by a wall of thunderous yet familiar sound. The word 'familiar' doesn't refer to my previous encounter with the band at the Princeville (where else?), but to their total lack of originality - which applies to vocals, guitar style, overall sound & image. However, they did turn in a fine, tight set & fully deserved the encore they received.

In a back copy of Sounds, I found this quote from Leppard's bassist, Rick Savage: "Basically, it's just down to the fact that we're all posers. We all want to go onstage, wear dinky white boots, tight trousers & have all the girls looking at our balls. That's us, that's it. We're arrogant bastards."

That was 6 months ago. Since then, the band've got a lucrative contract with Phonogram &'ve toured with Sammy Hagar & AC/DC. However, the show they put on at the university showed that their above-quoted philosophy has only strengthened, though they tended at times to get a little distant from their audience.

The set opened with 'It Could Be You' - a new song which demonstrated the band's musical maturity despite their average age being only 18. This was followed by the band's current single - 'Hello American' - a song in which Joe Elliot flaunts his high-pitched, almost strained vocals to good effect. 'When The Walls Came Tumbling Down' is perhaps the finest song of the set, combining a slow melodic opening with pure energy at its most refined & centred around a superb vocal hookline.

'Rock Brigade' features the dynamic & accomplished Rick Allen on drms - playing at a volume as audible as an express train running over your hearing aid whilst you're still wearing it.

The B-side of their self-financed EP which first established the band - 'Overture' - is a good indication of their versatility. It starts with Steve Clark on gtr & he's soon joined by other gtrist Pete Willis (on a Gibson Explorer - a perk from their 6-figure recording deal). This number would do Rush proud.

Numbers that followed like 'Answer to the Master', 'Sorrow is a Woman' & 'Good Morning Freedom' were all delivered with great professionalism & enjoyment by the band. The set wound up with 'Satelite' & 'Wasted', a great improvement on the poorly recorded version on their 1st single.

They returned to encore with 'Ride Into The Sun' & 'Getcha Rocks Off' - the latter destined to become a HM anthem.

The great thing about Leppard which makes Witchfynde appear ordinary is simply class. The band have earned a lot of success in a short time & it'd be tough if it went to their heads - not that I think it will. I predict that this year they'll headline at many major UK venues. Their first album 'On Through The Night' is out this month - I only hope that the production's better than on their previous offerings. Steve Brown

RECORDS + TAPES RECEIVED
reviewed by Nick Toczek

PRESS RELEASE (cassette of self-made live recording) Good quality recording - except for too strong bass response - with plenty of the feel of a live tape. Onstage, they're now very tight & offer an impressive spectrum of vocal & musical skill. The arrangements are good but I feel there's too much instrumentation, with none of the musicians seeming to let up for a moment. It makes for a very dense sound - which goes against current trends. None-the-less, it's high time they tried for a record deal.

DANCE CHAPTER (studio cassette) 'Anonymity' This is a 6-minute track (see band profile) which has a driving & insistently hypnotic power. A most effective touch of phasing/blurring on both voice & instruments. An original & infectious sound that's highly original. There's a subtle build-up of intensity throughout that rivets the listener. Great ending too with double drumbeats on last few bars. I like this one very much.

RADIO 5 (pre-release cassette of single) 'Japanese Art' c/w 'True Colours'. Brit. rock seems obsessed with things Japanese. Anyway, this one's another winner. Excellent mixing has left a clean sound in which voices/instruments are all absolutely clear. A-side's good modern new wave/post-punk. B-side's even better - with good use of Roland 77 drum machine. An impressive vinyl debut for R5. Buy it - it'll be out this month.

ONE ADULT (studio-recorded demo cassette) For sheer recording quality, this is the best-produced cassette I've had yet. It makes my cheapo player sound like a TEAC reel-to-reel. One Adult play a very clever game. They can play Princeville (a die-hard heavy rock venue) one week & Palm Cove (punk/mod/new wave) the next - going down very well at both. They're at once hard & commercial / heavy & poppy. A lot of excitement in these numbers. An excellent vocalist. Unlike Press Release, they keep the sound uncluttered & the result is that they're quite simply one of the best bands in W. Yorks. No records out (why not??) so you'll have to catch them live.

VEX (rough home-made demo tape). Drum-machine, phasing on guitars, echo on vocals, etc. I've recently seen this band live & was impressed. On that showing, this tape doesn't do them justice. It's o.k., & at best has echoes of Dance Chapter's track (see earlier), but at worst it's too chaotic - with the instruments merely working against each other. Lyrics aren't too good, but the potential's there - it just all needs to be much tighter if they're after a good demo.

THE QUICK (rough home-made demo/rehearsal tape). Very poor sound quality, with the band just running through numbers in rehearsal. Most of the numbers sound as though they began life as medium-paced semi-melodic rock songs - though here they're hard & fast. I've mixed feelings. The band's out of tune & don't keep time too well, but they could be good fun live. 'Another Sunny Day's' the only stand-out number.

THE DISTRIBUTORS (single on unnamed own label) 'T.V. Me' c/w 'Wireless'. This is accomplished electronic pop. A-side reminds me of 'Warm Leatherette' by The Normal. It's got nice repeated bass patterns. It's cold fun. B-side is reggaefied electronics. Very clever. Again, the bass-player underpins it most effectively. Do listen to this. You'll either love it or hate it... Me? I don't hate it.

THE OSCILLATORS (single on Warren Records) 'Leonard Cheshire' c/w 'Fast Breeder Reactor'. 2 anti-nuke songs from a bunch of Mekons fans. Good enough but a bit basic. Slightly tinny mix doesn't help & the pace-changes are a bit irritating. They've a new one out soon - should be interesting.

CITY LIMITS (E.P. on the Luggage Label) 'Morse Code Messages' b/w 'If I had the Time' + 'Just can't say goodbye'. Really bright dance-pop in the Joe Jackson-Elvis Costello mould - though **not** one of those carbon-copy stunts that're rife. This is fresh & original. If they're lucky, one of the idiots on Radio One'll fall in fickle love with it for a week or two. That'd give them the deserved break. Is this a W.C.R. hit-pick?!

THE ADICTS (E.P. called 'Lunch With The Adicts' on Dining Out Records). Side One:- 'Easy Way Out' + 'This Week'. Side Two:- 'Straight Jacket' + 'Organised Confusion'. Outsiders, this comes all the way from Ipswich! They're another punk band... but streets ahead of most of their ilk. This stuff's got the same sparkle to it that makes (say) The Ramones records ever-popular. A most appealing cacophony. Reserve a table now.

No space for **gig round-up**: Best gig of Feb. was Costello/T-Birds/Rockpile at B'ford Univ.

Rock 'n' Roll Page

THE ELVIS MUSICAL

written by Brian Rushgrove

"There will never be another Elvis." says the perspiring look-alike in the white suit. True, but while his songs are still being sung he lives on.

After a successful three-year run at The Astoria Theatre, London, the award-winning smash-hit musical 'Elvis' finally hit Yorkshire & has just finished a two-week run at The Grand Theatre, Leeds.

The three main stars put in performances that were at times quite moving. Dave Ballard & Bo Willis who played the younger Elvis's were well supported by some shit-hot musicians & backing singers. They did a good job of recreating the sound of the early fifties in particular. But it was left to Bogden Kominowski as the mature singer to capture almost perfectly the powerful vocal style of the later Elvis Presley.

Musical Director, Kevin Robinson:- "Not all of the audience are rock-n-roll fans - though a lot do turn up in their gear to scream, shout & dance in the aisles. Some of those who grew up with Elvis as their hero seem to come along to see the younger ones going wild. They can probably remember how this sort of music used to cause riots when the likes of Haley first started touring. Others probably need reminding that they once got this involved themselves."

Bradford Rock'n'Roll Exhibition provided the display & juke boxes in the theatre. Our roving reporter from the exhibition spoke to Bogden, Bo & Dave, all of whom were quick to say that they were great Presley fans: "The musical's fantastic with marvellous audience participation. After its Leeds run, we'll be taking it to Scandanavia for six weeks & then back to this end of the country for a run of shows in Hull." Be there.

"FUNNY! IT FIT ME IN 1958"

The Bradford R'n'R Exhibition's been so popular in Leeds that it's been invited over to Hull when the musical's showing there.

CLASSIFIED ADS — 10p per word - ring Bradford 21867

Wanted. Dms + Gtr + Bass (17-20)... with own gear if possible... to form band... all types of rock → avant garde. Ring Shabbir (vocalist) on B'f'd 43178 any Thurs. 3pm - 7.30 p.m.

For Sale. 3 HMD p.a. amps (wattages = 30x30, 60x60 & 100x100 - total output = 380 watts). Also, MM electronic cross-overs. All rack-mounted. £150 o.n.o. Ring B'f'd 497092.

Microbe P.A. Hire. 100 watt individual 6-channel mix-down. Monitors + mikes + road crew = £15 + petrol. Ring B'f'd 497092.

Ld. Gtrist wanted for punk band TOTAL CONFUSION (see profile in W.C.R. 2). Experience unimportant, but must play fast. Ring Boredom on B'f'd 570750.

White Sounds - Planning a party? - Disco (twin deck, 50 watt) + D.J. available. Special prices for students. Leave message for Mo at Queens Hall, B'f'd, or ring B'f'd 3454 between 1-2 p.m.

Rhythm Gtrist wanted for Ulterior Motives - B'f'd band with single out & many gigs lined up. Ring Nick on B'f'd 21867.

Van + driver. Two available: one is Malc. on B'f'd 44428, other is Ken on B'f'd 683195.

Advertising puts hairs on yr chest — why not try it, lady?

Bradford's 'Shaft Drive' have 1st single due out this month - Steve Davis currently after new bassist & d'mer.

The Cat's Pyjamas, Morley St., B'f'd will stock singles by local bands - also any craft work — no, not Kraftwerk, you nurd... leather work, handmade stuff, etc. Go see them.

WOOL CITY ROCKWORD 3.

by Ken Turner.

(Grid contains partial entries: 18 across = EUGENIC; 25 down = TRAD)

Clues Across.

1. Arrives at party and completes local band. (5,3,5)
9. Idiot music for Warner Bros. cartoon. (5,4)
10. Arts I merge for Eastern music maker. (5)
11. Bring in the music with this! (5)
12. Confused Italian half ends Genesis number. (4)
13. Court or Cove? Orchestra or Club? (4)
15. Seen around church — marked up. (7)
17. Horizontal thinking? (7)
20. Closed then, but quite the reverse at this time. (3,4)
21. Money for musical instrument? (4)
22. Artist and National Trust together go mad. (4)
23. Once strung along with the Dominoes. (5)
26. NME writer — bit of a goer, I'm told. (5)
27. Rumoured to have seven small men in her band. (4,5)
28. Fewer from the Left Wing, perhaps. (9,4)

Clues Down.

1. Flour grinder, charged particle and Peter make successful records. (7,7)
2. South African female band sounds like a hit. (5)
3. Rolf Harris's keyboard. (10)
4. Spirits visited the Vaults? (7)
5. One trying to get a message to Rudee in particular. (7)
6. Not difficult in seas you know. (4)
7. Trap it, Rex, for one more journey! (5,4)
8. Patellas with first night nerves? (9,5)
14. Hid for free passage. (6,4)
16. Recovery the reason for a climb. (2,3,4)
19. 199 surround young lady for well known music. (7)
20. Idiot piece of drumming is vegetarian delight. (3,4)
24. Moving in her German river. (5)

Clued in!

Last month it was Sue Prince who won two and a half pounds of jelly babies for getting the first correct entry! She was thrilled beyond belief! But this month — would you believe it — nobody managed to send in an exactly correct entry!! So it's commiserations to STEPHEN BROWN who missed out again, and to TINA BARTROP (first timer?) who narrowly missed out on a tasty treat of a prize. I can see I'm going to have to make it easier for you, so this month's is the proverbial piece of cake. I've even written in the only word I had to look up in the Encyclopaedia Britannica! So there! Well, all I can say is best of luck with this month's crossword, and should you be lucky or have a good clued-in view of the local music scene, I'll be leaping on to your neighbourhood bar to present you with this month's personalised prize! Cheers, Ken.

Last Month's Solution

(Solution grid with visible entries including: FAVOURITE BAND, PART TIMER, ACTON, RADAR, USED SENSE, ISLANDER, PASS UP, GASSED, HALF RAIN, ANTIDOTES, AND IT, COMBO, EARTHWORM, MOST OF A MINUTE)

MY DOE SPITS ON HISSING SID!   SAVE 'WAGGONER'S WALK'!   COMPOST CORNER!

TEL 32721

JSG music

108B Main Street, Bingley.
Tel. 68843.

ACCESS & BARCLAYCARD WELCOME

Part exchange welcome –
amazing discounts.

MAIN AGENTS FOR
MOOG, GIBSON, LAB SERIES, KORG,
FENDER, RICKENBACKER, MUSIC MAN,
H/H, MARSHALL, PARK, M.M.,
CUSTOM SOUND, AMPEG, OVATION,
YAMAHA, LANEY, CRUMAR, PEAVEY,
ROLAND, CARLSBRO & lots more.
Custom P.A.'s up to 2KW
FULL H/H CONCERT P.A. IN STOCK.

Don't fly off the hanger 'cause you can't find what to wear — Come to THE CAT'S PYJAMAS

39 Morley St, BRADFORD

Also: Handicrafts and Second-hand RECORDS

Witch design

for All BANDS, MUSICIANS, and CLUBS...

We Are Specialised In DESIGNING:

★ ALBUM & SINGLE SLEEVES ★ POSTERS
★ T-SHIRTS ★ BADGES.

very Reasonable PRICES!

Contact or Leave a message for: MO
AT: ROOTS RECORD SHOP, 16, LUMB LANE, BFD 8).
OR:
RING BFD '34543', ONLY! Between 1—2 noon.

PALM COVE CLUB
Hollings Rd., Bradford 8. (tel. 499895).

LIVE BANDS EVERY FRI & SAT
(See gig guide on page 20 for details)

LICENSED BAR TILL 1am

Club also open throughout the week
9pm – midnight with reggae disco

Car park at rear
Pool tables
Good West Indian Food
New Wave, Mod, Reggae Jukebox

THE COMMUNICATIONS CENTRE

(a posh name for a basic facility)

offers 4-TRACK with DBX
at £3-50 p.h. + tape

Gear Includes:-

TEAC 3340, DBX, ITAM 10-4 desk,
LEVERS-RICH E200, REVOX B77,
ORBAN REVERB, FILTERS, GRAPHICS,
etc.

FULL D.I. + MIKES by AKG, CALREC,
etc.

RING ALF or MOYA on B'F'D 22769.

West Yorkshire Gig Guide — MARCH

T.B.A. = to be arranged. **✱** Palm Cove's B'ham Reggae Package = Barry Brown + Trevor Hartley + The Corner Shots + Natros. **◊** = Coda Music's guitar session at Splash One features several top-rate guitarists. Tickets from Coda, B'fd. **✕** = Leeds Univ.'s John Peel Extravaganza (local bands) Agony Column + Deadringer + The Switch + The Statics + Psycho + Foma + Paradiddle + Beans + Jazz bands. **†** = Princeville gigs are Sun. lunch.

NB All gigs correct when we went to press, but some'll change. Phone the venue to be sure of the gig.

Venues not listed in last issue include:- Gladrags Theatre Club, Leeds (Merrion St. Precinct, tel. 450992) + Staging Post, Leeds (tel. 735541) + Splash One (next to St. Benedicte's), Swarcliffe Ave, B'fd. + 14.

SAT 1 — HADDON HALL, Leeds = Switch. FFORDE GREENE, Leeds = Orphan. WHITE LION, Hudds. = The Limit. STAGING POST, Leeds = Red Eye. PALM COVE, B'f'd = Drug Squad. LEEDS UNIV. = Pretenders (sold out).

SUN 2 — VAULTS BAR, B'fd = Statues of Famous People + The Scene. HADDON HALL, Leeds = Side Effect. STAGING POST, Leeds = Tarot. WHITE LION, Hudds. = The Dots. FFORDE GREENE, Leeds = Mud. PRINCEVILLE, B'f'd = Spinoes.

MON 3 — WHITE LION, Hudds. = Sretemrellik (Special gig). VAULTS BAR, B'fd = Oral Sax. MARQUIS OF GRANBY, Leeds = Dance Chapter. FFORDE GREENE, Leeds = Crazy Cavan.

TUE 4 — VAULTS BAR, B'fd = Airkraft. FAN CLUB, Leeds = Sore Throat. ROSE & CROWN, Ilkley = Metal Fatigue.

WED 5 — B'F'D UNIV. = Dexy's Midnight Runners + The Nips. VAULTS BAR, B'fd = Middle 8. WHITE LION, Hudds. = House of Om.

THU 6 — QUEENS HALL, B'fd = Vex + Counterdance + support. GLADRAGS THEATRE CLUB, Leeds = Idle Rich. FAN CLUB, Leeds = Expelaires + Dance Chapter + Duo + Electric Tent Pegs. FFORDE GREENE, Leeds = Planets. LEEDS POLYTECH. = The Charlie Parkas + The Smirks. PRINCEVILLE, B'f'd = COACHHOUSE, Hudds. = Superstud.

FRI 7 — PALM COVE, B'f'd = The Solos + support. LEEDS UNIV. = John Peel Extravaganza. MARQUIS OF GRANBY, Leeds = Cuba. HUDDERSFIELD POLY. = Albertos + Smirks.

SAT 8 — STAGING POST, Leeds = Local Heroes. HADDON HALL, Leeds = Lucky Strike. FFORDE GREENE, Leeds = Japanese Toy. WHITE LION, Hudds. = Dawnwatcher. PALM COVE, B'f'd = Birmingham Reggae Package.

SUN 9 — VAULTS BAR, B'f'd = Shadowfax. FFORDE GREENE, Leeds = The Movies. HADDON HALL, Leeds = Middle 8. FAN CLUB, Leeds = The Cramps + Nightmares in Wax. WHITE LION, Hudds. = The News. COACHHOUSE, Hudds. = Teenbeats.

MON 10 — VAULTS BAR, B'f'd = Oral Sax. PRINCEVILLE, B'f'd = Silent Movie. FFORDE GREENE, Leeds = Jonny Reb & The Confederates. STAGING POST, Leeds = City Limits. ST. GEORGE'S HALL, B'f'd = Buddy Rich.

TUE 11 — VAULTS BAR, B'f'd = Vex. ROSE & CROWN, Ilkley = Elements.

WED 12 — B'F'D UNIV. = Nine Below Zero + support. WHITE LION, Hudds. = Or Was He Pushed.

THU 13 — GLADRAGS THEATRE CLUB, Leeds = Vex. FAN CLUB, Leeds = Psychedellic Furs + Spasms. FFORDE GREENE, Leeds = The Cruisers. PRINCEVILLE, B'f'd = Aftermath.

FRI 14 — PALM COVE, B'f'd = Vex + Parisian Axis. FFORDE GREENE, Leeds = Jab-Jab. QUEENS HALL, B'f'd = Mysterious Footsteps + Violation.

SAT 15 — HADDON HALL, Leeds = Red Eye. STAGING POST, Leeds = Local Brew. WHITE LION, Hudds. = Geneva. PALM COVE, B'f'd = Mirror Boys. FFORDE GREENE, Leeds = China Town + Glossy Mags.

SUN 16 — VAULTS BAR, B'f'd = Japanese Soldiers. COACHHOUSE, Hudds. = Crooks. HADDON HALL, Leeds = City Limits. STAGING POST, Leeds = Side Effect. FAN CLUB, Leeds = The Step. FFORDE GREENE, Leeds = Chickenshack. WHITE LION, Hudds. = The Dots. PRINCEVILLE, B'f'd = Buffalo.

MON 17 — VAULTS BAR, B'f'd = Oral Sax. SPLASH ONE, B'f'd = Crestas + Gary Boyle & friends + Helter Skelter. FFORDE GREENE, Leeds = Matchbox.

TUE 18 — VAULTS BAR, B'f'd = Total Confusion. ROSE & CROWN, Ilkley = White Lie.

WED 19 — WHITE LION, Hudds. = Graham Philpot's Eightpiece. LEEDS POLYTECH. = The Squire + support. LEEDS UNIVERSITY = Sad Cafe.

THU 20 — GLADRAGS THEATRE CLUB, Leeds = The Statics. FAN CLUB, Leeds = Akrylykz + Seventeen. FFORDE GREENE, Leeds = Dynamite. COACHHOUSE, Hudds. = Vardis. PRINCEVILLE, B'f'd = Limelight.

FRI 21 — LEEDS UNIV. (Lipman Building) = Agony Column. PALM COVE, B'f'd = Eaten Alive By Insects. FFORDE GREENE, Leeds = Cuba.

SAT 22 — HADDON HALL, Leeds = Agony Column. WHITE LION, Hudds. = The Guests. PALM COVE, B'f'd = Jimmy Lindsay. STAGING POST, Leeds = Dodgy Tactics.

SUN 23 — VAULTS BAR, B'f'd = Ulterior Motives. STAGING POST, Leeds = Shabe Appeal. HADDON HALL, Leeds = Alwoodley Jets. WHITE LION, Hudds. = Airkraft. COACHHOUSE, Hudds. = Killermeters. FFORDE GREENE, Leeds = Metro. PRINCEVILLE, B'f'd = 633 Squadron.

MON 24 — VAULTS BAR, B'f'd = Oral Sax. FFORDE GREENE, Leeds = Black Cat. MARQUIS OF GRANBY, Leeds = Switch. ST. GEORGE'S HALL, B'f'd = Stiff Little Fingers.

TUE 25 — VAULTS BAR, B'f'd = The Quick. ROSE & CROWN, Ilkley = Sturgeon Roe.

WED 26 — WHITE LION, Hudds. = Glossy Mags.

THU 27 — GLADRAGS THEATRE CLUB, Leeds = T.B.A. (Leeds band). FAN CLUB, Leeds = Slaughter & The Dogs + Klyngons. FFORDE GREENE, Leeds = Rhythm Hawks. PRINCEVILLE, B'f'd = Race Against Time.

FRI 28 — PALM COVE, B'f'd = Wolfrace. BANDSMAN, Brighouse = Mysterious Footsteps. FFORDE GREENE, Leeds = Limelight.

SAT 29 — HADDON HALL, Leeds = The Vye. ST. GEORGE'S HALL, B'f'd = David Soul. WHITE LION, Hudds. = Talisman. PALM COVE, B'f'd = Hustler St Band. STAGING POST, Leeds = T.B.A. ST. GEORGE'S HALL, B'f'd = Rose Royce.

SUN 30 — VAULTS BAR, B'f'd = Rhino. STAGING POST, Leeds = T.B.A. HADDON HALL, Leeds = Proposition 31. COACHHOUSE, Hudds. = T.B.A. WHITE LION, Hudds. = The Dots. FFORDE GREENE, Leeds = Deadringer. PRINCEVILLE, B'f'd = Jeddediah Strut.

MON 31 — VAULTS BAR, B'f'd = Oral Sax.

TUE 1 — VAULTS BAR, B'f'd = Trampus. ROSE & CROWN, Ilkley = (NO BAND THIS WEEK).

WED 2 — WHITE LION, Hudds. = Glass Rock.

THU 3 — BINGLEY ARTS CENTRE = Agony Column. GLADRAGS THEATRE CLUB, Leeds = T.B.A. PRINCEVILLE, B'f'd = Deadringer.

FRI 4 —

SAT 5 — HADDON HALL, Leeds = Dirty But Nice. WHITE LION, Hudds. = Geneva. FFORDE GREENE, Leeds = Kraken.

MARQUIS OF GRANBY, Eastgate, Leeds 2 (tel. 454480) was a late entry. Hope you can read all this — it's a bit messy! — Ed.

ISSUE #5

April 1980, 1,500 copies printed, 20 pages, A4, glossy cover, improved printing

My editorial for this issue hints at the manic, non-stop existence I was living during the time I edited WCR. Every issue involved securing and arranging advertising to pay for the printing, doing interviews, writing reviews, compiling the gig guide, sorting all the rest of the content, spending hours carefully writing and then drafting out every page, sorting artwork, etc. Then there was getting the printing done, collecting copies, distributing some to every outlet, going out night after night to sell copies in venues, and outside as people were leaving. There were countless other tasks related to WCR, its contributors, and readers. On top of this, I was gigging all over the country, organising it all, writing poetry, doing journalism for other magazines, etc., etc. The pace never let up. There were never enough hours in the day. I was constantly working late into the night and getting up early after too little sleep... and I was loving it!

Notes on bands profiled in this issue.

Leeds band, The Expelaires, had a huge influence on the local music scene. Their keyboard player, Craig Adams, went on to play bass with The Sisters of Mercy before becoming a founding member of The Mission (with fellow Sisters of Mercy departee, Wayne Hussey).

A few of the many singles and E.P.s I was sent. Some of these were released after 1981, but all feature musicians I knew or worked with while producing Wool City Rocker.

WHAT DOES YOUR BAND REALLY SOUND LIKE ?

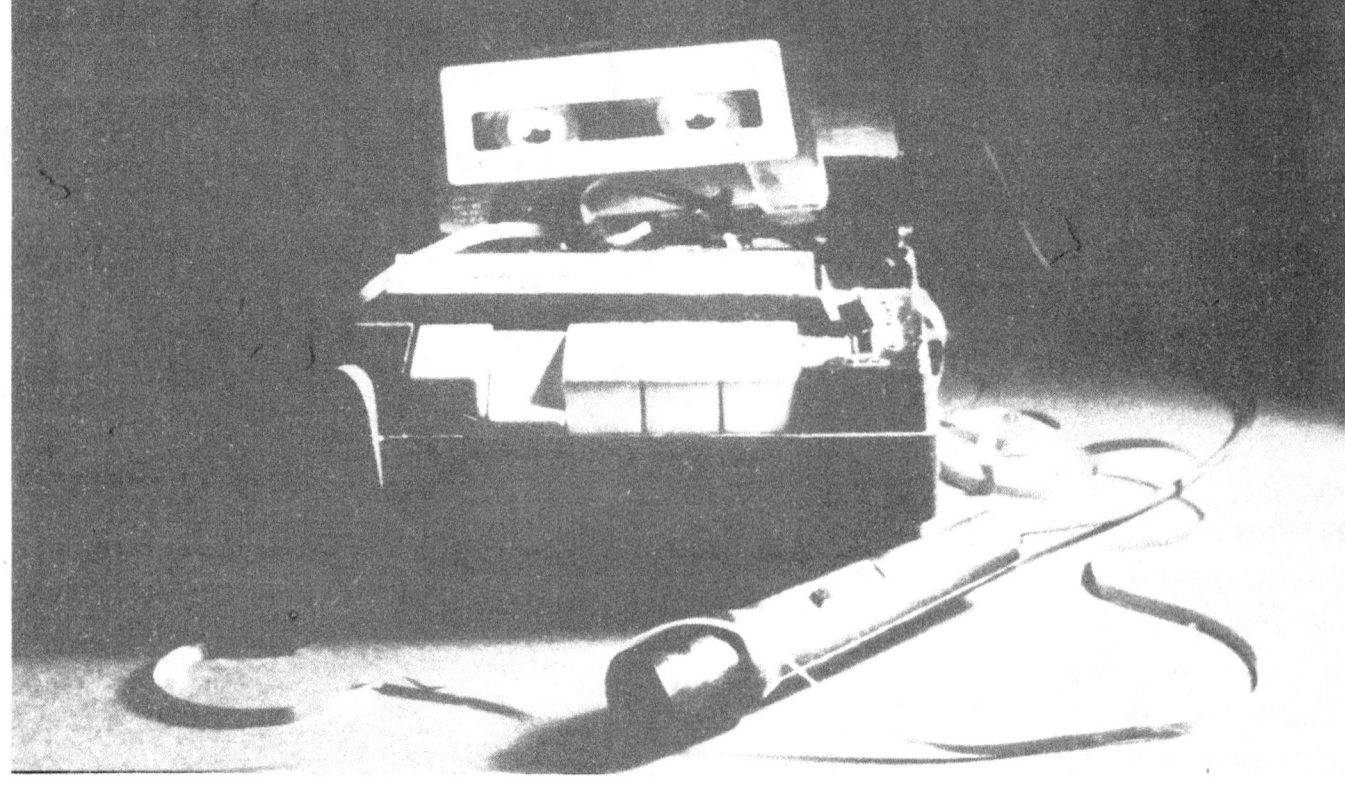

FIND OUT AT....

Friendly relaxed studio with top quality 8 track recording facilities

For details of studio rates and record distribution through the RAM Label phone **Leeds 446622**

RAM RECORDING STUDIOS

64 ARMLEY ROAD · LEEDS LS12 2DR
Telephone: 0532 446622 (2 lines)
(or Wakefield 67470)

THE ONLY FULL TIME PROFESSIONAL STUDIO IN LEEDS

The Wool City ROCKER

EDITORIAL

Another month, another issue... & at last the thing's beginning to take shape. This one's closest yet to being what I hoped to produce when I first started the mag. Still a lot of room for improvement - but it's getting better, isn't it? Keep sending in ideas, info., material, etc.

This one's been the hardest yet to compile - 12 hours of sleep in the past 5 days. Next time round I'll have to bring in someone else to help - maybe there'll be a full editorial board soon! Anyway, a big round of thanks to everyone who's contributed to this issue + all of you who read it.

As well as selling in shops round West Yorks., the mag is now being sold by various people round venues etc. Also, it's now available through both Rough Trade & Better Badges in London. God knows how I'll get next month's issue together - as well as doing a lot of gigs with my own band, I've got a week's work as visiting writer in Wakefield schools & I've also got 1,500 copies of my other magazine (a literary mag called The Little Word Machine) to distribute. Not to worry, it'll all get done somehow. You can look forward to a review of an L.P. called 'All my Geraniums are Bullet-proof' by Deep Freeze Mice on Mole Embalming Records (honest truth! - they're from Leeds & it's a good album).

Hope you're all going to come along to St. George's Hall, B'ford on May 3rd to see my band + Expelaires, Radio 5, The Scene, Shake Appeal, City Limits... 6 bands for only a quid! It's a Radio Leeds promotion & I'm organising it. We need your support - if this one's a success then there'll be others featuring local bands. Keep taking the tablets. I'm going to have a bath now.

Till May, then,
Nick Toczek

CONTENTS

```
Stan Engels' Cartoons......................... 12,14,16
3 Bands In Profile: The Switch, Muggins Blight & Knife Edge. 4
Band Profiles: Shake Appeal & The Expelaires................. 5
Featured Band: The Solos..................................... 6
Live Reviews: Geneva, Mysterious Footsteps & Idle Rich...... 7
Featured Band: 9 Below Zero.................................. 8
Look Back At Anger: Mods'n'Rockers '64 & '65................. 9
Band Aid: D.I.Y. Discs + West Yorkshire Venues.............. 10
Editor's Nowtz............................................... 11
Records & Cassettes Review.................................. 11
3 Bands in Profile: The Elements, Harsh Words & The Xpozez.. 12
Whiteman's Reggae........................................... 13
Reggae Choice............................................... 13
Letter: Coda Practice....................................... 14
Live Review: Coda Guitar Night.............................. 14
Letter: When The Hissing Stops.............................. 15
Demo Tapes.................................................. 15
Live Reviews: Dexy's Midnight Runners & The V.I.P.'s........ 16
Nowtz (Extra)............................................... 16
Live Review: Press Release.................................. 17
Rockword 4.................................................. 18
Eddie Cochran............................................... 18
Back Issues................................................. 18
West Yorkshire Gig Guide.................................... 20
```

EDITION No.5   APRIL '80

EDITOR: NICK TOCZEK

CONTRIBUTORS:
STAN ENGEL
KEN TURNER
BRIAN RUSHGROVE (cuttings)
KEITH E. RICE
MICK MARTIN
ANDY PROCTOR
ROB
WINSTON (Roots)
PHIL FOSTER
PAUL FROM CODA
+ ALL THE BANDS & VENUES...

TERMS OF SALE: 30p each direct to the public or 45p each by mail order from the address given below. Bulk orders of 15 or more copies can be had at the discount price of 20p each (so why not sell the magazine yourself at gigs, school, etc.?)

ADVERTISING RATES: Standard 3½" x 3½" box is £20 for first time of advertising, then £10 for subsequent placings. Colour, different size, special lay-out, etc. by arrangement.
Ring or write for advertising rates card & any other details.

EDITORIAL ADDRESS:

5 Beech Terrace,
Undercliffe,
Bradford BD3 0PY,
West Yorkshire,
England.
(tel. 0274-21867).

3 bands (plus name-checks for loads more)

researched & written up by Nick Toczek

THE SWITCH

Line-up: Tom Bliss (Voc/Kbds),
Pete Dowling (B.Voc/Dms),
Rob Lowther (B.Voc/Gtr),
Dave Turner (B.Voc/Bass).

FROM LEEDS

Tom Bliss, originally a folkie, turned to rock music in '77 when he formed The Cockpits with John Shepherd (ex-Sneakers) & Judy (now with all-girl band Straits). After experimenting with a 'new wave big-band' called The Neighbours, he played keyboards for a short time with The Squares (a Leeds band now signed to Sire) & also for Agony Column (now signed to Phonogram on their Back Door label). In January of this year he formed The Switch.

As a journalist, drummer Pete Dowling has worked for Beat Instrumental & has contributed pieces to Melody Maker & Sounds. He was drummer/guitarist with an experimental band called Performance Anxiety & writer/drummer with The Ambitions before joining The Switch.

The band's guitarist comes originally from Carlisle, joined Leeds band Sneakers until the band broke up in '79 when the rhythm section went off to join Roy Sundholm (feature on his band will appear in WCR soon - listen out for their forthcoming single 'Good Girls Don't Wear White' which should be a massive hit - ed.).

Dave Turner, the band's bassist, has been in a host of bands including Leeds bands Jobe St Day & Luigi Ana Da Boys.

All this info. was gleaned from the band's press release. Their demo cassette is reviewed elsewhere in this issue & they're now gigging regularly round West Yorks with a fast-growing reputation. Worth catching.

Contact: Tom Bliss on Leeds 751112

Muggins Blight   FROM SKIPTON

Line-up:- Ld.Voc = Liz Wilson; Rm.Gtr/Voc = Carl Dulling; Ld.Gtr = Mick Smith; Bass = Gary Holdsworth; Dms = Frank French.

"Johann Muggins was an infamous Skipton train robber who later became a sheep farmer in Australia, where he compiled 'The Muggins Catalogue of Rare Sheep Diseases' - but whilst doing so, he fell victim to the dreaded Blight." - at least, that's what the band tell me in their letter.

Johann Muggins was the name of a band that Carl & Mick were in back in '78. In July '79 they went on to form Muggins Blight, joined by Frank (formerly with Omen who are now called The Quick - see WCR 4) & Gary plus John Masters on lead vocals (John played bass 'Satisfaction' by the band Bubblerock).

The band released an EP on Look Records in Dec. '79 ('Mr Somebody' c/w 'They Go Up They Go Down' & 'Malcolm Where's The Talcum' (though for some reason the sleeve notes call the drummer Andy French). By the time the EP came out, John had already been booted out of the band (Oct) & Carl took over lead vocals until the arrival of Liz in Jan '80. She'd never been in a group before, coming from Settle where was a shepherdess(!). She'll be making her live debut this month.

Muggins Blight play new wave pop music & their set consists of original material except for the '67 Monkees hit 'Pleasant Valley Sunday'. They've been gigging round Keighley/Skipton but now plan to play elsewhere throughout Yorks.

In April, as well as having lined up several gigs, they've a recording session at JSG - though there aren't any plans yet for a second single.

Contact: Carl on Skipton 2838.

KNIFE EDGE

Line-up: Tim Knowles on Gtr + Charly Peace on Bass + Edge on Dms + Mark Sweeney on Voc + Dave Hall on management & steering wheel of van.

FROM LEEDS

The original Knife Edge was formed in '76 & included Tim & Mark + a different bassist & a drummer. It lasted for just over a year: "We played fast rock that was a bit rough & naive. It didn't go down too well, being a mixture of music that lacked any direction, but we were a new band then."

In Dec '77 they decided that they wanted to do something more solid & it just wouldn't work with the drummer & bass-player - "by then we were doing about 4 gigs a week & had begun to take it all more seriously". In Jan '78 Charlie came in on bass & they got in Rob Steeles (on loan from Luigi Ana Da Boys) as drummer - little knowing then that they spend the next 2 years using temporary drummers. Through '78 they did supports to major bands including No Dice (Leeds Poly, reviewed in Sounds), Penetration, Fabulous Poodles, Wreckless Eric, Bethnal, etc. For the last half of the year their drummer was John Shepherd (that's 3 shepherds so far on this page - all Wool City Rockers..!?). He had been with Sneakers & had just turned down an invitation to join Sad Cafe. He stayed for a few months, leaving to form his own band (Lucky Strike). Rob Steeles returned for a while, then John Kewley (ex-Jobe St Day, "a sort of Wishbone Ash band that'd been very popular around Leeds". Next up was Rick Potter (ex-Comix) who lasted from Nov '78 to Feb '79. They decided to call it a day. "Charlie wanted to leave (he joined Motivators for a while) & it was all getting stale anyway." Tim & Mark were left with a bunch of HP debts & decided to devote some time to song-writing.

In May, Charlie came back, but it took till Oct/Nov to find Edge. Their first gigs with the new line-up & new material was last month at the John Peel Extravaganza at Leeds Univ. They've got a whole bunch of gigs lined up for the next few months (more than most local bands) & are recording a single on 1st April: 'Favourite Girl' c/w 'Say You Will' (a double A-side on their own No Hessle Records label). It should be out in May.

Contact: Dave Hall (manager) on Leeds 741072.

Stop Press: out March 31st is 'Hicks From The Sticks'-The Pick of The Northern Rock Scene - an LP on Rockburgh Records that features Airkraft (Halifax), Expelaires (Leeds), Clock DVA (Sheffield), Music For Pleasure (Leeds), Nightmares In Wax (Liverpool), Ada Wilson & Keeping Dark (?), Modern Eon (Liverpool), Medium Medium (Nottingham), Radio 5 (Bradford), They Must Be Russians (Sheffield), Section 25 (Blackpool), Art Failure (Nottingham), I'm So Hollow (Sheffield), Wah Heat (Liverpool), Stranger Than Fiction (Leeds) & The Distributors (Wakefield). I've only heard 3 of the tracks, but if they're anything to go by then it should be an exciting & wide-ranging album. It'll be reviewed in WCR 6. The whole thing was compiled by Leeds rock writer Nigel Burnham (a.k.a. Des Moines of 'Sounds'.

Incidentally, 2 bands dropped from the album at the last minute were Dance Chapter (Leeds) &... Ulterior Motives (B'f'd)-shame!

2 Leeds (FIVE) bands
BOTH ON ROCKBURGH LABEL...

SHAKE APPEAL | THE EXPELAIRES

Contact: Charles Sheppard (manager) on Leeds 624731 ext. 268 (evenings).

"There's no politics - we're geared to audience reaction... It's enjoyment. We have fun on stage & want everyone else to have fun too."

"We're sort of heavy dance music - it's a full sound that could be commercial but generally we try to avoid it."

Contact: Craig (after 6) on Leeds 582813 or Paul on Leeds 772253 (leave a message if he's out).

interviews by Nick Toczek

Line-up: Fiona Mitchell (Voc), Mick Ingham (Gtr/B.Voc), Nigel Holleran (Kbds/B.Voc), Rob Wells (Bass/B.Voc), Dean Fearnsides (Dms).

In June '79 Shake Appeal formed &, from the outset, intended to work towards becoming full-time pro. They invited a friend, Charles Sheppard (who'd run clubs & discos in the past) to become their manager. Their debut gig was on 18th July at St.James' Nurses' Home in Leeds.

Gigs were fairly sparse during '79 (they did less than 20) but Charlie lined up a lot for the new year &, immediately prior to these, they spent a lot of time rehearsing, song-writing & generally tightening up the band. It's a common experience for bands to feel the need to readjust after having done their first few performances.

During Jan/Feb they did just short of 20 shows & planned to leave March free for recording. At an early Jan gig in Goole, they'd had a 'phone call from Des Moines about a compilation album of northern bands that he was putting together for Rockburgh Records (see Stop Press elsewhere in this issue) & they sent him a demo tape. He liked it & so they met up with him: "He told us about Rockburgh & Sandy Roberton who runs the label. Des sent the tape down to him & he took an immediate interest in us. In fact, when we did a gig at Haddon Hall, Leeds on 20th Jan, Sandy was there to see us." The result is that, rather than put them on the sampler, Roberton signed them (in March) to a long-term deal with Rockburgh - 3 singles & an option on an album in a year's time.

On 6th & 7th March they recorded the first of these singles at Matrix Studios in London, going back down the following weekend to remix it. "My Own Way" c/w "Not Interested" will be released on Rockburgh on 18th April.

About half of the band's material is written jointly by Mick & Fiona, the rest of the songs are either by Mick or Nigel. However, they are keen to point out that what really makes the numbers work is the arrangement on each - this being the work of the whole group as a unit.

Line-up: Paul Gregory (Voc), Craig Adams (Kbds), David Harper (Bass), Carl Harper - his brother (Dms), David Wolfenden (Gtr).

Paul, Craig & David W + Martin Edwards (Dms) & Sean Walker (Bass) formed the original Expelaires in June '78 & their 1st gig was supporting The Dodgers at The Fan Club (then at Roots, Chapeltown) when they "were a straight-ahead punk band - 1-2-3 ramalama". In late '78 Martin & Sean left, Carl + Mark Copson (Bass) joined them & the band began to move away from punk towards their present sound. They got a John Peel session in May '79 as a result of having given him a copy of a 5-track demo tape they'd recorded at September Sound, Hudds. They also gave a copy of the tape to Bill Drummond of Zoo Records (Liverpool) who signed them for one single (with option on 2 more after 6 months). "To See You" c/w "Frequency" (see reviews) was recorded at September Sound in July '79 & came out in October. "Of the 5,000 pressed, about half have sold - though we've yet to see any royalties. We've now left Zoo, mainly because they weren't really interested in us." "Then Mark put his arm through a window & badly injured himself so we had to find a stand-in. Dave volunteered." "Then Des Moines came to us about his sampler album. After that, we played at The Marquee with The Mekons & Sandy Roberton was there. He offered us a one-single deal on Rockburgh." 'Sympathy (Don't be taken in)' c/w 'Kicks' (recorded at Matrix) came out on 21st March.

"We've only done about 35 gigs in the 2 years - which is partly deliberate because we didn't want to get stuck on the local gigs circuit."

"The new single's about the most immediately commercial of our numbers. In the case of the single, our attitude's pretty cold-blooded. We want to show that we can produce stuff that sells so that we're in a strong position to bargain for our own say on a major recording contract in the future."

Martin Blowers runs 'Folk Club' (Thurs nights) on Westwood Hospital Radio (B'f'd 882001 ext. 264) & wants to record local folk acts for broadcasting - he can record live at folk clubs too. His home no. is B'f'd 672819

THE SOLOS

(SIX)

reviewed by Nick Toczek

LIVE...

Previously known as The Monos, The Solos did The Palm Cove, Bradford last month to the usual small audience that turns out whenever the venue risks putting on a good but little-known band from outside the area. Those who stayed away missed a good night. Scotland has been steadily putting out good bands for the past few years & this one's Edinburgh-based, with a single just out on Cobra Records. They play a mixture of rock reggae & pop that they term 'power calypso'.

The band are Winston, Nii Odoi, Quao, Oddoye (all one guy! - born in Ghana - on bass), David Michael Gray-Buchanan (from Leeds, on guitar), Brian O'Donnell (from Glasgow, on drums), Freddie Kande Fadiga King (from French Guinee, on vocals) & Jaimie McGregor Watson (from Canada, on guitar). Some mixture, huh?!

The sound at The Cove is hardly ever very good & theirs was o.k., though too bassy. The standout numbers early on in the set were 'One Way Love' (b-side of single) & 'Peking Shuffle' which got them their first round of applause. The band were all dressed in black-&-white & worked with an easy stage confidence & an obvious enjoyment of their own music that'd have been infectious if there'd been a good crowd. It's dance music but small audiences don't dance.

'Drums in My Head' has the frontman/vocalist working hard to generate audience-group rapport with good back-up vocals from rhythm guitarist Jamie Watson. 'Straining' impressed because of the chorus echo on guitar - an extraordinary effects unit that makes the guitar sound exactly like keyboards - you'd have to see it in action to believe it (or take a listen to the single & see if you aren't convinced that they must've used keyboards).

Throughout the set, bass & drums maintain a sharp, strong, danceable rhythm with the lead guitar doing a fine job of creating the peaks in each number, the catchy songs hinging on the dual vocals.

'Trouble That You Put Me Through' actually got a few people up & dancing, & to follow it: "Here's a number that you can all get up & dance to... it's called 'Secrets'". Despite the low-key response, the band are going all out to enjoy themselves up there & are putting a whole lot of energy into their set. "This is our new single. You've all got to go out & buy it. It's called 'Talking Pictures'. They were all up & dancing to this at The Hammersmith Odeon last night". (A joke - they played Laffayette's in Wolverhampton last night).

"This is our last number... We hope to be back in 1999 - & we'll dedicate this to the bloke who's been dancing & the woman with him & all the rest of you - it's called 'Psychic Eric'".

A few calls for an encore & they come back on. The vocalist's enthusiasm bubbles over & they bounce into a great fun number called (I think) 'Some People Say'. And that's it. They're not merely a good live band. There's musicianship, that vital spark of real orinality & they've a clutch of instant pop songs. It's been a good night's entertainment.

ON RECORD...

'Talking Pictures' - the a-side opens with that remarkable keyboard effect on rhythm guitar, setting a sort of see-saw rhythm that moves gradually into the background, returning towards the end of the song. This is a good modern sound & that I've not heard it on radio I can only put down to the current glut of singles plus the fact that the further north you are as a band, the harder it is to catch the London-based mass media. Side 2 opens with 'One Way Love' which is perhaps their strongest live number. Here, it's very good, but lacks the powered excitement of the stage version. 'Psychic Eric' - the 3rd track - is equally strong. The band's use of effects lends them a marginally electronic feel. Nice one.

JSG music

108B Main Street, Bingley.
Tel. 68843.

ACCESS & BARCLAYCARD WELCOME

Part exchange welcome - amazing discounts.

MAIN AGENTS FOR
MOOG, GIBSON, LAB SERIES, KORG, FENDER, RICKENBACKER, MUSIC MAN, H/H, MARSHALL, PARK, M.M., CUSTOM SOUND, AMPEG, OVATION, YAMAHA, LANEY, CRUMAR, PEAVEY, ROLAND, CARLSBRO & lots more.
Custom P.A.'s up to 2KW
FULL H/H CONCERT P.A. IN STOCK.

PALM COVE CLUB
Hollings Rd., Bradford 8. (tel. 499895).

LIVE BANDS EVERY FRI & SAT
(See gig guide on page 20 for details)

LICENSED BAR TILL 1am

CAR PARK AT REAR
POOL TABLES
GOOD WEST INDIAN FOOD
NEW WAVE & REGGAE JUKEBOX

This month: Rufaro, Hair Restorers, Hi-Fi Battle, Seventeen, Clint Eastwood, Knife Edge, Cimarons

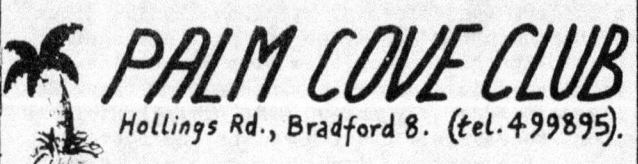

LIVE

GENEVA
THE WHITE LION
Huddersfield
(15/3/80)

The White Lion is a largish pub in the centre of Huddersfield - a good gig from a not too large band's point of view, with a well-defined alcove playing area reasonably visible to the audience. The booking policy is pretty eclectic, three bands per week (Sat, Sun, Wed), this week they range from H.M. to jazz to R & B. Tonight, it's Geneva from Huddersfield, a six-piece heavy metal outfit utilising bass, drums, lead, rhythm, keyboards/synth., & voice. They're young, have been gigging for about a year sporadically & have a single out in about six weeks.

The two sets the band plays consist mostly of heavy metal classics interlaced with four or five original numbers. The first set was an altogether unhappy affair, but things perked up in the second half when there was a degree of enthusiasm about that couldn't solely be put down to 'rent-a-crowd'. On the plus side, the band revealed themselves to be fairly competent musicians (though perhaps under-rehearsed) & managed to create a reasonably tight sound marred only by the few occasions when they failed to play in the same key. When they played their own material they showed a degree of compositional ability, particularly with 'Suicide' (the A-side of the single) a song with haunting keyboard/guitar accompaniment, lyrical drama & a neat power chord finale.

The real problem for the band has nothing to do with the minor slips that irritated them so much on the night. The sound tended to a sort of sameness & they lacked instrumental flair, there were sound problems (probably due to their lack of acquaintance with the PA) & there were straightforward mistakes. These minor difficulties can easily be remedied with time & experience. The real problem arises from the effect the seemingly endless number of H.M. classics (which outnumber the original songs 2:1) that the band plays has on what they do. If they're serious about becoming anything more than an anonymous pub band then the classics have to go. It's not just that the band failed to either do identikit reproductions or stamp their personalities on the songs (but that did happen), it's just that it's so easy to be tempted to play 'Since you've been gone', 'Smoke on the water', 'Back in the USSR', 'Johnny B. Goode' (cringe), etc., etc. There are lots of people who'll lap this up till the cows come home, boys, but it won't make you rich & famous. Perhaps that's a bit over the top, but, if the band are to become interesting (& rich & famous), they'll have to ditch the standards & work out an identity of their own, as well as a more powerful stage presence - it's symptomatic that they seemed to be playing for their ten or fifteen friends up front rather than for the rest of us. They're going, they've got the ability, but I wonder if they're serious.

- Phil Foster.

MYSTERIOUS FOOTSTEPS
& The Idle Rich
THE VAULTS BAR
Bradford
(17/2/80)

A Negatives concert used to be an experience: a jam-packed throng of punks wilding out to a straight-ahead powerhouse incarnation of '76 punk rock. But times change - even for Bradford punks. Singer Dave Wilcox didn't want to change & opted out; & now the remaining Negatives are Mysterious Footsteps (billed as 'Gunrunners' for this try-out gig), more a white reggae band than a hard-boiled punk outfit.

This was only the second gig under the new identity, & a goodly proportion of The Negatives' travelling fan club of thousands turned up, obviously expecting it to be the same as always. It wasn't.

With their opening number, the surprisingly melodic 'Tomorrow's World', the band served notice of the changes; & more than half of the set consisted of new material (written in the fortnight since Wilcox' departure), either melodic pop-rock or classy white dread. Of course it still sounded a lot like The Negatives. There was still the simple intensity of the old band & lots & lots of energy (courtesy of drummer Tino Palmer), but there were also more vocal harmonies & more lead guitar work. Bassist Bob Robinson took most of the lead vocals & made a good job of it too, but it was guitarist Pete Stobbs who took the vocal highlight of the night with a sensational touch of echo on 'White Dread'.

In comparison with The Negatives, Mysterious Footsteps garnered only muted audience response. It took their third song, the slow-burning 'Black Panther', to draw any real applause; & it was their seventh, 'I Wanna Be', before anyone was dancing. Towards the end of the set & for the encores, the band gave in to the expectations of their fans & trotted out some of the old favourites, including 'House of The Rising Sun', 'Love Is Not Real' & 'Stake Out'. Predictably, the Vaults' floor became a mass of heaving, swaying, pogoing punks wilding out - it was, after all, what they had come for!

The ex-Negatives are attempting a task of sizeable proportions in moving so radically from such a strongly-established identity & trying to take such a reactionary entourage of fans with them. However, the new band does work very well &, if given the time & the chances, may prove to be as successful as their illustrious predecessor.

Support band The Idle Rich also seem to have an identity problem in that they sometimes call themselves The Plates (see WCR 3). For tonight's show they were definitely The Idle Rich & played an energetic set that was anything but idle.

The band have a tight, powerful sound (largely due to the driving bass of Dez Staunton), a good vocalist in his brother Brendan, & an unusual drummer in 'Sid' Sidelnyk who seems to specialise in speed-of-light drum rolls! Unfortunately, Chris Scurrah played too much discordant guitar, spoiling some of the sparser moments - although he played the occasional nice fluid line.

However, the band's main problem seemed to lie in their material. After kicking off to a great start with 'Waiting For My Train', a power-socko piece of pop-rock, the rest of the set was a little on the bitty side - noted exceptions being the reggae 'Story of My Life' & 'Everybody Else Is In Love' which went through some rivetting time-changes.

On this showing, The Idle Rich were a good but flawed band who still have a lot of potential. Unhappy with the gig themselves, the band mean to tackle their problems. More substantial material & a stronger guitar line should see them develop into one of the city's better bands.

- Keith E. Rice.

AHA! BIT OF SPACE - HOW'S ABOUT BUYING Ulterior Motives' single - 'Another Lover' c/w 'Y'Gotta Shout' on Motive Music Records? From HMV, Roots, Cat's Pyjamas (B'f'd) or Scene & Heard, Univ. Record Shop (Leeds)... or direct from Wool City Rocker if you send a quid + your name & address... O.K?

NINE BELOW ZERO

the band

If the current blues revival is being spearheaded by The Blues Band, then Nine Below Zero (who headlined at Bradford University on 12th March to a disappointingly small audience - bad weather & near the end of term) are hard on their heels. They put in an excellent set of US urban blues standards plus original numbers.

From S.E. London, the band's current line-up is Dennis Greaves (voc/gtr), Pete Clark (bass/song writing), Mark Feltham (harp/voc) + Sticks Burkey (dms) - his 1st gig with the band, after only 7 hrs rehearsal.

Dennis & Pete were together in Stan's Blues Band (founded July '77) in which they were joined a year or so later by Mark Feltham. They played pubs initially, gradually working up to larger venues like Dingwalls, doing their own management/agency bit & holding down day-jobs. Then, in Oct '79, they met up with their current manager - Micky Modern, who looks & sounds very much like Jimmy Pursey of Sham 69 - & decided on the name-change.

I asked them about the problems of playing blues when musical trends - till recently - have been in other directions: "We've always believed in what we're doing. It's a matter of attitude & we've changed a few peoples' attitudes just by sticking with it."

Under Micky's wing, they started gigging heavily - "wherever & whenever we could" - & brought out thie live EP in Dec '79. So far they've shifted over 12,000 copies & it's still going strong - no mean achievement, especially when you consider that it's only in the past few weeks that they've received any media attention. The first 3,000 copies were pressed on Mickey's own M & L label & were all sold at gigs, then A & M picked it up, pressing a further 1,000 on M & L before releasing it on A & M. "Derek Green - the vice-president of A & M comes from South London & gets on well with the band - we owe him a lot for his support & backing." "They've really gone for it..." that's the band's motto & it might even be the title of the first album.

The standards & originals in the set are split about 50/50. "It's Chicago-style blues - Little Walter, Muddy Waters & anyone else like that - not white 60's blues." Since signing to A & M in Feb, they've been lining up a lot more gigs ("We're mostly a live band.") though this gig is only their 3rd outside the London area. They'll be going out this month (April) on their first nationwide tour.

The band's name comes from the title of a Sonny Boy Williamson number: "Muddy Waters does a better version of it." As a unit, they're totally self-sufficient, with their own van, p.a., etc. "We don't go over 2kw or use a lightshow or anything like that. The aim is to go out on a low running cost & simply play good music. It's a long set - up to 1½ hrs, but we're all working lads & believe in working for what we want."

Contact: Jean on 01-701-7462 or via A & M on 01-736-3311. (interview by Nick Toczek)

the record

EP opens with 'Pack Fair Square' - a rip-it-up full-throttle version of a number that'll be familiar to all fans of live blues. Great energetic stuff with fast hamonica to the fore. Next up is 'Rocket 88' - only slightly slower. It's the band's immaculate tightness & fine live feel that immediately impresses - that & the great harmonica solo that closes the first side. Turn over for a beautifully sensitive renition of the slow blues 'Last Night (I lost the best friend I ever had)' with Feltham taking the vocals & a fine guitar solo from Greaves, followed up by more good harmonica. The final number's Freddie King's eminently danceable rockin' blues 'Tore Down'.

The band's got the same feel for the blues that characterised the best of the early Stones numbers - but with far more musical agility than they had in those days. The recording quality can't be faulted either... if you like blues, you'll love these.

The band's back at the university soon - make sure the place is full next time!

"No politics. No poetry. No posing. Just good music..."

CLASSIFIED ADS/CLASSIFIED ADS/CLASSIFIED ADS....

BANDS - Problems getting to gig? Ring Dave on Leeds 741072. £10 under 50 mile round trip. 20p per mile over 50 miles. Fast efficient service. Big van (1½ ton Box).

DRUMMER NEEDED to join original-sounding band playing all own material. Ready to start playing now. Age, experience immaterial. Ring Ian on Cleckheaton 878664 or Victor on B'f'd 664188 (eve).

DRUMMER REQUIRED URGENTLY for studio album work & many gigs. Phone Nick: Pudsey 562077 between 6-8 pm or all day Wed.

IF YOU CAN PLAY THE GUITAR OR THE DRUMS reasonably adequately, please get in contact with Barry or Janet (ex-Remainz) or ring B'ford 34460 & leave a message or phone number.

VAN (35cwt) + DRIVER AVAILABLE for gigs or light removals. Cheap rates. Ring Malc on B'f'd 44428.

GUITAR PARTS FOR SALE - necks, bodies, pickups, etc. Also empty speaker cabs & other band bits. Cheap. Ring B'f'd 47088 or 43441.

CLASSIFIED ADS IN WOOL CITY ROCKER ARE 10p A WORD & YOU CAN RING THEM IN ON B'FORD 21867 OR WRITE TO 5 BEECH TERR., UNDERCLIFFE, B'FORD, BD3 OPY, WEST YORKS. ENCLOSING TEXT PLUS CASH OR CHEQUE OR P.O. (PAYABLE TO NICK TOCZEK).....

ARE YOU LEGAL, HONEST, DECENT ?... BORING SOD!

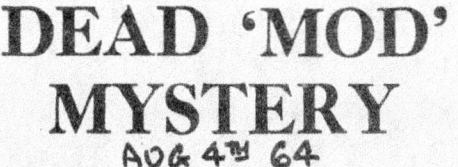

DEAD 'MOD' MYSTERY
AUG 4TH 64
More arrests after seaside violence

100 TEENAGERS RIP HANDLES OFF TRAIN

A BOY in "Mod" clothing who was found dead on the beach at Hastings early yesterday after Sunday's violence was still unidentified late last night. None of the many teenagers who were asked if they knew him could name the boy, aged between 15 and 17.

Mr. Donald Brown, Chief Constable of Hastings, "At present I have an open mind about his death." Chief Constable was giving a late night Press conference were 15 more arrests on the promenade, bringing the 48 hours to 74.

More than 100 "Mods" stormed off the Hastings at Charing Cross, London, station, the station foreman found bulbs removed doors in parts of the train—one carriage shades.

As all was reported quiet "Rocker" trouble blew up midnight they had arr police and gangs of y beach with drawn trunch

The dead boy at Hastin 5ft. 5in. tall, of medium build a small oval face. He had a small to the left of his jaw and a scar on his left hand. He was w blue jeans, a black T-shirt white long-sleeved pullover, yellow bathing trunks jeans.

Yesterday police separ large groups of teenag to drive them out o the second day runn the Metropolitan P the town to help

A police spo Yorkshire Post: " has undoubtedly hel Hastings fairly tr Although there had been d dents, the number of t showed how successful the a had been.

Mr. Brown said there had been "sporadic disturbances" between the old town, at the east end of the Hastings promenade, and the pier. But, he added: "Nothing has got out of hand."

GANGS BROKEN UP
Youths driven out

Some of the youths sent f reinforcements from London, police stopped them entering town. Gradually, the youths driven out. The large gangs broken up into small groups and

Police were allowing th return to Hastings in tw threes to collect motor-cyc scooters. Meanwhile, holid strolled between the two teenagers, lay on the b enjoyed themselves.

It was estimated that 200 policemen patrolled most of the weekend another RAF transpor Northolt carrying a fu men on their way to r who had completed the duty in Hastings. At Brighton at Whitsun there wer 75 arrests. The lower number in Hastings seems to indicate that the police airlift operation has helped to check this new form of hooliganism.

50 REMANDED
Bail for girls

'Mods' and 'Rockers' in bottle clash with police
40 held at Marga'

Yorkshire Post London St PECIAL police patrol out at Margate (K ht after a day c ween "mods" and the police.

rty youths will At midnight said the fina xpected to b he trouble. thrown a e officers ed on , today ll of er' resort—outside an i 'c' screaming teenag marche'

AIRBORNE POLICE IN ACTION
AUG 3RD 64.
Teenagers held after 'Battles of Hastings'
MORE VIOLENCE LAST NIGHT

For the first time, Britain's airborne into action yesterday. They f Northolt, Middx., to Hastings between the Sussex resort Late last night there "Mods" and "R

75 ARRESTED BRIGHTON
MAY 19TH 1964
Extra police called to curb teenagers

HEAVY FINES ON 'LITTLE CAESARS'
Yorkshire Post Reporters

FORTY policemen went from Eastbourne to Brighton last night to help the local force to control unruly teenagers after a day of clashes in five girls were hurt in a skirmish involving n 1,000 youths. By 9 o'clock it was estimated ods or Rockers had been arrested.

owed the weekend scenes at Margate re shocked by fines totalling £1,900 ths. Dr. George Simpson, chairman of described them as "these long-haired, y little sawdust Caesars." [Report P. 7.]

ouths will appear in Court today charged est Undercliffe. Four van loads of police centre where a gang of 200 smashed s during a symphony concert.

e sent from Medway towns to the n after reports that large groups om the coast, were gathering eenagers carrying belts and they formed.

Gang battles at Hastings: 64 were arrested

WHEN police had added up the total arrests of "Mods" and "Rockers" after the weekend clashes at Hastings, they found they had arrested and charged 64 during the disturbances. Chief This total, the Constable of Hastings (Mr. Donald Brown), said, included 17 juveniles, and two girls aged 18. Some of them were charged with more than one offence.

The total included some who were arrested but not charged Among them was a 14-year-old girl who was given a "ticking off" before Parents at police headquarters and her Fifty were due to appear in court today, 25 adult defendants first and another 25-11 adults and 14 juveniles—later this afternoon.

Handcuffed in pairs
The first batch arrived at the court at Hastings Town Hall in a coach from Lewes Jail. They were handcuffed together in pairs. About 50 people stood on pavements opposite the court and watched them being taken inside. There were no demonstrations. The court public gallery was crowded. Four youths made a brief appearance at Margate Court to- day after last night's seafront skirmish. Mods and Rockers, were remanded on bail All four youths charged with being in posses- sion of an offensive weapon, a An 18-year-old Margate youth length of chain, and three other was charged with threatening behaviour

Yarmouth fines
When 13 youths appeared before Great Yarmouth magistrates today on charges arising from disturbances Yesterday's sea front Inspector John Cooper said the 2 p.m. yesterday and hr his fir hands and hordes of teen were infesting our front and s

The first night youths were all charged with using threatening behaviour likely to cause a breach of the peace. One of them, with a bad record, was sent to prison Three other youths were fined £10, two others £20, one £40, and one

GONE H

A taxi-driver said that had been quiet since the e lone. Many of the youths had one," he said.

The nuisance clashes began when

GANGS PROWL STREETS
Holidaymakers swept aside
BRIGHTON settled down to an uneasy calm yesterday after a morning of clashes between Rival gangs of Mods and Rockers. About 75 arrests were made by evening. Police reinforce Yorkshire Post London Staff from East Sussex West Sussex and Hastings colleagues to help their

Gangs prowled the streets, some of the Brighton continuing Chief batty for more Boroo Rocker Buckingham Brighton on Peacehaven Mon. groups there wer The Park was th Mondaythey there would be clash with demonstration their annual what Bank Holiday what normal on Bank Holiday sh

PLAIN CLOTHES
Plain clothes police be haired Mods and Ro crowds of rockers-he uncouth coffee f an

LOOK BACK AT ANGER!

SUMMERS '64 & '65

CUTTINGS ON LOAN FROM BRADFORD ROCK'N'ROLL EXHIBITION

BAND AID

TEN

D.I.Y. DISCS

SOME LOCAL RECORDING STUDIOS

<u>Cargo</u>, Kenion St, Rochdale (16-track) (524420)

<u>Look</u>, 38 Knowle Rd, Golcar, Huddersfield (16-track) (658895)

<u>J.S.G.</u>, Heaton, Bradford (8-track) (Bingley 68843/B'f'd 832187 or 491231)

<u>Ram</u>, 64 Armley Rd, Leeds 12 (8-track) (Paul on 446622)

<u>Communications Centre</u>, 21 Chapel St, Bradford (4-track) (Alf on 22769)

Most studios can offer you a package deal on pressing single & printing sleeve/label etc. However, you might (a) want to cut some corners (b) deal with the manufacturers yourself (c) try to put together a cheaper/better package for yourself... if so, read on....

Before you do anything else (a) send off to Better Badges (address below) for <u>Common Knowledge</u> (15p + postage per copy) - a mag for DIY record-makers: issue one covers production, issue two promises more + how to hit the media; (b) ask Rough Trade (address below) for their DIY fact-sheets (c) try to talk to a few bands who've done-it-themselves - learn from their mistakes - it's an expensive business!

MASTERING is the production of an initial lacquer (process also called 'cutting'). This is the original for the record. Ask for an acetate of this - will cost a couple of quid, but gives you a clear idea of what the record'll sound like. Expect to spend £50+. SLEEVES & LABELS need to be ready before the master goes for pressing as the whole process includes sticking on the labels & putting the discs into their sleeves. Good idea to design the sleeve yourself (pro designers charge £200 or so!). Labels have to be printed on special paper & there are several companies that handle such work. You can get records with blank white labels & white sleeves for little or no cost & do further packaging/presentation yourself - Common Knowledge No.1 covers this, but it's all very laborious & time-consuming & the end-product's not that professional-looking. Good packaging helps to secure orders from the distributor. PRESSING of the records is the most expensive job (about 15p each on 1,000, bit less if you have more done). You also have to collect them yourself. The labels & sleeves add up to 10p per copy to the price - depending on how luxurious you want it. DISTRIBUTION is the most important thing - no good sitting on 997 copies. Most of the small label distributors pay 45-50p per record - so don't overspend on recording & production! They then sell to shops for 60-70p a copy.

DISTRIBUTORS: (ring first & offer to send copy of single or cassette of forthcoming single - latter means you can get advance orders - most pay cash, some only do sale or return). RED RHINO (Adrian or Tony), 9 Gillygate, York (0904-36499) ROUGH TRADE (Sue or Richard Scott), 202 Kensington Park Rd, London W11 (01-727-4312) DEAD GOOD RECORDS (Andy Stephenson), 292-3 High St, Lincoln, Lincs. LN2 1AL (0522-38322) SCOTIA (Shak), 33-37 Jeffrey St, Edinburgh EH1 1DW (031-557-0029) PINNACLE RECORDS (Dave Roberts), Electron House, Cray Ave, Orpington, Kent (0689-25741) FRESH RECORDS (Alex Howe), 359 Edgeware Rd, London W2 1BS (01-258-0572). Half a dozen more next issue + record, sleeve & label manufacturers & more info.

BETTER BADGES (who also make badges & duplicate tapes) are at 286 Portobello Rd, London W10 (01-960-5513/4).

Continues in next issue... so buy it!

<u>More studios</u>:- <u>Box</u>, 119 High St, Heckmondwyke (8-track) (405681) + <u>Leader</u>, 209 Rochdale Rd, Greetland (8-track) (Elland 76161) also <u>Ric-Rac</u> (Leeds) + <u>September Sound</u> (Huddersfield) - neither listed with directory enquiries!

VENUES

Not a complete list - if you can plug some of the gaps then please get in touch... O.K., Joe, here we go..........

BRADFORD

<u>St. Georges Hall</u>, Hall Ings (man. Mr Rose 32514) (box office is 32513)

<u>Palm Cove Club</u>, Hollings Rd, B8 (Di/Robbie 499895) (or ask for Chris Groves if yr after gigs)

<u>Queens Hall</u>, College S.U., Morley St, B7 (392712)

<u>Vaults Bar</u> (College bar), Gt Horton Rd, B7 (392712 Vaults ext. day or 392713 evenings)

<u>B'f'd Univ</u>, S.U., B7 (gigs at S.U. & in Gt Hall) (Andy Dixon, Soc Sec on 34135)

<u>Royal Standard</u>, Manningham Ln, B8 (27898)

<u>Princeville WMC</u>, Princeville Rd, B7 (78845) (run by Brian McGrath, there Thur eve/Sun lunch)

Some of the disco clubs also have bands when it suits them. Recent ones include <u>Scamps</u>, <u>Gatsby's</u>, <u>Splash One</u>, <u>Maxim's</u> — try 'em - keep it live.

LEEDS

<u>Leeds Univ</u>, S.U. (various halls), Univ Rd, L2 (39071 Soc Sec for main gigs/Ents for smaller)

<u>Leeds Poly</u>, S.U., Calverley St, L1 (Soc Sec 30171)

<u>Marquis of Granby</u>, Eastgate, L2 (454480)

<u>Fan Club at Brannigan's</u>, 174 Briggate, L1 (446985) (gigs run by John Keenan)

<u>Haddon Hall</u>, Bankfield Rd, L4 (man. Shirley 751115)

<u>Fforde Greene</u>, Roundhay Rd, L8 (490984)

<u>The Peel</u>, 63 Boar Lane, L1 (455128)

<u>Staging Post</u>, Swarcliffe Ave, L14 (735541)

<u>Royal Park</u>, Queens Rd L6 (785076)

<u>Cosmo Club</u>, Francis St, Chapeltown, L7 (624138?)

<u>Wigs Wine Bar</u> - wherever that is.... (Jubilee Hotel?)

HUDDERSFIELD

<u>Hudds Poly</u>, S.U., gigs at Gt Hall, Queensgate (Soc Sec on 38156)

<u>White Lion</u>, Cross Church St (22407)

<u>Coachhouse Club</u>, 78-81 King St (20930)

Seem to remember a club called <u>Cleopatra's</u> having bands on sometimes - is that in Hudds...?
+ <u>Albion Hotel</u> (new venue), New St. (24200)

ILKLEY

<u>Rose & Crown</u>, Church St (607260)

<u>Ilkley College</u>, S.U. (Soc Sec 607768 - never in)

Also available for hire is a room in <u>The Listers Arms</u>, Skipton Rd (bit expensive - bid her down - room holds about 120+) (608698).

YEADON

<u>Peacock Hotel</u>, Harrogate Rd (Rawdon 502416)

BINGLEY

<u>Bingley Arts Centre</u> (available for hire - 7982)

KEIGHLEY

<u>Temperance Hall</u> (new venue - no bar!) (603621)
+ <u>Kings Head</u> (new venue), South St (604660)

HALIFAX

<u>Good Mood Club</u> (regular venue but ex-directory!) (try 68905...)

HARROGATE

<u>Adelphi Hotel</u>, Cold Bath Rd (63334)

Also <u>Connaught Rooms</u> & <u>Cock & Castle</u> have bands occasionally.

WAKEFIELD

Seen bands advertised at <u>Tiffany's</u>, Southgate (76215) also at some place called <u>Unity Hall</u>. Must be plenty of others. (75719)

SKIPTON

<u>Devonshire Hotel</u>, Newmarket St (3078)
+ <u>The Rugby Club</u> seem to have bands on sometimes.

This page was researched & compiled by Nick Toczek.

EDITOR'S NOWTZ

Invited along to see Ram Studios in Leeds. They've only been going since last year, but the set-up's impressive & they're full of ideas for the future - of which one is an LP (financed by the bands/distributed & promoted by Ram). First one's on the way already with tracks by Side Effect, Gimmix, The Cat, The Forst, The Beans, etc. (more on this next issue). A 2nd album's already being planned. Hear some recently recorded tracks by The Beans & Motivators - sounded good. Others recording there include You, Dance Chapter, The Confessors, etc. Using their rehearsal studio are Expelaires, Moonstone, The Brain & Twisted Nerve (latter being Paul Mirror's new band - he ran a few gigs at Glad Rags before skinhead/BM violence & other problems stopped them).... Malcolm Day (a.k.a. Fairplay) moving out of Bradford's Royal Standard in mid-April (to The Bluebell in Shipley). He says that he doubts that the venue'll carry on taking bands after he's out. He hopes to do a final gig before he goes - may well be either U.K. Subs or Cockney Rejects with Shagnasty (good name!) in support - gig might be on April 12th or sooner. He told me that Adam & The Ants have dumped vocalist (Adam) & taken on a new Adam who's none other than one Malcolm McLaren (how come the bad guys always win thru??) ... Scamps (Bradford) now running a Tuesday rock club (admission free/bands paid expenses only). Paul (manager) is on 26001 - let's hope (a) it works well & (b) he'll soon be able to pay fees... sad to hear that One Adult have lost their vocalist & that the whole band's future's in doubt... BBC Radio Leeds' Metrognome rock prog. gets better & better - & they're now doing recording sessions (1st 5 bands invited in this month are Shake Appeal, Spider Blues Band, The Scene, Ulterior Motives & one other now being booked). They're also promoting a concert of local bands at St.Georges Hall, B'f'd on May 3rd featuring 6 bands for a quid in (see Gig Guide) - be there!... Pennine Radio also toying with ideas of doing more for local rockscene but need more encouragement - so write to them with ideas of your own... N.B. both Bob Preedy's rock show (Pennine) & Metrognome will play tapes by local bands - just send them in... John Farquhar (who's been running The Vaults Bar - which is now fully booked through to Sept!) is now also running events at the much larger Queens Hall over the road - so maybe they'll now get turn-outs of more than a dozen when bands are on there... letter from a Leeds band co-op 'Centrepoint'. They run gigs, share tasks like fly-posting, use some of the profits from gigs to go towards materials to build their own studio. They're also producing a Leeds fanzine called 'Centrepages'. The bands include 'This Is It'. You can contact them on Leeds 490749... letters back in Jan from Ian Copley & Diane Fairfax - both of whom thought that the first 2 issues plugged my own band too much - they're right, sorry (see, I didn't even name it!)... also in Jan (I'd no space for Nowtz in Feb or March issues) a nice letter from Rugby from Column 88 - a band who rate Bradford as one of the best cities in the country for rock bands to play & "raved about Bradford's rockscene to Ramones, Dammed, Chelsea, etc."- nice one!... I've already mentioned Centrepages - other local fanzines worth reading are Townbeat (Hudds) & Damaged Goods (Harrogate) - both of which cover gigs & bands around W.Yorks. Townbeat's at c/o Peace Works, 58 Wakefield Road, Aspley, Hudds. & Damaged Goods is at Cockstone Hill Farm, Goldsborough, Knaresborough, HG5 8NT (TG's 20p, DG's 30p... no more space... send me any news that you think'll fit in Nowtz... hi to Mandy in Aussie.

RECORDS & CASSETTES
Reviewed by Nick Toczek

THE EXPELAIRES (single on Zoo Records). A-side: 'To See You' has haunting hollow guitar & keyboards + a fast rhythm section give this number a slightly 'Eastern mystical' flavour that's very reminiscent of The Doors. Repetitive vocals add to this impression. Whilst not an outstanding song on first hearing, it's one that sneaks much closer to you on repeated listenings. B-side: 'Frequency' opens with dms/kbd/bass - & again it's very much like The Doors. I like the way the raw guitar steps in & then out again. Nice fade-out to only kbds at the end. They've a second single just out on Rockburgh.

THE VYE (pre-release copy of single on Dead Good Records, with lyric sheet - out c.25th April). A-side: 'Five Hours 'Til Tonight'. This'll get a lot of airplay. It's instantly appealing rock with some fine kbds-work & a catchy hook. Good use of echo on the drums. Like The Knack, they cleverly sit somewhere between m.o.r. pop, heavy rock & polished modern music. The right choice for their long-awaited first release. B-side couples 'Right Girl, Wrong Time' with 'Staying In Bed With The 'Phone'. The first is a slowish pop ballad that's good, if a little dated. Chorus lifts it above the average. Second up is a sophisticated jazz-influenced number that I suspect would sound a lot more ordinary without the neat arrangement that they've put on it. It's a bit like some of Quantum Jump's numbers. In terms of sheer musical accomplishment, The Vye are streets ahead of most local bands - though their work is progressive rather than innovative. (A-side recorded at Sept. Sound, Hudds./B-side at Pollen Studios, nr. York).

DAWNWATCHER (acetate of forthcoming single on own label - should be out by now). It's a double A-side: 'Spellbound' c/w 'Hall of Mirrors'. The first is a good heavy metal number with a nice rough mix to it & hardworking guitars/keyboards that make for a more melodic sound than on most contemporary HM discs. The second is a much more atmospheric piece. It's 6 mins long with kbds to the fore & an excellent fast-picked lead break All told, a single that's bound to please fans of the band & HM freaks in general. It should earn the band a good bunch of new fans as well.

THE BEANS (single on Ram Records - the label's first release). It's a shame to see a good band reducing their chances by having a non-descript name coupled with a rather bland record sleeve. That said, this single's well worth a listen. The A-side, 'No Boys For You', is a real grower with an appealingly sexist lyric. It's the one out of this month's batch that I've been playing again & again. On the other side are 2 numbers - 'Pressure' is a slowish reggaed pop song with deceptively simple drumming, while the oddly-titled 'Ravel It Up' is the weakest of the 3, but OK all the same. (Recorded at Ram Studios, Leeds - where one of the band works).

THE NEAT (single on Neat Beat Records). Picked the disc up myself in the reduced-price rack. A-side's 'Hormones In Action (In My Heart)' which, whilst biologically inaccurate, is a 60's Beatles-ish light pop song. B-side's 'Take Your Chance' which is even more like early Beatles. No year given on this record, but I'd guess they were aiming at the power-pop/flop market that preceded mod revival (i.e. late '78/early '79). It's OK, but pretty forgettable. (Recorded at Ric-Rac Studios, Leeds).

THE SWITCH (cassette of 2 tracks).'OK So I Blew It' is a poppy rock song - the sort of thing that would probably do better on the US singles market than on ours. 'Trick Of The Night' is a bit more original, has more character to it. Kbds/gtrs/voc blend to good effect. A pleasant pair of songs.

The Vye are at The Adelphi Hotel,Harrogate on April 18th.

3 Bands in profile...

THE ELEMENTS (FROM KEIGHLEY)

Voc = Jayne Tretton; Gtr = Stan Greenwood; Bass = Trotwood; Sax/Backing Voc = Spud Taylor; Dms = Stuart Lilley.

In October '79 Stan, Rog & Spud joined forces with Simeon Warburton (R.Gtr/Voc) & Dave Feary (Dms) to form a band called System. They rehearsed but, before they were ready to do any gigs, Simeon left & was replaced (in Nov) by Jayne. They changed the band's name to The Elements, debuting at The Beeches Hotel, Keighley (4th Feb '80) - "& it was a good one... we were pleased with it". A couple of weeks later, Dave left the band to be replaced by Stuart & the current line-up was together for their second booking - at The Woodhouse Hotel, Keighley. Since then, they've done gigs at The Rose & Crown, Ilkley & Morton Institute (nr. Keighley). They've a fair number of bookings now lined up for April & May - including The Kings Head, Keighley; The White Lion, Huddersfield; The Temperance Hall, Keighley & Bingley Arts Centre (last 2 with Ulterior Motives).

I asked them to describe their music: "It's new wave with a jazz-influenced sax that's a cross between Didier Malherbe & Laura Logic." (Malherbe is French for bad grass - so I guess that makes it Sax & Drugs & Rock'n'Roll...).

Their immediate plans are to get more gigs round the area - the aim being to get the band in shape & also get enough money to buy more p.a. gear. They also plan to get into a studio fairly soon to do a demo tape.

Their current stage set is about 50% original material + cover versions of songs by Bowie, Joe Jackson, X-Ray Spex, The Banshees & a couple of '60s numbers like 'You Really Got Me' & 'Let's Dance'.

I thought it might be interesting to get each member of the band to name their 2 all-time favourite tracks - so here they are:-
Trotwood's: 'Star' (off Bowie's Ziggy Stardust LP) + 'Liar' (Pistols); Stan's: 'Clash City Rockers' (Clash - the number that gave this mag its name!) + 'Peter Gunn' (Duane Eddy); Spud's: 'Elemental Child' (Tyrannosaurus Rex) + 'Oh Bondage - Up Yours' (X-Ray Spex); Grok's (manager): 'Lady Eleanor' (Lindisfarne) + 'Si Tu Doit Partir' (Fairport Convention); Stuart's: 'Freebird' (Lynard Skynard) + 'Sin City' (AC/DC); Jayne's: 'Breaking Glass' (Nick Lowe) + 'Coffee Home Ground' (Kate Bush)... quite a mixture!

Contact: Spud (daytime) on Keighley 607366.
(interviewer: Nick Toczek)

Harsh Words (FROM BRADFORD)

Gtr/Kbds/Bass/Voc = Gary Quinn; Gtr/Kbds/Bass/Voc = Paul Deighton; Bass/Gtr/Voc = Allan Hollins; Dms = Paul Mitchell.

Some 5 years ago while at Bradford's Carlton G.S., Gary started a band called Ocean which went thru the usual personnel changes in its early life. Paul Deighton joined as bassist shortly after the band's inception, & about a year later Allan took over on bass, with Paul picking up lead guitar.

The band then drifted onto the Working Men's Club circuit, using a succession of drummers. Playing 2 or 3 times a week, the band eventually got fed up with doing the latest chart hits demanded by their audiences & having the handful of original songs in the set ignored. By mid-'79 they'd had enough & decided to quit the W.M.C. circuit to sort out a new musical direction.

They rehearsed for about 6 months, recruiting Paul Mitchell as regular drummer along the way, & worked up an all-original set (written by Gary & Allan). Under the new name of Harsh Words, they've played a smattering of gigs this year & recorded a demo tape at J.S.G. which has been hawked round London collecting interest at A & M & Virgin among others. (Another trip to the capital is planned shortly, to hassle further for a deal).

Influenced by the likes of Genesis, The Beatles, Jefferson Airplane/Starship & Steely Dan, Harsh Words play an elaborately-constructed but hard-edged melodic rock with a skill that only years of regular gigging can bring.

Contact: Paul Deighton on Bradford 676608.

(interviewer: Keith E. Rice)

THE XPOZEZ (FROM HUDDERSFIELD)

I've not met them, but they write:- "The Xpozez played their second gig recently at The Albion in Huddersfield & seemed to get a good response from the crowd.

We are a punk band & were formed in early '79 after 2 years of grovelling for money to buy equipment. Tez & Nog first put down 2 tracks in a bedroom, but they were scrapped.

We went through various line-ups until we thought we had the right members - then Batey pulled out & left us with Heppy who had been standing in for him. Trimble had earlier replaced Nel in the line-up. Then the numbers just flowed out. We don't believe in long-drawn-out solos, going more for rhythm.

The tracks that stand out most in our set are 'Systems Kill', 'Skitzofrenia', 'New Law' & 'The Sack' although the 3 covers we do also go down well.

Our latest line-up is: Voc = Tez X; Bass = Trimble; Guitar = Nog; Drums = Heppy; Tea = Jayne (a real name at last! - ed); Biscuits = Dave Ellis.

If anyone wants to contact us they could ring Hudds 662008 or Hudds 664386. We want more gigs."

REGGAE

WHITEMAN'S REGGAE: DUB MADE EASY AND YOUR WORRIES SOLVED

My adventures with reggae began with The Wailers' 'Burning' & the first Virgin Front Line sampler - 69p at the time. 'Burning' was fairly basic & not too difficult for a rock addict. Front Line I found forbidding, for a time. Opened by The Mighty Diamonds' engaging singalong 'Right Time', it quickly turned into a menacing &, at first, jarring mesh of dub effects, impossibly gruff voices declaiming mystical slogans & rhythms previously unknown north of Brixton.

Rhythms were & are the key. Once you have heard the music as it was intended to be heard, very loud (but not distorted) in a dim smokey room filled with people, you begin to understand that reggae is - like R & B, from which it sprang - rude, aimed straight at the pelvic region. There are great singers, great arrangers & great producers but they are the icing on the rhythm-cake. Bass & drums are the mainstay & the best records are those that exploit, display & bounce off the basic rhythms.

This is where dub comes in. Non-reggae people frequently ask "What is dub?" (What is religion? What is sex? What is Tetleys? etc.) Easiest to explain by playing some - loud, of course! Dub is instrumental reggae that has been tampered with by the producer. He may blank out certain tracks, bring forward others, add his own - anything is permissable so long as the basic rhythm is allowed to thunder on with as little interruption as possible. So dub may vary from an almost identical instrumental version of a song to an unrecognisable & joyous cacophony of police sirens, steel bands, barking dogs & muttered patois underpinned & often obliterated by heart-stopping bass & drums like rifle-fire. This sounds like a chamber of horrors to the reggae novice but, as with the best things in life, practice makes perfect.

You may be interested in reggae & not know where to start. The best reggae is imported, pressed from "recycled tupperware" (quote John Peel), hideously expensive & usually comes complete with a different label & artist for every record, producers still holding the main vote over what is released in Jamaica. Having found it (not easy) & bought it (not cheap) you may not like what you get. So the best thing is to start with easy-to-get-hold-of full-of-credits British releases. Samplers are the easiest & most obvious way. There are good & bad.

The only person playing reggae on the radio regularly is John Peel & then not much worth listening to tho'.

Most <u>Bob Marley & The Wailers</u> records are pretty classy & easy on the untrained ear.

<u>Burning Spear</u> - not very accessible at first but majestically satisfying eventually (sounds like a sex-aid ad.).

<u>Lee Perry</u> - a producer & occasional singer. Legendary - sometimes with reason.

<u>Augustus Pablo</u> - producer & melodica player. Mostly instrumental & just about unique. A very personal taste.

<u>Mikey Dread</u> - producer, singer & relatively new name. One good LP & some fair 12" singles.

<u>Culture</u> are a distinctive vocal trio. LP - 'Two Sevens Clash'.

Reggae enthusiasts will probably declare I've missed out the best but, as with all music, choice is always personal.

Finally, reggae - under one name or another - has been going as long as 'rock' & deserves as much respect. Even in its most inflated & overblown aspects it never approaches the absurd pretentions, posing & posturing of rock's ego-maniacs.

- ROB

REGGAE CHOICE * REGGAE CHOICE * REGGAE CHOICE * REGGAE CHOICE * REGGAE CHOICE * REGGAE CHOICE

'Are We A Warrior' - I Jahman   'Cultural Roots' - Dean Frazer
'Deeper Roots' - Mighty Diamonds   'Africa Stand Alone' - Culture
'Lover Rock Vol.2' - Various Artists   'In The Light' - Horace Andy

- Roots Record Shop

CODA PRACTICE
(fanmail)

It's not often I feel motivated to write to the press, either music or straight, but I'd like to set the record straight with a few Bradford bands. Being an avid reader of your comic, I've twice noticed in interviews (Beats Working & Idle Rich) that £7.99 a throw for Coda's rehearsal room is considered a bit steep.

Well, let me tell you a story... Once upon a time, when we decided to open a rehearsal room, we didn't have much second-hand gear around so we put our own personal gear up there - Barry's double Ludwig drum kit & Avedis cymbals, my Fender 2x15 cab & Marshall 4x12 & Peavey Classic combo & a Marshall 50 watt top to name but a lot.

Within a month or so the Fender cab was blown, the kit was wrecked, the output transformer in the Peavey was blown, two Avedis cymbals had been nicked, & some bastard stole the valves from the back of my amp & if I ever catch him I'll wring his bleeding neck.

This state of affairs has carried on for 2 years now, with varying degrees of success to the wreckers & thieves.

The room is now covered in graffiti, the acoustic tiles have been ripped from the walls & the gear has degenerated until it's barely working. Generally speaking, the room is a shithole.

In the beginning, the charge was £1-00 per hour with all the gear provided right down to drumsticks & guitars & leads etc. which continued to disappear at an alarming rate.

Why, you may ask, didn't we do something about it? There are very few alternatives. Closed circuit TV? A little bit expensive &, although viewing would be better than the usual crap on TV music shows, someone would have to be paid to sit & watch it every night. Check the room before the band leave the premises? Again, impossible with only one person in the shop at night.

Why not just give it up as a bad job, I hear you ask? Well, for some perverse reason, we feel that someone has to provide encouragement & facilities for local bands, facilities which are sadly lacking in Bradford. Having seen the way some bands started off bashing out a few tunes at Coda, it's good to see that they've turned out to be damned fine bands - like The Negs (sorry, Mysterious Pawprints) & my own favourites, Agony Column & Radio 5 all of whom are worth seeing at any time. More recently, we've had in up-&-coming bands like Idle Rich, Beats Working & Total Confusion, all of whom are serious about their music & rehearsing & show promise of things to come.

The bands who rehearse here seem to split into 2 categories. The first are the serious bands like the ones mentioned (& others). The second category consists of bands who come to make as loud a noise as possible (not just new wave bands, either!!) on someone else's gear cos if they did it at home their parents or neighbours would have them shot. They think that by virtue of the fact that they've paid for a rehearsal room they can physically & electronically abuse someone else's gear & room, invite 43 mates in for a party at the same time, rip off bits of kits & amps, mics, leads, plugs, etc. etc. & generally display as much interest in creative music as the programme controllers of Radio One. These bands had better think again before they ring up to book another rehearsal. Which category do you fall into? And is your band's name scribbled on the drum heads in the rehearsal room?

Rehearsal rooms in London are amazing - all top-class gear, pool tables, Space Invaders, coffee machines, etc. The prices are so outrageous that most Bradford bands would have to do a month residency at The Vaults Bar to afford an afternoon's rehearsal in there. It's the same story everywhere - 'you gets what you pays for'.

We are faced with three simple alternatives:-
1) Clean up the room, decorate it & generally tart it up, put good class gear up there & charge a ridiculous rate for it, thus cutting out the bands who desperately need a rehearsal space.
2) Keep it as it is, but who wants to rehearse in a shithole anyway?
3) Give it all up as a bad job & say it's just too bad that bands that may just get somewhere won't have a chance.

Since last April, providing the rehearsal room has cost Coda Music at least £700.

Your suggestions are welcome. I've already rambled on too long, so I'll shut up. The choice is yours, music lovers. Think about it.

Coda Guitar Night
at Splash 1, B'ford. Mon. 17th March.

GARY BOYLE & FRIENDS/RICHARD HARDING & THE CRESTERS

It was a blind date for me. Splash 1 - the basement with a bar & a Space Invaders - was an unusual setting for a guitar night, & when Gary Boyle took the floor with his friends I was pleased that though I'd lost at Invaders, I was obviously going to hear some good music. Gary (gtr), Paul Birchall (kbds), Gary Culshaw (dbl & elec bass) & Graham Dean (dms) played an excellent set of 7 numbers lasting over an hour. There were 3 Chick Corea numbers, including his amazing 'Spain', & the others were centred around Gary's guitar, some brilliant piano, & a smattering of Stanley Clarke-like bass. Altogether good jazz, fast-moving & smooth, from a new band with an obvious wealth of stage experience.

A break with the disco in half-swing led to Richard Harding playing 3 lovable guitar solos - including 'People' & a rateable 'Dancing Cheek To Cheek' - as an intro to The Cresters, for whom he plays guitar & mouths thank-you's into an invisible microphone. The Cresters being an experienced club band, they got the audience (of a hundred or so) going with medleys of famous tunes like 'The Stars & Stripes', 'West Side Story' & 'When You Wish Upon A Star', finishing off with Brubeck's standard 'Take Five'. Their encore was deserved - they tried hard - even though Gary Boyle's band had played well to a seemingly frozen audience & got none.

All in all it was a fun evening, even down to the fact that I fell into a road works hole on the way home! Cheers, God - & thanks to Coda.

- Ken Turner.

(Surely 'West Side Story' is a film/musical - does he mean 'Maria' or maybe 'There's a Place For Us'? ... must've been that fall - ed)

OPEN LETTERS DEPT. PRESENT

"...... when the HISSING stops......"

"It was the Obnoxious Whippets and the Pluggs here last night."

"Oh yeah? Any good?"

"No, crap! Couldn't hear meself drink"..... That could be the sort of conversation you'll hear after quite a few gigs. And it's not really so surprising that the bulk of local talent is labelled "crap" when the gear they use leaves so much to be desired. Nomatter how much talent there is on stage, the wall of white noise achieved by a heavy mix in an attempt to disguise poor equipment will do anything but improve a performance. I have no doubt that the talent is there, as is the enthusiasm, but the gear is frequently not there.

The answer could be an "equipment pool" — or in other words, if an amp. (for example) is not being used for one evening by the band which owns it, another band could "borrow" it for their own use, and accept responsibility for the amp. for that night. In short, all sorts of gear can effectively be "shared" although, of course, the problems are numerous. Would any owner be willing to "lend" his gear? Will the end result be that more bands improve — or will they only squabble over damage done to gear? Is it possible that the system could be centralized so that the right gear could be found for any band if and when they need it? And initially, the most important question of all ..... has any one of you tried this idea before? Did it work?

Why not write to the Rocker with your opinion, or ideas. Is the whole thing feasible? Then when the hissing stops... who knows?...

Ken Turner.

DEMO TAPES reviewed by Nick Toczek.

<u>KNIFE EDGE</u> (a 9-track cassette that includes one of the tracks on their imminent single). The band play poppy rock music & are fronted by a skilled & distinctive vocalist. The music is distinguished by them putting a guitar to the fore that has a lot of bassy distortion - appealing, if slightly over-used. Above all, though, it's the song-writing that makes this band. There's not one duff number on this demo. Couple that with their go-ahead manager/roadie (Dave Hall) & you've got a formula that seems a cert. for success. One track - "She's Got Control" is the current No.1 on the W.C.R. office (my front room) playlist.

<u>THE ELEMENTS</u> (8-track cassette). While Knife Edge have been on the scene in one form or another, for years, The Elements are a new band - so any comparisons would be naff. The band feels right & the sax-player beefs the sound out well. They're very like X-ray Spex. What The Elements display most strikingly is an abundance of potential. ie. The tape's O.K., but more gigging & experience & they'll leave it way behind. The girl singer's voice has still to realise its full dimensions, but it's a good one. Same applies to the arrangements & cohesion between the different instruments. A whole lot of good ideas, but still raw. Give them 6 months & they should really begin hitting highs.

<u>DANCE CHAPTER</u> (2-track cassette recorded at Ram Studios). Not everyone's music, this, but I go for it. 'Anonymity' got a good review in last issue. These 2 tracks are similar - & that's my only reservation. I'd like to have heard the band injecting a little more variety into these songs, at least as far as the overall sound is concerned. That said, here's a pair of songs that bridge the gap between experimental & popular rock - with the emphasis on the former. The sound is blurred & carries a lot of bass. Dms/bass set up a series of regular rhythms over which the guitar plays riffs. A hypnotic, drawn-out vocal gives the whole a sinister tension.

BETTER BADGES
PRODUCTION PRICES

UNDER 500
1. ALL SMALL RUN PRICES INCLUDE VAT
2. ARTWORK MUST BE CORRECT SIZE
3. REDUCTION OF B/W ARTWORK £1
4. MORE THAN ONE DESIGN IN EQUAL QUANTITIES IS OK

D.I.Y./ ONE OFFS - 1¼" & 2¼"
20p each + 10p P&P

UNDER 100 - 1¼" & 2¼" Colour Xerox
10 off - £2.50 + 10p P&P
30 off - £6.60 + 20p P&P
50 off - £10.00+ 50p P&P

100 OFF   B&W   Colour
1" 1¼" 1½" -£11   £13 + 50p P&P
2¼" - - - -£13   £15 + £1 P&P

500 & OVER
1. PRICES EXCLUSIVE OF VAT & CARR.
2. ARTWORK ANY SIZE, MUST BE COLOUR SEPERATED
3. ALL DESIGN WORK EXTRA
4. 3 WEEKS DELIVERY

SET UP 1st colour £10
       extra colours + £15

MAKE UP 1"   1¼" 1½" 1¾" 2¼"
500 -   £25 £25 £30 £30 £35
1000 -   £35 £40 £45 £50 £60

ALWAYS EXTEND DESIGNS BY ¼" DIAM. FOR WRAP-AROUND.

286 PORTOBELLO ROAD
LONDON W10 960 5513

DEXY'S/v.i.p.'s

LIVE — March 5th at B'ford Univ. — reviewed by Andy Proctor — **LIVE**

Dexy's Midnight Runners - a Birmingham-based 8-piece outfit - are Kevin Rowlands (gtr/voc), Al Archer (gtr), Jim Patterson (trom), Pete Williams (bass), J.B. (sax), Steve Spooner (alto sax), Andee Leeke (kbds) & Growk (dms). Donkey jackets & woolly hats are their trade mark. Their music has a powerful soul feel to it, major influences being Geno Washington, George Benson & a host of other 60's soul artists. They mix soul with their own ideas & produce a new type of music that's not a revival of 60's soul. Ska is old news - best swap your parkas for donkey jackets before the prices go up. Dexy's are definitely not just a fun band. They take their music very seriously. Anti-poser, genuine feeling & total dedication is what they try to put over. They prefer doing it the hard way, playing small venues all over the country. They have just done a 44-date tour. (Kevin Rowlands, I must say, has changed since his days in The Killjoys).

> **Telegraph & Argus**
> **Thursday, March 27, 1980**
> At the Shearbridge public house in Great Horton Road, Bradford, in conversation with customers he said he was a detective constable injuring into the Ripper case.

Dexy's came on at 10.30 & by that time the place was quite full. After the first few numbers the audience started to move with the music. The band really put a lot of effort into the gig & when they all came up to the edge of the stage the atmosphere was almost menacing. Powerful conviction to their music is certainly the impression I got. Even if you didn't like the music, you had to admire the way it was put over. Some of the songs weren't memorable, but these were overshadowed by an otherwise sparkling performance. They went down really well, 2 encores no less. It was a short performance of about 40 minutes - deliberately so, because the band reckon the atmosphere is lost & people get bored if they play for too long.

What I don't understand is what pleasure you lads get out of going round in mobs all dressed the same, armed and looking for trouble...

If you like ska then you'll probably like The Dexy's, it's the sax. The band believe their type of music "will become much bigger than ska ever was/is". With a teenage generation who missed out on 60's soul & now want to hear it, they may be right.

The debut single 'Dance Stance' was good & their current single 'Geno' is even better. Definitely one for your collection. Thanks to J.B. for the Dexy's information.

The V.I.P.'s are Jedrzej Dmochowski (gtr/voc), Guy Morley (gtr/voc), Andrew Price (bass) & Paul Shurrey (dms). The band got together at Warwick Univ. 2 years ago, but have only been playing seriously for 9 months. They play 60's beat/rock'n'roll in a commercial T.O.T.P. style. It's the type of music they like & that's why they play it - not just because they can't think of anything else. They reckon they are a fun band but they "take the fun seriously".

Their stage act was quite lively, plenty of enthusiasm but without any real power. Most of the songs they did were your average Radio One pop but they did do a couple of good numbers. The reception they got from the sparsely filled Communal Building was very tame. After about 20 minutes into the set they did covers of 'Hippy Hippy Shakes' & 'Wipe Out' to try & make a better atmosphere - it didn't work & they didn't get an encore. The band's musical ability wasn't anything special except for the drummer who was excellent.

Personally, I thought they weren't serious at all. They seemed to be mainly out for a laugh & the audience came second. To get any widespread success they will need a better-constructed set & to direct their enthusiasm to writing more original material. To be fair (if it's possible), it was only their second night supporting The Dexy's. They came onto the tour at short notice & had no time to prepare for it. Their music isn't everyone's pint of Whitbread, but if you like fun pop music they're o.k. With enough publicity they could go far (don't quote me) - if Squeeze can find fame playing pop, why can't other bands? Their 3-track E.P. 'Causing Complications' is worth a listen. Thanks to Paul for information on the band.

Bradford Printshop

SILKSCREEN

You can print your own posters for cost of materials

We can print and design posters at reasonable prices

For details Phone 22518

THE COMMUNICATIONS CENTRE

(a posh name for a basic facility)

offers 4-TRACK with DBX at £3-50 p.h. + tape

Gear Includes:-

TEAC 3340, DBX, ITAM 10-4 desk, LEVERS-RICH E200, REVOX B77, ORBAN REVERB, FILTERS, GRAPHICS, etc.

FULL D.I. + MIKES by AKG, CALREC, etc.

KING ALF or MOYA on B'F'D 22769.

Nowtz (Extra)

Good (French) rock programme on Sunday afternoons at about 1300m. Long wave. On 30th March it included Slits, Chords, Revillos, Steppenwolf, early Who, Cramps, Madness, Simple Minds, Heart, Bob Seeger, Pretenders, Flying Lizards, Lambrettas, etc... Action in Keighley: Kings Head now doing regular gigs. Also, Keighley Rock Club at Temperance Hall. Also Downtown Club rumoured to be restarting... Radio 5 release 'True Colours' c/w 'Animal Connections' on Rockbrough in early April & their own single 'Japanese Art' c/w 'True Colours' on Airplay Label withdrawn due to poultry pressings - may repress this month...

PRESS RELEASE

live... **ROSE & CROWN, ILKLEY** — REVIEWER: MICK MARTIN *live...*

It was a shame that only a few of the people of Ilkley knew of Press Release. Had more been alerted to their talents, a medium-sized audience could quite easily have been a packed one.

The band opened at a fast pace in the shape of 'Away'. Tricia Cusack, vocalist, did justice to a number which had a good lyric & more rhythm & melody than many of the so-called sensational smash hits that we hear all the time; & the band performed with a degree of enthusiasm not always present in groups playing smaller venues.

Next up was the band's offering on our fair isle's unemployment, 'Off The Job', which incorporated the dual rhythm guitars of Niall McDonough & Paul Everett (who doubles on keyboards on some numbers) with an attractive lead solo from the former.

Unfortunately, the evening was not without the odd technical hitch. The second guitarist's amp kept playing up & there was a brief stoppage while the experts struggled frantically with the problem. The band seem to be dogged by trouble** but it usually works out fine in the set. This was true of tonight as Mick Rennard, the band's bassist, explained that not only had his own amp packed in during the soundcheck, but at about 7.30 there had been a 20-minute power cut which caused a few hearts to flutter.

Back to the set & a rousing well-constructed rock'n'roll number called 'Violent Times'. To follow this was "Reggae Ship", an expression of the band's opinion of reggae. It's enough to say that one line goes: "ain't no substitute for rock 'n'roll". It was a nice little variation on the standard reggae beat. Then came what was undoubtedly the pick of a fairly good bunch. An instrumental, mainly showing off the skills of Niall on guitar, it bore the charming title of 'Pigs That Fly & Go Dead'. This was their newest number & a good example of the variety of music Press Release perform. This brought the first set to an end & the crowd, now growing in number, showed their appreciation.

Half an hour later, the second set began with another number which possessed the individual qualities apparent in the band's songs. This was 'Who Killed Music?", a reference to the punk/new wave explosion of '77. 'Money Makes Money' followed, after which things were slowed down a little by a song simply called 'This'. 'Bottles' & 'Better Now' went down well with the audience which, by now, was quite impressed. Nobody objected to hearing 'Away' again &, because of the favourable response they had been getting throughout the set, they came back to perform a blues jam which they hadn't intended doing to begin with. Drummer, Chris Parker, said they had not rehearsed it properly & that none of the band knew it that well.

Of the numbers performed, 3 stuck in my mind: 'Away', 'This' & the instrumental 'Pigs That Fly & Go Dead'. The last 2 showed the band to be influenced, in my mind, by the likes of Santana & P.F.M., but were none the less enjoyable of it. 'This' is in the Genesis mould - being similar in style to 'Many too Many'.

Points against Press Release, although quite few, cannot be ignored. There is still a great deal of room for improvement, though tonight mistakes were at a minimum. I feel that perhaps they are too heavily influenced by other bands which may stop them from getting a sizeable following of their own. I find myself asking if they would sell records, given the chance to do them. A lot depends on the new material. The set at present is however very accessible & they are well worth seeing in concert.

****

**STOP PRESS (Release):- Since this gig, the band have split up due to personal commitments & differences. The word is that the bassist is reforming the band & that, of the old line-up, Tricia & Paul have both left.

HARD LINES
64a Notting Hill Gate
London W11 - 229 4919

The Vaults
VARIED LIVE ENTERTAINMENT 4 NIGHTS A WEEK
JAZZ & POP — ROCK & FOLK
TRADITIONAL HAND-PULLED ALES • BAR SNACKS • ADMISSION FOR LESS THAN THE PRICE OF A PINT
HEAVY METAL — WHITE DREAD
BRADFORD

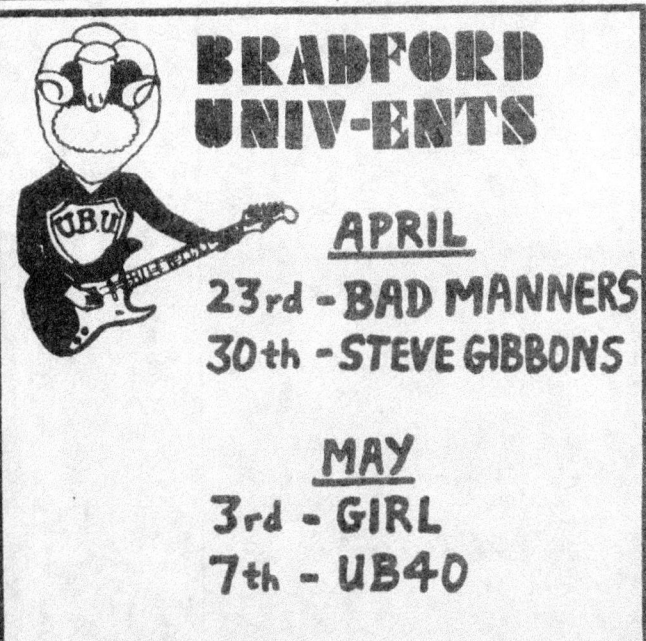

BRADFORD UNIV-ENTS

APRIL
23rd - BAD MANNERS
30th - STEVE GIBBONS

MAY
3rd - GIRL
7th - UB40

(SLIGHTLY SMALLER, BUT JUST AS COMPLICATED... WOOL CITY ROCKWORD 4. by Ken Turner. See below for last month's solution.

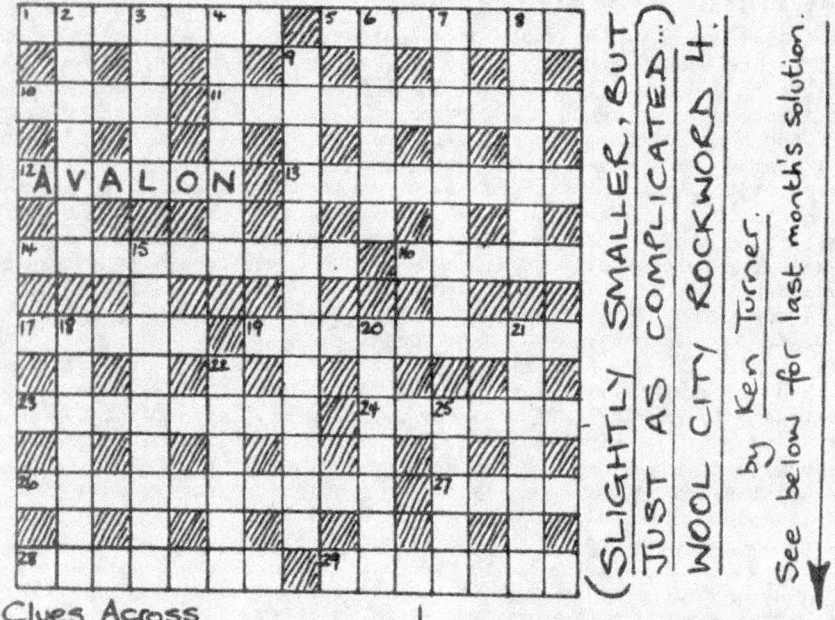

Rockword 3, this was, so who was the winner?.....
3 WINNERS - Marian Fenoughty + Steve Brown + Mick Fearnley...
Cheers till the next time!
Ken

Clues Across.
1. M-murder awful percussionist? (7)
5. Label in black and white. (3,4)
10. Roma becomes bridge player. (4)
11. Necessary items - often naked? (10)
13. Dislike one way to do it. (8)
14. Angry exchange puzzle. (9)
16. Pour water over point in rise. (5)
17. Food musical babies eat? (5)
19. One plus one. (6,3)
23. Bad show for American dice? (4,4)
24. Corned beef protector? (6)
26. Gamble on more than.... (3,4,3)
27. ..... uneven chances. (4)
28. As American coinage climbs. (7)
29. Do to end terrible uneven music? (3,4)

Clues Down.
2. Takes away those not wanted. (7)
3. Leeds University initially ram abstract wall painting. (5)
4. The same at last. (4,3)
6. In now interesting season. (6)
7. Boot boys, not thick, but sensitive! (4,5)
8. Red Noise Column. (7)
9. Same old numbers asked for. (5,8)
15. Adolph's instrument. (9)
18. Band waiting in the bushes. (7)
20. Point of no return reached. (2,2,3)
21. Didn't kill the beast, merely started the clock! (5,2)
25. No-one else's belongs to me - so it must be. (2,3)

Back Issues

Wool City Rockers Nos. 1-4 are still available at 30p each + 15p postage & packing...

No.1 Vex + Violation + The Scene + Deadringer + Press Release + Remainz + Ulterior Motives + Negatives + Shaft Drive, etc.

No.2 Eaten Alive By Insects + Mephisto Waltz + Radio 5 + White Spirit + Total Confusion + Silver Screen Girls + Shadowfax + Salford Jets + Planet, etc.

No.3 Agony Column + Hustler St Band + Another Wrist Action + Excel + The Plates + Beats Working + Scum + Trampus + Limelight + Japanese Soldiers, etc.

No.4 Mysterious Footsteps + Gary Glitter Interview + Coast To Coast + Cameras in Cars + Silent Movie + Def Leppard + Little Brother + The Quick + Elvis Costello + Side Effect + Dance Chapter + One Adult + Witchfynde + Dawnwatcher, etc.

ALL HAVE LOTS OF INFO, CARTOONS, PHOTOS, FEATURES, NEWS, ETC.

{SPECIAL OFFER DURING APRIL - ALL 4 ISSUES (1-4) FOR A QUID!!}

EDDIE COCHRAN...
Twenty years ago this month - on April 17th 1960 - Cochran, one of the most influential figures in the early days of rock music, was killed in a car crash. Below is the report of his death that appeared in the local press on the following day :-

Crash death of Eddie Cochran

SECOND US 'ROCK' SINGER INJURED

AN American Rock 'n' Roll singer, Eddie Cochran (20), died in St. Martin's Hospital, Bath (Somerset), yesterday afternoon after being in a car crash near Chippenham (Wilts) early in the day.

The condition of another American "Rock" singer, Gene Vincent (21), who was also injured in the crash, was said at the hospital to be "fair."

Cochran and Vincent had ended a week's engagement at Bristol and were on their way to London Airport to fly to Los Angeles after a 12-week tour of Britain.

Hit lamp standard

When their car hit a lamp standard, the passengers—who also included Miss Shelley Sharon (20), a friend of Cochran's, and Mr. Patrick Thompkins (29), of St. James's Road, Camberwell—were thrown out. The driver, George Martin, of Blackthorne Road, Hartcliffe, Bristol, was unhurt.

All five were taken to Chippenham Hospital and later all except Martin were transferred to Bath.

Vince Eager, the 19-year-old British Rock 'n' Roll singer, who was due to fly to Los Angeles with Cochran and Vincent, was told of the accident at London Airport. He cancelled his flight and left by car for Bath.

West Riding visits

Reginald Brace writes: Both Eddie Cochran and Gene Vincent made recent appearances in the West Riding. They starred in a Rock 'n' Roll show at the Gaumont, Bradford, on January 30, when Mr. Vincent walked off stage in the middle of a song because of constant barracking from a section of the audience. They also topped the bill at the Empire, Leeds, for a week at the beginning of March.

Cochran, who was born in Oklahoma, is estimated to have travelled 30,000 miles and performed before more than three million people. Vincent, a native of Norfolk, Virginia, is a former boiler tender in the United States Navy. He was one of the Rock 'n' Roll pioneers with Bill Haley and Elvis Presley.

BOB PREEDY PRESENTS

PENNINE ROCK
TWO HOURS OF THE BEST OF ROCK MUSIC....
7.00 P.M   WEDNESDAYS

Pennine Radio 235m MW & 96.0 VHF Stereo
THE SOUND IS ALL AROUND.

 28 Church Bank, Bradford 1. (tel. 307433)

MUSICAL INSTRUMENTS — SALES + HIRE + EXPERT TUITION ON GUITAR, BASS, DRUMS, KEYBOARDS + REPAIRS

REHEARSAL ROOMS + RECORDING & VIDEO STUDIOS + LIVE RECORDINGS FOR BANDS, GROUPS, ARTISTS.

P.A. HIRE (100 - 3,000 watts) + CREW and TRANSPORT. (P.A. Rig :- 30/2 Allen & Heath + RSD & BGW Amps + Shure & AKG & Beyer Mikes).

Agents for :- Marshall, Ludwig, Carlsboro, Ovation, Premier, Olympic, Tama, Ibanez, Pearl, Beyer, A.K.G., Korg, Peavey, Gretsch, Slingerland.

JUST IN !! LARGE STOCKS OF IBANEZ GUITARS FROM £150 - £700.

J.S.G.
8-TRACK STUDIO
Bradford

Allan & Heath 16 x 8 mod. III
Tascam 80/8
Revox B77   Space Echo
MXR Stereo Graphics
AKG Shure Electrovoice Calrec Mikes
Resident Producer

RECORD PRESSING

Rates: £7 per hr. + tape
£50 per 8 hr. day + tape

Tel. Bingley 68843 or B'f'd 832187
also B'f'd 491231

GRASP THIS MONEY SAVING OPPORTUNITY!!!
Annual Stocktaking SALE
Starts SAT. 5th APRIL

Kitchens BRADFORD

Keyboards

New Yamaha CS5	£199
New Yamaha CS30	£575
New Hohner C.P. duo	£399
New Hohner Globetrotter Piano	£195
Wasp Synth	£205
Yamaha CP20	£595
E-H Miers Synth	£95
S/H Jen SK2000	£125

New Guitars

Left Hand Gibson S.G.	£399
Aria Pro II 245	£175
Aria YS 300	£175
Aria RS 850	£175
Eros Bass	£65
Left hand Gibson Les Paul	£575
Anniversary Les Paul	£595
S.R.D. hand made custom 1225	£850

Plus full range of Fender electrics at the best possible prices — call in and see for yourself.

New Amps

H.H. 12 channel Mixer	£350
LAB 9 Combo 520	£275
LAB L2 Amp/Cab 567	£295
M.M. 12/2 Mixer 315	£250
Maine 200w Slave 212	£175
Maine Artiste Amp 295	£225
Fender Super twin 704	£350
Fender twin Reverb	£375
Fender M.M. Bass Combo	£95
Fender PA 100 Amp	£175
Fender Powered Mixer 640	£375
Kitchens PA Amp & Reverb 175	£140
Randall 120w Mixer 531	£275
Custom 150w Mixer Amp 244	£175
Yamaha S100 2 x 12 Combo 395	£295
Yamaha 2 x 12 Cab 199	£135

30% Reduction on Fender Jumbos: Classics
25% Reduction on Landola Jumbos:
15% Reduction on Yamaha Jumbos: Classics

A large Selection of Reduced Drum kits — Including Slingerland, Rogers, Premier, Ludwig, Beverley.

LARGE SELECTION OF SECONDHAND AMPS, CABS, AND GUITARS.

BRADFORD 26 North Parade. Tel. 23577
Also at LEEDS, BARNSLEY, NEWCASTLE, HUDDERSFIELD

West Yorkshire Gig Guide
APRIL 1980

All gigs listed here are correct at time of going to press, but some may alter. If you're keen to catch a particular band then you can always ring the venue on the day to be sure (see Band Aid page for phone numbers). Abbreviations: TBA= to be arranged, TBC=to be confirmed, HM=Heavy Metal, R'n'R=Rock'n'Roll. If you know of other West Yorks. venues that I ought to be listing here, then please ring me (B'ford 21867) & let me know. Thanks. Have a good month. N.T.

TUE. 1
- VAULTS BAR, B'F'D - Trampus.
- KINGS HEAD, K'L'Y - The Elements.
- FAN CLUB, LEEDS - The Switch.
- THE PEEL, LEEDS - Talisman.

WED. 2
- ROYAL PARK, LEEDS - Dirty But Nice.
- WHITE LION, HUDDS - Glass Rock.
- UNITY HALL, W'FIELD - Gang of 4 + Au Pairs.

THU. 3
- PRINCEVILLE, B'F'D - Deadringer. BINGLEY ARTS CENTRE - Agony Column
- ROYAL PARK, LEEDS - Stormy Monday + Cheap n' Nasty + Deep Freeze Mice.
- FAN CLUB, LEEDS - Killing Joke (TBC) + Motivators
- COACHHOUSE, HUDDS - H.M. night (TBA)
- THE PEEL, LEEDS - Spider Blues Band.

FRI. 4
- THE PEEL, LEEDS - John Taylor Quartet (Blues).
- FFORDE GREENE, LEEDS - Kyro.

SAT. 5
- STAGING POST, LEEDS - QVRM. HADDON HALL, LEEDS - Dirty But Nice.
- PALM COVE, B'F'D - Hi Fi Battle (with 2 reggae sound systems).
- WHITE LION, HUDDS - Geneva. ALBION HOTEL, HUDDS - The Zipps
- ROYAL PARK, LEEDS - Spinoes.
- FFORDE GREENE, LEEDS - Kraken + The Originals.

SUN. 6
- MARQUIS OF GRANBY, LEEDS - The Neat. STAGING POST, LEEDS - Convix.
- PRINCEVILLE, B'F'D (lunch) - Kyro. FFORDE GREENE, LEEDS - Japanese Toy.
- VAULTS BAR, B'F'D - City Limits
- WHITE LION, HUDDS - The Scene.
- HADDON HALL, LEEDS - Metal Fatigue.

MON. 7
- VAULTS BAR, B'F'D - Oral Sax.
- ROYAL PARK, LEEDS - Shake Appeal.
- PALM COVE, B'F'D - S.O.S. Band.

TUE. 8
- VAULTS BAR, B'F'D - Side Effect.
- THE PEEL, LEEDS - Talisman.
- ROSE & CROWN, ILKLEY - Jeddediah Strutt.
- FAN CLUB, LEEDS - Silver Screen Girls + support.

WED. 9
- THE YORKSHIREMAN, SKIPTON - Muggins Blight.
- ROYAL PARK, LEEDS - Alibi.
- WHITE LION, HUDDS - The Elements.
- VAULTS BAR, B'F'D - Beats Working.

THU. 10
- TEMPERANCE HALL, KEIGHLEY - The Elements + Ulterior Motives.
- PRINCEVILLE, B'F'D - Vardis. QUEENS HALL, B'F'D - Hustler St. Band
- FFORDE GREENE, LEEDS - Yakety Yak (R & R)
- FAN CLUB, LEEDS - Chelsea + Red'C'. ROYAL PARK, LEEDS - Spinoes.
- THE PEEL, LEEDS - Spider Blues Band. COACHHOUSE, HUDDS - H.M. (T.BA)

FRI. 11
- FFORDE GREENE, LEEDS - Dodgy Tactics.
- RUGBY CLUB, SKIPTON - Muggins Blight.
- PALM COVE, B'F'D - Rufaro.
- THE PEEL, LEEDS - John Taylor Quartet.

SAT. 12
- STAGING POST, LEEDS - Dodgy Tactics. FFORDE GREENE, LEEDS - Money.
- HADDON HALL, LEEDS - Lucky Strike.
- PALM COVE, B'F'D - Seventeen. QUEENS HALL, B'F'D - The Quick
- ROYAL PARK, LEEDS - Proposition 31.
- ALBION HOTEL, HUDDS - Treatment.

SUN. 13
- MARQUIS OF GRANBY, LEEDS - The Elements. FFORDE GREENE, LEEDS - Girl.
- PRINCEVILLE, B'F'D (lunch) - Spider. COACHHOUSE, HUDDS - Bodysnatchers
- VAULTS BAR, B'F'D - Mysterious Footsteps. FAN CLUB, LEEDS - T.B.C.
- STAGING POST, LEEDS - Jeddediah Strutt. WHITE LION, HUDDS - The Dots.
- HADDON HALL, LEEDS - Coast To Coast.

MON. 14
- ROYAL PARK, LEEDS - Side Effect
- VAULTS BAR, B'F'D - Oral Sax
- FFORDE GREENE, LEEDS - Flying Saucers (R'n'R)

TUE. 15
- ROSE & CROWN, ILKLEY - Ulterior Motives. FAN CLUB, LEEDS - Air Raid.
- BLACKAMOOR'S HEAD, PONTEFRACT - Knife Edge.
- VAULTS BAR, B'F'D - Harsh Words.
- THE PEEL, LEEDS - Talisman.
- KINGS HEAD, K'L'Y - Muggins Blight.

WED. 16
- ROYAL PARK, LEEDS - Shake Appeal.
- WHITE LION, HUDDS - Press Release (?).
- ST. GEORGES HALL, B'F'D - Sham 69 + support.

THU. 17
- ST. GEORGES HALL, B'F'D - B.A. Robertson + support.
- TEMPERANCE HALL, K'L'Y - Violation + support.
- FAN CLUB, LEEDS - Crass + Poison Girls. COACHHOUSE, HUDDS - HM(TBA)
- PRINCEVILLE, B'F'D - Slender Thread.
- ROYAL PARK, LEEDS - Fama. THE PEEL, LEEDS - Spider Blues Band.

FRI. 18
- ST. GEORGES HALL, B'F'D - Def Leppard + Magnum + Shadowfax.
- FFORDE GREENE, LEEDS - Arctic Lite Rocksearch '80 (semi-final).
- PALM COVE, B'F'D - Hair Restorers.
- THE PEEL, LEEDS - John Taylor Quartet.

SAT. 19
- PALM COVE, B'F'D - Clint Eastwood (reggae). HADDON HALL, LEEDS - The Vye.
- ROYAL PARK, LEEDS - Jeff Jackson & The Huns.
- STAGING POST, LEEDS - Breaker. ALBION HOTEL, HUDDS - Terminal 3.
- WHITE LION, HUDDS - Airkraft.
- FFORDE GREENE, LEEDS - Witchfynde.

SUN. 20
- MARQUIS OF GRANBY, LEEDS -
- PRINCEVILLE, B'F'D (lunch) - Speedy Bears. FAN CLUB, LEEDS - T.B.C.
- STAGING POST, LEEDS - Breaker. FFORDE GREENE, LEEDS - Eric Bell
- COACHHOUSE, HUDDS - Purple Hearts. WHITE LION, HUDDS - Speedy Bears.
- VAULTS BAR, B'F'D - Spinoes. HADDON HALL, LEEDS - Glossy Mags.

MON. 21
- VAULTS BAR, B'F'D - Oral Sax. MARQUIS OF GRANBY, LEEDS - The Syndromes.
- ROYAL PARK, LEEDS - Coast To Coast.
- FFORDE GREENE, LEEDS - Pole Cats (R'n'R).
- ST. GEORGES HALL, B'F'D - Genesis.

TUE. 22
- ROSE & CROWN, ILKLEY - Ertix.
- VAULTS BAR, B'F'D - Talisman.

WED. 23
- ROYAL PARK, LEEDS - Side Effect.
- SCAMPS, B'F'D - Violation.
- WHITE LION, HUDDS - Shader.
- B'F'D UNIVERSITY - Bad Manners.
- VAULTS BAR, B'F'D - Vietnamese Babies (by any other name!)

THU. 24
- TEMPERANCE HALL, K'L'Y - Mysterious Footsteps.
- THE PEEL, LEEDS - Spider Blues Band. PRINCEVILLE, B'F'D - Diamond Head
- ROYAL PARK, LEEDS - Tom Egan's Ready. COACHHOUSE, HUDDS - HM(TBA)
- FFORDE GREENE, LEEDS - Shades (R'n'R).
- LEEDS POLYTECH - The Mo-dettes.
- FAN CLUB, LEEDS - Subway Sect.

FRI. 25
- PALM COVE, B'F'D - Knife Edge.
- THE PEEL, LEEDS - John Taylor Quartet.

SAT. 26
- STAGING POST, LEEDS - Spider Blues Band. ALBION HOTEL, HUDDS - Xpozez.
- WHITE LION, HUDDS - Jeddediah Strutt. HADDON HALL, LEEDS - Classics.
- GOOD MOOD, HALIFAX - Mo-dettes. FFORDE GREENE, LEEDS - The Vye.
- HUDDS POLYTECH - Martha & The Muffins.
- ROYAL PARK, LEEDS - Dirty But Nice.
- PALM COVE, B'F'D - Cimarons.

SUN. 27
- MARQUIS OF GRANBY, LEEDS - Coast To Coast. VAULTS BAR, B'F'D - This Is It
- FFORDE GREENE, LEEDS - Supercharge. WHITE LION, HUDDS - The Dots.
- COACHHOUSE, HUDDS - Mo-dettes. STAGING POST, LEEDS - The Neat.
- PRINCEVILLE, B'F'D (lunch) - Stallion. ST. GEORGES HALL, B'F'D - Madness.
- HADDON HALL, LEEDS - City Limits.

MON. 28
- BRADFORD UNIVERSITY - ? Surprise guests?
- FFORDE GREENE, LEEDS - Jonny & The Roccos (R'n'R).
- ROYAL PARK, LEEDS - Paradiddle.
- LEEDS UNIVERSITY - The Only Ones.
- VAULTS BAR, B'F'D - Oral Sax.

TUE. 29
- ROSE & CROWN, ILKLEY - The Vye.
- VAULTS BAR, B'F'D - Silent Movie.
- KINGS HEAD, K'L'Y - T.B.A.
- THE PEEL, LEEDS - Talisman.

WED. 30
- LEEDS UNIVERSITY - Wild Horses. VAULTS BAR, B'F'D - Roger Sutcliffe.
- BRADFORD UNIVERSITY - Steve Gibbons Band.
- ST. GEORGES HALL, B'F'D - Undertones + The Moondogs.
- WHITE LION, HUDDS - Rod Mason.
- ROYAL PARK, LEEDS - Middle 8.

THU. 1
- PRINCEVILLE, B'F'D - Sledgehammer.
- ROYAL PARK, LEEDS - The Defects.
- COACHHOUSE, HUDDS - H.M. (T.B.A.)
- THE PEEL, LEEDS - Spider Blues Band.

FRI. 2
- PALM COVE, B'F'D - Oral Sax.
- THE PEEL, LEEDS - John Taylor Quartet.
- COSMO CLUB, LEEDS - The Skatalites.

SAT. 3
- ST. GEORGES HALL, B'F'D - Radio 5 + Ulterior Motives + The Scene + Shake Appeal + Expelaires + City Limits
- ROYAL PARK, LEEDS - Spider Blues Band. B'F'D UNIVERSITY - Girl.
- WHITE LION, HUDDS - Rabstallion. ALBION HOTEL, HUDDS - Private Dicks.
- HADDON HALL, LEEDS - The Clients. STAGING POST, LEEDS - Knife Edge.
- PALM COVE, B'F'D - Dillinger.

SUN. 4
- PRINCEVILLE, B'F'D (lunch) - Private Dicks. VAULTS BAR, B'F'D - Proposition 31.
- STAGING POST, LEEDS - Dick Smith Band.
- HADDON HALL, LEEDS - The Switch.
- WHITE LION, HUDDS - Shake Appeal.
- FFORDE GREENE, LEEDS - The Insiders.

MON. 5
- VAULTS BAR, B'F'D - Oral Sax.
- ROYAL PARK, LEEDS - After Dark.
- FFORDE GREENE, LEEDS - Crazy Cavan + Rockabilly Rebels (R'n'R).
- TEXTILE HALL, B'F'D - Fashion Show with live band(s).
- MARQUIS OF GRANBY, LEEDS - Shattered Doll.

TUE. 6
- ROSE & CROWN, ILKLEY - Muggins Blight.
- VAULTS BAR, B'F'D - Rhino.

ISSUE #6

May 1980, 1,500 copies printed, 20 pages, A4, glossy cover, improved printing

As a consequence of my workload, this issue finally emerged two weeks later than it should have, but it was the smartest edition to date.

Notes on bands profiled in this issue.

I love bands with daft names. Two such outfits feature in this issue. The first was one of the two best-named bands in Bradford at that time. Eaten Alive By Insects vied with Policeman With A Loaf Of Bread for the city's top band-name status. The second was Leicester combo The Deep Freeze Mice (not that great a name, but wonderful when paired with their album's title and label) because their debut LP, *My Geraniums Are Bulletproof*, was released on Mole Embalming Records. What's not to love about that? Read my review of it and enjoy the fact that the titles of the tracks are equally wacky.

PALM COVE CLUB
Hollings Rd., Bradford 8. (tel. 499895).

LIVE BANDS EVERY FRI & SAT
(See gig guide on page 20 for details)

LICENSED BAR TILL 1am

CAR PARK AT REAR
POOL TABLES
GOOD WEST INDIAN FOOD
NEW WAVE & REGGAE JUKEBOX

This month: JEDRELL BANK. PERFORMANCE. THE SOLOS. STALLION. RADIO 5. THE GUESTS. CORNER SHOTS. MOVEMENTS. fashION Show. S.O.S. BAND. + others

---

JSG STUDIOS
8 Track Studio
RECORD PRESSING
Bingley 68843
Bradford 832187

---

235 Pennine Radio

BOB PREEDY PRESENTS

PENNINE ROCK
TWO HOURS OF THE BEST OF ROCK MUSIC....
7.00 P M   WEDNESDAYS

Pennine Radio 235m MW & 96.0 VHF Stereo
THE SOUND IS ALL AROUND.

JSG music

108B Main Street, Bingley.
Tel. 68843.

ACCESS & BARCLAYCARD WELCOME

Part exchange welcome —
amazing discounts.

MAIN AGENTS FOR
MOOG, GIBSON, LAB SERIES, KORG,
FENDER, RICKENBACKER, MUSIC MAN,
H/H, MARSHALL, PARK, M.M.,
CUSTOM SOUND, AMPEG, OVATION,
YAMAHA, LANEY, CRUMAR, PEAVEY,
ROLAND, CARLSBRO & lots more.
Custom P.A.'s up to 2KW
FULL H/H CONCERT P.A. IN STOCK.

RAM RECORDING STUDIO
64 ARMLEY ROAD, LEEDS LS12 2DR.
tel. Leeds 446622 or Wakefield 67470.

SPECIAL OFFER TO W.C.R. READERS

£100 Gives You: 10 Hours in our 8-track studio to record a 3-song demo tape.

Plus: the ½-track stereo master - yours to keep.

Plus: 10 cassettes of the songs.

THIS OFFER WILL RUN THROUGHOUT MAY AND JUNE - BUT DON'T DELAY - BOOK NOW TO BE SURE OF GETTING IN WHILE THE OFFER LASTS!

the HMV shop
5 Cheapside, Bradford. tel. 28882.

This space cost us £10 so PLEASE!! come to our shop & select something from our extensive range of rock, reggae, new wave, jazz records + the hundreds of badges, patches, posters, record care accessories, etc. and buy it to justify our expenditure.

P.S. We also run a fast ordering service.

EDITORIAL

This issue's very late, coming out 1½ weeks into the month - this due to all the work involved in running the local bands' Spring Rock Special at St. George's Hall, B'f'd. The gig drew over 1,000 people - which makes me wonder why it's never been done before at that venue. Reviewers came from the national music press (N.M.E, Musicians Only & Record Mirror) as well as from the T.&A. Print strikes permitting, you'll be able to read the reviews in mid-May.

Next issue will be a double one for June & July, thus giving me the chance of grabbing a break & pausing to plan out the mag's future.

Other news: I've been asked to write for Musicians Only & so hope to be able to give some nationwide coverage to the West Yorks. scene. If the number of new venues becoming available to bands in this area is anything to go by, then the scene really is expanding fast - an encouraging trend in these times of Tory silliness.

Keep on contacting me about bands, gigs, venues, sales outlets for W.C.R. & any other info. that you think might grab me.

Come what May; June & July... till then don't visit embassies,
yours, Nick Toczek. 8th May '80

Edition 6. May 80.

Editor:- Nick Toczek

Contributors:-
- Nick Toczek
- Kev Hopgood
- Ken Turner
- Stan Engel
- Keith E. Rice
- Steve Brown
- Albert Rutherford
- Andy Proctor
- Ron Shirt

TERMS OF SALE: 30p each direct to the public or 45p each by mail order from the address given below. Bulk orders of 15 or more copies can be had at the discount price of 20p each (so why not sell the magazine yourself at gigs, school, etc.?)

ADVERTISING RATES: Standard 3½" x 3½" box is £20 for first time of advertising, then £10 for subsequent placings. Colour, different size, special lay-out, etc. by arrangement.
Ring or write for advertising rates card & any other details.

EDITORIAL ADDRESS:
5 Beech Terrace,
Undercliffe,
Bradford BD3 0PY,
West Yorkshire,
England.
(tel. 0274-21867).

A WEST YORKS. TOP TWENTY

This is my own, entirely subjective, selection from the records & cassette tapes in my collection - most of which have been sent in for review in Wool City Rocker. It's very much a choice of current favourites & will probably be totally different in a couple of weeks. False modesty prevents me from including 'Record On A Radio Show' by Ulterior Motives (from the tape of our Radio Leeds recording session). If I've not had a cassette (or record) from your band then send me one. I'll probably invite someone else to listen to my collection & draw up another chart in a couple of months. Meanwhile, here is mine:-

1. 'She's Got Control' KNIFE EDGE unreleased demo tape.
2. 'Photographs' SILVER SCREEN GIRLS A-side of single on Siren Records.
3. 'Can't Get You Out Of My Mind' KAY RUSSELL home-recorded demo tape, unreleased.
4. 'Where Were You?' MEKONS A-side of single on Fast Records.
5. 'Outskirts' EATEN ALIVE BY INSECTS unreleased demo tape.
6. 'Getting Nowhere Fast' GIRLS AT OUR BEST B-side of single on Record Records.
7. 'No Boys For You' THE BEANS A-side of single on Ram Label.
8. 'Violent Times' PRESS RELEASE unreleased live demo.
9. 'I Met A Man Who Spoke Like An U.C.C.A. Form' DEEP FREEZE MICE track on 'My Geraniums Are Bullet-Proof' album on Mole Embalming Records
10. 'Hey Girl' THE SCENE A-side of single on Hole In The Wall Records.
11. 'We're From Bradford' THE NEGATIVES unreleased demo track.
12. 'Really Into You' SHADOWFAX A-side of single on Bradford Records.
13. 'Darkness' STRANGER THAN FICTION B-side of single on Ellie Jay Records.
14. 'True Colours' RADIO 5 A-side of single on Rockburgh Records.
15. 'Anonymity' DANCE CHAPTER unreleased demo tape.
16. '5 Hours 'Til Tonight' THE VYE A-side of single on Dead Good Records.
17. 'To See You' THE EXPELAIRES A-side of single on Zoo Records.
18. 'Hall Of Mirrors' DAWNWATCHER A-side of single on Dawnwatcher Records.
19. 'T.V. Me' THE DISTRIBUTORS A-side of single on ? Records.
20. 'I'm In A Mess' THE FORST track on 'The Art of Solving Problems' album on Ram Label.

NEAR MISSES:-
- 'Morse Code Messages' - CITY LIMITS (A-side of single on Luggage Label).
- 'Trousers' - ONE ADULT (unreleased demo tape).
- 'Head In The Clouds' - ADA WILSON & KEEPING DARK (A-side of single on Rockburgh).
- 'Don't Tell Me' - THE STATICS (unreleased demo tape).
- 'My Own Way' - SHAKE APPEAL (A-side of single on Rockburgh Records).

Another Pretty Face

Their letter...

Hi Nick, as promised, here are the singles plus photo (sorry it's a dreaded Virgin press pic but it's all we have) & here's a brief run-down on the band.

Mike Scott (voc/gtr) & John Caldwell (gtr) knew each other back home in Ayr, zigzagging in & out of various bands both together & apart (White Heat, The Aaargh, The Mood, Vince Whirlwind & The Hypocrites, Karma) until they moved to Edinburgh for university life. Deciding this was a waste of time, they formed Another Pretty Face (taking the name from a gloriously defunct New York outfit) with two other Ayr exiles These were Crigg (ex-Mood drummer) & James Geddes (a.k.a. Vince Whirlwind!) on bass - the place Edinburgh, the time March '79. One gig later, a single 'All The Boys Love Carrie' c/w 'That's Not Enough' was recorded with William Mysterious (ex-Rezillos) who played saxaphone & co-produced. Julie Burchill made it 'single of the week' in NME & the band toured intermittently with The Revillos. Spotted in London by Virgin Records (boo hiss... a theatrical aside), APF were signed up on Nov.1st '79. Both Crigg & Jim had since departed (as well as temp. bassist Ray Gunn) to be replaced by drummer Steve McLaughlin (ex of little-known local worthies The Cubs) & bassist Willie Kirkwood (ex even lesser-known Station 6). A new single with Branson's buffoons 'Whatever Happened To The West' c/w 'Goodbye 1970's' (again produced by Mysterious) failed to excite the media (despite a few Radio 1 plays) or Virgin, though we think it has a great garage-band appeal.

After mucho hassles & disagreements ('artistic control', huh!), Virgin let us record an album with Only Ones' bassist Alan Mair at the controls. They hated the result. This is because:-
(i) they wanted a 'house producer' like Dave Batchelor, Bill Price, Mick Glossop etc., even though they agree most of them tend to be homogenised; (ii) it wouldn't appeal to the American market (big deal!) like Interview & Jane Aire etc.; (iii) it contained no likely single - nor should it... by contract it was specified that we wouldn't allow previous singles to be put on albums, nor allow album tracks to be released as 45's. Just because Blondie & The Police do this very successfully doesn't mean that it doesn't STINK LIKE HELL.

So then (penniless) we went on tour with Stiff Little Fingers who were very helpful in most ways. When they found out that Virgin had not paid the tour 'buy-on' but that we'd had to pay it ourselves, SLF gave us the whole £2,500 (! - ed.) back. They also encouraged us a lot & were pretty friendly, even nick-naming us Another Fine Mess.

Right now we are planning to secure release for an album + single with a like-minded company. Hopefully we'd also be able to gig constantly & meet lots more fans. We do not set ourselves up (or apart) as messiahs - rather we wish to act as catalysts to encourage Individualism & Belief.

ROCK'N'ROLL IS IN THE HANDS OF FOOLS
Do Something About It!

Cheers, Johnny Waller (Manager, APF)

MUSICIANS ONLY, April 26, 1980.
BRADFORD: Vaults Bar — Oral Sex.

Their singles...

'All The Boys Love Carrie' c/w 'That's Not Enough' (New Pleasures '79). A-side's Bowie-esque punk. Rough mix, but it's a strong vynyl debut. B-side spins to another good rocker - while it comes across as slightly tepid on record, this should be a strong number live. It's really down to the lead guitar work which is skilled but totally predictable. 'Whatever Happened To The West' c/w 'Goodbye 1970's' (Virgin Records '80). A-side... Kev: "Mmm, I like this... has a driving beat on it." Virgin were wrong to dismiss this one. It's a good single, though a different producer might have been able to pull out a stronger & more discernable band identity from the sound they create. Weird opening to the B-side a they blow their punk credibility with a slow & heavy Elton John piano + vocals. Jesus, it's a ballad - complete with a smokey sax solo mid-way through the number. It's O.K., but unexpected here. Kev: "Yeah, a record for 2 o'clock in the morning."

Reviewed by Nick Toczek & Kev Hopgood.

THE COMMUNICATIONS CENTRE
(a posh name for a basic facility)

offers 4-TRACK with DBX
at £3-50 p.h. + tape

Gear Includes:-

TEAC 3340, DBX, ITAM 10-4 desk,
LEVERS-RICH E200, REVOX B77,
ORBAN REVERB, FILTERS, GRAPHICS,
etc.

FULL D.I. + MIKES by AKG, CALREC, etc.

RING ALF or MOYA on B'F'D 22769.

CLASSIFIED ADVERTS.

GUITARIST LEAD/RHYTHM & HARP WANTS TO JOIN/FORM BAND WITH R'n'B, REGGAE, NEW WAVE INFLUENCES. DEDICATED MUSICIANS ONLY. MESSAGES AT 833973 or 834404 for MALCOLM.

LEEDS RECORD COLLECTORS FAIR SUNDAY MAY 18th ASTORIA CENTRE, ROUNDHAY RD., HAREHILLS (by FFORDE GREENE PUB) + 11am-5pm. OVER 50 STALLHOLDERS FROM ALL PARTS OF THE COUNTRY + ALL TYPES OF RECORDS (EXCEPT CLASSICAL) PLUS BOOKS, MAGS, POSTERS, BADGES,etc. ADMISSION ONLY 30p FOR INFORMATION RING LYNN UNDERWOOD ON:- LEEDS 687572.

ROCK DRUMMER AVAILABLE. STUDIO & GIGGING EXPERIENCE. RING NICK ON BRADFORD 34558. (9am-5pm only).

Bradford Printshop

SILKSCREEN

You can print your own posters for cost of materials

We can print and design posters at reasonable prices

For details
Phone 22518

LIVE REVIEWS

AIRKRAFT +Friends — White Lion, Hudds. April 19.

I was expecting to see a couple of sets from one of West Yorkshire's rising stars (NME notwithstanding). Halfway through the evening I began to wonder if I'd lurched into some bizarre joke. Airkraft had brought some chums with them, whom they let loose on stage. First up were the duo Type Appeal, then Forty Bouncing Belgians (an impromptu grouping of Type Appeal, half of Airkraft & a lady in a black leotard), leaving Airkraft a meagre 45 minutes at the end.

Type Appeal were a duo alternating on gtr & bass, adding synth & tapes on occasion. They manifested a truly bizarre concoction of styles. Musically they encompassed Ottway & Barrett (of a somewhat muted variety), Gang of Four (ditto), reggae, Kraftwerk & a nondescript play-in-a-day blandness. Lyrically they evoked a sort of art school adolescent alienation. Visually they utilised Gary Numan (black shirts), Sparks, Charlie Chaplin, sundry bits of Michael Crawford, with lots of righteous grimaces & fluttering eyelashes thrown in for good measure. If, after all that, anybody should wonder why I'm taking them seriously, it's because they actually seemed to be serious. e.g. the chorus of 'Putting on Style': "Putting on style/It's just a facade/If I didn't have my mask/Life would be so hard". I bet Jean-Paul Satre's turning in his grave. I nearly was. They didn't go down very well with the audience, a rugby club outing & drunk (but happy) Huddersfield Town fans.

Since Forty Bouncing Belgians were playing numbers they claimed not to have rehearsed, I won't bother to review them. Suffice it to say that firstly the young lady in the leotard seemed unusually self-concious & secondly I never thought I'd live to see the day that 'Heroes' would be done a la Status Quo.

At 10 o'clock Airkraft took the stage. Luckily they were worth the wait. They're three-quarters from Halifax & one quarter from Brighouse - Steve Greenwood on bass, Sean O'Connell dms, Chris McParland & Simon Jones gtrs. Things seem to be moving for them at the moment - they've a single out - 'Moving Target', a track on the 'Hicks From The Sticks' compilation album - 'Moving Rhythms' & have been getting a good bit of national airplay.

They kicked off at a blistering pace which was maintained throughout the set, in the course of which they revealed themselves to be well rehearsed & musically confident. They're a song-centred band & it's here their strength lies. Apart from XTC's 'Radios in Motion' & a distinctively arranged version of 'I'm a Believer', they played entirely original material. The words were rather difficult to hear, but a band that can put together a song about somebody's infatuation with Joyce McKinney can't be all bad. At times the words seemed to have a romantic Pete Shelleyish edge to them. The music is a pretty distinctive amalgam. For a start, the band utilise 3 fairly good vocalists in strong permutations which obviously give them a decent amount of depth in this department. The rhythm section is as tight as hell, moving between driving funk & XTC'x versatile chopping & changing. Again, XTC's presence, along with that of the Buzzcocks, is oticeable in the chording & licks, the former for example in the introduction to 'Science Fiction' & the latter in 'Joyce McKinney'. Solos were short, to the point & invariably well-played. It never seemed that anything was played that wasn't necessary, the songs rarely straying much over 3 minutes in length. These factors combined with the tight arrangements are a pretty solid basis for the band to work on. But it did seem to me that there was room for improvement. In particular, the set suffered slightly from a uniformity of pace. I'm sure that, with the inventiveness they've obviously got, the band wouldn't find it all that difficult to work in some interesting slower passages. In fact they showed they could do something in this direction with the 'Hicks From The Sticks' track. I've also got a sneaky feeling that there's a shortage of rehearsed material (which might have had something to do with the debacle that went down before they played). Given the amount of effort they put into each arrangement though, that's understandable.

Definitely a mixed evening. In ancient Greece they used to have people deliberately compose bad verse to show up the good stuff by contrast. I wonder if Airkraft have hit upon a not-so-new marketing technique.
— Phil Foster.

OR WAS HE PUSHED... White Lion, Hudds. March 23.

This was a gig I was looking forward to, having read good reports of the band in Townbeat (Hudds. fanzine - not in action at the moment). It started quite reasonably enough, but went downhill quickly. Singer Mick Massey is, I believe, a local rock 'personality'. He is also an extremely irritating singer, which spoilt what little appeal the band had for me. However, the fact that other local rock 'personalities' were in the audience meant that the band received a flattering reception - after all, that's what the music business is all about, isn't it, chums? The outsiders in the audience seemed almost oblivious to the band, & carried on talking as if nothing was happening. The band made little or no discernible attempt to remedy this - apart from Mr Massey, they have virtually no stage presence, &, apart from the drummer, limited musical ability.

It's no fun going through life looking like an Australian...

The songs went on & on, & I got more & more bored. Each time they hit on a nice instrumental break, the singer came back in & ruined things. I went into the back room while the encores were going on, but I gather there were a few of those too. A bitter disappointment, I'm afraid. I hope 'Huddersfield's leading rock venue' isn't just becoming a mutual admiration society.
— Ron Shirt.

SPINOES — Vaults Bar, B'f'd. April 20.

I was late - very late. What could I say to my wife? Darling, I've been beaten up again! Let's face it, she's credulous as hell. A punk stopped me in the street. He said, "You got a light, mac?" I said, "No. But I've got a dark brown overcoat."

Enough said. But when you're on stage, if you can't tell jokes - don't! Spinoes' vocalist had this seemingly overwhelming desire to tell crude jokes badly. However, apart from that & his Eddie & The Hot Rods front-stage stance which makes him look a punk (he isn't) the gig was tremendous fun. For a kick-off some dirty rat had half-inched Spinoes' van, including half their stage set-up. So, with a depleted p.a. & only one microphone (perhaps that's why he clung so desperately to it?), the band got through a ten-number set, mainly blues/rock orientated. With gusto is the only way I can describe how they thundered into the classic 'Born To Be Wild', & they thrashed lovingly through a number called 'Meatheads' (any relation to Blockheads, lads?). Before ending the set with more blues, they'd taken more classics like 'Wheels On Fire' & 'Summertime Blues' by the throat & delivered 'I'll Never Drink Again' & 'If You Don't Like What I'm Doing' with a certain grace to a good-humoured, receptive audience. The Vaults Bar was full & the encores were deserved. No-one objected to a repeat of a number done

LIVE REVIEWS

SPINOES (cont.)

earlier in the set, & it went down well the second time around. All in all, chaps, I'm sorry I was late & missed the first couple of numbers, because although the band faltered once or twice musically (which I'll put down to lack of gear & their use of a relief drummer) & I didn't like the jokes, the evening was in the end just jolly good fun. Whatever Spinoes lacked because of p.a. or presentation, they made up for in enthusiasm. You might not make your fortune that way, but you can give the punters a good night out.
Hope you get the van back.

The Zipps →

AGONY COLUMN / CHEAP 'N' NASTY / THE STATICS — Bingley Arts Centre, April 3.

Arriving late at the venue, I found I'd missed the first band on the bill (The Statics) which was a drag as I'd heard a couple of tracks by the band & had been keen to see them in action. Apparently they'd gone down quite well with the surprisingly small audience of about 150. As if that wasn't enough, I'd also missed most of Cheap 'n' Nasty's bright set. Their last three numbers were of tight, fresh & bouncy pop-rock. This Keighley 4-piece (gtr & voc/bass/kbds & voc/dms) are very polished with a deal of professional stage confidence. If you can imagine Billy Joel gone raunchy rocker, then you'll have a rough idea of their appeal. The kbds set the strong melody lines while the drummer supplies an equally strong range of dance rhythms. Bass & gtr then fill out the sound - with the latter adding neat-but-not-too-flash-or-overlong lead breaks here & there. They came back on for only one encore (the audience wanted a second). 'Dressed To Kill' was an impressive finisher. You'd enjoy this band - look out for them.

A twenty minute wait for bill-toppers Agony Column (who've a single, their second, long overdue from Back Door & now set for release at the end of May). The Arts Centre's an excellent & under-used venue with good acoustics, a full lighting rig, a licenced bar & an easy atmosphere.

Agony Column opened with the forthcoming single 'Love In The Head' which is a strong number but they were still getting into their stride & so it came over as slightly weak. Next up was 'Good Grief' (B-side of their first single on Tyger Records) & this came over well. The band offer clean post-new-wave rock with dual harmonies on this number's catchy chorus. Their accessible, distinctive guitar sound is the outfit's main strength - the clever & creative lyrics running a close second. The 3rd song, 'I Wanna Be Your M.P.' (M.P. = missing person) is exciting & aggressively Costello-ish with a nice short guitar break mid-way. 'Party Piece' which followed is another really strong slice of pop. The band have improved immeasurably since I last caught them in action (Queens Hall, B'f'd in late '79) - & I was impressed then! They're now not just a good new music band, but are very tight &

compulsively danceable - qualities that were lacking in their Queens Hall set. 'Free Love' was introduced by the vocalist as: "a very serious, dynamic & moving ballad". It is a little slower, but still intensely rhythmic. (All the intro's are put over neatly with an ever-present tongue-in-cheek humour). But this is too slow for the band's punchy style & seems weakish. Next one, please... "This is the premiere for a completely new song. It's shit-hot is this... if only I could remember it. It's called 'Blow The Man Down'". And it is good - Agony Column at their best - i.e. fast, confident, intense & highly energetic. Then 'I'm Not Waving But Drowning' (which is a quote from West Yorks. poetess Stevie Smith who shared - she's dead now - birthdays with me = 20th Sept.... interesting stuff, eh, readers??). This is an impressively complex piece of song-writing/-arranging with regular pace-changes & a slow build-up via various rock-n-reggae rhythms to a really exciting finish. The beautifully-titled 'What Has He Got That I Haven't Got Apart From You' is another winner. "Now we're going to do a little reggae-foxtrot: 'Black Is Scared'". Their dancing out front. "Well, someone down here was asking for fast numbers - from here on in I can promise you it's nothing but..." (he pauses & grins) "... a disappointment..." (a second pause) "...with the possible exception of the number after next!" Then they go into 'Love Is A Blanket Expression' (& there's a dirty joke somewhere in that title).

I had to go out into the foyer at this point to sell last month's Wool City Rocker (hot off the press that evening) & so missed the titles of their last three numbers (which included a couple of encores. I recognised '(I Had It All) Worked Out' which was the A-side of their first single - a much improved version of the record. And I was told that one of the others was called 'I've Got Performer Trouble' (another dirty joke?).

Three excellent bands - so what's wrong with all you stop-at-homes? The place should've been full.
— Nick Toczek.

TAKE 3 TYPES OF ROCK: POP, JAZZ & PUNK....

The Zipps (Leeds/B'ford)

Line-up:
Spark = Bass/Backing Vocs; D.J. = Gtr/B.Vocs; Simon Sharp = Dms; George Little = Voc. *(Interviewed by Nick Toczek)*

The Zipps have only been in action since early '80, having done 4 gigs - The Beehive in W'field, The Albion in Hudds., Batley Town Hall & The Royal Standard in B'f'd. They'll have done a 5th (at Queens Hall, B'f'd) by the time you read this, with others lined up during summer at The Beehive, The Vaults (B'f'd) & The White Lion (Hudds.).

All have been in various local bands in the past & George's claim to fame is that he played the punk, Andy Ferocious, in the rock musical 'Oz Iz OK' (with music by The Howard Ellis Band) which had a run at The Alhambra, B'f'd & also at Leeds Civic Theatre. It was a popular show, but lack of capital called a halt to plans to take it down to London.

Average age 20, they describe themselves as a new wave pop band. Well organised - especially for such a new outfit - they've got a room in the cellar of a club in Leeds where they've the gear permanently set up for rehearsals. They already have badges printed &, on 9th May, will be going into September Sound Studios (Hudds.) to record a demo tape. This demo, together with some carefully designed publicity, will then be going out to record companies in the hope of swinging a deal for the band. They are keen to get a deal with a company (they'd like it to be A & M) rather than do an own-label job.

They write all their own material & describe their stage presentation as visual - with loud colours & high-energy movement. They've no specific influences, but aim at a commercial sound: "It seems to work well in that audiences enjoy us & no-one's yet come up after a gig saying that we sound like anyone else."

Contact: Dave Johnson (D.J.) on B'f'd 637634.

Middle 8 (B'ford/Leeds)

Line-up:
Dave Cass = Kbds/Voc; Steve Pollard = Gtr; Mick Collins = Bass/Bass pdls/Voc; Neil Raper = Dms. *(Interviewed by Keith E.Rice)*

Dave & Mick started off together in G.P.O. about 4 years ago, playing jazz-rock in the style of Genesis, Camel, Yes & Weather Report. During the band's lifetime, they accrued a good reputation, an excellent demo tape which was listened to with interest by record companies approached, & eventually Neil as their regular drummer.

G.P.O. became Middle 8 about a year ago when Dave, Mick & Neil joined up with Steve, formerly with an out-&-out rock band, Bastille. Predictably, the new band rocks a lot more than its predecessor, although the jazz influence is still very powerful. With an all-original set, written almost entirely by Dave, the band have slowly but surely been winning over initially-reluctant rock audiences & are now hoping to break onto the university circuit.

They have recently recorded 5 numbers at JSG in Bradford, & hope to have their popular instrumental 'Countess Of Lyme' released by either Pye or Dead Good Records in June; that will be followed by an E.P. headed by 'Carry on Nigel' in August.

Middle 8 are probably one of the most technically accomplished bands gigging in West Yorkshire at present. All but Steve are full-time musicians; all of them work in dance bands when Middle 8 is inactive & have done prodigious amounts of live & studio session-work.

Contact: Dave on B'f'd 687881 or Mick on Leeds 757662.

TERMINAL 3 (B'ford)

Line-up:
Dom = Voc; Nev = Ld gtr/Voc; Kenny = Bass; Mick = Dms. *(Interviewed by Nick Toczek)*

Dom & Nev had been rehearsing with a band they called Bloody Minded when they decided to form Terminal 3. The band came together in Feb. & have done 3 gigs - all in B'f'd - 2 at Scamps, 1 at Queens Hall. At the first of these, they only did 3 own numbers + covers of songs by Crass, S.L.F., Slaughter & The Dogs & U.K. Subs. They're now busy writing more of their own songs & dropping some of the covers. By the time this has been printed, they'll have clocked up a 4th gig (at Albion, Hudds.) & they're lining up more - including a support to Mysterious Footsteps & Delta 5 at B'f'd Univ. With more gigs, they hope to build up the sort of punk following that The Negatives used to pull.

"Most of our songs are pretty hard punk - though we've just added a new (reggae) number called 'Ban The Bomb' & also do a semi-reggae called 'Iron Fist' that was written by Nev & a friend, Steve Parkin. A guy called Turkey wrote a couple of our lyrics for us - though mostly it's Kenny & Dom who do the lyrics & Nev who writes all the music. Our own songs are going down well in the set - that's why we're doing more. Terminal 3 at Heathrow is for international departures & Mick likes airports."

Contact: Dom/676101, Nev/576558 or Mick/601971.

- IT WAS BAD ENOUGH WHEN THEY GOBBED ON BANDS, BUT THIS IS RIDKULOUS!!

BAD MANNERS

ONE GIG, TWO REVIEWS

B'F'D UNIV., 23 APRIL

Bad Manners are Fatty Buster Bloodvessel (Doug Trendle) - vocs, Winston Bazoomies (Alan Sayag) - vocs/mouth organ, Louis Alphonso - rm.gtr, David Farren - bass, Martin Stewart - kbds, Brian Chew-it - dms, Andrew 'Marcus Absent' Mason - sax, Chris Kane - tenor sax, Gus (Hot Lips) Herman - trumpet.

Bad Manners are a N.London-based 9-piece & in my books are the nuttiest & funniest of the ska revival bands. The rather large Doug formed the group about 5 yrs ago as Stoop Solo & The Sheet Starchers. Two years ago, their numbers peaked at 16 members. Slimming down to 9, they then began in ernest. In the early days, their music was more R'n'B/reggae orientated, but they progressively moved deeper into ska.

It's only since Christmas that the band have been playing full-time - it being then that they signed a record deal with Magnet. Although they are definitely a ska band, they have retained their roots. The music has an R'n'B/Caribbean edge to it, shown by their versions of 'Woolly Bully' & 'Lip It Fatty'. These roots set them apart from other ska revivalists as being original.

The band came on at 10.30pm, the support band having pulled out at the last minute without time for a replacement to be found. The first number 'The Magnificent 7' was done without Fatty. He came on for the second number 'Woolly Bully' which was magic. Doug's size & his amazingly long tongue (which was constantly displayed) make a stunning focal point for the band. Other excellent tracks were 'Ne-Ne Na-Na Na-Na Nu-Nu', 'Lip Up Fatty', 'Holidays', 'The Killer', 'King Ska/Fa', 'Can't Help You' & the most amazing version of 'Monster Munch' you could ever imagine. This unusual bunch of characters dance & loon about on stage, are great to watch & even better to dance to. No politics, no social commitments, just plenty of posing & really good fun music.

They got a really good reception, rightfully receiving two encores - the first of which included 'El Pussycat' & 'Ne-Ne Na-Na Na-Na Nu-Nu', while the second (they could've done a third) was 'Woolly Bully' played fast - perhaps the best number of the night.

Their brass section is one of the best in the business & it blends really well with the mouth organ. What they lack in musical brilliance, they certainly make up with lots of effort & energy. The band were a bit disappointed with the turn-out, but it didn't stop them putting everything into the performance.

Their single 'Ne-Ne Na-Na Na-Na Nu-Nu' hasn't done as well as it should have done, but there's still time. The album 'Ska'n'B' from which most of their set comes is really good & received excellent reviews in the national music press.

18 great songs, a loony full-filled performance, lots of dancing & an electric atmosphere. Live ska at its best by Bad Manners.
- Andy Proctor.

University has Bad Manners! Shock Horror Probe! Rasp, Yelp, Bellow, Poot, etc... Well, it wasn't quite like that. In fact, after-thoughts like "You've seen the poster - now meet the flesh. All of it!" & so on. I was, to say the least, apprehensive at the idea of such a confrontation. That is, until I arrived. Having made up my mind to sidle neatly up to the dressing room door & introduce myself with a nervous "Hi", & possibly a step backwards, I was about to knock when suddenly, & without prompting, the door was opened by - not a jolly giant of a man - but a young lady! Gasp, sighs of relief. "'Ello", she said, &, not that I'm usually this forward with ladies, I found myself asking "Hello, can I come in?" Indeed, in we went, but not to find things rapidly in preparation for the gig. The only real sign of musical life was Andrew Mason (saxophonist) licking reeds in a corner of the room while deftly cracking a bottle of Stella Artois. The others (namely Prince Nutty & Chalkie) informed me that the support band hadn't arrived & the lads in the band were playing pool.

The band are at their best on stage, I was told, despite rumours of practical jokes galore & spontaneous outbursts of kleptomania when they're about, so off I dutifully went to watch & listen. The turn-out for the gig wasn't encouraging, & I expected more bodies to arrive later. They didn't, but of course had Bad Manners appeared on TOTP prior to the gig (they appeared on it next day - ed.) it would have been vastly different. As it was, however, if you weren't there, quite simply you missed a treat. Bad Manners potively flew onto stage & super ska took over. After a swift burst of 'Woolly Bully', Fatty (or is it Buster?) tried to dedicate the next number to a mate of his, presumably Norman or something, but it must have been nerves that made it come out as "This one's for you, Ne-Ne Na-Na Na-Na Nu-Nu!" Never mind, eh, because it was superb. Then that was followed by something for everyone - Big Shots, Scarfaces, Monsters, Fatties, more Woolly Bullies & even Pussy Cats! I loved the neat version of the old Dave & Ansel Collins hit 'Double Barrel' too. In short, it proved difficult & unnecessary to judge each number seperately. There seemed little point once the audience were whipped into a frenzy, & the band got them going with a rapid-fire & constantly excellent set. The overall sound was crisp, brilliant & exciting, & I especially liked the wailing saxaphone. (Maybe that's what Stella-impregnated reeds do for you?). Anyway, the crowd, still disappointingly small, but having enough fun for a thousand, demanded more when the music stopped, & for a moment it almost seemed as if the set was to be played again in full! We should be so lucky, but I was more than pleased to have lived through it once! Nice show fellas. Cheers - & I hope Norman buys the single & the album.
- Ken Turner.

RINKY TALES PRESENT: Life in Snot Town

- TERRIFIC!
- HOW'S YOUR MUSIC GOING?
- I JUST DISCOVERED SOMETHING THAT'LL REVOLUTIONISE THE MUSIC SCENE.
- LISTEN
- TWANG!
- THAT'S GREAT! WOT'S IT CALLED?
- GASP!
- I CALL IT A CHORD.

2 WAKEFIELD BANDS
(both on Rockburgh's 'Hicks From The Sticks')

Ada Wilson's Keeping Dark

Had a package through the post from this band, so what follows is gleaned from that.

Keeping Dark centres around Ada Wilson (ex-Strangeways) on gtr/vocs, Pete Morton (ex-Just Frank & Strangeways) on dms & Steve Smith (ex-Just Frank) on bass/vocs. Another regular member is Dave Whittaker (who, as Music For Pleasure, wrote & performed 'Human Factor' on Rockburgh's 'Hicks From The Sticks' album) on pno/organ. Other musos who occasionally join in are Furb (vocs/harmonica) + Ian Nelson (sax) + Gough Snape (special effects) + Maggie Coen (violin).

The band's first vynil action was a single, self-financed & released on Ellie Jay Records late last year. 'In My Quiet Room' c/w 'I'm In Control Here' was a November single of the week in Sounds. The recent follow-up (on Rockburgh Records) is 'Head In The Clouds' c/w 'It Doesn't Have To Be' - the A-side of which also features on 'Hicks From The Sticks'.

Contact: David Oddie (manager) on W'f'd 255803.

The Singles: 'In The Quiet of My Room' c/w 'I'm In Control Here'. 1st side opens with drum machine. Add melancholy vocals/strummed acoustic gtr/hand-claps/violin. Oddly '60s early Pink Floyd sound. Later on there's kbds, & still the drum machine underpinning it all. 2nd side has just acoustic gtr. + vocals. Short-haired hippie folk-rock. Daevid Allen-ish. Clean production on this anachronism. Ada doing his own thing out of time. Oh, & it's on Ellie Jay Records '79.

'Head In The Clouds' c/w 'It doesn't Have To Be'. Maybe we've got it all wrong & it really isn't 1980. Ada's now taken up a fuller & more poppy band sound & has become Hollies/Beatles. This'll be a smash hit during summer '65 &, as such, it's a highly commercial single with sax/kbds /tambourine filling out the sound on the A-side. B-side's similar. Rockburgh '80. (Nick Toczek + Kev Hopgood)

Stranger Than Fiction

S.T.F. are Steve Kennet (voc/gtr), brother Stuart Kennet (dms), Glynn Banks (bass) & Norman Pierce / Sean McKernan (both on synths).

The original band formed about 18 months ago with the first 3 listed above + a rhythm guitarist who soon left, being replaced by Terry Costello on synth. This line-up recorded the band's only single to date, but Terry left after about 9 months - "He didn't really fit in with us - didn't even look right for the band." Norman was a rhythm guitarist (ex-Psychic Volts, an outfit from Dewsbury) & Sean's always been with us, helping out as a roadie/sound engineer. "For the type of stuff we do, we needed synth operators rather than kbds players, so it wasn't too hard to work them both in on the songs. This is now done & the band have just started gigging again with recent gigs in W'f'd, Sheffield & Barnsley. These have gone well & they're pleased with the new line-up.

The single - "Into The Void" c/w 'Darkness' was self-financed & released on Ellie Jay Records in a pressing of 1,000. It was recorded a September Sound last September - "About the time we did Leeds Sci-Fi Festival." It got little reaction from the music press (a one-line mention in NME) but John Peel played it. They've sold about 800, mostly at gigs & without any distribution deal. It still sells well & they should sell out soon.

A phone call from Des Moines about 'Hicks' prompted them to send him a demo tape of 5 songs done by Steve, Stuart & Glynn (with Steve doubling on kbds - the whole recorded in a small garage studio) &, with no time for them to rerecord numbers, they let him take the demo version of 'Immortal In Mirrors' for the album - so they're now not too pleased with the quality of the track as it appears on the record.

In early May, they're going into Cargo Studios to record a second single - probably 'Losing You' c/w 'Touch & Go' or 'Chameleon' - Des Moines having offered to secure them a deal.

They aim at a commercial electronic sound - but not too commercial. "There's a good melody-line to all the songs. Most are written on gtr, but the final product has synths up front, with the gtr actually dropped completely from a couple."

For the immediate future, they're after gigs plus a recording & management deal. Din-Disc have just recently expressed an interest in the band. They do see themselves as both a live & recording band: "We always seem to get a good reaction live. The music's danceable, ranging from weird jerky insect dances (Chameleon), though more poppy synth songs to eerie mysterious songs (Ice Age)."

Contact: Steve on Royston 3992. (Interview: Nick Toczek)

The Single: 'Into The Void' c/w 'Darkness' (Ellie Jay Records). A-side is synth-based electronic rock. Android boogie. It's much more danceable than most Ultravox/Numan type music, mainly due to the absence of a drum-machine. B-side opens with mechanical sounds... [illegible] ...again in the darkness. (Nick Toczek + Kev Hopgood)

BAND AID

Last month's issue contained the first 'Band Aid' page (listing venues throughout W.Yorks & giving some info. on D.I.Y. record production. It seemed popular, so I'll try to make it a regular feature. In fact, I'm planning to produce a northern bands' handbook at the end of the year which will have in it all the general info. I've gathered that'll be useful for groups, managers, etc. Look out for more about this in forthcoming issues. Meanwhile, here's this month's page:-

D.I.Y. DISCS

I listed some local recording studios in last ish. The next step is to get a master laquer cut - ie to transfer the recording onto disc.

You may have noticed that, scratched into the area between the grooves & the label on a lot of small label/independent records are the words 'A Porky Prime Cut'. This guy (real name George) has a reputation for doing a good job. He used to work for Master Room, 59 Riding House St., London W1. (tel. 01-637-2223/4) but has now moved to IBC Sound Recording Studios, 35 Portland Place, London W1. (tel. 01-637-2111). The cutting engineer that I've dealt with & found very helpful is Brian East of Spectrum Sound, 127 Ashford Road, Bearsted, Maidstone, Kent. (tel. 0622-3891). Others you might try include Trident Recording Studios, 17 St. Annes' Court, London W1. (tel. 01-734-9901); Tape One Studios, 29/30 Windmill Street, Tottenham Court Rd, London W1P 1HG.(tel. 01-580-0444/5/6); Pye London Studios, 17 Gt. Cumberland Place, London W1. (tel. 01-262-5502). There are others, but these should be enough to give you some choice. Reckon on paying about £40 + an extra £5 or so for an acetate (it's optional, but I'd highly recommend that you have one done - it's a disc that you can play only a few times with a light needle, but it's the only chance you'll get to listen to the disc before you pay for the pressing - if it's not right, then you can stop here & maybe remix your studio tape or check for a mastering fault).

While this is being done, you should also be having labels & sleeves printed. The pressing plant will require masters, labels & sleeves before they go ahead with pressing - this because the pressing, labelling & inserting into sleeves is one through process. The printing of labels is a specialised job because of the odd shape of labels & the glue used. Likewise with sleeves because of the awkward folding & gluing process. Consequently, these tend to come a bit expensive. For labels, try Shalford Press, 85b Bradford Street, Braintree, Essex, CM7 6AU. (tel. 0376-21125/26110); Peter Gray (don't have the address) (tel. 01-464-0828); Harrison & Son Ltd., Printing House Lane, Hayes, Middlesex. (tel. 01-573-3828). However, you can cut corners here. Most pressing plants will put on plain white labels free of charge - you can them use either a rubber stamp or have stickers printed if you're prepared to put in the time in adding the info. to each record individually - not recommended if you want the thing to look at all 'professional'. Sleeves are done by Delga Press (the main ones), Dingwall House, 8 Marlborough Road, Bromley, Kent, BR2 9NH. (tel. 01-460-0112). Others include Uniprint, 117 Euston Road, London W1. (tel 01-388-1559); Hannibals (no address), (tel. 0533-695413); West 4 Record Covers, West 4 Tapes & Records, 169 Chiswick High Rd., London W4 2DR. Supply your own artwork/design if you can. Play about with ideas before deciding on a final cover - you'll have to live with it & rely on it to sell your record for you. A good photo, letraset lettering, the help of a friend who can do a good cartoon or drawing, etc. are all worth considering. If you can afford extra for a card cover, they always look better than paper covers. Good idea to go for bright colours & an eye-catching design so that people notice it in a record shop display. Make sure the group's name is clearly legible so anyone who's hear of you can easily spot it. If you send off tape, sleeve design & labels on the same day, they should all be ready within about three weeks. Arrange for all of them to be delivered direct to the pressing plant, but do ask to see proofs of labels & sleeves to check for any errors before they're actually printed up.

Next month I'll cover pressing & the legal & copyrighting angle. After that I'll give some info on getting reviews, airplay & general media coverage.

Finally, for those of you already with singles out or in the pipeline, here are some more distributors (I gave about half a dozen last month):- Spartan, London Road, Wembley, Middlesex. (01-903-4753/6); Mojo (reggae), 94 Craven Park Road, Harlesden, London NW10; Virgin Records Retail Ltd., 32 Avonmore Road, Avon Trading Estate, West Kensington, London W14. (tel. 01-603-4588).

Thanks to Rough Trade, Common Knowledge & the band Scritti Politti for most of the addresses. Do read the info in WCR 5 - much of which ties in with the above (back issues are 45p inc. postage from me).

SERVICES

P.A. Hire. Several bands do regular p.a. hires - in Leeds Bradford area these include Agony Column (up to 1,000 watts - tel. B'f'd 664885 or Leeds 460679), Shadowfax (tel. Bill Chapman on Pudsey 576991) & Trampus (I don't have their number, but they're in The Vaults Bar most evenings). Coda & JSG (see adverts) both do hires on a wide range of gear. J.C. P.A. Hire are supposed to be very good, cheap & efficient (ring Chris on Royston 3267 or John on Royston 3231). For up to 2,000 watts, ring Neil Brewer P.A. Hire on 0254-667463 (home) or 0254-56563 (work).

Lighting. Sweat Lighting & Effects are at 6 Field Head Lane, Illingworth, Halifax, HX2 9JL. They're good & cheap. (Ring Dave Fryer on H'f'x 247331 or Chris Rodziewitz on Brighouse 718092).

Transport. You can usually find a whole list of self-drive hire companies in yellow pages (let your fingers do the roadie-ing) &/or the local paper. Also in the local paper will be a list of driver-&-van hires (under light removals, with the best list appearing on Fri/Sat - cut these out & file them for quick reference - you never know when you might need them). We (Ulterior Motives) use Malcolm Douglas (B'f'd 44428). Dave Hall (manager/roadie for Leeds band Knife Edge is also available most nights on Leeds 741072).

So that's it. Next month on this page I'll also be doing a feature on publicity - covering posters, leaflets, stickers, badges, radio & press gig guides (including WCR's!), etc. Few gigs are properly publicised & as a result bands play to smaller audiences than they need to, venues often fold due to lack of attendance & we all lose out. I hope that some of my ideas might help to reduce these problems at your gigs.

Room for one last note here. If you've any ideas on info. that you'd like to have included in future 'Band Aid' pages then please get in touch - I'll happily try to research & collate any useful details.

VINYL & TAPE REVIEWS
45's, 33's and Tapes

45's

GIRLS AT OUR BEST: Getting Nowhere Fast c/w Warm Girls (Record Records '80). We put the 2nd side on first - the one that everyone seems to be treating as the A-side. It's good distinctive post-punk with Judy Evans (vocs) sounding like Annie Halsam (of Renaissance) improbably drafted into The Banshees. The other side's more of a John Peel Show track. I prefer it, Kev's less keen. It's a grower - I like the record more each time I he r it. This was single of the week in NME a couple of weeks ago, but don't let that put you off. The band's from Leeds - I believe they're a session group that includes a Mekon.

SHAKE APPEAL: My Own Way c/w Not Interested (Rockburgh '80). A-side has bouncing, mildly reggaed guitar plus Fiona Mitchell sounding mid-Atlantic. Blondie meets Pretenders for a likeable pop-song that should serve to earn this Leeds band some airplay & media attention. B-side is faster & more aggressive, but more monotonous too - Kev & I weren't that interested either.

RADIO 5: True Colours c/w Animal Connections (Rockburgh '80). A-side: Kev points out that the intro's just like Bryan Ferry's 'Dance Away'. Effective use of their Roland 77 drum machine throughout, with the full band only coming in for brief chorus sorties. I've heard this song often (live, on B-side of 'Japanese Art' their own-label single released last month & on 'Hicks From The Sticks') & I like it very much. Kev was less keen on first hearing. B-side: Fast chopped rhythm gtr. & vocals. Kev:"Like The Buggles gone heavy." Interest ng discordant guitar break using long-delay echo effect. Kev: "An interesting single but it won't make No.1." R5 are currently Bradford's band-most-likely-to.

BAD MANNERS: Ne-Ne Na-Na Na-Na Nu-Nu c/w Holidays (Magnet '80). We were given this a their recent B'f'd Univ. gig. Put the B-side on first. It's dancing ska with brass section to the fore. Nothing much to distinguish it from the rest of this ilk. A-side's one we both like. The band have really mastered this style of music & can inject the same infectious & loony sense of fun into it that Madness achieve. Deserves to be more than a minor hit.

-listened to be Kev Hopgood & Nick Toczek

Two more arrived after Kev had gone home to Huddersfield - so here's my solo reaction to each:

SILVER SCREEN GIRLS: Photographs c/w Silver Screen Girls (Siren Records '80). I've seen SSG live twice (Vaults Bar & B'f'd Univ) &, for a band supremely confident in their own ability, found them disappointing in the extreme... but here's the vindication. This is an remarkably fine single. Both the songs powerful with excellent arrangements & good mix of sound. Living up to their glam-rock/fem-rock image, they really do pick up where The New York Dolls left off. This is heavy instant pop that's tight as hell with powerful 4-part vocals, driving rhythms & melodic strength. A-side guests Alan Bailey on kbds & he injects just the right extra texture. B-side's as good - well-paced with good guitar-work. SSG are from Bradford.

RICH WILDE: The Lady Wants To Be Alone c/w The Lady Wants To Be A Clone (Dead Good Records '79). Rich, who seems to come from somewhere in the direction of Hull, is credited with vocals, synth sisers & 'treated' percussion. No other musicians involved. A-side has a clockwork drum rhythm fed with spoken vocals (Ferry-style) & melody kbds. Slight phasing - especially on vocals & drums works well. A good if slightly unimaginative slice of electronic pop. B-side has much more to it. Phased electronic jazz traffic overlaid with piano - a bit like an up-dated 'Wade In The Water'. Look out for this guy - this single might have slipped through the net unnoticed, but a couple more could see him sneaking into the public's fickle affection.

Tapes

THE STATICS: White Sound + Don't Tell Me... (recorded at Ric-Rac Studios, Leeds in Dec '79). A Leeds combo who're linked with Deep Freeze Mice (see album review). If you like your pop to be percussive & repetitious then you'll go for this band. Loud bass, drums & chanted vocals are livened up by a variety of kbd/electronic sounds overlaid. That's 'White Sound'. Similar can be said of the 2nd track - though it's much more appealing with a good poppy melody & reggaed danceability. If it's to be a single, then this should be the A-side.

KNIFE EDGE: Favourite Girl + Say You Will (recorded at Ram Studios, Leeds & set for release as a single on their own No Hessle label in a couple of weeks). A-side has strong driving gtrs. & a catchy tune that sticks with you. Main line on which it really scores points is the stand-out vocalist. This can't fail to get airplay & may even get into the small labels charts. B-side's strong too, but broken up a little too much by its rhythm changes.

CITY LIMITS: No Regrets + Dancing In The Heat (recorded at Ric-Rac for release as a single on own Luggage Label in a few weeks). This'll be the band's 2nd single & is good pop, though very much in the Joe Jackson/Elvis Costello mould. Both sides are good enough to get them airplay & to sell well. Neat & professional. I'd not be at all surprised to see this release securing a major label contract for the band.

THE SOFT CELL: Facility Girl + Bleak Is My Favourite Cliche + Occupational Hazard + Penthouse Pet + Persuasion. 5 tracks of electronic pop with drum machine + kbds + vocals + electronic effects. Differs healthily from most electronic efforts in that it has variety - not the heard-one-track-&-you've-heard-them-all syndrome. It's a curious mixture - some of it gets through, other bits become boring before they fade away. I often wonder why so much of this music lacks direction - maybe because there's no developed market to dictate terms. It seems to depend a lot on basic handling of machinery to produce rhythms + use of sound effects to add variations, often with poor performance poetry for lyrics. The Soft Cell are good at what they're doing & it is genuinely interesting, but they too have fallen into the trap of letting the electronics stand in wherever human originality & inspiration run a little thin. From Leeds, they're gigging round the area. I'd be interested to see whether their audiences react to the music. Most electronic music events that I've been to tend to induce lethargy & I'm sure that this is down to the performers rather than the musical sources. If electronic music is a branch of pop/rock then surely it should be exciting, shouldn't it? Maybe someone out there'd like to reply to the above.

-tapes listened to by Nick Toczek

2 × 33⅓ = 66⅔

HICKS FROM THE STICKS

Much-vaunted compilation album of northern bands - just under half of them from from W. Yorks. Here's a track-by-track breakdown:-

Side 1:
1) Airkraft's 'Move In Rhythm' is one of the LP's most immediately commercial tracks - its avant garde new wave feel is produced via an odd amalgam of standard pop outtakes rather than any real originality. (2) Expelaires' 'Sympathy (Don't Be Taken In)' is distinguished by the Doors-ish kbds/basslines/repeated vocals that're typical of the group. A-side of their current Rockburgh single, it isn't as good as their earlier Zoo single called 'Frequency'. (3) Clock DVA offer 'You're Without Sound'. Their reputation as an experimental new wave band has got them a considerable underground/cult following. This is an interesting piece of crossover commercial weirdness with a hint of electronics. (4) The first exciting track on the album is Music For Pleasure's 'The Human Factor'. Good catchy electronic rock that's rhythmic without being boring/fast without being monotonous. Good one. (5) Nightmares In Wax sound like late 60's freaks on 'Shangri-la' Peel'd play this once for old time's sake & then dump it. So would I. Main fault is simply that they try to pack in far too many disjointed ideas. It doesn't gel & the whole mess tastes of hippie failure. (6) Ada Wilson & Keeping Dark have 'Head In The Clouds' which is classy mid-60's copy-pop with brass section, kbds, tamb, etc added for extra spice. In fact, the song works much better as a sampler track than as a single in its own right (see singles reviews). (7) Modern Eon's 'Choreography' is ok but, like a lot of the weaker tracks on this LP, it's ordinary where it should be exciting & repetitive where it should be inventive. (8) Ditto for 'Them r Me' by Medium Medium. This begins promisingly, stagnates after a minute or so, & then just seems to go on, & on for ages. It's a positive relief when the needle arm lifts off.

Side 2:
9) Radio 5's 'True Colours' is very catchy & stops soon enough to leave you wanting more. It's fresh & fun & I like the skillful use of the lyrics (swerve /deserve). See also singles reviews. (10) They Must Be Russians (aren't the names of all these bands good!) ask 'Where Have I Seen You' & set me wondering why it is that so many northern bands are so doggedly churning out thinly-disguised 10-year-old rock songs. This sounds like a song off a duff Country Joe & The Fish album. (12) Art Failure have 'Gimmick' on offer. More monotony here, but I do actually like it this time. Shame that it's trapped on side 2 amongst a bunch of substandards. (13) And we get 'I Don't Know' by I'm So Hollow & they really don't know... Take X-Ray Spex or Souxie & Banshees & slow them down to half speed. Dance music for the disabled. Oops! I've missed out (11), though with good reason. It's Section 25's 'After-Image'. Pass me the P.I.L.s, I've got a headache! This is boredom given a good production job & flattered by some ok musicianship. I wonder if the other 24 sections are as likely as this is to start The Yawn as the new in-thing? (14) Hot atmospheric dance-pop from Wah! Heat in the form of 'Hey Disco Joe'. Fronted by some great basslines, with drum machine & powerful vocals. The combination is strong enough to make sure that this number works well. But it goes on about one-min. too long & has a mess for a finish. (15) Stranger Than Fiction: 'Immortal In Mirrors'. Hell, this is a good band! (See also p.9 for feature & single review). I love this track. Appealing vocals backed neatly by gtr versus kbds. A real winner (& it's only a rough demo recording that was never intended for release!). Watch out for this combo, they deserve a bigger bite of the rock apple. (16) A speeded-up rip-off of The Normal's classic synth-song 'Warm Leatherette' is provided by The Distributors. But 'TV Me' is a good song in its own right - so the LP ends well.

Summary: Tracks 4, 9, 12, 15 & 16 would've made a great e.p. Tracks 1, 2, 3, 6, 7, 14 are ok as sampler tracks, but I hope that the bands have better stuff than than this in their sets. Tracks 5, 8, 10, 11, 13 are the pig-shit. All told, an interesting album, with a few startlingly good tracks - & I suppose that's the best you can expect from a compilation. Even the original 60's best-seller (CBS's 'Rock Machine Turns You On') which persuaded the music biz that samplers were good money-spinners contains a deal of dross among its tracks.

MY GERANIUMS ARE BULLETPROOF

A brave venture, this. Deep Freeze Mice release not their own single, but their own LP on Mole Embalming Records. And the whole thing's highly original with gallons of quirky appeal. Track-by-track then:-

1) Kbds that sound like electronic spinet + a tune with nursery rhyme simplicity + oddly sung-&-spoken lyric (like an improved Peter Perret of Only Ones fame). 'Radio Yoghurt' is a strong & tasty opener. Airwaves in a carton. (2) 'I Vote Conservative ('Cause I'm In Love With You)' is addressed to Maggie T. The Not Sensibles also have an M.T. love song & I wrote one for a band I used to be in back in '76 (mine ended: "...she'll give me an election & come at the top of my poll!"). (3) 'Emile Zola' has Franglais lyrics that mention this literary frog. The song ends with a delectably unbearable gtr solo. (4) On this side of the LP, I like tracks 1, 4, 5, 6 in particular. So 'Phyllis is a Protozoa' is fine by me. (5) 'Embalming Fluid Future'. My mummy likes this one (weak Egyptian joke). It's a slow reggae with a sax break. Weird as ever & twice as likeable. For those into words, this one tells a horror story that's got all the subtle charm of a blood-stained breadknife. (6) 'I met a man who spoke like an UCCA form'. This is a classic track. I love it passionately & I don't know why. Is it because (a) it's odd (b) I'm odd (c) it ends abruptly (d) I know what an UCCA form is & have a degree in Industrial Metallurgy (true) (e) I've met the same bloke (f) I was that man? Marks awarded for correct answers only & deducted for wrong ones. Discuss the last sentence & the next one. This is no way to write a review.

Side 2: One long mainly-instrumental track called 'The Octagonal Rabbit Surplus'. It's new wave avant garde classical music injected with pop extracts & a variety of sounds & noises produced physically & via processed electronics. It's totally different from the A-side (from any A-side, in fact). Odd little snatches of catchy rhythm are there only long enough for you to start getting into them before they vanish without trace, a new regime of sound stepping in. If I like this side less, then it's only because it's deliberately elusive. Ten mins of semi-classical non-rock, then a toilet flushes (literally) & a gtr break leads into a 30-sec. burst of rocksong that's then sucked off (!) into the void & there's a solo session for the drummer - on cymbals, no drums. 1½ mins of this & we slip back into the rocksong ("I'm really nice, You're really nice, He's really nice,"etc. - great philosophical lyrics!). Another flush of the toilet & we're off again, this time on kbds.... Buy this bunch of bulletproof blooms for cold rodents. They come from Leeds. You'll be surprised.

By the way, while we've on the subject of Moles & Franglais, when Soft Machine split in half in '71, Robert Wyatt formed a band of his own. French for Soft Machine is Machine Mou so his band was Matching Mole!

CLASSIFIED XTRAS Guitar & Bass Tuition. Jazz, Rock, Blues. Beginners to advanced. Leeds area. Phone Leeds 689062.
LEAD GUITARIST (Experienced) requires position in rock band into Rainbow, Bebop Deluxe, etc. Ring Niall on Bfd 498597.

SABREJETS

A package has come through from Newcastle band The Sabrejets - press releases/photo/new single & covering letter. The letter says that they're trying Wool City Rocker because "We don't get any coverage in the London music press 'cos we're based up here". So here's a page on them....

A 4-piece, namely Diesel La Fume, Kid Glover, Remo Reeds & Antoine Legris, they don't catagorise their music, but have been described as an 80's R&B/rockabilly band, though their influences extend into country, cajun, jazz & Latin American forms. Remo, on drums, is the latest addition - with the others doubling on various instruments including saxes, congas, guitars, maraccas & harmonica.

Their first single, 'Radioland' c/w 'Ace Cafe' & 'Caldonia' was released in '79 by Blueport Records & was played regularly on Radio One (John Peel, Paul Burnett, etc.) & got into Time Out's Top Ten.

In recent months, the band have toured with The Darts & The Pirates on their northern dates as well as going out as part of the Blueport Records package shows round the college circuit up north & also down to London for two shows. During the Bedrock Festival in their home town, they topped the bill at The Guildhall.

At the end of last month, Blueport Records released the band's second single, 'Voodoo Cave' c/w 'At The Quayside',(see review below) & the band have lined up a tour of the North-east & Scotland during May. After that, they're hoping to line up some gigs on the continent where their first single became quite popular.

The band can be contacted through Mike Maurice at Blueport Records on 0632-812377.

Diesel La Fume   Kid Glover

Their Single...

'Voodoo Cave' c/w 'At The Quayside' (Blueport Records '80). The A-side is a rather uninspired rock number that sounds slightly hippie/sixties-ish, though the fast-played congas opening is effective & there's some nice sax. It's the guitar that really screws it up - that & the overall monotony. The B-side, however, is a great little number which is a cross between Kursall Flyers & Darts. It's appealing pop with a strong hook & a nice touch of self parody. It's about the band's singer writing to film stars (Brigitte Bardot et al) inviting them to come & stay with him: "Well, it's not as if I'm just another joker in a bar at The Quayside/ I'm Diesel La Fume the famous rock & roll star at The Quayside/But every screen goddess I've written to yet/Thanks me for the letters & she sends her regrets/Says she's never even heard of The Sabrejets or The Quayside." Should have been the A-side.

Reviewed by Nick Toczek & Kev Hopgood.

Nowts...

Following close behind Rockburgh's Northern bands compilation comes one even closer to home. At the end of this month Ram, the Leeds studio/label will be releasing 'The Art of Solving Problems'. All tracks recorded in the studio by local bands, most of them based in Leeds. It features 2 tracks each by 6 bands: The Forst, The Motivators, Side Effect, Gimmicks, The Cat, The Beans. I've heard a cassette of the album & it's got some excellent tracks (full review in next issue). If you buy the album, you'll also get several freebies with it. The whole thing promises to be well worth grabbing. And for a final touch of added interest, the cover design is by WCR's resident cartoonist, Stan Engel.

More recording news. Agony Column's new single 'Love in The Head' will be out on Phonogram's Back Door label this month. Here in Bradford, Jonathan Howard's Kirk Enterprises will be putting Bradford groups onto vynyl - starting with Mysterious Footsteps (ex-Negatives) who're in the studios (Cargo) this month recording tracks for a June/July single release in a first pressing of 2,000 copies. Other interested bands who've got studio standard cassettes can send them to JH at 5 Kenmore Road, Wibsey, Bradford 5.

Aries Enterprises (Jules, who manages Hustler St. Band, Little Brother & Willy Becket) are in conflict with Palm Cove Club over events that took place after their gig there in March - a nasty argument with neither side prepared to back down. Looks like legal action, so I can't say more.

Town Beat, the Hudds. fanzine, has folded (at least for the present, though it may reappear in a few months). Some of the work lined up for the issue that failed to appear is in this issue of WCR, as are some of the cartoons by their guy Kev Hopgood.

Scamps (B'f'd) now in regular action as a rock venue one or two nights a week. Royal Standard (B'f'd) now under new management & the manager may be taking bands, but not punk. Temperance Hall (K'l'y) no longer having bands following complaints about noise levels. The Crown in Ivegate (B'f'd) had punk bands Violation & Total Confusion on one night last month - makes a change from their usual bill of strippers & topless barmaids... or does it?

Damaged Goods, the fanzine coming out of Harrogate area, has been silent for some months now - is WCR the only mag left in W.Yorks?

New issue out now of my other magazine - The Litt Little Word Machine(No.11). It's a literary periodical (perfect bound, full colour cover, real typesetting, etc.- much smarter than WCR!). 88pages of prose, poetry, reviews, articles & info. on the international small press lit. scene. It's only 80p (+ 15p postage) direct from me at WCR's address.

I'm still after more outlets for WCR so if it's not on sale in your area & you think you know of a possible outlet, then please give me a ring. Also, if you think you'd like to try selling some copies yourself then just get in touch. You get them at ⅓ discount & so stand to make 10p on every copy you sell - should pay for a few beers if nothing else.

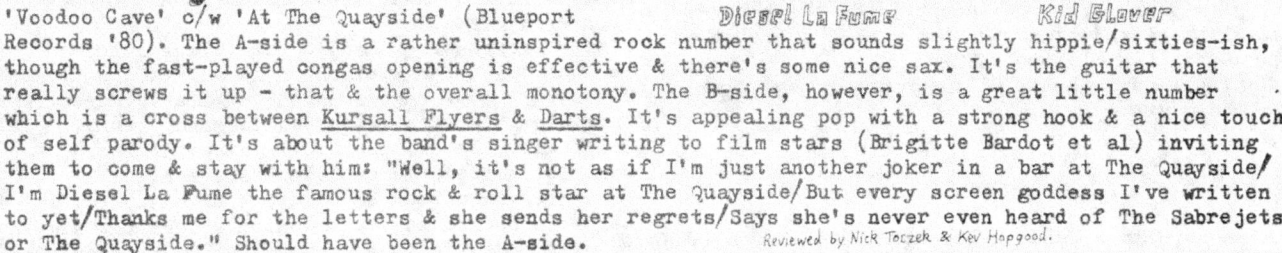

Sandy Robertson in 'Sounds' singles reviews section back in May '79. This was the debut of The Specials, the first single from 2-tone & it's B-side was 'The Prince', the first single from Madness. How wrong can one man be?! He still works for Sounds.

THE SPECIAL A.K.A. 'Gangsters' (2 Tone) If this represents the future of anything, then I will eat one of Pete Silverton's exotic sandwiches while baring my privates to the entire secretarial force of Hi Fi For Pleasure. That may appear to be a potentially stupid and vulgar piece of self-promotion, but so is 'Gangsters'. Like an MoR TV theme mixed in with despicable 'pink' reggae. If you don't agree, then give the Special AKA all your money, pronto.

── Right you are, mate, here are 4 more for yr scrapbook ──

Goff Jackson and THE HUNS (from Leeds)

Line-up: Mik Bridgman (Vocs/Gtr), Pete Cahill (Bass/Vocs), Dermot Quigley (Gtr), Mogs (Alto Sax), Dave Lee (Dms).

Their letter reads: "Born over several pints in the Leeds Univ. bar in the early summer of '78, Goff Jackson & The Huns, then comprising Pete & Mik with Howard Rogers & Egly on guitars, played their legendary first gig at the university at the end of the summer term. Guest superstar drummer John Diamond joined the band on the afternoon of the gig &, having received a tumultuous (if stunned) reception, the band promptly broke up, with Mik, Howard & Egly leaving Leeds.

Howard returned to Leeds in '79 &, finding that he was living 100 yards from Pete, formed Huns Mk II with him. Saleem Gazdar was drafted in on 2nd guitar, John returning on drums & Mik commuted from Birmingham to play the gigs in summer '79 at the university & at The Royal Park. Flushed with success, the band broke up again.

Pete & Mik spent the autumn of '79 writing songs & looking out for suitable Huns. The present line-up came together in spring '80 & played their 1st gig at The Royal Park in April. The Huns are hoping not to split up this time & are intending to play their brand of fractured-rhythm bottie-waggling (I didn't write this - ed!) music at any venues that will have them."

Contact: Dave (Leeds 623306 evenings or Otley 464056 daytime).

TOXIC (from Ilkley)

Line-up: Chris McLaughlin (Gtr), Tim Dawson (Bass Gtr), John West (Voc) & Mick Lister (Dms).

Another letter. This one reads: "We started in Nov '79 (having all been friends for a long time), but didn't have enough gear to really get going properly until Xmas. After this, we started seriously practicing & writing songs. Chris writes the music & Tim writes the words, then we make minor adjustments as a group. We do as few covers as possible because we find them boring.

The music we make is a sort of punk/rock combination. We're all into different kinds of music which keeps it interesting for us.

We did our first gig at Skipton Town Hall with The Defects & Vacant a while back, taking 30-40 people with us on the strength of them having watched us practice, heard our tapes or heard of us by word of mouth. We were very pleased with the reaction we got to our set.

In the near future we hope to do a few supports, perhaps at our school & maybe promote something with The Defects at a local youth club. We liked Violation's idea of an open-air punk festival in Bradford.

Contact: Tim (Ilkley 608925).

Side Effect (from Leeds)

Line-up: Tony Hall (Ld Voc), Jon Bedford (Kbds/Voc), Bruce Wilson (Gtr/Voc), Steve Pearson (Bass) & Dave Maud (Dms).

Side Effect were formed in April '79 when Bruce & Tony joined the remnants of Leeds outfit Black Dogs. (Before Black Dogs, Dave & Steve had played in Knife Edge).

With 3 of the band having played together for some time, the new outfit was able to start gigging shortly after forming. Playing driving melodic rock with some complex, jazzy arrangements, they have managed to build up a regular & devoted following in the year they've been gigging.

They've recently recorded some numbers written by Jon (the band's driving force) at Ram Studios, & at least one of these will appear on Ram's upcoming compilation album of Leeds bands. Other tracks, including stage favourites 'Voyage' & 'Pin-Striped Suit', will appear on a Side Effect E.P. released by Ram in June. At the moment, the band are playing as many West Yorks. gigs as possible to build up their following.

Summing up the band's attitude towards what they're doing, Tony says, "We are a collective outfit & we don't make a penny from the band. Our aim is just to entertain & enjoy ourselves."

Side Effect's outward-looking attitude is reflected in the way they have done a considerable amount of p.a. work for other Leeds bands such as Middle 8, The Neat & The Beans.

Contact: Jon (Leeds 751744).

The City Limits (from Leeds)

Line-up: Ted Waite (Ld Voc/Rm Gtr), Anthony Peart (Ld Gtr/Voc), Paul Hartwood (Bass) & Colin McCaig (Dms).

They've been together with this line-up for 4-5 months. Before that, they worked as a 5-piece for approx. 3 years.

Their first self-financed single** was released earlier this year & almost sold out in the first 2 months (a few copies left - available direct from Stuart Rhodes, manager, 21 Manor Terr., Headingley, Leeds, LS6 1BU - price: £1.15 inc. postage; title: 'Morse Code Messages').

They've since been back into Ricrac Studios in Leeds to record the follow-up - though the aim is to sign a deal with a company rather than put it out themselves.

The band lean towards a commercial pop sound, trying to be dancy, yet retaining an air of technicality & so please the audiences & themselves. "At the moment we're talking with a couple of record companies but nothing is definite & we're happy enough to keep plodding along."

Contact: Stuart (Leeds 757929).

** 1st single reviewed in W.C.R 4.

ULTERIOR MOTIVES MAYPOLE MUSIC EXPEDITION (Northern Rock-Pop!)

- SAT. 3 MAY - ST. GEORGE'S HALL, B'F'D. (with 5 other local bands - see gig guide)
- SUN. 4 MAY - BLACKAMORE HEAD, PONTEFRACT.
- THU. 8 MAY - QUEENS HALL, B'F'D. (with New Age)
- SUN. 18 MAY - HADDON HALL, LEEDS.
- SAT. 24 MAY - ROYAL STANDARD, B'F'D.
- MON. 26 MAY - MARQUIS OF GRANBY, LEEDS.
- THU. 29 MAY - BINGLEY ARTS CENTRE. (with The Elements)

Northern Rock-Pop!

APRIL AT PRINCEVILLE!!

HEAVY METAL — REVIEWER: STEVE BROWN. — **HEAVY METAL**

This modest haven of metal mayhem, which has seen bands such as Saxon, Bethnal & Samson serve their apprenticeships, is at present benefiting from the strongly revived interest in Heavy Metal & is putting on some of the best bands in the country. April was no exception & produced some fine performances.

The first of these came from Dedringer, a Leeds-based band who make regular appearances at Princeville & always prove to be great crowd pullers. The diminutive Jonny Hoyle on vocals is well suited to HM but is by no means the focal point of the band. All too often my attention drifted away from the music as a whole & Hoyle as frontman, to the two wildmen of the outfit - Neil Hudson on guitar & especially the crazed Lee Flaxington who wields his Ibanez Flying V to great effect.

Numbers early in the set such as 'Direct Line' & 'She's Not Ready' confirmed the tightness of the band. Their brash, hard rock music is very commercial & the band as a whole most versatile. Audience participation was always in evidence, not only in the multitude of possessed headbangers at the front, but also during the choruses of songs like 'Runaway' & 'Lazy Sunday'. Quite deservedly, the band received two encores, the 2nd of which was AC/DC's 'Whole Lotta Rosie', a version which was however rather tame & revealed the band's weaknesses.

Overall it was a fine set from Dedringer with some impressive guitar work from the dual Gibson Les Pauls of Neil Hudson & Al Scott. Kenny Jones (Dms) & Lee Flaxington were invaluable, despite a rather suspect mix on their instruments. The band will be back at Princeville soon & I suggest you make an effort to be there.

Seven days later came the turn of another local band, Vardis. The impression I got from this 3-piece outfit was that it was simply a one-man show. Steve Zodiac, guitarist, vocalist & the band's songwriter, is a talented musician especially with his powerful rhythm work. However, I felt he was let down somewhat by the bass guitarist & drummer partly due to the bad sound mix. At times though they functioned perfectly as a unit & showed themselves to be following in the style, be it purposely or not, of Motorhead, which in my opinion does them credit. Zodiac, although a fine guitarist, is not cut out to be a singer & the band would certainly benefit from a powerful vocalist. The best two songs they performed were the two tracks on their current single - well worth buying.

There was nearly no band at all the following week. Apparently Eric Bell & his band had a spot of engine trouble somewhere near Stoke on Trent, but finally arrived at about 9.30. Unfortunately, it took some time to bring the band's sound anything near respectability. At times the band sounded more like Robin Trower than Trower himself. An indication of Bell's past connections with Thin Lizzy came with a weak version of 'Whisky In The Jar' which was applauded more in recognition of the song rather than for the way it was delivered. The high spot of a dullish set was Thin Lizzy's old stage fave 'The Rocker' which was well-executed though spoilt by an indifferent lead solo.

If this was something of an uninspired evening, then it was more than made up for the following week when Diamond Head made their first appearance at Princeville. Their reputation & excellent debut single had drawn a full house. They opened with 'Helpless', the B-side of their single & a brilliant number delviered with boundless energy. The band's set showed them to be the best to have visited Princeville since Saxon's last gig there. Their posters proudly display a quotation from Sounds which runs: 'the biggest new prospect in heavy rock since Led Zeppelin' &, although this is perhaps a little over the top, Diamond Head have definitely got what it takes. Sean Harris is one of the best frontmen/vocalists I have ever encountered & he creates an excellent rapport with the audience - especially with those head-banging at the front as he enthusiastically joins them. It took Brian Tatler a while to show what good effect he could create from his Flying V but it was well worth waiting for. The band's enthusiasm at times tended to overshadow their music, but the sound was brilliantly controlled by drummer Duncan Scott. Diamond Head have an album entitled 'Lightning To The Nation' in the pipeline which will include numbers like 'Trick Or Treat', 'Streets Of Gold', 'It's Electric', 'To Heaven From Hell', 'Play It Loud' & 'Am I Evil?', all of which are superb & I greatly look forward to hearing it. Two encores once more, the 2nd of which was called 'Sweet & Innocent' & was the best song of the set.

This climaxed a great month of HM music at Princeville, not so much with a bang but more with an explosion.

LEEDS UNIVERSITY'S UNION RECORDS

HUGE REDUCTIONS

Over 2,000 items at cost price!!!
Plus at least £1.00 off all full-price L.P's

SALE ON NOW

E.M.I. Record Tokens accepted at 10% discount on list price.

SHOP IN BASEMENT OF UNION BUILDING
OPEN: MON-FRI 9.30a.m.-5.00p.m.

LEEDS UNIVENTS PRESENT

MAY ENTERTAINMENTS

TUE. 6	ROY HARPER	(£2.00)	R.S.H.
FRI. 9	MAGAZINE	(£2.00)	R.S.H.
FRI. 16	IVOR CUTLER	(£1.00)	Debating Chamber
SAT. 17	BRAND X	(£1.85)	R.H.S.
SUN. 18	AVERAGE WHITE BAND	(£2.50)	Refectory
SAT. 31	JOE JACKSON	(£2.50)	Refectory

Ents. Secretary, Andy Kershaw.

3 LIVE REVIEWS.

BABY TUCKOO
Vaults Bar, B'f'd. 13th April.

Among those who know, Sak (gtr) & Smiggs (bass) have a reputation that goes before them something like the prow of a battleship. Thus, it was no surprise that their first Vaults Bar gig (& only the band's 3rd public outing) pulled in a near-SRO audience which included a goodly number of musicians come to check them out.

That S&S deserve their immense reputation at least partially is in no doubt. Smiggs provides the very heaviest of foundational basswork yet remains flexible enough to avoid ever sounding turgid; on top of this Sak executes his near-perfect mastery of the guitar, playing fast or economically as appropriate & making delightful use of occasional wah-wah or feedback. And in Baby Tuckoo, S&S have a potentially good band. Steve Horton is a dynamic vocalist & a good frontman; & Marc Schofield is a powerful drummer whose work is only marred by his sometimes allowing flashy rolls & cymbal-work to come before keeping basic time. Put together, the 4 members of Baby Tuckoo create a solid but shifting wall of sound that throbbed with excitement & drew one of the most enthusiastic responses I've seen in months from a Vaults' crowd.

However, some of the very reasons that Baby Tuckoo went down so well at the Vaults also show the very definite limitations of their concept. They played 2 sets of AC/DC & Deep Purple covers, all at a standard HM fast boogie pace. (They justify the use of cover versions in the same way as U.S. MOR songstress Linda Ronstadt; i.e. it's better to do covers than have a set of self-composed inferior songs.) Of course, this sent the headbangers apeshit - & they did do excellent versions of 'Highway Star', 'Somebody Get Me A Doctor', 'Whole Lotta Rosie' (complete with audience "Angus" chant) & 'Burn' among others - but it made for inevitable boredom for anybody other than total HM freaks, & it means that the band have no identity of their own.

Baby Tuckoo have a lot of potential, but if S&S ever want to graduate beyond beginners' & no-hopers' venues like the Vaults, then they're going to have to form their own strong identity - including writing some of their own material, adding something original to cover versions, & learning to vary pace & intensity. Significantly, one of the most interesting numbers of the night was Slade's 'Gudbye T' Jane' - at least it sounded very different to the original.

-Keith E. Rice.

HARSH WORDS
Vaults Bar, B'f'd. 15th April.

The band opened up with the synthesiser pounding out its heart which neatly led into 'Problem Page', a number co-written, I believe, by Allan Hollings & Gary Quinn. This was loud & proud, as was their next 'Gambling Song' which would probably have had them dancing in the aisles at The Rainbow Theatre, not to mention The Hammersmith Odeon (you have mentioned it - ed.).

The introduction of Paul Deighton playing piano swiftly led us into 'Class Distinction' & 'My Music'. Coupled with the synth, it seemed to slice the room in half (neatly, though, I might add).

'Thought I saw Somebody' slowed things down a bit & I think they probably needed it. However, 'Could be Doing Something Better at Home' soon restored Allan's (the bassist) energy. (I'm sure he was plugged into a generator somewhere!!).

Next came a number he'd written entitled 'I Think I Love You'. It was dedicated to someone somewhere, but he never said who! A good elaborately well-constructed hard-edged melodic rock number (see W.C.R. No.5; Keith E Rice)it was. So were 'Busy Man' & 'It's Alright' which gave everyone a chance to seep gently into the realms of reality again. Nice commercial songs, these. 'Wild Horses' was no exception, nor was 'I Didn't Know (that you loved me)'. The band exchanged instruments throughout the set, Allan on gtr/bass, Gary & Paul on kbds/gtr/bass & all 3 using their larynxes somewhere along the line & they never collected £200 for passing 'Go'.

They finished their hour-long set with 'Why Don't You Chain Me Down?' (perhaps dedicated to Joyce McKinney) & 'Cut It Down', a number about the hassle of recording in studios. 'Problem Page' was a reprisal & I'd swear they heard it across the water.

Paul Mitchell on drums shouldn't go unnoticed either. He, like the rest, gave all. The John Bonhams & Phil Collins of this world eat your hearts out - You ain't seen nuthin' yet!

O.K., so maybe I'm slightly biased. I have actually had the pleasure of seeing the band before (somewhere in Leeds where you needed to fight through the crowd to see them). However, they brought their own brand of explosive rock coupled with the lightshow into the city. All young record labels take heed, Harsh Words could be a profitable partnership for a marriage. After all, they're only hard-working boys who want to rule the world.

-Albert Rutherford.

THE NEWS
The Albion, Hudds. 15th March.

The gig got off to a bit of a limp start with a song called 'Romantic Rendezvous' & stayed pretty flaccid all night. Nothing much to get excited over here.

After overcoming some hassle or other with their amp, they got into their second song 'She Loves You Jimmy', or something like that. Quite a nice song with a good bassline. Things stayed lukewarm with 'Dead End Boy', another danceable ditty, then froze totally with 'Worn You Out', a boring, monotonous, tedious song with no muscle at all.

The News seem to be another band into doing 60's pop &, like a lot of other bands, they don't quite pull it off. Whatever happened to punk? - why are bands nowadays so bloody nice?!!

Anyway, on with the review. The fifth song was 'It's Alright Now' followed by 'Second In Your League', both pretty unremarkable. The next song, 'Dancing Alone', I remember quite liking, nice use of hook lines. After this mild treat came another crashing disappointment called 'Captain Dan Dare' - Yeuk!! Bloody awful. At this point I decided to go home, so I don't know if they did anything of note after I left, I doubt it. Why am I such a miserable sod?

-Kev Hopgood.

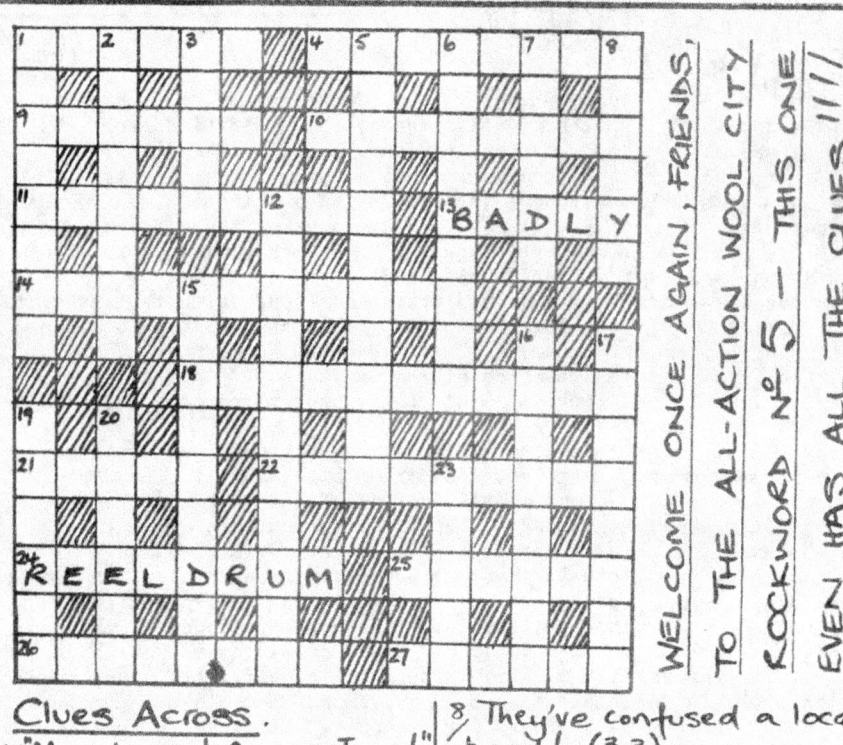

WELCOME ONCE AGAIN, FRIENDS, TO THE ALL-ACTION WOOL CITY ROCKWORD No 5 — THIS ONE EVEN HAS ALL THE CLUES !!!!

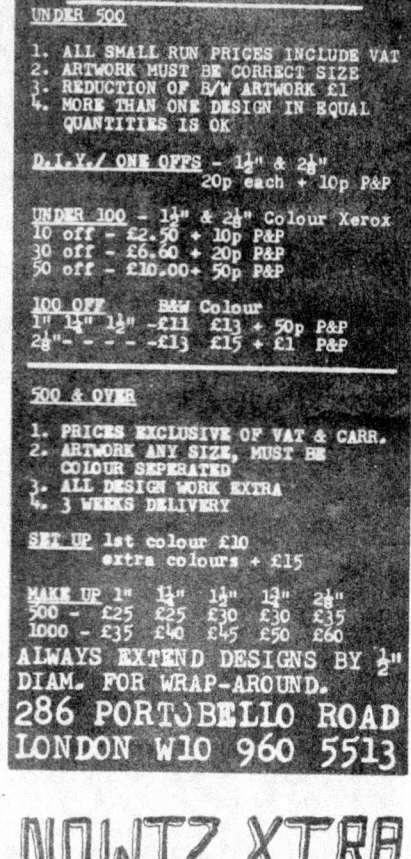

Clues Across.

1. "My, oh, my! Boy am I —!" from Sad Cafe. (6)
4. Tiny piece added to drill, perhaps. (5,3)
9. Ancient fellow, Ian Dury's dad? (3,3)
10. A cute car, being precise! (8)
11. Coarse Les makes earthenware. (9)
14. Slim ruler, male, intelligent creature. (8,3)
18. Where Brazil might be, concisely speaking. (2,1,8)
21. The Police collectively. (5)
22. Not cruise revised! Not a 14! (9)
25. Ill feelings to 1000 before her in Wonderland. (6)
26. Parts of Keighley band. (8)
27. Lost when angry or drunk, perhaps. (6)

Clues Down.

1. Where the Rocker comes from. (4,4)
2. Sid's cat I move - vicious! (8)
3. Wipe out. (5)
5. Rodent's T.V. club not up to much? (6,5)
6. Bad old sun destroyed noisy groups! (4,5)
7. Bruford's band that no housewife would buy? (5,1)
8. They've confused a local band! (3,3)
12. Without banking facility? Definitely not. (2,2,7)
15. Sharp Leeds band. (5,4)
16. Dimes ELO spent for tunes. (8)
17. Attack Lennon's fingers and paint, I hear. (8)
19. Leeds v-venue comes across...
20. ..... more than colourful. (6,6)
23. I judge, angry. (5)

Solution to Rockword No 4.
And despite missing clues to it, we have prizes to give to:-
John Cattanach from Pudsey.

NOWTZ XTRA

Brian McGrath, who runs heavy rock gigs at Princeville, B'fd on Thursdays & Sundays (latter at lunchtime) is hoping to start up on Monday nights with non-heavy bands. Splash One, B'f'd (next to Bonepart's) is now running regular Tues. night live gigs - mostly of electronic bands. The Crown, Ivegate, B'f'd is now taking band bookings. Trampus blown out of their support booking to Saxon at St. George's Hall, B'f'd. when they turned up late with their gear.

SPLASH ONE, manager (eddie) on B'f'd 323339

When you're thinking of recording

Masters or Demos you'll need a studio with a reputation for good sounds, good engineers, and a friendly relaxed atmosphere.
A studio with the facilities you want, 16 track or 8 track available by the hour or on day bookings. The effects you'll need like Flanging, Echo, Reverb, A.D.T. Noise Gates, Compressors, Harmonisers, Dolby 'A' etc., and a studio area with room to breathe.
A studio because of its unique sounds, attracts bands from all over the British Isles, Germany and Denmark, and a studio that doesn't charge the earth.

16 track £15 per hour   8 track £9 per hour
16 track £130 per day   8 track £75 per day
(10 hours)   (10 hours)

ONE FREE HOUR TO SET UP IN,
NO OVERTIME CHARGES. WHEN YOU'RE THINKING OF A STUDIO LIKE THIS YOU'RE THINKING OF

RECORDING STUDIOS

Ring us at
ROCHDALE (0706) 524420

KENION ST., ROCHDALE, LANCS., ENGLAND

ULTERIOR MOTIVES BADGES — black & white — 1½" enamel
5 Beech Terrace, Undercliffe, Bradford, BD3 0PY.
includes 10p postage...
30p by post from Wool City

CODA MUSIC
28 Church Bank, Bradford 1. (tel. 307433)

MUSICAL INSTRUMENTS — SALES + HIRE + EXPERT TUITION ON GUITAR, BASS, DRUMS, KEYBOARDS + REPAIRS

REHEARSAL ROOMS + RECORDING & VIDEO STUDIOS + LIVE RECORDINGS FOR BANDS, GROUPS, ARTISTS.

P.A. HIRE (100 - 3,000 watts) + CREW and TRANSPORT. (P.A. Rig:- 30/2 Allen & Heath + RSD & BGW Amps + Shure & AKG & Beyer Mikes).

Agents for :- Marshall, Ludwig, Carlsboro, Ovation, Premier, Olympic, Tama, Ibanez, Pearl, Beyer, A.K.G., Korg, Peavey, Gretsch, Slingerland.

JUST IN!! LARGE STOCKS OF IBANEZ GUITARS FROM £150 - £700.

IT'S THE WEST YORKSHIRE GIG GUIDE FOR THE MERRY MONTH OF MAY 1980...

THU 1
- PRINCEVILLE, BRADFORD = Sledgehammer.
- ROYAL PARK, LEEDS = The Defects.
- THE FAN CLUB, LEEDS = Holly & The Italians + The Motivators.
- QUEENS HALL, BRADFORD = Backslider.
- FFORDE GREENE, LEEDS = Knife Edge.

FRI 2
- PALM COVE, BRADFORD = Jedrell Bank.
- COSMO CLUB, LEEDS = The Skatalites.
- FFORDE GREENE, LEEDS = Rocker.

SAT 3
- ST. GEORGES HALL, BRADFORD = Radio 5, Ulterior Motives, The Expelaires, The Scene, Shake Appeal + City Limits.
- ROYAL PARK, LEEDS = Spider Blues Band.
- BRADFORD UNIVERSITY = Girl.
- WHITE LION, HUDDERSFIELD = Rabstallion.
- QUEEN'S HALL, BRADFORD = Coast To Coast.
- HADDON HALL, LEEDS = The Clients.
- FFORDE GREENE, LEEDS = Cadillacs.
- PALM COVE, BRADFORD = Black Stallion.
- ALBION HOTEL, HUDDERSFIELD = Private Dicks.
- STAGING POST, LEEDS = Knife Edge.

SUN 4
- PRINCEVILLE, BRADFORD (lunch) = Private Dicks.
- STAGING POST, LEEDS = Dick Smith Band.
- VAULTS BAR, BRADFORD = Proposition 31.
- WHITE LION, HUDDERSFIELD = Shake Appeal.
- HADDON HALL, LEEDS = The Switch.
- FFORDE GREENE, LEEDS = Writz / The Insiders.
- UNITY HALL, WAKEFIELD = Magazine + Manicured Noise + Stranger Than Fiction.
- BLACKAMORE HEAD, PONTEFRACT = Ulterior Motives.

MON 5
- MARQUIS OF GRANBY, LEEDS = Shattered Doll.
- VAULTS BAR, BRADFORD = Oral Sax.
- FFORDE GREENE, LEEDS = Crazy Cavan + Rockabilly Rebels.
- ROYAL PARK, LEEDS = After Dark.
- ST. GEORGE'S HALL, BRADFORD = Saxon + Trampus.
- QUEENS HALL, BRADFORD = Shadowfax + Silver Screen Girls.

TUE 6
- ROSE & CROWN, ILKLEY = Muggins Blight.
- VAULTS BAR, BRADFORD = Rhino.
- LEEDS UNIVERSITY = Roy Harper.
- KINGS HEAD, KEIGHLEY = Omen.
- BLACKAMORE HEAD, PONTEFRACT = Blush.
- QUEENS HALL, BRADFORD = Backslider + Japanese Soldiers.
- SCAMPS, BRADFORD = Coast To Coast.
- SPLASH 1, BRADFORD = Soft Cell + electronic disco.

WED 7
- LEEDS UNIVERSITY = The Blues Band.
- WHITE LION, HUDDERSFIELD = Mysterious Footsteps.
- ROYAL PARK, LEEDS = Knife Edge.
- VAULTS BAR, BRADFORD = Poetry In Motion (Little Brother + Willy Beckett + Hustler St. Band).
- BRADFORD UNIVERSITY = UB40.
- QUEENS HALL, BRADFORD = Middle 8 + Oral Sax.

THU 8
- PRINCEVILLE, BRADFORD = Slender Thread.
- QUEENS HALL, BRADFORD = Ulterior Motives + New Age.
- FAN CLUB, LEEDS = Cuddly Toys + Y?
- VAULTS BAR, BRADFORD = Doncaster Arts Co-operative.

FRI 9
- LEEDS UNIVERSITY = Magazine + Bauhaus + The Statics.
- QUEENS HALL, BRADFORD = Dirty Jed's Blues Band + The Klingons.
- PALM COVE, BRADFORD = Radio 5.

SAT 10
- STAGING POST, LEEDS = The Vye.
- WHITE LION, HUDDERSFIELD = Heritage.
- HADDON HALL, LEEDS = Agony Column.
- BRADFORD UNIVERSITY = Brand X + Bruford.
- QUEENS HALL, BRADFORD = Mysterious Footsteps + support.
- ALBION HOTEL, HUDDERSFIELD = Willful Damage.
- PALM COVE, BRADFORD = Corner Shots + Movements + reggae sound system (a B'ham package).

SUN 11
- PRINCEVILLE, BRADFORD (lunch) = Street Fighter.
- STAGING POST, LEEDS = Vogue.
- FFORDE GREENE, LEEDS = Sledgehammer.
- HADDON HALL, LEEDS = The Statics + Deep Freeze Mice.
- WHITE LION, HUDDERSFIELD = The Dots.
- VAULTS BAR, BRADFORD = Hustler St. Band.
- BLACKAMORE HEAD, PONTEFRACT = (T.B.A.)

MON 12
- MARQUIS OF GRANBY, LEEDS = Gimmix.
- VAULTS BAR, BRADFORD = Oral Sax.

TUE 13
- ROSE & CROWN, ILKLEY = Side Effect.
- VAULTS BAR, BRADFORD = The Elements.
- BLACKAMORE HEAD, PONTEFRACT = Dirty Stopouts.
- KINGS HEAD, KEIGHLEY = Agony Column.
- SCAMPS, B'F'D = Contax.
- SPLASH ONE, B'F'D = Vex.

WED 14
- VAULTS BAR, BRADFORD = Knife Edge.
- WHITE LION, HUDDERSFIELD = Evasive Action.

THU 15
- PRINCEVILLE, BRADFORD = Dawnwatcher.
- UNITY HALL, WAKEFIELD = Mike Harding.
- FAN CLUB, LEEDS = Nik Turner's Inner City Unit + Eyes At Risk.
- QUEENS HALL, BRADFORD = Knife Edge.

FRI 16
- UNITY HALL, WAKEFIELD = The Only Ones + Wasted Youth.
- HUDDERSFIELD POLYTECHNIC = It's A Roadshow.
- PALM COVE, BRADFORD = Performance.

SAT 17
- STAGING POST, LEEDS = Red Eye.
- WHITE LION, HUDDERSFIELD = Glossy Mags.
- HADDON HALL, LEEDS = Shake Appeal.
- LEEDS UNIVERSITY = Brand X + Bruford.
- BRADFORD UNIVERSITY = Mysterious Footsteps + Terminal 3 + War Babies.
- ALBION HOTEL, HUDDERSFIELD = (T.B.C.)
- PALM COVE, BRADFORD = The Guests.

SUN 18
- PRINCEVILLE, BRADFORD (lunch) = TBA.   BLACKAMORE HEAD, PONTEFRACT = Crash Alley.
- STAGING POST, LEEDS = Luigi Ana Da Boys.
- HADDON HALL, LEEDS = Ulterior Motives.
- VAULTS BAR, BRADFORD = Treatment.
- WHITE LION, HUDDERSFIELD = Torpedoes.
- ST. GEORGE'S HALL, BRADFORD = After The Fire.
- LEEDS UNIVERSITY = Average White Band.
- FAN CLUB, LEEDS = Monochrome Set.

MON 19
- MARQUIS OF GRANBY, LEEDS = Electric Tent Pegs.
- VAULTS BAR, BRADFORD = Oral Sax.

TUE 20
- ROSE & CROWN, ILKLEY = Dirty But Nice.
- VAULTS BAR, BRADFORD = Local Heroes.
- KINGS HEAD, KEIGHLEY = Tokyo Rose.
- BLACKAMORE HEAD, PONTEFRACT = The Zipps.
- SCAMPS, B'F'D = Coast To Coast.
- SPLASH ONE, B'F'D = The Soft Cell.

WED 21
- WHITE LION, HUDDERSFIELD = Coast To Coast.
- VAULTS BAR, BRADFORD = Red Shift.
- ST. GEORGE'S HALL, BRADFORD = Iron Maiden (B'f'd Univ. Event).

THU 22
- PRINCEVILLE, BRADFORD = Buffalo.
- FAN CLUB, LEEDS = Teardrop Explodes + support.
- UNITY HALL, WAKEFIELD = Girl + support.
- SCAMPS, BRADFORD = S.O.S. Band.

FRI 23
- PALM COVE, BRADFORD = The Solos.
- BRADFORD UNIVERSITY = Ulterior Motives + others.

SAT 24
- STAGING POST, LEEDS = The Switch.
- WHITE LION, HUDDERSFIELD = The Forst.
- HADDON HALL, LEEDS = Dick Smith's Band.
- ROYAL STANDARD, BRADFORD = Ulterior Motives.
- ALBION HOTEL, HUDDERSFIELD = Evasive Action.
- PALM COVE, BRADFORD =

SUN 25
- VAULTS BAR, BRADFORD = Mysterious Footsteps.
- PRINCEVILLE, BRADFORD (lunch) = Devil's Answer.
- STAGING POST, LEEDS = Side Effect.
- WHITE LION, HUDDERSFIELD = The Dots.
- HADDON HALL, LEEDS = The Vye + Metal Fatigue.
- BLACKAMORE HEAD, PONTEFRACT = Rockabilly Rebels.

MON 26
- MARQUIS OF GRANBY, LEEDS = Ulterior Motives.
- VAULTS BAR, BRADFORD = Oral Sax.

TUE 27
- ROSE & CROWN, ILKLEY = Agony Column.
- VAULTS BAR, BRADFORD = Middle 8.
- KINGS HEAD, KEIGHLEY = The Elements.
- BLACKAMORE HEAD, PONTEFRACT (T.B.A)
- SPLASH ONE, BRADFORD = Idle Rich.

WED 28
- WHITE LION, HUDDERSFIELD = The Passage.
- VAULTS BAR, BRADFORD = The Vye.
- BRADFORD UNIVERSITY = George Melly & John Chilton's Feetwarmers.
- UNITY HALL, WAKEFIELD = U.K. Subs + support.

THU 29
- BINGLEY ARTS CENTRE = Ulterior Motives + The Elements.
- PRINCEVILLE, BRADFORD = China Town.
- UNITY HALL, WAKEFIELD = The Human League + The Scars.
- FAN CLUB, LEEDS = Local bands (TBA).

FRI 30
- LEEDS UNIVERSITY = Cousin Joe From New Orleans.
- ST. GEORGE'S HALL, BRADFORD = Adam & The Ants (: Adam Ant + new band).
- PALM COVE, BRADFORD = S.O.S. Band.

SAT 31
- STAGING POST, LEEDS = City Limits.
- WHITE LION, HUDDERSFIELD = Geneva.
- HADDON HALL, LEEDS = The Switch.
- LEEDS UNIVERSITY = Joe Jackson.
- ALBION HOTEL, HUDDERSFIELD = Knife Edge.
- PALM COVE, BRADFORD = (T.B.C.)

SUN 1
- PRINCEVILLE, BRADFORD (lunch) = Kyro.
- VAULTS BAR, BRADFORD = Shake Appeal.
- STAGING POST, LEEDS = Convix.
- WHITE LION, HUDDERSFIELD = The Guests.
- HADDON HALL, LEEDS = Side Effect.
- FAN CLUB, LEEDS = Robert Fripp & The League of Gentlemen.
- BLACKAMORE HEAD, PONTEFRACT =

MON 2
- VAULTS BAR, BRADFORD = Oral Sax.

TUE 3
- ROSE & CROWN, ILKLEY = The Quick.
- VAULTS BAR, BRADFORD = Disco Students.
- KINGS HEAD, KEIGHLEY = Chainsaw.
- BLACKAMORE HEAD, PONTEFRACT =
- SPLASH ONE, BRADFORD = Countenance.

N.B. FFORDE GREENE (Leeds) & COACHHOUSE (Hudds) aren't answering the phone. I rang each of them about 10 times!

N.B. (T.B.C.) = To Be Confirmed; (T.B.A.) = To Be Arranged. Look out for Burnley bands Not Sensibles + Tiger Tails at Scamps, B'f'd on Wed 4th June.

ISSUE #7

June/July 1980, 2,000 copies printed, 20 pages, A4, ace cover

This issue spans two months, mainly to allow me time to breathe, eat, and sleep. Love the cover design by Mo Maklouf. Though still subtitled 'West Yorkshire's Rockscene Monthly', WCR was now being distributed via the independent music distribution cartel jointly created by Red Rhino (based in York) and Rough Trade (based in London). Through them, WCR was being supplied to music shops throughout Britain and even overseas. With this in mind, I was already broadening the coverage of the content, hence the three-page (12-14) feature 'Looking At Lancs.'.

Notes on bands profiled in this issue.

This issue includes two great bands from Leeds that never quite gained the acclaim they deserved. They were The Mirror Boys and Knife Edge. Page six sees two key Leeds recording studios - Ram and Ric-Rac - promoting what each regards as some of the best tracks by bands they've recorded. It's an indication of just how huge the Leeds music scene was becoming. The same could be said of the scene in Bradford, and elsewhere across the north of England.

The Wool City ROCKER

WEST YORKSHIRE'S ROCKSCENE MONTHLY

JUNE–JULY 1980
DOUBLE ISSUE
No. 7

30p

- LUCKY STRIKE
- MIRROR BOYS
- SAXON
- GOD AND THE DEMI-GODS
- THE QUICK
- GLOSSY MAGS
- GIRL
- TREATMENT
- FLYING SQUAD
- LOCAL HEROES
- CAMERAS IN CARS
- HEAVEN 17
- THE ZIPPS
- SHEILA AND THE POO FLAPS
- TIZWAS
- OSCILLATORS
- MO-DETTES
- THE SUBLIMINAL CUT
- KNIFE EDGE
- TWISTED NERVE
- BACK HOME
- THE NOT SENSIBLES

SEX PISTOLS' FILM REVIEWED

2-month gig guide • looking at lancs • fanzines

RIC~RAC SOUND STUDIO

What have all these groups groups got in common?

They have all recorded with us, and that was when we were only a part-time studio.

We are now full-time with what is probably the best-equipped 8-track studio in Yorkshire.

So Why Don't You Give Us A Try?!

FOR FURTHER DETAILS SEE INSIDE BACK COVER OR RING LEEDS 633717

RIC~RAC SOUND STUDIO

CODA MUSIC
28 Church Bank, Bradford 1. (tel. 307433).

MUSICAL INSTRUMENTS – SALES + HIRE + EXPERT TUITION ON GUITAR, BASS, DRUMS, KEYBOARDS + REPAIRS

REHEARSAL ROOMS + RECORDING & VIDEO STUDIOS + LIVE RECORDINGS FOR BANDS, GROUPS, ARTISTS.

P.A. HIRE (100 – 3,000 watts) + CREW and TRANSPORT. (P.A. Rig :- 30/2 Allen & Heath + RSD & BGW Amps + Shure & AKG & Beyer Mikes).

Agents for :- Marshall, Ludwig, Carlsboro, Ovation, Premier, Olympic, Tama, Ibanez, Pearl, Beyer, A.K.G., Korg, Peavey, Gretsch, Slingerland.

WE CAN NOW SUPPLY ANY VINTAGE AMERICAN GUITAR – RING FOR QUOTE

PALM COVE CLUB
Hollings Rd., Bradford 8. (tel. 499895).

LIVE BANDS EVERY FRI & SAT
(See gig guide on page 20 for details)
HALF-PRICE ENTRY BEFORE 10.30 p.m.!!
LICENSED BAR TILL 1am

CAR PARK AT REAR
POOL TABLES
GOOD WEST INDIAN FOOD
NEW WAVE & REGGAE JUKEBOX

FORTHCOMING REGGAE NIGHTS INCLUDE THESE MAJOR ACTS :-
June 15th. – Clint Eastwood.
June 28th. – Cygnus.
July 5th. – Jab Jab.
July 12th. – Ranking Dread.
July 26th. – Eugene Paul & Samantha Rose.

RUSH! Now For Rush Tickets

the HMV shop

T SHIRTS MANY DESIGNS £2.99

100's Of Albums Only £3.99

Falling Rock

5 CHEAPSIDE BRADFORD 28882

The Wool City Rocker

EDITORIAL

Later than ever with this issue which covers June & July to give me time to get back to publishing at the start of the month instead of midway through it! Issue 8 will cover August & September (because most of you'll be on holiday & so two issues would not sell too well). Then, come October, we'll be back to monthly issues.

As threatened, we're expanding W.C.R... Circulation's up from 1,500 to 2,000. We've 3 pages on Lancs. (more in next issue) & will soon be covering all of Lancs. & all of Yorks. Ah, the power! Actually, it's due to you who buy & read the mag. - hope you'll keep with us. There should be a rock magazine covering the north of England & based up here. That's the role I'd like to see W.C.R. playing.

Is there anyone out there who's got a car & would accept a few quid for spending 2 days driving me round Leeds/Bradford area putting copies of WCR in the shops? It'd be a pair of days every month. Please ring if you can help out.

2 pints of lager & a packet of crisps, please!! 2 pints of lager & a PACKET OF CRISPS PLEASE!!!

LUV, Nick Toczek (20/6/80)

Issue Number 7. JUNE & JULY '80.

The editor's Nick Toczek who also did layout & wrote most of the mag, typed it all up, etc. However, the following also did their bit:-
Mo Maklouf of Witch Design who did the cover. Stan Engel & Kev Hopgood who did the cartoons. Plus scribes Ken Turner, Phil Foster, Steve Brown, Mick Mitchell & Ady Steele. Special thanx to Gris Boojum (ex-TownBeat), Gaynor, Ken, The Elements, Dave Hall & you!

TERMS OF SALE: 30p each direct to the public or 45p each by mail order from the address given below. Bulk orders of 15 or more copies can be had at the discount price of 20p each (so why not sell the magazine yourself at gigs, school, etc.?)

ADVERTISING RATES: Standard 3½" x 3½" box is £20 for first time of advertising, then £10 for subsequent placings. Colour, different size, special lay-out, etc. by arrangement.
Ring or write for advertising rates card & any other details.

EDITORIAL ADDRESS:
5 Beech Terrace,
Undercliffe,
Bradford BD3 OPY,
West Yorkshire,
England.
(tel. 0274-21867).

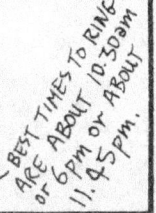
BEST TIMES TO RING ARE ABOUT 10.30am or 6pm or ABOUT 11.45pm.

CONTENTS/DISCONTENTS...

1 = Mo Maklouf's cover.
3 = You are here! + A Wool City Rocker →
4 = SAXON + MIRROR BOYS + TISWAS.
5 = Discs & Demos Reviewed.
6 = Ram's Album + Ric Rac's Cassette.
7 = GIRL + BROKEN HOME + GLOSSY MAGS + SHEILA & THE POO FLAPS + GOD & THE DEMI-GODS + Classified Adverts.
8 = SEX PISTOLS' film + MO-DETTES + LUCKY STRIKE + Stan Engel Cartoon
9 = TWISTED NERVE respond to TREATMENT when they get THE SUBLIMINAL CUT
10 = June Gig Guide + Bradford, Leeds & Huddersfield venues.
11 = July Gig Guide + other W. Yorks. venues + N. Yorks. venues.
12 = N.E. LANCS. MUSICIANS' COLLECTIVE + 3 Fanzines + Stan Engel Cartoon + Ivor Cutler slogan + Elephant. } Looking At Lancs.
13 = FLYING SQUAD + NOT SENSIBLES + Kev Hopgood Cartoon + T.& A. cutting.
14 = LOCAL HEROES + STURGEON ROW + TERMINAL MUSIC.
15 = HEAVEN 17 + Nowtz + Missed Discs.
16 = VeNews + Fanzines.
17 = Nowtz + Stan Engel Cartoon.
18 = Ken Turner's 6th Rockword + Band Aid.

SAXON — St. George's Hall, Bradford. 5th May 1980.

Under the name Son Of A Bitch, this band had graduated with first class honours from the circuit of clubs like Bradford's Princeville, so I was looking forward to a powerful set from them. I was not disappointed. 1,300 metal devotees turned up, on the strength of their incredible second album 'Wheels Of Steel', to witness a metal nearer molten than simply heavy, as Saxon strove for musical excellence & achieved it without a hint of complacency.

The band comprise guitarists Graham Oliver & Paul Quinn, bassist Steve Dawson, drummer Peter Gill along with vocalist Biff Byford who is not only a remarkable character both on & off stage, but also a mighty singer with a fine range.

Opener 'Motorcycle Man' was delivered with a degree of professionalism which only comes after years of hard work. Unfortunately midway through 'Still Fit To Boogie' a complete power cut stopped Saxon in their tracks & saw them scurry to the wings. It was a rather embarrassed Biff who apologised for the 5-minute interval & the song was restarted. However, despite the calibre of the next two numbers, it was not until '747 (Strangers In The Night)' the new single, that the audience's enthusiasm was totally restored. The rest of the set was free of incident & passed by all too quickly. 'Backs To The Wall', 'Freeway Mad', 'Stallions of The Highway' & 'Streetfighting Gang' went down a storm; even 'Frozen Rainbow' sounded fresh & exciting in a performance which gave no respite to the entranced head-bangers.

Encores were a formality & the evening's events were brought to an end by a stunning 'Machine Gun' featuring guitarist Graham Oliver emulating his axe-hero Jimi Hendrix to great effect (thus proving that "the more it grinds, the more it whines"). The rising mushroom of thick red smoke climaxed a spectacular performance, indicating without doubt that Saxon are here to stay.

I spoke with Graham Oliver after the show & was quite taken aback by his quiet nature which had me wondering whether this was the same guy I had seen smashing his SG against the sides of the PA. Open & unpretentious to interview, he told me of the band's extensive commitments at home & abroad. After the British tour, it's on to Europe to do some festivals before returning to complete an album for release in November for which they're still writing material. At home again, they hope to be on the bill for festival at Crystal Palace on August 9th (along with Judas Priest, Ted Nugent, Krokus, Tygers of Pan Tang & possibly AC/DC). They're doing Loch Lomond festival on June 22nd (with Ian Gillan, Krokus, Lindisfarne & The Only Ones). They have also been asked to be special guests on the bill at Stafford Bingley Hall on July 26th when headliners will be Motorhead. Graham was, however, somewhat sceptical about the planned American tour with wildman Ted Nugent, but it's only a matter of time before they bridge the Atlantic & storm the USA.

Saxon must be one of the hottest properties in the business yet their hospitality after the show was quite out of line with the accepted image, as jokers of the band - Biff &, especially, Steve Dawson - warmly entertained the fans who stayed behind.

I cannot understand the narrow-minded people who simply dismiss Saxon as unoriginal. It's quite ridiculous. And, certainly, no-one can begrudge them their new-found success. In my opinion, having seen them as Son Of A Bitch at Princeville, this success is well overdue.
— Steve Brown.

MIRROR BOYS — Jenks' Bar, Blackpool. Thu. 22 May '80.

Line up: Sax/Voc = Junior (Graham Aierth), Ld Gtr/Voc = Geoff Clout, Bass/Voc = Graham Cardy, Dms = Mit Lims (Tim Mills of fellow Leeds band The Neat).

It's 8.45 in Jenks & the gig is very much like a leap back in time with about 25/30 people all looking like '74/'76 Hippies. Now's the time for the band to come on. They all look good, with each member very much a character in his own right. They open with a number called 'The Android Song' that's very tight & well performed, obviously hoping to impress with a nifty sax solo in there. We're now into the third song - a number with similarities to something by Talking Heads. The last song of the first set was 'Disco Music' with lyrics like "Suck my cock, it's Blackpool rock" leading into James Brown's 'Sex Machine' which seemed to be a bit of a joke amongst the band. People were wondering which way to take them. (Orally?? - ed.)

Second set, & the band are late - the D.J. becoming impatient. I think the band were just waiting till more people arrived. The audience now numbers 100/150 including members of Blackpool band The Fits. They open this set with 'At Tiffany's' ("Everybody's enjoying themselves but me...") which is an excellent catchy number, but the sound's gone off a bit with the bass a bit too loud so it masks Geoff's fine guitar work. Second number, the sound much better & things now warming up. Mit Lims on drums has definitely come on since last I saw him (& if he takes my tip, he should stay with this outfit). Fifth number, 'I Don't Wanna Be 20', possibly a good single, went down well & won over the punters. So the set's going fine - then comes the disappointment as they start to repeat material from the first set but, as most people missed them first time around, they go down well - especially 'Disco Music' with added extras like a song from The Sound of Music & some yodelling from Geoff. So this tight nifty set ends amid shouts for more. They encore with an a cappella song that comes over well, leading back into 'Disco Music' (plus bits of 'King Of The Road' & a general jam... "Disco music go away/this is what we like to play..."). A good

A good band. They've a single out soon. So take a tip from me - go & see them if you get a chance.
— Barry Lights.

TISWAS — Huddersfield Polytechnic 16th May '80

On entering the Poly it was made blatantly clear what the Tiswas team had in mind. A large polythene sheet covered the entire arena &, with the words "The Four Bucketeers" written on the backcloth, a night of slapstick was lying ahead. But what else? Whilst I was driving to Huddersfield, I was trying to imagine what sort of show I was going to see. As it turned out, they didn't perform for a pre-teenage audience, most certainly not like the Saturday morning chaos. As Chris Tarrant said, "The average age of viewers is 25 with an I.Q. of 4." (Nuff said).

The performance started late with the appearance on stage of Chris Tarrant, John Gorman & Bob Carolgees. Chris began to mutter in his smooth manner &, due to a bad PA system (which thankfully improved soon after) I missed half of what he had to say, but I think he was giving a briefing on the programme to follow.

"Where's Sally James? N'yuk, n'yuk." seemed to be coming from everyone around me (including myself). She eventually appeared (this is what they want) to the usual cat-calls, wolf-whistles & cries of "Drop 'em, Blossom!" & "Show us y'tits!" with Chris mimmicking the audience reaction. John Gorman rang up the speaking clock to prove to us that they do the show live & it wasn't a recording - fair enough. The show then got under way with a song - "A is for A" (repeat), "L is for long" (repeat) "S is for strong... etc. until we got "A long strong black pudding up my great (Margaret) Thatcher" - original anyway.

As the show went on, we were entertained by Bob & Charley The Monkey who sang a song & told jokes. Then a request was made for a girl to come up from the audience & kiss Charley. As soon as this was done, Chris came on with his wig & a little red book for a 'This Is Your Life' on the unsuspecting victim from the audience. She took to it well & showed great emotion when introduced to her 'stage' father, 'Bishop Gorman' & fellow prostitute friend Sally James - & did that raise a cheer, with Sally clad in a low-cut waistcoat, fishnet tights & a mini-mini shirt.

Bob Carolgees came on next & rattled off a bevvy of blue jokes, followed by John Gorman in a 'Smello' sketch (complete with stink bombs in his pocket). Then the interval, which was a relief cos me bum was aching after sitting cross-legged on the floor.

The legendary Spit - the punk dog - was next to grace the stage, thrilling the audience with his gobbing antics - except for one who cried out "Why doesn't he spit?" "Why don't you piss off?" retorted Spit's master. (Ah, don't you just love professional finesse??? - ed.).

The 'Masked Poet' & side-kick presented some fluent four-line 'sonnets' before giving way to the ever-popular (but monotonous) 'Compost Corner' ("Compost Corner!" - thank you) which gave two lunatics from the audience the chance to get covered in all sorts of muck, custard pies from 'The Phantom Flan Flinger' & various other assortments of Tiswas gunge.

Sally James appeared (we thought she'd gone home) to complete the foursome on stage, who then gave us a rendition of a raucous football crowd song entitled 'Far Canal', an audience-participation number that went down well - work out why.

For the encore there was the inevitable 'Bucket Of Water Song' during which the polythene sheet served its purpose. The song was well mimed until Sally James opened her gob in the wrong place, but we all got wet so I suppose it didn't really matter.

They're a really talented bunch, with the exception of Sally James whose talent is purely physical - & she knows it.

An excellent show, but I did feel sorry for the mother who brought her ten-year-old daughter to the show. It wasn't the nice little kiddies show that she expected... Is that what they want?
— Mick Mitchell.

SPIT SPAT HERE

THE VERY LATEST RECORDINGS

DISCS (INCLUDING RECORDS)

CAMERAS IN CARS/4-track EP (IN CINC RECORDS '80). This Bradford band's D.I.Y. single has good packaging with an attractive sleeve that opens up to give lyrics, photos, track & recording info. Side A: 'Time Bomb' Synth. intro. that leads into vocals which are shouted rather than sung, sounding like a Yorks. John Otway or John Cooper Clarke. It's a good song in a rough, anti-melody way. 'Avoid A Void' is a bit monotonous for most people's tastes — though it does have that something which holds your attention. Side B: 'Bright Boy' has a good guitar intro. & the song's a good one — best on the EP — but it's too long or else should have more variety to it. 'The Author' is too long & good, but also goes on for far too long. The whole is quite good, but also for the band & good value at 99p.

ALWOODLEY JETS/33⅓ EP (LOOK RECORDS '80). Side one: 'Heaven Can't Wait' has good vocals on a pleasant song. Keyboards & guitars are fine. Drums are a bit too plodding & heavy — otherwise, a good number. 'Long Time Lonely' is another appealing song in which I like the seesaw guitars & reggae touches — & again, the vocals are powerful. But the plodding drums are still there offering too little variety. Side two: 'Crash-n-Burn' features some good guitar-work & is another heavy pop song. The music's commercial, but dated. 'Hearts' has the same drumming yet again. Hell, it's ruining this EP for me. This last number has solo vocals that are powerful & as impressive in their own way as were the mixed vocals on the first number. What's on offer here is a set of fairly ordinary commercial rock songs that the band put over well.

Touring Holland in June then 2 weeks of London gigs in early July + Japanese tour in the pipeline

THE OSCILLATORS/Taking Harrogate By Yawn (Yawn Products '80). A-side: 'Marilyn Brown' is a number that really grows on me — has a great 'Na-Ni-Na, Na-Ni-Na-Ni-Na-Ni, Na-Ni-Na, Na-Ni-Na' chorus chant. This is a vast improvement on 'Leonard Cheshire' — their earlier single (reviewed in WCR4, etc.). B-side: is 'E-Boat' which is a bit more mannered, but still likeable in a slightly tedious way.

YOU/the night & music (Ram Records). Side A: 'Wreckers Song' is rock/punk cross-over. The band's not bad, but the recording's none too hot... & nor's the vocalist whenever he makes the mistake of trying to hold a note for any length of time. I like this song, though, especially close to 'When you Cry' is an altogether weaker song that runs dangerously close to 'All roads lead to Gotham City'. 'Autopsy' is an odd, macabre dirgy tune, screams, etc. 'Thinking of You' doesn't cut it with me either. Again, it's slow & lacks fun. 'Your Face' is a slow ballady opening followed by a speeding up of the whole pace. The slow piece spotlights the singer's thin voice & the song itself isn't for me. A disappointing EP with a rough sound that is probably simply due to this Leeds combo squeezing too much onto a 7-inch disc (over 5-minutes per side is just about certain to adversely affect the sound quality).

Bradford punks Violation have a single due out at end of July.

KNIFE EDGE/'Favourite Girl' c/w 'Say You Will' (No Hassle Records '80). This is an excellent single. It has an exciting feel, a catchy pair of songs, good lyrics. Knife Edge must be one of the most commercial bands on the West Yorks. rock circuit. Buy this — you won't regret it.

Best-selling local band single in June (according to Radio Leeds).

UNRELEASED DEMO TAPES

THE ZIPPS/3-track demo recorded at September Sound in Huddersfield by this Bradford band. 'Flying So High In The Sky' is white reggae-pop that's too sugary for its own good — reminding me of The Banana Splits or one of those late sixties bubblegum groups (1910 Fruitgum Co., etc.). 'Since You Went Away' is more of a straight rock song, with more weight to it, but it's less fun & tends to go on a bit. 'Black & White Movies' is Boomtown Rats meet Elvis Costello & so it's ultra-palatable Elvtown Ratello. So, a fun demo, but nothing to chase after.

THE QUICK/3-track demo tape: 'Motor Car' is a new one on me — a good song. 'Now She's Gone' has less immediate appeal, while 'The Train' is pure 60's pop (Gerry & The Pacemakers, Tremeloes, Freddy & The Dreamers, Billy J. Kramer) with the added bonus of quite a clever instrumental reggaed final verse. I wasn't keen on their first (home-made) demo (see WCR 4 for review) but this 2nd one is much better. From Keighley, The Quick're fast-becoming a band to watch.

C.B.S. have told The Quick to change their name because of U.S. early punk band (now defunct) with same name & vinyl out on C.B.S.

THE TOXICS/8-track demo. Almost all my namesakes, the members of this Ilkley outfit are still at school. They are, on this showing, very clearly a raw 77-ish punk band — primitive &, kind of good enough. Like Angelic Upstarts & relative new-comers of their hards Rejects. Whether they can carve a niche there for themselves remains to be seen. Certainly they work up a good hard wall of punk guitar that should make them a popular live outfit.

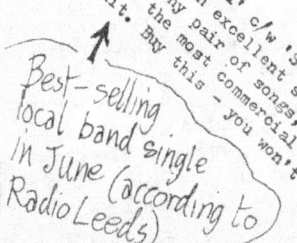

Dirty but Nice

DIRTY BUT NICE/3-track that this Leeds outfit recorded at Ric Rac in April. They're musicians more than they are rock stars, so you get very polished music that's almost sterilised — hyper-arranged with thin coating of jazz notes. You'll gather that this sort of music is a bit too cold & calculated/premeditated for my own tastes — no guts or raunch to it. But, my prejudices aside, they are certainly good at what they do... so much so that I almost like their classy work on a track called 'Chinese Takeaway', really do like 'Mr. Fixit', but find the final track — 'I Don't Understand' — contrivedly unpleasant... or maybe it's just that I don't understand!

page 5.

THE ART OF SOLVING PROBLEMS - LEEDS' 1ST COMPILE ALBUM
released late in May on Ram Records!

Six bands, two tracks each go to make up this Leeds album. It's not one that I was altogether sure about on first listening, but I like it much more after several replays. With one exception (The Cat) these are all local pub rock bands &, with all recorded in the same studios, they fit togther surprisingly well - overcoming the major problem with sampler albums, that of the various tracks being at odd with each other. Obviously, as a low-price showpiece for the studio, this should pay dividends for Ram, but it's also a very concrete way in which they can help local rock. I'd have thought that other studios could do much the same. Incidentally, the sleeve design (the acknowledgement got missed out by the printer) is by WCR's own cartoonist Stan Engel. And now the album track-by-track:-

1/1 The Forst/'I'm a Mess'. Most punky track on the album & also one of the most infectious. Mildly amusing lyric (a dig at punk individuality cult) adds to its immediacy. I think I'm right in saying that the band come from Wakefield & so are the only ones on this album who aren't actually from Leeds - though they play there regularly.

1/2 The Motivators/'Miss Demeanours'. Would just be a good but ordinary rock number if it weren't for the quite clever insertion of mechanical/Devo-ish instrumental bursts. Like many of these tracks, this one is better 3rd/4th time around.

1/3 The Gimmicks/'(He's Only) 25'. I've never seen this band or heard their work before, but everyone tells me they're good. This song backs up that opinion, being nicely balanced between light pop & commercial rock.

1/4 The Cat/'Heather Weather'. This guy sings & plays the instruments himself, multitracking to get it all in. Unlike the others, this therefore lacks the excitement that is generated by a bunch of people getting off on mutual enthusiasm - & it shows. The whole song plods along with a dreariness that makes it a non-starter - doesn't even sound as if it comes from the same studio!

1/5 Side Effect/'Chain Reaction'. Good chorus, but the guitar/keyboards sound on breaks & verses is a bit dated. Don't like the song's ending either.

1/6 The Beans/'Clouds Over The Moon'. I liked this band's single (also on Ram) & this track maintains the standard. They're a good white reggae band. Extra marks for use of two voices on the final verse. Also for spot-on tight rhythm thoughout.

2/1 The Beans/'Getting On The No.9'. This one's not reggae - just a great piece of pop music with a lot of neat touches to keep it interesting from start to finish.

2/2 Side Effect/'Pin Stripe Suit'. One of their popular stage numbers (if you've seen them, you might better remember it for the chorus of "Don't let your love tie you down"). This has grown to be my favourite track on the album. As soon as it finishes, I want to hear it again. Commercial enough for them to release as a single.

2/3 The Cat/'The Evil Way'. There's a heavy rock feel to this - except where it's off-set by flute-like synth. The R.S.P.C.A.'s gonna get me for cruelty to The Cat, but this is just another tedious yawn.

2/4 The Gimmicks/'Three Separate Worlds'. It's ok, this - but that's all. I can take or leave it. Really, it needs something more to lift it a bit. There's a distinct lack of enthusiasm that suggests the band have been playing this number either too much in the studio or else just had it in their stage set for too long & the spark's gone out of it.

2/5 The Motivators/'An Eye-Opener'. Reggae with an excellent lyric. The song itself is very slightly too laid-back for my tastes. And why do so many of these good Leeds pub bands seem to have lead guitarists who play very ordinary pre-'77 rock-guitar breaks? A good number for all that.

2/6 The Forst/'Doing Nothing With My Life'. More new wave than punky this time. Odd spoken bit in the middle that doesn't quite work. This song keeps putting me in mind of The Boomtown Rats (& that's no bad thing) - though it's not quite as inventive nor as immaculately tight as that notorious crew. Still, they're a band I'll be watching with interest.

So, as a sampler, how does it do for its artists? Well, booby prize of a can of Whiskas goes to The Cat. Can Side Effect dump their boring material & put together a whole set as good as 'Pin Stripe Suit'? I doubt it. A lot of people seem to think that The Motivators are a good bet for bigger things in the rock world. Their two tracks here leave me in some doubt that they can come up with songs that have that vital touch of individuality. The Gimmicks are, by all accounts, a great pub band. If so, they should settle for that. It puts them head & shoulders above most local bands, whilst being shoved onto a larger stage may well kill them stone-dead. The Forst certainly have something special, but I'd want to see them live before speculating on their chances as a lot'll depend on how well they put it over on stage. That leaves The Beans. They're an excellent studio band (should be, with one of them actually employed as an engineer at Ram). With determination & the right back-up, they're the ones I'd back to win through.

With the album comes a small poster made up from photos of the bands plus a lyric sheet. At around 2½ quid, it's a good bargain - one I can recommend.

RIC RAC DEMO TAPE
- specially compiled for W.C.R. by Mick Robson of Ric Rac - not available to the public.

The Switch/'Can't Stand Still'. Apart from a weak talk-over bit in the middle & a totally predictable guitar break, this is fun. Lots of woops, shouts & spicy percussion plus a powerful hook. Not at all what I expected from this band - a pleasant surprise.

The Clients/'Killing Time'. They're the only outfit on here who're not from Leeds (Harrogate, in fact). Good vocalist plus an interesting guitar sound (cross between Dire Straits & Shadows) with a tight fast rhythm section. Good, though the song's a bit samey.

Dodgy Tactics/'Can't Blame Me'. This is white reggae that's about the police but not like The Police - it's much more solid & draws more on black reggae for its influences. This band is really good - the whole feel is intense, fun & compulsively danceable.

The Cat/'Lizzie'. Purrr, so we meet again! The note here says that the guy is called Bernard Pitts & he plays all instruments except drums - this number's mostly synths/vocals. It's much better than his tracks on the Ram sampler, but I'm still not converted - too gloomy & serious.

Bob & Baz/'Counting Out Time'. Multitracked vocals/instruments from two guys who used to play bass & guitar in Strangeways & later in Cuba. This is exciting use of a good studio to realise some neat ideas. Bit overlong for anyone who's not on their wavelength; spoken lead voc. + Simon-&-Garfunkel-ish back-up vocals & off-reggae rhythms with smooth layer of percussion. Idiosyncratic's the non-committal way to describe it.

Dodgy Tactics/'Boys in Blue'. Same theme, but pop-rock, not reggae. Good lyrics again... though you might not think so if you're a cop! Keyboards & drums work together well on this one.

The Clients/'Modern Lovers'. Is a catchy modern pop song. Good back-up vocals that're underused. Unspectacular instrumental break midway. The rest is great. It's a song that - with a bit more work - could be massively commercial.

The Switch/'Nothing's Sacred'. Good production can't always save an ordinary song with a weak chorus from being just that. The band are good, but the feel is tame & a bit wimpish. The drum sound in Ric Rac is always outstandingly good - & is here.

The Cat/'Non Connexion'. Nine lives, but losing a few on this page! This is the best of the four tracks - the music is strong, but the vocal bulldozes through the number.

There are two further tracks both written & sung by Chris Morris (ex Paper Lace), with backing vocals & music by him, Dene Michaels & Mick Robson (who runs the studio). The first is a good slice of disco music, the second an M.O.R. ballad - both with immaculate production.

Ric Rac is an excellent & versatile studio - physically a bit cramped, but otherwise hard to fault. If you want any further reassurance of this, listen out for Cuba's 'Wireless World' on Ariola (due out soon). It's very rash of to make such a prediction, but I'll be disappointed if it's not an enormous hit - & that's a number that was very much the product of the studio.

WITCH DISCO HIRE!
Run your own disco... full rig for hire with twin deck plus mic. 40% discount for students...
For full details ring Bradford 34543 between 1-2 p.m.

girl + broken home
University Bradford 3rd May '80

For some inexplicable reason, Bradford's quota of metal fans decided to stay away in numbers for this promising event. In fact when support band Broken Home appeared about 9.30 pm the audience was sparse to say the least. None the less, the band soldiered on to perform an extremely enjoyable set of medium paced rock n' roll which was clinically executed and quite original. briefly the band comprise Dicken, vocals/guitar, Peter Crowther, bass (both ex Mr. Big), Rory Wilson, guitar, Graham Pleeth keyboards and ex Gillan drummer Pete Barnacle. Tonight was only their second ever gig but they proved to be very tight and well balanced and I am sure they stand a good chance of commercial success. The songs 'Stop Looking at Me', 'Jerusalem', and 'Shot Over Hill' all worked well with their distinctive almost Geddy Lee like vocals of Dicken prominent. The best songs of the set were firstly 'Death Boy' a great rocky number and the band's newly released debut single 'Death of Gog', which is littered with some dynamic power chords with subtle piano contrasts. The only nagging doubt I have about Broken Home is simply image as they appeared to lack that all important stage presence. However, if Genesis man Tony Smith sticks with 'em They can't go wrong and I look forward to the forthcoming album released on June 6th.

Girl were a different proposition all together. I must admit I had my doubts about them before they came on. Two inauspicious TV slots (OGWT & TOTP) and the rather patchy debut album 'Sheer Greed' which contains some really brilliant songs but is let down sadly by songs such as 'Passing Clouds' and 'Things to Say'. Thankfully, their live performance belied the bland production of the album and Girl proceeded to shatter any preconceived ideas I had about them with some driving HM which sent the by now considerably larger crowd into raptures of delight. The twin guitars of Phil Collen and Gerry Laffy are the mighty basis around which Girl is built and contrasted with the adequate depth provided by Simon Laffy's bass and Dave Gaynor's Drums, they create an overall potent sound Frontman Philip Lewis really enjoys himself on stage as though the punters are the people he wants to be with, and the stage is the place he likes to be. Off stage he appeared rather depressed and somewhat subdued as he returned to his upper class entourage, headed by one Baroness Fiona de Fex-Janniers who quite eagerly filled my notebook with information (though mainly about herself) and she insisted on me mentioning her as the future Mrs. Lewis.

It's difficult to know whether their effeminate image turns people away in any great numbers, but there is nothing effeminate about the sweat they work in delivering such gems as 'My Number', 'Hollywood Tease' and their two quite breathtaking covers, firstly the Kinks classic 'You Really Got Me' and 'Do You Love Me' of Kiss.

One important thing is their favour as they continue their quest for world recognition is that Girl are quite unmistakeable, both in image and sound. Their spot on the UFO tour has no doubt been invaluable and I can only see them progressing - for the time being at least.

Finally a pointer to local bands may lie in the same way in which Girl signed to Jet Records. Philip Lewis explained how they scraped the cash together to make a video in a small studio in Muswell Hill and on its delivery to Jet they were snapped up immediately. Moreover, the video cost a total of about £250, much less than cutting a disc. —Steve Brown.

GLOSSY MAGS
WHITE LION huddersfield. 17th May '80

As Alan Whicker would probably say, an evening of distinct & contrasting halves. First, The White Lion for Glossy Mags. Let's not beat about the bush, I found this really 'orrible. Rumour has it that they're 'new wave' which I take to mean a refined poppy music inspired by punk but not tied down by its limited format - e.g. Costello, Police. What we had here, by contrast, was a sort of lifeless, multi-purpose aural wallpaper, borrowing all the external characteristics of new wave whilst carefully sucking out any vitality that might lie therein. Glossy Mags is, no doubt without them knowing it, a good name for them, all lifeless 'sophisticated' titilation, jet set angst & reproduction posters. They're a five-piece - rhythm, lead, bass, drums, keyboards/synth. The numbers are usually about love, mainly lost, in a plethora of regrets & world-weary resignation. Apart from a couple of balladish things, the set was mainly up-tempo with bits of jazz & shuffle thrown in along the way, invariably competently played with an air of cultured indifference - or was it just boredom? What stick in the mind are the very precise guitar solos (note-for-note reproductions of things played 100 times before?) & the single-line synth passages - oh god, those synth passages. You know, the sort of things they have on those ghastly travel programmes on TV, playing behind pictures of Aryan surfers & obese secretaries from Birmingham drinking Watney's Red Barrel... At times they wandered into a kind of castrated (on both the musical & the lyrical level) Elvis Costelloish sort of thing with a sixties throwback feel about it. To be fair to the band, the majority of the audience seemed quite pleased with it all. It put me in mind of Gerry & The Pacemakers. When we're fifty & going to Beastly Variety Club they'll have this sort of stuff as background music for the bingo games. New wave? New Faces, more like.

The first set was enough for me, so I set off for The Albion to find out what "To be confirmed" were like. Now that's another story altogether. —Phil Foster.

Sheila & The Poo-Flaps / God & The Demi-Gods
PALM COVE CLUB Bradford. 17 MAY '80

At 50p, the gig was a giveaway. It was a benefit for one-parent families in the area & was billed as The Earwigs + God & The Demi-Gods. The Earwigs, being Barbara Canter (bass), Danny Nuttall (dms) & Alex Bilenko (gtr) - all ex-Klingons - with Jeremy Stein (gtr) & Steve Wood (kbds), decided at some point prior to the gig to rename the band Sheila & The Poo Flaps. (They've since changed the name again - to Olga & The Communists, though Danny tells me it'll change again soon - take a back seat, Spizz! - ed.) It was a new name for a trial gig, testing how well the new band fit together. In fact, they didn't play badly at all, the most notable of their numbers being the reggae ones, given stage presence by Jeremy's fronting of the band on guitar. But overall, their performance was overshadowed by the earlier set done by God & The Demi-Gods, I thought, so I sought out a Demi-God for a few words.

Tim Nuttall (dms), Victor Vaselenko (gtr), Roger Greenslade (gtr/voc) & Buzz (bass) played a rivetting set of staccato guitar & distortion to a well-held drum rhythm. Cataclysmic stuff! "We play anti-music," I was told, "even to the point of hating playing it & hating ourselves for playing it." No gig satisfaction there, but I suspect that whatever motives the band have for playing - love, hate or indifference - they will in the end enjoy the confusion & interest they create. I especially liked 'Rock & Roll Ballet' but was impressed throughout, despite the fact that I couldn't hear any of the lyrics, which I'd hoped to hear after a reference to early Floyd by a Demi-God. Apparently, the band paly infrequently, only when they feel they have to, so they've no idea when the next gig would be. I'll be watching. —Ken Turner.

← most pretentious statement of this issue.

FAVOURITE GIRL From KNIFE EDGE
nohesslerecords F001
+ Available from most record shops xxx+

CLASSIFIED ADS.
10p per word. Ring Nick on B'f'd (0274) 21867.

NOVICE DRUMMER requires permanent evening practice room. Will pay modest rent if necessary. Tel. Keith on B'f'd 392503.

AIRBEAT RECORDS DISTRIBUTORS. Barry Lights, 48 Crystal Rd, Blackpool, Lancs. Tel. (0253) 46503. Sneakers 4-track cassette (Abt Cass 1), Titles: 'Oh Fay', 'Oh Buddy Holly', 'All Winter Long' & 'Prickley Heat' now available. Send £1-25 + 25p p. & p.

VOCALIST (no previous experience) wants to join/form pop & rock band. Very keen. Anyone interested please contact Keith Noe, 7 Barnard House, Saffron Drive, Alerton, Bradford.

BAND TRANSPORT. Cheap & reliable. Ring Malcolm on Bradford 44428. Also available of light removals, shifting gear, even pianos!

ULTERIOR MOTIVES badges. 2-inch enamel in fabulous black & glorious white. 30p (inc. postage) from Wool City Rocker.

Sex Pistols' Great Rock 'N' Roll Swindle Reviewed

Never mind the bollocks, here's the... who? Good question. Some of you may remember the appearance in 1977 of a combo named The Sex Pistols whose existence more or less amounted to a finger in the eye of anything within poking distance, including its own ugly little visage. Before their inevitable demise, they exerted not a little influence on contemporary music & then vanished in a puff of suicide/murder/legal action/recrimination of which this film constitutes just one small part.

Behind it all, the film would have us believe, were the machinations of that latterday Machiavelli, Malcolm McLaren, whose strategy for world domination involved the creation of a band whose main strength lay in their ability firstly to convince friend & foe alike that their existence constituted a threat to western civilisation as we know it & secondly, as a consequence of this, to prize huge amounts of money from record companies determined to turn this collapse into the ringing of cash registers. By way of a combination of actual footage of events (musical & otherwise), cartoon & scripted action, McLaren gleefully details the minutiae of the process in the context of a potted history of the band's antics. There's the careful creation of the band (as ugly & untalented as possible), generation of a mystique by wholesale manipulation of the media & record companies, the cynical manufacture of shock/horror events. McLaren puts particular emphasis on his modified version of the 'keep-'em-waiting' concept of performance - viz. play as little as possible, preferably not at all. Thus fans were encouraged to trek across country to see gigs the band had no intention of playing. Amidst footage of the band playing (?) all their goodies, there're cartoon versions of vomit at Heathrow & fux & loathing at A & M Records, Sid Vicious lapsing into Jeckyll & Hyde when he forgets to don the macho-rebellious persona he's supposed to project, much running round on Brazillian beaches with Biggs & his Nazi friends & much much more. If you're a woman, you might complain about being portrayed as merely a collection of orifices to be entered in various directions, but you can't satisfy (I-ed.) all the people all the time.

Well, what does it all mean? It means that we've been had. This circus constitutes about as much of a threat to western civilisation as The Muppet Show. In fact, it actually embodies all the seedy aspects of human folly that it so joyfully points its finger at. Whoever was responsible for sanctioning the final 'product' (in effect, Richard Branson, I would imagine) would have us believe that anybody who thinks that modern music can amount to a serious articulation of discontent is deluding themselves. The film is a stinking, heaving mess of cynicism - presumably in accord with what actually happened - an unconcious but self-regarding attempt to illustrate the idea that whatever we might do to change our lives is just another aspect of the disease masquerading as the cure, a thesis crudely encapsulated in the image of effigies of the band dangling by their necks from a gallows at the beginning of the film.

A parable of our times? Probably. But more like Hollywood histrionics reincarnated with a cockney accent, the dying grunt of a bunch of jaded, cynical old men flogging a dead horse.
— Phil Foster.

THE MO-DETTES
THE GOOD MOOD CLUB, HALIFAX. 26/4/80.

You've probably heard of The Mo-Dettes even if you haven't seen them yet. They're an all female four-piece from London with a single out at the moment called 'White Mice' which seems to be getting some airplay. They certainly seem to inspire a certain amount of devotion, a bunch of admirers of a mod/skin inclination had hitched all the way up from London to see them.

In musical inclination the band are basically R-&-B/pop - imagine a simplified version of Dr Feelgood (just imagine it????) & strictly up-tempo & you won't be far off the mark. Oh yes, they wear kilts & pencil skirts & ladybird's antenae. From this it's clear we are in for A GOOD TIME. And what's wrong with that, you ask? Nothing, I reply, er..... nothing at all.

I didn't get any of the titles of the songs apart from 'White Mice' & 'Paint It Black' (not an original, I hasten to add). Nor did I cop for much of the lyrical gist - the vocals were pretty much back in the mix, so much so that even the introductions disappeared into the audience background mumble. I've a feeling that it won't have worried them unduly - everybody jumped up & down in the right places & the band's friends from London got up on stage & sang along on a Beatles song, the title of which eludes me at the moment. I do remember the Stones number sounding very much, I imagine, as it would do if played by a bunch of Zulu drummers.

Profound they aren't, but considering the audience reaction (not once did I hear anyone say "gerremoff"), they've probably had greater social effect than all the pseudo-philosophical vapourising of the Genesis/Yes ilk rolled together simply by getting up on stage & playing. End of lecture.
— Phil Foster.

LUCKY STRIKE
The Warehouse, Leeds. 9th May 1980.

I was gazing into the 'control room' where the console, record decks & assorted equipment could have come straight out of a recording studio. Mike was staring through his glass pigeon-hole at the dance floor. There were no laser-beam lights, no mirrored suits, just the drifting sounds of the music Mike had picked to lead into the appearance of Lucky Strike on stage. It all struck me as rather odd, but then Mike is no ordinary fellow. He runs The Warehouse, which everyone in the area now knows as a very good discotheque, the reputation of which is about to change slightly owing to the appearance of a few local bands. The setting is almost perfect for a small concert, with the band on a stage flanked by bars & seating areas & the dance smack dab in the middle of the place. The acoustics are good too. The basic idea is that instead of just a disco, which really only blossoms into life when the pubs close, Mike will put a local band on from 9-11pm three nights a week or so, with no charge at the door & the drinks at pub prices until 10.30pm. So the band is free, the drinks much the same price as elsewhere, & if you should decide to stay after 11pm, the disco follows as soon as the band finishes. Mike doesn't yet know whether it's working or what effect it'll have on the disco, but he's giving it a try with the likes of Spider Blues Band, Helter Skelter &, tonight, Lucky Strike.

It was the first time I'd seen the band in action. Everyone in the band was wound up, ready to play, but their stage experience wouldn't let all the tension go straight away. They moved smoothly into 'Surrender To The Rhythm' & had the fairly sparse audience tapping their collective feet & moving closer to the stage & onto the dance floor from the start. As a few more folks arrived & moved in for a better view & a place at the bar (in some cases!), Grom announced that the set was to be split into two, with a suitable break about halfway. This is the usual arrangement, apparently, so as not to wear the band out too quickly & (I imagine) give the bar staff a chance to catch up with themselves around 10.30! Classic R-&-B & soul was the order of the day for us, as Lucky Strike ran through 'How Sweet It Is', 'We Gotta Get Out Of This Place', 'Stand By Me' & so on, finishing the first half of the set on 'Midnight Hour'. John Shepard's drumming, I thought, was the basis for a hard driving sound with Grom Kelly fronting the band well, & handling the introductions with ease. I do hear that Grom plays harp too, but in this case he was completely overshadowed by Roger Pond-Jones, the guest harmonica-player, who must be one of the biggest blokes playing on the local scene. He positively threw himself into 'Hoochie Coochie Man' at the start of the second set & was always on side of stage mouthing lyrics & aiding the rhythm with a bit of thigh-slapping (his own, honest!) when he wasn't included in a number. Having him as guest was a neat move that gave the band a smart, fluid touch, & the extra punch when a song demanded it. All in all, very capably handled, lads. John told me that they have their off-days, as does any band, so go & see them on a good one. The band are playing for the fun of it, so the more of you who go to see them, the more fun there'll be for all, & the better the band will be. (That applies to most bands, as anyone who's been part of a small, embarrassed audience at a gig that failed to develop much atmosphere will know only too well - ed.)

Although The Warehouse as a venue is limited in its range by Mike's personal choice of bands, it's a great setting - somewhere new & interesting for local music-lovers, as well as would-be disco-freaks. An intriguing combination!
— Ken Turner.

Twisted Nerve

<u>Line-up</u>: Paul Mirror (vocs/lyrics), Steve Gregg (gtr/bkg vocs), Steve Wardle (gtr/bkg vocs), Andrew Felton (dms) & Nick Hay (bass).

Back in Sept '79 the two Steves began looking around for others to form a band, eventually met up with Paul in Jan '80 & had the full band line-up by late Feb. They then spent two months rehearsing & writing songs at Ram Studios in their home-town of Leeds before making their public debut at The Marquis of Granby on 26th May (on a double bill with Bradford's <u>Ulterior Motives</u> - another name-check, heh! heh!)

They played Boston Spa on 31st May & have July gigs at Seacroft Hotel & The Royal Park in Leeds, with a couple of dates lined up back at The Marquis in late summer.

On 28th June, the band is booked into Ram to record a demo tape (with Dave Whittaker of the band <u>Music For Pleasure</u> coming in as producer).

When I interviewed them, the band volunteered a bunch of personal rock histories. Here are the edited highlights... Steve Wardle was previously in a band called <u>The Mess</u>. Nick Hay lived down in Croydon until '78 & was in a number of London's early punk bands with such exotic names as <u>Hairy Balls & The Masturbators</u> + <u>Truss</u> (which Nick describes as a support band!) + <u>The Failures</u> + <u>The Rubbers</u> + <u>Rampant Syphillis</u>... y'know, sometimes I worry about today's youth - when I was a lad we never used words like rampant. Andy says: "I was in a band called <u>Bio-Feedback</u> & we played just one gig for which we only had 30 minutes' rehearsal. There were three of us - no bass-player, but no-one noticed that!" Paul Mirror has been involved in music for about 6 years & has done over 200 gigs. <u>The Mirrors</u> was the first band for which he wrote all the songs & their line-up also included Dave Whittaker (already mentioned above). Steve Gregg once played guitar in a play, but this is his first band & the gig at The Marquis was his first ever. Also at the interview was a friend of the band called Merrick who has the distinction of having been the band's manager for about two hours (he tried & failed to get them a gig at Wig's Wine Bar so they sacked him). He once had piano lessons from a neighbour.

The group write all their own songs - usually starting with a set of lyrics by Paul. "My lyrics are mostly sexual politics plus a couple of topical songs (like 'Oil!' which is about the Ayatollah) but I avoid taking any specifically political stances." Often Paul also comes up with the rough outline of a melody. The band as a whole then hammer out the complete song that won't just be a straightforward basic pop song - "We like to use a mixture of rhythms & melodies so that the song's a bit more complex than just verse/chorus/verse/chorus." Paul says that the eventual aim is to develop a new approach to the standard 2-guitar line-up.

<u>Contact</u>: Steve Wardle on Leeds 673701. Paul on Leeds 652464.

from an interview by Nick Toczek.

TREATMENT

<u>Personnel</u>: Ali White (ld voc/some rm gtr), Phil Russell (ld gtr/bkg voc), Rodger Massiah (b gtr/bkg voc), Clive Worley (organ/Wurlitzer pno), Pete Hunt (dms).

<u>Music</u>: They've been compared with <u>Roxy Music</u>, <u>Talking Heads</u>, <u>XTC</u> & <u>Captain Beefheart</u>, seeing themselves as one of the bands emerging from the new-wave era with a different kind of pop/rock that is catchy & accessible without being instantly disposable. In the early days, the band worked at mixing new-wave, reggae & jazz/funk influences - an uneasy blend at first, but one that they now feel gives the group its own distinctive style. Live, they do a set of 18 numbers drawn from a constantly evolving repertoire which has included over 50 original regularly-performed songs. They attach a lot of importance to the lyrics which they feel are better than most - a claim backed up by a report in the local press which summed up the band's strengths as: 'good catchy choruses, a really tight rhythm section, & excellent lyrics'. Song titles include: 'Safe & Sound', 'Fatal Attraction', 'Pop Gigolo', 'All Your Favourite Flavours', 'Minutes To Go', 'Ego Voyeur', 'Dog The Mind' & 'Another Jungle'.

<u>Background</u>: The nucleus of the band met at Huddersfield Polytechnic (where two were students & one a lecturer in psychology/sociology) & have been together for two years gaining experience by playing in pubs, clubs & colleges throughout the region.

<u>Contact</u>: Manager (Paul Wess) on Huddersfield 46970.

from their publicity leaflet

The Subliminal Cut

<u>The group</u>: Hugh Gubbin (voc), Hugh Morley (gtr), Chris Jackson (kbds), Mick Bunnage (bs), Graham Summers (dms). (Mick & Graham are both also in <u>Deep Freeze Mice</u>).

The band formed as <u>The Statics</u> in Feb '79 & have played mostly around Leeds, about twenty gigs in all - supporting bands such as <u>Magazine</u>, <u>Mekons</u>, <u>Agony Column</u>, <u>Screams</u>,

HUGH GUBBIN gets his foto'd face into W.C.R. while the rest of THE SUBLIMINAL CUT have to make do with name-checks.

<u>Crisis</u>, <u>Donkeys</u>, etc. In Dec '79 they recorded two tracks at Ric Rac Studio in Leeds (see tape review in WCR6) which were intended for release as a single but they didn't have the money to release it & "anyway, we felt after the recording session was over that the tracks were a bit flat & lifeless but that's probably because it was our first time in a studio. I think that we did the best we could & any other band would have done about the same under the circumstances. It was something we had to go through, so it wasn't wasted."

One of the main problems that the band feel they are currently facing is one that they have in common with numerous local outfits. "Unless you're doing a support at The Fan Club or The University, it's hard to draw more than 50/60 people to a gig. So it's a priority for us to get out of Leeds for gigs if we want to reach a reasonable number of people. It was good supporting <u>Magazine</u> as they drew the kind of audience that seems to like us - but we couldn't draw them in such numbers in our own right. It's a drag that those gigs are few & far between. There's a club recently opened in London - The Moonlight - that's intended as a showcase of bands from The Provinces, so maybe we'll get a gig there. We'd like to play Sheffield, Manchester, etc. but a lot of clubs seem to be closing down & the others aren't keen to risk booking bands like us who've not had extensive media coverage. Also, the fact that our music's slightly different from standard rock & pop means that gigs are harder to find. Most people who go to gigs don't like to be offered anything that they've not heard before."

I asked them about plans for vinyl... "We feel that we now have a more clearly-defined musical direction as a group, but we've no money to do it ourselves. There's a chance, though, that we might get one side of an E.P. on Mole Embalming Records (with <u>Deep Freeze Mice</u> on the flip), though that's still very much in the air at the moment."

Any other hassles...? "We need management & a phone - it's a real problem not being on the phone at all."

The interview ended here, but a letter arrived two days later:-

"Dear Nick, after the interview we suddenly realised that we hadn't said much about the music. Most bands interviewed in the W.C.R. seem to treat the music as incidental & we don't want to do that.

The main points are these. We like to vary our arrangements & avoid the obvious & contrived. One aspect of this is the absence of conventional solos ('White Sound' is an exception). Creating atmosphere & feeling is more important than displays of technical skill.

It is important to be open to new ideas, & difficult to build up the confidence to use them. When bands start worrying about showing influences, or whether audiences like their music, is where we believe most of them go wrong, though sometimes it's hard to avoid.

Likewise, we want people to have to think about the lyrics, as opposed to being spoon-fed with clichés. Making things easy can make things worse.

Obviously there's too much here for a W.C.R. article, but we hope you can use some of it. (Wrong - ed.) We will be sending some photos in the near future. Cheers, Graham Summers. P.S. How about a regular letters page in W.C.R.? More feedback, we say."

Finally, the name-change to <u>The Subliminal Cut</u> was partly because the band's very different nowadays & so they felt a change of name was needed. Also, <u>The Statics</u> was rather non-descript & anyway there were several other bands with the same or similar names (e.g. <u>The Statistics</u>, <u>The Ecstatics</u>, etc.).

You can contact the group at 46 Ashville Avenue, Leeds 6, which is the address of Mole Embalming Records as well.

THE NEW LOO GUIDE — JUNE '80 — A FEW things to do...

SUN 1
- Fan Club, Leeds = THE LEAGUE OF GENTLEMEN + MARTIAN SCHOOLGIRLS.
- Vaults Bar, Bradford = MONEY.
- Fforde Greene, Leeds = HELTER SKELTER (jazz rock, weekly residency)
- Marquis of Granby, Leeds = CHINA TOWN.
- Staging Post, Leeds = CONVIX.
- Haddon Hall, Leeds = SIDE EFFECT.
- White Lion, Huddersfield = (lunch) COAST TO COAST / (eve) THE GUESTS.
- Princeville, Bradford (lunch) = KYRO.
- Warehouse, Leeds (lunch) = BEST FRIENDS.

MON 2
- Fforde Greene, Leeds = DYNAMITE.
- Marquis of Granby, Leeds = SPINOES.
- Princeville, Bradford = STREETFIGHTER.
- Royal Park, Leeds = SNAKEBITE.

TUE 3
- Vaults Bar, Bradford = BABY TUCCOO.
- Rose & Crown, Ilkley = THE QUICK.
- Kings Head, Keighley = CHAINSAW.
- Splash One, Bradford = COUNTER DANCE.
- Oddfellows Arms, Bradford = BEATS WORKING.
- Scamps, Bradford = COAST TO COAST.
- Warehouse, Leeds = SPIDER BLUES BAND.

WED 4
- Vaults Bar, Bradford = CHINA TOWN.
- Unity Hall, Wakefield = SAXON + TYGERS OF PAN TANG.
- White Lion, Huddersfield = PRIVATE DICKS.
- St. George's Hall, Bradford = DAVID ESSEX.
- Bradford University = THE VAPOURS + support.
- Royal Park, Bradford = NIGHT TRAIN.
- Warehouse, Leeds = HELTER SKELTER.

THU 5
- Rose & Crown, Ilkley = CHAINSAW.
- Queens Hall, Bradford = BEATS WORKING.
- Fan Club, Leeds = U2 + FASHION.
- Fforde Greene, Leeds = LONE STAR.
- Princeville, Bradford = WHITE SPIRIT.
- Royal Park, Leeds = TALISMAN.

FRI 6
- Unity Hall, Wakefield = TOYAH + THE RENT BOYS.
- Fforde Greene, Leeds = DICK SMITH BAND + THE ELEMENTS.
- Palm Cove, Bradford = SANCTION.
- Cleopatras, Huddersfield = ADAM & THE ANTS + MARTIAN DANCE.
- Royal Park, Leeds = WHITE EAGLES (resident Friday jazz band).

SAT 7
- Albion Hotel, Huddersfield = RHINO.
- Seacroft Hotel, Leeds = CONVIX.
- Fforde Greene, Leeds = VERNON & THE G.I.'s.
- Haddon Hall, Leeds = LUCKY STRIKE.
- White Lion, Huddersfield = JEDEDIAH STRUTT.
- Palm Cove, Bradford = SUGAR MINOT + TONY TUFF + BLACK ROOTS BAND.
- Royal Park, Leeds = NEW KING SNAKES.
- Cleopatras, Huddersfield = COCKNEY REJECTS.
- Staging Post, Leeds = GVRM + support.
- Queens Hall, Bradford = TRAMPUS.

SUN 8
- Vaults Bar, Bradford = TALISMAN.
- Leeds University = THE SPECIALS + THE BODYSNATCHERS.
- Fforde Greene, Leeds = JAPANESE TOY.
- Haddon Hall, Leeds = LUIGI AWA DA BOYS.
- White Lion, Huddersfield = THE DOTS.
- Princeville, Bradford (lunch) = SIDE EFFECT.
- Royal Park, Leeds = HELTER SKELTER.
- Staging Post, Leeds = SHAKE APPEAL.
- Warehouse, Leeds (lunch) = BEST FRIENDS.
- Blackamore Head, Pontefract = JEDEDIAH STRUTT.

MON 9
- Marquis of Granby, Leeds = KNIFE EDGE.
- Princeville, Bradford = JEDEDIAH STRUTT.
- Royal Park, Leeds = DODGY TACTICS.

TUE 10
- Vaults Bar, Bradford = MIDDLE 8.
- Rose & Crown, Ilkley = SHAKE APPEAL.
- Kings Head, Keighley = COAST TO COAST.
- Fforde Greene, Leeds = MATCHBOX.
- Scamps, Bradford = JAPANESE SOLDIERS.
- Oddfellows Arms, Bradford = VINYL DINERS + BEATS WORKING.
- Warehouse, Leeds = SPIDER BLUES BAND.

WED 11
- Vaults Bar, Bradford = THE MODERATES.
- White Lion, Huddersfield = 633 SQUADRON.
- Royal Park, Leeds = GOFF JACKSON & THE HUNS.
- Warehouse, Leeds = HELTER SKELTER.
- Polish Club, Halifax = MYSTERIOUS FOOTSTEPS + local bands.

THU 12
- The Warehouse, Leeds = KNIFE EDGE.
- Fan Club, Leeds = THE PHOTOS + THE VYE.
- Fforde Greene, Leeds = GINGER BAKER.
- Princeville, Bradford = DEDRINGER.
- Royal Park, Leeds = BLIND DATE.

FRI 13
- Bradford University = PRESSURE SHOCKS + ULTERIOR MOTIVES + THE PRESS + PLEXUS.
- Unity Hall, Wakefield = THE BEAT + THE AKRYLYKZ.
- Fforde Greene, Leeds = DEDRINGER.
- Palm Cove, Bradford = THE ELEMENTS.
- Leeds University = SLADE + SHAKE APPEAL + CITY LIMITS + THE SWITCH + SPIDER BLUES + BLUES EXPRESS + THE VYE + CONFESSOR + GARY BOYLE + NERVOSA + AGONY COLUMN.
- Royal Park, Leeds = WHITE EAGLES.
- Cleopatras, Huddersfield = ECHO & THE BUNNYMEN + support.

SAT 14
- Albion Hotel, Huddersfield = PROPOSITION 31.
- Queens Hall, Bradford = THE ZIPPS.
- Seacroft Hotel, Leeds = DIRTY BUT NICE.
- Fforde Greene, Leeds = BLUE EYES + PASSPORT SMILES.
- Haddon Hall, Leeds = SHAKE APPEAL.
- White Lion, Huddersfield = GLOSSY MAGS.
- Palm Cove, Bradford = CLINT EASTWOOD.
- Royal Park, Leeds = LUCKY STRIKE.
- Huddersfield Polytechnic = KILLERMETERS + SMALL HOURS + E.M.F.
- Staging Post, Leeds = DEVOTION.

SUN 15
- Fan Club, Leeds = PINK MILITARY + guests.
- Fforde Greene, Leeds =
- Haddon Hall, Leeds = KNIFE EDGE.
- White Lion, Huddersfield = TREATMENT.
- Princeville, Bradford (lunch) = RED EYE.
- Royal Park, Leeds = HELTER SKELTER.
- Staging Post, Leeds = DODGY TACTICS.
- Warehouse, Leeds (lunch) = BEST FRIENDS.
- Blackamore Head, Pontefract = DIRTY STOPOUTS.

MON 16
- Fforde Greene, Leeds =
- Marquis of Granby, Leeds = SPIKE.
- Princeville, Bradford = TRAMPUS.
- Royal Park, Leeds = THE GIMMICKS.
- Warehouse, Leeds = FAD GADGET.

TUE 17
- Vaults Bar, Bradford = ULTERIOR MOTIVES.
- Splash One, Bradford = MEPHISTO WALTZ.
- Rose & Crown, Ilkley = BLACK FERRET STOMP.
- Kings Head, Keighley = 633 SQUADRON.
- Scamps, Bradford = KNIFE EDGE.
- Oddfellows Arms, Bradford = MYSTERIOUS FOOTSTEPS + BEATS WORKING.
- Warehouse, Leeds = SPIDER BLUES BAND.

WED 18
- Vaults Bar, Bradford = NIGHTSHIFT.
- Unity Hall, Wakefield = BUDGIE + VARDIS.
- White Lion, Huddersfield = 7 YEAR ITCH.
- Royal Park, Leeds = TREATMENT.
- Warehouse, Leeds = AGONY COLUMN.

THU 19
- Rose & Crown, Ilkley = THE VYE.
- Queens Hall, Bradford = NIGHTSHIFT.
- Fan Club, Leeds = COCKNEY REJECTS + KIDZ NEXT DOOR.
- Fforde Greene, Leeds =
- Princeville, Bradford = DAWNWATCHER.
- Royal Park, Leeds = SIDE EFFECT.

FRI 20
- Fforde Greene, Leeds =
- Palm Cove, Bradford = JEDRELL BANK.
- St. George's Hall, Bradford = WHITESNAKE.
- Royal Park, Leeds = WHITE EAGLES.

SAT 21
- Albion Hotel, Huddersfield = ALL OVER THE CARPET.
- Seacroft Hotel, Leeds = CONVIX.
- Fforde Greene, Leeds =
- Haddon Hall, Leeds = THE VYE.
- White Lion, Huddersfield = THE FLOOR.
- Palm Cove, Bradford =
- Royal Park, Leeds = DIRTY BUT NICE.
- Staging Post, Leeds = DAWNWATCHER.

SUN 22
- Fforde Greene, Leeds = THE JERKS.
- Haddon Hall, Leeds = CITY LIMITS.
- White Lion, Huddersfield = THE DOTS.
- Princeville, Bradford (lunch) = BLACK FERRET STOMP.
- Royal Park, Leeds = HELTER SKELTER.
- Staging Post, Leeds = LIMELIGHT.
- Warehouse, Leeds = BEST FRIENDS.
- Blackamore Head, Pontefract = PROPOSITION 31.
- Vaults Bar, Bradford = SHADOWFAX.

MON 23
- Fforde Greene, Leeds =
- Marquis of Granby, Leeds = MOTIVATORS.
- Royal Park, Leeds = GOFF JACKSON & THE HUNS.

TUE 24
- Vaults Bar, Bradford = THE ZIPPS.
- Rose & Crown, Ilkley = HEAVEN SEVENTEEN.
- Kings Head, Keighley = THE SHEDS.
- Scamps, Bradford = THE VYE.
- Oddfellows Arms, Bradford = IDLE RICH + BEATS WORKING.
- Warehouse, Leeds = SPIDER BLUES BAND.

WED 25
- Vaults Bar, Bradford =
- White Lion, Huddersfield = R.I.F.
- Royal Park, Leeds = SPIDER BLUES BAND.
- Gallop Inn, Harrogate = THE MIRROR BOYS.

THU 26
- Fan Club, Leeds = ECHO & THE BUNNYMEN + guests.
- Fforde Greene, Leeds =
- Princeville, Bradford = JAVELIN (ex-STRAY).
- Royal Park, Leeds = AFTER DARK.
- Mitre, Knaresborough = HEAVEN 17.

FRI 27
- Unity Hall, Wakefield = GARY GLITTER & THE GLITTER BAND + CUDDLY TOYS + PARIS NINE + GUY JACKSON.
- The Gate Hotel, Leeds = THE AMAZING GUFFSTRUT.
- Adelphi, Harrogate = HEAVEN 17.
- Fforde Greene, Leeds = SASSAFRASS.
- Palm Cove, Bradford = THE SCENE.
- Royal Park, Leeds = WHITE EAGLES.
- Leeds University (refectory) = SUPERCHARGE.

SAT 28
- Albion Hotel, Huddersfield = ROUGH JUSTICE.
- Seacroft Hotel, Leeds = THE AMAZING GUFFSTRUT.
- Fforde Greene, Leeds = DEVOTION.
- Haddon Hall, Leeds = RED EYE.
- White Lion, Huddersfield = THE LIMIT.
- Palm Cove, Bradford = CYGNUS.
- Royal Park, Leeds = GLOSSY MAGS.
- Staging Post, Leeds = LUCKY STRIKE.

SUN 29
- Vaults Bar, Bradford = MYSTERIOUS FOOTSTEPS + STUFFED BADGERS.
- Fforde Greene, Leeds = JAVELIN.
- Haddon Hall, Leeds = ALWOODLEY JETS.
- White Lion, Huddersfield = (lunch) COAST TO COAST / (eve) B-MOVIE.
- Princeville, Bradford (lunch) = T.B.A.
- Royal Park, Leeds = HELTER SKELTER.
- Staging Post, Leeds = 2TV.
- Warehouse, Leeds (lunch) = BEST FRIENDS.
- Blackamore Head, Pontefract = KNIFE EDGE.

MON 30
- Fforde Greene, Leeds =
- Marquis of Granby, Leeds = HAIR RESTORERS.
- Princeville, Bradford = J.G. SPOILS.
- Royal Park, Leeds = STORMY MONDAY.

VENUES IN BRADFORD
- Princeville (tel. 78845)
- Palm Cove (tel. 499895)
- St. George's Hall (tel. 32513 (box office) / 32514 (main))
- Vaults Bar &/or Queens Hall (tel. 392712)
- Scamps (tel. 26001)
- Oddfellows Arms (tel. 611944)
- Bradford University (Students' Union) (tel. 34135)
- Splash One (tel. 32339)

VENUES IN LEEDS
- Fan Club at Brannigan's (tel. 446985)
- Staging Post (tel. 735541)
- Warehouse (tel. 468287)
- Royal Park (tel. 785076)
- Fforde Greene (tel. 493471) -new number-
- Marquis of Granby (tel. 454480)
- Cosmo Club (ex-directory)
- Leeds Polytechnic Students' Union (tel. 30171)
- Leeds University Students' Union (tel. 39071)

VENUES IN HUDDERSFIELD
- Haddon Hall Hotel (tel. 75115)
- Seacroft Hotel (tel. 645984)
- Gate Hotel (tel. 658802)
- Coachouse Club (tel. 20930)
- White Lion (tel. 22407)
- Albion Hotel (tel. 24200)
- Cleopatras (tel. 24510)
- Huddersfield Polytechnic Students' Union (tel. 38156)

Try this Programme

JULY '80 GIG guide

TUE 1
- Vaults Bar, Bradford = COAST TO COAST.
- Rose & Crown, Ilkley = AVALON HIGHWAY.
- Kings Head, Keighley = BACKSLIDER.
- Scamps, Bradford = (T.B.A.)
- Oddfellows Arms, Bradford = THE SCENE + BEATS WORKING.
- Warehouse, Leeds = SPIDER BLUES BAND.

WED 2
- Vaults Bar, Bradford = STRANDID.
- White Lion, Huddersfield = TRAMPUS.
- Royal Park, Leeds = TREATMENT.
- Speakeasy, Wakefield = TAROT.

THU 3
- Queens Hall, Bradford = STRANDID.
- The Peel, Leeds = THE AMAZING GUFFSTRUT.
- Fforde Greene, Leeds = (T.B.A.)
- Princeville, Bradford = WITCHFYNDE.
- Royal Park, Leeds = FLYING SQUAD.

FRI 4
- Fforde Greene, Leeds = THE FABULOUS POODLES + support.
- Palm Cove, Bradford = THE GUESTS.
- Royal Park, Leeds = WHITE EAGLES.
- Thurscoe Hotel, Thurscoe (nr. Pontefract) = TAROT.

SAT 5
- Albion Hotel, Huddersfield = (T.B.A.)
- Seacroft Hotel, Leeds = (T.B.A.)
- Fforde Greene, Leeds = THE FABULOUS POODLE + support.
- Haddon Hall, Leeds = DICK SMITH BAND.
- White Lion, Huddersfield = TREATMENT.
- Palm Cove, Bradford = JAB-JAB.
- St. George's Hall, Bradford = DEXY'S MIDNIGHT RUNNERS + THE BLACK ARABS + THE UPSETS.
- Royal Park, Leeds = CONFESSOR.
- Staging Post, Leeds = SPIES.

SUN 6
- Vaults Bar, Bradford = SHAKE APPEAL.
- The Cherry Tree, Leeds = KNIFE EDGE.
- Fforde Greene, Leeds = (T.B.A.)
- Haddon Hall, Leeds = THE NEAT.
- White Lion, Huddersfield = THE DOTS.
- Princeville, Bradford (lunch) = BABY TUCKOO.
- Royal Park, Leeds = HELTER SKELTER.
- Staging Post, Leeds = MIDDLE 8.
- Warehouse, Leeds (lunch) = BEST FRIENDS.
- Blackamore Head, Pontefract = PRIVATE DICKS.

MON 7
- Fforde Greene, Leeds = (T.B.A.)
- Marquis of Granby, Leeds = FLYING SQUAD.
- Princeville, Bradford = VARDIS.
- Royal Park, Leeds = GOFF JACKSON & THE HUNS.

TUE 8
- Vaults Bar, Bradford = BEATS WORKING.
- Rose & Crown, Ilkley = TALISMAN.
- Kings Head, Keighley = RHINO.
- Scamps, Bradford = (T.B.A.)
- Oddfellows Arms, Bradford = STURGEON ROW.
- Warehouse, Leeds = SPIDER BLUES BAND.
- Birdwell Club, Barnsley = TAROT.

WED 9
- Vaults Bar, Bradford = 156 BAND.
- White Lion, Huddersfield = MIRROR BOYS.
- Royal Park, Leeds = KNIFE EDGE.

THU 10
- Arts Centre, Bingley = KNIFE EDGE + THE GIMMICKS.
- Fforde Greene, Leeds = WITCHFYNDE.
- Princeville, Bradford = SPRING OFFENSIVE.
- Royal Park, Leeds = THE SWITCH.

FRI 11
- Fforde Greene, Leeds = (T.B.A.)
- Palm Cove, Bradford = SPLASH.
- Royal Park, Leeds = WHITE EAGLES.
- Newton House, Wakefield = TAROT.

SAT 12
- Albion Hotel, Huddersfield = (T.B.A.)
- Seacroft Hotel, Leeds = BREAKER.
- Fforde Greene, Leeds = (T.B.A.)
- Haddon Hall, Leeds = SIDE EFFECT.
- White Lion, Huddersfield = KNIFE EDGE.
- Palm Cove, Bradford = MOVEMENTS + RANKING DREAD.
- Royal Park, Leeds = JOHN OTWAY (free entry with copy of current single).
- Staging Post, Leeds = KNIFE EDGE.

SUN 13
- Vaults Bar, Bradford = THE QUICK.
- Fforde Greene, Leeds = (T.B.A.)
- Haddon Hall, Leeds = LUIGI AMA DA BOYS.
- White Lion, Huddersfield = E.II.R.
- Princeville, Bradford (lunch) = OXYM.
- Royal Park, Leeds = HELTER SKELTER.
- Staging Post, Leeds = LOCAL HEROES.
- Warehouse, Leeds (lunch) = BEST FRIENDS.
- Blackamore Head, Pontefract = (T.B.C.)

MON 14
- Fforde Greene, Leeds = (T.B.A.)
- Marquis of Granby, Leeds = CITY LIMITS.
- Royal Park, Leeds = TWISTED NERVE.
- Vaults Bar, Bradford = CHINA TOWN.

TUE 15
- Vaults Bar, Bradford = CONTAX.
- Rose & Crown, Ilkley = PROPHET.
- Kings Head, Keighley = CITY LIMITS.
- Scamps, Bradford = (T.B.A.)
- Oddfellows Arms, Bradford = VINYL DINERS + BEATS WORKING.
- Warehouse, Leeds = SPIDER BLUES BAND.

WED 16
- Vaults Bar, Bradford = THE NEW KING SNAKES.
- White Lion, Huddersfield = LOCAL HEROES.
- Royal Park, Leeds = KNIFE EDGE.
- St. George's Hall, Bradford = THE SPECIALS + support (unconfirmed).

THU 17
- Queens Hall, Bradford = BACKSLIDER.
- Fforde Greene, Leeds = (T.B.A.)
- Princeville, Bradford = DICK SMITH BAND.
- Royal Park, Leeds = ROUGH JUSTICE.

FRI 18
- Fforde Greene, Leeds = (T.B.A.)
- Palm Cove, Bradford = THE GUESTS.
- Royal Park, Leeds = WHITE EAGLES.

SAT 19
- Albion Hotel, Huddersfield = SERGEANT FURY.
- Queens Hall, Bradford = TREATMENT.
- Seacroft Hotel, Leeds = SLIDER.
- Fforde Greene, Leeds = (T.B.A.)
- Haddon Hall, Leeds = CITY LIMITS.
- White Lion, Huddersfield = DAWNWATCHER.
- Palm Cove, Bradford = (T.B.A.)
- Royal Park, Leeds = SIDE EFFECT.
- Staging Post, Leeds = TAROT.

SUN 20
- Vaults Bar, Bradford = TREATMENT.
- Fforde Greene, Leeds = (T.B.A.)
- Haddon Hall, Leeds = VYNYL DINERS.
- White Lion, Huddersfield = THE DOTS.
- Princeville, Bradford (lunch) = ORIGINALS.
- Royal Park, Leeds = HELTER SKELTER.
- Staging Post, Leeds = THE NEAT.
- Warehouse, Leeds (lunch) = BEST FRIENDS.
- Blackamore Head, Pontefract = TAROT.

MON 21
- Fforde Greene, Leeds = (T.B.A.)
- Marquis of Granby, Leeds = SIDE EFFECT.
- Royal Park, Leeds = MUGGINS BLIGHT.

TUE 22
- Vaults Bar, Bradford = CORRIDORS.
- Rose & Crown, Ilkley = KNIFE EDGE.
- Kings Head, Keighley = MYSTERIOUS FOOTSTEPS.
- Scamps, Bradford = (T.B.A.)
- Oddfellows Arms, Bradford = ULTERIOR MOTIVES + BEATS WORKING.
- Warehouse, Leeds = SPIDER BLUES BAND.

WED 23
- Vaults Bar, Bradford = STACKS.
- White Lion, Huddersfield = THE QUICK.
- Royal Park, Leeds = THE ZIPPS.

THU 24
- Fforde Greene, Leeds = (T.B.A.)
- Princeville, Bradford = MONEY.
- Royal Park, Leeds = BACKSLIDER.
- Turk's Head, Batley = TAROT.

FRI 25
- Fforde Greene, Leeds = (T.B.A.)
- Palm Cove, Bradford = (T.B.A.)
- Royal Park, Leeds = WHITE EAGLES.
- Kingsley Farmers' Club, Kingsley (nr. Pontefract) = TAROT.

SAT 26
- Albion Hotel, Huddersfield = ULTERIOR MOTIVES.
- Seacroft Hotel, Leeds = BREAKER.
- Fforde Greene, Leeds = (T.B.A.)
- Haddon Hall, Leeds = RED EYE.
- White Lion, Huddersfield = THE LIMIT.
- Palm Cove, Bradford = EUGENE PAUL + SAMANTHA ROSE + support.
- Royal Park, Leeds = THE SWITCH.
- Staging Post, Leeds = (T.B.A.)

SUN 27
- Vaults Bar, Bradford = TRAMPUS.
- Fforde Greene, Leeds = (T.B.A.)
- Haddon Hall, Leeds = THE VYE.
- White Lion, Huddersfield = (lunch) COAST TO COAST / (eve) THE NEWS.
- Princeville, Bradford (lunch) = MEAN STREET.
- Royal Park, Leeds = HELTER SKELTER.
- Staging Post, Leeds = KNIFE EDGE.
- Warehouse, Leeds (lunch) = BEST FRIENDS.
- Blackamore Head, Pontefract = (T.B.C.)

MON 28
- Fforde Greene, Leeds = (T.B.A.)
- Marquis of Granby, Leeds = TALISMAN.
- Royal Park, Leeds = KNIFE EDGE.

TUE 29
- Vaults Bar, Bradford = TAROT.
- Rose & Crown, Ilkley = METAL FATIGUE.
- Kings Head, Keighley = STACKS.
- Scamps, Bradford = (T.B.A.)
- Oddfellows Arms, Bradford =
- Warehouse, Leeds = SPIDER BLUES BAND.

WED 30
- Vaults Bar, Bradford = CITY LIMITS.
- White Lion, Huddersfield = THE GUESTS.
- Royal Park, Leeds = METAL FATIGUE.

THU 31
- Queens Hall, Bradford = CITY LIMITS.
- Fforde Greene, Leeds = (T.B.A.)
- Princeville, Bradford = STREET FIGHTER.
- Royal Park, Leeds = AGONY COLUMN.

N.B. End of July gigs not all available at time of going to press (T.B.A. = To be arranged) — ring venues to check bookings.

OTHER W. YORKS. VENUES
- Arts Centre, Bingley (tel. 7982)
- Rose & Crown, Ilkley (tel. 607260)
- Unity Hall, Wakefield (tel. 75719)
- Tiffany's, Wakefield (tel. 76215)
- Kings Head, Keighley (tel. 604660)
- Blackamore Head, Pontefract (tel. 702345)
- Good Mood, Halifax (ex-directory)
- Devonshire Hotel, Skipton (tel. 3078) (occasional gigs)

VENUES IN N. YORKS
- Adelphi Hotel, Harrogate (tel. 63334)
- Cock & Castle, Harrogate (tel.)
- The Mitre, Knaresborough (tel. Harr. 863589)

BE WARNED! IT'S LIVE rock

LOOKING AT Lancs.

NORTH-EAST LANCS. MUSICIANS' COLLECTIVE

It was a misty day in August when Simon Lanzon gave me a lift back from Deeply Vale. He was holding the Not Sensibles fanzine that was holding to remind me of an interested local musicians. So on a Wednesday night a fortnight or ??? came along to a meeting of interested local musicians. The initial curious musicians. M.P.A.A.* Gallery. The initial assemblies were a rather chaotic, but out of the old M.P.A.A.* Gallery. The initial this was forged some semblance of order.

Our first problem was that of organising a venue. The Union Hotel in Colne (which had played host to The U.K. Subs through a couple of months previously), we had found a working men's coming up. The new landlord was keen to up-management & the pub a chance of image. However, a change of image in Nelson that was very enthusiastic in the pub as a Blackburn band now signed to E.M.I.) meeting (a Blackburn band now signed to E.M.I.) club in Nelson to about 15 events ranging from Stiffs, a local trad. H.M. freaks. Since then Bender) blossomed into something since then small house of punks & H.M. freaks. Since then this venue has in this venue has in

The main organisation of this venue has in fact gone through vigorous change. Spider & this fascinating month under the banner of 'Z' this fascinating one-man promotions whilst the Musicians' Collective played host to (Gary Boyle's Straightforward punk through jazz-rock by Michael Burrell) H.M. (Violation & Total Confusion).

Enterprises, has run the Collective's management. The nights, its own promotions there on one Friday also under this imagery & also holds every month when The Collective's gigs is also under 'Z' Enterprises a local, last month when The Collective & Poison enough of this 'Z' last month when The Collective & Poison fruits of the stage jointly brought Crass & Poison fruits of 'Z' Enterprises mag. - ed.) Bendigeidfran Sablon (O.K.') ed.)

Girls to Nelson to a jampacked night out. This mag. Girls also becoming an established night out, this also being organised by Rob Cortine & Dale Myers.

Another venue, The Inn Place, at Burnley, is also being organised by Rob Cortine & Dale Myers, two local punks.

Another problem was that of the inexperienced bands being organised finding the p.a. equipment, but being partly by the co-operation of bands in lending equipment. This has being solved by the bands can get their expensive p.a. system for Collective bands in lending of the bands in order to find quantities of expensive & had problem of hiring & hiring p.a. system in order to find could get by them a policy of hiring gear to the Collective by lending to having & a backline the collective by in lending the company of having a beat only for the Collective a p.a. system the company that we hire from. Collective are unbelievably helpful. They work for a pittance of a fee & genuinely believe in the all figs. L.D.P.A.*, leaves the company that we hire from. Collective are unbelievably helpful. They work for a spirit of The Collective.

Collective bands, particularly The Not Sensibles have played as far out as Newcastle, Liverpool Erics (recently closed down - ed.), Manchester Polytechnic & soon Bradford Scamps (cancelled due to management not being keen to have punks - ed.). Credit for the regular gigging is due to Simon Lanzon who has been the organising genius as well as founding father of NELCOL. We also have our own fanzine, 'The Cat Ate The Dog's Dinner', edited by Gary Brown & a local rival 'Revolt in Style', edited by Andy Martins (hini'). 'Cat Ate...' works as a healthy alternative journal for musicians in this area. Copies of the fanzine are available for 15p plus p. & p. from M.P.A.A.*, 2 Hammerton Street, Burnley. Any articles sent in will also be printed.

Future plans for the Collective are heading towards establishing a record label (Snotty Snail) which is already well on its way with The Not Sensibles single 'Margaret Thatcher' & the forthcoming Tiger Tails single 'Words Without Conviction'.

Other future commitments involve establishing the Collective hut as a centre of operation to cut down our dependence on M.P.A.A. The results of our scheme have led to the formation of many new local bands & we are now looking forward to a new growth of expansive activity.

VENUES:-

Railway Workers: Simon Lanzon (21986/29513). Spider (34910)
Inn Plaice: Rob Cortine (35674). Quent (26386), Dale (32561).

BANDS:-
Not Sensibles (loony punks): Simon Lanzon (21986/29513).
Stiffs (classy punk): Tommy (Accrington 34835), Ian (Blackburn 61843), Phil (Blackburn 65147). Sunil
Red Stripe (new wave): Shaun (36648), Pete (56174).
Chimp Eats Banana (more loony punk): Marty (27570).
Tiger Tails (r'n'b punk): Marty (867703).

N.B. All nos. are Burnley (STD code 0282) except where listed as otherwise.
"M.P.A.A. - Mid Pennine Arts Association.

2 BURNLEY FANZINES

THE CAT ATE THE DOGS DINNER. No.7 (14 pages, 15p). Cheapo printing in black-&-white only, but it has plenty of news, info, reviews, cartoons, poems, lyrics, letters, etc. They publish everything submitted - go some's good, some's crap. A useful local mag (N.B. Not Sensibles use its pages to plug themselves even more than I use this mag to plug U!***or No**esi).

REVOLT IN-STYLE. No.2/March '80 (10 pages, 10p). 5 b-&-w sheets hand-written & cheaply printed with a staple in top left corner. Describes itself as 'Your Sarcastic Monthly', & has a lot of nice touches as 'Your Sarcastic Monthly/Sun journalistic styles. Also carries a pretty tough & don't say much. Also carries a take Titbits/Sun journalistic styles. That said, Cat Ate.../Not Sensies, laughs & that's the mag's strong point. The few reviews are letters & an interview with Simon Lanzon (of Cat Ate...) carries info. etc.). To be fair, R in-S is a punkzine described as Your Drastic Monthly - all good worthwhile incestuous stuff. No.8 is a self-lot of what Cat Ate meal & another REVOLVE IN-BILE No1 duplicate of R in-S No.21 It's called REVOLVE IN-BILE No1 the full typed Cat Ate meal & another - all good worthwhile incestuous stuff. No.8 is a self-described is edited by Andrew Martins from 30 Brunshaw Avenue, Burnley, Lancs., BB10 4LT. C.A.T.D.D. is from the address given in the article below & fanzine feature elsewhere in for other fanzines, see Blackpool Rox (below) & fanzine feature elsewhere in this issue.

KEEP AT IT

BLACKPOOL FANZINE...

BLACKPOOL ROX. No.6 (10 pages, no price on it). This is a strange 'zine. I can't decide how much of it is creative & imaginative layout & how much is just bad journalism & semi-literate ramblings. There are some very odd reviews & a lot more work's actually gone into creating the messy layout than it'd seem at first glance. Either way, it earns a few bonus marks for striving to be slightly different.

Photos, reviews, info, etc. on local bands & venues. Two main features are a WEIRD & almost incomprehensible interview with local outfit Section 25 & an interview (disjointed, but just about understandable) with a neo-Nazi outfit called War Crimes (formerly Final Solution) whose songs are all about killing Jews. Featuring these is bad journalism - there's a world of difference between freedom of speech & freedom of bigotry/persecution/racism. That's about all I've got to say about this mag. If you want to see it, it's from Anchorsholme Lane, Blackpool, Lancs. (tel. 852945).

As far as gleaning info from the mag about the rockscene in Blackpool, there's not much that I've learned - it does list two dozen local bands, giving the phone nos. of two of these - one of which is The Membranes who produce the mag. The main venue out there would appear to be Jenks Bar.

There's a guy out there called Barry Lights who used to be involved in the Leeds rockscene. He's been trying to organise gigs over there for West Yorks. bands. His address is 48 Crystal Road, Blackpool, FY1 6BS, Lancs. (See also in Classified Ads.). Anyone wanting to know more about the scene in the area could get in touch with him.

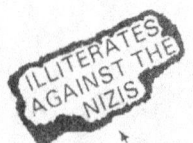

ILLITERATES AGAINST THE NAZIS

AN IVOR CUTLER SLOGAN

page 12.

2 Bands from Burnley

The Flying Squad

notsensibles

Dear Nick,
I phoned you on 29/4/80 after you were recommended by various venues in Leeds as the man who could get things moving for a new band. You asked for details, so here goes....
We are the Flying Squad, a five-piece Burnley-based band.
The members are:-
Gaz - lead vocal.
No.6 - guitar(Gibson S.G. Standard, Burman Pro 2000 combo.)
Gonzo Beard - guitar(Gordon Smith Gypsy II, Marshall Master Vol., Orange 4x12.)
Grouch - bass(Rickenbacker 4001, Marshall 100 Super Bass amp., various cabs.)
The Honey Monster - drums(Maxwin kit, Zildjian cymbals.)
A.K.G.and Shure microphones, 1 kilowatt P...

The band was formed at the end of '79 from the ashes of Barnaby Rudge & Beggar's Dog, both obscure bands from Burnley. The idea was to form a band with greater horizons than playing covers around the Burnley/Blackburn area, where people prefer to get drunk to music they already know rather than pay attention(and money!) to a band trying to do something original. For instance, we played a gig at Nelson Railway Workers', promoted by the local Musician's Collective to an audience of about twenty people, most of whom we know, showing the marked lack of interest in new bands in this area.
On the positive side, the best(and first!)gig that we played was at De La Salle College, Middleton, to a mixed audience of students, who gave us an enthusiastic reception much to the surprise of the college promoters, who said we'd be lucky if anyone eventurned up(apathy again!)
This is the only thing which is currently upholding morale in the band, so we could do with a few good gigs to help us regain our confidence.
To give you some idea of what we are about(besides listening to the enclosed tape), our influences range from Roy Orbison to the Clash(work that one out for yourself!)
If it's of any interest, our covers include such gems as Girl's in Action(Invaders),Larry Wallis' Police Car, and some well known numbers like Brand New Cadillac(Clash version) and Landlord(Police), though we aim to introduce original material to the set as each song is completed.
We have a few gigs lined up:-
June 4-Portland Bars,Manchester(Audition).
June 7-Spreadeagle,Ashton-under-Lyne,M'c'r.
June 20/21/22-Regent Hotel,Blackburn.
July 3-Royal Park Hotel,Leeds.
July 4-Commercial,Stalybridge.
July 7-Marquis de Granby,Leeds.
July 27-Bank Hall Miners,Burnley(lunchtime).
We can be reached at:-
0282-24015 No.6(ask for young Chris').
0282-29404 Gaz.

They've brought out two singles - 'Death to Disco' & '(I'm in love with) Margaret Thatcher', both on their own Redball Records label. The second of these went to no.5 in the Sounds alternative chart. I'm told that they've also got an album now out that's called 'Instant Classic'.
A fun & slightly anarchic band with a rough & raw sound, they've not had an easy time finding venues in their area that'll accept them. Several of their early gigs were prematurely terminated by management at the venues. Through The Collective (see opposite) they have helped to build up an active local scene in the Burnley/Nelson/Colne areas.
The band & The Collective had sizeable write-ups in The Guardian & The Artful Reporter last January & the band has regularly had good coverage in some of the national music papers - notably Sounds.
Having worked hard over the past two years in what was a very low-profile local rock scene, they've built up a solid following, but are still short of gigs outside their home county. They're currently trying to line up some Yorks. bookings & should be over here in the autumn. If recent reviews are anything to go by, they should be worth catching.

THE FLYING SQUAD'S DEMO TAPE...

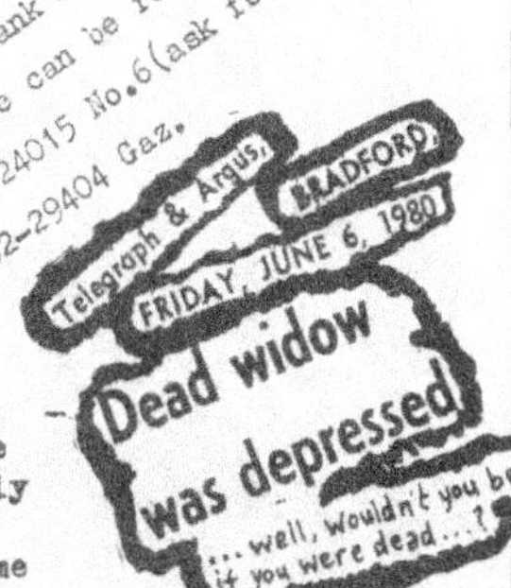

Telegraph & Argus, BRADFORD
FRIDAY, JUNE 6, 1980
Dead widow was depressed
...well, wouldn't you be if you were dead...?

This is a slightly rough demo tape which I suspect is the band's own work rather than a studio job. But it's good enough to give a taste of what the band's about.
'Water Street' is a straight rock song with white reggae & new wave garnishing on the top. While the song's fairly non-descript, the band do quite a nice job on it. The vocalist has a good but unremarkable voice & there's some interesting lead guitar for those who like to look for instrument-heroes in their bands. 'Shut Up' is much the same.
The band is tight & there's a bouncy touch to their songs that lifts them out of the dirgy just-another-northern-rockband mould. However, they're still a little too much in the traditional British guitar-based rock mould for my tastes, offering nothing that's particularly distictinctive or innovative. And, as for the Clash influence that their letter claims, I honestly can't hear it anywhere here. Next up is 'She's So Attractive'. I wish the drummer didn't make every number sound exactly the same! Otherwise, this is o.k. Finally, 'Something Wrong'. I like the guitar on this.
Overall then, this is a good straightforward commercial rock band, if a little dated in style. They seem to have problems accepting the fact that punk/new wave has changed the face of rock. Maybe they should aim more at H.M. & not try to straddle the chasm between '63 & '80. Anyway, they're gigging locally, so don't just take my opinion - go along & decide for yourself.

LOCAL HEROES

STILL LOOKING AT LANCS.

LIVE REVIEW

Local Heroes are a 4-piece band from Rochdale. Line-up is Alan Wild (gtr/voc), Flea (gtr/voc), Colin Schofield (dms), Ken Park (bass/voc) & they've been playing in their present form for about 8 months. They've & are currently engaged in a mini tour which, by the time you read this, will have seen them take in The Vaults Bar, Bradford. Poor advertising for tonight's gig has resulted in their playing to a very sparce audience of die-hard punks who are none too appreciative of what the band are up to - which is a shame because I think they are potentially very good.

Talking to the band, I discovered that they like The Jam, while I'm floundering around trying to make comparisons, Weller & co. are a jumping off point. They've got that Jam-like hard edge & vibrancy, but it's more complicated than that mainly because of the songs. The guitars lock together, very tight, but not mechanically so - brief solos, tight riffs, duetting, all in the context of melodically interesting songs underpinned by very solid work from the bassist & drummer. They exuded power & invention that prevent it from falling into the one-dimensional rent-a-rock that's so popular nowadays. The band was formed from an amalgamation of a punk band & a glam rock band & it's noticable that these distinctive styles play off against each other to good effect, complimenting in the single track 'Blast The Pop' with its punk musical noticeable 'melody' in the context of a decidedly un-punk influenced verse accompaniment.

It's a pity they played to such an unappreciative audience - they deserved better. It does seem to be the case that there are lots of high quality bands playing nowadays to no great effect. I hope that Local Heroes manage to find the ineffable something that gets them noticed & persuades their audiences to make the quantum jump from indifference to attentiveness.

— Phil Foster.

THE SINGLE

Blast The Pop. The song's fine, but has far too much bass on the mix as a whole, making it sound leaden rather than the bouncy & fresh goodish pop song it's intended to be. Tomorrow, this is a song that I'm sure it would also have been better with a much brighter mix on the sound, though the drums come through well. Live, here, they come up with a refreshingly commercial back of songs, the band live itself won't disappoint the fans who want to get the heavily against this I fear. However, it should sell very 30, catch the band live if you can. If you want to get the well at gigs & won't disappoint. disc. - a double A-side on Junior Records - it's available for £1 (plus 17p P. & P.) from Jack Kay, 389 Albert Royds Street, Rochdale, Lancs. OL16 3AE. Chenues/P.O.'s should be made payable to J. Kay.

STURGEON ROW

Letter + Record review + Cassette review

P.F.Clark, writing from Salford, encloses a 3-track cassette & a 4-track E.P. by his band Sturgeon Row. In the letter he says: "We recorded the E.P. at home on a TEAC 4-track & using a drum machine. This was at the beginning of 1979 when Sturgeon Row was an embryo. Most of the recording was done at Robert Wenn's home in Somerset. The mixing was done at Mushroom Studios in Bristol. We sold about 100 copies to friends etc. & gave away the same number as demos without much success. We still have a couple of hundred. I would be interested to know what you think of the E.P.

In September '79 we (Rob & I) got hold of a drummer (Geoff Dench) & the three of us moved up to Salford. We practiced madly for several weeks & arranged 6 or 7 gigs locally, & at Fforde Greene (supporting The Vye) & Haddon Hall. Unfortunately, about a week before our first gig, our transit van & all our musical instruments & PA/amps were stolen (value about £2,000). We managed to fulfill all our bookings, but were severely hampered by having to use borrowed gear etc.

In February, Geoff returned to Somerset. We were then without any gear & without a drummer BUT we didn't give up! We advertised in the local press & this resulted in the new Sturgeon Row (Paul Clark - gtr/voc, Rob Wenn - bass/voc, Eric Cruice - dms). We borrowed money from the bank & bought a couple of guitar amps. A few months of practicing & we have just received an insurance settlement on the stolen gear. This money was used to buy some good PA gear. We are now back on the road & the cassette is a sample of our current material. We are using this cassette as a demo at the moment & it has so far been received favourably by pub landlords etc. I hope you like it & can review it. Our only date in your area at present is Marquis of Granby on Mon 8th Sept.

You may have heard from/soon hear from Colin Robinson of Terminal Music & the group Night Visitors. I gave him your name & he told me he would be contacting you."

THE E.P. Side 1: 'Friction' has a vocalist who sounds remarkably like John Mayall on 'Bare Wires' or 'Laurel Canyon' but with the added asset of a vocal range that lets his voice drop a lot deeper. It's this voice that jumps out at you from the catchy & clean reggae backdrop. 'The Next Time' is a track I'm not as keen on. It sounds like an early 70's rock ballad with a Dire Straits guitar break. OK of its kind, I suppose, but a bit boring really. 'I Want You' (not the Dylan song!) opens with acoustic guitar. This is an awful folksy love ditty that I'd probably get to quite like if I listened to it too much - but I won't. This is so 'nice' with such trite lyrics that it'd even embarrass Paul McCartney. There's some unpleasant keyboard/synth work here too. (oops, forgot to say that it was 1st track on side 2). 'Just For Reference' has a blend of jazz/reggae/pop influences. It starts like it's going to good, but turns out to be too laid back & I can't say that the keyboard playing does anything for the band. The drum machine's used well though... but no, I'm going off this one. I like the first track, but the other 3 are just MOR mediocrity that's 10/15 yrs out of date & stripped bare of any excitement. Shame. The EP's on Rhopey Records & there's a free lyric sheet included.

THE CASSETTE. This is the more recent material & they've wisely opted for the more raunchy style of material that Paul Clark writes (tracks 1 & 4 on EP, with other 2 tracks by Rob Wenn). The result is a jerky, foot-tapping, staccato, reggae pop. I like 'Breakout' very much. Then comes a new version of 'Fiction' that's a vast improvement (both in arrangement & quality of recording). Finally there's 'City' which opens well with attractive guitar & has a good instrumental break, but the verses are too slow & the overall style is a little dated. Really, I reckon it's the lyrics & the way they come across that spoils this number for me. That said, it is an interesting tape & should serve its gig-getting purpose well - so look out for the band when they're in the area. Go have a listen - see what you think to them.

TERMINAL MUSIC

letter + cassette review

From Colin Robinson of Terminal Music comes the label's first release - a cassette album by 262 called 'for Fun & Profit'. He writes "262 are a purely recording unit & have already recorded a lot of material over the last year. They will probably have more bass/drums emphasis in their music, cream of which was used on 'for Fun & Profit'. The 4-track studio. 262 was recorded on two 2-track machines, but we are going to record the bass & dub/electronic reggae elements & more, Apart from running Terminal & playing in their music, member of Salford mod rock with reggae & new wave influences. We've played about 25 gigs in the last 6 months in the Manchester (literally) good quite a following. Our line-up features Janice Johnston Howie (voc), Andy due to the fact that we've got a bloody (literally) good Colin Robinson (dms), Rick Cooke (gtr), Tony White (bass) & Rich Souter Hieke & Rick Cooke (gtr), synths/tenor sax/blood capsules) & I stage show. Now played Leeds recently which was really impressive, the Bikini Brothers who went on to become the Tunes, & I was in a couple of bands including Paul Grainger, Spitfire - Night Visitors have come out very well. We have also at Cargo which have come out very well. We have just finished the Video used two of the tracks as soundtrack, we're really intend to plague these companies with a video album to use it to release our second album and possibly a light-hearted Terminal intend to release a series of cassette albums of Manchester region. The future ones should include a very reasonable price. The future ones should include a also Salford. P. & P., cheques/P.O.'s payable to 262 Robinson, 262 M6 5N3 & is available by mail for M6-M5 Salford.

'for Fun & Profit' by 262 (Terminal TCAS1) is the first release from Terminal Music, 133 Lower Seedley Road, Salford, M6 5N3 & is available by mail for 90p inc. P. & P., cheques/P.O.'s payable to C. Robinson.

This fills both sides of the tape to give an hour's playing time - good value if the overall product were a compilation album. As it is, there are no titles & no clearly defined tracks - mostly it's made up of snippets of musical doodling that's self-consciously 'different' & unconciously self-indulgent. For much of the time, almost all rhythm plus kiddy-tunes on a basic drum machine. There are a few good bits, but a first whole thing fed through an echo unit - almost too few. Sorry Colin, but better than this, zero creativity is offered. Let's hope for the release should have been a synth with the listener. There is no fun for the profit of any kind for the listener. Neither fun nor for the future Terminal things better than this, output.

HEAVEN SEVENTEEN - a band with commitment

This page was supposed to carry a large feature on a new Bradford band called Heaven Seventeen. However, when I came to type this up, I couldn't find the text of the interview or the photos that I'd filed away. So, with profuse apologies to them (& the promise that when I find them I'll run the feature as originally intended), here's a report on the group.

For several weeks, I'd been getting 'phone calls from some guy with a new band. He didn't want to meet up with me in a pub, but was insistent that I take time out to come down to their 'rehearsal studios'. I'd been putting it off because I knew it'd take up some time & I'd a million other jobs to get done. However, I eventually agreed to meet them in The Churchill, Bradford where my own band end up after rehearsals. Rehearsal over, I'd just got in a game of pool went they arrived. Five minutes drive in their tiny van & I'm being lead into an old warehouse, expecting to find a couple of tatty amps & a tape recorder stashed away in some cold backroom. Wrong!

Heaven Seventeen are 5 guys in late teenage who hold down dayjobs but have virtually given up a social life to become a rock band. Each of them (plus the two roadie/engineers) has sunk £1,000 of savings into buying gear. No rich relations, it's all their own money. With the result that they went to J.S.G. in Bingley & bought over £7,000-worth of gear. In a rented warehouse, they've set up one room for rehearsing, a second - adjoining the rehearsal room - for mixing & a third, a sizeable hall, is being done out so that they can use it to do showcase performances to invited friends of the band. When the conversion work's finished, they intend to have the rehearsal room/mixing room operative as a proper studio to serve the band. All this, & they've not yet done a gig!

The band's members have only been playing their instruments seriously for the past year or so &, as I listened to them running through a short selection of their original songs, there were a few rough edges; though the numbers are good, with a couple that I particularly liked. With the gear to give them an outstanding stage sound plus a well-rehearsed set (they work most nights for several hours) of promising self-written songs, they are a band that deserve to do well. They've had some bright posters printed. I suggest you look out for them. They've certainly worked hard enough to deserve an audience.

NOWTZ

July 7-12 I'm co-tutor on a residential course entitled 'Writing For Performance' that's open to anyone - writer, musician, lyricism, poet, etc. It's run by the Arvon Foundation at Lumb Bank in Hebden Bridge & there are special reduced rates for people living in Yorkshire - the whole week complete with bed & board is only about thirty quid. If you're interested, ring Hebden Bridge (042-284) 3714 & ask for full details.

There's a band called MOONWALKERS on at Bretton Hall, Wakefield on 26th June as support to NO DICE. They include a guy from Bradford (he wrote to me & asked me to mention it).

Oh damn! - this is a page for admitting inefficiencies - I've just realised that I've forgotten to include a pre-release review of Agony Column's single in the singles reviews section. Next issue-OK?

SLIPPED DISCS
(one's we should've reviewed but were never sent + a couple that predate W.C.R.)

ROCKABILLY REBS - E.P. (own label, '79). Rockabilly's what Matchbox are currently riding as they clock up a string of hits for themselves. Their nearest competition is an outfit called Whirlwind. If the genre takes off, then Bradford's reps, & a popular outfit in the local W.M.C.'s, are Rockabilly Rebs. Their EP consists of 4 tracks - 2 their own, 2 covers of standards. The A-side offers their own 'Boot Hill Boogie' which has just the right guitar sound & is fronted by a good vocalist. Being a blend of country & rock'n'roll, it's easy to see why this cuts it in the clubs. 2nd track is a fairly good version of 'Ain't Nothin' Shakin''. Turn over for 'One Way Train' which has an irresistable steam-train rhythm coupled to a catchy walking bassline. Neat guitar break too. Finally, there's a good version of 'Alabama Shake'. I'm a mug for this sort of stuff - love it. I'm told they've another release in the pipeline - will look out for it with interest.

KILLERMETERS - 'Twisted Wheel' c/w 'SX225' (Gem, '80). Back in the mid-sixties, The Twisted Wheel was the Manchester club to which mods travelled miles for all-nighters. The Huddersfield superstars come up with a good mod song here that's got a Geno Washington guitar sound + the party feel that's on Secret Affair's singles. Slightly bland & derivative, but a fine single for all that. It would have probably got into the lower reaches of the nation's charts if it'd had more airplay. B-side's also good - maybe even better than the A. I sure you all know that an SX225 is a Lambretta scooter (I think 225 refers to the number of mirrors &/or pendants it'll take).

THE DONKEYS - 'What I Want' c/w 'Four Letters' (Rhesus Records,'79). This is a powerful piece of driving new wave pop that got a lot of airplay & was plugged heavily in the music press. It should've made them popstars... but it didn't. Rough justice, it's a bloody good single &, rereleased on a major label, could still do it for them. As that's unlikely, unless you can pick this up in the second-hand racks, you'll just have to take my word for it. B-side's nearer to raw punk - a bit heavy-handed, but with an interesting mixture of vocals.

THE JERKS - 'Cool' c/w 'Cruisin' (Again)' (Lightning '78). The second single from the band that John Keenan (manager of The Fan Club, Leeds) described as Leeds' first punk band. A-side is odd. Neither one thing nor the other, it mixes punk vocals with melodic keyboards, standard rock guitar & basis drumming. It's alright, but no big deal. B-side is a bit ordinary except for the keyboards. Oh, & I like the use of the back-up vocals on the last couple of lines.

JOHN POTTER'S CLAY - E.P. (Nighthawk Records '79). I was interested to come across this because Jerry Clark of the Bradford band Coast To Coast mentioned playing on this, though he never even got a copy himself (see profile of C. to C. in W.C.R. 4). Four tracks, with Jerry on guitar (mostly rhythm) on all but 'Down The Line'. First up's 'Seaside Sally' which is R'n'B with a happy-go-lucky feel to it. 'Sister Sunshine' is slightly more bluesy (esp. the keyboards on the verses). Flip for Roy Orbison's 'Down The Line' (only cover version on the E.P.). This is a Jerry Lee Lewis type of number, complete with rattle-along barrelhouse boogie piano that's nicely echoed by the guitarist. 'No Use Hanging Around' has a bit more of a rough pub rock feel to it. Again, the piano's great.

Has anyone got any records by local bands that they might sell? I'm trying to build up a comprehensive collection. Ring me on 21867 (Bradford) if you've any offers - Mick Toczek

VE·NEWS

Credits

ODDFELLOWS ARMS, 696 HARROGATE ROAD, BRADFORD (tel. 611944) is a good new venue that needs your support. Bradford band Beats Working have persuaded the landlord to let them use his new club room (known as Oddie's Music Room) for a new wave music night every Tuesday. A brand new extension on the pub, the room holds over 200 people & has a large stage, lighting, etc. Beats Working lay on a p.a. each week + new wave disco. They do a half-hour set early on in the evening & then have a guest band for the main spot. At 30p in, this is very good value. Bands booked or being booked for the coming weeks should include Ulterior Motives, Mysterious Footsteps, The Idle Rich, The Scene Agony Column, The Switch, etc. The club runs every Tuesday, 7.30-10.30pm. The pub's just next to Eccleshill Baths (on the Thorpe Edge, Greengates or Apperley Bridge bus routes - ie routes no. 629, 632, 633 & 635). Bands wanting to do the gig should contact Gareth (B'f'd 390089 after 6pm) or Richard (B'f'd 638141) both of whom are in Beats Working.

THE TAVERN IN THE TOWN, WESTGATE, BRADFORD 1 (tel. 25008) is trying out bands from the end of June on Friday & Saturday nights. Again, if this venue is to be a success (& not revert back to the dreaded disco!) then it'll need your support. Some of the bands that'll be invited to do gigs there include Counterdance, Vex, Mephisto Waltz, Man Ray's Haircut (good name for a band!), Mysterious Footsteps & others. Interested bands should leave a message in the pub for Jack, who's the guy running the programme of bands.

THE MITRE in Knaresborough is a small pub venue that's being run by a member of Harrogate band Vynyl Diners. More details about this in next issue, but if you're impatient you can ring the pub on Harrogate 863589 - the guy who runs the gig is called Andy, whose band has the distinction of having the same infectious initials as Val Doonican!

QUEENS HALL in Bradford (now under the control of John Farquhar - who runs the Vaults Bar - as far as band dates are concerned) is starting to feature live bands on a more regular basis. John is keeping the venue open at weekends all through the summer (as it's the college students' union, it usually closes for the summer). He is hopeful that there will soon be a change in the terms of the licence so that the general public can be admitted (currently it's restricted to members & their guests - a limitation that's been the kiss of death for the past few years. Let's hope this venue soon regains some of its former popularity.

THE WAREHOUSE in Leeds (tel. 468287) - formerly an ultra-trendy disco - seems to be moving into live music in a fairly big way, with plans to feature bands on several nights each week. Already, they've given Spider Blues Band a Tuesday night residency, have Best Friends every Sunday lunchtime & Helter Skelter (who already have a Sunday night residency at The Royal Park) look like taking Wednesday nights. Other nights will have bands doing one-off gigs. Bands interested in securing gigs there should get in touch with Mike, the owner, by phone or else by calling in person at the club.

CLEOPATRA'S in Huddersfield has opened up to major punk bands on Fridays &/or Saturdays. These gigs are being booked in by Ray Rossi, manager of Slaughter & The Dogs. It looks like Huddersfield is fast becoming the only town in this area that has several weekly punk venues (the other notable one there being The Albion). But the city already has its name engraved in the annals of punk history by being the last town in England to host the Sex Pistols (Xmas '78) before they went to The States & there split up - J.R. going to ~~Dallas~~ (oops) P.I.L. & S.V. heading off to play bass for Presley, Holly, Hendrix, Joplin, Morrison, etc.

PALM COVE in Bradford continues to feature local bands, but is also expanding its programme of top-line reggae acts. So, it looks like there's at last a regular venue for live reggae in the area... not before time!

Debits

THE ROYAL STANDARD in Bradford is now under new management. It's large music room has a good stage &, until recently, served as a major punk venue in the city. The whole place is getting a face ift at the moment, but will probably be back in action in early autumn. However, the manager's very wary of rock bands & certainly doesn't want to continue with punk He plans to try Country-&-Western, etc. Let's hope he'll have rock bands at least a couple of nights a week. Should be a good venue if so because there'll be a steak bar in the room to the left as you walk into the pub. With food, drink, rock & pool what else could you ask for...?

THE PEEL in Leeds has changed hands & the new guy doesn't seem interested in continuing with bands - anyway, the brewery are converting the downstairs room, so it's not available any more.

SPLASH ONE in Bradford is giving up its Tues. night electronic music disco-&-band programme. It's not proved popular with regulars in the club & nor has it drawn many punters from outside. Mephisto Waltz (17th June) will be the last to play it.

by NICK TOCZEK

FANZINES

Fanzines - the D.I.Y. equivalent of what were in the sixties & early seventies termed 'alternative' press - have sprung up in vast numbers since the punk/'77 movement against the m.o.r. rockscene; Sniffin' Glue, Mark Perry's 'zine, having lead the field.

Here are some that've come through the mail to me recently - there'll be others covered in future issues. In previous issues I've mentioned Damaged Goods (Knaresborough) & the now-defunct Town Beat (Huddersfield). On page 12 of this issue are mentioned Blackpool Rox & the 2 'zines from Burnley, Cat Ate The Dog's Dinner & Revolt In-Style.

Total Disdain No.1. 10p for 10 sheets typed one side & stapled together. Clash, Killermeters, Mick D'Chaucer & reviews, articles, etc. No big deal, this. A bit messy & few new ideas, though some of it makes quite interesting reading - expect much more of future issues if it's to justify its existence. Certainly no replacement for Townbeat. From an unspecified address in Huddersfield.

Lens Nos.1-10. (full set from Spring '77 to date). Began at 15p, up to 20p since no.8. Wakefield's irregular rockzine has local scene + a few bigger names in each issue. Layout's interesting & varied (within the limitations of cheapo printing - just black on white paper, sheets stapled together). Also has poems, fiction, etc. Good use of fotos, but some awful line drawings. A Lens Special - 45 British Groups From The New Wave is an interesting idea with foto of each band + a short write-up. Shame that the write-ups aren't up to much in places. However, at 20p it's still excellent value. Most issues are now sold out. Ed. Mick Herrington, 24 Peterson Road, Wakefield (tel. 62934).

Vague Nos.1-4. Some 20p, others 25p. Covers Wiltshire (with what???) & comes from 'Butcombe', Castle St., Mere, Wilts., BA12 6JF. Editor is Tom (real name Steve Thomas). I like this one very much indeed. Most important of all is that it has ambition, with each issue being a vast improvement on the previous ones. No.4 is almost handsome. Usual mix of local bands + some nationals/internationals. I like the weird cartoons. If you wanna see this one, I've some copies - send 50p & you can have all 4 issues by return of post.

All The Poets Vol.2. In which a bunch of old hippy poets hide their words among a whole lot of good artwork & some nice bright colours - which doesn't change the fact that the words are more crap than poetry. The editorial on the inside back cover is a cry for a return to the good old positivism of America in the fifies.... yeuch! It's 30p from 77 Templars Ave., London NW11.

And here are 4 reviewed by self + Ken Turner...

Shake 7 (15p - write c/o Rough Trade, 202 Kensington Park Road, London W11). Mod mag that's quite good. Interviews & reviews that are readable if a little dumb at times. Interestingly, not as blinkered as the mod label might suggest - this issue has interview with Spizz & reviews include The Beat & they like Nine Below Zero. No gig guide, so it's more what has been than what will be... but so's the whole Mod movement, innit?

Tales Of Dayglow comes from Steve, 92 Kenwyn Drive, Neasden, London NW2 7NU. It's 20p & is one of the better ones. Comments & reviews from all angles - some direct opinions, but mainly observation. Interestingly written - good journalism. Plenty of variety for the reader, including ultra-sick cartoon & a creepy story. Features Slaughter & The Dogs, U.K. Subs (R.I.P.), Capt. Sensible, Mysterons, Pretenders, J.J.Burnel, etc.

The Poser No.5. A photozine. A good idea. Just photos (of gigs in 1st 3 months of '80 - a selection of pictures from each of 5 gigs - Clash, Flowers, Slits, Au Pairs, Pink Military). Also one article per issue on taking photos - this time it's 'Developing Your Own Films'. Most of the photos in here are black-n-white, but there's interesting use of colour wash on some. Capturing of the sense of live action in these photos is great. Done by Neil Anderson, 4 Palmerston Crescent, London N13 & printed & published by Better Badges at 25p + 15p P&P.

No Easy Answers No.1. is from 56 Grangemill Rd., Bellingham, London SE6. Punkzine - punk music/politics/art/anti-style. Features a Crass interview plus Poison Girls, Cyclon B, record reviews/gig reviews/lyrics/etc. Chaos used to good effect in the layout - plenty to read here for your 25p. Ken quite likes it, I think it's great. How about you....?

More fanzines in future issues - if you're travelling round the country, do look out for regional music mags like these - there's now one in almost every town. Most a cheaply-done duplicator efforts, but that's not to say they don't have something interesting to say. Touring bands should contact local fanzines - write-ups in them are often more likely to be read by rock fans/punters in the area than (say) local newspaper or even nation press coverage. They offer an alternative to the national muzak press that's smaller in circulation but far more accessible & much less likely to twist what you say &/or try to sell you as half a million things that you aren't/weren't/never will be.

...& so, people, we come - once again - to the end of another page with space enough to say hello to Mandy in Aussie. Now get off this page, you cur

N.B. A wide selection of fanzines is available from (a) Better Badges, 286 Portobello Rd., London W10.(01-960-5913/4) or (b) Rough Trade, 202 Kensington Park Road, London W11. (01-727-4312) - ring or write for their lists of available mags.

page 16.

NOWTZ

Written & compiled by Nick Toczek.

BBC Radio Leeds is taking its rock programme, **Metrognome**, off the air during summer - using 'the cuts' as an excuse. That's the bad news... with last show going out (5.45-630pm) on Wed 25 June. The good news is that on Wed 2 July (6.30-8.30pm) there is a special rock programme to see in the summer in which the entire two hours will be devoted to local bands - DON'T MISS IT. Also, for bands doing gigs during the summer, carry on sending in dates because the Metrognome team are going to make sure that the gig guide is slotted into other programmes - in fact, they are hoping to start a daily rock music diary slot to help maintain some local rock coverage. As you'll see from the advert. on the back cover, Eel Pie (Pete Townsend's record co./studios/video team/etc.) will be up in Bradford in July giving local bands a chance, for £100, to get a sound-&-vision video tape of their stage act. The two main points here are (a) with video as the coming thing, many bands are already using it to get the big guys interested (it's cheaper than numerous badly-paid showcase gigs in London where invited music press/record co. reps/etc. fail to turn up) so it looks like a good thing to get into & (b) with their usual rates fixed at £253, this really is a cheap offer. What you get (according to leaflets in front of me & 'phone conversations with Eel Pie) is one hour of set-up/sound-check time followed by an hour of recording. It's an 8-track recording that can be done live or can use you miming to a studio recording or can use a mixture of pre-recorded & live takes for the sound. Visually, you get a full-colour video film using three cameras. So, if you're in a band & can muster £100 between you, it sounds like a good idea. With basic editing & cost of the tape included, there shouldn't be hidden extras - & it should only cost a further £10 to get second cassette of the type that'll show through a home TV video machine - hire one of them & you can watch yourself on TV at home - bring back Crossroads, all is forgiven! Leeds band The Squares (who're excellent live) have a new single 'Oh, Buddy Holly' due out in late June on Airebeat Records. Around same time Mirror Boys (also Leeds) have 'Captain Scott at Tiffany's in a Jumble Sale Soup' out on Wortley Road Records (it's a 3-track e.p. of 'At Tiffany's' c/w 'Jumble Sale Soup' & 'Captain Scott' - which goes some way towards explaining the ludicrous title!). Also onto disc in June are Agony Column (see review of pre-release cassette elsewhere in this issue). Bradford club band Ocean have a single out in June that contains two of their own songs. Also on the club circuit, Rockabilly Rebs are planning to bring out a second disc (see review of their first elsewhere in this issue). Best new band name award goes to the punk outfit who're on at Albion, Hudds. on Sat 22 June (see gig guide). Went into Ric Rac Studio in Leeds & caught Cuba doing the finishing bits on 'Wireless World' which will be their next single on Ariola Records - & I think it's excellent. The studio's quite small (it's in a converted cellar) & has just gone full-time after a few years as a part-time studio. It's the best gear of any 8-track studio in the area & has a totally committed & involved engineer in Mike Robson (who also owns the place & lives above it) - an experienced musician himself, he makes a point of trying to understand what each band's about so that he's working with them - more like an extra member of the group than an outside engineer/producer. Certainly, Cuba & Shake Appeal (who were in the week before Cuba) have not found better than him & Ric Rac - & both bands have had quite a lot of studio experience. Two dead record shops: Scene & Heard in Leeds & Pearsons in Bradford. The two had the same owners &, appear to have been losing money. Shame to see them go. More & more people in the music biz seem to be taking an interest in Bradford as being a place that's likely to grab the nation's rock focus some time very soon. John Peel & Pete Townsend are among them. One dead band... in case you've not yet heard, Bradford's Radio5 split up at the end of May. They'd just put in an excellent Peel session & looked all set for bigger things. The various members should be reappearing with new outfits in the not-too-distant time to come. John Parker's words-&-music show 'For The Price Of A Pint' is at Bradford's Theatre In The Mill for 4 nights (17th-20th June). 7.30 start @ 45p in. Guests include Rufaro & poets Little Brother & Willy Beckett. Cassette distribution: young guy called Neil O'Connor writes to say that he intends compiling a catalogue of D.I.Y. cassettes currently on sale & is keen to hear from anyone selling them. He also welcomes ideas, info., etc. His current plan is to distribute the catalogue as a free insert in fanzines, etc. Sounds like a good idea. He can be contacted at 135 The Hough, Northowram, Halifax, HX3 7DH. Whilst on the subject of cassettes, I hear that there's a company setting up with recording gear & a fast tape copier as a mobile, touring gigs recording bands & offering instant cassettes of the gig to punters as they leave - only works for bands not signed to a label, but should be an interesting development.

BETTER BADGES
PRODUCTION PRICES

UNDER 500

1. ALL SMALL RUN PRICES INCLUDE VAT
2. ARTWORK MUST BE CORRECT SIZE
3. REDUCTION OF B/W ARTWORK £1
4. MORE THAN ONE DESIGN IN EQUAL QUANTITIES IS OK

D.I.Y./ONE OFFS - 1½" & 2⅛" 20p each + 10p P&P

UNDER 100 - 1½" & 2⅛" Colour Xerox
10 off - £2.50 + 10p P&P
30 off - £6.60 + 20p P&P
50 off - £10.00+ 50p P&P

100 OFF B&W Colour
1" 1¼" 1½" - £11 £13 + 50p P&P
2⅛" - - - - £13 £15 + £1 P&P

500 & OVER

1. PRICES EXCLUSIVE OF VAT & CARR.
2. ARTWORK ANY SIZE, MUST BE COLOUR SEPERATED
3. ALL DESIGN WORK EXTRA
4. 3 WEEKS DELIVERY

SET UP 1st colour £10
extra colours + £15

MAKE UP	1"	1¼"	1½"	1¾"	2⅛"
500 -	£25	£25	£30	£30	£35
1000 -	£35	£40	£45	£50	£60

ALWAYS EXTEND DESIGNS BY ½" DIAM. FOR WRAP-AROUND.
286 PORTOBELLO ROAD
LONDON W10 960 5513

Well I don't know how your dad's gonna take it Charlie.... he was dead set on you coming into the family racket....
Stan Engel

THE COMMUNICATIONS CENTRE
(a posh name for a basic facility)

offers 4-TRACK with DBX
at £3-50 p.h. + tape

Gear Includes:-

TEAC 3340, DBX, ITAM 10-4 desk, LEVERS-RICH E200, REVOX B77, ORBAN REVERB, FILTERS, GRAPHICS, etc.

FULL D.I. + MIKES by AKG, CALREC, etc.

RING ALF or MOYA on B'F'D 22769.

RAM RECORDING STUDIO
64 ARMLEY ROAD, LEEDS LS12 2DR.
tel. Leeds 445044* or Wakefield 67470.

Basic Rates = £8·50 per hour.

£80 for a 10 hour day

SPECIAL OFFER:- 10% discount on production of this advert.

N.B. 445044 is a new phone no.

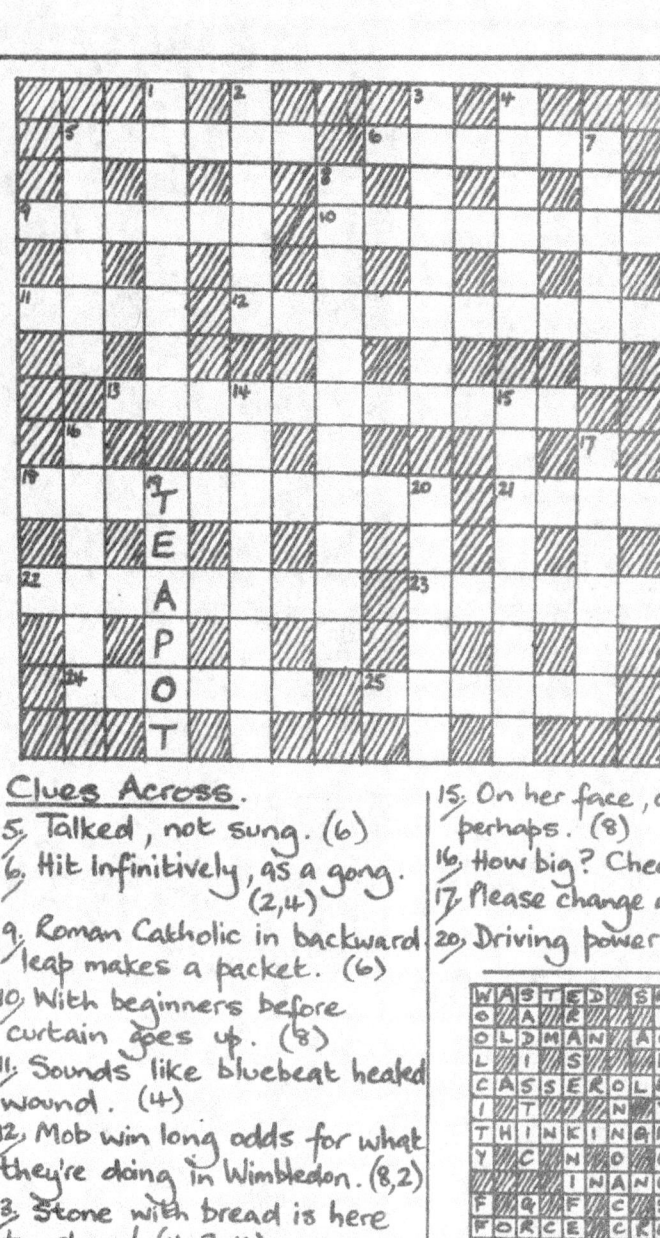

HI, THERE! THIS IS STEP-ON-A-SLUG PRODUCTIONS WELCOMING YOU TO THE WOOL CITY ROCKWORD No XI!!! (number six, bonehead! oh, sorry, will he ever learn?)

Clues Across.
5. Talked, not sung. (6)
6. Hit Infinitively, as a gong. (2,4)
9. Roman Catholic in backward leap makes a packet. (6)
10. With beginners before curtain goes up. (8)
11. Sounds like bluebeat healed wound. (4)
12. Mob win long odds for what they're doing in Wimbledon. (8,2)
13. Stone with bread is here to stay! (4,3,4)
18. Time hasn't run out. It's..... (4,3,4)
21. Adopt 5 down to attract attention. (4)
22. Comb take-away for my support? (2,4,2)
23. Right of admission to course.(6)
24. Bad bands, but mainly jokes, attract plenty. (6)
25. Put with 19, under breakfast. (3-3)
15. On her face, or on my collar, perhaps. (8)
16. How big? Cheers! (2,4)
17. Please change at the wheel? (6)
20. Driving power. (6)

Clues Down.
1. Gig nothing! This is classical! (8)
2. Colour Donovan mellow. (6)
3. Without basement, can't be a pub. (2,6)
4. Guitar man. (6)
5. Mr. Engel leads church! That's how he stands. (6)
7. Well known moron. (6)
8. Tom'N'Ted came, roughly told us how gig went. (11)
14. I hear you, Dave Edmunds. (8)

Solution to Rockword 5
No-one got it right, so no prizes! Keep trying, eh? Cheers, Ken.

BAND AID
Only a small Band Aid section this time - bigger one next issue.

Primarily for new bands &/or managers, here's a bit on actually marketing your outfit. You should devote some cash to printing costs. What you'll need is (a) the means to sell the band to promoters, agents, record co's, etc. (b) the means to let the public know you exist & where to catch you live.

Business publicity. Cheapest is just phone calls/letters pushing the group. A phone is essential for them to contact you. Letter-headed note paper impresses better than ordinary paper — these can be hand-done & copies run off at any instant-print shop or small printer's. But beware, prices vary enormously, so shop around. Get info. sheets run off giving line-up + basic info. on the band. Business cards are also useful. Photos of the band help too - especially with getting good press coverage. N.B. Buy a copy of 'Exchange & Mart' (from any good newsagent) - there are low-cost publicity services & printers of every kind advertised in there. Companies like Walkerprint do package deals offering you photos, letterheads, posters, stickers, etc. to promote your group. A sample tape (cassette) of the band (home-recorded, live, in a studio) will help get gigs & record co. interest (unless it's bad-quality or your band's poor!).

Street publicity. Free gig guide listings in national & local music press, local papers, local radio; posters: hand-done, duplicated or printed; leaflets; stickers & badges - I'll be listing media addresses/phone nos. in next ish. Exciting stuff, this rock'n'roll, isn't it!!

SHIT! THERE'S NEVER ENOUGH SPACE - I'D LOADS MORE TO SAY BUT....

cont. →

QUEENS HALL
BRADFORD

FOR THE FIRST TIME EVER OPEN EVERY THU. + FRI. + SAT. NIGHT THROUGHOUT THE SUMMER FEATURING LIVE BANDS & DISCOS.

Also, some dates available for private functions - contact John Farquhar, manager on 392712.

MEMBERS' NOTICE

REGGAE! SOUL! CALYPSO! FUNK!
16 LUMB LANE, BRADFORD 8.
ROOTS RECORD SHOP
Posters, hats & clothes. African hairstylists.
TEL. Bradford 32721.

Bradford Printshop

You can print your own posters for cost of materials

We can print and design posters at reasonable prices

For details Phone 22518

RIC~RAC SOUND STUDIO

How would you like to record on equipment like this...?

SOUNDCRAFT 1" 8-TRACK + DBX
REVOX 377   } ½-track
BRENELL T19
    CUSTOM DESK
NAKAMICHI CASSETTE DECK
MASTERROOM STEREO REVERB
KLARK TEKNIC DN70 DIGITAL DELAY
   "   "   DN71 HARMONISER
   "   "   DN34 ANALOG DELAY/FLANGER
   "   "   DN22 GRAPHIC EQ
AUDIO & DESIGN SCAMP RACK
    NOISE GATES/EXPANDERS
    COMPRESSORS/LIMITERS
    DYNAMIC FILTERS
QUAD/TANNOY/AURATONE MONITOR SYSTEM

BELL STEREO FLANGER
AUDIO DEVELOPMENTS COMP's./LIMITERS
NEUMAN/AKG/ELECTROVOICE MIC's.

All this for the basic price of £10 per hr. which is the same price as any ordinary 8-track studio. Reduced rates for 10 hrs. or more. Ring Mick on Leeds 633717.

WE ALSO HAVE RECORDS PRESSED AND RELEASED ON OUR OWN "LUGGAGE LABEL".

RIC~RAC SOUND STUDIO

EEL PIE

MOBILE

will be in BRADFORD

JULY 21st - 25th
we invite LOCAL BANDS
TO RECORD

SOUND / VIDEO

PACKAGE DEAL
- Combined 8 Track & 3-Colour Cameras
- 60 min. Video Cassette

£99 inc.

Bookings & Details   RING — Kendall, on

BRADFORD 42096

When you're thinking of recording

Masters or Demos you'll need a studio with a reputation for good sounds, good engineers, and a friendly relaxed atmosphere.
A studio with the facilities you want, 16 track or 8 track available by the hour or on day bookings. The effects you'll need like Flanging, Echo, Reverb, A.D.T. Noise Gates, Compressors, Harmonisers, Dolby 'A' etc., and a studio area with room to breathe.
A studio because of its unique sounds, attracts bands from all over the British Isles, Germany and Denmark, and a studio that doesn't charge the earth.

16 track £15 per hour	8 track £9 per hour
16 track £130 per day	8 track £75 per day
(10 hours)	(10 hours)

ONE FREE HOUR TO SET UP IN,
NO OVERTIME CHARGES. WHEN YOU'RE THINKING
OF A STUDIO LIKE THIS YOU'RE THINKING OF

RECORDING STUDIOS

**Ring us at
ROCHDALE (0706) 524420**

KENION ST., ROCHDALE, LANCS., ENGLAND

8-TRACK - £50 per eight hr. day!
4-TRACK - £40 "   "   "   " !

JSG STUDIOS
· 8 Track Studio ·
RECORD PRESSING
Bingley 68843
Bradford 832187

Fully Equipped Studio

Using Tascam, Allen Heath, Revox, Roland, Quad, A.K.G., Calrec, etc., etc.

FREE

USE OF ANY OF THE FOLLOWING EQUIPMENT

Polymoog, Minimoog, Fender Rhodes Suitcase, Hammond X5 Organ, Moog Taurus Bass Pedals, ARP Salina String Machine, Clavinet D6, Mellotron, Premier Drums, Kramer 5000 Dmz Bass, Accoustic Piano & Guitars + numerous effects.

ISSUE #8

August/September 1980, 1,900 copies printed, 20 pages, A4, another ace cover

In my editorial, I offer several excuses for this issue coming out two weeks late. I always struggled to find the money to pay the printer. That's what made producing WCR a constant uphill struggle. Note that I couldn't afford a glossy cover on this edition. However, another great cover by Mo Maklouf made up for that. Incidentally, during the 1980s, Mo designed album covers for Misty In Roots and for other acts on their label, People Unite.

Personal Notes on bands profiled in this issue.

Rockabilly Rebs (page 6) were the live band at Gaynor's and my engagement party at The Palm Cove. Ian Anderson, keyboard player with Heaven 17 (page 12), was the photographer at our wedding.

Gaynor & Nick

Which studio did Dedringer use to get a contract with Dindisc, along with Orchestral Manouvres; and which studio did the Gang of four use for their contract with EMI? Radio 5 and Aircraft with Rockburgh, I.Q. Zero with Logo, Excel with Polydor Music for Pleasure with DJM? And which studio has just recorded the new Fall album & single and a Heavy Metal compilation album for Logo records, released in September? The new Manchester Collective album and recordings by DAF from Germany, Mini Pops from Belgium, Girls At Our Best, Stranger Than Fiction, Joy Division, a new album from Ada Wilson, the Buzzcocks in during August and a single from Dalek I, R n' B group the Cheaters, Durutti Column, Beats Working, and the Donkeys new single, the Killermeters and Danse Macabre? Heavy Metal bands Buffalo, Turbo, Rhab Stallion, Streetfighter, Scorched Earth, Jededdiah Strutt, Oxym & Warrior; the Comsat Angels and I'm So Hollow, Mysterious Footsteps, the Oscillators and an album with the Not Sensibles?

The Studio all these bands recorded at was—

and whether you're mastering or making demos you've got all the same facilities on 16 track or 8 track, Digital Delay, Anolog Delay, Harmonizers, Echo Plate, Tape Echo, Stereo Flangers, Spring Reverb, Noise Gates, Compressors etc. plus our Soundcraft desk with sweep EQ and JBL monitoring and that great unique Cargo sound. The price for a day booking on 16 track is just £14 per hour for a 10 hour day or £16 per hour for less time, and on 8 track it's only £8 per hour for 10 hours or £10 per hour. The only extras are the ¼" tape at £10 for a full reel and £5 for half a reel and VAT. There are no overtime charges, no tape hire charges and we're open 24 hours 7 days a week, so you can record day or night at no extra cost and we've got a pub next door,
So call round or give us a ring, and we'll see you soon......

Recording Studios
Kenion Street
Rochdale
Lancs   (0706) 524420.

The Wool City ROCKER

Issue Number 8.
AUG. & SEPT. '80.

EDITORIAL

12/8/80.

Hello, yr. editor here, hope yr. having a good sunny summer (ke! he!). Just heard new JAM single - isn't it *great*, if a bit Beatles/M.O.R. Buy Mysterious Footsteps fab 4-5!! This'll sorta drift around, doubling as NOWTZ. First off, sorry this issues almost 3 weeks late. Mostly this is because I've not had the money to do it, also because of printer's summer holidays & my flu. Please help out by ⓐ buying this if you haven't already, ⓑ by asking for it in your local shops & encouraging them to stock it if they don't (ring me if you can suggest possible outlets), ⓒ subscribe if you have any difficulties getting issues (mail order is 50p a copy or £4-50 for 10 issues = 1 year), ⓓ advertising if you're a big rich organisation (rates card on request), ⓔ selling copies yourself (wonderful discount terms). Do go along to FUTURAMA 2 - the full line-up's amazing (see advert on p.9). I'm now also writing a rock column for Yorkshire Arts Association's monthly "The Month In Yorkshire" (1st article will be in "October In Yorkshire"). Also, Musicians Only have asked me to put together a 2-page feature on rock in Bradford. I'll be doing that in early Sept. - ring me if you've any info./ideas/suggestions. There's a notice on the railings outside St. Mary's Catholic Chaplaincy (opposite my local, the exotically-named Cock & Bottle) which just reads: "PLEASE DO NOT." - that's Catholics for you! Also, a large poster every Saturday on the door of The Belle Vue, Bradford says: "Stripper - entry 15p"... the obvious remark'd be sexist! Gleaned from letters (wasn't room for a letters page, sorry):- ① Problem, vocalist with Bradford punx The Hanged wrote re their forthcoming E.P. due in a week or two on their own Crypt Label. ② Local punk bands Chronic & Living Dead are setting up own Apathy Label - punk bands write to A. Farrow, 12 Hayfield Close, Baildon, W. Yorks. Also, Living Dead soon have a cassette L.P. out on X-Centric Noise Tapes Ltd., % A. Thompson, 17 West End Rd., Hull, E. Yorks. Andy Farrow also sent me an enthusiastic review of Chronic's recent gig at Guisley Town Hall - but I'm reluctant to use reviews by friends of the band being covered - outside reviewers tend to be more interesting to read & (obviously) more objective. ③ Skipton's Gips sent me a badge (thanx!) & some info. on themselves - must interview them soon - if you think it's hard getting gigs round Leeds/Bradford or elsewhere round W-Yorks., try being a Skipton/N. Yorks. band... you'd get to feel like an unemployed shepherd signing on in central London! Odd incomplete review of Blackpool punx The Fits at Salvation Army on Fri 11th June - don't even know who sent it!! They sound like a fine basic punk group. ④ Gris Boojum of % Peaceworks, 58 Wakefield Rd., Aspley, Huddersfield, W. Yorks, HD1 3AJ would like to hear from anyone who was at the gig at Ivanhoe's, Hudds. on Xmas Day '77 (Sex Pistols, as if you didn't know!) - especially anyone who photo'd or taped any of the proceedings. He's planning a book or at least a pamphlet on the gig & will answer all letters & return any material lent to him. ⑤ Paul Chapman of Huddersfield has got a new band called Votre Militaire - 5-piece with female singer & ditto bassiste. Debut gig = Hudds. Rugger Club - 17 Aug. ⑥ The Vye have broken up - expect 2 off-shoots, one called New Opera. Also, The Scene change guitarists, add kbds & become Buddy Valenteen & The Lonely Hearts. The Killermeters drop a guitarist & change their name soon. CRASS to play Cleo's (Hudds) & Panache (B'f'd) in October. Gris Boojum (see address earlier) launches Snark Music at end of Aug. with a cassette L.P. of 15 Hudds. area bands: OR WAS HE PUSHED, GUESTS, TREATMENT, GENEVA, JAB JAB, THE NOISE, GLOSSY MAGS, GENTLE IHOR, E2R THE FLOOR, THE EXTRAS, PRIVATE DICKS, TRIANGULAR HOUR + 2 others + a 20-page booklet & a badge, all for less than £2! Also, around end of Sept., Mundane Music is releasing an L.P. (vinyl disc!) of 10 or so local bands "Owt For Nowt" - will include O.W.H.P. Guests, Treatment, Jedeadiah Strutt, etc. Now piss off onto page 4! Luv & Sunshine, Nick Toczek

Rock 'n' Roll-call:-

1 = Mo Maklouf's cover design.
3 = ICI.
4 = Violation.
5 = Princeville/Huddersfield/Rip Offs.
6 = Most of Rockabilly Rebs. (↓)
7 = Gabriel Gets Phil'd In etc. + Rebs. cont'd by Phil Foster.
Ate = Cuba, Lucky Strike, W.C.Rhists.
9 = Live: Treatment/Fab.Poo's + Profiled: Warlord. FUTURAMA2
10 = Aug.GIGS + Band Aid (playlet, prayer, gig publicity).
11 = Sept.GIGS + Useless Addresses/Useful Cartoons.
12 = Guy Jackson + Heaven 17.
13 = **NEW SINGLES**
14 = Gawpin' at Lancs: Manchester/Salford.
15 = Bradford Rock 'n' Roll Exhibition.
16 = **C.30 cassettes C.90 GO** (called 'Only A Northern Song')
17 = Mick Picks The Loch.
18 = Ken's X-word + Fanzines, news sheets, comix, etc.

Editing, typing, layout, most of the contents, most of the distribution, etc. by NICK TOCZEK.

Other contributions from:-
MO MAKLOUF   KEITH E. RICE
STEVE BROWN   PHIL FOSTER
KEN TURNER   BARRY DAWSON
KEV HOPGOOD   STEVE CAIRNS
MICK MITCHELL DAVE PARKINSON
GRIS BOOJUM   COLIN ROBINSON
PAUL CLARK   PIP NANA

Thanks to ANDY CAIRNS for loan of a better typewriter than mine & to GAYNOR for being herself. Hello to MANDY in Aussie & John Peel at The Beeb.

TERMS OF SALE: 30p each direct to the public or 50p each by mail order from the address given below. Bulk orders of 15 or more copies can be had at the discount price of 20p each (so why not sell the magazine yourself at gigs, school, etc.?)

ADVERTISING RATES: Standard 3½" x 3½" box is £20 for first time of advertising, then £10 for subsequent placings. Colour, different size, special lay-out, etc. by arrangement.
Ring or write for advertising rates card & any other details.

EDITORIAL ADDRESS:
5 Beech Terrace,
Undercliffe,
Bradford BD3 0PY,
West Yorkshire,
England.
(tel. 0274-21867).

BEST TIMES TO RING ARE ABOUT 10.30am or 6pm or ABOUT 11.45pm

VIOLATION

The Bradford punk band, Violation, had a write-up in the first issue of WCR. At that time, they'd done on public gigs. Here's what's happened in the eight months since then....

The band's line-up remains unchanged (Aky on dms, 'Oxfam' Harry on voc, Mick on gtr, Barry on Bass). It was the trio of Aky, Mick & Barry (+ assorted friends) that waited for me in The Manville. Pints in, cigs lit & formalities aside, they let me choose some photos & then began to talk about themselves.

The band's first two gigs were both at Palm Cove, & both with The Negatives & Total Confusion: "On the first gig we were first band on & went down well, so at the second one, we went on after Total Confusion - but Harry had laryngitis so it was difficult, though we still seemed to go down well."

Aky's determination & dedicated enthusiasm has always been a major driving force in the band. By persistent 'phoning, he secured support spot to The Clash at St.George's Hall, Bradford as the band's third gig! No mean achievement "It was a bit of a rip off. We got lousy treatment from the roadcrew who just weren't interested in us at, so we got no proper soundcheck, were only allowed to do a half hour set, had to bring all our own gear & only got paid £25. The Clash's thing of saying that they want to help other bands just isn't true - more like they want an inexperienced band with a bad sound as the support so that they look better when they go on. However, it was go to do. We were surprised at the really good reception that we got - the fans were great. Also, it got us a big feature in The Telegraph & Argus."

"We did the Railway Workers, Nelson with The Quick as our support. The gig went well but everything went wrong on stage - strings broke, fuses blew, etc. After that we did Queens Hall & Scamps in Bradford & then The Albion, Huddersfield. At Scamps, we amazed the manager (& ourselves too!) by getting over 250 people in on a Wed. It was our best gig so far. However, the London management of Scamps have since decided that they don't want punks in their clubs, so we can't do it again. The Albion went well too - we're back there on a rebooking on 12th July." (Ya missed it, reader! - ed.).

"We used to rehearse at Coda, but we had hassles with them & anyway couldn't afford to pay for every rehearsal so we've now moved into a mate's cellar with our gear. We've put money into doing it up so we're low on funds now, but it's been well worth it. Once we've got more cash, we'll do a studio demo - in the meantime, we're hoping for a chance to do a session for Pennine Radio (that'd give us a demo to send out too)."

Songwriting: music by Barry, lyrics by Harry. "It is still basically punk, though with touches of new wave." Barry: "We've the power of a punk band but we like to think that we refine it a lot - sort of like Wire but more powerful." Aky: "But we still like to think of ourselves as being a punk band - & we still play to & for punks."

"Gigs are very hard to get - partly because we're punk, partly because there are so many bands & so few venues. And we can guarantee to bring along at least 3 or 4 vans of fans to every gig." They feel that a deal for management might help, but would prefer to keep on doing their own. Asgard, the major London-based agency is interested but want the band to be more successful first.

Contact: Aky on Bradford 71793.

page 4.

H.M.'s Princeville: summer cruisin'

Whatever image Princeville WMC conjures up in the mind of those yet to visit, this venue still remains an impressive platform for heavy rock at its finest, & did so even through the punk/new wave explosion of '76/'77. Once again, this remarkable tradition came through late June & all of July unblemished as some of the top HM outfits in the country succeeded in bringing capacity audiences to their feet.

June's programme was closed by last-minute replacements Streetfighter, a 4-piece band from Blackpool who specialise in reproducing HM classics. With accurate executions of numbers like 'Space Station No.5', 'Jailbreak', 'Emerald', 'Highway Star', & 'Rocky Mountain Way' to name but a few, they provided sufficient ammunition to keep the headbangers at the front constantly active. The ability of each of the individual members is unquestionable, although commercial success will obviously always elude them (ironically enough, I thought the best song of the set was their own 'Streetfighting', simply because it suffered no comparison with the original). Perhaps the greatest hinderance to the band lies in their bass guitarist whose resemblance to Phil Lynott in both vocal & playing style (black Fender Precision et al) is too close for comfort. However, at this level, Streetfighter will never be out of work & I look forward to seeing them here again soon.

Witchfynde are now considered one of the most prominent up-&-coming HM bands, although a great deal of their reputation is built entirely around their single 'Give 'em Hell', an obvious necessity for any budding record collection. A full house was treated to a powerful set, rich in excitement if not originality. Witchfynde revel in this sort of atmosphere &, as the set proceeded, the band completely obliterated my previous criticism (see WCR4). 'Gettin Heavy', 'Do It', 'Do You Believe What You Read in The Stars?' & 'I Woke Up Screaming' were all excellent & were heavily dominated by some eyecatching (don't you mean earcatching?!-ed.) drumming & powerful guitar work from Gra Scoresby & Montalo respectively. Naturally, 'Give 'em Hell' gained the best response from the knowledgeable audience who can be hard to please at times but can certainly appreciate an excellent band like Witchfynde.

The following Thursday was, for me, one of total depression as I found myself at the other end of the country & thus was unable to see the return of Diamond Head, one of the finest HM bands to emerge for a long time. By all accounts they were outstanding &, at the Vardis gig on 17th, there were plenty of Diamond Head T-shirts on view. For Vardis therefore it was a case of follow that, but they're local favourites & audience reaction & respect were never in doubt. However, after previous performances here, I had dismissed Vardis as no-hopers clinging onto the lower rungs of the ladder of fame. Since then of course, a recording contract has come their way & the band are in the process of recording a live album. Consequently, Vardis have acquired high quality equipment in abundance which, along with the excellent mix, produced a superb sound with bass & drums sounding crystal-clear against the unique sound of Steve Zodiac's guitar. This was the first time I had seen Vardis play as a unit rather than as individuals at times working against each other. Their record company's interest in them is, on this showing, well-founded indeed. 'Destiny', 'Situation Negative' & '100mph' complete with extended over-the-top lead solo in true metal tradition, all went down a storm, yet for me the best songs of the set were both new numbers, firstly 'The Lion's Share' & secondly 'Let's Go' soon to be released as the band's next single. Encores included the excellent 'If I Were King' throughout which even Steve Zodiac's voice sounded good, but I still stick to my opinion that Vardis would vastly improve by employing a strong singer/ frontman to bring out their full potential. Despite this, Vardis turned in an overall brilliant set, the only criticism being its length; just 40 minutes excluding their two encores. On a final note, Vardis have been given support slot on the forthcoming Hawkwind tour & will also support The Plasmatics on their solitary British date in London.

July's programme was closed by Leeds band Red Eye turning in a commendable if uninspiring set. The good sound & the band's musical ability were often overshadowed by some dreadful vocals which did anything but set the crowd alight, yet musically Red Eye are very competent & at times exciting, especially when they unleash dynamic power chords & intricate dual guitar breaks from the twin Gibson SG's - as in 'Motorcycle Dreamer'. The set contained a number of covers of which ZZ Top's 'Tush' & Joe Walsh's 'Rocky Mountain Way' were dealt with quite well, but their handling of AC/DC's 'Let There Be Rock' & 'Whole Lotta Rosie' were terrible (Bon Scott, God bless him, must have turned in his grave) & the applause that they received for the latter was more out of recognition for the song that its execution. This was an inconsistent set by Red Eye with many conspicuous faults which may decrease with time; but, like Vardis, Red Eye need a singer up front who can at least hit a few true notes, in order to consolidate their line-up.

Princeville's bill for August looks just as inviting & potentially mindblowing with the returns of White Spirit & Limelight to name but two. ~ Steve Brown.

Boojum Bags 7!... Huddersfield SAT. 14th June '80.

The times are a-changin' in Huddersfield, not so many months ago I would have been pushed to find two bands playing in the town on a Saturday night. However, on this night I clocked up seven groups in four venues, although I had to employ some judicious sprinting!

Here is a brief look at the evening.

1. The Guests (Poly). Snappy pop from a four-piece that includes a sax. Self written material played with style & some intelligence - i.e. knowing when to use effects such as echo & when not to. As I have written elsewhere, I still feel sure lead singer, Dave Haigh, could beat Elvis Costello at his own game. This is a Huddersfield band that deserves your attention.

2. Glossy Mags (White Lion). They don't cut it with me, though they do have a strong local following in tow. The sound is too cluttered & confused to be pop with a sting. Take a listen to The Guests, boys, to see how economy does have its virtues.

3. Proposition 31 (Albion). I found this embarrassing. When they started, they were before a reasonably attended bar room. When they finished, punters were thin on the ground, having found the upstairs bar a better proposition.

These grown men gave us a display of crass stage mannerisms with some dodgy rock thrown in. Only a version of 'I'm so Bored with The USA' relieved the monotony. I think 'I'm so Boring in Morley' would be safer, gents.

4. E.M.F. (Poly). A recording ska band who will last as long as....

5. Xpozez (Cleopatras). Three months ago they were no-hopers, but now they KNOW what they are doing. Their brand of punk, derivative of The New York Dolls (though not their image) & The Art Attacks, hits between the eyes.

A dozen fast, two minute songs espousing the Crass philosophy showed that some of us are still riding on '77.

6. The Killermeters (Poly). Their first home town gig since losing a guitarist, but they haven't lost their sound, which is described by some as 'fresh' & others as 'limp & tired'.

This style of mod cannot give them a living for much longer unless their forthcoming first LP surprises everybody & revitalises the mod market.

7. The Vibrators (Cleopatras). I'm not sure how many members of the band are from the '77 line up, but no matter, the image is preserved as clean punks.

Audience reaction was slight to the new material, it being both unfamiliar & second rate. An attempt at vocal harmony on 'Sweet Sweet Heart' (from the first LP) was a sad disappointment, but the magnificence of the two 1977 singles 'Baby Baby' & 'London Girls' was undiminished - perhaps it was just good to hear them again. -Gris Boojum.

...& Chisholm Gets Ripped Off! Harrogate SAT. 12th JULY '80.

Ironically, The Rip Offs' gig at The Cock & Castle (supporting The Mirror Boys) could have been one of the town's swansong rock events; for, as gig venues in the town close under financial pressure, Harrogate's two dozen or so bands are finding dates hard to come by. Meanwhile, like Roman revellers before the city's fall, gig-goers thoroughly enjoyed the line-up at The Cock.

Bradford punk poet Little Brother made one of his infrequent visits to Harrogate to entertain a packed hall in his own inimitable satirical style.

The Rip Offs are a newly-formed 8-member Harrogate band already making an impact in the area.

Fun & unconventionality are the band's main aims, as evidenced by such songs as 'Michael Rowed The Boat Ashore' & a stylised version of the Batman theme-tune.

The Rip Offs are brothers Martin & Nick Hutchinson (grt & bass), brothers Gary & Dave Kinder (voc & dms, the latter for absentee Dave Howitt), Dave Hanks & Pete Richmond (gtrs) & backing vocalists Caroline Barrett & Rachel Nash.

High-points in a varied & disverse set were 'I'm A Shark', a fishy little number with a floating bass line (these puns are awful, well done, John - ed.) running through it to give a desert island flavour & 'Hello, Hello', a teenage love ballad.

A Lene Lovich touch was added by backing vocalists Caroline & Rachel & the group was held together throughout by rock-steady bassist, Nick, standing out of the limelight at the back of the stage. ~John Chisholm reviewed.

ROCKABILLY REBS
interviewed by Nick Toczek

"ROCKABILLY RULES U.K.!"

The band first formed under this name in November '77 — long before Matchbox charted with the song of the same name — so they're not just recent bandwagon jumpers.

The original line-up was Boyd Greensmith (rm gtr), Paul Harrison (dms), Richard Thorne (b) & Garry Strain (ld voc/gtr). This lasted till early '79 when Boyd & Rich left. For the next year, they went through various line-ups, including a spell with no bassist & a short stint with a sax player (until the band decided to drop some rock'n'roll numbers that were in their set & go for pure rockabilly — & hillbillies didn't have saxes). Since Jan'80 Paul & Garry (who long ago gave up playing gtr & just does voc: "I was a lousy guitarist.") have been working with Graham Kearns on bass & Nigel Hope on guitar — a stable & easy-going unit. It was this bunch + manager that I met for a Sunday lunchtime drink in Bradford's chic hostelry The Cock & Bottle.

I enjoyed this interview more than any other I've done to date. They've got an infectious sense of fun — my local doesn't have many people with cowboy gear, Gene Vincent badges & 50's hairstyles — & those that do come in don't usually pass round jelly babies...

In between the goonery, I did manage to find out a bit about the band. I've not seen the band live, but reviewed their EP in the last issue of WCR. "It reached no.2 in the R'n'R chart in Sounds." "We recorded it with Dean Scholey on guitar & Martyn Lynch on bass — that was back in July '79 — Martyn's now lead guitarist with Johnny Storm & The Hurricanes (& before he joined us he was with Namesake who released 'Rockabilly Blues' on Box label back in '76)". I asked them a bit more about the band's own E.P. — specifically the recording of it — how they got the distinctive countrified early rock sound. "We wanted a genuine live sound — not a studio-produced multi-tracked & processed product. There are no overdubs, it was all done in one straight take. And the only effect is some echo, nothing else. That's how we'll always be." They've turned down offers of auditions for TV programmes such as 'Oh Boy' & 'Let's Rock' because it would've involved miming on stage & the band are adamant that they will only ever go for a genuine live recording or nothing.

Their current live set is pure rockabilly plus a few obscure R'n'R oldies (b-sides & album tracks). The only original songs are the two on the E.P. but they are writing new material at the moment. "The real problem is to come up with new tunes that aren't standard 12-bar, but at the same time aren't as much of a blatantly commercial sell-out as (say) Matchbox do."

It turns out that Nigel, who looks the odd one out with his glasses, beard & moustache, used to be in Bradford heavy rock bands such as Black Cat Yard

continued on page 7

RIC~RAC
SOUND STUDIO

12 KIRKDALE AVENUE

LEEDS LS12 6AP   TEL. 633717

IF YOU WANT A TOP QUALITY DEMO OR MASTER TAPE RECORDED ON THE VERY BEST OF PROFESSIONAL RECORDING EQUIPMENT.

IF YOU WOULD LIKE TO RECORD IN A COMFORTABLE STUDIO WITH EASY ACCESS FOR LOADING AND PARKING.

IF YOU NEED SOMEONE WITH THE MUSICAL AND TECHNICAL EXPERIENCE TO BRING OUT THE BEST IN YOU AND YOUR MUSIC AND WHO CARES MORE ABOUT QUALITY AND YOUR SATISFACTION THAN HOW MUCH THEY CAN MAKE OUT OF YOU.

THEN RING MICK ON LEEDS 633717 to ARRANGE A CALL FOR A COFFEE AND A LOOK-ROUND.

We have recorded masters for:—
ARIOLA EMI SIRE and GRANADA TV
also numerous custom pressings on our own
LUGGAGE LABEL.

RIC~RAC
SOUND STUDIO

Gabriel gets Phil'd in 3rd time round

Peter Gabriel's third album has become something of an event - he's been acclaimed both on the air & in print & it has been hailed as a masterpiece by no less an 'authority' than Derek Jewell of The Sunday Times - so I thought I'd have a listen & see what all the fuss was about - having been, in the dim & distant past, a 'fan' of Gabriel myself & feeling him to be quite an amiable fellow.

The tracks on third are mainly of two sorts. On the one hand there are 'Intruder', 'No Self-Control', 'I Don't Remember', 'Family Snapshot', 'Lead A Normal Life' & 'And Through The Wire', all of which, to some degree, explore states of personal obsession & isolation. On the other, 'Not One of Us' & the much acclaimed 'Biko' are more politically inclined. 'Games Without Frontiers' neatly unites these concerns. A heavily introspective, but brief, instrumental - 'Start' - is thrown in for good measure. The explicit humorous touches that marked much of his work with Genesis as well as his earlier solo efforts are noticeably played down & the music underlines this bleaker perspective.

The most immediately noticeable aspect of the album is the violent, thrusting & at times nerve-grating nature of much of the music on hand. This is effected in a variety of ways. Firstly, rhythm is invariably pushed to the foreground. This is built on the foundations of a drum sound which is cymbal-less, very thick set, relying much on the use of tom-tom & bass drum, at times primitive, restless, lurching & driving. This is accentuated by some pretty hair-raising bass lines from both bass & synthesiser & some of the raunchiest rhythm guitar I've heard for a while (particularly noticeable here is Paul Weller's contribution on 'And Through The Wire'). Over the top, some buzz-saw guitar licks, neat, frenzied sequencer loops & def synthesiser & voice effects & vocal arrangements all contribute to the air of urgency & confusion. At times, by contrast, the music manifests restraint, simplicity & directness as, for example, the arrangement of 'Lead A Normal Life' built up on a sequencer loop & a single-line piano figure, or the spartan drum beat & bagpipe (! Paul McCartney eat your heart out) backdrop of 'Biko'. As ever, Gabriel's capacity for producing a well turned melody & an immediately accessible hook-line is present - apart from 'Biko', 'Lead A Normal Life' & the instrumental, almost every track is easily a potential single. Anybody looking for solo histrionics will be disappointed: everything is subordinated to the goal of well crafted, totally integrated pieces of music - guitar work, for example, from Bob Fripp is in evidence (& as Fripp-like as ever) but strictly bound by its content & augmentative rather than obtrusive.

All of which was pretty much to be expected - Gabriel's musical abilities are undoubted. But the album does leave me dissatisfied - not for musical reasons, mainly for inadequacies in the lyrics. Obviously, for certain artists it would be unfair to be so concerned with the words, but with Gabriel it's pretty clear that they're an important part of the whole so they should stand up to consideration at length. They mar the work for me simply because they attempt to project a significance not actually present & which Gabriel does not seem to have been able to create.

The first track, 'Intruder', is a monologue by a murderous voyeur; the music & words are intended to convey the twisted aspects of his psyche, but almost immediately, in the third line, Gabriel loses track of what he's up to & has him utter: "I know where to find precious things in your cupboards & drawers" when in essence a voyeur/murderer is not concerned with valuables as such, but with the fetishes that fire his libido which could be shoes, photographs, underwear, but certainly not cash & jewelry. When he does get back to his subject it's more in the abstract & lifeless terms of a national health psychiatrist than in the compulsive manner of a monomaniac: "The sense of isolation inspires me... I like the touch & the smell of all the pretty dresses you wear". This lack of feeling for the subject & a tendency to fill in with stock clichés pervades most of the album. Take 'Biko' for example: "You can blow out a candle/But you can't blow out a fire/Once the flame begins to catch/The wind will blow it higher". However much the view that justice will prevail has succoured the hearts of the oppressed, it does not, unfortunately, appear to be borne out by the facts of history as countless groups of people & individuals who have gone to the wall would testify - at best, the belief is comfort in a hopeless situation, at worst an obstacle to effective action. These inadequacies reach their nadir in 'Family Snapshot' - a portrayal of a Lee Harvey Oswald type character who's about to assassinate an important political figure. Again, when he's not reporting the events & stock actions which constitute the stereotyped concept of this situation - "The streets are lined with camera-crews/Everywhere he goes is news" - Gabriel resorts to psychological clichés: "I want to be somebody/You were like that too/If you don't get given you learn to take/And I will take you". Perhaps the song wouldn't be so bad if it wasn't for the awful conclusion - we discover the murderer is motivated by a desire to gain the attention he had not had as a child due to the break-up of his parents' marriage.

It's unfair not to mention that in places the lyrics are pretty good. Take 'Family Snapshot' again. The chorus - "I'm shooting into the light" is neat, pointing up the way the hero is shooting to the attention of the public by shooting down the good aspect of himself. Or 'And Through The Wire', a song about the ambiguities & frustrations of a love relationship where wire is telephone wire, cage wire, trip wire, electric wire, barbed wire, etc. - images which concretely point up the complexities. 'Games Without Frontiers' also stands up to pretty close scrutiny. For the main part, though, I think Gabriel not only encapsulates the profound human mysteries of obsession, isolation, violence & madness in trite formulae, but also fails to convincingly portray them. His vision is buttressed by a cocoon of music (excellent in itself) which gives it emotional plausibility, but it remains aesthetically & intellectually unsound. And I wonder if this is because Gabriel is not so concerned with the issues he raises as he would have us believe. "All you people in TV land/I will wake up your empty shells/Peak time viewing blown in a flash/As I burn into your memory cells..." sings the assassin in 'Family Snapshot', yet it could as easily be Gabriel singing straight at his audience. It seems to me that he is as much concerned to act the role, much romanticised, of the alienated outsider as to understand the grisly reality - & you'll find that kind of thing done far more honestly by the likes of Judas Priest. But with far less skill - you pays yer money & takes yer choice.

Rockabilly Rebs. (continued from page 6)...

& Goodnight Vienna (with his wife): "I wasn't into tuneless new wave, but did want something different from heavy metal. In this music I _really_ get a chance to play guitar &, though it was a long way from what I imagined I'd be doing, I'm totally hooked on it now. Within the 12-bar framework, there's a lot of melody & it offers endless possibilities for a guitarist. I now use a very clean guitar sound where I used to use a heavy metal drone." The others told me that it's his guitar-work & heavy rock background that make the group sound distinctively different from other rockabilly combos. They're a club band, but are keen to try gigs in rock clubs &/or on the college circuit.

Too tall? Balding? Sexual hang-ups & anal acne? Missed an issue of W.C.R.? Car won't start? No milk this morning? All your worries are over! Astonishing medical breakthru! Back issues available (50p each incl. p&p.) from W.C.R., 5 BEECH TERR., UNDERCLIFFE, BRADFORD, BD3 0PY, W. YORKS.

cuba

I first bumped into Cuba at Ric-Rac Studios in Leeds a few weeks ago when they were recording their second single - Wireless World - which is to be released by Ariola. The pre-release tape is reviewed elsewhere in this issue. I was going to interview the band, but we were all too busy, so Dave Parkinson (kbds/voc & songwriter) sent me a copy of a hypothetical grilling of himself by me, so what follows is:-

A FAKED INTERVIEW WITH CUBA'S DAVE PARKINSON:

NT: How did the band get together?
DP: I used to play kbds & write for The Sneakers. That band fell apart in mid'79 - a very frustrating time - the agency folded, we smashed up our van, recorded a single for Phonogram (Teenagers in Love) which they didn't release. Eventually, our gtr, bass & drums left to join The Roy Sundholm Band. In the interim, we'd recorded a demo with a girl singer Ellie Gant, at Ric-Rac, which I produced. Unfortunately she turned out sounding like a D.Harry clone, so after the rest of the band split I got to know Josie (voc) & Phil (dms); rerecorded their tracks onto the demo & sent it off to record co.s in desperation. Straightaway, Nomis (the A&R company for Ariola) picked up on it & offered us a deal with album options - wacko! we thought.
NT: I hear they released that demo, unaltered, as the first single (Furtive Winks/Valkyrie of Love:Ariola AHA561).
DP: Yeh. They couldn't believe it was done on 8-track I've produced demos for other bands at Ric-Rac (like Shake Appeal, The Mirror Boys & The Neat) & reckon it's the best 8-track outside London. You couldn't hope to work with a more sympathetic & helpful engineer than Mick Robson. Now he's gone full-time, I'd recommend Ric-Rac to any band wanting a class demo.
NT: The second single's a bit different - why did you stick with Ric-Rac for it?
DP: Well, there are drawbacks in mastering a single on 8-track - e.g. we had to bounce down 2 gtr tracks + 2 synth tracks onto 1 track - but we got an excellent raunchy sound. It's so easy to submerge your musical personality in a bigger studio - not so at Ric-Rac.
NT: So when's the 2nd single being released by Ariola?
DP: Har-di-har. Let me say we're very down on Nomis & Ariola. Basically they're full of shit. They haven't 2 brain cells to rub together. They failed to promote the first single & they've no idea what to do with the 2nd. What with the recession hitting the music biz, they're all shit-scared to commit themselves to anything - it means putting their jobs on the line...
NT: (after DP has expounded at length on the above topic) OK, what's the current line-up then?
DP: Well, after we signed to Ariola, we drafted in Bob & Baz (b & gtr) from the defunct teeny-pop band Strangeways. After heavy rehearsals, on the eve of our first gig, they made a 'tactical withdrawal', but we're still good mates -they're ace musicians & writers. We got onto our new guitarist, Graham Turner, through Ade (Agony Column's sound engineer) - to whom many thanks. Graham & Paddy Kogan (bass player with The Squares) played on the 2nd single, but we've just got permanent bassist, Mac - so the new line-up is yours truly plus:-

- The Rt. Hon. Josephine Kennington-Kennington on lead larynx. As soon as I met her I became enchanted by her phenomenal pair of lungs. A former deb., she astounded the party set by arriving at her coming out ball on a Triumph 750 (honest!).
- Mac on bass. Rumoured to be a long-lost relative of the Mactavish of Mactavish. Plays a Rickenbacker with a customised lower cutaway to accommodate his enormous dangling sporran.
- Gorgeous Graham Turner (who used to go out with my cousin Vicky - ed.) on guitar. Actually Bill Nelson's smarter brother (clock those pallid, pinched features!). He gives guitar lessons at Coda (plug), but we don't hold it against him.
- Phil Parkin on drums. A former trainee hod-carrier, he flunked the exams & became a demolition expert. In fact if you listen to Wireless World, you'll realise he's not actually playing drums - we taped him knocking down an outside toilet.

NT: Finally, what about 'musical policy' (as they say) for the future?
DP: Well, with Sneakers I wrote mainly commercial pop songs. I still have a penchant for really crass pop (like the B-side of the 2nd single), but we're becoming very, very different - a whole lot more adventurous. My ideal band, I think, would be an amalgam of The Human League, Joy Division, Weather Report, Desmond Dekker, Charlie Drake & Nervous Norvus. We'll be working with Bill Nelson in Autumn - so that should produce some goodies. Also, Phil & I recently worked with The Mirror Boys, live & on their single & were quite influenced by their song-writing approach.
— UNINTERVIEWED BY NICK TOCZEK.

Contact: Mark Saunders (manager) on Wakefield 70211 (work) or 0904-703706 (home).

LUCKY STRIKE

Line-up: Grom Kelly (voc/harp), Peter O'Grady (kbds/voc), Ian Booth (tenor sax), Mick Robinson (gtr), Chris Swindells (bass/voc), John Shepard (dms) & Roger Pond-Jones (guest harp).

The band's history is as long as it is involved, but to be as brief as possible, those of us who remember Spiral Highway will know of Grom & John. John joined with Peter in Owl, & Chris & Mick were playing in Martha's Graveyard. Chris branched out into country-rock when he joined Ten-legged Friend, & some very short-lived bands ensued, such as Dear John with Ian & Peter playing. John meanwhile, having left Sneakers, phoned Grom to see whether Lucky Strike was feasible. After 6 months or so of loose arrangements, the band reached its present form, & it was Peter who listed some songs, saying "Let's play these". A fixed line-up in the band with a variable but neatly arranged set brought requests for more gigs. The band as a principle, however, are playing just for fun. They've been around long enough to know better than to proclaim themselves stars of any magnitude. They're just good musicians playing good-time R&B & soul music. They don't play hits - or rather if they do, the hits are mid-60's ones played with real feeling. The band like the audience to have a good time, & if they went to dance, so much the better. Lucky Strike are based in Leeds, but might venture further.
— INTERVIEWED BY KEN TURNER.

Contact: John Shepard on Leeds 756070.

W.C.R.TISTS...

Stan Engel ~ our regular cartoonist since issue 1 ~ has done the cover design for Ram Records' compilation album "The Art of Solving Problems".

Kev Hopgood ~ our other cartoonist has a comic strip mag. 'Crisis'. No.1, just published, features the 1st part of The Rise & Fall of Johnny No-one. It's great value at only 15p + s.a.e. from Kev at 101 Manchester Rd., Sleithwaite, nr. Huddersfield, W. Yorks. Get it!

Mo Marlouf (foto'd above) ~ designer of the covers of W.C.R's Nos. 4,7 & 8 ~ has just spent 10 days training with Hipgnosis (the famous London design co. whose work includes L.P. covers for Pink Floyd, Led Zepplin, 10cc etc. He's a graphic design student at Bradford College & will be social secretary next year.

ALL 3 ARE AVAILABLE FOR ANY COMMISSIONS & ARE OPEN TO OFFERS & IDEAS. CONTACT THROUGH W.C.R. (address/phone no. in front of mag.)

Two Cuban heels, one with a severe dose of Parkinson's disease.

LIVE IN LEEDS x2

Andy S. gets a bit of personal TREATMENT

This is the age of live music, eh? Well, will someone please tell that to all the narrow-minded little jerks who will be going along to see City Limits, Side Effect & Agony Column in the coming weeks at The Marquis. All the above-named groups are good - but so are Treatment. So why the total lack of human activity tonight? If it wasn't for myself & my mate, the audience would have numbered NIL.

O.K. - so there were no advertisements in the local paper, no posters around the town, & the Dallas repeats were just starting on BBC2 - but surely, after filling The Royal Park & packing The White Lion in the previous week, surely they are justified a greater audience than just two people!

Despite the empty spaces, & the obvious feeling of despair through the entire band, they all got up on stage & dished out a very professional 13-song set. Opening with 'Birth Certificate', the immediate & lasting impression was that this was going to be a very very good set - & it was! 'You Really Got Me' & 'Ego Voyeur' followed up & the catchy little riffs & choruses showed that despite the massive lack of audience, this was going to be no practice session.

'Safe & Sound', 'Now You See Me, Now You Don't' & 'Jesus Wants Me For A Sunbeam' proved to be the highlight of the evening. They typified the excellent quality of this pure-pop set, & this band, given just a tiny bit of luck, may just make it.

I'm sorry it's a kind of patchy review, but with only two people there (& one of them suffering from a cold) it was hard to put this gig into any kind of perspective. However, this is a good band, so I want all the able-bodied people who read this to get off their bums & go & see them - right?!

-reviewed by Andy Stevens

FAB POOS & their DINKY DOOS

Line up: Tony de Meur - ld.voc/ld.gtr; Richie Robinson - bass/voc; Bobby Valentino - violin/gtr/mandolin/voc; Bryn Burrows - drum.

The Fabulous Poodles are a band everyone seems to like, but no-one goes overboard on them. They were formed in mid-76 when the remnants of The Poodles, Tony & Bobby were joined by Richie & Bryn. They came to the attention of many whilst supporting Tom Petty on his tour of America, & have since always seemed to be on the fringe of something big. They are a very tight rock'n'roll band with an extraordinary knack of being able to captivate any audience & then proceed to keep them engrossed in a whirlwind set.

'Suicide Bridge' opened the evening, with 'Chicago Boxcar' following up, sounding for all the world like a very early Stones number. It was clearly evident at this early stage that the band genuinely enjoyed their music (a state of mind which is sadly lacking in many of today's top groups) & a crowded Fforde Greene warmly appreciated an hour of nothing but 100% effort.

The first two of five new numbers on the set list proved to be the highlights of a set which contained no bad songs, yet never produced the spark to set the whole thing alight. 'Poison Pen' & 'Package Deals', the new numbers, along with the band's personal favourite 'Talking Trash', made the effort on the Poodles' side all worthwhile.

With the two 45's available on Pye 'Bionic Man' & 'Wonk Shy' offered to round off the night in fine style, I set off home very worried: The Fab Poos' new material suggests that they are indeed heading for something big, but I have a nagging doubt that someone might just beat them to it!

-reviewed by Andy Stevens.

unCLASSIFIED ADS

EXPERIENCED PRODUCER LOOKING FOR BANDS WITH IMMINENT STUDIO WORK - DEMOS OR DISCS. DON'T WASTE MONEY HOPING FOR A GOOD END RESULT... BE SURE OF ONE. FOR FURTHER DETAILS, RING LINDSAY ON LEEDS 623306.

VOCALIST/GUITARIST SEEKS MUSICIANS TO FORM BAND. MODERN STUFF, ENTHUSIASM MORE IMPORTANT THAN EXPERIENCE. CONTACT: JOHN, 40 GEORGE ST., MILNSBRIDGE, HUDDERSFIELD.

RAM REPAIR SERVICE. ALL GROUP GEAR FIXED & FIDDLED WITH AT THE STUDIO REPAIR SHOP. PHONE LEEDS 445044 FOR DETAILS

CLASSIFIED ADS. ARE ONLY 10p per word
SELL GEAR, FIND MUSOS, OFFER
SERVICES, ETC. - YOU KNOW IT MAKES ~~MEMONEY~~ SENSE!

!! FUTURAMA 2

QUEENS HALL, LEEDS

SAT. 13th SEPT. SOUXIE & THE BANSHEES, BILL NELSON, ROBERT FRIPP & BARRY ANDREWS' LEAGUE OF GENTLEMEN, SIMPLE MINDS, U2, WASTED YOUTH, CLOCK DVA, ALTERED IMAGES, MODERN ENGLISH, BLAH BLAH BLAH, MIRROR BOYS, VENA CAVA, ACROBATS OF DESIRE, Y?, MUSIC FOR PLEASURE, DISTRIBUTORS, SOFT CELL, GUY JACKSON, EATEN ALIVE BY INSECTS.

SUN. 14th SEPT. GARY GLITTER, ATHLETICO SPIZZ 80, PSYCHEDELIC FURS, HAZEL O'CONNOR'S MEGAHYPE, 4BE2's, YOUNG MARBLE GIANTS, SOFT BOYS, DURUTTI COLUMN, CLASSIX NOUVEAUX, BRIAN BRAIN, BLURT, NOT SENSIBLES, DESPERATE BICYCLES, FRANTIC ELEVATORS, FLOWERS, BOOTS FOR DANCING, VICA VERSA, ARTERY, NAKED LUNCH, HOUSEHOLD NAME.

Also LAZERS, VIDEOGAMES, STALLS, etc.

!! FUTURAMA 2

TICKETS:- £6 per day or £10 for both days
AVAILABLE FROM:-
JOHN KEENAN, P.O. BOX HH9, LEEDS LS8 1AN.
+ HMV Bradford + VIRGIN & JUMBO in Leeds

WARLORD

Line-up: Stephen 'Stef' Erdos - ld voc/rm gtr; Steve 'K.K.' Davis - ld gtr/bkg voc; Keith Graham - ld gtr/kbds; Mick Noonan - bass/bkg voc; Ian Shaw - dms.

Warlord are the successors to Shaftdrive (see WCR's 1 & 3), a Bradford-based heavy metal outfit of much potential, who split at the beginning of the year in acrimonious circumstances. While drummer Pete Emmonds has been in & out of Trampus & bassist Rick Ironmonger played with Beezer Bob & The Brainwaves before finding a new home with Vex, Steve & Keith decided to keep their lead guitar partnership together & build a new band.

Things began to fall into place for the two guitarists when Keith was invited to rehearse with Stef & Mick & subsequently got Steve involved. As well as hitting it off musically, they found themselves relatively free of the ego trips & personality clashes which had destroyed Shaftdrive; by the end of February the four had agreed to form a band together & began writing new songs & rehearsing intensively while seeking a drummer.

Mick is a classically-trained & first linked up with Stef some four years ago, teaching him to play guitar. They ran a band called Paradox during the latter half of '78, weaving a curious line between new wave & Motorhead-style HM. Following Paradox's demise, Stef & Mick simply rehearsed & auditioned for close on a year. Hearing of the Shaftdrive split, they first asked Rick to play bass for them, but he vascillated & in the meantime Mick decided to apply his own considerable talent to learning bass. They then made the connection with Keith & Steve.

Under the name of Bloody Sunday, the new band made its debut at Queen's Hall during the Bradford Festival in April, with Japanese Soldiers' John Binns standing in on drums, & were well received. A few days later the same line-up played at Scamps in Bradford; following which the four principals went back to rehearsing & auditioning.

They met their future drummer at Scamps when he, in a state of considerable inebriation, caused a scene by attempting to jam with the understandably reluctant Backslider! The band met Ian again the following night in The Vaults Bar, discovered that he was in fact a drummer of some experience, & asked him to rehearse with them.

With Ian in place and under the new name of Warlord, the band played at Scamps again in late June & followed that with a particularly successful set at The White Lion, Huddersfield. No, with the advice of ex-Azel bassist Barry More (who is also acting as soundman), they are lining up a series of late summer gigs.

Inevitably, Warlord's sound is similar to that of Shaftdrive - especially as they include 3 old numbers ('Trees', 'Solitary' & 'No Return') in the present set - but the new band insist that their sound is more clearly defined:-
"It's a lot faster than Shaftdrive was. We've stopped trying to please both punks & bikers. We're just aiming for the heavy metal audience. A lot more skill has gone into it."

~ written & researched by Keith E. Rice

Contact: Stef on B'ford 31930.

AUGUST '80

If in doubt, just stay home & watch telly — when the bomb drops, whether you went to a gig in Aug/Sept. '80 won't matter a whole lot, will it?

Date	Gigs	Date	Gigs
FRI 1	Cleopatra's, Huddersfield = ATHLETICO SPIZZ 80 + support. Fforde Greene, Leeds = LIMELIGHT.	**SAT 16**	Mitre, Knaresborough = NOSFERATU V. Royal Park, Leeds = NIGHT TRAIN. Palm Cove, Bradford = ODESSOS. Haddon Hall, Leeds = KNIFE EDGE. Funhouse Bar, Keighley (lunch) = MYSTERIOUS FOOTSTEPS. Fforde Green, Leeds = T.B.A. White Lion, Huddersfield = THE GUESTS. Staging Post, Leeds = AGONY COLUMN.
SAT 2	Thirsk & Sowerby Institute, Thirsk = ROCKABILLY REBS. Staging Post, Leeds = DEVOTION. Castleford Trades & Labour Club = TAROT. Royal Park, Leeds = REDEYE. Princeville, Bradford = ADDICTION + SELECTIVE FORCE. Funhouse Bar, Keighley (lunch) = THE QUICK. Haddon Hall, Leeds = THE ZIPPS. Fforde Greene, Leeds = THE INVADERS + DODGY TACTICS. White Lion, Huddersfield = GLOSSY MAGS.	**SUN 17**	Huddersfield Rugby Club = VOTRE MILITAIRE. Haddon Hall, Leeds = THE SWITCH. Vaults Bar, Bradford = STYROS. Fforde Greene, Leeds = T.B.A. Sandmartin, Airdale, Castleford = TAROT. White Lion, Huddersfield (lunch) = PRIVATE DICKS; (eve) = DOTS. Princeville, Bradford (lunch) = WILLFUL DAMAGE. Dock Green, Leeds = AMAZING GUFFSTRUT. Palm Cove, Bradford = JED'S BLUES BAND. Staging Post, Leeds = ALWOODLEY JETS + THE MOSS. Panache, Bradford = ABRASIVE WHEELS.
SUN 3	Vaults Bar, Bradford = SWAKARA. Staging Post, Leeds = REDEYE. Princeville, Bradford (lunch) = CONFESSOR. Royal Park, Leeds = 156 BAND. Palm Cove, Bradford = JED'S BLUES BAND. Panache, Bradford = DISCHARGE. Fforde Greene, Leeds = DEVOTION. White Lion, Huddersfield (lunch) = PRIVATE DICKS; (eve) = THE POTS.	**MON 18**	Royal Park, Leeds = NOSFERATU V. Arts Centre, York = VINYL DINERS. Marquis of Granby, Leeds = MIDDLE 8. Speakeasy, Wakefield = TAROT. Fforde Greene, Leeds = YACKETY YAK. White Lion, Huddersfield = ORAL SAX.
MON 4	Tiffany's, Leeds = MIRROR BOYS + LITTLE BROTHER. Marquis of Granby, Leeds = TWISTED NERVE. Thurnscoe Hotel, Barnsley = LIMELIGHT. Roundhill Club, Castleford = TAROT. Fforde Greene, Leeds = LITTLE TONY & THE TENNESSEE REBELS. White Lion, Huddersfield = ORAL SAX. J.P. + A.T.N.	**TUE 19**	Vaults Bar, Bradford = NOSFERATU V. Palm Cove, Bradford = THE JAZZ ROCK BAND. Rose & Crown, Ilkley = BUTB. Kings Head, Keighley = THE SYSTEM (formerly JOHN DOE).
TUE 5	Vaults Bar, Bradford = MIDDLE 8. Palm Cove, Bradford = THE JAZZ ROCK BAND. Rose & Crown, Ilkley = THE ELEMENTS. Kings Head, Keighley = PYRAMID. Royal Park, Leeds = ROUGH JUSTICE.	**WED 20**	Vaults Bar, Bradford = ACCELERATORS. Speakeasy, Wakefield = TAROT. White Lion, Huddersfield = THE FLOOR.
WED 6	Vaults Bar, Bradford = WARLORD. White Lion, Huddersfield = THE ZIPPS. Royal Park, Leeds = MIDDLE 8.	**THU 21**	Princeville, Bradford = E.F. BAND. White Lion, Huddersfield = T.B.A. Royal Park, Leeds = SLIDER. Fan Club, Leeds = BAUHAUS + film show.
THU 7	Fforde Greene, Leeds = GIRLS SCHOOL + NOSFERATU V. Princeville, Bradford = LIMELIGHT. Palm Cove, Bradford = THE KLINGONS. Fforde Greene, Leeds = GIRLS SCHOOL + MUNROES. Royal Park, Leeds = SLIDER. Fan Club, Leeds = PETER HAMMILL + NEW OPERA.	**FRI 22**	Cleopatra's, Huddersfield = T.B.A. Palm Cove, Bradford = T.B.A. Fforde Greene, Leeds = RAY CAMPI'S ROCKABILLY REBELS.
FRI 8	Cleopatra's, Huddersfield = SLAUGHTER & THE DOGS + NOT SENSIBLES. Fforde Greene, Leeds = JAB-JAB. Unity Hall, Wakefield = ULTRAVOX + MODERN MAN.	**SAT 23**	Comrades Club, Bedale = ROCKABILLY REBS. Staging Post, Leeds = T.B.A. Seacroft Hotel, Leeds = TWISTED NERVE. Royal Park, Leeds = NEW KING SNAKES. Palm Cove, Bradford = TONY TUFF & band. Haddon Hall, Leeds = CONFESSOR. Funhouse Bar, Keighley (lunch) = T.B.A. Fforde Greene, Leeds = WHITE SPIRIT + STILL EARTH. Dacre Village Hall (nr Harrogate) = OSCULATORS + NOT SENSIBLES + COLLUSIONS OF ROMANCE + others. White Lion, Huddersfield = PRIVATE DICKS.
SAT 9	Progressive W.M.C., Burnley = ROCKABILLY REBS. Staging Post, Leeds = MUNROES. Trades & Labour Club, Castleford = BLUSH. Royal Park, Leeds = ALIBI. Palm Cove, Bradford = PAT KELLY + backing band. Funhouse Bar, Keighley (lunch) = SYSTEM. Haddon Hall, Leeds = AGONY COLUMN. Fforde Greene, Leeds = CHEATERS + GRAFF SPEE. White Lion, Huddersfield = TALISMAN.	**SUN 24**	Seacroft Hotel, Leeds = TWISTED NERVE. Haddon Hall, Leeds = SIDE EFFECT. Vaults Bar, Bradford = KYRO. Fforde Greene, Leeds = RAM JAM BAND. Blackamore Head, Pontefract = TAROT. White Lion, Huddersfield (lunch) = WAMMAKK JAMMERS (eve) DOTS. Princeville, Bradford (lunch) = CHAIRS. Dock Green, Leeds = AMAZING GUFFSTRUT (lunch). Palm Cove, Bradford = JED'S BLUES BAND. Staging Post, Leeds = DODGY TACTICS. Panache, Bradford = SHATTERED DOLLS. Royal Park, Leeds = CONFESSOR. Fan Club, Leeds = RICO.
SUN 10	Vaults Bar, Bradford = TALISMAN. Fforde Greene, Leeds = E.F. BAND. Staging Post, Leeds = DEDRINGER. White Lion, Huddersfield (lunch) = MIDDLE 8; (eve) = 7 YEAR ITCH. Princeville, Bradford (lunch) = STILL EARTH. Dock Green, Leeds (lunch) = AMAZING GUFFSTRUT. Palm Cove, Bradford = JED'S BLUES BAND. Staging Post, Leeds = DEDRINGER. Panache, Bradford = THE NOT SENSIBLES. Fan Club, Leeds = MERTON PARKAS + BEATS WORKING. Haddon Hall, Leeds = SHAKE APPEAL.	**MON 25**	Marquis of Granby, Leeds = ADA WILSON & KEEPING DARK. Fforde Greene, Leeds = DEDRINGER. Royal Park, Leeds = THE SWITCH.
MON 11	Marquis of Granby, Leeds = AGONY COLUMN. Roundhill, Castleford = LIMELIGHT. Fforde Greene, Leeds = RWT ROCKERS. Royal Park, Leeds = GOFF JACKSON & THE HUNS.	**TUE 26**	Vaults Bar, Bradford = THE GUESTS. Palm Cove, Bradford = THE JAZZ ROCK BAND. Rose & Crown, Ilkley = SYSTEM. Kings Head, Keighley = XPOZEZ.
TUE 12	Vaults Bar, Bradford = THE PRESS. Palm Cove, Bradford = THE JAZZ ROCK BAND. Scamps, Bradford = VEX. Rose & Crown, Ilkley = JOCK HUNTERS FIG. Kings Head, Keighley = KNIFE EDGE.	**WED 27**	Vaults Bar, Bradford = OPTIC NERVE. White Lion, Huddersfield = BACKSLIDER.
WED 13	Vaults Bar, Bradford = ROUGH JUSTICE. Yarborough Club, Doncaster = TAROT. White Lion, Huddersfield = CONFESSOR.	**THU 28**	Wombwell Reform Club, Barnsley = LIMELIGHT. Princeville, Bradford = RACE AGAINST TIME. Royal Park, Leeds = GLOSSY MAGS. Fan Club, Leeds = T.B.A.
THU 14	Princeville, Bradford = ALEC JOHNSON BAND. Royal Park, Leeds = KNIFE EDGE. Fan Club, Leeds = WASTED YOUTH + ACROBATS OF DESIRE.	**FRI 29**	Cleopatra's, Huddersfield = BAD MANNERS. Palm Cove, Bradford = T.B.A. Fforde Greene, Leeds = DICK SMITH BAND.
FRI 15	Gate Hotel, Leeds = NOSFERATU V. Cleopatra's, Huddersfield = T.B.A. Palm Cove, Bradford = THE SCENE (farewell gig). Fforde Greene, Leeds = TURBO. Fan Club, Leeds = MO-DETTES + support.	**SAT 30**	Stone Chair Variety Club, Halifax = ROCKABILLY REBS. Staging Post, Leeds = T.B.A. Good Mood Club, Halifax = DEDRINGER. Royal Park, Leeds = KNIFE EDGE. Trades & Labour Club, Castleford = LIMELIGHT. Funhouse Bar, Keighley (lunch) = THE ELEMENTS. Palm Cove, Bradford = SPLASH. Haddon Hall, Leeds = LUCKY STRIKE. White Lion, Huddersfield = T.B.A.
		SUN 31	Dudley Hill & Tong W.M.C., Bradford = ROCKABILLY REBS. Haddon Hall, Leeds = LUCKY STRIKE. Vaults Bar, Bradford = PROPOSITION 31. White Lion, Huddersfield (lunch) = MIDDLE 8 (eve) = AIRKRAFT. Princeville, Bradford (lunch) = NEW KING SNAKE. Dock Green, Leeds = AMAZING GUFFSTRUT. Palm Cove, Bradford = JED'S BLUES BAND. Staging Post, Leeds = THE NEAT. Panache, Bradford = SAIGON (electronic, not punk). Fan Club, Leeds = T.B.A.

It's... BAND AID

↑ ↑ ↑ ↑ ↑ ↑

John Peel: "What's Band Aid about this time?" "OH LORD ABOVE, PLEASE Attila The Nun: "Publicising gigs." STOP ALL WAR & FEED THE Queen Mother: "Charming, utterly charming." STARVING & MAKE TONIGHT'S J.P. + A.T.N.: "Happy birthday, ma'am!" GIG A SELL OUT... AMEN"

Ideally, here's how to do a complete money-is-no-object publicity campaign for your band:

① General posters saying that your band's coming/gigging round the area/fab 'n' groovy/available for funerals & christenings/whatever — i.e. bright posters that keep yr band's name around even when yr not gigging. These & all other publicity should have the band's name writ large in standard logo form (i.e. always write it the same way). NB. Fly posting's illegal - so do it yourself! ② Spray/chalk stuff about the band wherever you can & put up/hand out printed stickers - more illegality. fun, huh?! ③ Design/have designed some headed notepaper (do the master copy in black on white paper & take it to a cheap printer to get copies run off on coloured paper). Use this for all your press releases. ④ 1st press release = letter saying the band exists, who you are, what you're doing, where you can be contacted - keep it concise but lively & interesting. Mail to: NME, NMN, Sounds, RM, MM, MO, ZZ (addresses opposite) + local fan zines/rock mags (& + a few outside your area too - Rough Trade & Better Badges stock most fanzines) + local newspapers/weekly advertiser, etc. + local radio & T.V. stations (addresses from library or specific newsmen, DJs or producers who might be interested - if in doubt, ring to ask who might take an interest in rock) + Radio One (addressed to specific DJ or his producer c/o BBC Radio One, Broadcasting House, London W1A (AA). This 1st press release can also go to anyone else (agency, record co, etc) that you hope to seduce with yr musak. You can include photos, stickers, badges, business cards, etc. ⑤ Oh yes - get Better Badges or some other co. to do your badges. ⑥ And get business cards run off. ⑦ 2nd press release (sent out 2 weeks before start of month in which you've a bunch of gigs lined up) - list gigs in coming month (& yr tour) & enclose live photo(s) + repeat of basic info about band (2/3 lines or so) - most important that this goes to newsdesk/news editor on national/local media. ⑧ Posters listing all gigs lined up to go up throughout area your touring - especially in/around venues, with appropriate venue highlighted in the list - looks impressive. ⑨ 3rd press release - to go out 2 weeks before the gig, listing it & any other gig(s) in that week - this release being addressed to the gig guide & sent to weekly national music papers, radio programmes, etc. ⑩ Posters to go up/be sent out 2 weeks before the gig - this time just advertising the specific gig. ⑪ Leaflets run off & distributed (in venues, music shops, record shops, libraries, up in shop windows, etc.) + handed out to treadies (!) - these to list gigs, give a bit of info on band, press quotes (the good ones!) etc. ⑫ More posters to go up every 2 or 3 days until gig ⑬ Talk about the gig(s) wherever you get a chance - word of mouth is best publicity of all. ⑭ Any extra, gimmick, idea to further hype yourselves, the gigs, the venue, the band, etc. DO AS MUCH OF THIS AS YOU CAN AFFORD, PUT IN A GOOD GIG, GET FAMOUS. AWFUL, ISN'T IT !!!

scribbled by... Nick Toczek (again!).

SEPTEMBER '80

On 20th Sept. I'll be 30 years old & will be blowing out the kandels at The Royal Park with my band. Be there! See how OLD I look!

MON 1
- Marquis of Granby, Leeds = TELEGRAPH.
- Fforde Greene, Leeds = FREDDIE FINGERS LEE.
- White Lion, Huddersfield = ORAL SAX.
- Royal Park, Leeds = WOOLLY DRUNKS.

TUE 2
- Vault's Bar, Bradford = NEW KING SNAKES.
- Scamps, Bradford = HARSH WORDS.
- Palm Cove, Bradford = THE JAZZ ROCK BAND.
- Rose & Crown, Ilkley = CITY LIMITS.
- Kings Head, Keighley = CHAINSAW.

WED 3
- Vault's Bar, Bradford = SEVEN YEAR ITCH.
- White Lion, Huddersfield = VOGUE + AMAZING GUFFSTRUT.
- Royal Park, Leeds = GOFF JACKSON & THE HUNS.

THU 4
- Princeville, Bradford = SLENDER THREAD
- Fforde Greene, Leeds = ANGELWITCH.
- Royal Park = AGONY COLUMN (pending confirmation)
- Fan Club, Leeds = BRIAN BRAIN (a.k.a. Martin Atkins ex-P.I.L.) + TEMPORARY TITLE.

FRI 5
- Palm Cove, Bradford = NEW ULTERIOR MOTIVES + TWISTED NERVE.
- Cleopatra's, Huddersfield = T.B.A.

SAT 6
- Bowling Club, Ripon = ROCKABILLY REBS. Funhouse Bar, Keighley (lunch) = T.B.A.
- Palm Cove, Bradford = S.O.S. STEEL BAND.
- Haddon Hall, Leeds = SHAKE APPEAL.
- Fforde Greene, Leeds = CIRCLES.
- White Lion, Huddersfield = GLOSSY MAGS.
- Staging Post, Leeds = THE MUNROES.

SUN 7
- Walton Miners' Welfare, Castleford = ROCKABILLY REBS. Fforde Greene, Leeds = STRAY.
- Vaults Bar, Bradford = SIDE EFFECT. White Lion, Huddersfield (lunch) = PRIVATE DICKS : (eve) = DOTS.
- Princeville, Bradford (lunch) = ROUGH JUSTICE. Dock Green, Leeds = AMAZING GUFFSTRUT (lunch).
- Palm Cove, Bradford = JED'S BLUES BAND. Royal Park, Leeds = MIRROR BOYS.
- Panache, Bradford = THE WILD BOYS + THE SAMPLES. Staging Post, Leeds = TALISMAN.
- Haddon Hall, Leeds = DODGY TACTICS.

MON 8
- Marquis of Granby, Leeds = STURGEON ROW.
- Roundhill Club, Castleford = DEDRINGER.
- Fforde Greene, Leeds = FLYING SAUCERS.

TUE 9
- Scamps, Bradford = NEW ULTERIOR MOTIVES + HEAVEN SEVENTEEN.
- Vault's Bar, Bradford = STUFFED BADGERS.
- Palm Cove, Bradford = THE JAZZ ROCK BAND.
- Rose & Crown, Ilkley = BACKSLIDER.
- Kings Head, Keighley = THE ELEMENTS.

WED 10
- Vault's Bar, Bradford = THE WALL.
- White Lion, Huddersfield = T.B.A.

THU 11
- Princeville, Bradford = DEDRINGER.
- Fforde Greene, Leeds = LUTHER MASSON BLUES BAND.

FRI 12
- Cleopatra's, Huddersfield = T.B.A.
- Palm Cove, Bradford = GREGORY ISAACS' package.
- Kings Hall, Ilkley = CHAINSAW + JEDEDIAH SKRUFF.

SAT 13
- Barnsley Civic Hall = LIMELIGHT. Royal Park, Leeds = SPINOES.
- Palm Cove, Bradford = T.B.A. Funhouse Bar, Keighley (lunch) = T.B.A.
- Haddon Hall, Leeds = AGONY COLUMN. Queens Hall, Leeds = FUTURAMA 2 (day 1)
- Fforde Greene, Leeds = CHEVY. Souxie & Banshees / Bill Nelson / Robert Fripp/U2
- White Lion, Huddersfield = THE GUESTS. Simple Mindy/etc. SEE PAGE 9 FOR FULL DETAILS.
- Staging Post, Leeds = T.B.A.

SUN 14
- Ledley W.M.C., Huddersfield = ROCKABILLY REBS. Panache, Bradford = THE WALL.
- Vault's Bar, Bradford = T.B.A. Haddon Hall, Leeds = LUIGI ANA DA BOYS.
- Staging Post, Leeds = LIMELIGHT. Fforde Greene, Leeds = QUARTZ.
- Princeville, Bradford (lunch) = SPIDER. White Lion, Huddersfield (lunch) = MIDDLE 8 : (eve) = HARLEQUINS.
- Palm Cove, Bradford = JED'S BLUES BAND. Queens Hall, Leeds = FUTURAMA 2 (day 2) Gary Glitter/Sprzz/P.Furs/etc.
- Dock Green, Leeds = AMAZING GUFFSTRUT (lunch)

MON 15
- Marquis of Granby, Leeds = NEW ULTERIOR MOTIVES.
- St. George's Hall, Bradford = SECRET AFFAIR.
- Sandmartin, Airdale, Castleford = TAROT.
- Princeville, Bradford (FREE CONCERT!!) = STORM TROOPER.
- Fforde Greene, Leeds = GENA & THE ROCKIN' REBELS.
- White Lion, Huddersfield = ORAL SAX.

TUE 16
- Kings Head, Keighley = NEW ULTERIOR MOTIVES.
- Vault's Bar, Bradford = CRAFTY AVENUE.
- Scamps, Bradford = OPTIC NERVE.
- Palm Cove, Bradford = THE JAZZ ROCK BAND.
- Rose & Crown, Ilkley = TOKYO ROSE.

WED 17
- Vault's Bar, Bradford = RABSTALLION.
- White Lion, Huddersfield = NEW KING SNAKES.
- Royal Park, Leeds = KNIFE EDGE.

THU 18
- Princeville, Bradford = WHITE SPIRIT.
- Royal Park, Leeds = ACCELERATORS.

FRI 19
- Cleopatra's, Huddersfield = T.B.A.
- St. George's Hall, Bradford = SHAWADDYWADDY.
- Palm Cove, Bradford = BUDDY VALENTEEN & THE LONELY HEARTS (ex-Scene).

SAT 20
- Royal Park, Leeds = NEW ULTERIOR MOTIVES. Staging Post, Leeds = KNIFE EDGE.
- Tingley W.M.C., Leeds = ROCKABILLY REBS. Funhouse Bar, Keighley (lunch) = T.B.A.
- Palm Cove, Bradford = T.B.A.
- Haddon Hall, Leeds = ALWOODLEY JETS.
- White Lion, Huddersfield = TREATMENT.
- Seacroft Hotel, Leeds = AMAZING GUFFSTRUT.

SUN 21
- Princeville, Bradford (lunch) = BABY TUCKOO. Fforde Greene, Leeds = TYGERS OF PAN TANG.
- Fforde Greene, Leeds = DEDRINGER. White Lion, Huddersfield (lunch) = T.B.A. : (eve) = THE DOTS.
- Blackamore Head, Pontefract = TAROT. Dock Green, Leeds (lunch) = AMAZING GUFFSTRUT.
- Palm Cove, Bradford = JED'S BLUES BAND. Staging Post, Leeds = CUBA.
- Panache, Bradford = T.B.A. Royal Park, Leeds = HELTER SKELTER.
- Haddon Hall, Leeds = RED EYE.

MON 22
- Marquis of Granby, Leeds = STRANGER THAN FICTION.
- Vault's Bar, Bradford = ULTERIOR MOTIVES.
- Fforde Greene, Leeds = BLACK JACKS.

TUE 23
- Scamps, Bradford = THE ELEMENTS.
- Vault's Bar, Bradford = DISCO STUDENTS.
- Palm Cove, Bradford = THE JAZZ ROCK BAND.
- Rose & Crown, Ilkley = PROPHET.
- Kings Head, Keighley = NEUTRAL ZONE.

WED 24
- Vault's Bar, Bradford = CONTROL VOICE.
- White Lion, Huddersfield = THE SHEDS.
- Royal Park, Leeds = DISCO STUDENTS.

THU 25
- Princeville, Bradford = T.B.A.
- Fforde Greene, Leeds = ATOMIC ROOSTERS.
- Fan Club, Leeds = SPLIT ENDZ.

FRI 26
- Cleopatra's, Huddersfield = T.B.A.
- Polytechnic, Huddersfield = THE DANCE BAND.
- Palm Cove, Bradford = T.B.A.
- Fforde Greene, Leeds = DISCO STUDENTS.

SAT 27
- Castleford Trades Club = TAROT. Funhouse Bar, Keighley (lunch) = T.B.A.
- Palm Cove, Bradford = T.B.A.
- Haddon Hall, Leeds = A NEW OPERA (ex-Vye).
- White Lion, Huddersfield = 7 YEAR ITCH.
- Staging Post, Leeds = T.B.A.
- Royal Park, Leeds = LUCKY STIKE.

SUN 28
- Vault's Bar, Bradford = MYSTERIOUS FOOTSTEPS. White Lion, Huddersfield (lunch) = ORAL SAX :
- Princeville, Bradford (lunch) = TOKYO ROSE. Dock Green, Leeds (lunch) = AMAZING (eve) = PRESS GANG.
- Palm Cove, Bradford = JED'S BLUES BAND. Staging Post, Leeds = 7:10 (formerly Alibi). GUFFSTRUT.
- Panache, Bradford = T.B.A. Fan Club, Leeds = U2.
- Haddon Hall, Leeds = KNIFE EDGE.

MON 29
- St. George's Hall, Bradford = GILLAN.
- Marquis of Granby, Leeds = VINYL DINERS.
- Princeville, Bradford = ROCKER.
- Kings Head, Keighley = PROPOSITION 31.

TUE 30
- Vault's Bar, Bradford = MIDDLE 8.
- Scamps, Bradford = NEUTRAL ZONE.
- Palm Cove, Bradford = THE JAZZ ROCK BAND.
- Rose & Crown, Ilkley = KNIFE EDGE.

SEACROFT HOTEL, LEEDS - I phoned 3 times - on 3rd time, manager told me he couldn't be bothered to read me the gigs & didn't care whether he was listed or not - don't blame me, I voted Labour....
ALBION, HUDDERSFIELD - manager away till 18th Aug. Bands on after that, but relief manager didn't know which or when. Ring pub on Hudds. 24200.

USELESS ADDRESSES

WEEKLIES
1. New Musical Express, 3rd Floor, 5-7 Carnaby St., London, W1V 1PG. (tel. 01-439-8761). News Editor & Gig Guide: Derek Johnson.
2. Musicians Only, 2nd Floor, 143 Charing Cross Rd, London, WC2. (tel. 01-734-2139/2166/2231/2226) News Desk: Steve Wall // Gig Guide: Jeff Hammer or Neil Hooper.
3. Sounds, 40 Long Acre, London, WC2E 9JT. (tel. 01-836-1522). News Editor: Hugh Fielder // Gig Guide ('Steppin' Out'): Susanne Garrett.
4. Record Mirror (Same address, phone no., staff as Sounds)
5. New Music News, 14 Rathbone Place, London W1P 1DE. (tel. 01-637-7991/2/3 or 01-580-6104). News Editor: Brian Harrigan // Gig Guide ('Scene Ahead'): Sally Payne.
6. Melody Maker, 24-34 Meymott St., London, SE1 9LU (tel. 01-261-8000). News Editor: John Orme // Gig Guide ('Look Hear'): Chris Hayes.
7. Zig Zag, 118 Talbot Rd, London W11. (tel. 01-221-7422). Editor: Kris Needs (monthly, no gig guide).
8. Rough Trade, 202 Kensington Park Rd, London W11 (tel. 01-727-4312).
9. Better Badges, 286 Portobello Rd, London W10. (tel. 01-960-5513/4).

This cartoon will never get off the ground...

Guy Jackson & one Heather Wibbley drink my coffee & sit in my chairs - must be the start of another WCR interview. It is. Here's what I found out.

G.J. & sometime side-kick, Rob Metcalf began live life as a duo called The Wibbley Brothers - first in school shows about 4 years ago. They entered Pub Entertainer of The Year, getting to the London finals: "then we failed abysmally, but it got us our first pro engagement - 4 nights doing a spot between records at Jingles, a London disco. We got paid off after the 3rd night - not a great start!" That was back in Xmas/New Year '78/'79.

Prior to this interview, I'd had - though the post - G.J.'s demo tape of some 24 tracks, some live, others home recorded. There are a couple of poems done (inevitably) in JCC style, several poems done to guitar & a whole bunch of songs done variously to guitar/drum machine, etc. - with Mr Metcalf & Ms Wibbley in there for guest appearances. It's a most interesting tape, with G.J. coming across as a skilled lyricist/poet & a versatile performer-songwriter. Personally, I feel a shorter demo with 'Raincoats', 'Northern Soul', 'Social Parasite' & maybe two others on it would be more effective - easier to listen thru & consistently impressive. The 3 named numbers would make a great first single/EP.

Back to the interview. Living in London (well, Bushey in Herts, actually) during holidays & at Leeds Univ. during term time, he's been gigging mostly in the two cities - with a few others on the college/univ circuit (Oxford, Leicester, York, Nottingham) - often as a support solo act to a major touring band. In this capacity, he's worked with Delta 5, Gary Glitter, The Photos, 9 Below Zero, The Wimps (with whom he actually plays guitar occasionally as well), Otway & Barrett, etc. He has more gigs lined up in Leeds during September & is hoping to do a set of appearances around universities during freshers' conferences.

For the past 12 months, he's been waiting for some songs to be released on The Wimps' own label Sniff, but it doesn't look like that'll materialise. Red Rhino (York label) were interested, but since that initial interest haven't said any more. However, he's hoping that the current demo & the work that it's getting him on the live scene will generate some interest elsewhere that'll lead to a recording deal.

Contact: ring 01-950-1491.

Guy Jackson finds a guitar in a park litter bin, tries it on for size in a nearby street & then tries to persuade Bearded Baker & Son to put up the dough to make him a popular music star.

GUY JACKSON

HEAVEN 17
an everyday tale of ungigging...

H.17 are: Ian Tilliard (voc), Mark Tighe (gtr/b.voc), Ian Anderson (pno/org/b.voc) Nick Hiles (bass/b.voc), Tony Horsfall (dms).

The band's members have been friends since '77 & the band came together gradually over a year or so, with the group actually together & beginning to rehearse by Sept '79. There was a bit about the band in WCR7, here's a catalogue of their gigging experiences - interesting in that it highlights many of the factors which effect most new bands trying to break into the local pub rock circuit.

The band's first booking was at The King's Head in Keighley, but - due to a mix-up - not on the pub's rock night. The manager & the regulars (aged about 50 for the most part) were expecting some sort of m.o.r. cabaret duo. "We got our mixing desk as far as the door & were turned away." Lesson one. Make sure that you & the management clearly understand what each of you means by 'music'.

Their 2nd gig was at The Adelphi Hotel, Harrogate. "Having agreed on the gig, we began to worry when, one after another, 4 bands phoned us to say they were supporting us. When we contacted the venue to check things out, we were told that the guy who'd booked us (the manager) had done a bunk. The new manager said we were down in his diary as 'a dance'. The whole thing was so confused that the gig had to be 'postponed', but we're anyway not too keen to try for another date there - no-one seems to know who's running what there." Lesson two. Try to make sure that you can rely on whoever books you - get the gig confirmed in writing &/or keep in regular contact with the venue between the booking & the gig itself.

3rd was at Rose & Crown in Ilkley. "We actually did this gig! It went down quite well with the crowd & we were pleased with it." Lesson 3. Don't let the bad ones put you off - if you're any good at all, you'll at least win a few!

4th gig was at The Mitre in Knaresborough. "15 people turned up & we lost money quite heavily as we were booked on a door-money deal. However, we were determined to enjoy the gig & it did go quite well - was a bit of a party & we were able to let rip - albeit in a small way." Lesson 4. Before accepting a door-money deal, check out how popular the venue is, whether sending posters, doing fly posting, etc. will help.

Further gigs are being lined up, but the band are finding it really hard to get bookings. Lesson 5. There are half a dozen bands chasing every gig going - i.e. too many bands for too few venues & this area has far more venues than most. And there's no easy answer to that.

I've listened to a couple of demo tapes by the band & have heard a few live numbers in their rehearsal studio. The band's music is very Manchester new wave in style - mostly Buzzcocks, but also Joy Div/Fall. Kbds really excellent, imposing appealing melodies on insistent oppressive background rhythms. There are good slowed instrumental breaks in some of the songs & throughout they constantly generate a mesh of overlapping rhythms behind Shelley/Devoto-ish vocals.

Contact: Andy on 587045 (eve)

DISCS SUSSED & DISCUSSED

CUBA (Leeds/B'f'd) 'Furtive Winks' c/w 'Valkyrie of Love' (7"45rpm on Nomis Music '80). Off-beat pop in which the complex masquerades as the superficial. Steve liked the B-side with its Pauline (of Penetration, RIP) vocals & heavier guitar work. I loved the weird rushed vocals on the A-side & we both agreed that the song was quite refreshingly original, without obvious influences. See tapes received for review of forthcoming follow-up.

AGONY COLUMN (Leeds/B'f'd) 'Love In The Head' c/w 'Free Of Love' (7"45rpm on Back Door '80). A fast, tight outfit firmly rooted in progressive new wave, but with pre-'77 influences too. Good songs on this long-awaited 2nd 45, tho' slightly disappointing as single-material. I still feel that the band should aim at album market, not this. They need more time & space to get their music across than 2 3-minute bursts like this.

LIMELIGHT (Mansfield) 'Metal Man' c/w 'Hold Me, Touch Me' (Future Earth '80). Double A of mild-mannered metal from one of the finest live bands on the HM club circuit. 2 good numbers that lose much power on this weak production. Excellent songs, immaculately executed, but limp vocals on 1st side - a fast early Rainbow-ish no. - & a rather poppy treatment on side 2. It's hard to see who'll buy it - too soft/light for HM fans, too cliched for pop. Steve wants 'Man Of Colours' on their next single.

OCEAN (B'f'd) 'Don't Want You To Love Me' c/w 'I Must Be Dreaming' (Little Black Plastic '80). Highly commercial MOR pop with strong late-'60's folk-rock undertones given a clean & balanced production by JSG Studios. A club/cabaret band, Ocean have come up with a single that'll do well in that sort of market. More variation of pace & texture could've given the numbers a bit more punch.

MIRROR BOYS (Leeds) 'Capt. Scott' 'At Tiffany's' (in a) 'Jumble Sale Suit' (7"45rpm on Wortley Road '80). A trio + 2 from Cuba guesting on dms/kbds. 'Tiffany's' is a good if slightly drab song. 'JSS' is far more catchy - a pop song with bouncing dms/kbds/sax & neat use of vocals on the chorus when only dms back them. The brief 'Capt. Scott' is best of the 3, distinguished by slightly weird vocs & kbds. All the numbers are danceable & fun.

MYSTERIOUS FOOTSTEPS (B'f'd) 'Like They Do In The Movies' c/w 'White Dread' (7"45rpm on Yeti '80). Ex-Negatives (minus Dave Wilcox) come up with reggae. Steve:"What I admire about this band is that they play within their ability, thus ensuring that what they do, they do well - though I'm not impressed with these songs at all." Nick: "I like these - especially for the catch chorus lines. Of all the records we've got here, 'Movies' is the one that sticks in my head. The recording quality's fine (Cargo Studios). My only criticism is the lack of variety. They latch onto a good riff & don't let go for even a bar or two."

MIDDLE 8 (Bradford) 'Misadventure' c/w 'Countess of Lyme' (7" 45rpm on JSG '80) Jazz-rock outfit, they offer 2 instrumentals on their vinyl debut. Steve: "The A-side successfully recreates the sound of Colliseum II (circa 'Wardance'/'Electric Savage')." B-side is like a TV theme tune. Musicianship is much in evidence - especially on gtr/kbds - with the whole enhanced by a fine studio job from JSG.

DEDRINGER (Leeds/Bradford) 'Sunday Drivers' c/w 'We Don't Mind' (7"45rpm on DinDisc '80). Arrived the day after Steve was round to review with me - shame, he'd have liked it. I do too. It was panned by all on a recent Roundtable (Radio One), even Biffed by Saxon's singer... & they were wrong! It's well recorded heavy commercial rock with a powerful double chorus - most of all, it sounds exciting. Other side's more predictable, but equally good. DinDisc look set to become fashionable & Dedringer'll go with them.

SLAUGHTER & THE DOGS (Manchester) 'I'm The One' c/w 'What's Wrong Boy' + 'Hell In New York' (7"45rpm on This Records '80). Seminal punks still after the big chance. A-side is an attractive slice of raw rock/punk crossover. Flip for 2 tracks that're more heavy than punk. Like U.S. Pistols or English N.Y.Dolls. Very basic, but everything here suggests that there's plenty of life in the old dogs yet. Could catch the HM punk market (Motorhead, Damned...)

THE CHEATERS (Manchester) 'Triple A' (3-track 7"45rpm EP on Prefab '80). Described as R'n'B, it opens disappoint disappointingly with a crappy pop song that's got a weak football-terraces chant for a chorus. 'Baby What You Want Me To Do' is the classic Jimmy Reed number - good, but Rockpile beat all comers in this neck-of-the-woods - but it's Steve's favourite track. I go for the closer 'From The Hip' which is pure '63 R'n'B & I was 13 years old...

INSTANT AUTOMATONS (Scunthorpe/Grimsby) 'Peter Paints His Fence EP' (6 tracks at 33⅓rpm on 7" on Deleted '80). Steve hates it/I like it with a couple of definite exceptions: 1st track's good, 2nd is self-indulgent & bad, 3rd is a slightly pretentious Numan piss-take (clones & robots in the lyric). What's meant to be parody/put down also smells a little like they've been drawn into it themselves. Over for 4th - a likeable poem to music 'People Laugh At Me Cos I Like Weird Music'. Then More loony fun with 'John's Vacuum Cleaner' & even Ste en likes the lyric! Ends with Peter's fence getting an instrumental respray & harmonica on heavy echo delay is most effective. Very amateur/fun.

THE HITMEN 'She's All Mine' c/w 'Slay Me With Your 45' (7" 45rpm on Urgent '79) + 'OK' c/w 'That's Not Me' (as before but '80). Their 1st 2 singles. First is new wave vocals combined with pop melodies - but it's the distinctive gtr sound that grabs you with its original phrasing & odd slide technique. 2nd single is more poppy & consequently less original - but add the excellent mix/production job (Rockfield 24-track) & you've got a much more marketable commodity. Swings & roundabouts...

CIGARETTES 'I Can't Sleep At Night' c/w 'It's The Only Way To Live (Die)' (7"45rpm on Dead Good '80). Comes with a poster of Maggie T. dubbed: 'Britain's Nuclear Threat'. 2 anti-nuke songs (I think, but lyrics are hard to hear). A-side's a sort of Undertones-meet-Buzzcocks that's not instantly catchy, but quickly grows on you. B-side's similar, but less listenable.

B-MOVIES 'The Soldier Stood Alone' c/w 'Drowning Man' & 'Soundtrack' (7"45rpm on Dead Good '80). Another Pete Shelley vocalist. Recorded in the same studio as Cigs, the band sound much the same - even more Buzzcocks than The Buzzcocks! Only different in that they've kbds to the fore. Again, vocals are irritatingly hard to hear - but there's a good songwriter here.

KOSE-A-BII 'Funk Wave' c/w 'Love Me Tonight' (12"45rpm on Variety '80). NY label for NY black disco band who're visiting B'f'd, where 2 of band were born. Live, they've been putting in immaculately tight & varied sets that put disco-dismissers in the same league as The Flat Earth Society. Here, they come up with a couple of good but standard disco nos., neither of which give much indication of the band's overall scope.

TUXEDO MOON 'Scream With A View' (4-track 12"45rpm EP on Pre Records '80). Steve Brown finds his namesake her on synths/saxes/vocs - but dissociates himself from him entirely. This is San Franciscan experimentation & is not a taste the 2 S.B.'s share: "They appear to be a band who merely play with sound." I disagree (again!). Having been none too keen 1st time, I've since played this several times & am impressed with the processed sounds & the atmospheres that they generate. Neither pop nor rock, it's rooted in jazz & electronics, with each of the 4 musicians playing an impressive range of instruments. Good one.

PALM COVE CLUB

Hollings Road, Bradford 8. (Tel. 499895)

Every Friday:	**Rock Bands** (with bar from 7.30pm–1am)
Every Saturday:	**Reggae Bands** (with bar from 9pm–1am)
½ price admission before 10 pm.	
Every Sunday:	**Jed's Blues Band** (with bar from 7.30pm–10.30pm) pub price beer
Every Tuesday from Mid-August onwards **Live Jazz-Rock** (with bar from 9pm–midnight)	

STOP PRESS: FRIDAY 12th SEPT: GREGORY ISAACS

CODA MUSIC

28 Church Bank, Bradford 1. (Tel 307433)

MUSICAL INSTRUMENTS—SALES + HIRE + REPAIRS
+ EXPERT TUITION
ON GUITAR, BASS, DRUMS, KEYBOARDS

REHEARSAL ROOMS + RECORDING & VIDEO STUDIOS +
LIVE RECORDINGS FOR BANDS, GROUPS, ARTISTS.

P.A. HIRE (100-3,000 watts) + CREW and TRANSPORT.
(P.A. Rig:—30/2 Allen & Heath + RSD & BGW Amps
+ Shure & AKG & Beyer Mikes)

Agents for:—Marshall, Ludwig, Carlsboro, Ovation, Premier, Olympic, Tama, Ibanez, Pearl, Beyer, A.K.G., Korg, Peavey, Gretsch, Slingerland.

WE CAN NOW SUPPLY **ANY** VINTAGE
AMERICAN GUITAR — RING FOR QUOTE

THE COMMUNICATIONS CENTRE

(a posh name for a basic facility)

offers 4-TRACK with DBX
at £3.50 p.h. + tape

Gear Includes:—
TEAC 3340, DBX, ITAM 10-4 desk,
LEAVERS-RICH E200, REVOX B77,
ORBAN REVERB, FILTERS, GRAPHICS, etc.

FULL D.I. + MIKES by AKG, CALREC, etc.

RING ALF or MOYA on Bradford 22769.

GAWPIN' AT LANCS.– MANCHESTER

BANDS:

Night Visitors. A 5-piece band that performs modern rock with electronic, reggae & new wave influences. See WCR7 (p.14) for fuller info on this outfit.

262. An experimental music outfit that records but does no live work. Also featured in WCR7 (see p.14 for info on band & review of their cassette).

Sturgeon Row. A 3-piece outfit that was also featured on p.14 of WCR7. They've an E.P. & a cassette out.

Strandid. A 3-piece Jam-like outfit from Salford. Lively stage act, pretty professional. Recently they supported The Cramps at Manchester Poly. (I saw them at Queens Hall, Bradford last month & enjoyed their set – tight & powerful, though the on-stage presence wasn't to good – ed.).

Two Tone Pinks. Good so-called mod band. Play a few cover versions. Have a 4-track cassette called 'Verbal Cock-ups' out at the moment. (The name was picked before The Specials' Two Tone Label stole our nation's heart away – ed.).

Pure Product. Excellent, weird, funky band. 5-piece (voc, gtr, gtr/sax, bass, drums). Ace rhythm section. Single out on Streets Ahead label.

Backroom Boys. Had a single out on RSO as The Tunes. 5-piece (voc/gtr, kbds, gtr, bass, dms). Costelloish sound. Making an album at Cargo at the moment. Worth seeing.

The Images. Very young mod band. Very realistic impressions of early Who, Small Faces, etc. Great fun!

Matinee. Good 3-piece. Very tight, great drummer – in fact they're all good players. Bit like The Jam in places.

The Trend. Tight, poppy band – bit like The Salford Jets but better. Getting popular now, with gigs in London & singles on MCA.

There are loads more bands in the area of course, such as A Certain Ratio, Armed Forces, the remains of Joy Division, The Freshies, The Things, The Worms, The Photographs, Thunder Boys, etc.

GIGS:

The Millstone, Thomas St. (off Tib St.).
Puts bands on regularly in upstairs room. Band takes door money. Run by Clive of The Twisting Ferraris – contact him through the pub.

Portland Bars, Piccadilly Plaza.
Bands on most nights of the week. Free to get in, band gets £25. Audition night Wed.

Cyprus Taverns, Princess Street.
Bands on Sunday nights – run by Manchester Musicians' Collective.

Beach Club, at Oozit's Club, Newgate St., Shudehill. New venue, bands & films every Wed. until 2am. Quite a good place.

Kim Philby Club, at Deville's, Lloyd St.
Quite well-known bands on on some Thursdays.

Band on the Wall, Swan St.
Popular jazz club which puts rock on on Mon.

The Ardri, Coupland St. (off Cambridge St.).
Big club, rock on Thurs.

– phone nos. from directory enquiries (192).

FANZINES:

City Fun. Usually fortnightly. Similar format to Wool City Rocker. Main Manchester fanzine. Contact Neil on Glossop 62798 or City Fun, c/o New Hormones, Newton Buildings, 50 Newton Street, Manchester.

Output Terminal. New Terminal Music fanzine/info sheet featuring reviews of Night Visitors & 262, Night Visitors gig lists, other Salford/Manchester band info., etc. To be sold at Night Visitors gigs.

Radcliffe Times. Not a fanzine(!) but reporter Paul Campbell is great for reviewing tapes, gigs & so on & is a mine of information. Contact him through The Radcliffe Times, 40 Church St., Radcliffe, M26 9SQ.

Photophobia. Scrappy little fanzine, comes out every six weeks or so. Address is 9 Egerton Grove, Chorley, PR7 2HQ.

There are other Manchester fanzines such as **Flying V** (HM), but I don't know much about them.

– compiled for W.C.R. by Colin Robinson of Night Visitors, 262 & Terminal Music
with help from Paul Clark of Sturgeon Row.

page 14.

C30·C60·C90·Go!

BLUSH: 'Totally Up' (a 6-track tape released on Venal Tapes, Cell 002). Heavy melodic pop that combines the best of commercial new wave (Blondie/Jam/Squeeze) with the across-the-board type of rock appeal that, say, The Motors achieved. Notably there's a good heavy gtr sound with well-used effects plus impressive back-up vocal harmonies to a Joe Jackson/Ian Page lead vocal. Every song's a potential single, with inventive arrangements & full marks to Ric-Rac for a top quality production job. Only real reservation is that, like The Jags, & a million other bands they've a would-be Elvis Costello on vocals - good but too derivative. The cassette's £1-99 from manager Steve Musson, 6 Green Lane, Mansfield, Notts. The band themselves are from the Wakefield area.

CUBA: 'Wireless World' c/w 'Frankie' (pre-release tape of single due out on Ariola). Leeds/Bradford band with another Ric-Rac recording. I'm totally sold on the A-side. Other side's a straightforward 60's-ish popsong. Steve rightly points out a strong parallel with The Tourists - it's there in the overall sound, but more especially in the vocal (which he thought was Annie Lennox at first). Steve: "Vocals are a bit samey throughout, making the choruses sound weak. Also, the same basic plodding drumming on both tracks is more & more noticeable as you listen - irritatingly so."

POLICEMAN WITH A LOAF OF BREAD: 20-track demo tape (home-produced) from this Bradford Dadaist combo (sent along with this cartoon, a selection of weird paintings & various other oddments). Steve (after 1st 3 tracks): "Well... I think I can confidently predict that they're not destined for commercial success." So we listen to 20 anti-songs from this successor to Scum (see WCR 3) & the lead vocal proves to be unremittingly & relentlessly awful. Somewhere here is an attempt to come up with something other than the usual commerical pop dross. Mostly they only offer another dross from a different kitchen - though throughout there's a real sense of direction & strong hints of real creative originality (with inventive lyrics) but they've a long way to go. A couple of years & they could be influentially avant garde. Steve: "Makes Joy Division sound like Boney M!"

TAROT: 5-track studio demo from these Pontefract heavy rockers. Steve: "This is more up my street - though it's not exactly the best. They've played Princeville a couple of times & went down ok, but not great. There's good & bad HM - this falls somewhere between. It's good to hear forceful gtr, but there are a lot of standard influences here. There's no doubting their musical ability & the tightness of the band, but - now they've been together 18 months - they should try to develop a more distinctive sound of their own otherwise their chances of furthering their careers in the music biz must remain slight."

NIGHT VISITORS: 5-track release on Terminal Music (or is this just a demo for me?). Ring Andy on 061-789-2686 if you're interested. Some excellent commercial sounds spoiled by suspect harmonies over the excellent female lead vocalist (who sounds not unlike The Photos' Wendy Wu). On most tracks there's also a synth that's too prominent. 'Playing The Pool' was a good number (no synth or backing vocals on it) with added sax-appeal. Overall, these Mancunians show good variation in pace & melody on a tape which would be significantly improved by better production. Their complex & occasionally jazzy arrangements work well most of the time, but in several places the musicians actually work against, rather than with, each other.

AN ITCH: 4 tracks done as a demo on a portable cassette recorder in the guitarist's front room. It's a very rough recording so there's a bad imbalance between the instruments & an atrocious vocal sound so the band are hard to assess accurately. It seems to be marginally experimental rock that doesn't come across. It's a bit boring. Title of 2nd song sums them up on this showing: 'Mediocrity Kills'. However, they seem to be a new outfit, so we'll reserve judgement till we can review a gig or hear a better recording.

VINYL DINNERTIME: A DISC COURSE

VINYL DINERS: 3 track cassette: 'Germany', 'On The Box' & 'Starbeck' - available at gigs or ring John (manager) on Harrogate 889384. Punky new wave pop with vocal harmonies (male lead voc + 2 female back-up vocs) that give them an overall sound rather reminiscent of Rezillos/Revillos. Extremely catchy & instantly enjoyable. We're both very impressed.

RIC-RAC STUDIO: various artists recently in the studio (specially compiled by the studio for WCR). Side One: THE NEAT. The whole of this side of the tape is devoted to a selection of their light, 60's-style pop w ich isdone well, with good harmonies & overall arrangements that are pleasing. In addition, this recording captures the band's bubbly sense of tacky fun. However, the songs are rather weak with melody lines that are predictable &/or very derivative. '78=powerpop, '79=mod, '80=this stuff. Rock on, Tommy! Side two: THE EMMAUS (4 tracks), CHRIS MORRIS (2 tracks), THE GRUMBLEWEEDS (1 track). First up is some deliberate & considered rock with disc-style drumming & hypnotic guitar. Not poppy or immediate - quite the reverse, it's fairly restricted - but most appealing. Cold, hard & interesting - they use repeated riffs without becoming boring. Parallels with Joy Division, but less doomed & gloomy. Chris Morris (ex-Paper Lace) joins with Mick Robson (owner/engineer at Ric-Rac) to come up with two of Chris' own songs to immaculately produced, M.O.R. disco formula. Excellent of their kind, but ultra-bland from the viewpoint of a rock fan. Steve: "The sort of thing that EMI'd sign up straight away". Finally, we've The Grumbleweeds' slice of pure 50's rock. Again, the production's excellent. Sax, gtr, vocs all sound totally authentic. As a bonus there's exciting use of echo on the drums. However, Steve still thinks that the band are at their best with their more familiar humorous material.(Try them on Radio 2 - Sun or Fri nights).

VEX: demo recorded at Cargo on April 29th '80. Tracks: 'Iwojima'/'Mercenaries'/'Cybernetics'/'Reply'/'Switch Me On'. Experimental synth-based Bradford outfit with a new line-up. They sound a bit like O.M.I.T.D. - ie they're at the poppy end of electronic eccentricity. This is much better than their previous demo (WCR 4). Best track is 'Mercenaries' First & last tracks also have appeal, but we didn't like the other two at all. This contrasts strongly with the band's own preferences - so I guess we're on different tacks. They rate 'Reply' as the best track (it's the worst) & dismiss 'Switch Me On' as a mess (which it's not). Chacun son gout - whatever that means!

~ Nick Toczek & Steve Brown.

V.D. & Blush (well, wouldn't you??) - these 2 win top marks this ish. Give them a (dose of) clap. While Ric-Rac gets a special mention for production quality.

LEEDS RECORD COLLECTORS' FAIR
at THE ASTORIA CENTRE, ROUNDHAY RD., HAREHILLS (by Forde Greene pub)
11am-5pm on SUN. 31st AUG.   Admission: 30p
Over 60 stall-holders from all parts of the country + all types of records
Also, books, magazines, badges, posters, etc.
FOR FURTHER INFORMATION RING LYNN UNDERWOOD ON LEEDS 687572.

Sweet Palace Restaurant

629 Leeds Road, Bradford. Tel. (0274) 666060.

EAT IN and TAKE-AWAY SERVICE

Specialists in CURRIED CHICKEN, KEBAB, TIKKA and all kinds of Asian Foods.

Open daily from 9 a.m. until 4 a.m. the following morning.

HOME DELIVERY BY TAXI CAN BE ARRANGED TAXI CHARGE PAYABLE

Proprietor: Mr. M.A. Bajwa.

10% DISCOUNT ON ALL STUDIO PRICES

(Only With This Advert.)

police..regatta&outlandos...£3-50 each
whitesnake..ready'n'...£3-50
bob marley..survival...£3-50
LKJ...bass culture...£3-50
jam..in the city..£3-99
michael jackson..off the wall..£3-50
motorhead...overkill&bombers...£3-50 each
joy division....both £3-99 each
clash..london calling..£3-50
ac/dc..if you want blood.....£3-99
joan armatrading..me,my etc...£3-50

the HMV shop — WHILST STOCKS LAST

MICK PICKS THE LOCH...

This was the 2nd Loch Lomond rock festival & the organisers are hoping this will be a regular event in the Scottish rock calendar, & it certainly was very popular & managed to attract a lot of big bands. Despite all this, the organisation left a lot to be desired (especially when compared to Reading). For example, on arrival you're collared £2 to park the car, £13 for your weekend ticket, then a further £1 to set up y'tent a good 400 yards (it could have been further) awayfrom y'car, & all this is a good mile walk up a country lane away from the actual arena.

Upon every entrance to the arena, you were frisked for carrying any kind of drink & any found in your possession had to be discarded at the gate. "I suppose it prevents people getting pissed & causing trouble", I thought, until I saw a tent inside the ground selling nothing but Skol at great expense.

On to the show (at last) & the first major band to make an appearance were Stiff Little Fingers. Good news is that Jake Burns has still got a sore throat & his gravel-pit vocals were in fine form. With the usual raw agression, they hammered their way through 'Suspect Device', 'Alternative Ulster' & 'On The Edge' etc. in fine style. I was just disappointed at the shortness of their set, ¾ hour, followed by an interval of an hour before we saw the vivacious Annie Lennox hit the stage with The Tourists. This was greeted by a barrage of Skol cans flying towards the stage which soon took the sting out of Annie's tail & therefore resulted in a very mediocre, half-hearted performance. Mind you, I really enjoyed the haunting rendition of 'Loneliest Man In The World'.

To finish off the Saturday night, the band we were all waiting for - The Jam - & they didn't let us down. They were tough & agressive, especially after Paul Weller gave the small section of the audience their last warning for slinging cans of Skol. (Fortunately, it worked).

A marvellous set which comprised of 7 of their 10 singles, plus several B-sides (including the excellent 'A Bomb In Wardour Street' & 'Down In The Tube Station') & also the best part of the 'Setting Sons' album. "This next song is about what's happening to you lot." snarled Paul Weller (referring to can throwing element), "It's called 'Going Underground'". And they really launched into the song with great feeling backed up by Foxton's solid bass & Buckler's steady beat, they executed the number in fine style.

By now I'd had my money's worth, & Sunday was still to follow.

Sunday arrived with a farewell to the rowdy punks & mods & a greeting for the peaceful rockers, hippies, etc.

I woke up too late to see Wild Horses, much to my disgust, but arrived in time to see the pseudo hard man band Krokus (from Switzerland, which seems like a good excuse). They got away with a set which appeared to comprise of about two chords distorting loudly, the occasional lead break consisting of two notes suspended for as long as possible, & some prawn (avec hairy chest) screaming his balls off. Why they went down well, I just don't know.

Lindisfarne provided a break from the heavy metal & produced a fun set that was appreciated by all (except those who decided it wasn't cool if they weren't shaking their heads). 'Lady Eleanor', 'Run For Home' & 'Fog On The Tyne' were especially well received.

Next was the old war horse of head shaking, tonsil rattling & groin guitar fame, Ian Gillan. This was an incredibly short set including 'Sleeping On The Job' & 'Mr. Universe' but surprisingly no 'Vengance' (1st single). Gillan leered & grinned at the audience: "I think we need a little smoke", he said, leaving the stage for Bernie Tormé to do his 5 minute intro. It wasn't till Tormé finally struck the first 3 immortal chords that the vast majority present realised that we were in for one of the rock classics of our time, 'Smoke On The Water', then the heads started shaking as the rest of the band rejoined Tormé, John McCoy bouncing about like a space hopper & making his bass look like a banjo.

Saxon were as boring as their Swiss counterparts, Krokus, with the addition of the guitarist spending the last ten minutes of the set rolling around the stage (as if The Alien was trying to escape from inside him) & throwing his guitar about, collecting as much feedback as possible. "Pure talent!!"

Finally came the big moment, Wishbone Ash. It appeared after about ½ hour that they had run out of material & were repeating themselves, so much so that I became bored, bought a hamburger & went home.

~earwitnessed by
MICK MITCHELL

UNKLASSIFIED ADS. (10p per word - ring or write it in).

→ EXPERIENCED PRODUCER Looking for bands with imminent studio work. Demos or discs. Don't waste money just hoping for a good sound- be sure of one. For further details ring Lindsay on Leeds 623306.

→ VOCALIST/GUITARIST seeks musicians to form band. Modern stuff, enthusiasm more important than experience. Write: JOHN, 40 GEORGE ST., MILNSBRIDGE, HUDDERSFIELD

N.B. This is a quote from Blackpool Rox itself (I'm just rendering unto Caesar...)

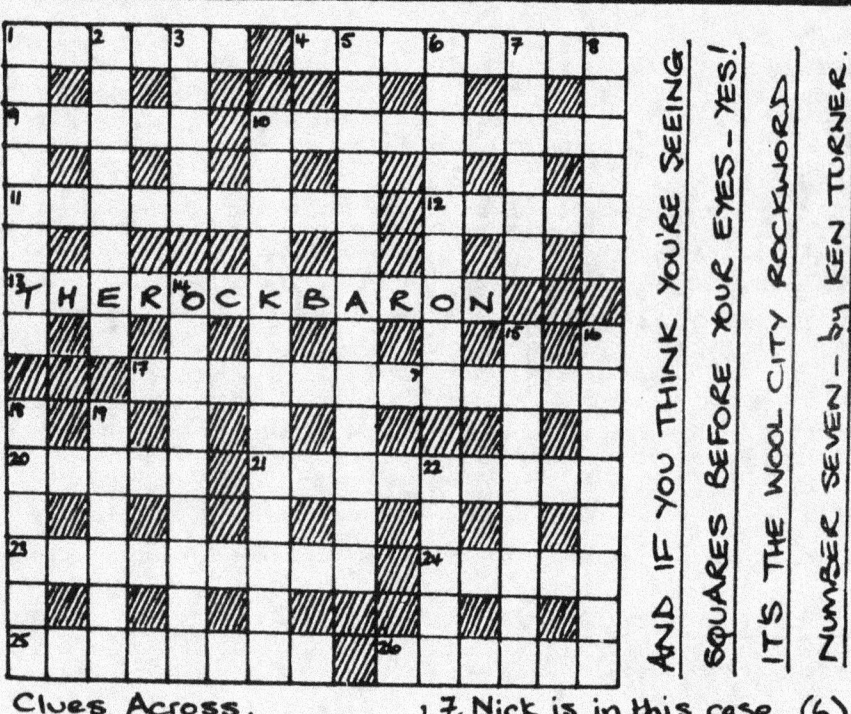

AND IF YOU THINK YOU'RE SEEING SQUARES BEFORE YOUR EYES—YES!
IT'S THE WOOL CITY ROCKWORD NUMBER SEVEN — by KEN TURNER.

Clues Across.

1. What Lord Sutch did. (6)
4. D'y'ken the master (of the turntable)! (4,4)
9. Fly-boy Edward played. (5)
10. We are now, and Kate Bush was once. (9)
11. According to Einstein, this band existed. (6,3)
12. To be played energetically, this. (5)
13. Song of love, French. (6,1-5)
20. Me, frugal? That is to say ..... (1,4)
21. To chill? No! Arrange to cover embarrasment. (4,5)
23. Selling millions of records or breaking Olympic ones. (5,4)
24. I am ed., making papers etc.. (5)
25. Actual recording, in studio terms, perhaps. (4,4)
26. Wounds extensively...... frightens. (6)

Clues Down.

1. Shoo felines for beat group! (4-4)
2. Turner (compiler) and editor in short, come back. (8)
3. Dery's ex.. (5)
5. Cold turkey? Getting warm! (4-5,4)
6. and 22. Reviews for Wool City Rocker, jokes? (5,3,1,5)
7. Nick is, in this case. (6)
8. Illuminations underneath the 16's? (6)
19. Heard and eaten in Jenks' Bar, Lancs.? (9,4)
14. The best kind of sensation? (9)
15. Motivated philanthropist. (2-6)
16. Wary Chas. rebuilt tunnels. (8)
18. Stiff little one. (6)
19. Queen, Elizabeth that is. (6)
22. See 6.

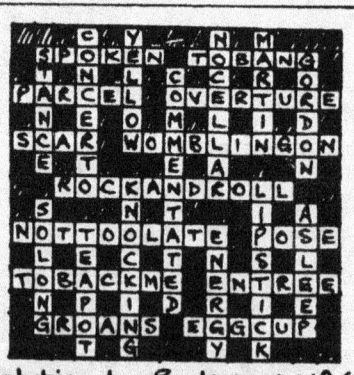

Solution to Rockword No. 6.

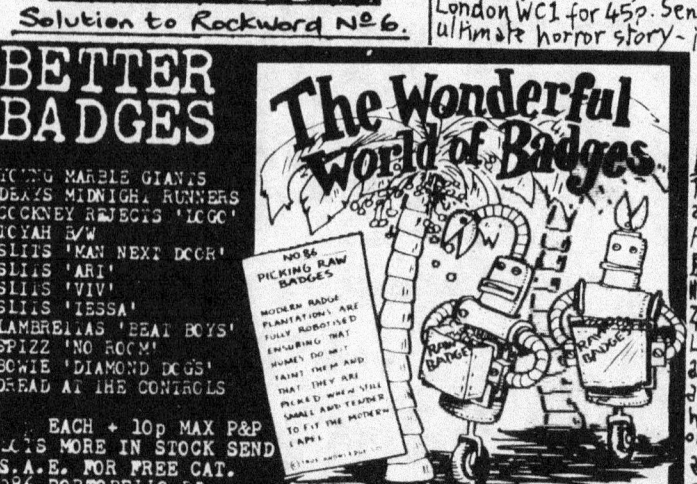

Fanzines, news sheets & comix!

Page 3
ed. Robert Galeta, 1 Sunningdale, Bradford 8, W. Yorks.
Magazine of writing, drawings, photos, interviews, articles, etc. No 1 is just out. Fascinating variety. Liked the drawings, enjoyed Cory Harding's prose poems. Also has interview with fashion designer Paul Smith, feature on the band Metabolist, 2 politico-poems by someone called Nick Toczek..... 40p. Support your local mags!

The Gargoyle & The Nosey Neighbours Supplement Vol. 2
from: 6 Queen St., Mytholmroyd, W. Yorks. HX7 5HN. It's a duplicated punkzine. Letters, cartoons, gig reviews, news, etc. Bit scrappily put together, but has plenty in it - incl. Adam & Ants, Cockney Rejects, etc. Only 15p - try it.

A Bit of Culture
1st 3 issues (March, May, June '80) 10p 10p 15p
from: Keef, Crispin & Neil, 38 Water End, York (Tel. Keef on 58395).
Teenzine - by & for anyteen-yr-olds. And a good one it is too... impressed with this - lots of enthusiasm & good ideas.

Cassette Survival: life without vinyl.
from: Protag, Low Farm, Brigg Road, Messingham, Scunthorpe, S. Humberside DN7 3RH.
A catalogue of 100's of cassettes available from dozens of low-budget indies. Free from address that's also home of Deleted Records. Another essential - send for it (encl. s.a.e. to cover postage costs).

Vague No. 5 (June/July '80). ed. Tom,
'Butcombe', Castle St., Mere, nr. Salisbury, Wilts., BA12 6JF. One of the best fanzines around. Lotsa stuffing crammed into it's slightly messy pages. Occasionally self-indulgent, but never predictable.

Protest & Survive
32-page booklet from CND, 29 Great James St., London WC1 for 45p. Send off for it - the ultimate horror story - it'll scare the shit out of you - & so it should.

Also Free Radio Flyer (10p from
P.O.B.35, Well, Salop) - anti-BBC newsheet promoting alternatives.

Free Festivals 1980
from Stone, 45 Westwood Hill, London SE26 6NS - a leaflet about/from an organisation that has loads of leaflets on offer for free - about running festivals etc.

BEATEN TO THE PUNCH (Geoff on York 51872) free single sheet a pilot for possible mag. BLACKPOOL ROX No 7 (10p), 87 Anchorsholme Lane, Anchorsholme, Blackpool, Lancs. "hastily pasted together street fanzine don't buy this." "(sic)

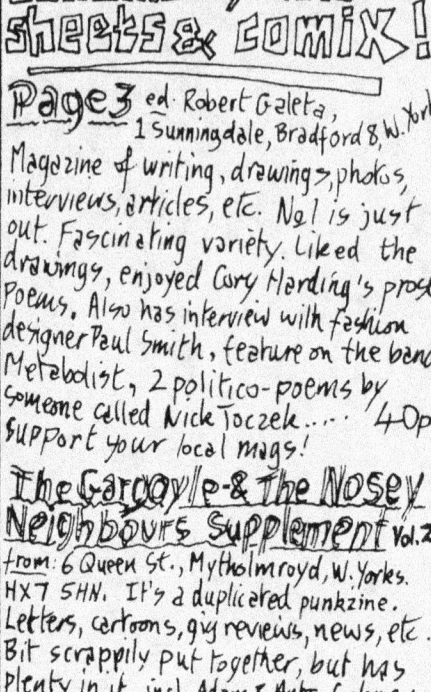

page.18.

BRADFORD COLLEGE
QUEENS HALL & VAULTS BAR

TRADITIONAL ALES

From 1st. Sept. 1980 an extensive selection of hand-pulled traditional ales will be available at both of these venues. These will include:-

- SAMUEL SMITH'S
- TIMOTHY TAYLOR'S
- THEAKSTONS
- SCOTTISH & NEWCASTLE

For all enquiries about either venue ring Bradford 392712.

8-TRACK - £50 per eight hr. day!

Fully Equipped Studio

Using Tascam, Allen Heath, Revox, Roland, Quad, A.K.G., Calrec, etc., etc.

USE OF ANY OF THE FOLLOWING EQUIPMENT

Polymoog, Minimoog, Fender Rhodes Suitecase, Hammond X5 Organ, Moog Taurus Bass Pedals, ARP Salina String Machine, Clavinet D6, Mellotron, Premier Drums, Kramer 5000 Dmz Bass, Acoustic Piano & Guitars + numerous effects.

BOOK NOW

ISSUE #9
October 1980, 2,100 copies printed, 20 pages, 25cm x 17cm, smaller

This issue sees WCR subtitled 'Yorkshire's Rockscene Monthly' (rather than West Yorkshire's). While sales were going well, I was stubbornly determined to keep the cover price at 30p, as it had been from the outset. Distribution, whether through friends and supporters buying bunches of copies at a discount, or big distributors like Red Rhino and Rough Trade taking hundreds of copies at an even bigger discount (because they had to make something, and so did the shops to which they distributed it), I saw less and less of that 30p cover price. Most of WCR's (i.e., my) meagre income came from advertising revenue. Collecting that wasn't always easy. The most lucrative advertising space in WCR was the back cover. That space in issue 8, as you'll have just seen, had been taken by Ray Rossi for a full-page advert for the Manchester band he managed, Slaughter and the Dogs. Getting the payment from him proved very challenging. For the full story about that, you'll again have to wait for my soon-to-come book *My Life Sentences*. I desperately needed that money to pay for issue 9, but it wasn't forthcoming. Meanwhile, I was also struggling to pay my mortgage and other household bills at 5 Beech Terrace.

Our printer for the first eight issues was Orient Press, a very helpful and encouraging Asian-run Bradford press based just off Forster Square, on Canal Road. However, by issue 9, I simply didn't have the funds to pay for printing up front. The situation threatened to end WCR at No.8. However, John Tempest (old school-mate and good-egg Bradfordian man-about-town) came to the rescue, offering to print the mag more cheaply and even to wait for full payment until I'd sold some of the copies he'd printed. Issue 9 did appear, albeit in a smaller size, but at a lower printing cost. I'd designed each page to fit on A4, so the print size was smaller, but the quantity of content was no less. I designed the cover for this issue, its theme being how men view women.

When John Tempest came to collect the print-ready pages late in the evening of 28 September, he found me still working on the final pages. Did he complain? No. He sat down with me, and we co-wrote the reviews of fanzines that appear on page 18. As the cryptic note down the side of the page explains, we finished the issue at 4.11 a.m. on 29 September, and he went off with the pages to print the mag and deliver finished copies back to me less than 48 hours later. John, you were a true friend! N.B. Respect for the man. John founded (in 1984) and still runs The Bradford Soup Run, which provides food and care to the homeless in Bradford. He also spent years as (Psycho Surgeon's frontman), Wild Willi Beckett's campaign manager whenever he stood as The Monster Raving Loony Party candidate in Bradford elections. For several years, John also managed the career of famed Bradford illusionist, escapologist, and magician, Shahid Malik. John liked WCR because he played guitar and sang. I still own a copy of the single he released in the 1970s.

Notes on bands profiled in this issue.

Ian Anderson's Futurama photographs (page 10) show some of the key acts, but miss the one I most remember. That was Manchester band The Frantic Elevators, with a red-haired frontman whose extraordinary voice blew everyone away. They were low on the bill, but amazing. He was Mick Hucknall, later to front Simply Red and carve his own solo career.

LEEDS UNIVENTS PRESENT

Wed. 1st Oct. **Stiff Package** = 5 bands: ANY TROUBLE + JOE 'KING' CARASCO & THE CROWNS + DIRTY LOOKS + THE EQUATORS + TEN POLE TUDOR.

Sat. 4th Oct. **Rory Gallagher**
Fri. 17th Oct. **The Tourists**
Sat. 18th Oct. **Rockpile** (with Dave Edmunds & Nick Lowe)
Mon. 27th Oct. **Loudon Wainwright III**
Wed. 29th Oct. **John Martyn** (with band)

Also, next month's fare includes:—
Sat. 8th Nov. **Darts**
Sat. 15th Nov. **Steel Pulse**
Sat. 22nd Nov. **Iron Maiden**
Sat. 29th Nov. **Hazel O'Connor's Megahype**

Tickets: available 9.30-5 (weekdays) from University Union Record Shop in the Union basement and (evenings/weekends) from the Porters' Lodge in the Union entrance or on the door on the night of the gig. N.B. YOU DON'T HAVE TO BE A STUDENT TO GET IN TO THESE GIGS.

LEEDS UNIVERSITY'S UNION RECORDS
ALL ALBUMS AT DISCOUNT PRICES

We now sell tickets for all Leeds University concerts & are booking agents for Leeds Playhouse & The Grand Theatre, Leeds.

SHOP IN BASEMENT OF UNION BUILDING   OPEN: MON-FRI 9.30am-5.00pm

---

HUDDERSFIELD POLYTECHNIC

Great Hall Queensgate Hudds.

October Bookings...

Sat. 4th Oct. = **Otway & Barrett**
Fri. 24th Oct. = **Linton Kwesi Johnson**
Fri. 31st Oct. = **John Martyn Band**

TICKETS ON SALE IN THE TRAVEL OFFICE IN THE STUDENTS' UNION BUILDING (10am - 3.30pm, weekdays). OR ON THE DOOR ON THE NIGHT.

RING HUDDERSFIELD 38156 FOR INFO. ON TIMES, PRICES, ETC.   OPEN TO THE PUBLIC

Editorial

What a month September's been! I've spent most of the time trying to get together enuf money to save me from having to sell this mansion. I'm still here, so it looks like the pressure's easing a bit. Somewhere between last editorial & this, I became 30 yrs. old. The week before, I spent 2 days at Futurama, running a stall with Gaynor, Gris Boojum (ex-Townbeat & currently chief mogul of Snark Records!) & Ian (say 'cheese'...click!) Anderson, selling my wares. Blasted my ears to shreds, forgot what sleep meant, bunged up my nasal tubes with glue fumes & generally enjoyed myself. Current line-up of Ulterior Motives did 3 of our 6 publicised gigs & called it a day. Ann (vocals) is forming an acoustic band, Martin (dms) is off to university, Mick (gtr.) is forming his own heavy-ish rock band, Dave (temp. backing vocs) will be joining some band here or in Preston where he's starting at the Polytech. Self + recent newcomer Neil (bass) + sundry others will form a new outfit - so we're not gone yet!! Look out for the new band in November/December. New printer + this has been a low budget rushed job. As I write this, I've no idea how the mag'll turn out - probably with slightly smaller pages. Hope you still like it. In the wider world, Lennon's in the studio - hope he's not doing stuff he'll live to regret... but who am I to suggest he's too old?! The Police come up with a predictable single, The Buzzcocks copy old Kinks' tune, The Stones (despite national music press slagging off) come up with their best single in ten years, poor old John Bonham goes off to drum for Ded Zepplin & Hendrix beat him to it by 10 years. As if that wasn't enuf, the fox that lived over the back from Beech Terrace (& used to bark & howl every night) got itself run over in Killinghall Rd. - poor thing. Chewing gum goes up to 10p & typewriter ribbon go up by over 30p to £1-30! By the way, no review of Futurama here - it was covered in all the music papers, with my 1,500 words on it appearing in Musicians Only. Same issue had a foto by Ian Anderson (who's incidentally kbds. with Heaven 17) & a review of B'f'd's Warlord by Steve Brown - look out, M.O., it's a W.C.R. take-over!

Some of you might've read a load of crap in Sounds about the death of live rock in Bradford-Keighley area, with all venues closing their door to bands due to a noise-level limit of 86 decibels. The truth is that B'f'd council have banned bands from Keighley Leisure Centre because of noise (nearby neighbours complained) & because of some violence & general healthy vandalism at recent gigs. Effectively, Bingley Arts Centre is (temporarily) unable to book bands. That's all! Source of Sounds crapola report is the same guy who splashed the inaccuracies across the pages of his employers' rag - Keighley News - namely one Tim Tate. The main result of this masterly piece of journalistic irresponsibility is that at least one Keighley pub venue, fearing police raids & other hassles, has closed its doors to rock bands this month. I spent an hour & a half talking to council officials last week & found out that no action against pub or club venues is planned or even anticipated. It's high time that Tate & cohort Mike Morris did a proper job as rock writers/reporters or else gave up. Meanwhile, their writing has closed one of Keighley's only remaining venues. — Nick Toczek (it says here) 29th Sept '80

Contents

There's the usual mixed bunch in here. Ian Anderson gets a page of **Futurama Fotos**, Stan Engel & Kev Hopgood have **Kartoonz**, some of the featured bands include **Distributors** (interviewed), **Vibrators** (live-ish), **Nosferatu V** (in profile), Keith Rice on **Swakara**, Mick Mitchell went to **Reading Rock '80**, Tino Palmer enjoyed **Gregory Isaacs**, I interviewed local producer **Lindsay Frost**, there's the usual Yorkshire **Gig Guide**, there are reviews of **L.P.'s, Singles, tapes & fanzines**, there's stuff on ex-Vye outfit **New Opera**, some chat with **Surfin' Dave**, plus **Chinatown, Knife Edge, The Neat, Blush, Force Nine, Pete Mayhem** eating catfood, **Jedediah Strutt, Tarot, Lou Reed** & much more!

page 3.

SACRE BLEU, MON BRAVE, C'EST NUMERO NEUF!

SUBTITLES: ISSUE NINE. OCTOBER '80.

Editing, interviewing, layout, cover design(?), most of contents, libel, etc. by NICK TOCZEK.

Other contributions from:-

STEVE BROWN	KEITH E. RICE
KEN TURNER	MICK MITCHELL
STAN ENGEL	KEV HOPGOOD
TINO PALMER	JOHN TEMPEST
ANDY STEVENS	JOHN ROW
GEOFFREY BALLPOINT	MARC NICHOLLS

& I've probably missed out a couple, but it's long after whatever the time was long ago & I'm falling asleep doing this scribbling.

Bit of space here so I'll use it to ask you to give me a phone call or write to me if you can give me the name/phone no. of any shop that might sell this mag. Thanx in anticipation...

TERMS OF SALE: 30p each direct to the public or 50p each by mail order from the address given below. Bulk orders of 15 or more copies can be had at the discount price of 20p each (so why not sell the magazine yourself at gigs, school, etc.?)

ADVERTISING RATES: Standard 3½" x 3½" box is £20 for first time of advertising, then £10 for subsequent placings. Colour, different size, special lay-out, etc. by arrangement.
Ring or write for advertising rates card & any other details.

EDITORIAL ADDRESS:
5 Beech Terrace,
Undercliffe,
Bradford BD3 0PY,
West Yorkshire,
England.
(tel. 0274-21867).

BEST TIMES TO RING ARE ABOUT 10.30am or 6pm OR ABOUT 11.45pm.

Jedediah Strutt

Jedediah Strutt is a rock band from Halifax. All the members are 18 & the band was formed while they were still at school. They're much influenced by Free, Hendrix & Lynyrd Skynyrd. They've now been gigging for almost a year, not without hassles.

Early on, they had all their gear nicked & so had to save up to replace it.

Basically a four-piece (gtrs, bass, dms) they tried out a keyboard player (ex-Bolyn), did a couple of gigs with him but decided that he didn't fit & so he moved on by mutual agreement.

For the past seven months, they've been gigging regularly & are currently touring clubs. However, with two of the band unemployed, money's very short & they're after a few short tours supporting name acts.

The band have a track on 'New Electric Warriors' (Logo Records) which is the newly-released sampler album of northern heavy rock bands. Their line-up is: Dave Lister on guitar, Paul Farrell (maneating plant, it says here) on drums, Jim Callan on bass & Andy Wood (from whose letter this info was lifted) on guitar. Contact: Andy on Halifax 66410.

Stop Press:- I'm told that Jedediah Strutt have been signed by Chrysalis!

A Few Words About The Vibrators At Dolly Gray's In Wakefield 15 September 1980

There were only a few in the audience. (Why?) The band tried very hard. Well rehearsed. Tight but not too precise. Presentation (ie what they did on stage - actions) predictable and ordinary (head back, top teeth biting bottom lip, rocking from one leg to the other, bending guitar strings, bending very low from waist whilst hanging onto microphone stand, aggressive etc etc). The music was written for bass guitar, drums, lead guitar, rhythm guitar, lead vocals and harmony vocals. It sounded like a lot of other rock/pop music. The lyrics seemed to be about every day occurences and experiences. The tempo was usually fast. The mix was very clear and not too loud - easy to listen to. There didn't seem to be any special or distinguishing qualities about the whole performance. The band attempted to engage the audience. A few people danced. The atmosphere was dull. Most people seemed to be bored and unresponsive. The band continued to put a lot of effort and energy into what they were doing. The total situation was hopeless. Is there any enthusiasm in Wakefield?

by Geoffrey Ballpoint

LIVE in Wakefield
Vibrators
Vibrators
Vibrators
Vibrators
Vibrators
Vibrators

TAROT

Dear Nick, here follows the 'TAROT' profile:- Tarot was formed 18 months ago in Doncaster and there is no change in the original line-up. The band members are:- Pete Alenby (vocals), Brian Redfern (bass), Malcolm King (guitar/vocals) and Andy Simpson (drums).

The first 6 months they worked the Northern club circuit, mainly playing at mid-week concerts catering for rock audiences. They only worked this circuit with one aim in mind to amass a certain amount of money to acquire an impressive P.A. and light show.

They now write and perform mostly their own brand of heavy metal material. Although the band is based in Doncaster, they rarely play their own town, extensively travelling up and down the country - working venues in Yorkshire, in fact anywhere where there are people who enjoy rock music, plus many venues in Newcastle, Blackpool, Bridlington, Scarborough, Birmingham, Nottingham (Romeo & Juliet's, Doncaster).

Tarot has supported such bands as Deff Leppard (Newcastle Mayfair), Fischer Z (Newcastle Poly.), The Jags. They have just finished recording 5 tracks (information on these can be obtained from the band) which are now with Des Moines of Sounds magazine, Radio Leeds and a major recording company in the States. The next step is that the tapes will do the usual rounds of the A.&R. men in London in search of that long awaited deal. And that was it...

contact:- Brian Redfern, 65 Ravensmead, Purston, Pontefract, W.Yorks. (tel. Pontefract 72777).

A man and woman appeared in the dock together at Bradford Crown Court yesterday charged with wounding each other.

Rumbold set about Thompson with an axe she kept under her pillow, while he was asleep in a chair at her home.

Thompson who has previous convictions for violence, was alleged to have wounded Rumbold on an earlier occasion with a bread knife.

She was said to have been stabbed in her chest and stomach and to have been cut on her fingers when she tried to grab the knife.

The couple were said to have had a stormy relationship.

from T.& A., Bradford - Oct. '80.

UNDERSTATEMENT OF THE YEAR!!

"No, I'm not trying to tell you I fought a war for people like you...."

"Until now, I didn't know there were any people like you.."

BRADFORD UNIVERSITY

4TH	BAD MANNERS	GH
6TH	WEAPON OF PEACE	CB
8TH	THE PHOTOS	GH
11TH	SLADE	GH
15TH	THE Q TIPS	CB
18TH	THE SKIDS	GH
22ND	FISCHER Z	CB
25TH	"SON OF STIFF TOUR"	GH
29TH	THE INMATES	CB

COMING IN NOVEMBER AND DECEMBER,

GARY GLITTER, BOSS

THE CURE,

AND MANY MORE!!!

TICKETS FROM H.M.V. RECORDS AND STUDENTS UNION SHOP

CB...Communal Building
GH...Great Hall

FOR FURTHER DETAILS CONTACT
BD. 34135 Ex. 42
MARION FOUNTAYNE

OCTOBER 1980

DISTRIBUTORS

An interview with Mick Switzerland - their man in Wakefield...

In Feb '80 the band released a first single on their own Recorded Sound label. Titles were 'Wireless' c/w 'TV Me'. A second, 'Lean On Me' c/w 'Never Never' came out on Sept 5th on the York-based Red Rhino Records label.

Q What's the band doing at the moment?

A In October we'll be recording some demos - rough versions of the numbers in our current set. We'll then choose the next single from those - to be released in the New Year, almost definitely thru Red Rhino again. Then for November we're trying to line up a Northern tour for ourselves & The Rhythm Clicks - a Newcastle band who're also signed to Red Rhino. Although the other 3 members of Distributors live in London, we've a strong Northern identity - mainly because I do a lot of the promo work from my Wakefield address.

Q You've said that you're not after signing to a major label or even getting outside management, so is that degree of independence important to the group?

A Yes. We're 4 very strong individuals with similar, but diverse musical backgrounds that bring in elements of experimental, freeform, dub, jazz & other influences, as well as MOR pop. I mean, you can't dismiss Abba, Cliff & The Shads, even (say) Matt Munro on the one hand, or punk, Bowie, synth music, the rise & rise of reggae & other recent influences on the other. As a 4-piece, we come together with a whole bunch of separate ideas & tend to write out of group improvisation. Improvising is a big factor. It's there in our live work - a good gig being one in which we're listening to one another more than to ourselves. The lyrics in particular are often last-minute improvisations - the lyrics of 'Wireless' for instance only came up in the recording studio itself. The lyrical spontaneity is often a bit like reggae toasting - the way the DJ's do off-the-cuff talk-overs. And the music goes through a whole load of changes before we come up with a definitive version - though even that can still change, sometimes into a completely new song.

We're very happy sticking with a small friendly label like Rhino that doesn't dictate terms to us & takes a real interest. As for management, we could do with a London guy to handle a lot of the promo footslogging work - though we'd ideally want him to come in as a fifth non-playing member of the outfit with exactly the same financial commitments & benefits as the 4 of us.

Q So how about your own individuality? Your musical involvement covers playing in the band, producing in the studio for other bands, songwriting, admin & promo organisation, & solo work. What do you want personally out of these beyond variety for its own sake?

A I'd like The Distributors to be able to work with the minimum of hassles; to do live gigs, compose & record, changing & developing as a unit of 4 individuals without too many worries about money, promotion & all the usual limitations of the record industry, music business & overdrafts.

With the outside producing I want to be an effective catalyst through my ideas & knowledge of studio technology. I don't want to interfere. George Martin was a great producer for The Beatles & a host of other sixties acts. And Eno, as a producer, is low profile in a very big way. What he did for Talking Heads was just great. I've watched him work in a studio & have been really impressed with his subtlety - he doesn't change anything, but makes all the difference.

The composing's random. I don't write songs. I go into the studio & see what I come up with - so it's a creative process that I allow to happen. I just want it to continue.

The business side is incidental. I do a lot of the hassling now, but would gladly drop it if someone else came in to do it - that'd be the fifth member I mentioned earlier.

The solo work was there long before Distributors started & will be there after the band's finished. All of us in the group have very solid projects of our own - musical & otherwise.

- interviewed by Nick Toczek (23 Sept 80).

page 5.

REGGAE   REGGAE   REGGAE

GREGORIAN CHANCE

Tino Palmer reviews Gregory Isaacs as the Ja. Reggae star tries to hit gold here in U.K.   PALM COVE, BRADFORD 12/SEPT/80

Fri night at Palm Cove - coachloads of fans arrive from Leeds for the reggae event of the year in Bradford.

Support band AREMA are from London & deliver an energetic 50 minute set. Watch out for this band because they are very good - their harmony work was great & they sounded tight. (Trouble reared its head all the way through the gig with a crackle in the P.A., but it wasn't too bad). At times, Arema sound much like Steel Pulse which is no bad thing, & they tell me they're bringing a single out in 3 months or so. Buy it!

11.25 & ROOTS RADICS BAND saunter onstage & start playing. After 5 minutes, they stop & the road manager (I presume) walks on to present to us "straight from Kingston, Jamaica, the great, great superstar Gregory Isaacs", & the cool ruler hits the stage - natty indeed in 3 piece suit & gold chain.

The vocals suffered in the first number but perked up for the next two - 'Storm' with a touch of off-key keyboards & 'Slave Driver' (one of my faves) which was also featured in the hilarious film 'Rockers'.

From then on the whole place was in the palm (ouch!) of his hand. Unfortunately, sometimes the vocals & keyboards went duff. When you could hear the organ though, it was very Harry J.-ish (he over-dubbed on the new LP) & there were some great echoed flourishes. 'Mister Cop' from the Extra Classic album involved a throaty singalong from the audience - I wonder why?! Some numbers from the Lonely Lover album came up - 'Tune In' (which most people know, as it's been out on 12" for ages) & 'Poor & Clean' ("I would rather live poor & clean than live rich in corruption").

Towards the end, 'Soon Forward' & 'Border' surfaced for air - Gregory giving the mike to the front rows for the chorus of the latter, & finally at 12.50 leaving the stage after one encore, for the Roots Radics to play us home, & finish a 75 minute set beautifully.

So, Gregory Isaacs has signed to an English label & should now be more widely available. He has a distinctive voice, perfectly suited to his predominantly lover's rock reggae, & I would hope to see him get to be as easily acceptable to the public as Bob Marley. A good gig, all in all.

Man of the match, Brian? Apart from Gregory's voice, it would have to be Arema's drummer - marvy, kidz!!

LEEDS RECORD COLLECTORS' FAIR
at THE ASTORIA CENTRE, ROUNDHAY RD, HAREHILLS (by Gipton Greene pub)
11am-5pm   Sun. 9th Nov.
With 60 stall-holders from all parts of the country - all types of records. Also, books, magazines, badges, posters, etc.
FOR FURTHER INFORMATION RING LYNN UNDERWOOD ON LEEDS 687572.

LURID IN CONTEXT
LOU REED IN THE 80'S

'Growing Up In Public' (Arista, Spart 1131)
the album reviewed by Marc Nicholls

In 1978 Lou Reed recorded Street Hassle, an album which might yet be viewed as the creative high-point in a long but unpredictable career on the fringes of popular music.

In a decade which charted his decline from uncompromising cult hero to a position totally at odds with the very real developments which dominated the 70's middle years, Street Hassle was a most unexpected treat. It had dignity, power, conjured images every bit as powerful as those of the early days when Reed would hang around the Factory, trading his unnerving monologues against the instrumental naivety of the prototype Velvet Underground. A myth which has since hung like a millstone around his neck. A yardstick to measure him by... relentlessly and without thought.

Since the release of Street Hassle we have been offered the enterprising live double Take No Prisoners, last summer's uneven The Bells, and now Growing Up In Public, the first new Reed product of the 80's and in some respects the most interesting of this vinyl quartet.
Interesting because here we witness the final stage in a transition which has occupied the man since days spent treading the boards as definitive 'Rock n Roll Animal' to those of present status, unashamedly middle-aged, closer to the traditions of Sinatra than the VU and its attendant projects. Reed was never blessed with a 'voice' in the accepted sense, yet rarely before has he demonstrated such an enviable ability to twist words, slur phrases, to utilise vocals so effectively as a means of communication whilst detracting nothing from the musical excellence which makes this album a success.

The band is much the same as that which worked on Reed's recent albums and live shows and is once again in perfect sympathy with the guy's unbending, individual approach. Ellard Boles in particular contributes some fabulous bass guitar, while Michael Suchorsky's drums are precise and inventive. Reed meanwhile swaps smack for psychology, laces it with a whole bunch of witty, tricky couplets and finally delivers the package with the kind of teasing sophistication previously held latent. On Keep Away he promises:

"I swear I'll keep away from dignity and pride/I'll keep away from abstracts I'll keep it all inside/I'll just wrap me up in butter and melt me on a shelf/I'll fry in my own juices, I'll become somebody else".

This playful semi-autobiographical mood dominates much of the record. The guy gets tender on Think It Over, bitchy on So Alone, wryly amusing on The Power of Positive Drinking:

"And then some people drink to unleash their libidos/and other people drink to prop up their egos/it's my burden man, people say I've the kind of face you can trust... And some say that liquor kills the cells in your head/And for that matter so does getting outta bed/When I exit, I'll go out gracefully, shot in my hand..."

And so it continues. Though lacking the primitive urgency of those classic early discs, Growing Up In Public substitutes a professional intrigue, Reed's flirtation with jazz, a set of eleven finely-crafted songs... like the man says:

"Well you said that you wanted to dance/ so now we're gonna dance..."

The Neat - Staging Post 31/8/80
More reviews about chocolate & mic stands

The Gimmicks proved to be a very able support to The Neat. They play a younger & more modern style of music & show there is hope in the younger bands of Leeds. They gave their catchy set a thorough airing &, despite the odd flat vocal sequence & an accident with one of the drummer's microphones, went down well with a moderately full Stging Post. However, these goings on with the microphones were later to be conclusively surpassed.

In seeing Ray Romance's (urgh, what a name) exuberance in leaping off the stage, it became obvious that he had not been paying attention at the sound check where any fool would have noticed that this blatant act of showmanship would result in the noticably short guitar lead pulling the top amp to the ground. This it promptly did &, in retrieving it, Ray managed to knock over the same, already battered, mic stand. He later explained however that these acrobatics werenot intentional - he just fell off the stage!(New Rhythm Guitarist Wanted.. ?)

I did enjoy seeing the various pieces of expensive equipment being projected through the air , but I enjoyed more the wonderful sound of The Neat. Their mid-sixties image & music is far from out of date. Tonight, as usual, they put in a set which turned this gig into a party.

They are not however, simply for the people to take as dumb entertainment. Their music is serious stuff, & with E.M.I. following up their demo with interest, I would be the last person to follow the crowd & dismiss them as past it. With such songs as 'Clean Cut Kids', 'C.P. Operator', 'All Or Nothing' & especially 'Good Looking Girls', they danced away a great night.

With a couple of Beatles covers in their encores, their material is clearly influenced by The Fab Four. However, our little Fearsome Foursome make the audience remember THEIR songs, not the familiar stuff. This is all enhanced by the natural sense of fun which flows from them & which is curiously contagious, with the audience catching most of it!

They opened their set with a number recently done by The Rubinoos in '77 - 'I Wanna Be Your Boyfriend", & as well as the above highlights, included their possiblenew single 'Hold Me' & the old Squares/ Sneakers number - 'Buddy Holly'. Dave Parkinson of Cuba gueasted with them on keyboards, providing a melodic extra.

Not surprisingly, I like The Neat & tonight was another in a string of consistently good gigs. So, dear reader....... they are not boring, past it, dated or sameish...... they're Neat.

- Andy Stevens.

CLASSIFIED ADVERTISING IN WOOL CITY ROCKER (readership now over 10,000) STILL COSTS ONLY 10p PER WORD. IF YOU'RE SELLING GEAR, LOOKING FOR 2nd HAND GEAR, AFTER MUSICIANS OR A BAND, RUNNING A MAG, STARTING A VENUE, SELLING DISCS, RUNNING A DISCO, HIRING OUT YOUR P.A., PRINTING POSTERS, PHOTOGRAPHING BANDS, DOING VAN HIRE, etc. WHY NOT USE US. RING NICK (ed.) ON 21867 OR WRITE TO: 5 BEECH TERRACE, UNDERCLIFFE, BRADFORD, BD3 0PY? (cheques/P.O.'s payable to Nick Toczek).

Good Sax Player Wanted for Bradford band. Recording sessions and gigging. Ring: Bradford 33531.

Female vocalist/songwriter seeks musicians to form acoustic band. Write or ring: c/o W.C.R. (address/phone no. given above).

Musicians wanted to form reggae band. Anyone interested ring Bradford 668260.

Shaftesbury Fender copy guitar with case £60. 30 watt valve amp & 100 watt crescendo speaker £60. Ring: Leeds 584846.

Back Issues of Wool City Rocker available at 30p each plus 15p postage - don't forget to enclose your name and address with order!

NEXT ISSUE WILL MARK ONE YEAR OF WOOL CITY ROCKER'S EXISTENCE - BUT THERE ARE MORE IMPORTANT THINGS THAN THAT IN THIS WORLD (CAN'T THINK OF ANY AT THE MOMENT BUT...)

BANDAID BANDAID BANDAID BANDAID BANDAID BANDAID BANDAID BANDAID BANDAID BANDAID BANDAID

⚡LIVE ON STAGE !⚡

When my band, Ulterior Motives, played The Royal Standard with Idle Rich as support, one of the support band got a bad shock due to faulty earthing on his guitar amp. A week later, when Coda did PA for The Scene at Palm Cove, Paul from Coda got a shock plus burns. Cause: faulty earthing of gear. Last month, Motives played Scamps with Heaven 17 in support. I got two shocks & a couple of H17 got the same. The earth on the plugs in the club was live - so the outer casing of all the gear was live, even when it was switched off. The manager called in an electrician immediately &, though it seemed ok, the band there the following week fared even worse, with two of the band sustaining quite serious shocks. The venue is safe now, but this bunch of accidents goes as a severe warning. ALWAYS CHECK YOUR GEAR. The commonest problem is with amps. If they're not properly earthed, a guitarist who has his hands on the guitar strings earths himself through the p.a. if he takes hold of a mic or even touches it with his lips. This KILLED Stone The Crows lead guitarist at a gig a few years ago! A good few others have gone the same way. RULES: (i) Know your gear & check it or get it checked regularly. (ii) Bands should invest in a circuit tester - for a few quid you can save yourself the cost of blown gear, a bad fright & perhaps even your life. (iii) Felt or sponge baffles which fit like caps over the heads of mics also help. Keep music live, but keep musicians alive!

LAW 'n' ORDER...

Hustler Street Band (now known as New Model Army) took Palm Cove to court for non-payment of fees following a very acrimonious disagreement/argument at the end of a gig they did there a couple of months ago. They won. Bands & organisers please note the following points. (i) A verbal contract is legally binding &, if a band performs as arranged, then the venue has to pay the agreed fee, regardless of the subsequent behaviour of members of the group or their management. (ii) The band were awarded gig fee plus costs in bringing the case to court & say that the whole thing was easily done - they took legal advice, but actually represented themselves in court. (iii) They hope other bands who have trouble getting their full fee after doing a gig will follow their example in using the law to make sure of getting what's rightfully theirs. Finally, when going to court, dress well, be polite & play the game their way - it might not be your idea of fun, but it'll make all the difference between winning or losing the case.

John Farquhar's no longer bars manager (Vaults Bar & Queens Hall). The students union of Bradford College have 'suspended' him & it seems highly unlikely that they'll reinstate him. It's a shame to see him go when he's worked so hard, booking in almost every band in the area over the past couple of years. As he may be taking action for a claim of unfair dismissal, I can't really say much more at the moment. June is now bars manageress & Mo Maklouf, college social secretary is booking bands for the two venues (tel. 392712). His first gig was Creation Rebel at Queens Hall (end of Sept) which pulled a huge crowd - a success marred slightly by one of the bar staff being injured in a dispute with one of the band over his right to an after-hours drink. Again, with legal action pending, I can't say more.

BAND PROFILE — A NEW OPERA

Their letter reads: A NEW OPERA is the band formed by Dave Albone & Andy Tillison, formerly of Leeds band THE VYE. Although this band have only just started to work as a full-time unit, the idea was floating in the atmosphere well before the Vye split. Originally it started out with Andy having a jam with Jonathan Bousfield & Anthony Haller from Otley-based group Metal Fatigue (in later days Media F). These first jams & ideas were collectively titled New Opera. However, because of Vye/Metal Fatigue commitments, nothing came of the project. The next step was a ludicrous series of low key gigs with daft names - Lance Toughnall's Eurasiatic Moose was one. By this time Dave from the Vye on drums & his brother Simon had replaced the original rhythm section. Rick Eager from the Vye was next to fall into the turmoil - & THE NEW OPERA did a few sporadic performances supporting Metal Fatigue & the Vye. (Confused yet? - I am!). Mick McFling succeeded to the guitar post &, after the Vye split, A NEW OPERA kicked off. Now, to add Quentin Churchill on lead vocals (ex Media F, etc.) the band had succeeded in completely confusing everyone.

Once the cofusion had been sorted out, the band could concentrate on their music rather than their personnel, & the result could be described as odd. Influenced heavily by the new wave of progressive (not HM) rock, they are determined to play music, synthesiser influenced, that is not necessarily dreary, monotonous or robotic. There is much percussion work, all of the members having things to hit as well as their normal instruments. Complex quasi-jazz patterns leap into new wave thrashes, which in turn move into atmospheric synthetic ramblings or tribal rhythms. Can't really describe it well enough. But if you expect the Vye you're in for a shock.

The band are optimistic, their set is different. They want to say something worthwhile, & they want to bring out their emotions. It's just that these guys have got really weird emotions -they're all HAPPY!

Line-up: Andy Tillison (kbds/voice/bad gtr/perc), Mick McFling (good gtr/perc/glissando gtr), Quentin Churchill (ld voc/perc), David Albone (dms/perc) & Simon Albone (bass/voice/perc + accessories).

Contact: Leeds 623306.

PALM COVE CLUB
Hollings Road, Bradford 8. (Tel. 499895)

Every Friday:	Rock Bands (with bar from 7.30pm—1am)
Every Saturday:	Reggae Bands (with bar from 9pm—1am) ½ price admission before 10 pm.
Every Sunday:	Jed's Blues Band (with bar from 7.30pm—10.30pm) pub price beer
Every Tuesday:	Live Jazz-Rock (with bar from 9pm—midnight)

STOP PRESS: HEAVY METAL EVERY FRIDAY (7.30-10.30) pub price beer + late bar. Diamond Head, Witchfynde, etc. -see gig guide.

BAND AID: producing

An interview by Nick Toczek with local studio producer Lindsay Frost on why all bands using a studio need a producer.

Several thousand bands have, in the past two or three years, released singles on their own labels. they've spent hundreds of pounds apiece & most are dissatisfied with the end-product. In many cases, it comes down to the studio engineer not understanding what the band was after. On major labels this problem is much reduced by the presence of a producer whose job is to bridge this gap. His fee is a small extra to the overall cost, yet very few independent bands use one. Hence this interview...

Lindsay Frost has been playing instruments since he was eleven. He started on clarinet, moving on to sax (which he played off & on for six months in The National Youth Jazz Orchestra), then keyboards (on which he's done session work, composes & arranges), then drums (on which he's done a lot of gigging - notably for The Out whose single 'Who is Innocent' was released first on Rabid & later on Virgin). He was musical director for The Northern Jazz Orchestra for two years & has done regular writing & arranging in his various ventures for the past few years It's worth adding that he didn't really want all this gen. included in the article, but I felt it it was useful to show that he's not just some goon who fancies his chances as a self-appointed record producer.

Q. What brings you to Leeds?
A When 'The Out' folded a year ago I was invited up here by a friend who'd got a club cabaret band. It looked like the chance of a regular wage, but didn't work out. By Xmas, we'd split up.

Q. So why producing?
A. I did a lot of sorting out after that. I'd done some producing in Manchester & contacted Ric-Rac to see if there was a chance of work through them. I did a demo there with Adrian Fuller & later did a recording with him at September Sound which came out as a single. Then I co-produced some demos for The Grumbleweeds, doing keyboards, drums & sax for them as well. Since then, I've been in touch with Bob Miller at Ram Studios & have done some work on his own material. Through him, I hope to be doing more work at Ram.

Q. What kind of producing are you after now?
A. Any bands at all. The only proviso is that they must be committed to their music. I enjoy most styles - almost anything, in fact. It's just that I like to get very involved & so need the same degree of commitment from the band.

Q. What do you see as being the role of a producer?
A. Primarily, he acts as a middleman between the band & the studio engineer. Bands usually come into the studio with a fairly clear idea of the kind of sound they want. In fact, this is essential if they don't want to waste time & money - their money. But they have probably worked very hard on their material & as a result will have lost some of the freshness that was originally there. An outsider - the producer - should be able to reinject some of that. In addition, a good producer can also help with the arrangements. He can tidy up the parts - especially where each musician comes in & where he finishes. And the band will probably not have a working knowledge of the studio & the available effects, so he can help out here too. Finally, it's worth pointing out that it's no longer good enough to come up with rough demos for major record deals. The companies want & expect demos of master quality - ie ones from which they could make an immediate _pressing_. All their own bands will have used producers & this is what the newcomers have to compete with.

So, are you going into a studio? If so, do give a bit of thought to using a producer. Lindsay's one of several who are available. Use one who knows the studio in which your recording. Invite him along to gigs &/or rehearsals. Try to get across to him exactly what you're after in terms of overall sound. Most are keen to do the work & won't rip you off. If they believe in what they're doing, they may well go for a straight percentage deal on the end-product or settle for a reasonable fee. It's always negotiable. If you want a professional result, it helps to set about the job in a professional manner.

Contact: Lindsay on Leeds 623306.

BLUSH

From Pontefract, the band are: Kevin Hickling on vocs, Len Barker on gtr, Steve Brough on bass & bkg vocs, Nigel Sykes on dms & Johnny Brown on gtr & bkg vocs.

Describing their music as 'fusion pop' & their financial state as parlous, they're a new wave band who play most of their gigs on the club circuit. I'd arranged to meet up with them after having heard & very much liked their demo cassette (see WCR 8).

Though the band has made quite a bit of money, it has all been ploughed back into the venture & so the members all have day jobs (& one unemployed).

"We've lost a lot of money recently through our pa & our van. The pa is an HH rig. When it works, it can be surprisingly good, but again & again since we got it we've had it blowing. It's been back at the factory more than it's been out on the road with us!"

"And our van blew up, costing us £1,000. Then there are agents' commissions, tax, overheads, etc. & with gaffa tape at £5 a roll in some shops, we don't come out with profits!!"

The line-up's been together for 2 years without changing. Working the clubs, they play a lot of cover versions - though they stress that these are their own arrangements & not just straight copies. And they only do songs that appeal to the band in the first place. The covers are partly because the crowd expect & want songs they know as well as the group's own numbers & also because 1½ hrs is a long time to play if you're just doing your own songs, so the covers pad it out & make it more varied. However, they're now finding that more & more of the crowd they pull is coming along to hear their own songs. In fact, their high energy new wave has pulled _too_ big a crowd at a couple of venues & they've been unable to go back because the staff 'can't cope'.

Manager, Steve Musson, put up the money for their demo. "We spent 8 hours working through the night in Ric-Rac". The demo's got EMI & CBS interested in the band, & also Mick Rea (brother of Chris) at Magnet. Those labels have promised to send along someone to catch the band live. The band feel that they're at their best live & so have high hopes for a deal in the near future.

In the immediate future, they're keen to do more supports to touring bands & get in as much gigging exposure as they can.

Their demo is on sale at gigs & is certainly proving to be popular. They've sold 400 in the past two months.

Contact: 0623-34747 (Steve Musson, magager) or Johnny on 0977- 43567.

SURFIN' DAVE

Line up: solo.

David Coleman (a.k.a. Surfin' Dave) moved from Bournemouth to Leeds in September to see Futurama 2 & to write songs: "You can't write rock'n'roll in a place as 'nice' as Bournemouth."

In the last 12 months he'd tried & failed to form a band down there (couldn't find a singer & kept changing drummers & guitarists): "Everybody who could play was already in a band & there weren't many of them anyway." So he decided to go it alone & did a couple of dozen supports to local bands in the Bournemouth/Poole area.

About six months ago, Ronnie Mayor (ex-Tours & now with Da Biz) formed Small Operations, an independent record label, initially to release a single by The Contacts (from Poole). This was followed by a single from Da Biz, with a 3rd due any time now from a solo synth-player called Paul Chambers. The 4th release will then be a Surfin' Dave 3-track single (God willing): "That'll be some time early next year. Meanwhile, I hope to form a band up here – probably a 4-piece with me on rhythm guitar (I tend to 'chang' my guitar) & vocals. We'd be doing late 50's/early 60's rock'n'roll in the modern idiom... sort of Jonathan Richman. I love Jan & Dean, The Beachboys & so on."

"When we were forming/trying to form the band, it was to do new wave pop – which wasn't what I was writing. That's why I eventually solo & why I now want to form a rock'n'roll band – which is the sort of music I've always been into. Something along the lines of a fast & very danceable Ray Campi is how I imagine it.

Dave is currently keen to get in some solo supports on the local pub/club/college circuit & would also like to hear from other musicians.

Contact:- S.D. at 121 Gathorne Terrace, Leeds (phone currently out of order). —interviewed by NICK TOCZEK.

P.S. Surfin' Dave is a genuine nickname not an assumed one. i.e. He does go Surfin' & got given the name to stop people confusing him with all the other Daves.

NEXT MONTH'S ISSUE... An interview with Split Enz, info. on scottish band The Freeze, Halifax's Private Dicks, Lancs. outfit 7 Year Itch, albums by 9 Below Zero, Myofist, R.A.F + loadsa local stuff & more. Plus one year of W.C.R.

NOSFERATU V

(pronounced 'vee' - it stands for vampire - 'Nosferatu, Spirit of Evil' was the first vampire film back in the early 20's).

They're a Leeds heavy rock band. Line-up is Tony Passmore (bass/voc), Steve Hoyle (dms/vocs), Bob Collinson (gtr/voc), Paul Barnett (ld. voc. & screams). They've since added a second guitarist, Nick Tyler. The band's been gigging round here (Bradford/Leeds) for a few months. Their first 3 gigs were a run of try-out dates at The Italian Club, Leeds Rd., Bradford. They've since done another dozen gigs & are currently taking time out to get a proper (Gothic) stage show together. "We want people to come to see us as well as to hear us". They do 2 covers: Saxon's "747, Strangers in the Night" & Motorhead's "Bomber". The rest of the set's original material. "We're working on a 15 minute medley of standards & will be adding Sabbath's "Paranoid" for the new set."

A £200 p.a. repair + money spent on repairing their lighting rig (which fell over) took the money that they'd intended using on a studio demo around now, but they hope to do one soon. More bad luck (guitarist on holiday) meant that they had to turn down the chance of supporting Girls School at The Fforde Grene in Leeds. A similar support to White Spirit was lost when the gig got cancelled due to White Spirit's last minute Reading Festival booking.

I asked them about their music: "It's powerful progressive rock. We tend to drive from the back, so it's strong on drums & bass. And we don't go in for long boring solos, just short ones with the emphasis on melody. That's the essence of our music: driving drums + solid bass backing, melodic guitar. Add screamed vocals & that's us."

"We go on stage to enjoy ourselves & we don't let up for a minute. That way, we reckon the audience will pick up on it & enjoy themselves." They did a rough video a few weeks ago at The Gate Hotel, Seacroft & will be in the recording studio after a run of October gigs. —INTERVIEWED BY NICK TOCZEK.

When you're thinking of recording

Masters or Demos you'll need a studio with a reputation for good sounds, good engineers, and a friendly relaxed atmosphere.
A studio with the facilities you want, 16 track or 8 track available by the hour or on day bookings. The effects you'll need like Flanging, Echo, Reverb, A.D.T. Noise Gates, Compressors, Harmonisers, Dolby 'A' etc., and a studio area with room to breathe.
A studio because of its unique sounds, attracts bands from all over the British Isles, Germany and Denmark, and a studio that doesn't charge the earth.

16 track £16 per hour	8 track £10 per hour
16 track £140 per day	8 track £80 per day
(10 hours)	(10 hours)

NO OVERTIME CHARGES. WHEN YOU'RE THINKING OF A STUDIO LIKE THIS YOU'RE THINKING OF

RECORDING STUDIOS

Ring us at ROCHDALE (0706) 524420

KENION ST., ROCHDALE, LANCS., ENGLAND

MAJICK PLASTIC TIME: SINGLES/E.P.'s

BEAT PUMP - '5 Month Plan E.P.' on Slow Lorries Records. A 3-piece who give 5 tracks that're Joy Division + drum machine. Rhythmic monotony with elusive charm. It succeeds because of the good songs, effective mix & neat bits of overdubbing. A good one from Wakefield... next!

TIGER LILY - 'Monkey Jive' c/w 'Ain't Misbehavin'. 1975 recordings by the band that later became Ultravox (Dennis Leigh aka John Foxx & co.), though you'd be hard pressed to recognise them here. The local boy & his former mates must find it a bit embarrassing. The songs are OK, but very dated & devoid of originality. File under collector's curiosity - more dead than good. On Dead Good Records who could surely have come up with a worthy newcomer rather than trying to cash in on the band's later reputation.

DISTRIBUTORS - 'Lean On Me' c/w 'Never Never' on Red Rhino Records. York label for 2nd single from Wakefield/London band. Like the vocals on the A-side, but the song relies on a weak bass riff + too thin guitar + predictable & too simple drumming. There's no meat here. B-side is more appealing with its choppy percussion. Must try harder next term.

MEKONS - 'Snow' c/w 'Another One' on Red Rhino Records. Leeds band on their third label. Masters of professional amateurism. It's either pretentiously awful or gloriously uncompromising, depending on the shape of your ears. Mine are latter-shaped & I love every shakey chord that this band has etched on disc. They never did kill Dan Dare & probably never will, but I still read every episode. Is this review too obscure?

RHYTHM CLICKS - 'Short Time' c/w 'Lies Don't Talk' & 'chains' also on Red Rhino. O.K., despite trite lyrics delivered like Shakespearian amateur dramatics. Weakish songs, but bass & keyboards fight bravely against the tide. Alas, poor Yorick. Exeunt.

THE EXPLOITED - 'Army Life' c/w 'Fuck The Mods' & 'Crashed Out' from The Exploited Record Co. (Red Rhino distribution). Skinhead punk. Totally clichéd. Fuck, wank, shit lyrics (with backing vocals from 'The Fuckits'). One of the best pure punk records I've heard in ages. 3 years too late to make the band stars, but still fucking good. From Edinburgh.

THE HITMAKERS - 'Keep On Proving It' c/w 'Tell Her I Love Her' on Surrey Sound Records. The sort of thing that makes me wish I had a radio programme of my own. Buddy Holly meet Wreckless Eric. Timeless pop. Why isn't this getting massive airplay? It's distributed by Pinnacle if you want to go out & order it.

JOY DIVISION - 'Incubation' c/w 'Komakino' on Factory Records. Out for a few months now, but I only got hold of a copy recently. This is the flexi-disc that you could've picked up for free just after Ian Curtis topped himself. The instrumental 'Incubation' comes in two parts that are really different songs - hammered typewriter percussion get gtr. on the first, kbds on the second. They've typically frozen hard appeal. Other side features Curtis' doomy despair with spacey bass and (almost) disco drumming. About as cheerful suicide itself. Sad. Mancunian, of course.

THE FREEZE - 'Paranoia' & 'For J.P.S.' c/w 'Psychodalek Nightmares'. Their '79 single. Good mixture of influences (punk, new wave, sixties psychodelia) that's too careful to be pop. Another good Edinburgh band doing themselves credit on their own A1 Records label. Nice try & warmer than their name suggests. Can't dance to it, but it's quite good to sit still to.

THE FREEZE (again) - 'Celebration' c/w 'Cross-over' also on A1 Records. The current single. First side is a foot-tapper for a (slightly dreary) celebration. Too samey, though there's a nice game of spot-the-piano to round it off. Flip side reminds me of Country Joe & The Fish. I used to like them. So I quite like this too. Think of a word... austere.

TYPE - 'Bright Green Angels' c/w 'Won't You Be Mine' & 'Fast' on Broken Records. She sounds like Siouxsie. They come from Loughborough. She sound just like Siouxsie. In the early, more punky days. 2nd track's better than the A side. Oh, yes, I'm enjoying this. A tasty bunch of songs, but they should've done a pic sleeve if they wanted to sell the thing.

CONTACTS - 'Young Girls' c/w 'Boyfriend' on Small Operations. Pop from Poole (in Dorset): "Young Girls do it so much better... when they're sixteen years old." or turn over for same tune reworked with a lyric that moans about boyfriends "they really get me down now, they hang around now... they don't leave any for me". Heavy stuff, huh? Forgetable.... there! I've forgotten it.

DA BIZ - 'On The Beach' c/w 'This Is No Audition'. Same sort of cruddy lyric: "Can't wait till the summer comes" leading into sexual fantasy. Same goes for the B-side. However, it's powerful, slightly Ramonesy pop with some nice gtr./dms. Quite catchy.

ALBUM: Back-Stage Pass

A punk sampler issued by Supermusic P.A. Hire (odd, that) & marketed & distributed by Red Rhino.

SLAUGHTER & THE DOGS open with their oldie 'Where Have All The Boot Boys Gone?' It's a bit rusty, but acts as a good opener. COCKNEY REJECTS don't do much for me. 'Wanna Be A Star' is a typical Rejects bash, with Stinky (vocs) sounding like a juvenile Max Bygraves telling his story. CYANIDE are good & 'Fireball' is a bit like a male Runaways at their best. U.K. SUBS are disappointing on the very ordinary 'Emotional Blackmail (part 1). The short (part 2) is more like it. There's a heavy metal guitarist hidden among their punkarama. MANUFACTURED ROMANCE have 'You' - a song that gains strength just before it finishes (!). Then comes the classic 'Murder of Liddel Towers' by ANGELIC UPSTARTS. One of their best songs & it still works wonders two years on. A great piece of convincing protest. EXPLOITED's 'Crashed Out' (see singles review above) fits well here. Last up on side one is STIFF LITTLE FINGERS' 'Closed Groove' - the first track that's not straight punk - more like a chanted poem with some sparse dm/bass/gtr. back-up. Not their best, but an interesting track for all that.

Stinky opens side two with: "Freedom? There ain't no fuckin' freedom!" & his band break into one of their better songs - 'Police Car'. Good one next from S.L.F. in 'Barbed Wire Love'. I like the line: "You set my armalite" & the doo-wop break that immediately follows it, but the real strength is the chorus line of the song's title. BOB DE VRIES vies with Descartes in a philosophical punk ditty with the irrefutable logic of its title: 'I'm Me'. Then ANGELIC UPSTARTS return to their fave theme of 'Police Oppression'. MANUFACTURED ROMANCE get 'Long Distance Love' off the production line. Their vocalist has an interestingly distinctive voice of a type I last heard from 60's chanteuse Billy Davis. Another good one follows from SLAUGHTER & THE DOGS with their 'I'm Mad'. Three left to go, first of which is ANTI PASTA's 'No Government' - which is a bit too rough-edged even for this anthology though it does drive along apace. CYANIDE score full marks again with 'Mess I'm In', leaving U.K. SUBS to wind up the party with 'New York State Police' in typically punky style.

There haven't been many good punk samplers. 'Live At The Roxy' & the Anglo-American 'New Wave' (the one that included Patti Smith's 'Piss Factory' & Richard Hell's 'Love Comes In Spurts') are the only ones that spring to mind. 'Back-Stage Pass' ranks alongside these. It has surprisingly few duff tracks & several stand-outs. Worth getting if this is your music & you've not already got too many of the tracks on singles.

ALBUM: Bouquet of Steel

A 15-track sampler of new music bands from in and around Sheffield on Aardvark.

ARTERY's 'The Slide' is an odd number in that it features the whole band only playing percussion + vocals. It's a powerful feature of their stage show, but isn't quite as impressive here - maybe why they're remixed the number for imminent single release.

B-TROOP's 'Peroxide Romance' is somewhere between a sixties pop ditty and Revillos, given a new music feel via synth & chopped guitar-work. A very appealing song.

COMSAT ANGELS, who look like they're being lined up for the big hype to stardom, offer 'Ju Ju Money' - a song that's OK but that's all. The arrangement is singularly lifeless & unimaginative. Disappointing, I expected much better.

DISEASE come up with 'Psychobin'. Droning guitars & a singularly unpleasant vocal drone/shout. It speeds up half way through, giving it a bit more bounce & helping it to finish more quickly.

FLYING ALPHONSO BROTHERS wing in with a slice of pure sixties pop 'Video Date'. The sound very like The Salford Jets.

I'M SO HOLLOW have 'Touch'. It's a very standard formula with the droning lifeless guitars (or could equally have been synth) & flat vocals. Another lump of disappointment from a band who should've been better than this.

MUSICAL JANEENS (& OTHER PARTY GAMES) have 'Glen Miller & his contemporary intimacies meets the musical janeens uptown with a packet of jellies & a caribbean monolith' except that they spell it Glenn, don't they? That apart, the title's about a silly & throwaway as the track which is more of a studio doodle. Quite entertaining, though.

NEGATIVES 'Was It The Night' comes out a pleasant but absolutely ordinary dated pop song. (Not to be confused with former Bradford punx of same name). Did I say punk...?

REPULSIVE ALIEN's 'Say & Do' is indeed punk. Very short, less than 2 minutes. Full of life & energy. Fun.

SCARBOROUGH ANTELOPES with 'Here We Go In Indigo' cleverly blend standard pop with new music influences. It's catching, you know.

SHY TOTS have been persuaded to speak up on 'Robot Maid'. More pop. OK but relies too heavily on the one-line-repeated-because-it's-good musical formula.

VEILED THREAT give us 'Torch'. Pull back the veil & there's no great threat. This is O.K. but, like so many of the tracks on here, it's unexciting. Quite interesting, but doesn't even try to grab you.

VENDING PACT go on a bit too long on 'Secret Thinking'. It's an average-to-good synthed number.

de tián's 'Chorale' really tries hard. Using echo on chanted vocals & no instruments, they produce a kind of monks-in-a-monastery pop. Full marks for trying to be different. Quite high mark for the outcome of their effort.

Y? surprise with 'End of Act One'. Live, they're posey & boring. Here, though, they pack a bit of punch & are an impressive closer.

I've been fairly hard on some of these bands. For a local sampler it's varied, generally well-recorded & makes for good overall listening. There's an excellent glossy book enclosed that covers all the bands on the album (photos, profiles, discographies) plus numerous other bands from around South Yorkshire. If you're interested in local rock & want to pick up on a sampler that includes a few bands who're bound to go on to bigger things, then this is definitely for you. Give it a listen.

Album: Tattoo Hosts Vision On

Ada Wilson + Ian Nelson (brother of Bill, I think) + Dave Whittaker (also of Music For Pleasure) come up with an excellent & varied selection of songs on their manager Dave Oddie's own label. Wakefield suddenly seems to be alive with good music.

It's a shame that Wilson overstretches himself on spoken poem-to-music 'Shattered, Unspoken'. He's no great poet & it comes over like

MAJICK PLASTICK (episode two)...

something being read out of a sixth-form magazine. The previous track 'Fantasy Island' has the man at his best - doing good contemporary rock, here given a pulsing tribal rhythm & the whole song delivered with panache & a touch of humour.

Between these two extremes, Ada Wilson (this is really his show) uses electronics, electric & acoustic guitars & studio effects to get over musics; ably backed up throughout by the other two on keyboards. Eerie atmospherics with careful use of echo typify the songs & the drum machine is employed well through about half the songs - as a supportive effect rather than an apology for a missing drummer.

The instrumental 'Red Pictures' effectively blends keyboards (Whittaker) & sax (Nelson) on a slow jazzy tune that grows on me. While the next number, 'Empty Building' has more raunchy sax on a song that harks back (in musical feel) to the early-mid seventies.

Generally, it's the range of styles & influences that impresses most. The three of them fight hard against slipping into any single style or 'sound'. An excellent & exciting first album from Wakefield's self-appointed cult-figures who seem to be spending 1980 showing that they really can deliver the goods.

If Ada Wilson stays clear of poetic aspiration & keeps a careful eye on the risk of trying to drag too much of a '65-'75 sound behind him into the '80's, then he's definitely a force to consider. I hope this album does grab him a slice of the limelight.

cassettes : cassettes : cassettes

ROCKABILLY REBS: demo tape of 10 tracks recently recorded a Box Studios. The band come up with a remarkably authentic 50's rockabilly feel which totally infectious. Echo + tinny guitar/cheap amp sound + clicking drumsticks & that odd slack-string bass sound all contribute. Featured in last issue, they've since been signed to EMI, so you may soon hear this for yourself. 2 of their own nos. plus 8 covers, the whole lot recorded in 5 hours! Nothing innovative here, but they pull out every possible cliché & do it all with slick professionalism. It's great fun & still 100% commercial. (Leeds/Bradford band).

HEAVEN 17: 11 track demo tape of songs that remind me of Buzzcocks with keyboards. There's the same combination of rhythmic monotony & an overlayed pop melody - a formula that can be traced back to bands like The Doors. Here, though, it's in a 1980's format. Bleak & insistent. On this showing, I'd say the band's best path would be to aim for cult status rather than compromise & chartdom. The Fall/Cure/ Pop Group/Slits/P.I.L. market would, I'd guess, accept them without demanding too many drastic changes from their current approach.

MUGGINS BLIGHT: A vast improvement on their single, this 3-track demo has the band emerging as a powerful pop-punk crossover outfit with immensely appealing songs that're quite well arranged (though I'd like to hear the band less drums-dominated than they are here). Good female vocalist & an appropriately distorted guitar. Why isn't this band regularly gigging outside their hometown area? (Skipton)?

ARTERY: 4 tracks from this Sheffield band from which their next 2 singles will be taken. Includes the remix of 'The Slide' - their track on the Bouquet of Steel album (see earlier review). A good band with a very distinctive sound'n'style that's both contemporary & original. I'm a little unsure about the production job here. It's a very clean mix, but also very flat - too cold & colourless by far. The band had much more texture & warmth than this when I saw them live at Futurama.

FORCE NINE: 2-track demo from a hard-driving rock outfit whose sound is very Led Zep. An impressive band for all that, with a high-pitched, high-powered vocalist as their up-front asset. 'Force Nine' is an out-&-out rocker, while 'Carbon Copy Man' is equally heavy, but it's spiced out with some neat guitar (+ effects). Tape echo delay works particularly well on this second number. The tape's got into the Sounds H.M. chart this month. If you like good HM, try this - you can get it from 12 Morris Crescent, Ribbleton, Preston, Lancs. (Preston 791220 for price, etc.)

TWISTED NERVE: Very good quality demo that shows this Leeds new-pop band at their best. Paul Mirror's a strong vocalist/frontman & a better lyricist than most. Clarity + carefully used echo give this recording real depth. I particularly like 'Heroes' which stands out as a good song both here & in the band's live set.

B. TROOP: An oddly misleading name for a band you might expect to be HM. This Doncaster outfit have a bouncy commercial pop that's built round sax & kbds. This 5-track tape is the first release (at £1-00) from Hotshot Records. It should, by the time you read this, have been followed up by a single ('Junior' c/w 'Espionage a go go' - both on this cassette) costing £1-25 inc. p&p. I particularly like 'Espionage...' with its bouncy drms & synth interspersed with thick layers of sax. You can find Hotshot at 5 Auckland Rd., Doncaster, S. Yorks. (tel. 0302-2050) & you can find B Troop also on 'Bouquet of Steel'.

NYLO KLINIK: A London band fronted by a guy whose writings have gone into my other magazine (The Little Word Machine). In an appealing blend of modern musics they offer 2-tone rhythms, semi-experimental electronics on kbds & predominantly new wave vocals that vary between Costello & Geldoff - though that's not to do the lead singer justice. He's also got a very versatile voice & comes in with plenty enough to convince the listener of his individuality & strength. Couple of the songs are a bit too long, but they're a powerful unit & I imagine they really cut it live.

THEIR CRIMES COMMITED: (I assume they mean 'committed'). A 12-track tape released as a cassette LP. by Cinema Product, 9 Egerton Grove, Chorley, Lancs. One side live (& very rough at that) the other a studio production. The live tracks are semi-electronic (gtrs/drm machine/kbds/drms/etc) with a very flat vocal that's more of a sub-Numan drone. It's hard to judge the live show on this quality of recording - a few good songs + a fair wack of monotony. The studio work includes a slowed-down track that sounds good but is over-long. That sort of sums up this tape. Too few good ideas & those that there are tend to be overused.

THE ELEMENTS: Keighley new wave outfit of guitars & sax + female vocalist. 4 good tracks that underline the variety of material that the band write (three of them have each contributed songs here) The band have since changed vocalist (taking in Tricia Cusack, ex-Press Release). This tape's been on sale at gigs & is available for £1 + postage from 182 Highfield Lane, Keighley, BD21 2HU.

STILL EARTH: Doncaster H.M. outfit with a 4-track demo recorded in July '80 at Planet Studios. The first song opens with a very standard guitar riff in heavy early 70's mid-Atlantic rock style. The whole thing goes on. They're good, I suppose, but it's all hopelessly dated & totally lacking in the slightest spark of originality, with atrociously trite vocals to boot. Shame to see good musicians waste their time on such rubbishy material.

PETER MAYHEM: Tape entitled 'Glamour in Squalor'. Extracts from his gay shows including electronic rock (synth/drm machine/vocals/etc) + taped interview on toilet sex in London + other bits of chat etc. The rock is a cross between Numanesque electronics & freeform electronic rambling with spoken/ chanted vocals that're hard to make out. Mixed feelings. The tape quality's poor but there are some neat ideas here & the interview is totally over-the-top & amorally amusing. Whole thing ends with a girl talking about vibrators & finally demonstrating how the tiny silver anal vibrator gives her an almost immediate orgasm!

HIDEAWAYS: home recorded demos from this Ilkley group who keep changing their name. Not bad quality of recording. The band play mainstream pre-punk U.K. rock. Lotsa textbook chord progressions. Can't imagine many audiences wanting this stuff nowadays. Some nice melody lines but...

Record & cassette reviews by Nick Toczek.

BETTER BADGES

100 BADGES

1½" black & white

£13-50 inc. p.& p.

s.a.e. for production price list & other details.

286 PORTOBELLO ROAD
LONDON W10 960 5513

page 13

Doncaster heavy rockers Still Earth have been together for 4 years, having built up a considerable following in South Yorkshire. The foursome - Andy Smith (bass), Keith Henson (voc), Nige Westmoreland (dms) & Roy Broughton (ld gtr) are now touring extensively throughout Yorkshire & beyond, both in their own right & as support to the likes of White Spirit & Limelight. Their recently recorded demo of four tracks done at Planet Studios is reviewed as a cassette elsewhere in this issue.

Contact: Ray on Doncaster (0302) 59979)

Letter in from Rockabilly Rebs (Leeds/Bradford band featured in WCR8) to say that they came second in their heat, but so impressed Vic Lanza (panellist & gen. manager of EMI) that he signed them to the label &, if all goes well, there should be vinyl of the band on general release fairly soon. NB The group's just been in Box Studios, Heckmondwyke, see cassette reviews.

In the same contest, Knife Edge (Leeds band featured in WCR5 & given a live review elsewhere in this issue) won their heat. Manager, Dave Hall, phoned me to say that the band were through to the next round & assured of a track on a sampler album from the record co.

EMI/Tetley Supergroup Contest at Compton Arms, Leeds.

Thanks to Richard Bradney of Cross Gates Leeds for his letter enthusing about The Other Switch, describing their music as a compound of 10cc & Supertramp, with a flavouring of Camel (!). Tom Bliss of that same combo also wrote to say that The Other Switch (who're from Leeds), are sick of discovering more & more same-name bands, are calling themselves The Other Switch. Rob Lowther (gtr/voc), Tom Bliss (voc/kbds), Dave Turner (bass/voc) & Pete Dowling (dms) number Sneakers, Squares, Performance Anxiety, Cockpits, Neighbours, anada Boys & The Ambitions among their Luigi collective previous bands - virtually a catalogue of Leeds pub bands of the past 5 years! So, if you like your music Camel-flavoured or simply want to catch a dose of good musicians, try The Other Switch.

Contact: Tom on Leeds (0532) 751112 (= Haddon Hall minus 3!)

Force Nine are a Preston-based heavy metal band (see photo & cassette review elsewhere). Their line up features Mick Burland on dms, Alan Sagar on bass, Martin Jay on lead gtr & singer Dave Wills: average age twenty.

Like most pro HM outfits, they've a full stage show that included 700w PA, full lighting, special effects, sound & lighting crew, etc.

All the members have ben in other bands before coming together in F9. Their manager, Dave Booth, writes that the band's after gigs at the moment, a good agent in the near future & a record deal in the long term.

Contact: Dave Booth/Dave Slater on Preston 791220.

Put words to the cartoon & send to KARTOON KAPTION KOMPETITION, 5 Beech Terrace, Undercliffe, Bradford, BD3 0PY. Winner(s) will be printed in our amazing Xmas issue. Don't forget to include your name & address.

Peter Mayhem, whose cassette of performance sound-tracks & live recordings is reviewed elsewhere in this issue, writes: "I have worked as a performance /cabaret artist for about 3 years. To finance my work, I have worked in London as a rent-boy & porn model which in turn gives me plenty of inspiration for performance material. I shall be performing around the area in the autumn with my show 'Glamour in Squalour'. I use a backdrop of film & porn slides, wear many fab frocks & at the climax actually eat a can of cat-food. I describe my show as 'Frocks & Cocks & loadsa Shocks'. For info write to Lowlife Productions, c/o 27 Leicester Grove, Leeds 7, Yorks." (But can he catch mice. .?)

THE COMMUNICATIONS CENTRE

(a posh name for a basic facility)

offers 4-TRACK with DBX
at £3.50 p.h. + tape

Gear Includes:—
TEAC 3340, DBX, ITAM 10-4 desk,
LEAVERS-RICH E200, REVOX B77,
ORBAN REVERB, FILTERS, GRAPHICS, etc.
FULL D.I. + MIKES by AKG, CALREC, etc.

RING ALF or MOYA on Bradford 22769.

Knife Edge - Staging Post 20/9/80

Line Up: Mark Sweeney - lead vocals; Tim Knowles - lead guitar/backing vocals; Charly Peace - bass guitar/backing vocals; Edge - drums.

"We believe we are the best band in Leeds." That's quite a statement to live up to. The band in question - Knife Edge - set about convincing me. 'Street Credibility' echoes round The Staging Post & immediately you are forced to take notice of this band. They want to be looked at, taken notice of & above all, appreciated. They love playing to an audience & to get involved with their feelings. As Mark Sweeney lurches off the stage & screams at an audience who don't really know what to expect next, you just can't help feeling sorry for the bands who stand as though there has just been an explosion at the Super Glue factory. Exuberance abounds as they crash through 'Girl Trouble', 'Take A Shot', 'Fighting In The Chapel' & 'New Love'.

The first thing that struck me about Mark Sweeney is his remarkable resemblance to Jimmy Pursey. (Well, I think so!). He also portrays many of the oratorical qualities of the above Mr.P. The songs too are all very much 'doing it for the kids' numbers, all about being young & having 'street credibility'. They are full of energy & deliver their set in this manner.

Sweeney relieves himself (!? - ed.) of his jacket for the second set &, now newly adorned with head headband, goes through such numbers as 'Say You Will', 'She's Got Control' & 'I Go Wild'.

The rest of the band are completely engrossed in their music. They are somewhat detatched from the eccentricity of Mr. Sweeney but are however essential to the band's sound. They all have individualistic habits & it is by no means a case of Mark Sweeney being backed by Knife Edge. Tim Knowles excellent guitar work shows up particularly in 'I Go Wild' & 'Distress SOS' whilst all the time Edge & Charley contribute with a solid punchy rhythm.

Knife Edge are a band you just can't afford to miss.

They may not have entirely convinced me about their being the best band in Leeds, but they certainly are very close to that pedestal. They are verging on sheer excellence & it is my firm belief that they will go on to much greater things. (P.S. You read it first in W.C.R.). (Third, actually, They got written up well in Sounds a couple of years ago by Des Moines & in Musicians Only a couple of months ago by me - ed.).

— Andy Stevens.

CHINATOWN

A suspect mix & inadequate PA system did little to overshadow an enjoyable set from the much improved Chinatown. Musically their sound was hard-edged & cutting, well-rehearsed & deftly played. The set itself was of good songs, marred all too often by unnecessary & clumsy guitar solos, a crime of which both guitarists were guilty. Vocalist Steve Pragnell possesses a quite original high-pitched voice, but fails to use it to its full range. In addition, excessive echo &, at times, the rough mix further masked his voice.

'Time Will Tell' was by far the best song of the set & is a composition of newly recruited guitarist Danny Gwilym. It's a marvellously atmospheric piece with a refreshing, irresistable hook that's both simple & effective. The band wisely followed this by a number in complete contrast, 'Short & Sweet', a quick-fire rocker which lived up to its title. Chinatown's trump card & possible passport to success lies within the ability of drummer Steve Hopgood who dominates both sound & stage with his huge kit. His solo during 'Rock'n'Roll Legend' is well worth seeing &, in terms of musical ability, he stands head & shoulders above the rest of the band. The set was motoring along nicely before it crashed headlong into two terrible cover versions, UFO's 'Doctor Doctor', & Cheap Trick's 'I Want You To Want Me', both of which should be left well alone.

On the whole, their two encores were well deserved despite the low calibre of one or two songs such as 'It Could Happen To You' & their namesake 'Chinatown' (not Thin Lizzy's), which was particularly dull & uninspired.

As was shown by their performance, it's not all there yet but there is certainly no shortage of potential. The band's hometown of Portsmouth is famous for one particular 'Victory', maybe Chinatown are on target to become the second; just maybe.

- Steve Brown.

---

compere: Nigel Schofield of Pennine Radio

Folk Evening - Wed. 22 Oct. at Old Paris Restaurant

with records on sale & prizes to be won.

BOB PEGG + ROGER SUTCLIFFE + JOHN CAREY & LIZ JENKINSON + TIM MOON + MASON'S APRON + OTHERS.
+ poetry & humour from Nick Toczek (who?).

all proceeds to World Wildlife Fund. 75p inc. free supper

LIVE! LIVE! MUSIC MUSIC

AT....
The Queen's Hall
and
THE VAULTS BAR

we Have....
*Best Hand-Pulled Traitional Ales in Town!!

Bradford College
Students' Union
Queens Hall
Morley Street
Bradford BD7 1BW
Tel. (0274) 392712/3/4

Sweet Palace Restaurant

629, LEEDS ROAD   BRADFORD 3

Telephone (0274) 666060

Specialists in CURRY CHICKEN, KEBAB, TIKKA and all kinds of Asian Foods

Calling bands, students and anyone else who wants a sample of a good curry with a wide range of tasty starters and sweets. The **SWEET PALACE** offers all these at very reasonable prices. We are situated within two minutes drive from the centre of Bradford (on the left before Killinghall Road traffic lights).

WE PROMISE YOU EFFICIENT SERVICE AND A TASTY MEAL

Open daily 9 a.m. - 4 a.m.   Proprietor: Mohammad Afzal Bajwa

Swakara at The Vaults Bar, Bradford.

Swakara must be one of Bradford's most unjustly neglected bands. Having gigged all over the north & midlands for the past three years, they have built a small but fanatically-devoted following to whom their name is almost hallowed. Yet it must also be noted that they have detractors who label the band as nothing more than a Hendrix rip-off.

Certainly, from conversation with various of the Vaults audience, it became apparent that Swakara do produce an extreme polarisation of opinion. Many loved their music, but quite a few detested it & were at a loss to understand why the band were called back for two encores.

Basically, Swakara are a heavy-metal power outfit - consisting of the Wilkinson brothers, Paul (gtr/voc), Keith (bass/voc) & Bryan (dms), & lead vocalist Jonathan Byrne - whose sound is firmly rooted in the late 60's. Their music is dense & pyramiding; a cluttered & fuzzed cacophony of the same megaheaviness as The Beatles' "Revolution" topped with Hendrixian guitar pyrotechnics, all performed with skill & panache. Chuck Berry's 'Johnny B. Goode', their opening number, set the style & pace for the rest of the set: stomping along like a herd of buffaloes & flawless in performance, some intricate bass riffing on the changes, a space for jamming, & miles & miles of flashing guitar - some of it played by the teeth. Body-sweating music to set the mind reeling.

Of what followed, the covers stood out more (& were better received) than the originals - although 'Change Our Ways' carried a nice little shuffle beat & the steady 12-bar 'Blues Jam' was the one real variation in the set. Purple's 'Hush', Steppenwolf's 'Born To Be Wild', the "Angus!"-chanted anthem of HM 'Whole Lotta Rosie', & 'Jumping Jack Flash', among others, were worked well into the band's style & socked to the audience. A few walked out, groaning; those who stayed loved it & got progressively more enthusiastic.

So Swakara have found a niche, worked up a style & developed an audience; but the style is derivative & the audience is limited - & the reason is Paul Wilkinson. There is no doubting the man's tremendous ability as a guitarist; rather, it is his obsession with mimicking Jimi Hendrix' guitar-playing & stage mannerisms that is so limiting; bringing applause from those who are Hendrix fans & the 'rip-off' tag from those who are not. Before the show, Paul told me that he was aware of the problems created by the too-strong Hendrix association & was trying to steer the band away from that image, yet twice he had them leave him alone on stage to play solo on 'Star Spangled Banner' & the 'Electric Ladyland' opening; the first was overlong & had even the most fervent a little restless before the rest of Swakara came back on to take it into a dazzling 'Purple Haze', while the second was the perfect introduction to Dire Straits' 'Sultans of Swing' - ironically, the number which found Paul & his cohorts taking the most chances.

There can never be another Jimi Hendrix. He was a totally unique combination of outstanding musicianship, self-indulgent experimentation, bizarre showmanship, & self-parodying macho bravura. Treasure his music & take fistfuls of ideas from it, but don't copy because it simply can't be done. Swakara put on a good show that indicated they have the potential to develop their own, very strong identity; hopefully, they will do it.

— Keith E Rice.

RIC-RAC SOUND STUDIO

12 KIRKDALE AVENUE

LEEDS LS12 6AP   TEL. 633717

IF YOU WANT A TOP QUALITY DEMO OR MASTER TAPE RECORDED ON THE VERY BEST OF PROFESSIONAL RECORDING EQUIPMENT.

IF YOU WOULD LIKE TO RECORD IN A COMFORTABLE STUDIO WITH EASY ACCESS FOR LOADING AND PARKING.

IF YOU NEED SOMEONE WITH THE MUSICAL AND TECHNICAL EXPERIENCE TO BRING OUT THE BEST IN YOU AND YOUR MUSIC AND WHO CARES MORE ABOUT QUALITY AND YOUR SATISFACTION THAN HOW MUCH THEY CAN MAKE OUT OF YOU.

THEN RING MICK ON LEEDS 633717 to ARRANGE A CALL FOR A COFFEE AND A LOOK-ROUND.

STOP PRESS:- We are now able to offer facilities for recording full video demo tapes to go with studio sound recordings.

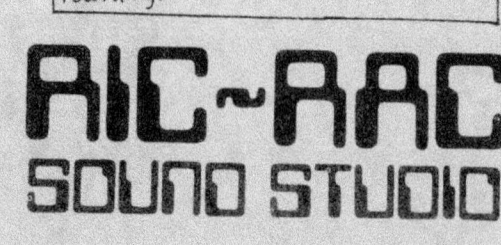

Reading Rockfest '80
Reviewed by Mick Mitchell

For all you readers of the NME, here's an account of the <u>musical</u> happenings of the weekend which were never mentioned in that inferior comic.

This is the weekend when approximately 30 bands take their coveted places on rock's most prestigious stages, & a weekend of heavy metal lay in store. 'Old wave' bands such as Whitesnake, UFO, & Gillan lined up against the 'new wave' bands such as Def Leppard, Iron Maiden & Praying Mantis.

FRIDAY - &, as always, I arrived late to hear the strains of the young pretenders from Switzerland, Krokus (see Loch Lomond review in last issue of WCR) although, to be fair, they sounded a lot more powerful & were certainly an improvement on their Scottish gig. This was probably due to the use of far superior equipment & the fact that I'm now more familiar with them.

Moving up the bill from last year come Gillan. I'm pleased to say that they played 'Vengeance' this time, plus the usual 'Mr Universe', 'Smoke...', etc. One of my favourites is 'If You Believe', which was apparently 'knocked together' by Bernie Tormé during a jamming session, the guitar at the beginning sounds incredibly like Hendrix. A scrappy show, but top of the bill next year perhaps?

Now here's a guy who's been around a while - Rory Gallagher playing his 3rd Reading & his 2nd headliner, still wearing his lumberjack gear. With Rory, anything goes, starting off with hard driving rock through to the blues, R&B & country music. Playing a range of instruments from the old faithful Rosewood Strat to Dobros, acoustics, mandolins & a variety of other electric guitars. If you don't like his carefree music, you must appreciate the talent & versatility.

Well, that's Friday over, & it's off for the usual 'rip 'em off priced' hamburger.

SATURDAY - & the sun's out which makes it a good day for lying around, getting pissed on y'crate of Watney's & listening to the day's offerings (or falling asleep in some cases).

Not surprisingly, people did fall asleep (myself included) because bands such as Broken Home, White Spirit & Grand Prix weren''t exactly awe-inspiring &, between the 3 of them, they couldn't come up with one classic which would make you want to wake up & listen.

Samson were the first band to make an impact on Saturday, a large cage surrounding the masked drummer made people sit up & watch out of sheer curiosity. The music began to pick up & vocalist Bruce Bruce gradually managed to attract the attention of the audience. Still, nothing to write home about.

Pat Travers managed to get the place going by playing music that was more cultivated than just a 3 chord thrash that we'd been so used to up to now. By this time it's getting darker & the audience are on their feet. Anticipation of the last two bands was creeping in (neither of which I'd heard before).

Iron Maiden (with their witch doctor-type symbol) made me think we were in for something <u>really</u> heavy & evil, & they certainly were loud & heavy, but no great sign of the evil. A solid sound, a bit of agression, but I'm sure they're capable of better things.

UFO really caught my eye (& ear) &, as I enthused about them afterwards, some bloke told me it was the worst gig he'd seen them do. I can't wait to hear a good one. Songs like 'Doctor Doctor', 'Rock Bottom', 'Shoot Shoot', 'Too Hot To Handle' & 'Lights Out' stood out like VD in a convent on a day of really stale music. Vocalist Phil Mogg reminds me of Rod Stewart in the way he struts & prowls around on here. The heavy image is dampened slightly by the 'pretty boy' looks of guitar/vocalist Kevin Heybourne.

Get y'Newcastle Brown out 'cos next come Geordie band Tygers of Pan Tang, better than the average HM band, plenty of potential, I particularly liked 'Suzy Smiled'.

Magnum brought a large following from Brum & managed to bring the audience to their feet, God knows why, I found them utterly boring & repetitive.

Budgie passed by with a reasonable response, but the next band to appear were a real surprise. At the last minute Blizzard of Oz (thankfully) pulled out & in came the old skinhead rockers from Wolverhampton - Slade, as elegant & raucous as ever. I've never seen anything like it; for the first (& only) time during the weekend, the place was set on fire & ripped apart by this band who captivated every single person present. (What about the married ones? - ed.).

Oldies such as 'Mama Weer All Crazee Now', 'Cum on Feel The Noize', 'Get Down & Get With It', plus new ones such as 'When I'm Dancing, I Ain't Fighting' & 'The Wheels Ain't Comin' Down' were among those that came off best of all. Anything after Slade was pure anticlimax. I'd love to see these guys back on top.

During the Slade (& not only Slade's) set, a can flinging fight took place, fun for some, dangerous for those whose heads were cut open, surely this is something we could do without next year.

Like I said, after Slade, everything was an anticlimax. Def Leppard played a mediocre set, & the big boys Whitesnake (Coverdale, Paice & Lord) were so incredibly boring. To be honest, I think I was in a minority here, but they certainly didn't live up to my expectations. They went down well. Perhaps people were making the most of the last band they'd hear from a weekend with only a few highlights & only one real surprise.

Yet again I walked out & looked for a hamburger & had to settle for a kebab. Got back to m'tent & some prick was playing Genesis (ugh!!) full volume in the tent next to me - ah well, there's no rest for the wicked. No John Peel <u>this</u> weekend! So what? I only missed the football results and, as the badges proclaimed, "John Ceel's a Punt".

After a whole weekend of HM, I reflected on how boring & clone-like the music was, but I suppose it's like any style of music, 90% of it's trash, but when it's good, it's <u>bloody</u> good.

Ian Gillan opened his heart & summed up why people from all over the continent make the pilgrimage to this 3 day spectacle by saying: "The spirit of festivals survives here, & no-one (pause) not one person can take that away". Never a truer word spoken; if the music wasn't all that brilliant, the spirit certainly was.

SUNDAY -& the weather's still good. Sledgehammer pass without notice, but following them are Praying Mantis & here we have a 'down the bill' band who shocked & impressed the 30,000-strong crowd. They should have been high up on the bill yesterday & livened up Stagnant Saturday.

Praying Mantis play HM with a melody which makes a change & makes them stand out from the other MOR bands. They sound like a mixture of Boston, Lizzy & Aerosmith.

"It's been my life ambition to play Reading" muttered vocalist/guitarist Tino Troy, & what better way to fulfil such a dream with the first encore of the day (a rare occurrence). Watch out for them, they're gonna be big.

Angelwitch follow. Not only have they a 3-piece Motorhead type line up, they have a Motorhead type sound, a bit rough but plenty of headbanging to be

---

CASSCORD
MAIL ORDER RECORDS AND TAPES

SINGLES for 40p inc. Bowie, Devo, Subs & Others
SINGLES for 75p inc. AC/DC, Marley, Iron Maiden, Numan, Costello, Beatles + more! ★ **Black Sabbath Albums** all £2.40 (double £2.95) ★ Other Albums from £1.20-£2.95 ★ CASSETTES from £1.49-£2.99 (Culture, Ultravox, Gabriel, SAHB, Marley, BeBop, Parker, Nugent, Allman Bros + many more!!)
A SELECTION OF 8-TRACKS from £1.10-£3.80 and FANTASTIC SAVINGS on RECORDS & CASSETTE CLEANERS & ACCESSORIES. ★ ★ ★
SEND FOR CATALOGUE—(25p discount on orders £5 or over with this ad)

CASSCORD
7 GLENLEE ROAD, LIDGET GREEN, BRADFORD 7, W. YORKSHIRE

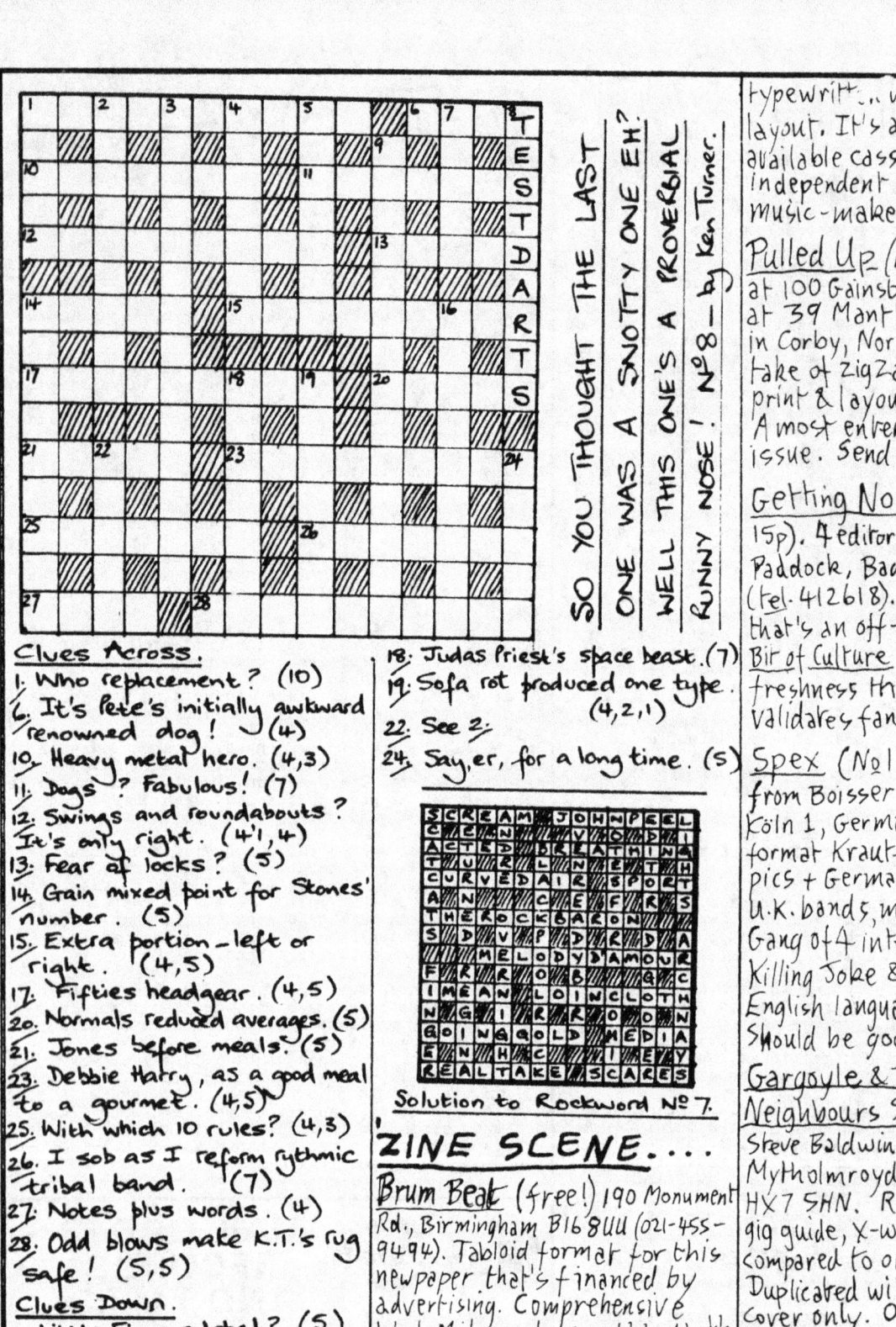

SO YOU THOUGHT THE LAST ONE WAS A SNOTTY ONE EH? WELL THIS ONE'S A PROVERBIAL RUNNY NOSE! Nº8 — by Ken Turner.

Solution to Rockword Nº7.

Clues Across.
1. Who replacement? (10)
6. It's Pete's initially awkward renowned dog! (4)
10. Heavy metal hero. (4,3)
11. Dogs? Fabulous! (7)
12. Swings and roundabouts? It's only right. (4',4)
13. Fear of locks? (5)
14. Grain mixed point for Stones' number. (5)
15. Extra portion – left or right. (4,5)
17. Fifties headgear. (4,5)
20. Normals reduced averages. (5)
21. Jones before meals. (5)
23. Debbie Harry, as a good meal to a gourmet. (4,5)
25. With which 10 rules? (4,3)
26. I sob as I reform rythmic tribal band. (7)
27. Notes plus words. (4)
28. Odd blows make K.T.'s rug safe! (5,5)

Clues Down.
1. Little Fingers label? (5)
2. and 22. Dizzy Gillespie doing the same as Gabriel! (7,2,1,4)
3. To reach a high standard. (2,6,3,3)
4. 10's headgear? (3,4)
5. Beaureaucratic decisions reversed for trouser design. (7)
7. Steel heartbeat makes reggae music. (5)
9. Not up to much. (4,3,7)
14. O age grips flowing note after flowing note! (9)
16. Cloud cover or nights produce these. (4,5)
18. Judas Priest's space beast. (7)
19. Sofa rot produced one type. (4,2,1)
22. See 2.
24. Say, er, for a long time. (5)

ZINE SCENE....

Brum Beat (free!) 190 Monument Rd., Birmingham B16 8UU (021-455-9494). Tabloid format for this newspaper that's financed by advertising. Comprehensive West Mids. rock monthly that's modelled on the national press. Good but ultra-straight.

Lens (No11, 20p). 10 Sherwood Grove, Wakefield (tel. 63780). Eds Ian & Mick have been doing this local mag. for a few years. Has features on local bands plus a few big names + letters + reviews. Gary G. + Toyah + Vapours + Human League, etc.

Strange Sounds (No.1, 20p). Gordon Hope, 24 Cowper Mount, Leeds LS9 7BB. A tapezine — typewritten with scattered layout. It's a catalogue of available cassettes from independent experimental music-makers.

Pulled Up (No.1, 10p). Charlie at 100 Gainsborough Rd. or "me" at 39 Mantlefield Rd. (both in Corby, Northants.) Nice piss-take of ZigZag for cover. Good print & layout. Plenty of variety. A most enterprising first issue. Send for it (enclose s.a.e.!)

Getting Nowhere Fast (No1, 15p). 4 editors, 13 Foxthorn Paddock, Badger Hill, York. (tel. 412618). Varied fanzine that's an off-shoot of York's Bit of Culture. Has plenty of the freshness that immediately validates fanzines.

Spex (No1, 2.50 Deutchmarks from Boissereestrasse 4, 5000 Köln 1, Germany. Smart, large-format Kraut-zine. Lotsa good pics + German text. Features U.K. bands, mostly. The Cure, Gang of 4 interview, Joy Div., Killing Joke & other new music. English language edition planned. Should be good.

Gargoyle & The Nosey Neighbours Supplement (No.3, 15p) Steve Baldwin, 6 Queen St., Mytholmroyd, nr. Hebden Bridge, HX7 5HN. Reviews, features, gig guide, x-word, etc. Scrappy compared to others under review. Duplicated with fotos on front cover only. O.K. for a local 'zine.

Riot/Clone souvenir handbook 50p from Dave Floyd, 1 Normanhurst, Feltham Hill Rd., Ashford, Middlesex (tel. 45017). Expensive, but interesting idea. It's the history of a (defunct) band.

Apathy (No1, 25p). Bradford punk zine from 22 Heaton Grove, Frizinghall, Bradford 9. Covers local punx Violation, Chronic, Living Dead. Enthusiastic but rather thin first issue. Fun & anarchy. Punk for punx. I like it.

J.S.G. Music Shop

108B Main Street, Bingley. Tel: 0274-568843

(Open till 9 pm every Monday and Thursday; Friday and Saturday till 5.30 pm)

FOR THE BIGGEST SELECTION OF GROUP GEAR AT THE LOWEST POSSIBLE PRICES

In the Guitar and Amp shop choose from:

Gibson, Fender, Washburn, Guild, Ovation, Rickerbacker, WAL, Lincoln, Peavey. full HH Concert Rigs, HH Performer, HH VS, Marshall, MM, Custom Sound. Carlsboro, Laney, Vox, Roland, 1,000 watt Rigs ready to go.
Mics by: AKG, Shure and Beyer.
Accessories by: Electroharmonix, Boss, Dod, Vox, etc.

In the Keyboard Department:

Wurlitzer, Moog, Roland, Rhodes, Korg, Hohner, Crumar, etc.

ALL THIS **PLUS** HIRE SERVICE, REPAIRS, HUGE SELECTION OF USED GEAR AND WE BUY FOR CASH

8-TRACK - £50 per eight hr. day !

Fully Equipped Studio

Using Tascam, Allen Heath, Revox, Roland, Quad, A.K.G., Calrec, etc., etc.

USE OF ANY OF THE FOLLOWING EQUIPMENT

Polymoog, Minimoog, Fender Rhodes Suitecase, Hammond X5 Organ, Moog Taurus Bass Pedals, ARP Salina String Machine, Clavinet D6, Mellotron, Premier Drums, Kramer 5000 Dmz Bass, Acoustic Piano & Guitars + numerous effects.

Yorkshire Gigs In October 1980!!!

We. 1
- City Hall, Sheffield = U.F.O. + FIST. Royal Park, Leeds = TREATMENT.
- Polytechnic, Leeds = SECRET AFFAIR + THE STEP.
- Rotters, Doncaster = SKIDS + BOOKS
- University, Leeds = 'SON OF STIFF' PACKAGE.* / GUY JACKSON.
- University, Sheffield = FISCHER Z.
- White Lion, Huddersfield = CITY LIMITS.

Th. 2
- Limit Club, Sheffield = REVILLOS. Royal Park, Leeds = 156 BAND.
- Fan Club, Leeds = U2. Princeville, Bradford = PARALEX.
- St. George's Hall, Bradford = SPECIALS + SWINGING CATS + STRAY CATS.
- Northern General Hospital, Sheffield = STILL EARTH
- Dragoon, Maltby = CARL GREEN & THE SCENE
- Polytechnic, Leeds = LAMBRETTAS.
- Fan Club, Leeds = U2 + MUSIC FOR PLEASURE.

Fr. 3
- Lead Mill, Sheffield = DEAD KENNEDYS + U.K. DECAY. Royal Park, Leeds = JAZZ
- Polytechnic, Sheffield = 9 BELOW ZERO. Palm Cove, Bradford = DIAMOND HEAD.
- Crucible Theatre, Sheffield = CHRIS BARBER'S JAZZ & BLUES BAND.
- Wombwell Reform, Barnsley = LIMELIGHT (1st night)
- Cosmos, Leeds = BLACK SLATE.
- Cleo's, Huddersfield = DISCHARGE + E POZEZ + BEYOND THE GRAVE.
- Fforde Grene, Leeds = BRICK MARINE.

Sa. 4
- University, Leeds = BAD MANNERS. Royal Park, Leeds = RED EYE.
- Wombwell Reform, Barnsley = LIMELIGHT (2nd night). Palm Cove, Bradford = BLACK STALLION.
- University, Leeds = RORY GALLAGHER
- Huddersfield Polytechnic = OTWAY & BARRETT.
- St. Johns College, York = THE KICKS.
- White Lion, Huddersfield = TALISMAN.
- Haddon Hall, Leeds = THE OTHER SWITCH.

Su. 5
- Fan Club, Leeds = ECHO & THE BUNNYMEN. Staging Post, Leeds = THE MUNROES.
- St. George's Hall, Bradford = TOURISTS + BARRACUDAS. Fforde Grene, Leeds = THE DANCE BAND.
- Unity Hall, Wakefield = SKIDS + BOOKS. Palm Cove, Bradford = JED'S BLUES BAND.
- Fforde Grene, Leeds = DANCE BAND.
- Fan Club, Leeds = ECHO & THE BUNNYMEN + THE SOUND.
- White Lion, Huddersfield = PRIVATE DICKS(L) / BREATHLESS (eve).
- Haddon Hall, Leeds = DODGY TACTICS. Princeville, Bradford (lunch) = RABSTALLION

Mo. 6
- University, Bradford = WEAPON OF PEACE.
- Romeo & Juliet's, Doncaster = DANCE BAND
- Royal Park, Leeds = GLOSSY MAGS.
- Fforde Grene, Leeds = FLYING SAUCERS.

Tu. 7
- Polytechnic, Leeds = JOHN COOPER CLARKE & PAULINE MURRAY (ex-PENETRATION) with INVISIBLE GIRLS.
- St. George's Hall, Bradford = PRETENDERS + TEN POLE TUDOR. Limit Club, Sheffield = CIRCLES.
- City Hall, Sheffield = OZZY OSBOURNE'S BLIZZARD OF OZZ + BUDGIE. Unity Hall, W'field = THE PASSIONS
- Top Rank, Sheffield = SKIDS + BOOKS. Rose & Crown, Ilkley = STACKS.
- Rotters, Doncaster = XTC. Royal Park, Leeds = CHRISTO.
- Scamps, Bradford = NOSFERATU V. Palm Cove, Bradford = PATCHWORK (Tall Rock)
- Limit Club, Sheffield = FISCHER Z

We. 8
- St. George's Hall, Bradford = 'BATTLE OF THE BANDS' Heat. White Lion, Huddersfield = RHINO.
- University, York = SKIDS + BOOKS. Royal Park, Leeds = ROUGH JUSTICE.
- Top Rank, Sheffield = ALVIN LEE + CHEVY.
- Lee Mount Club, Halifax = CRASS + POISON GIRLS
- University, Bradford = THE PHOTOS.
- Cudworth Village, Barnsley = LIMELIGHT.
- Polytechnic, Huddersfield = OR WAS HE PUSHED + THE GUESTS + TREATMENT + ALL OVER THE CARPET

Th. 9
- Limit Club, Sheffield = ECHO & THE BUNNYMEN. Princeville, Bradford = CRAFTY AVENUE.
- Polytechnic, Sheffield = 'SON OF STIFF' PACKAGE*
- Cosmos, Leeds = NOT SENSIBLES + THIS IS IT + WOLFRACE.
- Fan Club, Leeds = THE ALLIES + IKON.
- Royal Park, Leeds = TWISTED NERVE.
- Palm Cove, Bradford = AGONY COLUMN.

Fr. 10
- Polytechnic, Leeds = Q-TIPS + RELUCTANT STEREOTYPES.
- Unity Hall, Wakefield = THE SKIDS + THE BOOKS
- Cleo's, Huddersfield = CRIBBS + POISON GIRLS
- Royal Park, Leeds = JAZZ.
- Fforde Grene, Leeds = MORE.
- Palm Cove, Bradford = STORMTROOPER.

Sa. 11
- Queens Hall, Leeds = U.F.O. + FIST. Staging Post, Leeds = STILL EARTH.
- Staging Post, Leeds = STILL EARTH. Royal Park, Leeds = DIRTY BUT NICE.
- University, Bradford = SLADE.
- City Hall, Sheffield = JOE JACKSON + LINCOLN THOMPSON & THE RASSES. Fforde Grene, Leeds = PRISONER
- Cleo's, Huddersfield = FRONTLINE HIFI (disco) + WOLFRACE BAND.
- White Lion, Huddersfield = GLOSSY MAGS.
- Haddon Hall, Leeds = LUCKY STRIKE.

Su. 12
- Blackamore Head, Pontefract = RHABSTALLION. Princeville, Bradford (lunch) = J.G. SPOILS.
- Fan Club, Leeds = FLATBACKERS + IMPOSSIBLE MEN.
- White Lion, Huddersfield = MIDDLE B (L) + THE WASPS (eve)
- Haddon Hall, Leeds = LUIGI ANA DA BOYS.
- Staging Post, Leeds = AGONY COLUMN.
- Fforde Grene, Leeds = THE WOFFLERS BAND.
- Palm Cove, Bradford = JED'S BLUES BAND.

Mo. 13
- Genevieve's, Sheffield = ATOMIC ROOSTER + FLEK. Royal Park, Leeds = TOKYO
- University, York = BLUES BAND.
- Antonio's, Barnsley = THE ODDS (1st night)
- Romeo & Juliet's, Doncaster = LIMELIGHT.
- Marquis of Granby, Leeds = KNIFE EDGE
- The Sweatbox (Italian Club, Harris St) Bradford = CRASS + POISON GIRLS
- City Hall, Sheffield = HAWKWIND + VARDIS.

Tu. 14
- St. George's Hall, Bradford = SCORPIONS.
- Limit Club, Sheffield = WEAPON OF PEACE.
- Antonio's, Barnsley = THE ODDS (2nd night).
- Scamps, Bradford = CONFESSOR.
- Rose & Crown, Ilkley = DODGY TACTICS
- Palm Cove, Bradford = PATCHWORK.

We. 15
- University, Bradford = Q-TIPS + RELUCTANT STEREOTYPES.
- Royal Park, Leeds = RHABSTALLION.
- Antonio's, Barnsley = THE ODDS (3rd night).
- Marquis of Granby, Leeds = MIRROR BOYS + TECHNICIANS.
- White Lion, Huddersfield = THE FLOOR.
- Royal Park, Leeds = RABSTALLION.

Th. 16
- Limit Club, Sheffield = Q-TIPS + RELUCTANT STEREOTYPES.
- Dragoon, Maltby = CARL GREEN & THE SCENE.
- Royal Park, Leeds = DODGY TACTICS.
- Princeville, Bradford = CITY SLYK.

Fr. 17
- City Hall, Sheffield = PRETENDERS + TEN POLE TUDOR.
- Polytechnic, Huddersfield = INMATES + DEAF AIDS.
- University, Leeds = TOURISTS + BARRACUDAS.
- Cleo's, Huddersfield = COCKNEY REJECTS.
- Royal Park, Leeds = JAZZ.
- Palm Cove, Bradford = EFFIGY.

Sa. 18
- University, Bradford = SKIDS. Royal Park, Leeds = THE OTHER SWITCH.
- Polytechnic, Sheffield = INMATES + DEAF AIDS. Palm Cove, Bradford = NATURAL PROGRESSION + SHAKATONE HIFI.
- University, Leeds = ROCKPILE + GARY MYRICK & THE FIGURES.
- St. John College, York = WEAPON OF PEACE.
- Trades & Labour, Castleford = LIMELIGHT.
- Haddon Hall, Leeds = KNIFE EDGE.
- Cleo's, Huddersfield = JUDGEMENT + LITTLE WICKED HIFI (disco) White Lion, Huddersfield = WHAMMA JAMMA.

Su. 19
- Fan Club, Leeds = KILLING JOKE + AU PAIRS.
- White Lion, Huddersfield = PRIVATE DICKS (L) + JEANNE HAAN BAND (eve).
- Haddon Hall, Leeds = AGONY COLUMN.
- Staging Post, Leeds = SHAKE APPEAL.
- Palm Cove, Bradford = JED'S BLUES BAND.
- Princeville, Bradford = T.B.A. (lunchtime).

Mo. 20
- City Hall, Sheffield = SCORPIONS (day 1).
- Thurncoe Hotel, Thurncoe = THE ODDS.
- University, York = LINCOLN THOMPSON & THE RASSES
- Royal Park, Leeds = TWISTED NERVE

Tu. 21
- City Hall, Sheffield = SCORPIONS (day 2). Palm Cove, Bradford = PATCHWORK.
- Polytechnic, Sheffield = ROCKPILE + GARY MYRICK & THE FIGURES.
- Rotters, Doncaster = UB40.
- Warehouse, Leeds = SOFT BOYS.
- Birdwell, Barnsley = LIMELIGHT.
- Scamps, Bradford = RED EYE.
- Rose & Crown, Ilkley = AGONY COLUMN.

We. 22
- University, Bradford = FISCHER Z.
- Royal Park, Leeds = KNIFE EDGE
- White Lion, Huddersfield = PROPOSITION 31.
- Royal Park, Leeds = KNIFE EDGE.

Th. 23
- Polytechnic, Leeds = UB40.
- Princeville, Bradford = LIMELIGHT.
- Fan Club, Leeds = WAH HEAT + FRANTIC ELEVATORS.
- City Hall, Sheffield = ROSSINGTON COLLINS BAND + STRAIGHT EIGHT.
- Royal Park, Leeds = THE OTHER SWITCH.
- Princeville, Bradford = LIMELIGHT.

Fr. 24
- University, Sheffield = ERIC BLAKE.
- Polytechnic, Huddersfield = LINTON KWESI JOHNSON.
- Cleo's, Huddersfield = T.B.A. (punk).
- Royal Park, Leeds = JAZZ.
- Palm Cove, Bradford = TAURUS.

Sa. 25
- University, Bradford = 'SON OF STIFF' PACKAGE.* Fforde Grene, Leeds = GRACE.
- Cleo's, Huddersfield = LINCOLN THOMPSON & THE RASSES.
- White Lion, Huddersfield = THE GUESTS.
- Haddon Hall, Leeds = THE NEAT.
- Staging Post, Leeds = DODGY TACTICS.
- Royal Park, Leeds = 710.

Su. 26
- Top Rank, Sheffield = THE JAM + PIRANAHS. Fforde Grene, Leeds = DIAMOND HEAD.
- Princeville, Bradford (lunch) = STURGEON ROW. Palm Cove, Bradford = JED'S BLUES BAND.
- St. George's Hall, Bradford = MOTORHEAD + WEAPON. Princeville, Bradford (lunch) = WARLORD.
- White Lion, Huddersfield = JAZZ-T.B.A.(L) + 7 YEAR ITCH.
- Haddon Hall, Leeds = DALE HARGREAVES' FLAMINGO.
- Staging Post, Leeds = TALISMAN.

Mo. 27
- University, Leeds = LOUDON WAINWRIGHT III.
- Royal Park, Leeds = CONTROL VOICE.

Tu. 28
- St. George's Hall, Bradford = U.K. SUBS.
- Scamps, Bradford = THE WHIPS.
- Rose & Crown, Ilkley = CHAINSAW.
- Palm Cove, Bradford = PATCHWORK.

We. 29
- University, Bradford = INMATES + DEAF AIDS.
- Top Rank, Sheffield = BLUES BAND.
- University, Leeds = JOHN MARTYN BAND.
- City Hall, Sheffield = BUZZCOCKS.
- White Lion, Huddersfield = T.B.A.
- Royal Park, Leeds = OXYM.

Th. 30
- Warehouse, Leeds = Q-TIPS + RELUCTANT STEREOTYPES. Princeville, Bradford = MONEY.
- Polytechnic, Huddersfield = INMATES + DEAF AIDS
- City Hall, Sheffield = UB40.
- Dragoon, Maltby = CARL GREEN & THE SCENE.
- Fan Club, Leeds = ASSOCIATES.
- Royal Park, Leeds = DODGY TACTICS.

Fr. 31
- Polytechnic, Huddersfield = JOHN MARTYN BAND. Palm Cove, Bradford = H.M. (WITCHFYNDE?)
- Cosmos, Leeds = TRIBESMEN.
- University, Bradford = AU PAIRS + VIOLATION + reggae band.
- Cleo's, Huddersfield = JUNGLE MAN SHOW.
- Royal Park, Leeds = JAZZ.
- Fforde Grene, Leeds = DODECIAN ROCK.

*'SON OF STIFF' features ANY TROUBLE + JOE 'KING' CARRASCO & THE CROWNS + DIRTY LOOKS + EQUATORS + TENPOLE TUDOR.

LET ME KNOW ABOUT GIGS AND VENUES — I'M NOT PSYCHIC! RING NICK ON BRADFORD 21867 OR WRITE TO ME. (that's me!)

Abbreviations: TBA = to be arranged; (?) = to be confirmed; HM = heavy metal; (L) = lunchtime gig. Enough space here to put in some VENEWS....
Please note that FFORDE GRENE in Leeds will be closed for alteration from 13th - 24th Oct. A new punk venue in Bradford may well have been found in THE ITALIAN CLUB, Harris St (off Leeds Rd) — it'll be known as THE SWEATBOX & opens on 13th of this month with Crass + Poison Girls (gigs are being run by Aky of Violation who's available on Bradford 571793). Ronnie Corboz (who'd have been interviewed for this issue but he's never in!) is running booking for two new HM nights in Bradford — local bands will be on every Tuesday night (11ish onwards) at SCAMPS; while big names (starting with Diamond Head on 3rd) will be on at PALM COVE every Friday (opens 7.30 band off by 10.30ish, but bar till at least 1am. - beer at pub prices). KEIGHLEY LEISURE CENTRE now no longer taking rock bands, same applies, at least at the moment, to KINGS HEAD, KEIGHLEY & ARTS CENTRE, Bingley. Other venues to cross off are ALBION, HUDDERSFIELD which is no longer taking bands &, from the end of October for at least a month & maybe much longer, THE ROSE & CROWN, Ilkley where a new brewery hierarchy & financial cutbacks combine to call a halt to gigs while the brewery weighs up the money being made & lost on the Tuesday rock night. Oh, in issue 7 I give HADDON HALL's phone no. as Leeds 75115 - sorry, should've read 751115 - O.K? — Nick Toczek

ISSUE #10
November 1980, 2,500 copies printed, 20 pages, 25cm x 17cm

I guess that the most interesting aspect of this issue, which marked a full year of publishing, is on page eleven. Here you find my accounts for the year. These show that, at least financially, the magazine made a loss. As a committed anarchist, I never sought to make a profit. I just wanted a successful magazine. My main reason for publishing these figures was to prove to my critics and the Inland Revenue that I wasn't lining my pockets. A deficit of £223.50 over the year wasn't too bad. That worked out at a loss of roughly 61p per day. That was bearable. The problem was not the money, but the time that I had to invest in each issue. Around 40 hours per week, when I also had my own writing to do and a living to make from journalism and gigging, was more than exhausting.

Notes on bands profiled in this issue.

Impressed with the debut album by Split Endz (page 7), I went to see them and got to interview Tim Finn (whose bandmate and brother, Neil Finn, would go on to front Crowded House). I also interviewed the two of them for the UK weekly Musicians Only. The Finn brothers later told the editor of Musicians Only that I was the most knowledgeable journalist they'd ever met! That wasn't simply flattering; it actually earned me more lucrative, much-needed assignments for that journal. These enabled me to keep WCR going for a few more issues.

To read my stories about my early encounters with UB40 (page 16) and with U2 (page 17), you'll once more need to consult my forthcoming book *My Life Sentences*. Read the early piece on Ruby Turner (also page 17). I'd known her in Birmingham, and Frank Crow, who'd played guitar in the final line-up of Stereo Graffiti, went on to tour with her.

So now that your eyes are absolutely rivited to this bit here we will take this opportunity to tell you all about our shop. It's a record shop with lots of golden oldies, rock 'n' roll, punk, new wave, heavy - metal, progressive, rare records, imports, cassettes, singles and albums. We're always willing to do part - exchange or buy your collection from you if you're broke - if you've no wheels we'll collect. It doesn't matter what sort of records they are - give us a ring on Leeds 457765 or at home 075784 - 669, or call in to GEROL'S RECORDS, MERRION SUPERSTORE, LEEDS and have a chat and look around. - We could well have that elusive single or album that you've always wanted. See you soon

ROB & GERALD

GEROL'S RECORDS

MERRION SUPERSTORE LEEDS
(Tel: See above.)

EDITORIAL (o.n.o.)

So, reader, we meet again. Issue ten & a year since I set sail on the ludicrous rock'n'roll voyage.

You can read my full accounts on page eleven. Over 200 quid down on the year might not seem like success, but I'm not in it for the money (honest!). However, on the positive side, the mag. is now beginning to make a small profit & I'm starting to pay contributors at last. A big thanks to everyone who's worked for the mag. during the past year for little or no cash. Also, thanks to advertisers for using us & so making the whole thing financially possible. Thanks also to Mallett & Co (Chapel St, B'fd) who printed issues 1-8 & to Tempest & Cockcroft (Mariner's Drive, B'fd) who are the current printers. Both have put in long hours & been of invaluable help to me. Finally, a special thanks to everyone who's bought & read the issues & to all the shops that've stocked it.

For myself, I got a successful mag. out of the year's work. As a direct result of doing W.C.R., I'm also writing as a regular freelancer for the weekly national rock paper 'Musicians Only' & have a monthly rock column in Yorkshire Arts Association's 'Month In Yorkshire'. Both are available in well-stocked newsagents should any of you want to read even more of my opinionated ramblings. A new Ulterior Motives will be in the studio recording a second single (December, I hope) & some live gigs should follow. Two weeks ago I flew to Frankfurt for 3 days where I was booked to do some solo performances (5 in all). These were extracts from a one-man show with which I'll be touring in '81 & some of the pieces from this show will be published by Aquila Press in spring under the title 'Rock'n'Roll Terrorism'. There's more, but I'll suppress my enormous ego...

There's a bunch of new fanzines springing up round Yorkshire & it looks like we'll soon have a really active alternative rock press covering band activity in the county.

As regular readers will know, I'm always on the look-out for bands with imaginative names. This month, 'Sons of The Pope' add theirs to a list that already includes Bradford's 'Eaten Alive By Insects' & 'Policeman With A Loaf Of Bread' & Huddersfield's 'All Over The Carpet'. Any more contenders...?

Kay Russell (ex-Ulterior Motives & my co-editor on issues 1 & 2 of W.C.R.) is now in the band Fassbinder-Russell. They've a single out this month on Criminal Records. I've not heard it yet, but am reliably informed that it's kind to your ears. Listen out for it.

Y'know something? Doing W.C.R. is not without hassles. This past week I've (a) had the mag. banned in one of my regular shops, (b) been threatened with legal action for what I've written & (c) been threatened with being hospitalised for what I was planning to write. Beech Terrace is now surrounded by a 30ft barbed-wire fence with machine gun turrets at 3 inch intervals. Beyond these are a modest minefield, a pit of serpents & speakers that play the soundtrack of 'Sound of Music' whenever anyone comes within ½ a mile of my house.

Future issues of the magazine will be printed secretly & distributed at night by Securicor.

Robert Catesby, a Warwickshire squire. The leader of the plot was a Yorkshire man, Guy Fawkes. One of his friends

Guy Fawkes being arrested in a Cellar under the House of Lords.

Apart from that, life continues as (sub)normal. Light blue touch paper & stand well back. Don't eat duck eggs, next issue will be another 2-monther for Dec./Jan. Till then, then, Nick Toczek 28/10/80.

FIRST BIRTHDAY ISSUE NUMBER 10

No.10   **Nov. 1980**

Nick Toczek: edits; does design, typing, layout, lay-in, distribution, hassling; brews strong coffees & has two dogs & a cat to support; writes.

Stan Engel & Kev Hopgood: cartoonists.

Andy Stevens: writes.

Keith E. Rice: also writes.

Steve Brown: also writes as well.

Stuart Rhodes: also writes as well too.

BACK ISSUES: all are still available at 45p each (inc. p.&p.), though I'm already running low on issue No.7. Full sets of Nos 1-10 are on offer at £3·00 (post free) as a special "give a year of W.C.R. for Xmas" offer. I've also got copies of Ulterior Motives' single 'Another Lover' c/w 'Y'Gotta Shout' with a free enamel badge (£1·00 inc. p.&p.). Cheques payable to 'Nick Toczek' at the address at foot of this column.

THOUGHT OF THE MONTH:-
'Only a few shopping days to Armageddon'.

What you get: back cover has **Gig Guide** & some of the bands include **Speed** from Keighley, Bradford's **Vex**, Edinburgh's **Freeze**, **7 Year Itch** who're from Lancs, **Dale Hargreaves' Flamingos**, from Birmingham a pair of bands - **Wide Boys** & **Ruby Turner Band**, an interview with New Zealand's **Split Enz** whose L.P. also gets reviewed along with albums by **Prag Vec**, **9 Below Zero**, **Myofist**, **R.A.F.** Then there's stuff on **Shake Appeal** of Leeds & Halifax's **Private Dicks**. Add **Amazing Whipps** from Colne, Lancs. & **The Sofas** from Leeds. Andy Stevens spent a day with **UZ**, Keith E. Rice gets his teeth into **Handmade Goddesses** - a new all-girl Bradford band, Steve Brown interviewed **Limelight** (if he gets it to me in time!) & Stuart Rhodes outlines the agony & extacy of being a manager. There's no X-word because Ken Turner took a holiday, though he'll be back with an impossible one for Xmas. I review a bunch of fanzines + new books on **The Clash** & **The Jam**. There's a page of accounts for the first year. Cartoons from Stan & Kev. Reviews of cassettes by **Knife Edge** & **Rough Justice**. If there's space, I'll shove in my usual 'Nowtz'. Almost forgot to mention the single from **Methodischa Tune** & **Alan Whittle**'s cassette. There's probably more, but I can't think of anything else at the moment.

Use the magazine: get in touch if you're in a band, forming one, running gigs, have any ideas or suggestions, want any info, can suggest any possible sales outlets, want to contribute anything, think I ought to write up your favourite northern band. I try hard to keep the mag. open to all comers & I need your help if I'm to keep tabs on even a fraction of what's going on. The address/phone no. are opposite →

TERMS OF SALE: 30p each direct to the public or 50p each by mail order from the address given below. Bulk orders of 15 or more copies can be had at the discount price of 20p each (so why not sell the magazine yourself at gigs, school, etc.?)

ADVERTISING RATES: Standard 3½" x 3½" box is £20 for first time of advertising, then £10 for subsequent placings. Colour, different size, special lay-out, etc. by arrangement.

Ring or write for advertising rates card & any other details.

EDITORIAL ADDRESS:
5 Beech Terrace,
Undercliffe,
Bradford BD3 0PY,
West Yorkshire,
England.
(tel. 0274-21867).

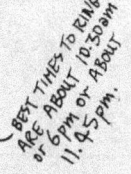

BEST TIMES TO RING ARE ABOUT 10.30AM or ABOUT 6PM or ABOUT 11.45PM.

HAND-MADE GODDESSES

Sandie Emmonds – ld vocs
Sharon Johnson – kbds/vocs
Maria Tarpy – bass/vocs
Carol Flanagan – gtr
Trudi Crook – dms

Hand-Made Goddesses are quite possibly Bradford's first all-girl heavy metal outfit; and they certainly make full use of their lush femininity – their stage clothes consisting of leather shorts, lace-up shirts and thigh boots. Yet despite this rather obvious appeal to the male erectile impulse, the "goddesses" rock out with a grinding power that totally belies the conventional image of the "gentle sex". And so far, so good; this combination of power-rock and blatant sexationalism has won a small but devoted (and how!) following.

H.M.G. began playing together earlier this year under the guidance of mentor Pete Emmonds, the infamous ex-Trampus drummer now with Baby Tuckoo, who is Sandie's brother and Maria's current paramour. They made their debut in May at Allerton Catholic Club under their original name of Phantasy and have since played a smattering of well-received gigs in local clubs and pubs. Bookings are on the increase and the girls expect a busy Autumn. There is also talk of recording a single, with Sandie's father putting up the readies; if they do it, H.M.G. would set up their own label and then look for a distributor.

The goddesses play early Seventies-style heavy metal, confessing Black Sabbath and (shock! horror!) Grand Funk Railroad as primary influences; however, they also admit to being greatly affected by the music of such new wavers as Cure and the Human League. Certainly their lyrics are in the mode of post-'76 pointedness, dealing with such topics as anti-fascism ("Pigs In Space"), disco violence ("Take The Rough With The Smooth") and prostitution ("Loose-Living Leper"). Trudi: "We believe that rock'n'roll should be fun, but there should be some meaning in the lyrics if anyone wants to take it further than basic enjoyment."

"And dressing sexy is part of the enjoyment – on both sides," adds Sandie, whose shorts once split on stage. ("Now, that was going farther than I had originally intended." Since then she has always worn knickers under her shorts.)

The question is: how long before "Sounds" discovers H.M.G.?

Contact: Sandie on B'F'D 570845   – Keith E. Rice

BETTER BADGES

100 BADGES

1¼" black & white

£13-50 inc. p.& p.

s.a.e. for production price list & other details.

286 PORTOBELLO ROAD
LONDON W10 960 5513

Editor's note - strange that I've never heard of this band before now! If I didn't know Keith Rice to be a man of high integrity (as are all of the clean-living youngsters who frequent The Vaults Bar) I might suspect that some deception was afoot here. As it is, I'll leave you to decide whether you believe in Goddesses or opt for healthy atheism in which they're hand-made on Rice-paper.

SPEED INTERVIEWED & PROFILED

Line-up: Daz (voc), Graham Mason (rm & ld gtr), Wayne Marshall (rm & ld gtr), Andrew Stonach (b), Colin Seward (dms).

Till 9 months ago, Andy & Graham were in a Keighley band together. When it then split up, they decided to form a new band. Colin came in on drums & brought vocalist Dazz with him. Steve Binns (called Elvis cos he was into r'n'r/rockabilly) was their 2nd guitarist, though he left after their first gig (supporting The Quick at The Vaults Bar in June of this year). That gig went well &, carrying on as a 4-piece, they did a few more gigs in & around Keighley, building up a good solid following. They've more gigs lined up (see gig guide) & are hoping to go into Cargo Recording Studio in March of next year to record 3 tracks.

Their music. Originally Andrew wrote the lyrics & Graham came up with tunes that were then arranged by the whole band. Andy: "But my lyrics weren't too hot – & I can't spell!" Dazz took over on lyrics. Their music's new wavish: "You can't really define it – piss rockers, Dazz calls us!"

"The Quick gave us a lot of help, especially at the start, showing us how to play, lending us gear & so on. Now we both of us help each other out with gear".

Initially, Andy & Graham played HM ("We were a bad Sabbath") but the arrival of Dazz & Colin really changed that. They now offer new wave with touches of reggae & pop – all of it original material.

Wayne Marshall, who's only been with the band of a few weeks, is already making a big difference – filling out the sound & working on the arrangements.

Having been helped by The Quick, they in turn are keen to help other Keighley bands. One in particular that they mentioned was 'Bovver & The Wombats' – a new Keighley band who're skinheads, most of them 6th-formers: "They do songs like 'Yobs with big boots who're really rather nice. They're ok – the whole thing's just a laugh to them. They've no money so they share our gear & we hope to be doing some gigs with them."

You can contact Speed by ringing Crosshills 32001 (Andy), Crosshills 35364 (Graham) or Keighley 606239 (Wayne).

– interviewed by Nick Toczek

The Freeze

Originally called 'Vortex', the band began life in '76 when they played own numbers & cover versions of well-known punk songs on the minimum of equipment but with a lot of energy. By '77, the 3 lead guitars had been honed down to one & there'd been a change drummer & a change of name. They were 'The Freeze'.

In early '78, with the drummer having proved unsuitable, they drafted in Graeme Radin & The Freeze as it is today really came into being. The only other change was in summer '80 when the four-piece became 5 with the addition of Tony Wallis on sax & guitar.

One of the best-known Scottish new wave bands who're not signed to a major label. Their EP ('In Colour') & a double A-sided single ('Celebration'/'Crossover') were both released on the Scottish indie, A.1. Records (see reviews in WCR 9).

In Scotland, they're a popular head-line band, drawing capacity crowds at 500-seater venues. They've also supported such bands as 'The Damned', 'Sham', 'SLF', 'Revillos', 'Skids', etc.

Line-up: Gordon Sharp (voc), David Clancy (ld gtr/synth/bkg voc), Tony Wallis (gtr/sax/synth/bkg voc), Keith Grant (b gtr/bkg voc) & Graeme Radin (dms). Also, 'Toke' who is lighting engineer & William Allison as sound engineer.

Contact: Alastair Allison (manager) on 050-684-4344.   (taken from press release)

Classified Advert. (10p per word - phone in on B'f'd 21867).
Professional Artwork for POSTERS, L.P. COVERS, etc. Ring Simon on Bradford 390943 for details & further info.

*   *   *   *   *   *   *

NOWTS bits bites 'n' bitches

IN 1938 REAGAN PLAYED THE LEAD IN A FILM CALLED 'ACCIDENTS WILL HAPPEN'... 42 YEARS LATER??!

'Phone call 2 weeks ago from a slightly miffed Tim Tate - rock journalist par excellence for the truly wonderful Keighley News. Upset about what I'd written last month in my editorial, he was drafting out the put-down in which he was going to tell me to leave rock journalism to the professionals like himself. He was "checking details" & wanted to know if he was right in saying that I was vocalist with... Mysterious Footsteps. Anyway, he promised to send me a copy of his article (which he didn't) & asked me if I'd print a letter from his editor. I said I would & he said it'd be through in a day or two. It's not in this issue because it never arrived. So that's professionalism, huh? Meanwhile, we all wait with trepidation for decibel meters to be installed in all the local pubs round Keighley-Bradford, as per his scare story. End of subject.

FIRST BASE: Centre for Unemployed Young People (c/o Tennant Hall, Blackman Lane, Leeds 2. tel. 445864) is an activities centre that should open later this month as a daytime coffee bar/youth club. As time passes, though, it's hoped to expand activities to cater for many of the needs of the young unemployed - with the emphasis on self-help. As part of their fund-raising, they've run two gigs (both in Leeds last month = Wolfrace + Not Sensibles + This is it at Cosmo's & Mirror Boys + Technicians at Marquis of Granby). Any bands prepared to do benefits or anyone who can help organise/run gigs or lend gear, print posters, whatever... please ring above no. & speak to Mart or Dave.

Letter from Hitch of 128 Otley Rd., Guiseley, nr Leeds (tel. Guiseley 77374 after 6p.m.). He wants contributions, tapes from bands, etc. for a new fanzine that he's launching. It's to be called SHINEY CALIPERS (tasteful!?). He's also hoping to bring out a compilation tape of local progressive new-wave bands. His own band is called 'Freefall' & they're looking round for gigs at the moment. Let's hope, with all that lot planned, he's 'Hitch' by name, but not by nature.

CONCERT FOR CHILE (Leeds Town Hall, 7.30pm Fri. Nov 21st). Leeds Chile Solidarity Campaign which is opposed to the government which first came to power with the '73 coup & has had a history of repression & torture is mounting this concert. It features the leading expatriot Chilean folk/protest group, Inti-illimani, & also the 'feminist' folk singer Frankie Armstrong. Good cause, fascinating music. Just the thing for a Chile November night. Starts 7.30pm. Tickets £2 from Central Library Leeds or Leeds University Students Union; 4th Idea Bookshop in Bradford, York Community Bookshop; Grass Roots, Manchester, etc.

Oops, correction to the editorial. Kay's band is called Fassbender-Russell (I think) & the first single, just to confuse things further, is released by the band under the name of The Sue Fassbender Band (Kay playing guitar).

P.S. Witcomb of Undercover Management writes to say that The Zipps (see WCR6) have undergone a ~~sex~~ name-change operation & will henceforth be called George Little's Cool In The Shade. Also, Mark Midgeley, their bass player, isn't. However, one Chris Hannah is.

Then the phone rang (does it ever not?) & Jock Cotton's voice told me that he (voc/gtr) + Don Hayes (bass) were keeping Bradford's Radio 5 going (the famed local 4-piece split up 3 or 4 months ago. With John Wallis in on Drums, they're currently revving up with a bunch of new songs & hope to be gigging in the new year. Watch these pages for further news on this one, Clive.

FINALLY:- Some gigs that missed the gig guide:- Propaganda Unlimited are promoting bands every Thurs. (late night) at Cosmo Club (a.k.a. Roots), Francis St, Leeds 7. 6th Nov. is 'Soft Cell' + 'If & The Questionaires'; 13th Nov is to be arranged; 20th Nov. is 'Vice Versa' + M.R.A.; 27th Nov. is 'The Swamp Children' + 'Eric Random'. Also in the bag are 'M.R.A.' + 'Household Name' at Leeds Poly Brunswick on Thurs. Nov. 6th & 'M.R.A.' + 'Household Name' (again) at Leeds Univ. in The Tartan Bar. (Propaganda are on Leeds 446694).

'Heaven 17' play Good Mood Club, Halifax on Nov 1st; Royal Standard, Bradford on Nov. 12th; Palm Cove, Bradford on Nov. 27th.

'Sharp Practice' play Wigs Wine Bar, Jubilee Hotel, Leeds on Nov. 22nd. & also are booked for the Dol Q Club, Marquis of Granby, Leeds on Nov. 12th.

'The Amazing Whipps' lose a gig - so you can't see them at Queens Hall, Bradford on Nov 21st.

That's your lot. Read the advert ↓ & then move on to sample the delights of page 6.
— NICK TOCZEK

NEVER TRUST A SLEEPING DOG

BRADFORD   the HMV shop   **LEEDS**

Watch out for Adam & The Ants' personal appearance at Leeds shop soon!!

UP TO 20 ALTERNATIVE CHART SINGLES at 99p

Includes: **JOY DIVISION, DEAD KENNEDYS, FAT GADGET, THE EXPLOITED, ADAM & THE ANTS**

BAND AID MANAGEMENT

A GUIDE FOR ALL LOCAL BANDS & WOULD-BE MANAGERS.

A manager is an important addition to a band & a good one is hard to come by. I'm sorry to say it, but they can't be found in Woolworths.

It's impossible to write a job description for a manager - he does just about everything that needs doing to keep a band together & working. He's like another member of the band & should be treated as such. I've been managing local bands for around five years now, so I feel I know what I'm talking about.

Before I go any further, if you're thinking of becoming the manager of a band for the money, then forget it because at the outset at least it's going to <u>cost</u> you money.

Quite a few bands have come up to me over the years looking for management & advice. One of the first things to remember is that a verbal agreement is legally binding & will stand up in court, so make sure that the person you employ can be trusted. Don't forget he's going to handle all your affairs including your cash. Not only does he help make the money, but he helps spend it as well - on things like posters, badges & other little items.

Another question I'm asked by groups is how much to pay the manager. Well, the answer is that you pay whatever you agree to. The average fee is 15% of gross takings, or you can work it so that you pay 10% of gross takings plus expenses. However you could strike lucky & find a friend to do the job for just expenses. The trouble here is that you must ask yourself if he can do the job properly. A manager has to be a man of many talents. He has to be able to sell your band to agents & promotors & sweet-talk landlords & their wives. To the manager you are a product & his job is to sell you - not only over the phone, but door-to-door. When he has sold your band for a night, he then has to organise the publicity & stir up some interest in the band. So, after he has informed the local radio stations & the national music press (spending more money), he starts on the fly posting & any other means of publicity that he can think of. Come the night of the gig, he should have found you that van that never arrives on time & double-checked never arrives on time & double-checked with the venue that you are still playing & not double booked. Then you are at the venue. He might have to take the door money & he's the one who has to face the landlord after the gig, smile nicely & grovel for another gig - & you've probably gone down like a ton of bricks.

The next night there's the whole show to repeat over again... & again... & again.

Well, I hope that's been of some help to you all. I'm now going to do some fly posting, so remember - Bill Stickers Knows No Fear.

Yours lovingly, Stuart Rhodes,
Manager of the lovable City Limits.

THE COMMUNICATIONS CENTRE

(a posh name for a basic facility)

offers 4-TRACK with DBX at £3.50 p.h. + tape

Gear Includes:-
TEAC 3340, DBX, ITAM 10-4 desk, LEAVERS-RICH E200, REVOX B77, ORBAN REVERB, FILTERS, GRAPHICS, etc.
FULL D.I. + MIKES by AKG, CALREC, etc.

RING ALF or MOYA on Bradford 22769.

SPLIT ENZ

PHOTOS BY IAN ANDERSON

TIM FINN: vocals, guitar, piano
EDWARD RAYNER: keyboards
NOEL CROMBIE: drums, percussion, noises
MALCOLM GREEN: vocals
NEIL FINN: guitar, vocals
NIGEL GRIGGS: bass

I interviewed Tim Finn of Split Enz a few weeks ago. Looking at that interview now, it seems to me that the actual questions are unimportant - they were only there to keep the man talking about his band & its music, which he did - so I'll dump them. Here's what he said:-

Tim Finn interviewed by Nick Toczek

"When we were last in England two years ago with the freaky clothes & hairstyles that Noel dreamed up, that weird image got overplayed at the expense of the music. We were on Chrysalis then. We were the right band for that label but, maybe, at the wrong time. Lack of a hit single drew a zero for us."

"Back in England this time round, it's all much more open - especially as far as the media's concerned. And there's so much good pop about now... it's great for us to be on the same label (A&M) as bands like Police, Squeeze & Joe Jackson."

"That quote where I said that we were ahead of our time two years ago is taken completely out of context. I was talking about the fact that we were revolutionary in our image in that we were totally asexual - the sort of band that it was safe to take your girlfriend to see (laughs). That was a mistake. Sex sells rock music - you've got to have a smidgen of it."

"It's good to sweat. It's good to work hard. That's what makes for a great band. You either thrive under the pressure or go down - we work better this way."

"When this UK tour finishes, we're off to USA for 5 weeks touring clubs. After that, we'll be back here in UK for a longer tour with a new single out. We'll be doing some European gigs too & should finish in time to be back in Australia for Xmas."

"We're from New Zealand, except for the rhythm section who're Pommies. But we've adopted Australia as the band's second home. We've had really big success there."

"Yes, there are some good new bands coming up over there. Ones that I like include Midnight Oil - a sort of pschedellic HM band who might be over here soon. The Reels might come over too - they're looking for good management at the moment. There's a band called The Flowers & Phil Judd who used to be in Enz has a band of his own now called The Swingers."

"For me, the essence of good rock'n'roll is heart. That's what wins through eventually. If you bring people's emotions to the surface & unite them... if you can do that then it's good. You can't just do it cold."

"Our music doesn't really have any politica

"Our music comes first & the lyrics are then put to it. There isn't much in the way of political content. That's probably because we come from Aussie where life's pretty good, so there's not the same insentive to get political."

BRADFORD UNIVERSITY NOVEMBER

SAT NOV 1	SIMPLE MINDS	GH
WED NOV 5	THE CURE	GH
WED NOV 12	U.2	CB
SAT NOV 15	THE PLANETS	GH
WED NOV 26	PRAYING MANTIS	GH
SAT NOV 29	LINTON KWESI JOHNSON	GH
WED DEC 3	THE STRAY CATS	CB
SAT DEC 6	GARY GLITTER	GH

TICKETS FROM H.M.V. RECORDS AND UNION SHOP. ANY ENQUIRIES PLEASE RING BRADFORD 34135 EX. 42 MARION FOUNTAYNE

PLUS DISCOS EVERY FRIDAY IN THE COMMUNAL BUILDING ----BAR TILL 12. ENTRY ONLY 40p.

GH = GREAT HALL
CB = COMMUNAL BUILDING

LEEDS UNIVENTS PRESENT

November 8 = DARTS (£3-25) + November 15 = STEEL PULSE (£2-00) + November 22 = IRON MAIDEN + December 3 = HAZEL O'CONNOR'S MEGAHYPE (£2-50) + December 6 = GANG OF 4 (£1-75) + December 13 = DIRE STRAITS (£3-50)

Tickets: available 9.30-5 (weekdays) from University Union Record Shop in the Union basement and (evenings/weekends) from the Porters' lodge in the Union entrance or on the door on the night of the gig. **N.B.** YOU DON'T HAVE TO BE A STUDENT TO GET IN TO THESE GIGS.

LEEDS UNIVERSITY'S UNION RECORDS

NOVEMBER SALE! OVER 2000 ALBUMS at 50p-£1-75

We now sell tickets for all Leeds University & Leeds Polytechnic concerts & for Leeds Playhouse & The Grand Theatre, Leeds.

SHOP IN BASEMENT OF UNION BUILDING   OPEN: MON-FRI   9.30a.m.-5.00p.m.

HUDDERSFIELD POLYTECHNIC

Great Hall Queensgate Hudds.

NOV 28 = GARY GLITTER
DEC 6 = STRAY CATS

Tickets on sale in the travel office in the Students' Union building (10am - 3.30pm, weekdays) also from Woods Music Shop, Huddersfield or on the door on the night.

RING HUDDERSFIELD 38156 FOR INFO. ON TIMES, PRICES, ETC.   OPEN TO THE PUBLIC

Limelight INTERVIEW

After turning up at Princeville on the off-chance that Limelight were playing - they were - I nipped backstage for just a quick chat & ended up staying 2 hours.

Currently promoting their single 'Metal Man' & awaiting the release of their debut album, with which they are really pleased, Limelight are finally getting through to the people that matter in the music business. With the support spot on the Saxon tour & an ambitious independent record company behind them, things are looking a lot rosier than they did during their brief spell with Decca Records.

Mike: "The last recording we did was about 7 years ago when we covered a song called 'Baby Don't Get Hooked On Me' by the American singer/songwriter Mack Davidson."

"How did you react to being called 'Decca failures' by Sounds?"

Mike: "I wouldn't say we were failures; we certainly had no publicity behind us anyway. In fact, Davidson put his own version out as a single shortly afterwards & that reached no.1 in America, so naturally our version was forgotten. We were nothing then anyway."

"What amount of freedom do you have with Future Earth Records? I know you wanted to record 'Man Of Colours' as the first single."

Pat: "Everyone wanted us to record 'Man Of Colours', so we expected it to really sell. However, we now realise the importance of airplay if we are intent on getting anywhere. 'Man Of Colours' is about 8 mins. long & therefore not really suitable for the radio, whereas 'Metal Man' has been picked up by many local independent stations although the major stations have avoided it, probably because of the poor production. Really, we could only put out 'Man Of Colours' if we were already established like for example Queen did with 'Bohemian Rhapsody'."

"So you're not particularly happy with the single?"

Pat: "Not really. We recorded it at September Sound Studios in Doncaster, a 16-track studio totally unfamiliar to us, where we just had one day to record both sides of the single. Ultimately we would like to re-record it."

"Before you actually signed to Future Earth a great deal of interest was shown in you by several major companies. ."

Pat: "Signing to F/E was a chance we didn't want to miss. The other companies interested in us kept asking for more material which never seemed to get us any further. We wanted something out on record because so many of the people who came to see us kept asking us to get something recorded. They were our first responsibility & will always remain so. CBS were particularly interested in us but we got the feeling that our say in matters of importance would be very limited. With F/E we have all the freedom we want."

"In that case, do you feel comfortable being pushed as a HM band?"

Glenn: "We find it really difficult to put ourselves in any particular bracket. Therein lies the problem. If people can't find a pigeonhole they tend to leave you alone."

Mike: "We fall somewhere between 2 markets,

like for example Rush. Don't get me wrong, I'm not putting ourselves alongside them musically, but they have completely overcome a similar problem & have bridged 2 markets which is really difficult to achieve but has to be our aim."

"Do you think the presence of cover versions in the set is helping or hindering your cause?"

Pat: "People do tend to remember the standards rather than our own songs, for example we had a review in Record Mirror a couple of months back & the reporter picked up on the only 2 covers we did that night & all he wrote about.

Personally, I think if you play cover versions well, then your own songs have got to stand up alongside them. I don't think 1 or 2 covers in the set will harm us. There are plenty of bands who have made it by doing the same. Eventually we will phase all of them out, but not just yet. Cover versions have helped us get into a lot of places though, & once in your own material gets established as well."

Obviously Limelight will be bracketed, analysed, classified & categorised. They show there is no substitute for talent &, in doing so, they shame other bands who deal only in the energy factor. I am willing to stake a lot on Limelight & I don't consider that a gamble. Limelight will be commercially successful.

- Steve Brown.

Album Out Now
"LIMELIGHT"
FER 008
Distributed by PINNACLE
On Tour with
SAXON

BRITISH TOUR DATES

NOVEMBER
20 - ST. AUSTELL LIDO
21 - TAUNTON ODEON
22 - SWINDON LEISURE CENTRE
23 - CHELMSFORD ODEON
24 - HEMEL HEMPSTEAD PAVILION
25 - WOLVERHAMPTON CIVIC
26 - CARDIFF SOFIA GARDENS
27 - SHEFFIELD CITY HALL
28 - SHEFFIELD CITY HALL
29 - BRADFORD PRINCE GEORGES HALL
30 - BLACKBURN KING GEORGES HALL

DECEMBER
1 - MANCHESTER APOLLO
2 - LIVERPOOL EMPIRE
3 - BRISTOL COLSTON HALL
4 - LEICESTER DEMONFORT HALL
5 - COVENTRY NEW THEATRE
6 - OXFORD NEW THEATRE
7 - IPSWICH GAUMONT
8 - SOUTHAMPTON GAUMONT
9 - DERBY ASSEMBLY ROOMS
10 - HANLEY VICTORIA HALL
11 - MIDDLESBOROUGH TOWN HALL
13 - EDINBURGH ODEON
14 - GLASGOW APOLLO
15 - DUNDEE CAIRD HALL
16 - NEWCASTLE CITY HALL
17 - BIRMINGHAM ODEON
19 - HAMMERSMITH ODEON

STOP PRESS: Dec. 12 - Carlisle Market Hall
Dec. 15 - Malvern Winter Gardens
Dec. 20 - Hammersmith Odeon

POSERS' CORNER

- DALE HARGREAVES
- THE AMAZING WHIPPS
- PRIVATE DICKS
- NINE BELOW ZERO

RIC~RAC SOUND STUDIO

12 KIRKDALE AVENUE

LEEDS LS12 6AP   **TEL. 633717**

IF YOU WANT A TOP QUALITY DEMO OR MASTER TAPE RECORDED ON THE VERY BEST OF PROFESSIONAL RECORDING EQUIPMENT.

IF YOU WOULD LIKE TO RECORD IN A COMFORTABLE STUDIO WITH EASY ACCESS FOR LOADING AND PARKING.

IF YOU NEED SOMEONE WITH THE MUSICAL AND TECHNICAL EXPERIENCE TO BRING OUT THE BEST IN YOU AND YOUR MUSIC AND WHO CARES MORE ABOUT QUALITY AND YOUR SATISFACTION THAN HOW MUCH THEY CAN MAKE OUT OF YOU.

THEN RING MICK ON LEEDS 633717 to ARRANGE A CALL FOR A COFFEE AND A LOOK-ROUND.

> STOP PRESS:- We are now able to offer facilities for recording full video demo tapes to go with studio sound recordings.

RIC~RAC SOUND STUDIO

WOOL CITY ROCKER: the first year

Thought up the name first (one night in Oct.'79, walking home from the pub). Decided it'd be a good name for a rock mag. Pilot issue came out on Friday 30th Nov.'79. First 2 issues were of Bradford Rockscene only & were co-edited with Kay Russell. She then left. Issues 3-8 covered West Yorks. Rock. Issues 9 & 10 cover the whole of Yorkshire. Interesting that the main criticism has been from people convinced that I'm raking in vast profits. In fact, I've lost money overall in the first year. However, I've enjoyed it immensely, am now set to become a press baron & should know better at my age.

Issue Number	Quantity Printed	Printing Cost (£)	Advert. Revenue (£)	Number Sold	Average Net Income Per Copy (£)	Sales Revenue (£)
1 (Dec.'79)	1,500	199-00	80-00	800	0-25	200-00
2 (Jan.'80)	1,500	213-00	90-00	700	0-22	154-00
3 (Feb.'80)	1,500	213-00	100-00	800	0-20	160-00
4 (March'80)	1,500	282-50	120-00	900	0-18	162-00
5 (April'80)	1,500	300-00	205-00	1,000	0-17	170-00
6 (May'80)	1,500	325-00	150-00	1,000	0-16	160-00
7 (June/July'80)	2,000	535-30	205-00	1,800	0-15	270-00
8 (Aug./Sept.'80)	1,900	595-00	280-00	1,700	0-14	238-00
9 (Oct.'80)	2,100	408-00	230-00	1,800	0-13	234-00
10 (Nov.'80)	2,500	485-00	330-00	2,200*	0-12	264-00*
		PRINTING COST FOR YEAR = £3,555-50	ADVERT. REVENUE FOR YEAR = £1,790-00			SALES REVENUE FOR YEAR = £2,012-00

* = estimated figure.

① From sales figures, it might seem that printing 1,500 each time rather than (say) 1,000 was extravagant. Perhaps so - kept hoping sales would shoot up. However, printing costs go mostly on setting up the printing & so the extra 500 of each only added about £40 to each bill. And back issues still sell to collectors etc..

② The relentless rise in printing costs is reflected in the improved quality of each successive issue + the increasing print run. Inflation also played a part. Change of printer & of size of copy dropped price by almost £200 with issue 9. The mag's always been 24pp.

③ Advertising rates haven't changed since the mag started (except for classified ads which were free for first few issues, then became 10p per word). The rise in advertising revenue has been due to the mag's growing reputation & effectiveness + me learning how to get advertising & just who to offer it to.

④ Number sold has gone up gradually & continues to do so as I find new sales outlets.

⑤ Average net income per copy has gone down steadily as ⓐ I've personally sold fewer copies (at 30p), ⓑ more copies have been sold through shops (at discount price of 20p to them), ⓒ up to 1,000 copies have gone to distributors (at 10p each for them to pass to shops at 20p each)

⑥ Sales revenue = no. sold × average net income per copy.

⑦ Overheads for year are 'phone bill (£250-00); stationary (£50-00); travel (for distribⁿ & interviews, etc.: £50-00); posters (£10-00); advert. rates cards (£15-00); postage (£60-00); fees paid to some contributors for special expenses (£35-00). Total overheads for year = £470-00

TOTAL INCOME = sales revenue for year + advert. revenue for year = £3,802-00
TOTAL EXPENDITURE = printing cost for year + overheads for year = £4,025-50
DEFICIT FOR FIRST YEAR = £223-50 ⬅

⑧ Each issue has taken an average of about 30 hr. to research & compile; 100 hr. to type, layout, paste up, etc; 60 hr. to distribute. Also, there are about 12 hr. spent on incidental work (giving out info, chasing up bad debts - hello, Ray Rossi (!), etc.). Total per issue = 202 hr. For yr. = 2020 hr. Per week (ie. 2020÷52‡) = just under 39 hr. That's a lot when it's loosing money! I've a living to make too via journalism (Musicians Only, Month In Yorkshire, etc) & work as a creative writer/performer.

‡ HOLIDAYS... WHAT HOLIDAYS ??
— NICK TOCZEK (22 OCTOBER 80)

THE WAREHOUSE

19-21 SOMERS ST.   LEEDS 1.   tel. 468287.

NOVEMBER DATES:-

Tues. 4th - **Comsat Angels**
(Melody Maker's best debut album of the year)

Wed. 5th - **Classix Nouveaux**

Sun. 9th - **Inversions / Inversions + Bodceian**
(LUNCHTIME)   (London Jazz-Funk Band)   (Leeds Reggae Band)

Tues. 11th - **7 Year Itch**

Wed. 12th - **Johnny Mars 7th Sun**
(top-rate U.S. blues band)

Sun. 16th - **Best Friends**
(LUNCHTIME)

Mon. 17th - **New Music**

Sun. 23rd - **Best Friends**

Tues. 25th - **Soft Cell**

Wed. 26th - **Night Doctor**
(10-piece ska & reggae band: ex-Marley)

!! STOP PRESS !!
STRAY CATS
THURS. DECEMBER 4th
"THE BEST NEW THING SINCE THE BEATLES & THE STONES!" - Mick Jagger

More top-line bands to be added: for details ring above number between 9a.m. & 2a.m.

page 12

250 years of rock   Doris Archer lives!

ELECTRONICALLY RECORDED...
...being the infallible verdict of Nick Toczek & Steve Brown.

9 Below Zero - Live at The Marquee
(released 1980 on A&M - no. AMLE 68515).

I caught this band live at Bradford University earlier this year (see WCR 5 for interview + review of E.P.). Steve saw them at Reading. We've both got a high opinion of their live set of raw all-out R'n'B.

This album has caught much of the atmosphere & intensity of the stage show with the audience response apparent not just between numbers, but throughout.

It's a generous collection too - 14 tracks (4 originals, 10 standards) & not a duff one among them. If you've any taste for R'n'B, then you'll be hard-pressed to find an excuse for not owning this. It's quite simply one of the best live albums of its kind in years. Mark Feltham's work on harmonica is the icing on the cake.

With many 'live' albums you find (a) that the tracks are the best of a whole series of recordings made during a tour - i.e. selected from numerous versions of each song & (b) that numbers have been 'tidied up' & even partially re-recorded in the studio afterwards. However, 'Live at The Marquee' is just what it claims to be - one concert (16th July 1980) with the band sounding just as they did on the night.

Prag Vec - No Cowboys
(released 17th Oct.'80 on Spec Records no. reSPEct 1 through Rough Trade)

Two years ago the band issued a 4-track E.P. on Spec (their own label). This L.P. is gleaned from sessions & live recordings done since then & includes a live version of 'Cigarettes' - one of the tracks on the E.P.

Off-beat pop & processed electronic music. Accessibly avant garde, the band have an excellent vocalist in Sue Gogan - Steve rightly compares her with Pauline Murray.

Unlike Gary 'play it again & again' Numan, Prag Vec don't work to any immediately recognisable patterns or formulae. While this makes it easier to listen to the album throughout, variety alone doesn't suffice. Their simplistic naivety has holes big enough to let boredom leak in - & it does.

I'd pick out about 6 of the 13 tracks as ones I'd want to listen to again. Steve picked out 'Third Person' as the only one he remotely liked.

The real point is that, had this been the first release by a relatively new band, it might have been promising. However, as the culmination of two/three years of working together, it's just not got enough to offer.

Split Enz - True Colours
(released 1980 on A&M no. AMLH 64822).

A special lazer-etched edition of the album! The single off this L.P. - 'I Got You' - has seen chart action this summer & so the album followed it into the L.P. charts... odd, when both were released back in January. Mostly, it's down to a combination of the band having come over here from Australia/New Zealand & A.&M.'s hard-sell dept.

I saw the band live at The Fan Club in Leeds. They were good. Here, many of the songs come over as much less dynamic/more processed. The album's a studio product. On stage, the modernistic percussion of Noel Crombie & keyboards of Eddie Rayner dominate. On the album, however, they take a back seat to the more dated guitar work.

Generally, songs & arrangements are good. Steve:- "They sound like a cross between Cheap Trick & the slushy chart pop of (say) New Musik or The Korgies - but I like Cheap Trick."

This is a good album of its kind, but both Steve & I have doubts about the band's future on the UK market. Their Antipodean successes come from a music derived primarily from mid-70's British rock - fine over there, but here...? For this band, a hell of a lot 'll hang on the next album.

R.A.F. - R.A.F.
(released 10th Oct.'80 on A&M - no. AMLH 64816).

Good band doing M.O.R. pop-rock. Quite varied - ranges from basic pop through to heavyish rock on the one hand, synthesised new music on the other. It's powerful, but there's nothing new here - just a singer-songwriter (David Valentine), his songs, his band. All talented, but the combination lacks identity & doesn't fit into any obvious category. Result is that he'll get ignored by the media - not my rules, but that's how the game has to be played nowadays. However, if you like keyboard- & guitar-based rock that's well played & slightly melodramatic at times, then give this album a listen.

MYOFIST - Hot Spikes
(released 10th Oct.'80 on A&M) no. AMLH 64823.

Last of the bunch sent by A&M. Cover & title suggest a heavy metal out-fit, but they're just an unoriginal powerpop combo trying to sound tough & hard. Weak & clichéd music coupled with bad, sexist lyrics. 3rd rate Canadian dross with few redeeming features. Add a faulty pressing that keeps sticking & it's a drag. They sing: "It was nice/We did it twice." We say: "It is shit/We don't like it."

Then Steve Brown went home, so singles & tapes are 'done' by me...

Singles:

METHODISHCA TUNE - Leisuretime c/w the twee googs (Eustone Records - no. T02 - 1980). Odd mix on the A-side has bass & drums upfront, guitar in background. Add vocals, backing vocals & a bit of sax. Put them all to a lazy tune. Not exciting, but distinctive. B-side's much better opens with guitar & tinny percussion. Bass is again inserted loud & clean. Vocals are hollow, & the whole is skeletal but insidious. It lasts less that 2 minutes. Remember the name. They're an interesting band. The single's distributed thru Rough Trade.

WIDE BOYS - Stop That Boy c/w Heart of Stone (Big Bear Records - no. BB 30 - 1980). A-side is buoyant, slightly ska pop. Guitar & organ work well together. Drums drive the number along well. The number reminds me of The Bodysnatchers (R.I.P.). B-side's an odd mixture of reggae & straight rock. A year ago, this'd have been a dead cert. for 2-tone-type airplay. Now it's a good debut from a band who're better musicians than these songs allow them to be.

RUBY TURNER BAND - Separate Ways c/w I Shall Be Released (Sunflower Label - no. SF1 - 1980: released thru Graduate Records). Via Graduate & with Bob Lamb (ex-Steve Gibbons & now producer for UB40) on production, this is a funky, jazz-influenced discodancer. Pleasant, but not a number that gives full rein to Ruby's enormous vocal talents. B-side is Dylan's song. Here, her voice is less straight-jacketed & she gives the number a sensitive interpretation. Catch this band live if you can - she's got magic.

tapes:

VEX - 3 demo/master recorded at Cargo in Rochdale. Titles: Stranger Station, (So This Is) Disco, Alien Emotion. The band gets better every time I hear them. Was impressed when I recently saw them live at Scamps, Bradford. They are rapidly proving themselves to be one of the city's best bands. Here, Cargo have done them proud. Their strong synth-based rock is given its full dimensions. Newcomers John Binns (ex-Japanese Soldiers) on drums & Rick Ironmonger (ex-Shaftdrive) on bass give the band extra punch, while Andy Tyson (vocals & synth) has lost all the nervous restraint that weakened their earlier work. Dave Pickard completes the sound with some tidy & unobtrusive guitar work. Look out for their debut single.

→ TAPES CONTINUED ON PAGE 14.

MORE ~~RED~~ BLACK TAPE... (continued from page 13).

7 YEAR ITCH - 'Oo Ya Ha' + 'I Wanna Make Ya'. Demo of 4th-coming single on their own label (out this month). First track has dramatic guitar-work, some beautiful high harmony work & a catchy hook-line ("Spend all my money getting out of my head"). Sixties West-Coast rock meets post-new wave (but only just). More fine guitar-work on the second track which is like a melodic/sophisticated Suzi Quatro. Two excellent songs that'll make a good debut single. Listen out for it - should earn some airplay. America would this band & Trans-Atlantic appeal is a rare rock commodity. Don't know where it was recorded, but the mystery studio did a fine job. Was it Cargo?

The Sofa - 'The Hat' + 'The Penny Drops' + 'The Ring'. First time in the studio for this band. First track's a pop song about a girl. Vocals sound slightly 'wooly' but otherwise it's O.K. Second track's a touch more distintive with nice pacing & the vocals well delivered - should have backing vocals on this sort of poptune. Aha! Track 3 has backing vocals on a line or two & they lift the song. Overall, an appealing demo - though there's nothing that jumps out & really grabs you. Guitar breaks could do with more work. Lyrics fit the songs well. Vocalist is good, but his voice is thinnish & needs back-up. Sofa, so good... Recorded Ric-Rac.

Rough Justice - 6-track cassette that's for sale (see below). They're a good heavy guitar band. Songs are dated but come over well & the recording quality's good 'n' clean. They're doing what they do do well. Will be an exciting band live. Can't fault the musicianship - there's some stunning lead guitar that's fast, melodic & rich. Only fault is that they work to a totally orthodox formula - i.e. it's music for the already-converted... but the climate's right for that at the moment.

Knife Edge - another on-sale 6-track. This one has the band's most popular live numbers given good studio production. I like this band, like their songs & like this tape. Neil Hooper slagged them off for this tape in Musicians Only. He was wrong. If songs send a shiver through me then I _know_ they're special.

Alan Whittle - 'Songs I Enjoyed Writing'. 10-track commercial tape from an acoustic guitarist-songwriter. American-influenced blend of blues, folk & country. He's an entertaining songwriter - relaxed & amusing, & a fine guitarist to boot. I found 'George Joseph Smith' & 'Big Red Sausage' the funniest... unsubtle in the extreme, but I still laughed. He also has some sensitive country ballads. Would have liked to hear some more of his guitar playing - maybe a couple of instrumentals. Alan's on 0773-812626.

KEV.

CLASSIFIED ADVERTS.
GUITAR TUITION - ALL STYLES. CHEAP RATES. WEEKLY OR TO SUIT. RING STEWART ON B'F'D 634858.
ECHO UNIT FOR SALE - SIMMS-WATT ECHO WITH TAPES & LEADS & FOOTSWITCH. £50 o.n.o. RING NICK ON B'F'D 21867.

We specialise in singles old and new and stock all the latest alburns

Jumbo Records 102 Merrion Centre Leeds LS2 8PJ
0532 455570

PRESS RELEASES, rare diseases, other bits & pieces...

PRIVATE DICKS

PRIVATE DICKS are from Halifax. They've a track on the Snark Music compilation album (on cassette, not vinyl) 'Only A Northern Song' & should have a single released early next year on a London-based label. They're a pure R'n'B band who're gaining a high reputation on the northern pub-rock circuit after about a year of hassles & hard work. Now, with the sudden growth in popularity of R'n'B, they're very optimistic about the chances of going fulltime pro in '81.

Their line-up is: Pete Cooke (voc/harm); Steve Whitehead (ld gtr/slide gtr); Dave Clay (dms/voc); Gus (bass) &, recent newcomer, Eddie Absent (sax).

Contact: Pete on Hx 202293, Gus on Hx 884887, Steve on Hx 68565 or write to John Sutton (manager) at 6 Elizabeth House, Cumberland Close, Ovenden, Halifax, W.Yorks.

THE AMAZING WHIPPS

Lancs band THE AMAZING WHIPPS mailed in a self-info package in which they describe themselves as a high energy, innovative R'n'B outfit with addition of funk & ska; a combination that they label 'a knockout Harvey Wallbanger of modern music'.

All 4 are in their early to mid 20's, each with several years of musical experience behind them. Mal Jackson (gtr/harmonica) is from Bradford (ex-Beezer Bob & The Brainwaves) & Charlie Caley (vocs/bass) was with Leeds bands Jobe St Day, Alwoodley Jets & Bombers. The other two members are Donna Maria Darlow (kbds) & Phil Sands (dms).

Contact: Dave Smith on 0282-812951 or by pen to Voxette Music Management, 11 North Ave., Barnoldswick, Colne, Lancs, BB8 6DE.

THE WIDE BOYS

2½ years ago, when I was living in Brum, there was a thriving pub-rock scene & I remember seeing early incarnations of THE WIDE BOYS - a loose collection of skilled local musos. Steve Maddox, then drummer with my own band, now plays keyboards with WB's. I owe a book to Martin Berry (voc/rm gtr) who used to be a bassist. Malcolm Smart (ld gtr) is an excellent guitarist who once did an acoustic set of classical pieces in a duo with Dave Carrol (then in Steve Gibbons Band)! Simon Smith (voc/rm gtr) was in WB's in the early days & is a dynamic singer. The other members are Steve Dolan (bass/bkg voc), Steve Fever (perc/voc) & Jim Bates (dms).

The band's got a track on the recent Brum compilation LP 'Bouncing in the Red' & have just had a single released on Big Bear Records (see reviews) which is attracting some airplay on Radio One. They're after gigs up north.

Contact: Jonah Wideboy on 021-449-1248 or write to 122 Church Rd, Moseley, Birmingham 13.

SHAKE APPEAL

A press release arrived. It reads:-
Leeds band SHAKE APPEAL are set to embark on a string of dates aimed at kids who don't look old enough to get into pubs. The mini-tour (growing larger by the day) is called 'A Chance To Dance', & offers just that to members of youth clubs & centres in Leeds & surrounding areas.

The show at each club or centre will consist of an hour's live performance plus disco (also supplied by Shake Appeal).

The idea came about when the band reluctantly agreed to a request by local community workers to take part in an event for children in a 'problem area'. The gig was a success, & the band enjoyed the spontaneity of the response, so it was decided that more of the same should follow.

This is largely an experimental tour so Shake Appeal hope to recover expenses only, with the hope that some new venues will be created along the way.

If you are a youth club organiser or member & would like the Shake Appeal Chance To Dance tour to visit your club, contact: Charles Shepherd (manager) on Leeds 624731 ext. 268.

DALE HARGREAVES' FLAMINGOS

The Vye, for four years one of the most popular groups on the Leeds pub-rock circuit, split up a few months ago shortly after the release of their first single (on Dead Good Records).

In last month's issue I wrote up one offshoot, New Opera. Dale Hargreaves, the band's singer/songwriter/frontman now re-emerges with his FLAMINGOS.

Performing new material plus a few old Vye numbers, they intend to carry on where the old band left off. Dale takes lead vocals & guitar, his fellow musicians being John Kewley (dms), Simon Hollis (bass), Jon Bedford (kbds/bkg vocs) & Richard Eager (ld gtr).

They'll be playing around the North during the next couple of months & are negotiating for a New Year tour in West Germany.

Contact: 0423 (Harrogate)-501019 or 01-481-4087.

UB40 + AFRIKAN STAR at Leeds University

by TINO PALMER

Outside Leeds University, a large truck is parked - reg. no. JAH 296V! An indication of the reggae to come our way.

Inside, a late start means the band stroll on at about 10.45 to a tape of 'Reefer Madness' (their own Egyptian reggae). Half way through, it stops & the band launch back into it - note perfect to the tape we'd just heard. Words of praise go to the sound crew - a great sound from a great mix where even Norman Hassans perc. could be heard clearly!

Surprisingly, some of the big hits came out first: 'King' (with weak vox), 'Food For Thought', 'I Think It's Going To Rain Today' (Randy Newman goes reggae!) & tracks from the LP & 12"er.

The new single was showcased; called 'The Earth Dies Screaming', it featured stunning lighting - smoke poured across the stage & blue sheet lighting bathed everything, producing an effect not unlike a horror movie.

An onstage fade with Brian Travers' sax leads into 'Burden of Shame', the lyrics biting through sharp & clear. The fast end section was accompanied by a brace of strobes to showcase Astro's fancy stepping. 'Little by Little' & 'Madame Medusa' were both introduced as "Rock Against Thatcher" numbers - bet that pleased the true blue cops in the audience (did they pay in?!) "...Rain Today" began just as the recorded version; Ali & Robin Campbell's voices echoed together - "Tin Can at my Feet" - wandering through the song. The band make good use of the echo especially on the sax & their use of onstage dub is refreshing. 'Signing Off' was the excuse to introduce the band - usually boring but Astro carries it off entertainingly (?!). For the first encore, Astro introduced an instrumental which "is the theme tune for a show going out on the BBC early next year." No title given though - enigmatic eh gang? "Madame Medusa" is extended & enjoys a healthy dub in the middle, with Astro jumping around like the "Legalise Cannabis" balloons in the audience. 'Food For Thought' & 'My Way Of Thinking' were aired again & finally they left the stage at 12.20. The lights go up & everyone troops home satisfied & fulfilled (sounds like a night in a brothel!)

A mention in despatches for support AFRIKAN STAR. A 9-piece 'progressive roots' band from Birmingham with their own Mikey Dread-type toaster, flautist (honest!) & dreadlocked dancer out front. They played a 50 min. set;- 'Cosmic Vibration' with its rub-a-dub style; 'Minority Struggle', 'Chaos' & 'Living in the System' (their single) all stood out & began the evening in good style.

I went to this gig hoping to find faults with UB40 but the way they present their show & the excellence of their sound - vital, I think, to the importance of their lyrics - makes this virtually impossible. If they come near again, be there or be somewhere else!

I learnt this weekend that while UB40 were onstage, drugs squad 'tecs raided their dressing room. The band arrived at the hotel at 1.30am, & 4 of them were nicked along with Afrikan Star with all of Afrikan Star & the entire road crew - 25 people in all. The moral (?!) of this story is... Don't let your support band smoke those strong Woodbines on stage!

TWO SINGLES BY BRADFORD BANDS

MYSTERIOUS FOOTSTEPS { 'Like They Do In The Movies' c/w 'White Dread' }

THE NEGATIVES { 'Love Is Not Real' c/w 'Stakeout' }

Available through Red Rhino & Rough Trade also 90p each direct from Kirk Enterprises, 5 Kenmore Rd., Bradford, BD6 3JH. (cheques payable to: J. HOWARD).

John Scheerer & Sons Ltd.

8 Merrion Centre, Leeds LS2 8NG.

Telephone 449592

We are main agents for Ibanez guitars, HH amplifiers, Tama and Premier drums.

We carry a comprehensive range of amps, drums, guitars and pedals—new and second hand.

COMPETITIVE PRICES

Part exchange always welcome

H.P. can be arranged

Also wide selection of brass and woodwind and repairs service on all instruments and gear.

Page 16

A DAY WITH U2
their beliefs, their hopes, their music.....

U2 - the same the world over; one letter, one number, no difference in France, Australia, Russia or America - U2 - unique. That is U2, they are unique.

They thrive on individuality. Their beliefs are their own, set firm in the direction of attaining attention & recognition. So, forget any comparisons with The Cure or anyone else whilst reading this - no one is like U2.

11.30 (Tick Tock?) & Bono stands on the monitors in front of the stage, his head brushing the ceiling, his eyes racing yet only staring at the middle distance.

U2 have come to Leeds for the third time in their career. In June this year The Fan Club was sparsely populated with about 50 inquisitive punters. Futurama followed in September with the eyes of 6½ thousand people from all over Britain on them - & here tonight, back down to earth, as only 100 or so line the walls of the same Fan Club. For me, U2's sheer brilliance deserves the attention of 6½ thousand EVERY time they play.

Their music on stage reflects their attitudes & beliefs off stage. Talking to them earlier on in the day, Bono's arms were flaying about characteristically, as he described in no uncertain terms what U2 are about. He cannot talk in an unfeeling way such is his commitment to the band: They come from Ireland & two years ago they said to the people there: "Look, we are U2, we are from your country, you must decide." And decide they did - U2 will become one of the best bands in Britain. That is the firm belief of their leader Bono - "We do not think in terms of failure, we have made it & will go further."

They aim to make themselves known the world over through the media - TV & radio. The greatest medium however is that of personal contact, in this U2 excel. They play for, and indeed along with, the audience. In fact, they become a part of the audience, yet with such individual feeling that by the end you know everybody in the band - from Bono's trancelike eccentricity to Adam's ice-cold emotions &, at times, almost shyness.

A moody opening number & a broken guitar string heralded the start of their set, but it all fell into place as Bono yelled out "11 o'clock Tick Tock" & U2 plunged into their first single. Amongst their set were "Stories For Boys" & "Electric Company" - both songs to listen for on their new album "Boy". "Touch" & "Things To Make & Do" - the B-sides of their only two British singles were highlights of a superb forty minutes which was a feast of a mixture of all that is U2. The personality, the moods, the exuberance, Bono's fine voice & exquisite crescendos of breathtaking U2 music.

U2, "Unique?" "Brilliant?" "Soon to become the best band in Britain?" U2 know, but you too can find out. Me? - well, I'm convinced.

U2 are:- Bono....Lead Vocals.
Edge....Lead Guitar/Backing Vocs.
Adam....Bass Guitar.
Larry...Drums.
         -Andy Stevens 5/10/80.
(I think he liked the band!-ed.)

CLASSIFIED ADS. (10p per word - phone-in service on 0274-21867).
BADGES - designed, printed & made up. Also **POSTERS & L.P.COVERS**. Contact: Grasshopper Printing Collective. Phone 0484-843879 for details. BADGES · POSTERS · L.P.COVERS · BADGES · POSTERS

"Try to think of it as just another aspect of international diplomacy, Beddowes...."
"I'll try Sir..."

ROUGH JUSTICE

Paul Edwards: voc (star find!)
Nick Downes: bass (ex-Proposition 31/Stress
Jeff Taylor: ld gtr (ex-Snoots/Luigi & DB)
Russ Middleton: ld gtr (ex-Stress)
Paul Graham: dms (ex-Actors/Stress)

Road crew: Cliff, Carl, Pete (paid in baked beans).

In typically restrained & modest style, Dave Hall (manager) writes:-

"They're a highly accomplished group of musicians fronted by a charismatic & energetic lead singer (faint traces of Freddie Mercury?) who provides the essential ingredients of excitement & aggression through his unpredictability on stage.

Russ Middleton & Jeff Taylor must be the best 2 guitarists in Leeds. (See what I mean?!-N.T.) They deliver the music fast & loud, seeming almost to duel with each other on stage.

Paul Graham & Nick Downes provide a meaty backing for the 3 frontmen who attack the audience with snarling guitars & screaming vocals, leaving them in no doubt that they have seen one of the best HM bands around.

Songs: lyrics by Paul, music by Russ.

The band have done 14 gigs to date, attracting a large following in Leeds, especially amongst the biking fraternity."

Contact: Dave Hall on Leeds (0532) 741072).

RUBY TURNER BAND

From a Graduate Records press release:-
"Ruby Turner was born in Jamaica 21 years ago. At the age of 9 she came with her family to England & settled in Handsworth, Birmingham. From school plays, she joined the city's Crescent Theatre Company. Her debut was a walk-on part in "Streetcar Named Desire" in which she sung a street song. More musical acting roles followed & in '77 she appeared in a rock operetta at The Edinburgh Festival (written by Gareth Owen - I used to drink with him when I lived in B'ham & was performing myself at the same festival - N.T.). Gareth was so impressed with her that he became her manager. They formed a band with Geoff Pearce as leader & were laying down a demo at Bob Lamb's studio when Graduate Records took an interest. They are now marketing & promoting the single (see reviews on p.13) released on her own Sunflower Label. A half hour show 'This Is Ruby Turner' was broadcast nationally on BBC TV a few months ago."

Contact: Dave Ingham at Graduate Records on (0384) 59048 & 211159.

Fanzines

Only 3 of them this time, but they are all interesting. First up is the second edition of Bradford's new punkzine **APATHY** still a bit expensive at 25p for ten black & white pages, but a much better issue than the first one. Discharge, Damned, Crass + some local groups. Lots of bad taste humour & generally anarchic fun. eg. On p2 it says in block capitals: "DON'T FORGET TO READ AKY'S ARTICLE 'IS PUNK DEAD' ON PAGE 5." Turn to page 5 & the entire article reads: "IS PUNK DEAD? IS IT FUCK!" As gripping as it's subtle, huh?. All correspondence to: Andy, 22 Heaton Grove, Frizinghall, Bradford 9. (... Heaton Grove? I lived at 7 Heaton Grove for the first 5 years of my life). So we move on, dear reader, to consider the merits & demerits of issue ten of **JAMMING**. 44 pages for 30p. & several of them printed in 2 colours, + a 4-colour cover. How do they do it? Must print it themselves. Mind you, it's taken them 9 months to get it together. Do buy it. There's lots in it & the mag's now available through H.M.V. It's been going for several years & has gone from strength to strength. And if you don't like it, don't blame me - I'm just the chambermaid. Finally, get out of the common market & read fanzine no 3... or, to put it another way, don't be Hague, ask for **Vague**. No.6 30p for 28 large pages into which a jungle of news, info, reviews, articles, etc is packed. Photos, cartoons, an extensive A-Z of fanzines, Pop Group, Crass, Devo, Cosmetics, etc. Bits of politics, anti-vivisection, more & more. Jamming comes from 5, Little Bornes, Alleyn Park, London SE21 8SD while Vague comes from Tom at 'Butcombe', Castle St., Mere, nr. Salisbury, Wilts., BA12 6JF.

A final word or two. All the above include stuff on Crass, who'd be in this issue of WCR except that I was stuck in the air above London airport (Heathrow) while they were setting up their gear to play in Bradford last month. The result was that I missed them (or they missed me - depends on how you see it).
— WRIT BY NICK TOCZEK.

Big Books Time

While I was in Frankfurt last month, I went round the Frankfurt (where else?) Bookfair. Stall N959 in Hall 5 was a display of publications from Pete Townsend's Eel Pie (of Video, recording studio, record label fame). I was given two of their recent rock books to review &, as they feature two of my favourites among the current crop of mega-bands, here's what I think of them.

The Clash - Before & After (£4·50). This is an album of photos by Pennie Smith with captions that are all quotes from the band's members. To their credit, The Clash held onto their 'street' principles longer than most other '76/'77 bands did — but the industry finally won them over via the money to buy clothes & other gear. ie. The Clash fell in love with pictures of themselves posing & acting out fantasy roles (rock rebels/U.S. gangsters/James Dean etc.). That said, this'd make a nice present for a Clash fan. Pennie Smith is one of the better rock photographers & her fotos capture much of the character of both band & individuals within it.

The Jam - The Modern World By Numbers (£3·95) This is a fairly thorough & well-researched history of the band written by Paul Honeyford & illustrated with a whole bunch of (mainly live) photos. Honeyford bases the book on Weller's outstanding lyrics & comes up with an informed & readable book.

Both titles are attractively laid out & produced. Eel Pie also publish a wide range of children's books & will also soon be bringing out Viv Stanshall's (ex-Bonzo Dog) novel... but is there anything that Eel Pie don't do?
— NICK TOCZEK.

8-TRACK - £50 per eight hr. day!

Fully Equipped Studio Using Tascam, Allen Heath, Revox, Roland, Tannoy, Quad, A.K.G., Calrec, etc.

USE OF ANY OF THE FOLLOWING EQUIPMENT

Polymoog, Minimoog, Fender Rhodes Suitecase, Hammond X5 Organ, Moog Taurus Bass Pedals, ARP Salina String Machine, Clavinet D6, Mellotron, Premier Drums, Kramer 5000 Dmz Bass, Acoustic Piano & Guitars + numerous effects.

JSG Music

YORKSHIRE'S LARGEST GROUP SHOP

108B Main Street, Bingley. Tel: 0274-568843

(Open till 9 pm every Monday and Thursday; Friday and Saturday till 5.30 pm)

FOR THE BIGGEST SELECTION OF GROUP GEAR AT THE LOWEST POSSIBLE PRICES

In the Guitar and Amp shop choose from:

Gibson, Fender, Washburn, Guild, Ovation, Rickerbacker, WAL, Lincoln, Peavey, full HH Concert Rigs, HH Performer, HH VS, Marshall, MM, Custom Sound, Carlsboro, Laney, Vox, Roland, Hill and RSD. 1,000 watt Rigs ready to go. Mics by: AKG, Shure and Beyer. Accessories by: Electroharmonix, Boss, Dod, Vox, etc.

In the Keyboard Department:

Wurlitzer, Moog, Roland, Rhodes, Korg, Hohner, Crumar, etc.

ALL THIS **PLUS** HIRE SERVICE, REPAIRS, HUGE SELECTION OF USED GEAR AND WE BUY FOR CASH

THIS GIG GUIDE IS IN AID OF 'ROCK AGAINST MYOPIA'

Remember, remember... The Gigs in November...

Sa 1	Cleopatras, Huddersfield = U.K. SUBS. Fforde Grene, Leeds = THE JETS (R'n'R). Royal Park, Leeds = KNIFE EDGE. White Lion, Huddersfield = SPEEDY BEARS. Haddon Hall, Leeds = SHAKE APPEAL. Seacroft Hotel, Leeds = THE ELEMENTS. Funhouse, Keighley (lunch) = KNIFE EDGE. University, Bradford = SIMPLE MINDS + MUSIC FOR PLEASURE.	**Su 16**	Haddon Hall, Leeds = KNIFE EDGE. Blackamore Head, Pontefract = TAROT. White Lion, Huddersfield = T.B.A. (lunch) / APPLE (eve) Warehouse, Leeds (lunch) = BEST FRIENDS. Windmill Youth Club, Rothwell, Leeds = SHAKE APPEAL. Princeville, Bradford (lunch) = SPIDER. Unity Hall, Wakefield = CAPTAIN BEEFHEART + COMSAT ANGELS. Royal Park, Leeds = 157. Fan Club, Leeds = NOT SENSIBLES + INFERNAL RACKET + 1 other. Vaults Bar, Bradford = ACCELERATORS Forge Inn, York = U.K. SUBS. Fforde Grene, Leeds = FABULOUS POODLES.
Su 2	White Lion, Huddersfield = MIDDLE 8 (L) + TREATMENT (eve). Princeville, Bradford = SPEEDY BEARS St. George's Hall, Bradford = JOE JACKSON. Blackamore Head, Pontefract = PRIVATE DICKS. Fan Club, Leeds = MONOCHROME SET. Haddon Hall, Leeds = SHARP PRACTICE. Theatre Club, Wakefield = B.A. ROBERTSON. Royal Park, Leeds (lunch) = 157. Unity Hall, Wakefield = SIMPLE MINDS + MUSIC FOR PLEASURE. Vaults Bar, Bradford = HEADHUNTER Warehouse, Leeds (lunch) = BEST FRIENDS. Fforde Grene, Leeds = GORDON ROWLEY'S NIGHTWING.	**Mo 17**	City Hall, Sheffield = O.M.I.T.D. Royal Park, Leeds = DODGY TACTICS. Skellow Grange, Doncaster = LIMELIGHT. Marquis of Granby, Leeds = HEAVEN 17. Unity Hall, Wakefield = SPLODGENESSABOUNDS. Vaults Bar, Bradford = LYM-BIK. University, York = CAPTAIN BEEFHEART Fforde Grene, Leeds = FLASH CATS (R'n'R). Warehouse, Leeds = NEW MUSIK. Princeville, Bradford = BABYTUCKOO + WARLORD. Haddon Hall, Leeds = WILD SMITH.
Mo 3	City Hall, Sheffield = ELKIE BROOKS. Queens Hall, Leeds = THE JAM. Haddon Hall, Leeds = STAGE B. Marquis of Granby, Leeds = DALE HARGREAVES' FLAMINGOS. Vaults Bar, Bradford = THE SHAKES. Fforde Grene, Leeds = RIOT ROCKERS (R'n'R).	**Tu 18**	Fieldhead Youth Club, Guiseley, nr Leeds = SHAKE APPEAL. Lion Inn, nr Castleton = KNIFE EDGE. Scamps, Bradford = JEDDEDIAH STRUTT. Marquis of Granby, Leeds = (T.B.A. - H.M.) St. George's Hall, Bradford = HOT CHOCOLATE.
Tu 4	Unity Hall, Wakefield = U.K. SUBS + CITIZENS Scamps, Bradford = KNIFE EDGE. Warehouse, Leeds = COMSAT ANGELS. Limit Club, Sheffield = MONOCHROME SET. Marquis of Granby, Leeds = RHABSTALLION.	**We 19**	White Lion, Huddersfield = BACKSLIDER Vaults Bar, Bradford = BABY TUCKOO. Polytechnic, Sheffield = RUTS D.C. St. George's Hall, Bradford = URIAH HEEP. Romeo & Juliet's, Doncaster = GIRLSCHOOL St. George's Hall, Bradford = URIAH HEEP. Polytechnic, Huddersfield = BARRACUDAS. Royal Park, Leeds = THIN RED LINE. Marquis of Granby, Leeds = (T.B.A.)
We 5	University, Bradford = THE CURE. White Lion, Huddersfield = ROUGH JUSTICE. Warehouse, Leeds (lunch) = CLASSIX NOUVEAUX. Marquis of Granby, Leeds = (T.B.A.) Vaults Bar, Bradford = SONS OF THE POPE.	**Th 20**	City Hall, Sheffield = SAD CAFE. Polytechnic, Leeds = ADAM & THE ANTS. Fan Club, Leeds = ANOTHER PRETTY FACE. Limit Club, Sheffield = BARRACUDAS Princeville, Bradford = CHINATOWN. Royal Park, Leeds = PRIVATE DICKS.
Th 6	Royal Park, Leeds = ROUGH JUSTICE. Cinema, Hebden Bridge = JOHN MARTYN + support. 68 Youth Club, York = SHAKE APPEAL. St. George's Hall, Bradford = SHAWADDYWADDY. Fan Club, Leeds = TEARDROP EXPLODES. Rose & Crown, Ilkley = DALE HARGREAVES' FLAMINGOS. City Hall, Sheffield = BARBARA DICKSON. Hallamshire Hotel, Sheffield = DANGEROUS GIRLS. Princeville, Bradford = (T.B.A.)	**Fr 21**	Polytechnic, Sheffield = HAZEL O'CONNOR. Splash One, Bradford = SHAKE APPEAL. Queens Hall, Bradford = THE AMAZING WHIPPS. Penthouse, Scarborough = BARRACUDAS. Royal Park, Leeds = WHITE EAGLES. Fforde Grene, Leeds = QUEEN IDA & THE BON TEMPS ZYDECO BAND.
Fr 7	Trinity & All Saints College, Horsforth, nr Leeds = SHAKE APPEAL. Fforde Grene, Leeds = RHABSTALLION. Tattoo, Scarborough = TEARDROP EXPLODES. Polytechnic, Leeds = COMSAT ANGELS. University, Leeds = V DISK. St. Stevens Hall, Steeton = SPEED. Polytechnic, Huddersfield = CLASSIX NOUVEAUX. Royal Park, Leeds = WHITE EAGLES.	**Sa 22**	University, Leeds = IRON MAIDEN. White Lion, Huddersfield = JEDDEDIAH STRUTT. Royal Park, Leeds = TREATMENT. Funhouse, Keighley = SPEED. Haddon Hall, Leeds = AGONY COLUMN.
Sa 8	University, Leeds = DARTS. Fforde Grene, Leeds = BARRACUDAS. White Lion, Huddersfield = GENEVA. St. Georges Hall, Bradford = BATTLE OF THE BANDS (Competition) FINAL * Fforde Grene, Leeds = BARRACUDAS. Haddon Hall, Leeds = ALWOODLEY JETS. Royal Park, Leeds = TALISMAN.	**Su 23**	Grand Theatre, Leeds = ELKIE BROOKS. Blackamore Head, Pontefract = RED EYE. White Lion, Huddersfield = MIDDLE 8 (lunch) / DOTS (eve) Royal Park, Leeds (lunch) = 157. Top Rank, Sheffield = ADAM & THE ANTS Princeville, Bradford (lunch) = PRIVATE DICKS. Fan Club, Leeds = JOSEPH K + ORANGE JUICE Haddon Hall, Leeds = LUIGI ANA DA BOYS. Staging Post, Leeds = THE AMAZING WHIPPS. Vaults Bar, Bradford = STAGE B (T.B.C.) Warehouse, Leeds = BEST FRIENDS (lunch) Fforde Grene, Leeds = TRIMMER & JENKINS.
Su 9	Top Rank, Sheffield = U.K. SUBS. Playhouse, Bradford = CAMERAS IN CARS + VEX + VENDINO PACT + POLICEMAN Staging Post, Leeds = KNIFE EDGE + TWISTED NERVE. WITH A LOAF OF BREAD + NICK TOCLEK + LITTLE BROTHER White Lion, Huddersfield = T.B.A. (lunch), DOTS (eve). Warehouse, Leeds (lunch) = BEST FRIENDS. Fforde Grene, Leeds = LIMELIGHT. Blackamore Head, Pontefract = WITCHFYNDE. Fan Club, Leeds = NEW HORMONES PACKAGE (LUDUS + 2 other N.W. bands). Vaults Bar, Bradford = SPEED Princeville, Bradford (lunch) = THE AMAZING WHIPPS. Haddon Hall, Leeds = THE OTHER SWITCH. Royal Park, Leeds = 157.	**Mo 24**	Royal Park, Leeds = KNIFE EDGE. Jasper's, York = DANGEROUS GIRLS. Haddon Hall, Leeds = YOU AND THE NIGHT AND THE MUSIC. Marquis of Granby, Leeds = THE SWITCH. Vaults Bar, Bradford = SWAKARA.
Mo 10	Rotters, Doncaster = HAWKWIND. Vaults Bar, Bradford = NEW MODEL ARMY. Horsforth Youth Club, Leeds = SHAKE APPEAL. Fforde Grene, Leeds = JOHNNY & THE ROCCOS (R'n'R) Top Rank, Sheffield = B.A. ROBERTSON. Romeo & Juliets, Doncaster = LIMELIGHT. Haddon Hall, Leeds = CONTROL VOICES. Royal Park, Leeds = GOFF JACKSON & THE HUNS. Marquis of Granby, Leeds = THE ESCORTS.	**Tu 25**	St. George's Hall, Bradford = GIRLSCHOOL Limit Club, Sheffield = SHAKE APPEAL. Warehouse, Leeds = SOFT CELL. Scamps, Bradford = MUNROES. Marquis of Granby, Leeds = (T.B.A. - H.M.).
Tu 11	Scamps, Bradford = ROUGH JUSTICE. Warehouse, Leeds = 7 YEAR ITCH. Marquis of Granby, Leeds = (T.B.A. - H.M)	**We 26**	Royal Park, Leeds = STURGEON ROW. White Lion, Huddersfield = RHABSTALLION / ELEMENTS Top Rank, Sheffield = GIRLSCHOOL University, Bradford = PRAYING MANTIS. Marquis of Granby, Leeds = Dol Q Club (with bands, fortnightly). Vaults Bar, Bradford = ORAL SAX (T.B.C.)
We 12	Polytechnic, Sheffield = CREATION REBEL. Royal Park, Leeds = GIMMICKS. University, Bradford = U2. Marquis of Granby = Dol Q Club (bands, every fortnight). White Lion, Huddersfield = VINDICATOR Vaults Bar, Bradford = ORAL SAX (T.B.C.). Rotters, Doncaster = B.A. ROBERTSON. Polytechnic, Leeds = NEW MUSIK. Warehouse, Leeds = JOHNNY MARS' 7th SON.	**Th 27**	City Hall, Sheffield = SAXON + LIMELIGHT. Fan Club, Leeds = WASTED YOUTH + BOYS WILL BE BOYS University, Leeds = BARBARA THOMPSON'S PARAPHENALIA. Royal Park, Leeds = AGONY COLUMN.
Th 13	St. Georges Hall, Bradford = B.A. ROBERTSON. Fan Club, Leeds = THE FALL. Princeville, Bradford = STREETFIGHTER. Royal Park, Leeds = AGONY COLUMN.	**Fr 28**	Polytechnic, Huddersfield = GARY GLITTER. Royal Park, Leeds = WHITE EAGLES. Penthouse, Scarborough = WASTED YOUTH Fforde Grene, Leeds = CRAZY CAVAN (R'n'R) Unity Hall, Wakefield = ROY HARPER + PATRICK FITZGERALD St. George's Hall, Bradford = SAD CAFÉ University, Leeds = Rag Extravaganza ** City Hall, Sheffield = SAXON + LIMELIGHT. Polytechnic, Sheffield = STRAY CATS.
Fr 14	Cosmos, Leeds = TRADITION. Fforde Grene, Leeds = TAURUS. Penthouse, Scarborough = BUDGIE. St. John's College, York = SPLODGENESSABOUNDS. Gaumont, Doncaster = URIAH HEEP. University, Leeds = OTHER SWITCH + NEW OPERA. Compton Arms, Leeds = KNIFE EDGE. Royal Park, Leeds = WHITE EAGLES.	**Sa 29**	University, Sheffield = IRON MAIDEN. Royal Park, Leeds = SHAKE APPEAL St. George's Hall, Bradford = SAXON + LIMELIGHT. Haddon Hall, Leeds = DODGY TACTICS. University, Leeds = HAZEL O'CONNOR. Trades & Labour Club, Castleford = ROUGH JUSTICE + GIMMICKS. Cleo's, Huddersfield = ASWAD. Fforde Grene, Leeds = SLENDER THREAD. White Lion, Huddersfield = TALISMAN. University, Bradford = LINTON KWESI JOHNSON.
Sa 15	University, Leeds = STEEL PULSE. Haddon Hall, Leeds = DALE HARGREAVES' FLAMINGOS Cleo's, Huddersfield = UNITY BAND + SHAKATONES Q. Royal Park, Leeds = DIRTY BUT NICE. White Lion, Huddersfield = TURBO. Fforde Grene, Leeds = FABULOUS POODLES. University Bradford = THE PLANETS. Civil Service Club, Shipley = THE ELEMENTS. Whigs Wine Bar, Jubilee Hotel, Leeds = TREATMENT.	**Su 30**	White Lion, Huddersfield = T.B.A. (lunch) / 7 YEAR ITCH (eve) Haddon Hall, Leeds = (T.B.C.) Fan Club, Leeds = (T.B.A.) Vaults Bar, Bradford = THE AMAZING WHIPPS. Princeville, Bradford (lunch) = OXYM Warehouse, Leeds (lunch) = BEST FRIENDS. Blackamore Head, Pontefract = DRAGSTER. Royal Park, Leeds = 157.

** (Fri. 28 at Leeds University) = local bands include: CONFESSOR, TAROT, STREETFIGHTER, HOOKER, DODGY TACTICS, SHAKE APPEAL, SPIDER BLUES BAND, STORMY MONDAY, OTHER SWITCH, & others.
* (Sat. 8 at St. George's Hall, Bf'd) = competition regional final includes: TREATMENT & others (phoned the organisers several times to ask which bands - was engaged every time).

Abbreviations: T.B.A. = To be arranged ; T.B.C. = To be confirmed ; H.M. = Heavy Metal ; R'n'R = Rock & roll.

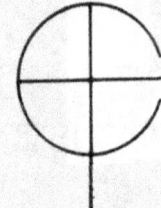

This magazine was printed by Tempest and Cockcroft, 9 Marriner's Drive, Bradford 9
Tel : Bfd. 43695. Happy Birthday W.C.R. !

John Tempest   Dave Cockcroft

ISSUE #11

December 1980 + January 1981, 2,000 copies printed, 20 pages, 25cm x 17cmm

I designed the cover for this issue and all the subsequent issues of WCR. In doing so, I particularly enjoyed my work on the cover of this issue, transforming Margaret Thatcher into a member of Adam and the Ants. Stealing NME's masthead (page 3) was also fun. If you count me, live reviewers, Stan the cartoonist, and Ken the crossword compiler, the WCR contributors now run into double figures!

Notes on bands featured in this issue. .

Gris Boojum's review of a Crass gig at Cleopatra's in Huddersfield (page 15) is arguably one of the best pieces ever published in WCR. Gris also reviews a gig by 7 Year Itch (page 14), whose only single bears witness to the fact that they were another West Yorkshire band that should've gone on to bigger things... but there were so many others with ace singles... Knife Edge, The Shakes, Delta 5, The Scene, Shake Appeal, Radio 5, etc.

Some more of the singles. A few of these were sent to me after 1981, but all feature northern musicians I knew or worked with while producing Wool City Rocker.

SO YOU WOULD LIKE TO HEAR YOUR GROUP ON RECORD

Kirk Enterprises calls all groups, solo singers, poets, artists and already established stars. We require groups for our new Warp Factor Two Compilation L.P.

WHAT'S IN IT FOR YOU?

50 L.P.'s for you to sell on your own, which won't be difficult once you've been round the group's family, friends and fans. We will bring the L.P. to the attention of all the major record companies. The L.P. will be released early in the new year.

ALL WE REQUIRE

Your studio quality master tape + £75 for one track or £140 for two tracks. (Two tracks = 100 L.P.'s for you).

SEND NO MONEY

Just write **ONLY** to the address below quoting your name, address, stating acceptance of the offer or your request for further information. Remember 1st come 1st served.

KIRK

KIRK ENTERPRISES

5 KENMORE ROAD
WIBSEY
BRADFORD
WEST YORKSHIRE

MYSTERIOUS FOOTSTEPS SINGLE
£0.65p P&P (FREE)

EDITORIAL...

THE MAN WHO TOLD THE TALE.

HI THERE, HUMANITY, HERE WE GO AGAIN WITH A TWO-MONTHER CUSTOM-BUILT TO DRIVE US HEAD FIRST INTO '81 VIA T.C.'s BIRTHDAY.

LOTSA GNUS (& A FEW RAINDEER) SO LET'S GET DOWN TO IT. EXTRA 1,000 COPIES PRINTED THIS TIME ROUND, GIVING TOTAL PRINT-RUN OF 3,500. PLEASE HELP BY LETTING ME KNOW IF YOU CAN SUGGEST NEW OUTLETS OR SELL COPIES YOURSELF. NEXT ISSUE (No 12) WILL INCLUDE A FREE FLEXI-DISC & WILL STAY AT 30p... HOPE YOU LIKE IT! HEY, I HEAR TELL THAT HUDDERSFIELD EXAMINER & OTHER LOCAL PAPERS HAVE INTRODUCED VICTORIAN CENSORSHIP - e.g. band adverts for local groups 'PRIVATE DICKS' HAVE TO BE PRINTED AS 'PRIVATE MICKS' & 'ORAL SAX' HAVE TO BE 'ORAL SAXAPHONE'!! WE HERE AT W.C.R. WANT TO EXPRESS OUR SOLIDARITY WITH THE PIONEERING CLEAN-UP WORK OF THE H.....FIELD EXAMINER. THE SOONER WE GET RID OF THE SORT OF PERVERTED & FOUL-MOUTH SHITTY LITTLE ARSEHOLES WHO USE WORDS LIKE 'SAX' & 'DICKS', THE SOONER WE'LL CATCH THE RIPPER & ACHIEVE GLOBAL DISARMAMENT. NOW FOR SOME BAND (as opposed to banned!) NEWS.... LEEDS' THE BEANS LOOK LIKE SIGNING TO CRIMINAL RECORDS.... ALSO FROM LEEDS ARE THE MOTIVATORS WHO'LL BE TOURING IN THE NEW YEAR & LOOK LIKE SIGNING TO THE PYE-LINKED CALENDAR RECORDS... KEIGHLEY'S THE QUICK HAVE CHANGED NAME TO THE SURVIVORS... BRADFORD'S RADIO 5 SOON TO RE-EMERGE AS A 3-PIECE, WITH ORIGINAL MEMBERS JOCK COTTON (voc./gtr.) & DON HAYES (bass) BEING JOINED BY JOHN WALLIS (dms).

YORKSHIRE T.V. ARE PILOT-RUNNING A NEW ROCK SHOW WITH 3 WEEKLY ½-HOUR SHOWS ON DECEMBER 5th, 12th & 19th AT 5.15 P.M. LOUSY NAME 'CALENDAR GOES POP'. ONLY ONE LOCAL BAND PER SHOW - MUSIC FOR PLEASURE (FROM LEEDS), VARDIS (FROM WAKEFIELD) & AROMATIC TOURS (FROM GRIMSBY - WINNERS OF 'BATTLE OF THE BANDS' HEAT AT ST. GEORGE'S HALL, BRADFORD). NATIONALLY ESTABLISHED GUESTS INCLUDE DOLLAR & B.A. ROBERTSON. A BAD START, BUT AT LEAST THERE'S PLENTY OF ROOM FOR IMPROVEMENT!! WRITE IN TO Y.T.V. & LET THEM KNOW WHAT YOU THINK OF THE PROGRAMMES & WHAT NEEDS DOING IF IT'S TO BECOME A WEEKLY SHOW IN '81.

VENUES: KINGS HEAD, KEIGHLEY RESTARTING GIGS (WITH RENEWED MUSIC LICENCE) IN NEW YEAR; FUNHOUSE KEIGHLEY (603796) HAS BAND EVERY SAT. LUNCH & IS STARTING MON. ROCK NIGHTS FROM 29th DEC; PHONE CALL FROM JOHN FARQUHAR (ex-bars manager, Queens Hall & Vaults Bar, Bradford) WHO IS LEAVING B'F'D TO TAKE OVER A SOUTH SHIELDS PUB - WISHES GOODBYE & THANKS TO ALL THE GROUPS WHO PLAYED HIS VENUES & HOPES THEY ALL FEEL THEY WERE FAIRLY TREATED BY HIM... HE KNOWS THAT ANY BAND THAT DIDN'T WAS USUALLY QUICK TO SAY SO!! ROSE & CROWN STILL NOT TAKING BANDS, BUT HOPING TO RESTART IN THE NEXT FEW WEEKS. SCAMPS, BRADFORD CLOSED FOR REFURBISHING. PALM COVE BEING REDONE INSIDE, BUT STAYING OPEN THROUGHOUT.

INCOMING PRINTED BITS... 'A BIT OF CULTURE' (fanzine from York) REACHES ISSUE No 4 & HAS PLENTY TO OFFER FOR COVER PRICE OF 10p - REVIEWS, INFO, FEATURES, ETC. VERY VARIED. THERE'S A 'HOW TO BE UNEMPLOYED' FEATURE FOR SCHOOL LEAVERS + A 2-PAGE SPREAD OF GRAFFITI ("If Margaret Thatcher's the answer, it must've been a very silly question!"). KNIFE EDGE HAVE DONE A SMART 4-PAGE BROCHURE ON THEMSELVES, DALE HARGREAVES HAS A BOOKLET (photocopied) OF HIS LYRICS, WHILE THE PATRIK FITZGERALD BAND HAVE PRODUCED BOTH. THE KNIFE EDGE THING IS DESIGNED TO SECURE GIGS FOR THEM & IS WELL PUT TOGETHER, IF A LITTLE TOO FORMAL. OTHER BANDS SHOULD FOLLOW SUIT IF THEY WANT TO BREAK OUT OF THE LOCAL GIGS TRAP. DALE'S LYRICS - INDIVIDUALLY RUN OFF TO ORDER ON A PHOTOCOPIER FOR 25p EACH. GOOD LYRICS OR PASSABLE-TO-POOR POETRY... AT BEST HE SHOWS SHARP INSIGHT, AT WORST CLICHED PREDICTABILITY. THE BOOK'S GOOD VALUE & HE'S CERTAINLY A BETTER WRITER THAN THE AVERAGE LYRICIST. PATRIK FITZGERALD'S 11 POEMS ARE EMBARRASSINGLY BAD... WHAT ELSE CAN I SAY? HE SHOULD STICK TO MUSIC MAKING! THE BAND'S BROCHURE IS EYE-CATCHING & EFFECTIVE.

MORE: 'ONE VOICE' IS BRADFORD'S NEW MONTHLY FOR THE CITY'S BLACK POPULATION. PRODUCED BY THE COLLEGE FROM TRINITY CENTRE. THE 1st ISSUE'S FREE & LOOKS LIKE AN INFORMATIVE COMMUNITY PERIODICAL.

THE STRUGGLING BAND - ANOTHER PRETTY FACE - HAVE A 4-PAGE COMIC/BROCHURE TO SELL THEMSELVES. ZAPPY, SHOULD GET THEM A FEW GIGS.

I'VE HAD TO HOLD OVER THE L.P. REVIEW TILL NEXT ISSUE (U2, DANCE BAND, MINIATURES, etc.) DUE TO LACK OF SPACE. OTHERWISE, IT'S ALL HERE. HOPE YOU LIKE IT.

FOLLOW THAT STAR, CAMEL-DRIVER! SEE YA NEXT YEAR. Nick Toczek.

NME WCR

5 Beech Terrace
Undercliffe
Bradford BD3 OPY
West Yorks.
Tel. 0274-21867

EDITORIAL
3rd Floor
5-7 Carnaby Street
London W1V 1PG
Phone: 01-439 8761

EDITOR
~~Neil Spencer~~ Nick Toczek

Deputy Editor ~~Phil McNeill~~
Features Editor ~~Tony Stewart~~
News Editor ~~Derek Johnson~~
Associate Editors ~~Charles Shaar Murray~~ ~~Monty Smith~~
Production Editor ~~Stuart Johnston~~
Special Projects Editor ~~Roy Carr~~

Staff
~~Paul Rambali~~
~~Max Bell~~
~~Danny Baker~~
~~Paul Morley~~
~~Adrian Thrills~~
~~Chris Bohn~~

Design
~~Carousel Crunch~~

Photography
~~Pennie Smith~~
~~Anton Corbijn~~

Contributors
~~Nick Kent~~
~~Fred Dellar~~
~~Tony Parsons~~
~~Julie Burchill~~
~~Angus MacKinnon~~
~~Chris Salewicz~~
~~Bob Edmands~~
~~Lester Bangs~~
~~John May~~
~~Penny Reel~~
~~Andrew Tyler~~
~~Ian Penman~~
~~Andy Gill~~
~~Paul Du Noyer~~
~~Graham Lock~~
~~Gavin Martin~~
~~Cynthia Rose~~
~~Vivien Goldman~~

Andy Darlington
Steve Brown
Ken Turner
Keith E. Rice
Gris Boojum
Mick Mitchell
Dave Shepherd
Ocky
Andy Stevens

Cartoons
~~Tony Benyon~~ STAN ENGEL
~~Ray Lowry~~

Research
Fiona Foulgar

New York Yorkshire
~~Joe Stevens~~
~~(212) 674 6024~~
~~Mick Farren~~
~~Richard Grabel~~

ADVERTISEMENT DEPT. Nick on 0274-21867.

P.J. Promotions presents
at
St. George's Hall, Bradford
on
Thursday 11th Dec. at 7.30p.m.

NEW ELECTRIC WARRIORS
HEAVY METAL MYSTERY TOUR
featuring 5 Yorkshire bands from the album 'New Electric Warriors'

**BASTILLE • RHABSTALLION
JEDEDIAH STRUTT • TURBO
• BUFFALO**

All tickets £2-00 (including V.A.T.) from St. George's Hall box office (tel. B'fd 32513)

LIMELIGHT

Album Out Now
"LIMELIGHT"
FER 008
Distributed by PINNACLE

On Tour with
SAXON

DECEMBER '80

1 - Manchester Apollo	11 - Middlesborough Town Hall
2 - Liverpool Empire	12 - Carlisle Market Hall
3 - Bristol Colston Hall	13 - Edinburgh Odeon
4 - Leicester Demontford Hall	14 - Glasgow Apollo
5 - Coventry New Theatre	15 - Dundee Caird Hall
6 - Oxford New Theatre	16 - Newcastle City Hall
7 - Ipswich Gaumont	17 - Birmingham Odeon
8 - Southampton Gaumont	18 - Malvern Winter Gardens
9 - Derby Assembly Rooms	19 - Hammersmith Odeon
10 - Hanley Victoria Hall	20 - Hammersmith Odeon

Album also available by mail order from Future Earth Records, 15 Darrington Drive, Warmsworth, Doncaster, S. Yorks. at £4.50 inc. P. & P.

SO, YOU THINK YOU KNOW ABOUT YORKSHIRE ROCK...

This competition is based on current & recent rock happenings in Yorks. &/or involving Yorkshire bands. Back issues of W.C.R. will help you with a few of the answers, but not all. Answer as many as you can & mail answers to 'Competition, 5 Beech Terrace, Undercliffe, Bradford, BD3 0PY, West Yorks. PRIZE = signed records by local groups + Professionals, Adam & Ants & many others.

1. There have been at least a dozen fanzines (locally produced rock mags) published in Yorkshire in the past year or so. How many can you name?
(a)   (g)
(b)   (h)
(c)   (i)
(d)   (j)
(e)   (k)
(f)   (l)

2. Several of the Yorkshire bands who've played the pub/club rock circuit include numbers in their names. Give the full names of the bands with the following numbers: (a) one, (b) seventeen, (c) thirty one, (d) six hundred & thirty three.
(a)   (c)
(b)   (d)

3. During 1980 about half a dozen sampler albums have been released which feature Yorkshire bands. Name the ones released on the following labels: (a) Rockburgh, (b) Logo, (c) Aardvark.
(a)   (c)
(b)

4. In 1980, a Leeds band released an LP on their own label. Name (a) the band, (b) the album & (c) the label.
(a)   (c)
(b)

5. In early 1980 an agent has to find one gig each for a mod., a punk, a HM, a reggae, a R'n'R & a commercial new wavish rock band. Booking one band into each of the following venues, he could be sure each would be at a place that regularly featured their type of music. Which band does he send to (a) The Albion, Huddersfield, (b) The Blackamore Head, Pontefract, (c) Palm Cove, Bradford, (d) The Coachhouse Club, Huddersfield, (e) Fforde Grene, Leeds, (f) Royal Park, Leeds?
(a)   (d)
(b)   (e)
(c)   (f)

6. Name the Sheffield band whose vinyl debut was a single with A-side lyrics that were about silkworms. They're now signed to Virgin.
Answer:

7. At which venues were the following events staged during 1980 (a) Futurama II & (b) Spring Rock Special?
(a)   (b)

8. One Yorkshire band released the same track as the B-side of one single, the A-side of another & had it included on an album, all three records being released during 1980. Name (a) the band & (b) the track.
(a)   (b)

9. There are rock shows on various local radio stations. Can you name those on (a) BBC Radio Leeds, (b) Bradford's Pennine Radio, (c) BBC Radio Sheffield, (d) Sheffield & Rotherham's Hallam Radio?
(a)   (c)
(b)   (d)

10. Name the band who've had singles out over the past couple of years on Fast Records, Virgin Records & Red Rhino Records.
Answer:

11. Shared band names. (a) Singles have been released in the past year by two Yorkshire bands called The Negatives. Name the home towns of both of them. (b) Side Effect & Side Effects are both Yorkshire bands. Name their home towns.
(a)   (b)

12. Def Leppard are a band who helped to pioneer the 1980 HM resurgence. They put out a 3-track EP on their own label before signing to a major label. Name (a) their own label, (b) the major label that they signed to & (c) the A-side of their first single for that label.
(a)   (c)
(b)

CONTINUED ON NEXT PAGE...

FAIRVIEW STUDIOS
WILLERBY — HULL

ARE INCREASING THEIR RECORDING FACILITIES FROM 8 TRACK TO:—

24 TRACK
FROM LATE DECEMBER 1980

OPENING RATE WILL BE £12.50 PER HOUR

FOR FULL DETAILS OF ALL OUR FACILITIES CONTACT:
(HULL) 0482-653116

Bradford Printshop

You can print your own posters for cost of materials

We can print and design posters at reasonable prices

For details Phone 22518

13. Graham Fellows went from Sheffield (via a Manchester label & a name-change) to 1980 chart success. Under what name did he find fame?
Answer:

14. Dead Good Records have recently released a single by Tiger Lily - a band with strong Yorkshire connections. The tracks were recorded in the mid-seventies & the band, under another name, have since had considerable record success. What was the name they adopted?

15. Ada Wilson, Ian Nelson & Dave Whittaker have collaberated to produce an oddly-named album. Name (a) the album, (b) Wilson's backing band & (c) the other band in which Whittaker plays keyboards (their best-known song is 'The Human Factor').
(a)   (c)
(b)

16. Name the home towns of the following HM bands. (a) Vardis, (b) Def Leppard, (c) Rhabstallion, (d) Tarot, (e) Dawnwatcher & (f) Dedringer.
(a)   (d)
(b)   (e)
(c)   (f)

17. A Leeds journalist who writes for Sounds has also compiled two sampler LPs of northern bands. Give (a) his name & (b) his pen-name.
(a)   (b)

18. Which Yorkshire groups released the following singles during 1980: (a) Twisted Wheel c/w SX 225, (b) Hey Girl c/w Reach The Top., (c) Getting Nowhere Fast c/w Warm Girls., (d) Into The Void c/w Darkness, (e) Mr Somebody c/w They Go Up! They Go Down!/ Malcolm Where''s The Talcum?, (f) Sunday Drivers c/w We Don't Mind, (g) Wheels of Steel c/w Stand Up And Be Counted, (h) Another Lover c/w Y'Gotta Shout, (i) Marilyn Brown c/w E-Boat, (j) Miracle c/w Home Is The Range.
(a)   (f)
(b)   (g)
(c)   (h)
(d)   (i)
(e)   (j)

19. Who (a) organises gigs at The Fan Club in Leeds & Wakefield Unity Hall, & also runs Futurama, the annual Leeds Sci-Fi Festival & (b) runs Aardvark Records in Sheffield & writes for Record Mirror?
(a)   (b)

20. B-Troop & Shy Tots are two bands who're featured on sampler albums from Aardvark & Future Earth. They also share the same home town (& it's not Sheffield). Where are they from?
Answer:

21. (a) What Yorkshire recording studio brought out an album in 1980 which contained two tracks each by six bands using that studio? (b) What was the album called? (c) Who designed its cover? (d) Name three of the six bands.
(a)   (c)
(b)   (d)

22. What bands released the following E.P.s (a) The Five Month Plan & (b) Capt. Scott At Tiffany's In A Jumble Sale Suit?
(a)   (b)

23. A memorable rock event took place in Yorkshire on 25/12/77. (a) What was the event? (b) At which venue did it take place?
(a)   (b)

24. What are/were (a) Logical Steps., (b) All Over The Carpet, (c) Pollen, (d) The First Fifteen Minutes., (e) The Sweatbox & (f) No Hessle?
(a)   (d)
(b)   (e)
(c)   (f)

25. Which bands are (a) Waiting For A Miracle, (b) available at $33\frac{1}{3}$ rpm & 100mph, (c) Travelogued? (All 3 are recent LP's).
(a)   (c)
(b)

26. Totale's Turn is a live album that features several tracks recorded at gigs in Yorkshire. Name the band involved.
Answer:

27. Anticipation & Mind Your Own Business were on singles by which Leeds band?
Answer:

28. (a) Whose car caught fire? (b) Who wants to know if you dream in colour?
(a)   (b)

GRASSHOPPER PRINTING COLLECTIVE

We can design and print your badges, posters, L.P.s and singles.
Badges made up by us.
Tel. 0484-843879.
23, Peel St., Marsden, Huddersfield.

COME IN FROM THE COLD!

4-track demos in (relative) comfort, £3.50 p.h. or £30.00 a day at
THE COMMUNICATIONS CENTRE
call Alf on Bradford 22769

Spend your Xmas holidays **SKIING** at Ram Studios in Leeds
£65 per 10 hour day
Those of you that won't be joining in the fun sod-off have a happy festive season.
And remember...

Ram Records
Ram Recording Studios
64 Armley Road Leeds LS12 2LG
Tel (0532) 44504

So now that your eyes are absolutely riveted to this bit here we will take this opportunity to tell you all about our shop. It's a record shop with lots of golden oldies, rock 'n' roll, punk, new wave, heavy-metal, progressive, rare records, imports, cassettes, singles and albums. We're always willing to do part-exchange or buy your collection from you if you're broke - if you've no wheels we'll collect. It doesn't matter what sort of records they are - give us a ring on Leeds 457765 or at home 075784 - 669, or call in to GEROL'S RECORDS, MERRION SUPERSTORE, LEEDS and have a chat and look around. - we could well have that elusive single or album that you've always wanted. See you soon

ROB & GERALD

ROCK 'n' ROLL RARITIES
PUNK and NEW WAVE
HEAVY and PROGRESSIVE
GOLDEN OLDIES
IMPORTS and COLLECTORS ITEMS
BLUES, POP, REGGAE etc.

GEROL'S RECORDS
MERRION SUPERSTORE LEEDS
(Tel: see above.)

Snark presents **Only a Northern Song**, a slice of west yorkshire

Available from tuned-in record shops or by mail order (£2.50 inc. p.&p.) from

SNARK MUSIC
c/o Peaceworks, 58 Wakefield Road, Huddersfield

Featuring tracks by:
THE GUESTS, TREATMENT, CHAPTER V, GENTLE THOR, BOOLEAN OPERATION, THE NOISE, GLOSSY MAGS, THE XPOZEZ, OR WAS HE PUSHED, JAB JAB, PRIVATE DICKS, L.E.D., TRIANGULAR HOUR, THE EXTRAS, THE FLOOR, BIG FAT WOMEN WOT CAN'T ADD UP, E2R

The whole package includes cassette, book, badge and balloon

ZANZIBAR at Scamps, Preston (11/11/80)

Line-up: Jon Thompson (gtr/ld voc), Mark Hanson (bs/voc), Viv Peters (kbds/voc), Fred Kelly (dms) & Dave Garstang (mixer).

Zanzibar, a 4-piece pro band who work in & around Preston, turned out to be something of a reviewer's nightmare due to their versatility. Inside 20 mins. we had heard heavy, commercial & contemporary rock, all with generous amounts of 3-part harmonies & impressive lead & synth breaks. Each song was different in style to the previous one, so they can't be classified in one bracket, & the faultless overall sound justifies their inclusion of their mixman in the line-up.

With songs like 'Last Night With The Boys' & 'Riding On The Road To Nowhere' they produced both British & American sounds with occasional shades of The Police & Graham Parker. Anyone still doubting their talent was corrected as Zanzibar executed an excellent, accurate version of Jeff Wayne's 'Fighting Machine'.

Pity that the set cooled off in the second half: 'No Time', 'Sooner Or Later' & 'Crying...' weren't special, but their final number 'Last Train' certainly was, & it set the sparse audience alight. If this or another of their good songs falls on influential ears, Zanzibar will find themselves in great demand.

A sad footnote to this report is that the band, as a result of playing this gig, were fired by a rival Preston nitespot 'The Moonraker' where they had held a weekly booking for the past 6 months.

Bitchiness like this is particularly sickening for a band whose only income is from playing gigs. Their most appropriate song that night was 'We Want More Wages'! Let's hope someone books them before they starve to death.

Contact: Mark on Preston 21563 or ring Blackpool 48407.

—DAVE SHEPHERD.

THE NEW HORMONES PACKAGE (9/11/80)
MUDHUTTERS + DIAGRAM BROTHERS + LUDUS
Fan Club, Leeds

The posters said 3 groups for £1-25 - not bad value - so off I went to The Fan Club. It was my first visit & I was struck dumb by the pathetic turn-out of 50ish for a band who'd done a much-acclaimed Peel session & got a page in the NME that very week

First on were The Mudhutters whom I didn't really listen to. Their set was about 8 songs strong & was of reasonable rock bordering on the new wavish.

But the moment most of the 50 or so had been waiting for emerged with The Diagram Brothers. What a refreshing change this band were compared with most groups of similar status. They seemed genuinely friendly towards us, the audience. The song introductions, all too rare nowadays, were interesting & informative. Although the singer has not been blessed with the most musical of voices, you could actually tell every word he sang.

The set ran up about 12 numbers & each got good applause. The single, 'Animals', really got the crowd going & had everyone... well, almost everyone ... well, some folk shouting the chorus. The only criticism is that the drumming sometimes tended to overshadow the guitars in the wrong places.

The songs tended to look at small things which affected the lives of The Brothers. Each song was treated with that unique brand of Diagram humour which helped result in some interesting titles like 'We Just Got An Electricity Bill For A Million Pounds' & 'The Pain In My Chest Is Better Now But I Shake A Bit'.

The audience demanded an encore but, due to the time, they didn't get one.

Next was Ludus, but I only saw them do 2 songs as I had to get my last bus.

yours, OCKY

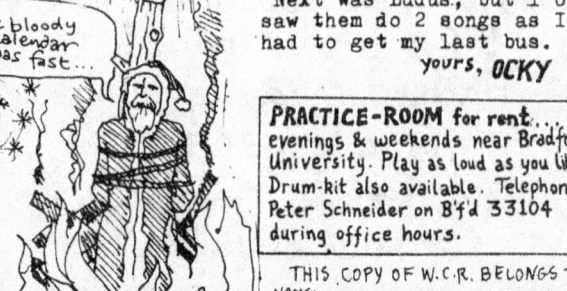

PRACTICE-ROOM for rent... evenings & weekends near Bradford University. Play as loud as you like! Drum-kit also available. Telephone Peter Schneider on B'fd 33104 during office hours.

THIS COPY OF W.C.R. BELONGS TO:-
NAME:
ADDRESS:

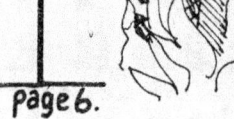

ONLY A NORTHERN SONG
Track-by-track through Snark Music's 17-band sampler cassette package of Huddersfield bands — reviewed by Nick Toczek.

This is an impressive compilation cassette that comes complete with well-printed booklet, badge & balloon (?!).

SIDE ONE:

① THE GUESTS / 'Impressing The Press'. And this pressman's fairly impressed by this palatable piece of lightweight 80's pop that's fresh & well-played.

② TREATMENT / 'Safe & Sound'. Passable song from this popular outfit, it's a new-rock ballad built round a regular bassline & keyboards rhythmic interplay with an appealing hook. Fast finish provides a neat closing touch.

③ CHAPTER V / 'Lucky Michael'. Jogging, early 70's rock arrangement on this one - pleasant, but undistinguished. I like the feel of this band much more than I like this particular song.

④ GENTLE IHOR / 'I've Fallen In Love With A Picture Again'. The first song that's remotely innovative, with its deliberately slurred & growly vocals chanted over an alternately strummed & picked electric guitar. He also has an interesting story in the accompanying booklet.

⑤ BOOLEAN OPERATION / 'Tune Me In'. This track's really fine. Keyboards plus processed vocals. Electronic pop that's quite accessible. Tasty, pass the ketchup, mother.

⑥ THE NOISE / 'The Bootleg Song'. Primitive punk push out guitar thrash outrage. I too was alive in '77 & look back with tender recall. Nice track. More ketchup!

⑦ GLOSSY MAGS / 'Did You Like My Card?' Melodramatic vocalist meets rock song with 2 reggae breaks & one awful HM-ish guitar break. O.K. overall, though the guitarist needs to cut his hair & listen new music. The song's a good one.

⑧ THE XPOZEZ / 'Skitzophrenia'. Bit of a tinny production that's like listening to the band through thick fog. Otherwise, this is a cheerless storm of punk aggression that's loveably awful. Gimme more! With red sauce, please.

⑨ OR WAS HE PUSHED / 'Singapore'. My favourite song on the cassette. Great pacing to this rock-reggae crossover number that's got attractive vocals & chorus. It's the sort of tune that lodges in the top corner of your skull & keeps emerging when you sit in the pantry polishing the silverware or slump on the toilet floor sterilising the needle in a match flame.

SIDE TWO:

① JAB-JAB / 'Randy Pony'. Legendary local reggae band at last get themselves into the logbook with this tasty slice of what they're good at - fun & danceable reggae with cheerful keyboards & a few novelty touches thrown in. Why hasn't this band got records out?

② PRIVATE DICKS / 'Private Dicks'. Jimi Hendrix rip-off to open (except that J.H.'s dick was never private... & nor were his privates!). This builds into a crusty loaf of R'n'B with obligatory harmonica breaks plus false endings galore. I'm enjoying this meal... another glass of ketchup, waitress!

③ L.E.D. / 'More than a Woman'. Sounds like it could've been recorded any evening in the past 15 years (& probably was) - ie. it's mainstream Brit-rock - though keyboards & bits of Spanish guitar help to make the paella less bland.

④ THE EXTRAS / 'Spacemen From Mars'. Late addition to the sampler. Slow & amateurish punk. It sounded awful at the start. Then I numbed to it. oops By the end it'd become almost enjoyable. Luckily, it finish before I'd time to start liking it.

④ TRIANGULAR HOUR / 'Public Enemy No.1'. Imagine a bass guitar walking down a long street at night. Drumsticks are following him, but every time he looks round, they duck into a doorway. He walks on & after a while the sticks are back. This happens several times. Guitars keep driving past. Finally, bass steps into the road & a speeding guitar runs him down. End of song. Strange!

⑥ THE FLOOR / 'What's your name?'. Punky pop. Catchy, & keeps the foot tapping on the band's name. Never did find out her name..... probably Floora.

⑦ BIG FAT WOMEN WOT CAN'T ADD UP / 'D.I.V.O.R.C.E.' Acoustic duo with own version of popular passtime. Funny with a sour edge.

⑧ E2R / 'Space Doubt'. Aha! Pure electronics - knew there was still something missing from this extraordinary variety of songs. Full marks to this

Boojum for this amazing mixture. This last one has very funny lyrics & is cleverly pieced together. Must be the first electronic band that smile a bit & could be mistaken for human beings! Lyrics are funniest if (Goddess forbid) you allowed yourself a few seconds of reckless mild sexism.

SINGLES
reviewed by Nick Toczek & Steve Brown.

THE NAUGHTIEST GIRL WAS A MONITOR - 'All The Naked Heroes' c/w 'Wax Museum' & 'West Street' (Aardvark Records - Steel 4). First track has dms/kbds that are very like those in Orch.Man's 'Enola Gay', except slower. Nick: "Good, but too one-paced throughout". Steve: "Always threatening to let loose with a faster beat, but never does. Totally boring simple song." Flip for a monotonous synthed instrumental followed by a second. Almost nursery rhyme tunes. Steve: "Music to fall asleep to... very quickly.

GIRLS AT OUR BEST - 'Politics' c/w 'It's Fashion' (Record Records - RR2). Follow-up to their much-vaunted debut single. Judy Evan's ultra-high choirboy vocals aren't to everyone's taste. For Steve, they ruin an otherwise excellent song. For me, they add an extra dimension to this irresistable slice of nouveaux-pop originality. Odd that the most effective instrument - the kbds - doesn't even get a credit on the sleeve. On the B-side, Judy alternates between her high voice & a more orthodox, Pauline Murrayish lower register. Another very appealing popsong.

STEPPING TALK - 'Alice In Sunderland' + 'Health & Safety' c/w 'Common Problem' + 'John's Turtles' (Eustone Records). This one's a year or so old & the band have recently (see review in WCR10) released a single as Methodischa Tunc. A-side starts with jangling guitar + lazy jazz sax that alternates with the male/female vocals that're slightly out of step with one another giving an odd hard-to-catch-the-words effect. Drums & bass provide some rhythmic stability, but the whole is fractured & verging on free-form. A welter of ideas here, with the distinctive vocal style particularly worth further development. B-side is less pleasant. 2nd track is an instrumental made up of single notes on a variety of instruments. It gets a bit too much on the ears.

DRINKING ELECTRICITY - 'Cruising Missiles' c/w 'Shaking All Over (dub)' (Pop Aural - POP 008). A-side is a single riff repeated & repeated (no vocals) with little variety. Steve finds it worthless - was still waiting for it to start when it finished. I enjoy it - sort of one-track robot disco. B-side's an electronic version of the Johnny Kidd & The Pirates piece of classic early rock, but it's almost unrecognisable (apart from the lyrics & a sneaked-in copy of the original guitar riffing near the end). Bit like Flying Lizards with more kbds. & less percussion, & it also lacks their instant quirky magic.

BOOTS FOR DANCING - 'The Rain Song' c/w 'Hesitate' (Pop Aural - POP 006). The first is an anti-melodic popsong with discordant guitars & vocals. Disappointingly ugly sound. Steve: Early XTCish, with the song dominated by quick-fire, non-stop lyrics & racing guitar for an overall interesting song, though I can't imagine it growing on me with further hearings". 2nd song. Nick: "I prefer this side. The vocalist's doing a nice job & the guitar-style is more suited to the rhythm. But, having seen & enjoyed this band at Futurama, I expected much more than this." Steve: "I don't like it & won't hesitate in dismissing it.

PATRICK FITZGERALD GROUP - 'Tonight E.P.' (Final Solution -FSEP001 -12"). An EP with 5 tracks: 'Mr & Mrs' + 'Animal Mentality' + 'Tonight' c/w 'A Superbeing' + 'Waiting For A Final Cue'. First is an OK poptune. Second is impressive with its haunting slow-fingered piano & vocals (both with echo) + strummed acoustic guitar. Third brings in electric instruments (kbds & rm.gtr.) for a moving poem/song with a domestic theme. Flip side is less appealing. It's first is of a one-beat drum intro to a non-descript tune the has the (presumably) desired effect of pushing the monotone staccato vocals to the fore. It reminds me of Tony Newley (who?). Last track was mystical gtr. sound + spoken vocals + wailing sax. Atmospheric but very late 60's (Country Joe & The Fish). P.F. moves away from his street-poet identity towards the arty (mildly) avant garde.

SUSAN FASSBENDER - 'Twilight Café' c/w 'Get Around It' (Criminal Records). A-side is a good commercial song with a repetitive, but insistent, funky feel. Should be a break in the verse-chorus pattern & the drums plod a bit, otherwise it's one of the best singles to've come out of Bradford in recent years. B-side is the best. Less commercial, but kbds, tight & driving vocals + harmonics on gtr. = 2 yo.

CHEERERS MUSIC STORE
(WHY TRAVEL? WE'RE HERE IN LEEDS CENTRE...)

AMP. DEPT. H|H MAIN DEALER.. MARSHALL, VOX, PEAVEY, M.M., RAVEN. McGREGGOR. WE ARE NOW 'TEAC' MAIN DEALERS. WEM, & JHS....

GUITAR DEPT. FENDER, GIBSON, IBANEZ MAIN DEALER, HONDO II, KRAMER, PEAVEY GORDON SMITH + VARIOUS SECOND HAND......

DRUM DEPT. PREMIER MAIN AGENTS, TAMA, SONOR, PAISTE ETC.

PART EXCHANGE AND PERSONAL LOANS AVAILABLE

TEL: 449692 — 9.00 to 5.30

8, THE MERRION CENTRE, LEEDS 2.

UNIVERSITY OF BRADFORD UNION

RICHMOND ROAD, BRADFORD, WEST YORKSHIRE BD7 1DP

SAT. JANUARY 24TH : LINDISFARNE
SAT. MARCH 7TH : SLADE
SAT. MARCH 14TH : PAULINE MURRAY

LOOK OUT FOR MORE!!

DISCOS DISCOS DISCOS START 16 JAN
PLUS DISCOS EVERY FRIDAY IN THE COMMUNAL BUILDING
---- BAR TILL 12. ENTRY ONLY 40p.

NON-STUDENTS WELCOME
TICKETS FROM H.M.V. RECORDS AND UNION SHOP. ANY ENQUIRIES PLEASE RING BRADFORD 34135 EX. 42 MARION FOUNTAYNE

Hi Friends
Try Roots Record Shop for the latest reggae records every week—even before they enter the music charts

ROOTS RECORD SHOP

16 Lumb Lane (near Morrison's city centre) Bradford 8.

Telephone No. Bradford 32721

MERRY XMAS AND A HAPPY NEW YEAR TO EACH AND EVERY ONE FROM JAH YOUTH AT ROOTS

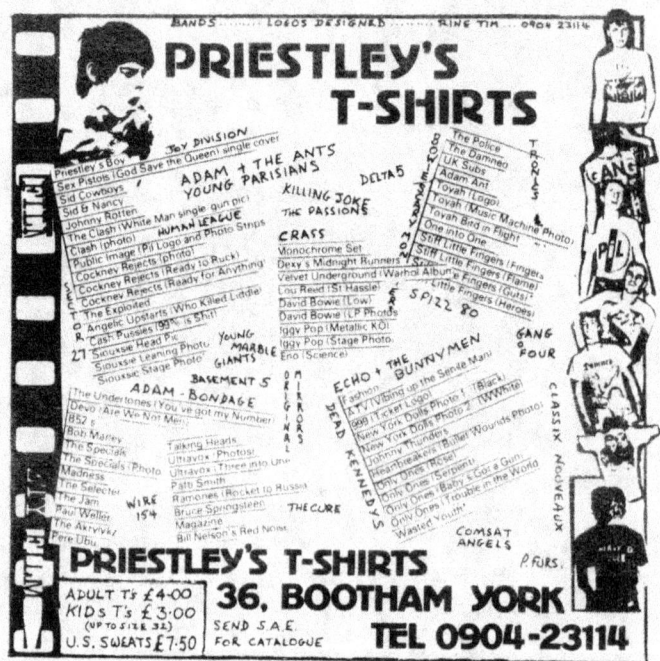

PRIESTLEY'S T-SHIRTS

BANDS LOGOS DESIGNED RING TIM 0904 23114

ADULT T's £4.00
KIDS T's £3.00 (UP TO SIZE 32)
U.S. SWEATS £7.50
SEND S.A.E. FOR CATALOGUE

PRIESTLEY'S T-SHIRTS
36, BOOTHAM YORK
TEL 0904-23114

AT LEEDS UNIVERSITY
LEEDS UNIVENTS PRESENT

3rd Dec = HAZEL O'CONNOR'S MEGAHYPE.
6th Dec = GANG OF FOUR
13th Dec = DIRE STRAITS
14th Dec = IAN DURY & THE BLOCKHEADS

NEXT TERMS BANDS SHOULD INCLUDE:-
U.F.O., THE BLUES BAND, THE STRANGLERS & many others

N.B. Students' Union card <u>not</u> necessary for admittance.

FOR TICKET ENQUIRIES & INFORMATION ON ALL OF NEXT TERM'S BOOKINGS RING UNION RECORDS ON LEEDS 44972.

UNION RECORDS
ALL L.P.'s AT DISCOUNT PRICES
plus SPECIAL OFFERS

N.B. We sell tickets for all Leeds University and all Leeds Polytechnic concerts. and are also agents for Leeds Playhouse & The Grand Theatre.

SHOP IS IN BASEMENT OF UNION BUILDING
OPEN MON-FRI 9.30am - 5.00pm

LETTERS FROM LOCAL BANDS...
SHARP PRACTISE (from Leeds)

Dear Nick,
we asked a 'rival' band member to put down a few lines about us rather than write something of our own.
Here is the result...

Dave Maud: drums. Martin Ward: bass. Pam Muller: vocals. Tony Rex: guitar. Duncan McFarlane: guitar/vocals.

The band play self-penned modern pop/rock. Their high standard of musicianship & melody is fast earning a good reputation & large following around the Leeds circuit.
Besides playing free gigs at Leeds Univ. (cancer research) & opening the Dol Q Club, they have played several gigs in Leeds schools along with the usual local venues.
'Catchy songs were thrown open to air by the exhilarating harmonies which swirled & lifted me two or three inches off the floor.'
- from review by Welk in Leeds Other Paper.
The band are now looking for possible venues outside Leeds.
Contact: Duncan on Leeds 782034.

THE SHAKES (from Keighley)

Hallo!!
The Shakes are a 5-piece pop group from Keighley, cultural centre of the cosmos. We have been through a bewildering array of names & personnel changes before settling with (left to right in the photo):-
Jeff (what a giveaway) gtr, back-up vox humanis.
Damian (do you like my shoes) gtr, back-up vox humanis.
Ashley (loric vilesilencer) lead vox, ad libs, raincoat.
Graham (lend me a pound) bass, back-up vox, silly noises.
Grubby John (I recognise your...) drums. obscenities, Renault 5.
 came together (literally) at a party in, in March, to celebrate the birth of n Van Stoates, famous Dutch Impression- painter & pederast.
Our music is an exquisite blend of The Beatles, XTC, The Undertones & The Spanish Inquisition. The resulting concoction closely resembles the mixture found down lampposts & in the gutters at closing time. Our gigs usually end up like a scene from 'Patton, Lust For Glory' with people dancing on tables, being sick in the ash- trays, etc. It's great.
Other than our chaotic presentation, our main claim to fame is that we have a seven stone roadie called Caligula who likes ~~getting pissed & being sick (lot of it about - ed... retch!), telling appalling jokes on stage~~
getting pissed, telling appalling jokes on stage & being sick (lot of it about - ed... retch!) in the van.
We're playing Palm Cove on Thurs 11th Dec, Funhouse Bar, Keighley on 27th Dec, & Ilkley College on 17th Jan. Be there or be square.
Contact: Keighley 69745 & ask for Zippo

THE MANAGEMENT OF
THE FORGE, YORK RD, TADCASTER
(tel. Tadcaster 833136)
are proposing to mount a regular & varied programme of LIVE ROCK starting in December. Ring for details.

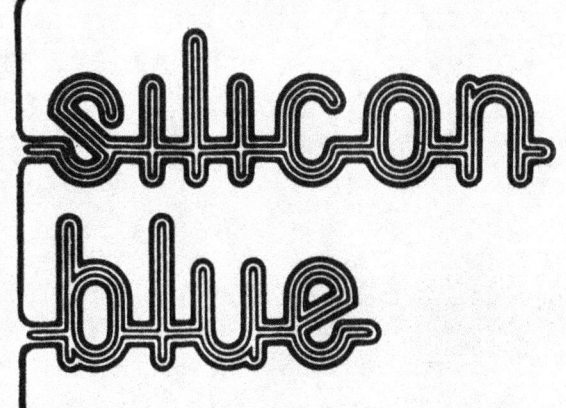

P.A. and SPEAKER MANUFACTURER

We build all group equipment, flight cases, etc.

Long term hire of sound installations also available

Custom built equipment. Component wholesalers and H/H Drivers at very competitive rates. Trade enquiries welcome.

SILICON BLUE LTD
HELEY DELL MILLS
ROCHDALE
LANCS.
tel: 0707-524828

1980 DISMEMBER 1980

MON 1
- Warehouse, Leeds = VICA VERSA. University, Sheffield = MYSTERY CULTS + LONG LANKIN.
- Fforde Grene, Leeds = FLYING SAUCERS. Fun House, Keighley = NEW MODEL ARMY + VIOLATION.
- Royal Park, Leeds = 710.
- Haddon Hall, Leeds = MADISON BLUES.
- White Lion, Huddersfield = ORAL SAX.
- Princeville, Bradford = BRICK MARINE + WARLORD.

TUE 2
- Limit Club, Sheffield = JOHN COOPER CLARKE + AMAZING WHIPPS.
- Community Hall, Grimsby = STRAY CATS + SEVENTEEN.

WED 3
- Royal Park, Leeds = GEORGE LITTLE'S COOL IN THE SHADE.
- University, Bradford = STRAY CATS + SEVENTEEN.
- Polytechnic, Sheffield = BLACK SLATE.
- University, Leeds = HAZEL O'CONNOR.
- Foggy's, Halifax = FEZ.
- White Lion, Huddersfield = OMEN.   Vaults Bar, Bradford = JAZZ NIGHT.

THU 4
- Warehouse, Leeds = STRAY CATS + SEVENTEEN. Princeville, Bradford = WHITE SPIRIT.
- Fan Club, Leeds = THE WALL + VIOLATION. Meanwood Hotel, Leeds = BEAST ON THE HILL.
- Limit Club, Sheffield = DANCE BAND. Wigs Winebar, Leeds = SPIDER BLUES BAND.
- Polytechnic, Leeds = BAD MANNERS + support.
- Palm Cove, Bradford = MO-DETTES.
- Penguin, Sheffield = HAZE.
- Royal Park, Leeds = PRIVATE DICKS.

FRI 5
- Unity Hall, Wakefield = SLADE.
- Fforde Grene, Leeds = BUDGIE.
- University, Sheffield = EDDIE & THE HOT RODS.
- University, Leeds = LIGHT OF THE WORLD.
- Royal Park, Leeds = WHITE EAGLES.
- Wigs Winebar, Leeds = DODGY TACTICS.

SAT 6
- College, Ilkley = AMAZING WHIPPS. Royal Park, Leeds = GOFF JACKSON & THE HUNS.
- Polytechnic, Huddersfield = STRAY CATS + SEVENTEEN. Wigs Winebar, Leeds = MOONSHINERS.
- University, Bradford = GARY GLITTER.
- University, York = XTC.   White Lion, Huddersfield = LEGAL AID.
- Tally Ho, Doncaster = KNIFE EDGE. Haddon Hall, Leeds = SHARP PRACTISE.
- University, Leeds = GANG OF FOUR.   Palm Cove, Bradford = ASWAD.
- University, Sheffield = OTWAY & BARRETT. Staging Post, Leeds = 710.

SUN 7
- Haddon Hall, Leeds = KNIFE EDGE. White Lion, Huddersfield = RAMURA(L) + DOTS(e).
- Fan Club, Leeds = GENERATION X + support.
- Princeville, Bradford (lunch) = AMAZING WHIPPS.
- Romeo & Juliet's, Doncaster = PIRANHAS.
- Staging Post, Leeds = MUNROES.
- Blackamore Head, Pontefract = CONFESSOR. Vaults Bar, Bradford = JENERATOR.
- Palm Cove, Bradford = JED'S BLUES BAND. Royal Park, Leeds = 156 BAND.

MON 8
- St. George's Hall, Bradford = STEELEYE SPAN. Vaults Bar, Bradford = REFLEX.
- Jaspers, York = VARDIS.
- Marquis of Granby, Leeds = KNIFE EDGE.
- Polytechnic, Huddersfield = HERE & NOW + support.
- Funhouse, Keighley = ELEMENTS.
- Royal Park, Leeds = YOU.   University, Sheffield = FATALES + MARK MY WORDS.
- Haddon Hall, Leeds = SPEED. Warehouse, Leeds = BOW WOW WOW 5.30 matinee + evening show.

TUE 9
- Limit Club, Sheffield = KILLING JOKE.
- Warehouse, Leeds = KNIFE EDGE + AXIS.
- Bentley Pavilion, Doncaster = HERE & NOW + support.
- Palm Cove, Bradford = PATCHWORK.

WED 10
- University, Bradford = MOTELS (to be TV'd for 'Rock Goes To College'). St. George's Hall, Bradford = XTC + MODERN MAN. Vaults Bar, Bradford = JAZZ NIGHT.
- University, Leeds = 9 BELOW ZERO + KNIFE EDGE. Cleopatra's, Huddersfield = DAMNED.
- Fforde Grene, Leeds = HERE & NOW + support. White Lion, Huddersfield = ORAL SAX.
- Warehouse, Leeds = ZIGGY HERO. Foggy's, Halifax = PRIVATE DICKS.
- Limit Club, Sheffield = Roy Wood's HELICOPTERS. Royal Park, Leeds = GIMMICKS.
- Polytechnic, Sheffield = STRAY CATS + SEVENTEEN. Central Halls, Grimsby = DEF LEPPARD.

THU 11
- St. George's Hall, Bradford = 'NEW ELECTRIC WARRIORS' mini tour. xx
- Limit Club, Sheffield = BAD MANNERS. Meanwood, Leeds = LOVE & REVENGE.
- Penguin Club, Sheffield = PRISONER. Wigs Winebar, Leeds = SPIDER BLUES BAND.
- Fan Club, Leeds = MO-DETTES.
- Palm Cove, Bradford = SHAKES + SPEED.
- Royal Park, Leeds = SPINOES.
- Princeville, Bradford = RACE AGAINST TIME.

FRI 12
- Polytechnic, Sheffield = SLADE.
- Penthouse, Scarborough = VARDIS.
- Palm Cove, Bradford = CUBA.
- Fforde Grene, Leeds = DEF LEPPARD.
- Polytechnic, Huddersfield = SKIDS + ON THE AIR.
- Royal Park, Leeds = WHITE EAGLES.   Wigs Winebar, Leeds = DODGY TACTICS.
- University, Sheffield = Xmas Party with STAN ARNOLD COMBO + GUY JACKSON + others.

SAT 13
- University, Leeds = DIRE STRAITS. Wigs Winebar, Leeds = HOTPOT BELLY BAND.
- Polytechnic, Leeds = THE SKIDS + ON THE AIR.
- College, Ilkley = AVALON HIGHWAY.
- Royal Park, Leeds = SHAKE APPEAL.
- Haddon Hall, Leeds = RED EYE.
- White Lion, Huddersfield = BUCK MOSEY & THE AUSTRALIANS.
- Fun House, Keighley = HEAVEN 17 (L).

SUN 14
- Haddon Hall, Leeds = GEORGE LITTLE'S COOL IN THE SHADE.
- University, Leeds = IAN DURY & BLOCKHEADS. Vaults Bar, Bradford = STUFFED BADGERS.
- Fforde Grene, Leeds = VARDIS.
- Palm Cove, Bradford = JED'S BLUES BAND.
- Rotters, Doncaster = DEF LEPPARD. Princeville, Bradford = CONFESSOR (L).
- Staging Post, Leeds = LOCAL HEROES. White Lion, Huddersfield = (T.B.A.) (L) + TREATMENT (e).
- Blackamore Head, Pontefract = TAROT.   Royal Park, Leeds = 156 BAND.

MON 15
- Top Rank, Sheffield = IAN DURY & BLOCKHEADS. Vaults Bar, Bradford = DIAL.
- Warehouse, Leeds = PYLONS.
- Fforde Grene, Leeds = FRANKIE MILLER BAND.
- Royal Park, Leeds = NEW KING SNAKES.
- Haddon Hall, Leeds = DRAGSTER.
- White Lion, Huddersfield = ORAL SAX.
- University, Sheffield = VENA CAVA + support.

TUE 16
- St. George's Hall, Bradford = IAN DURY & BLOCKHEADS.
- Limit Club, Sheffield = FRANKIE MILLER BAND.
- City Hall, Hull = THE SKIDS.
- Palm Cove, Bradford = BUZZCOCKS.

WED 17
- Polytechnic, Leeds = GARY GLITTER + support.
- Central Halls, Grimsby = STEVE HARLEY & COCKNEY REBEL + STRAIGHT 8.
- Foggy's, Halifax = VINDICATOR.
- Royal Park, Leeds = SHARP PRACTICE.
- White Lion, Huddersfield = TAROT.
- Cleopatra's, Huddersfield = BUZZCOCKS.   Vaults Bar, Bradford = JAZZ NIGHT.

THU 18
- Royal Park, Leeds = KNIFE EDGE (rushing on to Fan Club after).
- Fan Club, Leeds = XMAS PARTY with several bands ††
- Limit Club, Sheffield = SPANDAU BALLET (T.B.C.).
- Penguin Club, Sheffield = TOKYO.
- Princeville, Bradford = DEVOTION.
- Meanwood, Leeds = PROPELLORS. Wigs Winebar, Leeds = SPIDER BLUES BAND.

FRI 19
- Town Hall, Ossett = PIN-UPS + STRANGER THAN FICTION.
- Cleopatra's, Huddersfield = PYLON.
- Palm Cove, Bradford = SPINELS.
- Royal Park, Leeds = WHITE EAGLES.
- Wigs Winebar, Leeds = WHISKEY & ROG.

SAT 20
- Cleopatra's, Huddersfield = BURNING SPEAR (aka Winston Rodney).
- Palm Cove, Bradford = JAB-JAB.   Wigs Winebar, Leeds = PIN-UPS.
- Royal Park, Leeds = DIRTY BUT NICE.
- Haddon Hall, Leeds = AGONY COLUMN.
- White Lion, Huddersfield = NEW KING SNAKES.
- Fun House, Keighley = PYRAMID (L).

SUN 21
- Staging Post, Leeds = KNIFE EDGE + GIMMICKS.
- Queens Hall, Leeds = HAWKWIND + PRAYING MANTIS + support (inc. MICK TAYLOR guesting).
- Blackamore Head, Pontefract = LAUTREC.
- Palm Cove, Bradford = JED'S BLUES BAND.
- Royal Park, Leeds = 156 BAND.   Vaults Bar, Bradford = LOCALEROES.
- Haddon Hall, Leeds = CUBA.   Princeville, Bradford = WAMM (L).
- White Lion, Huddersfield = MIDDLE 8 (L) + DOTS (e).

MON 22
- Vaults Bar, Bradford = LOCALEROES + THE FEEL.
- Coachhouse Club, Huddersfield = 'ONLY A NORTHERN SONG' XMAS PARTY. **
- Warehouse, Leeds = Digital 'Disco' (with band - T.B.A.).
- Haddon Hall, Leeds = STAFF.
- White Lion, Huddersfield = ORAL SAX.

TUE 23
- City Hall, Hull = SAXON + LIMELIGHT.
- Limit Club, Sheffield = Q-TIPS.
- Palm Cove, Bradford = PATCHWORK.
- White Lion, Huddersfield = WHAMMER-JAMMER.

WED 24
- Palm Cove, Bradford = DIGNITY.
- Royal Park, Leeds = CONFESSOR + support.
- White Lion, Huddersfield = BREATHLESS.

THU 25
- CHURCHES & HOMES, YORKSHIRE - J.C. SUPESTAR'S BIRTHDAY GIG. (Bring a bottle!).

FRI 26
- Palm Cove, Bradford = QUAKER CITY (Sound system) + reggae band.
- Royal Park, Leeds = WHITE EAGLES.
- Haddon Hall, Leeds = DALE HARGREAVES' FLAMINGOS.
- White Lion, Huddersfield = SIMON LEGETT BAND (L) + WAMM (e).

SAT 27
- Funhouse, Keighley = SHAKES + SPEED (L). Wigs Winebar, Leeds = MILLSTONE GRIT.
- Royal Park, Leeds = KNIFE EDGE.
- Staging Post, Leeds = NO GOOD.
- Palm Cove, Bradford = NATRUS ROOTS.
- Haddon Hall, Leeds = DODGY TACTICS.
- White Lion, Huddersfield = PRIVATE DICKS.
- Princeville, Bradford = LIMELIGHT.

SUN 28
- Blackamore Head, Pontefract = STREETFIGHTER.
- Palm Cove, Bradford = JED'S BLUES BAND.
- Royal Park, Leeds = 156 BAND.
- Haddon Hall, Leeds = JONNY STORM & MEMPHIS.
- White Lion, Huddersfield = PRIVATE DICKS (L) + DOTS (e).
- Princeville, Bradford = STREETFIGHTER (L).

MON 29
- Royal Park, Leeds = HALF BROTHERS.
- White Lion, Huddersfield = ORAL SAX.

TUE 30
- Palm Cove, Bradford = PATCHWORK.

WED 31
- White Lion, Huddersfield = GLOSSY MAGS + guests.
- Wigs Winebar, Leeds = DODGY SPIDER BAND.
- Fforde Grene, Leeds = SPIDER.

** Only A Northern Song Xmas Party (Mon 22 Dec) = JAB-JAB, OR WAS HE PUSHED, THE GUESTS, GENTLE INJOR, BIG FAT WOMEN WHAT CAN'T ADD UP + others.
†† Fan Club Xmas Party (Thu 18 Dec) = KNIFE EDGE, ABRASIVE WHEELS, AN ITCH, GIMMICKS, IMPOSSIBLE MEN, MIRROR BOYS + 2 others.
xx 'New Electric Warriors' mini tour (Thu 11 Dec) = RHABSTALLION + SEDEDDIAH STRUTT + BASTILLE + TURBO.

NEW VENUE: Foggy's, George Sq., Halifax (every Wed. & possibly starting up on Mondays too. Run by John Sutton, 2 Grove Edge, Ovenden, Halifax. Tapes & info. to him if you want a gig.

FUN HOUSE, KEIGHLEY now doing regular rock. (Sat. lunch & Mon. night). Garth Cawood at the venue handles booking. KINGS HEAD, KEIGHLEY back in action again as a rock venue soon.

1981 PENURY 1981

THU 1	Royal Park, Leeds = CHARTER CAR. Meanwood, Leeds = ESCORT.	**SAT 17**	College, Ilkley = SHAKES + SPEED. Wigs Winebar, Leeds = NEW KING SNAKES. University, Leeds = U.F.O. Royal Park, Leeds = KNIFE EDGE. Haddon Hall, Leeds = DALE HARGREAVES' FLAMINGOS. White Lion, Huddersfield = RED EYE. Funhouse, Keighley = NEW OPERA (L).
FRI 2	Royal Park, Leeds = WHITE EAGLES. Wigs Winebar, Leeds = WHISKEY GROG.	**SUN 18**	St. George's Hall, Bradford = HAZEL O'CONNOR'S MEGAHYPE. Haddon Hall, Leeds = KNIFE EDGE. Palm Cove, Bradford = JED'S BLUES BAND. Royal Park, Leeds = 156 BAND. White Lion, Huddersfield = (TBA)(L) + WHAMMER JAMMER (e). Princeville, Bradford = MASK (L).
SAT 3	Queens Hall, Leeds = BLACK SABBATH + several other bands (VARDIS, A II Z) Royal Park, Leeds = SHARP PRACTISE. Haddon Hall, Leeds = LUIGI ANA DA BOYS. White Lion, Huddersfield = HALF BROTHERS. Princeville, Bradford = WITCHFYNDE. Funhouse, Keighley = SPEED (L). Wigs Winebar, Leeds = DODGY TACTICS.	**MON 19**	St. George's Hall, Bradford = U.F.O. Haddon Hall, Leeds = THE RUNNERS.
SUN 4	White Lion, Huddersfield = AMAZING WHIPPS (eve). Palm Cove, Bradford = JED'S BLUES BAND. Royal Park, Leeds = 156 BAND. White Lion, Huddersfield = (TBA)(L) + AMAZING WHIPPS (e) Princeville, Bradford = KYRO (L).	**TUE 20**	Palm Cove, Bradford = PATCHWORK. St. George's Hall, Bradford = SAXON + LIMELIGHT (rescheduled concert)
MON 5	Haddon Hall, Leeds = HOOKER.	**WED 21**	Foggy's, Halifax = STUFFED BADGERS. White Lion, Huddersfield = NO IDEA.
TUE 6	Palm Cove, Bradford = PATCHWORK.	**THU 22**	Royal Park, Leeds = GIMMICKS. Princeville, Bradford = (T.B.A). Meanwood, Leeds = (TBA). Wigs Winebar, Leeds = SPIDER BLUES BAND.
WED 7	Foggy's, Halifax = CHEATERS. White Lion, Huddersfield = CHAINSAW.	**FRI 23**	Royal Park, Leeds = WHITE EAGLES. Wigs Winebar, Leeds = (TBA).
THU 8	Limit Club, Sheffield = AFTER THE FIRE. Royal Park, Leeds = DODGY TACTICS. Princeville, Bradford = CHINATOWN. Meanwood, Leeds = (TBA) Wigs Winebar, Leeds = SPIDER BLUE BAND.	**SAT 24**	University, Bradford = LINDISFARNE. College, Ilkley = EIGA. Royal Park, Leeds = RED EYE. White Lion, Huddersfield = NEW KING SNAKES. Funhouse, Keighley = (T.B.A)(L) Wigs Winebar, Leeds = DODGY TACTICS.
FRI 9	Royal Park, Leeds = WHITE EAGLES. Wigs Winebar, Leeds = NEW KING SNAKES.	**SUN 25**	Palm Cove, Bradford = JED'S BLUES BAND Royal Park, Leeds = 156 BAND. Haddon Hall, Leeds = CHAINSAW. White Lion, Huddersfield = (TBA)(L) + DOTS (e). Princeville, Bradford = GENERATOR (L).
SAT 10	Royal Park, Leeds = RHABSTALLION. Haddon Hall, Leeds = PIN-UPS. White Lion, Huddersfield = TREATMENT. Funhouse, Keighley = MODES FOR MUTANTS (L). Wigs Winebar, Leeds = (TBA)	**MON 26**	
SUN 11	Palm Cove, Bradford = JED'S BLUES BAND. Royal Park, Leeds = 156 BAND. Haddon Hall, Leeds = NEW OPERA. White Lion, Huddersfield = (TBA)(L) + DOTS (e). Princeville, Bradford = ROUGH JUSTICE (L).	**TUE 27**	Palm Cove, Bradford = PATCHWORK.
MON 12	Jaspers, York = AMAZING WHIPPS. Haddon Hall, Leeds = ICON.	**WED 28**	White Lion, Huddersfield = CRAFTY AVENUE.
TUE 13	Palm Cove, Bradford = PATCHWORK.	**THU 29**	Princeville, Bradford = KRAKEN. Meanwood, Leeds = (TBA). Wigs Winebar, Leeds = SPIDER BLUES BAND.
WED 14	Foggy's, Halifax = PIN-UPS. White Lion, Huddersfield = GOFF JACKSON & THE HUNS.	**FRI 30**	Royal Park, Leeds = WHITE EAGLES. Wigs Winebar, Leeds = PIN-UPS.
THU 15	Limit Club, Sheffield = CLIMAX BLUES BAND. Royal Park, Leeds = ROUGH JUSTICE. Princeville, Bradford = (T.B.A.). Meanwood, Leeds = (TBA). Wigs Winebar, Leeds = SPIDER BLUES BAND.	**SAT 31**	University, Leeds = BLUES BAND. Haddon Hall, Leeds = RED EYE. White Lion, Huddersfield = TAROT Funhouse, Keighley = (T.B.A)(L) Wigs Winebar, Leeds = HOTPOT BELLY BAND.
FRI 16	Royal Park, Leeds = WHITE EAGLES. Wigs Winebar, Leeds = WHISKEY GROG.		GIG GUIDE ABBREVIATIONS :- (TBA) = to be arranged, (TBC) = to be confirmed, (e) = evening, (L) = lunchtime. **In next issue** - phone nos. of nearly 100 Yorkshire rock venues!!! FFORDE GRENE had answerphone machine on every time I rang. MARQUIS OF GRANBY had the phone disconnected or out-of-order. Many venues hadn't taken January bookings by the time we went to press.

The JAM + the Piranhas + the Nits at QUEENS HALL Leeds. Nov. 3rd.

Is this the Modern World? Was it the equipment, the mixers, or the venue? The latter two I would suspect. The reason for these questions is the poor quality sound we heard at this concert. The Jam singing completely out-of-tune is absolutely unheard of, but it happened on this night.

The Queens Hall is noted for its atrocious acoustics, but surely the guys controlling the mixers must also be held responsible for the poor quality sound. How they can sit there & listen to a mayhem of jumbled & distorted sound & not do anything about it, God only knows.

The only excuse that can be offered for the out-of-tune vocals is a totally ineffective fold-back system, where the boys obviously couldn't hear their own vocals.

Don't get me wrong, it wasn't like this throughout the set, just in the occasional number.

Faults apart, we were first of all offered on stage a London-based band named The Nits' An obnoxious looking cretin strutted on the stage wearing a 'dirty old mac' & posing with a can of beer in one hand & a fag in the other. He greeted us by staggering up to the mic., then sneered & uttered "Bleeach!!" Mmmm, heard that before? Yes, we'd been introduced to a clone of a certain Mr. John Rotten. Yawn!

As their set progressed, the crowd chorused "Pistols, Pistols!" to which our loveable vocalist demanded "Who wants The Pistols?".

A short interval was followed by the energetic Piranhas. They were welcomed by the audience chanting the refrain from their first hit single 'Tom Hark'. The stage was set for a lively evening. The audience were enthusiastic, the band were exciting.

All the members of this 6-piece band have outstanding personalities which come across & generate a warm & friendly atmosphere. They produced an excellent fun set & were well received by a normally hostile Leeds crowd.

After a long interval, Mr. Weller senior took to the stage to introduce his son's masterpiece, The Jam.

Kicking off with 'Thick As Thieves', the boys looked full of themselves. Twenty minutes later, after a few tracks off the new album 'Sound Affects', they weren't quite so full of it.

The bemused audience couldn't handle 20 minutes of previously unheard material (& the bad sound didn't help), so a quick burst of 'Modern World' soon put things right. This was followed by their last hit 'Start' which to me stands out as the best track on the new album but, with familiarity to the album, things might change.

Despite a few more hits & new material, things weren't going so well - & didn't the 3 of them know it? A subdued Paul Weller pleaded "It gets better..." & I must admit it did, not just because of the numbers they played, but I think the mixer finally decided something needed doing, improvement was made, but he never really pulled his finger out.

'When You're Young', & to me this is a classic lyrically: "That one's for kids who know where they're going, & this one's for the kids who don't." & we were blessed with 'Going Underground'. Everything else followed: 'Eton Rifles', 'Tube Station', 'Strange Town' & 'A-bomb...'. Three encores & the evening was complete.

"Hello, hooray, it's the price we pay for the Eton Rifles/Hello, hooray, I'd prefer the plague to the Eton Rifles."

—Mick Mitchell

REVIEW OF THE AUDIENCE AT THE CAPTAIN BEEFHEART/COMSAT ANGELS CONCERT AT UNITY HALL, WAKEFIELD
(16th Nov. '80)

Beefheart wit. "I eat bananas - but I ain't no monkey." Brandishing said fruit at heckler.

But generally speaking there's a simian quality about his audience, on the press-the-green-button-for bananas, press-the-red-button-for-voltage principle. Solitary heckler aside, it was Beefheart's audience. He expected - & received - unquestioning homage. Saunters on stage in floppy hat, bagged pants, pockets crammed & bulging with undisclosed goodies, plastic bag & sketchpad. Opens pad at page one - Pentel pen zigzag wander doodles, audience ovation. Sketchpad page two - slightly Jean Cocteau cartoon bullet-head figures & indistinct dialogue, audience ovation. Turns to back of sketchpad, blank cardboard held out for inspection, audience ovation (audience goes bananas?). A mild jest, perhaps even a mild Dada jest, but also a litmus test of audience credulity.

Long hair. Christ, I've not seen so much hair since Isle of Wight 1970. Grateful Dead buttons, & even sweat-bands in ratted (oft now-balding) foliage. And dope - don't bring your own, just inhale. Can this be 1980?

Comsat Angels are first up, identi-kit moderne, leather pants, Joe Strummer/Marlon Brando biker cap, synth burbles, sharp, fast, percussive. They press the red button & get the voltage. The audience don't connect, don't want to know, pointedly refuse to know. Sure I've seen better new bands, they are a mite imageless, less visually impressive & audially intriguing than other Sheffield bands who lack major label signings & reviews in Sounds (Clock DVA, Vice Versa), but they play their album well & deserve better. Beefheart makes sarcastic put-downs of what he calls 'new wave', audience laps it up, perhaps no longer even adulation of the derider as of their own perception. This is tedious, close your eyes, razor all preconceptions, ephemeral clutter & period sign-posts, & are the basic elements that different? Beefheart hasn't changed significantly since 1970. All the necessary components were there on his epic 'Trout Mask Replica' album, he's fattened some out, underlined here & there, re-arranged the punctuation, but the fragments of spaced-out chopped-up blues chording, methedrine stream -of-surreal lyrics & Howlin' Wolf vocals were present. The fact that the Magic Band personnel can change entirely yet the sound remain fundamentally the same surely indicates more than an element of formalisation. But after touring 13 years, that's inevitable, a slickness, a blurring of the Don Van Vliet with the Beefheart personna until even he don't know where the one ends & the other begins.

But what is important surely is that, if he stopped in '70, then the rest of Rock has only now got around to assimilating the full implications of 'Trout Mask', & that where he was then (& is now despite repetitions) is also where we find P.I.L., Residents, Ubu, Fall. What he should be doing is recognising this - not fighting it. The Comsats, if anything, come on more pop, more melodic; he more dissonant, adventurous, unconventional, if he but had the wit to realise it.

The audience also stopped dead, literally, in 1970, & don't venture one nanosecond beyond. Sample dialogue: "The Comsat Upstarts, never heard of 'em". "No, Comsat Angels". "Must be thinking of Angelic Upstarts. Never heard of them either". Smug insular laughter. Press the green button. A Beefheart poem about a woman taking a bath killed by a vagrant star from Saturn. Rapt attention. You wonder how they'd react to that same poem if anyone other than Beefheart wrote it. "Don't bore me, people" he warns. They're boring the shit outta me. A Beefheart poem from Replica on type-wrote script cigarette-burned & crumpled, incantation cut up by "SHUT UP" bellows aimed at the heckler at the back. Beefheart seems singularly perturbed by what is, after all, a regulation gig occurrence. Can't he tolerate such lack of homage? "If I was that clever, I'd flex my muscles at you" he howls flexing said muscles. Cue ovation.

Yet all this detracts from the music, no the spectacle, or the experience, or perhaps the total experience of Beefheart in full spate, when each facet of the disparate whole somehow gells into a multi-sensory phantasmagoria of euphoric absurdity, when the twains meet, when the merits or demerits of his lyrics, the complex simplicity of his scales, the idiot genius hick sophisticate mirrors no longer seem to matter, & it just IS, in perfect balance & rightness. He digs deep, the hallowed antiquity of 'Safe as Milk', the midstream stormer 'Big Eyed Beans From Venus' through to "Bat Chain Puller' & a stilted tele-prompter promo for 'Doc At The Radar Station', sprinkled with Zen Koan-like epithets aimed variously at Oedipal relationships, Reagan/Thatcher, "drums & percussion, percussion & drums, drums & percussion, percussion & opium & drums, drums & percussion".

Trouble is, I guess, Beefheart comes from a time when demarcation was crystal clear, there was us & them, hip & straight, aware & dead. Now there's a multiplicity of hip, each having relevance only to its peer group, no more Renaissance-man idea of complete knowledge of Rock totality. Cyclically each tribe has, or will have, its period of media glimmer. CND as next year's Two Tone for e.g. This gig is a minor regimental reunion masquerading as World War 1. And this gullible coterie of retired hippie sycophants are now lined up alongside the other, equally valuable/valueless subcultures of punk, soul rebels, poet-modernists, mod, rockabilly, etc. each with their own version of absolute truth. Comsat Angels deserve better. Beefheart deserves better, but somehow I guess the exact ratio of homage/homage-object suits him fine, & he don't want to wander into the big world outside clique adoration. Tough.

—ANDY DARLINGTON

BACKSLIDER
Vaults Bar, Bradford 26/10/80 by KEITH E. RICE

Y'know how it is: you just see too many bands in too short a time &, no matter how competent/good/interesting/promising/innovative/bloody-awful they are, it all begins to pall: especially for the reviewer, when it's as much a case of work as pleasure. Still, I had promised Backslider I'd review them so I turned up purely out of a sense of obligation. I was weary & dejected; I'd been up half the night at a party, I'd already reviewed one band that day (at a different venue), & my one true love had rejected me again (K.E.Rice's heart-rending autobiography continues in a future issue - there now follows a review of a band, ed.); & I was convinced that Backslider were a tuneless set

CONTINUED FROM P.

of no-talents I'd had the misfortune to hear about a year ago.

And you know what? I've not enjoyed a gig by a local band so much in ages! For starters I'd got them confused with another band. Not that Backslider are exactly the world's greatest musicians; in fact, they're indisputably amateurish. They were sloppy on on the changes; at times the guitars sounded slightly out of tune; the vocalist read his lyrics from a book on two numbers ; they fluffed openings & especially endings; & half the set the rhythm guitarist couldn't get his amp to work! Yet the sheer energy & enthusiasm they put into their music communicates above all else. It's almost a case of: they're having a good time & they'll be damned if the audience isn't going to have one too!

Initially, that audience didn't exist. The Vaults, after a long layoff (& we'll leave that political hot potato alone, thank you!), has only just started putting bands on again, & so the place was virtually empty when Backslider took the stage. Apparently undeterred, they played as if it were to a S.R.O. crowd &, by the time they came off, the numbers had increased quite dramatically.

Basically, Backslider play simple, melodic rock, falling into one of two idioms: either reggae or r&b - although they also did an AC/DC-type h.m. blast by the name of 'Go!' &, for encore, bluesmaster Albert King's 'As Time Goes By'. Their dub-influenced material is 'alright' & bassist Beany handles the simple steps immaculately, but it's at its most effective when considerably beefed up, as on 'Tonight's The Night'. Their reggae version of "All Along The Watchtower" was so slow it plodded & was the one duff number of the set - besides which , Gerard Wilkinson's aping of Hendrix' vocal mannerisms is not a good idea.

However, Backslider are a GREAT rhythm'n' blues band. Anthony Whitehead hits his snare drum as if it were his wife's lover's head, brother Andrew lets rip with numerous Chuck Berry-style guitar lines, & the whole band powers along like a bus going downhill without brakes! It's music you FEEL! Some of the sweatiest, foot-tapping, groin-swinging dance-alongers since the Feelgoods last played Bradford. Those Canvey Island degenerates are obviously a major influence on Backslider; & so are The Stones - 'Tease' with its walking bass & Wilkinson copying Jagger this time, was pure, early Glimmer Twins' product.

The aforementioned Mr. Berry is another primal influence & the band gave their own tribute to rock's greatest tax-dodger with 'Rock'n'Roll' - or, as it's usually called, 'Johnny B. Goode' - complete with genuine duck walk! However, the real killer of the show was 'Down & Out', an irresistable dance-alonger that had just about everybody on their feet; it just built & built, with guitarists Andrew Whitehead & Chris Khar playing in & around one another - it was one of those songs that really could have gone on all night.

Backslider have a long way to go in terms of proficiency, but they certainly have the right ideas about entertainment. See them; they're bound to put a smile on your face. They certainly put one on mine.

SEVEN YEAR ITCH — 25/10/80 — White Lion, Huddersfield

STOP PRESS: 'Seven Year Itch' have changed their name due to same-name London band who have just released an album. They are now called 'WHAMM'.

One becomes blasé about reports from friends & drinking companions on how good the band was that they saw last night; their judgements are usually coloured by the quality & quantity of beer consumed & whether they spent the night at the girl/boy -friend's house. I expect you can therefore imagine my reaction to: "That band, Seven Year Itch, were amazing. The pub was packed, with everybody having a good time & that girl singer's a piece of alright - you ought to have seen what she wasn't wearing - boy, they were good!"

By chance, I wandered into The White Lion, bored & fed up, to find Seven Year Itch (an awful name!) about to take to the stage & introduce themselves.

What am I doing here? Before us is the archetypal club band; dolly-bird singer, flat-capped & moustached guitarist with dreadful patter. I surrender my position (a standing space, the place is packed solid) & struggle towards the bar. The band starts. What is this? This is superb, the first number being 'Oo Ya Ha' with a simply dandy high harmony opening to meaty guitar work & the splendid phrase "Spend all my money getting out of my head".

Can one possibly imagine Fleetwood Mac, Rod Stewart, Eric Clapton & Blondie working together? The idea may be frightening but Seven Year Itch have made that manner of material work & they play it well - like that well-known drink, the effect is shattering. Ninety minutes whizz past & the audience have been left cooing "Oo Ya Ha" & calling for more. We had a good time.

Now read the first paragraph again.

— GRIS BOGRUM.

This is the first book to appear on The Jam, and has been written with their full co-operation, telling their story from start to "START!".

Illustrated throughout with over 60 black and white photographs (many never seen before) from Britain's top rock photographers.

The Modern World by Numbers
Paul Honeyford

112 pages; $3.95 ISBN 0 906008 22 0

Available from all good book and record shops, or in case of difficulty from the Magic Bus Bookshop, 10 King Street, Richmond, Surrey, for $3.95 (+ 75p p&p).

Please send me ____ copies of **The Jam** at $4.70 (inc. p&p).
I enclose cheque/PO. My Access/Barclaycard/Diners Club No. is

Name

Address

EEL PIE ROCK 'N' ROLL

Registered in England No. 1205 154

People in CRASS houses...
ANARCHY or ANACHRONISM?
10/10/80 Cleopatras, Huddersfield

Crass, the very name is liable to split any group into two bitterly divided camps. The main point of contention seems to be whether Crass is a rock band. The Crass organisation does produce records & tour around the provinces as a rock band is expected to do, but do they produce music when they are on stage?

Tonight at Cleo's the punk tribes are out on display, including a score who follow Crass across the land. Crass T-shirts, badges, armbands & patches are being sported & the mood is angry. The Poison Girls are ignored as they work through their set, the disco is met with jeers. I begin to wonder what any of us are doing here. Crass don't want to go on, not caring for the crowd, & I want to be going home as I keep imagining the imminent spilling of blood & the punks care about sod all.

Finally Crass take to the stage. It is difficult to say what was happening on stage as it all took place in darkness, but figures came & went, producing violent music. Hysterical? Angry? Paranoic? Revolutionary? Reactionary? Who am I to say..? The only line I could understand was: "Screaming babies, screaming babies!" Nobody else seemed to understand much either. There was some token pogoing at the beginning of each fast number, otherwise broad disinterest in the proceedings, except the two television screens flanking the stage & showing TV commercials, concentration camp inmates & home movies. WILL SOMEBODY EXPLAIN?

The significance of Crass to the audience is (I asked some members) limited to fashion, little or none of the political message sinking in. One band person said that Crass were greatly misunderstood by their audiences. When I suggested that Crass might one day be looked upon with nostalgia, in a similar manner to The Merry Pranksters, I was told that Crass was serious. That makes me think!

I shall remember Crass by their debut EP, 'The Feeding of the 5,000' - a basic statement of punk anger, powerful but hollow. I neither need nor want anything more. Is there any more?

—GRIS BOOJUM.

INVASION OF THE ANTPEOPLE!
ADAM & THE ANTS at Leed's Poly.
20/11/80

"So unplug the jukebox,
And do us all a favour,
That music's lost its taste,
So try another flavour
.... 'Antmusic'."

To say that Adam & The Ants were impressive in their appearance & their presence would be an understatement. The entire scene was magnificent; the large backdrop watching over the five warriors, the extravagant make-up, the theatrical clothes & the two drum-kits elevated above the stage at the back. Adam took a free role roaming the stage, controlling the tempo & beat with waving arms.

The drummers, Terry Lee Miall & Merrick, were the ones who impressed me above all. In front of them they had two identical kits. To see an excellent drummer is an experience but to see two of them working together so perfectly is something else. The introduction to many of the numbers, a pounding beat from both each with exactly the same movements & exquisite timing was like watching an immaculate display of synchronised trampolining.

'Dog Eat Dog', 'Kings of The Wild Frontier' 'The Magnificent Five' & their excellent new single 'Antmusic' were highlights of a set which was almost a complete run through of their new album, with two or three numbers from their first L.P. 'Dirk Wears White Sox' which is now celebrating one year without a break in the Sounds Alternative Chart.

Where The Ants could go from here is very hard to say. Their music is in no way pro progressive & only appeals to their own cult following. I would love to be proved wrong of course as such a band as this should be able to move with the times. Adam must obviously think differently as the fact that the last three singles were all included in the first five or six numbers must show that the band have great faith in the rest of their stuff.

Adam Ant is such a character however that I don't think he will ever lie down. He formed the band in 1977 & right from that date he believed in what they were doing. He's had more than his fair share of troubles with record companies, but all the time he has stuck to his guns in his belief that there is:

"No method in our madness
Just pride about our manner
Ant people are the warriors
Antmusic is their banner!"

Adam left the stage with his Fred Astaire-type cane in his hand waving it around as though putting a strange bewitching spell on the people below him. But, it may already be that he has..... he is already ruler of his own kingdom..... ruler of all his Ants.

—ANDY STEVENS

Photographs by Pennie Smith with passing comments by Joe Strummer, Mick Jones, Paul Simonon and Topper Headon.

"Being on the road with The Clash is like a commando raid performed by The Bash Street Kids. I hope this book gives you a bit of that feeling."
Pennie Smith

160 pages, 180 photographs, £4.50 ISBN 0 906008 23 9

Available from all good book and record shops, or in case of difficulty from the Magic Bus Bookshop, 10 King Street, Richmond, Surrey, for £4.50 (+75p p&p).

Please send me _____ copies of **The Clash/Before & After** at £5.25 (inc. p&p). I enclose cheque P.O.
My Access/Barclaycard/Diners Club No. is _____
Name
Address

EEL PIE ROCK'N'ROLL

Registered in England No.1205434

THE WAREHOUSE

19-21 SOMERS ST.   LEEDS 1.   tel. 468287.

December dates include...

Mon 1st = VICE VERSA   Thurs 4th = **STRAY CATS**

Mon 8th = BOW WOW WOW!!
MATINEE FOR 14-17 YR-OLDS AT 5.30 p.m. + EVENING SHOW WITH BAND ON AT 11.00 p.m.

Tues 9th = KNIFE EDGE + AXIS

Wed 10th = ZIGGY HERO

Mon 15th = PYLONS FROM USA... STABLEMATES OF THE B52'S

Mon 22nd = FUTURISTIC XMAS PARTY
WITH ELECTRONIC DISCO + MUSIC FOR PLEASURE

More dates being fixed for December & January - ring above no. between 9 a.m. & 2 a.m. for full details of times, prices and extra bookings that missed the copy date for this magazine.

LEEDS POLY UNION ENTS PRESENTS

in the new poly ents hall
Calverley St.   Leeds 1

Thursday 4th Dec. at 7.30 p.m. - **BAD MANNERS** + support [Tickets: £2-50]

Saturday 13th Dec. at 7.30 p.m. - **THE SKIDS** + support [Tickets: £3-00]

Wednesday 17th Dec. at 8.00 p.m. - THE XMAS BALL WITH THE ONE & ONLY **GARY GLITTER** + support
1am late bar at City Site & Brunswick Terrace [Tickets: £3-25]

MORE DATES BEING ARRANGED FOR JANUARY (RING FOR DETAILS)...

Tickets in advance from Leeds Poly Union (tel. Leeds 30171) or Leeds University Union Record Shop (tel. Leeds 39071) or on the door.

Turbo caught doing it live at The Good Mood, Halifax.

Do TURBO always stand like this & is it (a) because they do a lot of horseriding or (b) because they share some painful infection?

Recently featured on the 'New Electric Warriors' compilation album alongside the likes of more established rockers Vardis & Dawnwatcher, Turbo entertained a packed house with a well-balanced diet of melodic rock along with standard heavy metal 1980's style.

Obviously well-rehearsed, Turbo played within their ability thus keeping control over a fine set of numbers marred only by the inevitable 'obvious influences'. Although guitarists Ian Blackburn & Peter Mayhew together with vocalist Des Horsfall are the focal points of the band, their strength lies in the powerful rhythm section of drummer Chris Day & recent addition Chris Bartlett on bass (formerly with Bradford metalsters Trampus). Both are excellent musicians who give a rare depth to the overall sound, the quality of which is much sought after yet seldom achieved.

Outstanding song of the set was the epic 'Sunbird' which was particularly noticable for its atmosphere & subtle changes in pace, not unlike Def Leppard's 'Overture'.

'Assassin', 'Sirens', 'Electric Chair', 'War Heroes' & 'Running', the band's debut single (self-financed & worth a pound of anyone's money) are all songs in the same vein though not lacking in shape. With the acoustics doing the band no favours at all, it was only vocalist Horsfall who suffered within an otherwise creditable mix.

Turbo were very good indeed & have put a great deal of thought into their music, determined to be different, & I shall certainly see the band again. However, as for their chances of signing to a major company, I am - at least on tonight's performance - rather sceptical. Quite honestly, there are too many better bands ahead of them in the queue, most of whom won't get signed themselves. Even if they did get the deal they're searching for, their songs would need to be of a much higher standard for any chance of lasting success.

— Steve Brown.

LIVE MUSIC at **The Queen's Hall** AND **THE VAULTS BAR**

LIVE BLACK MUSIC Every Friday Night.

Heavy Rock + New Wave and Jazz Bands every: SUN. MON. WED.

Bradford College Students' Union
Queens Hall
Morley Street
Bradford BD7 1BW
Tel: (0274) 392712/3/4

GOSH! THIS IS IT! THE ONLY GENUINE WOOL CITY YULETIDE ROCKWORD No. 9. SO, WITH BITS OF HOLLY AND MISLETOE GRAFTED BETWEEN THE TEETH - BEST OF LUCK. Ken Turner.

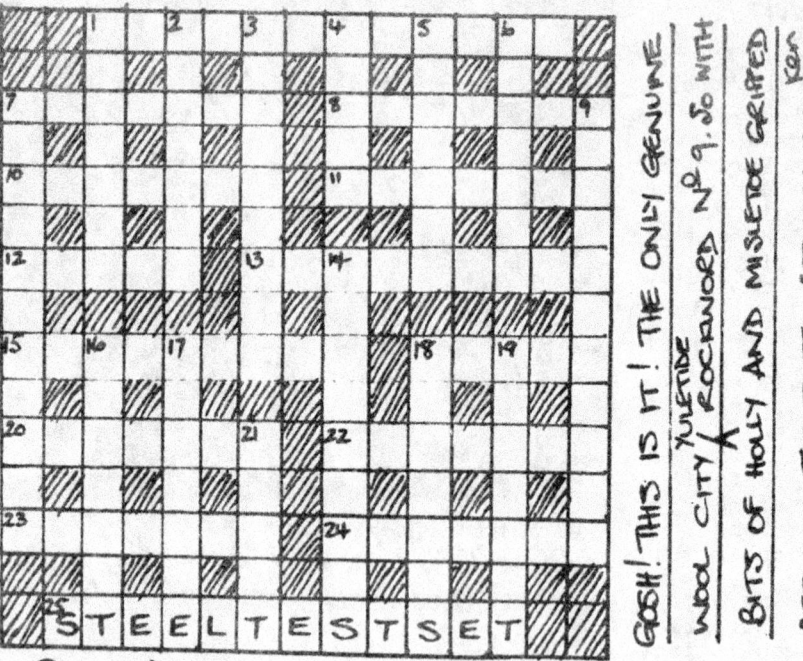

25. STEELTESTSET

Clues Across.
1. Rudolph's father, 24 hours later, on Dec. 25th? (9,3)
7. Smile — the booze has arrived. (5,2)
8. Tested, as 4 would have. (7)
10. and 11. Queue of what sounds like smokers fill money boxes. (4,3,7)
12. Do M.P.'s have one for Christmas? (5)
13. Bars dry in confusion? Offer him a drink. (6,3)
15. Whose branch brought to a head the gravity of it all. (5,4)
18. Baring of the flesh in the cheapest ripped clothes. (5)
20. Sips the brew for Greek dramatic poet. (6)
22. Wise men are part of the magic of Christmas. (3,4)
23. Feel for change and spout witticisms! (4,3)
24. Seasonal gathering of shop stewards? (7)

Clues Down.
1. First to turn up after the office party. (7)
2. Are Tory moves for the 'odd Teddy'? (4,3)
3. Food and drink available here in the evening. (6,3)
4. Scum and I mix. It's what this mag's for! (5)
5. The turkey is before the meal, and you are after. (7)
6. Puts sparkle into the morning after. (7)
7. Chill record buffet? (4,7)
9. Details of features. (11)
14. True spear makes openings. (9)
16. Here, now, for a gift. (7)
17. Blow up, not out! (7)
18. Promotion exercises? (4,3)
19. Rail set becomes seer of truths. (7)
21. Fatso goes back as he came. (2,3)

Solution to Rockword No 8.

Special Xmas & New Year Offer
10% OFF* ALL RECORDING PRICES ON PRODUCTION OF THIS ADVERTISEMENT

We would also like to wish everyone a very happy Christmas

*offer valid until January 31st 1981

CARGO RECORDING STUDIOS

Ring us at
ROCHDALE (0706) 524420
KENION ST., ROCHDALE, LANCS., ENGLAND

DEMO CASSETTES Reviewed by Nick Toczek.

RUSS VARLEY BAND: 2 SONGS - 'DEAR JOHN' & 'NEVER GONNA'. RUSS'S GRAVELLY VOICE EXPLODES ACROSS THESE TWO SELF-WRITTEN SONGS. BOTH ARE GOOD COMMERIAL HEAVY-EDGED ROCK, BUT IT'S HIS TRULY REMARKABLE VOICE THAT MAKES THEM STAND OUT. THE MIX IS NOT GREAT- VOICE TOO LOUD, BASS & GUITAR TOO QUIET, BUT IT'S A SMALL CRITICISM OF A FINE FIRST DEMO. RECORDED AT RIC-RAC, LEEDS (8-TRACK).

VIOLATION: A BUNCH OF IMPRESSIVE SONGS, ESPECIALLY THE FIRST FEW, ON THIS DEMO RECORDED AT THE COMMUNICATIONS CENTRE, BRADFORD (4-TRACK). A NEW VOCALIST SEEMS TO HAVE REALLY PULLED THIS BAND TOGETHER. BRADFORD'S LEADING PUNK OUTFIT, THEY'VE STILL SOME ROOM FOR IMPROVEMENT, BUT AKY'S DRUMMING & THE OVERALL TIGHTNESS OF THE BAND STAND OUT PARTICULARLY.

PAUL SZPYGIEL & FRIENDS (IAN NELSON-SAX/MARY NELSON -KBDS/MARTYN FOYE-DMS/STEVE SMITH-BASS/PAUL SZPYGIEL-GTR.& VOC.) WENT INTO CARGO STUDIOS, ROCHDALE TO RECORD THIS TRACK A FEW MONTHS AGO. THEY'LL BE BACK TO DO MORE IN A COUPLE OF WEEKS. THIS TRACK FEATURES UPFRONT BASS & DRUMS + SQUEEZED (AS OPPOSED TO PERCUSSIVE) KEYBOARDS ON AN ATMOSPHERIC & HIGHLY COMMERCIAL SONG. ALL VERY ORCHESTRAL MANOEUVRES... & GOOD WITH IT. THERE A TASTY AND ENTIRELY FITTING (BUT TOO BRIEF) SAX BREAK. I LIKE THIS BAND VERY MUCH INDEED.

BETTER BADGES
100 BADGES 1½" black and white
£13.50 inc. p.&p.
sae for production price list and other details.
286 PORTOBELLO ROAD LONDON W10 960 5513

8-TRACK - £50 per eight hr. day!

Fully Equipped Studio Using Tascam, Allen Heath, Revox, Roland, Tannoy, Quad, A.K.G., Calrec, etc.

USE OF ANY OF THE FOLLOWING EQUIPMENT

Polymoog, Minimoog, Fender Rhodes Suitecase, Hammond X5 Organ, Moog Taurus Bass Pedals, ARP Salina String Machine, Clavinet D6, Mellotron, Premier Drums, Kramer 5000 Dmz Bass, Acoustic Piano & Guitars + numerous effects.

JSG Music

YORKSHIRE'S LARGEST GROUP SHOP

108B Main Street, Bingley.   Tel: 0274-568843

(Open till 9 pm every Monday and Thursday; Friday and Saturday till 5.30 pm)

FOR THE BIGGEST SELECTION OF GROUP GEAR AT THE LOWEST POSSIBLE PRICES

In the Guitar and Amp shop choose from:

Gibson, Fender, Washburn, Guild, Ovation, Rickerbacker, WAL, Lincoln, Peavey, full HH Concert Rigs, HH Performer, HH VS, Marshall, MM, Custom Sound, Carlsboro, Laney, Vox, Roland, Hill and RSD. 1,000 watt Rigs ready to go. Mics by: AKG, Shure and Beyer. Accessories by: Electroharmonix, Boss, Dod, Vox, etc.

In the Keyboard Department:

Wurlitzer, Moog, Roland, Rhodes, Korg, Hohner, Crumar, etc.

ALL THIS **PLUS** HIRE SERVICE, REPAIRS, HUGE SELECTION OF USED GEAR AND WE BUY FOR CASH

FROM JANUARY 1st 1981
RIC~RAC Sound Studio

WILL BE THE FIRST 24-TRACK RECORDING STUDIO IN YORKSHIRE

Our new facilities include:—
NEW SOUNDCRAFT 16/24 DESK
NEW SOUNDCRAFT SCM 382
24-TRACK MACHINE
URSA MAJOR DIGITAL REVERB

8-, 16- & 24-track recording in extended studio area

AND WE'D LIKE TO TAKE THIS OPPORTUNITY TO WISH ALL OUR CUSTOMERS (OLD & NEW) A VERY PROSPEROUS NEW YEAR

For all studio enquiries ring Mick on Leeds 633717

ISSUE #12

December 1980 + January 1981, 2,000 copies printed, 20 pages, 25cm x 17cmm, free flexidisc

With this issue, WCR gains the new subtitle of 'The Northern Rockscene Monthly'. The flexidisc with this issue arose out of the blue. Shipley band Heaven 17, ambitious newcomers to the local music scene, offered this, their debut release, to WCR. It sounded great, and so I eagerly agreed. This, in turn, dictated the size and shape of the issue. What resulted was an odd mix with tiny print, but a package that was great value for 30p. The list of outlets (page 2) shows that WCR is not only available throughout Yorkshire but also has a strong presence in London and Lancashire. In addition, Red Rhino and Rough Trade were distributing copies elsewhere in Britain, as well as, albeit thinly, in Europe and the USA. The list of Yorkshire venues and their phone numbers (page 2) was widely used, particularly by bands.

Notes on bands featured in this issue.

The very punky Buzzcocks-ish *Somethings Wrong* on the flexidisc by Heaven 17 actually had a lot more wrong with it than the apostrophe missing from 'somethings'. On 13 March 1981, a Sheffield band using the same name released their debut single *(We Don't Need This) Fascist Groove Thang* on Virgin Records. Legal threats flew between the two bands for several months, during which time the Sheffield outfit, being on a major label, was climbing the ladder of fame. Eventually, the Shipley outfit, despite having been the first to use the name and the first to release a song, was forced to bow out and change their name to 1919, releasing the excellent proto-Goth single *Tear Down These Walls*.

Business card in plastic bag containing each copy

oooo COCKROACH MUZAK FOR SEXLESS PEOPLE

GRATUITOUS SEXISM

THE HOO-VETTES ON TOP OF THE POPS (miming the Hoover's not even plugged in!)

...Meanwhile, many miles away in a land called Yorkshire, the inevitable **FEBRUARY '81** issue of **WOOL CITY ROCKER** got its editorial. The inhabitants of that area would come to know of it as **ISSUE No 12**, & so it was...

This issue is different. I got bored stiff with the standard magazine format & therefore hope that the mag. will from now on take the form of some sort of package into which I'll shove whatever I think might be fun & interesting. If you've any ideas, then let me know. All that you require to successfully operate this issue are (a) one record player, (b) a wall & 4 drawing pins, (c) a magnifying glass (same one that you've used for the last 3 issues).

Did you see Bradford's Sue Fassbender on T.O.T.P.? I'll rashly predict that Bradford/Leeds trio The Donkeys will soon be on the same soap opera.

How did you do in the Yorkshire rock quiz in issue no.11? It wasn't easy, was it? You'll find the answers below. There's also a list of most of the current stockists of this magazine - sorry if I've missed any out. If any readers can suggest other possible outlets, then please ring me & I'll try to use them.

Hope you all had a good Xmas/New Year. Gaynor & I got engaged - thanks going to Palm Cove for party premises, Rob (of HMV) for D.J.ing, Rockabilly Rebs + Surfin' Dave for live musicing, Gaynor's family for the pressure cooker, Aunty Pat for the rolling pin, Heaven 17 for a large green paperweight in the shape of part of a man... etc.

Got a phone call from Kari Brown of The Wellington Club in Hull. She gave me the bad-taste-band-name-of-the-month: Lord Mountbatten's Bits & Pieces... & they've a single out - though I can't see it getting them onto T.O.T.P.! There's a sampler album of Hull bands due out soon. Kari's been kommissioned to kompile it for Koala Records & it'll be distributed through Pinnacle. Featured bands include London Boys (q.v), Baulk Mosaic, The Vets, Johnny Solo, Human Zoo, Sons of The Pope, Nyam Nyam, her own band Cool To Snog & several others. You have been warned!

With Reagan in power, how long before the hostages are begging to be allowed back into Iran?! There's a new venue in Leeds, but I forget its name (joke!).

Dead fish wearing shoes? Must be time to go. - March marches nearer, love & sex, Nick xxx

WOOL CITY ROCKER lives at...

5 Beech Terrace
Undercliffe
Bradford BD3 0PY
West Yorkshire
Telephone 0274 21867

where can also be found...
ALICE (a tabby cat)
SINBAD (a dark brown mongrel)
NICK TOCZEK (an editor)
SCRAPS (a b.&w. mongrel)

scattered around Yorkshire are...
STAN ENGEL (a cartoonist)
STEVE BROWN (a writer)
GEOFF CRUMACK (a photographer)
KEV HOPGOOD (another cartoonist)
ANDY SEVENS (a writer)
JOHN TEMPEST (photoer/writer)
KEN TURNER (X-worder/writer)
ANN & ANNE (a writers)
IAN TILLIARD (a cartoonist)
ANDY DARLINGTON (a big writer)

Musicians Wanted

DRUMMER urgently required for recording & gig commitments. BEEFHEART, BUNNYMEN & JOY DIVISION influences. Must be ambitious & dedicated. Rehearsal studio in Leeds area. Ring Martin on Wakefield 823944.

RADIO 5 want new drummer. For details ring Jock on Bradford 496272.

GUITARIST wanted for excellent pro band. Image essential. Phone Andy on 0535-32888 (evenings - 6-7.30).

Classified ads are only 10p per word. Ring them in or write...

YORKSHIRE & HUMBERSIDE GIGS
(other northern areas covered next month)

BRADFORD (0274-)
PALM COVE = 499894
UNIVERSITY = 34135
PRINCEVILLE = 518845
ST. GEORGE'S HALL = 32513 (Box Office)
QUEEN'S HALL =
VAULTS BAR =
† GATSBY'S = 28322
† SCAMPS = 26001
† TIFFANY'S = 24982/28975
† BIBI'S =
† ITALIAN CLUB (sweatbox)
BINGLEY ARTS CENTRE = 57982
† ROYAL STANDARD = 27898

HORNSEA (04012-)
FLORAL HALL = 2919

YORK (0904-)
UNIVERSITY = 413128
† THEATRE ROYAL = 23568
JASPER'S =
COLLEGE =

DONCASTER (0302-)
ROTTERS = 27448
ROMEO & JULIETS = 27858

LEEDS (0532-)
UNIVERSITY = 39071
POLYTECHNIC = 30171
WAREHOUSE = 468287
FAN CLUB at BRANNIGAN'S = 446985
COLLEGE = 392712
COSMOS =
AMNESIA =
ROYAL PARK = 785076
FFORDE GRENE = 490984
MEANWOOD HOTEL = 752165
STAGING POST = 735541
WIGGS WINEBAR (Jubilee Hotel) = 34172/38302
QUEENS HALL = 3196
MARQUIS OF GRANBY = 31250
HADDON HALL = 75115
GATE HOTEL = 658802
TIFFANY'S = 31448

KEIGHLEY (0535-)
FUNHOUSE = 603796
KINGS HEAD = 604660

ILKLEY (0943-)
COLLEGE = 607768/609010
ROSE & CROWN = 607260

BARNSLEY (0226-)
† CIVIC HALL = 203232

HUDDERSFIELD (0484-)
CLEOPATRAS = 24510
COACHHOUSE CLUB = 20930
WHITE LION = 22407
POLYTECHNIC = 38156
† ALBION = 24200
IVANHOES =

GRIMSBY (0472-)
CENTRAL HALL = 55796

SCARBOROUGH (0723-)
PENTHOUSE = 63204
† FUTURIST THEATRE = 60644

HALIFAX (0422-)
GOOD MOOD =
FOGGY'S =

PONTEFRACT (0977-)
BLACKAMORE HEAD = 702345

TADCASTER (0932-)
† FORGE INN = 833136

HULL (0482-)
THE ENDIKE HOTEL = 853211
CITY HALL = 20123
GROUCHO'S (Humberside Theatre) = 23638
UNIVERSITY = 42431
ORIENTAL HOTEL = 24927
WELLINGTON/BASEMENT CLUB = 23262
ANNABELLA'S = 59421
HESSLE TOWN HALL = 223111

SHEFFIELD (0742-)
PENGUIN CLUB = 385897
POLYTECHNIC = 738934
UNIVERSITY = 27704
LIMIT CLUB = 730940
TOP RANK = 21927
† BRINCLIFFE OAKS (Nether Edge) = 50624
HALLAMSHIRE HOTEL = 350740
THE ROYAL =
GEORGE IV = 344922
CITY HALL = 22835
THE PHEASANT =

WAKEFIELD (0924-)
UNITY HALL = 75719
† TIFFANY'S = 76215

Also, occasionally, gigs at Harrogate's Adelphi (0423-63334) & some others.

† = Not a regular venue

NB. Missing phone nos. are because phone nos. are missing.

O.K., SUCKERS, KRIZMUZ KWIZ LAID BARE...

(1) N.M.X. (Sheffield), LENS (Wakefield), SHINEY CALIPERS (Leeds), BIT OF CULTURE (York), TOWNBEAT (Huddersfield), IT'S DIFFERENT FOR GRILS (Sheffield), TOTAL DISDAIN (Huddersfield), DAMAGED GOODS (Knaresborough), APATHY (Bradford), GARGOYLE & THE NOSEY NEIGHBOUR SUPPLEMENT (Mytholmroyd), STRANGE SOUNDS (Leeds), GETTING NOWHERE FAST (York), BEATEN TO THE PUNCH (York), PINK FLAG (Sheffield), BATH BANKER (Sheffield), etc. (2) (a) ONE ADULT, (b) HEAVEN 17, (c) PROPOSITION 31, (d) 633 SQUADRON. (3) (a) HICKS FROM THE STICKS, (b) NEW ELECTRIC WARRIORS, (c) BOUQUET OF STEEL. (4) (a) DEEP FREEZE MICE, (b) ALL MY GERANIUMS (c) BULLETPROOF, (d) MOLE EMBALMING RECORDS. (5) (a) PUNK, (b) H.M., (c) REGGAE, (d) MOD, (e) R'n'R, (f) NEW WAVE. (6) HUMAN LEAGUE (1st single was 'Being Boiled'). (7) (a) QUEEN'S HALL, LEEDS, (b) ST. GEORGE'S HALL, BRADFORD. (8) (a) RADIO 5, (b) TRUE COLOURS - ("Japanese Art" c/w 'True Colours' - Airplay '80 deleted), 'True Colours' c/w 'Animal Connections' - Rockburgh '80 + a track on 'Hicks From The Sticks'). (9) (a) METROGNOME, (b) PENNINE ROCK, (c) SOMETHIN' ELSE, (d) HALLAM ROCK - dynamic, huh?! (10) THE MEKONS. (11) (a) BRADFORD & SHEFFIELD, (b) LEEDS & SHEFFIELD. (12) (a) BLUDGEON RIFFOLA, (b) VERTIGO, (c) WASTED. (13) JILTED JOHN. (14) ULTRAVOX. (15) (a) TATTOO HOSTS VISION ON, (b) KEEPING DARK, (c) MUSIC FOR PLEASURE. (16) (a) WAKEFIELD, (b) SHEFFIELD, (c) HUDDERSFIELD, (d) PONTEFRACT, (e) KEIGHLEY, (f) LEEDS. (17) (a) NIGEL BURNHAM, (b) DES MOINES. (18) (a) KILLERMETERS, (b) THE SCENE, (c) GIRLS AT OUR BEST, (d) STRANGER THAN FICTION, (e) MUGGINS BLIGHT, (f) DEFRINGER, (g) SAXON, (h) ULTERIOR MOTIVES, (i) OSCILLATORS, (j) COMSAT ANGELS - (respectively from (a) Huddersfield, (b) Bradford, (c) Leeds, (d) Wakefield, (e) Skipton, (f) Leeds/Bradford, (g) Sheffield, (h) Bradford, (i) Harrogate, (j) Sheffield). (19) (a) JOHN KEENAN, (b) MARCUS FEATHERBY. (20) DONCASTER. (21) (a) RAM, (b) THE ART OF SOLVING PROBLEMS, (c) STAN ENGEL, (d) MOTIVATORS/BEANS/THE CAT/SIDE EFFECT/GIMMICKS/FORST. (22) (a) BEATPUMP (from Wakefield), (b) MIRROR BOYS (from Leeds). (23) (a) SEX PISTOLS, (b) IVANHOES, HUDDERSFIELD - (last UK gig before Sid kicked it & J.R. took the P.I.L.S.) (24) (a) SAMPLER from FUTURE EARTH RECORDS, (b) HUDDERSFIELD BAND, (c) YORK RECORDING STUDIO, (d) E.P. on NEUTRON RECORDS (full title - '1980: The First Fifteen Seconds'), (e) PUNK GIGS AT THE ITALIAN CLUB, BRADFORD, (f) DAVE HALL'S LEEDS LABEL (Single: Knife Edge, Tapes: Knife Edge, Rough Justice). (25) (a) COMSAT ANGELS, (b) VARDIS, (c) HUMAN LEAGUE. (26) THE FALL. (27) DELTA 5. (28) (a) JOHN FOXX, (b) BILL NELSON. Next year's will be worse!

W.C.R's on sale at these OUTLETS....

J.S.G. MUSIC - BINGLEY
BARKBY'S (NEWSAGENTS) - BRADFORD
BOWES & BOWES (UNIVERSITY) - BRADFORD
COLLEGE SHOPS - BRADFORD
CAT'S PYJAMAS - BRADFORD
CITY NEWS - BRADFORD
H.M.V. - BRADFORD
MANVILLE - BRADFORD
PREEDY'S - BRADFORD
PRINCEVILLE - BRADFORD
ROOTS RECORDS - BRADFORD
ST. GEORGE'S HALL (box office) - BRADFORD
WOOLER'S (NEWSAGENTS) - BRADFORD
BRADLEYS RECORDS - HALIFAX
SCENE & HEARD RECORDS - HALIFAX
HEBDEN BRIDGE BOOKS
H.M.V. - HULL
(other Hull shops being added)
BOSTOCK'S RECORDS - HUDDERSFIELD
PEACEWORKS - HUDDERSFIELD
DISCOUNT RECORDS - KEIGHLEY
MUSIC EXCHANGE - KEIGHLEY
AIREDALE & WHARFEDALE COLLEGE - KEIGHLEY
BOSTOCK'S RECORDS - LEEDS
CORNER BOOKSHOP - LEEDS
GEROL'S RECORDS - LEEDS
H.M.V. - LEEDS
JUMBO RECORDS - LEEDS
LEEDS BOOKS
POLYTECHNIC UNION SHOP - LEEDS
UNIVERSITY UNION RECORDS - LEEDS
RAM RECORDING STUDIOS - LEEDS
RECORD GALLERY - LEEDS
RIC-RAC RECORDING STUDIOS - LEEDS
JOHN SCHEERER (instruments) - LEEDS
STAGING POST - LEEDS
VIRGIN RECORDS - LEEDS
BETTER BADGES - LONDON
COMPENDIUM BOOKS - LONDON
ROUGH TRADE - LONDON
RONDOLET RECORDS - MANSFIELD
REVOLUTION - SHEFFIELD
VIRGIN RECORDS - SHEFFIELD
RED RHINO RECORDS - YORK

Other distribution by:-
Barry Lights (BLACKPOOL)
Ken Turner (BRADFORD)
Dave Hall (LEEDS, etc.)
Dave Shepherd (PRESTON)

EXTRA OUTLETS
AMNESIA - LEEDS (NEW)
CARD CABIN - MYTHOLMROYD (omitted)

Please help me to add outlets. Just ring (0274-) 21867 & let me know of any outlets near you. - NICK

NICK TOCZEK'S WOOL CITY ROCKER No.12 FEB '81

LONDON BOYS are a Hull band who, to quote from their press release, play 'the music that people dance to - the speed of rock with the staccato reggae that eats your tapping feet, all bound in R&B.'

A short promotional video of the band is to be shot by local enterprise 'Off Balance Films' in the spring.

Andy and Rory write the band's material and share vocals and guitar-work, with Sarge on drums and Jon on bass.

They've a single 'Bleeding In My Heart' lined up for soon-come release on their own One Way Rec. label and are also recording two tracks for inclusion on a Hull compilation (see editorial of this issue) that's to be release on Koala Records in April.

You can contact the band through their manager, Malcolm Williamson, on Hull (0482) 842745.

This man has built his entire life around his uncanny, though superficial, resemblance to an American prison governor of the 1930s. The complete lack of convicted criminals in his bedsitter has embittered him.

HERESY, a three-piece heavy rock/blues band from Leeds, comprise Ian Bland(!) on guitars and vocals, Sim Parker on bass and vocals and Mark Platts on percussion and (it says here) assorted grunts.

Formed in mid-80, they rehearsed for six months during which time a guitarist and vocalist came and went.

Debut gig was at Royal Park in Leeds and they're at Froggies, Halifax on Feb.4, Royal Park on Feb.5, Speakeasy, Wakefield on Mar.2 &4. More being lined up.

There's a 3-track demo (recorded at Ric Rac) promised to me for review in next month's W.C.R.

Contact the band's manager via post office telephonic machinery on Leeds(0532) 751758.

MISTRESS describe themselves as a classic 3-piece (guitar, bass and drums) who play live and licking bitch rock.

Denny Gibson ('the bitch on bass and lead vocals') eats little boys for breakfast and was in the original all-girl band of the same name. With Andy Pharo on drums and Dean Kelly on bass, they also have bands like 'Bombers' and 'Jets' in their collective pedigree.

They've supported Madness, The Count Bishops, Hot Chocolate, Eric Bell Band, K.C. and The Sunshine Band and Little Bo Bitch - quite a mixed bag!

They've gigged on the continent and also zoomed down to London from their home town of Blackpool to headline at prestige metropolitan dives like Dingwalls, the Nashville and the Music Machine. Peel and Burnett have given Radio One airplay to their tapes and a recent Music Machine gig looks like it's secured them a management/agency/publishing deal on which the ink should be dry by the time you read this. And their drummer comes from Leeds...!

Agency: Wasted Talent (01-221-6136)
Management: C.A. Whitelaw, CAW Management on 01-851-3331 or 01-584-5622 (night) or 01-734-8211 (mornings) - what about afternoons?!

THE DONKEYS graze mostly around Wakefield. Yet another trio, they are Dave Owen (bass and vocals), Mark Wellham (drums) and Neil Ferguson (guitar and vocals). As a 4-piece (with Neil's brother, Tony on 2nd guitar) they came together around Feb. '79.

Their first single 'What I Want' c/w 'Four Letters' came out in Oct.'79 on the Manchester indie Rhesus Records. Deram then picked it up and it went to no.90 in the BBC charts, pulling a fair amount of airplay. They did some radio work as a result, including an 'In Concert' session. Deram promised a whole lot including an L.P., but it never materialised. Neil: "That was the first bitter experience." They then toured as support to Stiff Little Fingers: "We started as a pop band, then that tour turned us into a tougher-sounding band - we're now moving back towards being a pop/chart band."

Chris Dixon, owner of Rhesus, managed them-"The second bitter experience." He spent a lot of time telling them he was going to do great things for them, but little of the promised goodies ever materialised. 'As a result, they lost the impetus of the 1st single's action and the follow-up, 'No Way' c/w 'You Jane' didn't appear till the following May. Produced and engineered by The Ruts' producer Mick Glossop, it was released through low-key Phonogram subsid. Back Door - with very little promotion. It sold a mere 3½ thou. Neil: "It was a very professional job, but lacked power, especially at the bass end."

With Tony and the manager given the elbow, they've a new single 'Don't Go' c/w 'Living Legends' out on Rhesus (nominally, the thing being funded by John Brierley of Cargo Studios - where they do most of their recording).

Dave: "We now feel like we're starting afresh with this 3rd single and the band down to a 3-piece. There have also been delays while Neil's been setting up his own recording studio - Woodlands." (See advert on poster). "We're not going to let anything get in the way this time. We've been messed about too much by the sick attitudes of major companies and The Industry in general."

So they're now doing their own 'donkey-work'- self-managed and getting gigs for themselves, and preferring it that way, for the time being at least. They're also very happy to be linked with John Brierley who's straight with them.

Dave Owen is on Wakefield 893943.

PYRAMID are 'Eric' Hartley (guitars/vocals/synth), Jon Price (ld.vocals/harmonica), Ian Patrick (rm.guitar), Andy Dempster (bass) and Kev Collens (drums and percussion) - with sound engineer Richard Lloyd and Stuart Craven on lights and pyrotechnics.

Towards the end of '79 (minus drummer) the current line-up came together. 'Eric' and Andy had been together in a previous band, while Jon and Ian had both put in some time with 'Backslider'. By July '80, they'd put together a rough set and then acquired Kev (ex-633 Squadron etc.). By Sept./Oct. they'd gained a '1,000 watt p.a + Richard and Stuart to do the backstage work.

They played gigs at Kings Head, Keighley (too loud), Vaults Bar, Bradford, Ilkley College and Palm Cove, Bradford (too cold). The 'Eric' smashed his bike and broke his shoulder and two fingers (too painful!). That kept them out of action till mid-December.

Musical influences are diverse, with members of the band variously into folk (Jon), hard rock (Andy-"not H.M."!), psychedelia (Kev 'n' Jon), blues (Andy), pop/futurist ('Eric') - weird, huh!?

The resultant music is loud but not entirely heavy. 'No.7' is punkish. 'Won't Be Home' is a long folk/rock influenced piece. 'Wish You Wouldn't' is catchy pop. 'Crash Landing' - their forthcoming cassette-single - is a heavy rock tour de force ... so claims their letter; a point they re-emphasised in interview. "The problem is that we tend to be too varied for a lot of people - they like some, but not all of what we do, with different people liking different styles within our set."

"At the moment," said Kev, "we are up to our necks in debt over the p.a."

They plan to release the cassette as soon as they can afford it, and are after more gigs. "It's a problem when you can't get gigs in Leeds, for example, unless you've already done gigs in Leeds!"

With the exception of 'All Along The Watchtower' (Andy: "our version/accident of it") all the songs are their own, with lyrics by Jon and/or 'Eric' as the starting-point from which songs are then written by the group as a whole, in rehearsal.

Musical tastes aside the band see their close friendship and social life as a key factor in the group's stability. The three major things they have in common are space invaders, Hendrix and vindaloo with green chillis. Apparently these are necessary qualifications for Pyramid membership.

Contact: Andy on Bradford 565666 or 'Eric' on Bradford 391849 - both between 6p.m and 8p.m.

Snark Music*: 'It's only a Northern Song' Xmas Party.
Coach House, Huddersfield.
22:12:80 - foto'd & reviewed by John Tempest.

*Snark (snäk) - a mysterious, imaginary animal - created in 1876 by Lewis Carroll (1832 - 1898)
(In my encyclopaedia it comes between 'snare drum' & 'snarl')
104 years on ...

Why do reviewers categorise every band they review? As my New Year resolution I shall try to be more tolerant towards things that I don't know about. To that effect, if I don't describe the type of music a band plays maybe you'll go and find out for yourselves. Try it, you might be surprised. I was.

The GUESTS were very energetic (sometimes frantic), and enthusiasm reigned supreme - they kept banging their heads on the ceiling. As they were opening the gig they had the work to do, but in front of a partisan crowd they delivered the goods.

A sense of the theatrical (see drummer's eye) heralded the arrival of OR WAS HE PUSHED - they were determined to enjoy themselves - and made sure that others did too. (see pic of fan - no, he wasn't pushed.) Especially liked their 'Singapore'.

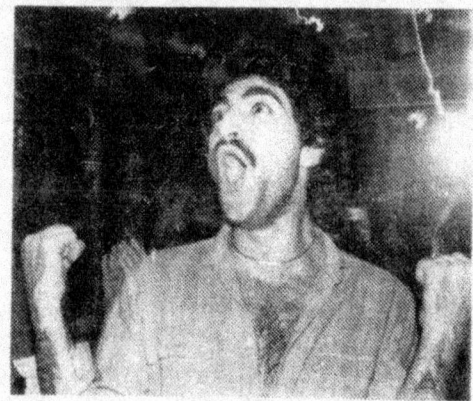

At every gig there are successes and failures. GENTLE IHOR attempted to be an anti - hero and succeeded as he left the stage after an extended tune up/sound check. Embarrassing; should learn to persevere. The show must go on. And so it did ...

Wot a name. Wot a performance. Lesser artists than BIG FAT WOMEN WOT CAN'T ADD UP would've whipped through their set and gone home. These guys were there, it was their stage, and they were going to entertain. Those who expected to dance, listened; those who expected to listen, joined in. An excellent lesson in communication and audience control.

O.K. O.K. They've been around for years - not with the same line up - but why haven't JAB JAB got further? They gave others a lesson in how to grab an audience and take them wherever they wanted. So polished and tight, and yet they still conveyed that impromptu 'come on and enjoy yourself' feeling. I did and I did.

Gris Boojum (head of Snark Music) presented a well balanced and prepared gig. So now the work really starts. The success of Snark Music and Gris's Chosen Few depends on the tape and acts being 'sold' to others. Will any or all of the Snark artists become household names? Will 'Boojum' later be mistaken for 'Bee Gees'? Yes to the former, doubtful to the latter. Just how it should be.

---

best because of the heavy sequencer rhythm and consequent hypnotic simplicity. **TAP 1** 4 tracks here: 'Psilisynthetique', 'Geiger Counter', 'How Do You Like This Angle' and 'Severed Wharves'. N: "This first track's a synth instrumental that's like a follow-up to the Doctor Who theme." A: "Riff-upon-riff construction that's again minimalist, but better than the previous tape." 2nd track. N: "This'd be a good theme tune for the televising of The First International 'Space Invaders' Players Contest!" 3rd and 4th tracks... A: "Generally, when he drops the rhythm in favour of random electronic work it's more like he's playing a game..." N: "...fun, but more like playing with sound effects than aiming to create a music." A: "I'd have liked him to have used a combination of rhythmic and random sound simultaneously. This is the better of the two tapes - not great musically, but what it lacks in skill, it scores as Art for Art's sake." N: "I'll play this as music to keep me alive while I'm putting W.C.R. together!"

These are 3 enterprising and useful cassettes. More are to follow from Tapir, and all the profits go toward a Collective for Bradford musicians - with a studio as the eventual target. Steve's first aim is to buy a fast cassette copier. So support Tapir and watch out for further product.

Other Stuff Sent In For Review...

Bit stuck for space, so here's an in-brief round-up (some help in reviewing these from Steve Brown and Alan Bailey). Hull's COOL TO SNOG sent a 4-track demo tape. Heavy phasing on guitar + high strident female vocals (reminiscent of Sue Fassbender/Delta 5/Girls At Our Best). They use the guitar+effects where other bands would use synth. "Satisfaction Week" is the best of this enjoyable quartet. The way the chords slide into one another is similar to Dance Chapter's excellent song 'Anonymity'. Alan Bailey's own band LOVERS INSPAIN demo has just one song. Free Ride is Alan's own composition (he played keyboards on Silver Screen Girls' single last year). It's funk-jazz with some really excellent work on guitar and bass. Crusaders music meets Ian Curtis vocals. Alan would have liked it to have come out even more funky - "should've been more like black soul than white soul". None-the-less, it's an excellent piece of polished music. THE RETURN OF JOHANN MUGGINS are the Skipton band formerly called MUGGINS BLIGHT (single last year). M.O.R. 60's pop with good melody lines and very good guitar, but merely functional drumming that's too restrained. Acoustic guitar and synth add variety. Easy to enjoy. ROCKABILLY REBS come up with a 14-track tape that'll be their first album (out this month). They rightly feel slightly disappointed with it. The bland production gets rid of a piece of their on-stage power and the songs come over as too similar. "Haunted House", "Caroline", their own "Boothill Boogie" and the final track "Rockabilly Angel" are among the good ones. It should easily sell to rockabilly fans (and Elvis fans), but they'll need better and fresher material to reach the pop market. NEW OPERA's demo from Ram Studios is bouncing keyboard new wave slightly marred by the flottish vocals. There's a biting sinister edge to their music and the playing's tight and convincing. A new band (off-shoot of The Vye), they're one to watch. Four singles that didn't fit into the singles reviews column... 3 are from The Donkeys who are a highly commercial pop band (see front-page feature). The first almost did it for them. The second would certainly have charted if it had been properly promoted. The third one, released at the end of last month, features "Don't Go" c/w "Living Legends". Steve doesn't rate it as highly as the first two, but I'm sold on it. I can't get the tune out of my head. If there's any justice, which there isn't, you should be fed this regularly by the goons who host "Radio One airspace". I also got sent a single by THE HORRIBLE NURDS "Consuming Passion" c/w "Personal Relationships" & I hated it. Bad punk with too-thin music and over-rough vocals. Nurds they surely are. Horrible the mix certainly is. PERE UBU's classic and influential early 78 album "The Modern Dance" has just been re-released by Rough Trade. The band's tense pacing and their original use of odd percussion/electronic noise/taped sound effects are coupled with David Thomas's unique voice. The experimental songs are intensely rhythmic and repetitive, comparable to Zappa/Beefheart/Residents. It's intelligent innovation - the apparent looseness never losing its firm grip on power rock. 3 years on, this album still retains its invaluable freshness. HARRY KAKOULLI's album "Even When I'm Not" (Oval Records) is a bunch of extremely catchy pop songs. He's former Squeeze bassist & this is the first time I've heard a bass solo played over another bass. Good production and his weakish but appealing voice ring through. The real winner, though, is the song quality with finger-click rhythms and Ian Dury/Jona Lewie immediacy that can't fail to grab you. This is a good album that should have been given the backing of a major label to promote it into the charts. MINATURES is an extraordinary compilation dreamed up by Morgan Fisher. 51 artists contribute one track each - none of them more than a minute long. The whole work gives the punter a chance to sample the off-beat indulgences of many of the leading popular creative artists of the past two decades. Contributors include: The Residents, Roger McGough, John Otway, Robert Wyatt, Andy Thunderclap Newman, Fred Frith, Neil Innes, Lol Coxhill, Steve Miller, Norman Levett (who?!), George Melly, Robert Fripp, Andy Partridge, Phantom Captain, Ron Geesin, Quentin Crisp, Ralph Steadman, R.D. Laing, Ivor Cutler, Martin Chambers, Dave Vanian, Metabolist, ½ Japanese, Mark Perry, David Cunningham, Kevin Coyne, Ken Cambell, Pete Seeger & numerous others. Infuriating/self-indulgent/delightful/exciting delete as applicable. LIMELIGHT's first album displays their musical excellence. Melodic heavy rock that features the outstanding guitar work of Glen Scrimshaw and the undoubted songwriting talent of brother Mike. Unlike most UK rock outfits their style is non-derivative. The ambitious arrangements that draw on transatlantic influences lend them potentially international appeal. The only real criticism is that they are firmly rooted in the musical tradition of late sixties acid rock. That said, there's a huge market for it and, on this showing, the band is set fair to tap it.

Tapir Product

STEVE WOOD, 2/4 KIPPING LANE, THORNTON, BRADFORD. (tel 0274-833059).

- TAP 2 - The 'Focus on Bradford' tape (live at Bradford Playhouse) at 75p
- TAP 1 - Sri Twill - 'The World of Paradiddle' (4 tracks) at £1.90
- TAP 3 - Sri Twill - 'Atom Bomb' c/w 'L.O.B.O.T.O.M.Y.' at 50p

Available by mail (enclose extra 10p for p. & p.) or from HMV, Bradford. 3 CASSETTES REVIEWED HERE BY ALAN BAILEY & NICK TOCZEK.

TAP 2 features various artists from a concert on 9/11/80. VEX Alan: "Vocals sound very cliched but the band's good - especially the guitar." Nick: "Yeah, they're one of the best in Bradford at the moment." A: "Good drummer too, & it's excellent for a live recording. Considering they've got an electronic identity, this is pretty musical. It's hard to draw comparisons - they've certainly got an identity of their own." N: "Rock-electronic crossover." A: "A bit repetitive though, the songs seem to be constructed more or less on one riff..." N: "...which shouldn't be the case with musicians of their calibre." A: "But the standard's consistently high throughout." NICK TOCZEK N: "My performance poetry/lyrics. I'll be touring later this year with a one-man show and this was a try-out of some pieces - not as good as I'd hoped." A: "It's very expressive - though 'Head Came Off' doesn't exactly stand up as poetry. It's the rhythm that holds each of them together. I like it." N: "I did it for fun. My band, Ulterior Motives, were asked to do the gig but couldn't, so I went along. I'd no idea it was being recorded." POLICEMAN WITH A LOAF OF BREAD A: "I don't really understand this sort of thing." N: "They take the piss out of everything - including themselves and the audience - it's Dada." A: "Proof that rhythm and melody aren't dead yet?!" N: "It's so atrocious that you've got to laugh. No redeeming features - which is what they're after." LITTLE BROTHER Poetry. A: "It's John Cooper Clarke with a Yorkshire influence. Very varied and non-serious in character." N: "Rhythm and rhyming lists that have humorous bite to them. His confidence carries the material really well." A: "In a lot of cases the subject-matter's cliched - 'Tit Week', 'In The Sun' and 'That World War III' one - but his style and rhymes are very individual." VENDINO PACT (guesting from Sheffield). A: "They sound like an everyday industrial band with little identity of their own." N: "We've been listening to Factory Records and once spoke to Ian Curtis..." A: "Vex did this sort of thing a lot better." N: "And with style and originality - which this band lack." CAMERAS IN CARS N: "Chopped punky electronics." A: "...with some impressive keyboards. The music's well-constructed and that guitar offsets the keyboards nicely - echo on the guitar is effective."

TAP 3 N: "Musical minimalism from Steve Wood on synth (with heavy sequencers) and vocals (with heavy echo/delay)." A: "When he uses variation, it sounds good, but he doesn't use it that often. Pretentious sci-fi lyrics in predictable new music vein." We both like Lobotomy.

PRINTED BY TEMPEST & COCKCROFT BFD. 43695 & 816478

BOW WOW WOW

The Warehouse in Leeds looks large with only a few dozen punters lined up against the walls like firing squad fodder. Pink Peg Slax - a young Leeds 50's rock/rockabilly 5-piece, put in a rather lifeless support spot that fails to impress. A new band, they've a good authentic early Elvis sound with a vocalist who looks the part - but they lack drive/excitement/presence. More experience and they could have something better to offer.

This is the matinee show (no drinks, under eighteens welcome) and marks the northern debut of Malcolm 'paedophile' McLaren's Bow Wow Wow - his first new venture since The Pistols went off (in his face). What I'd expected was a 90%-hyped/10%-talented bunch who'd probably be embarrassingly posey. Totally wrong!

Visually they're hot. Anabell in yellow dress (dress, mack, scarf, jacket) topped off with a pirate's hat. Matthew Ashman flicks a headful of tight white-dread beaded plaits and sports a white hollow-bodied and f-holed Gresch. He and bassist Leigh Gorman plunder the Shadows/Tornados sixties catalogue for a stack of gripping riffs. They're good musicians and the Shads rip-off is hard to spot behind Dave Barbarossa's stunning tomtom-'n'-bass relentless drum barrage. They hammer through a 40 minute set built out of the 8-track tape and their two singles. She skips, spins and bounces round the stage- a bundle of energy and infectious laughter; her odd squeaky voice brilliantly offset by the band's dense and bubbling rhythm c/w now-you-hear-it now-you-don't melody lines. Great band; great set.
-NICK TOCZEK

DIRE STRAITS at Leeds University

Mark Knopfler's in good form for this homecoming to his alma mater. He's relaxed with jokes and an easy friendliness to his between-songs chat.

In some ways once you've heard 'Sultana of Swing' you've heard most of what Dire Straits have to offer.....Dylanesque vocals walking hand-in-hand with that distinctive t(w)angy guitaring. Don't get me wrong, they're an outstanding band- just that the overall sound and the admittedly appealing melody on each successive song too often grows samey. That said, most else about this gig was near-perfect.

Sound mix, stage craft, pacing, musicianship, atmosphere - all high scorers. Also, while it's easy to view them as a guitar band - which they certainly are - that'd be doing them an injustice to the subtly unintrusive and multi-faceted keyboard action

Unlike many Superstar-status rock combos, they still work hard, enjoy themselves on stage and take risks. The 10 minute Dietrich/ Sally Bowles Kraut-cabaret constructed round 'Lace Boys' had more than a hint of hit-or-miss about it. They carried it off well in the end.

In a long and varied set, they constantly earn the enthusiastic applause that chases each number. More American than a planeload of Iranian exports, their music still has mileage in it, and the band'll be around for a good while yet.

Nick Toczek.

ARTERY severed by Nick Toczek

Third of the twenty bands on stage on the second day of Futurama II, the second annual Leeds Sci-Fi Festival, was Artery who did well to stimulate an enthusiastic response from the audience so early in the day. One number in particular stood out from the rest; 'The Slide' on which the whole band abandoned regular instruments and hit things instead. This all-percussion-and-vocals song is a riveting live number. You can see the band in the Futurama film which should go on general release in a few months.

A slightly muted version of The Slide is on the Aardvark Records sampler 'Bouquet of Steel' and a remixed version coupled with 'Unbalanced' is soon to be released as a double A-side single on the same label.

A demo tape and several phone calls put me on the Bradford-Sheffield line, dieseling down to the steel city for a hometown lunchtime pub interview with the band. Minus their bassist (working) but plus their Manager, Aardvark-meister Marcus Featherby, the band led me from BR to Tetleys.

Michael (guitar, percussion, sax and vocals), Simon (organ, percussion and vocals) Garry (drums and backing vocals) Mark (vocals, percussion and some offstage guitar) and Neil (bass and percussion) have been working together for the past eighteen months, first striking vinyl back in June '79 with a 3-track E.P. on Limited Edition Records. It has long since sold out. They describe it as having been a "good landmark for what we were doing then, but we don't use any of that material live anymore".

That first release was recorded without employing a producer. For the forthcoming single, they've enlisted the production services of Steve Hopkins. He's a side-kick of Mancunian independent whizz-kid Martin Hannett (a.k.a. Martin Zero) with whom he's been involved as co-member of the band Invisible Girls and also worked on Hannett's label - Rabid Records. The band members are divided over which side is more likely to swing some action their way. Meanwhile they wait impatiently for current hassles (the pressing plant going to the wall etc.,) to clear up and so let the single escape.

Live the band are unpretentious and unshowy, almost business-like in the way that they set about producing the sort of music that's earning them a name as distinctively original songwriters.

Mark: "Our sound's predominantly rhythmic - loud bass and percussion with guitar and keyboards both playing mostly rhythm".

Simon: "The guitar and organ both go through Carlsboro Super Stingray amps, so they merge well together".

Michael: "The Stingrays also provide some useful sound effects - they're why we sound like we do. Primarily, that amp gives the organ a sort of guitar sound".

Mark: "Neil doesn't use a bass amp for his guitar (a Fender Precision). He aims at a very distorted bass and finds bass amps too bland. He gets the sound he wants by putting it through an Orange Overdrive guitar amp".

Coming away from the interview I was left with strong impressions of both Mark and Michael. The former, as lyricist and most vocal member in interview,emerged as the band's main spokesman offstage just as much as he is on stage. Michael seemed the most jaded member and, whilst doubting his assertion that what he'd really like for the band is a full over-the-top show "with lightshow, strippers, fire-eaters...."(!), it did seem that his musical frustrations and short-fuse boredom will help prevent the band from ever slipping into a rut.

Rash predictions of imminent super-stardom are, more often than not, the kiss of death for a struggling band; and I don't anyway see Artery hitting such heights. What is true to say, however, is that they richly deserve a larger piece of the action than they're currently getting.

Contact: c/o Aardvark on Sheffield (0742) 669218.

the FAN CLUB
CLAIRE PLAYS THE RECORDS
Birmingham Road
CALL IN LOWER BRIGGATE LEEDS 446185
OPEN EVERY THURSDAY
Start 8.30pm — Close 1.00am
further enquiries: phone - 663252
ALL TICKETS ON THE DOOR
SUPPORT YOUR LOCAL GROUPS

SEE IT BEFORE IT HAPPENS!

THURSDAY 5th FEBRUARY - the PASSIONS plus REALLY!
New Single "I'M IN LOVE WITH A GERMAN FILM STAR"
members £1.25 non-members £1.50

THURSDAY 12th FEBRUARY - THE SOUND and Hokkies of Today
E.P. "PHYSICAL WORLD"
L.P. "JEOPARDY" - Single "HEARTLAND"
members £1.00 non-members £1.25

THURSDAY 19th FEBRUARY - U.K. DECAY with local lads the NOISE
Single "FOR MY COUNTRY" ON 'FRESH'
members £1.00 non-members £1.25

THURSDAY 26th FEBRUARY - THE CRAMPS
DON'T MISS THIS ONE!

SUNDAY 22nd FEBRUARY - JUDGE DREAD
SUNDAY 15th FEBRUARY - BAD MANNERS & the Boys

The 'FAN' goes into 'TIFFANY'S'
TIFFANY'S MERRION CENTRE LEEDS
Leeds (0532) 663252 or 31668/9

A BUNCH OF BIG ONES

Thursday 23/12/80. The Police are playing Bingley Hall. Saturday 17/1/81 - Echo and the Bunnymen have just walked off-stage at their secret Peak District gig. Between these two events lie 602 miles, 64 musicians about 40 oranges and countless hours of lost sleep.

So the day before Christmas Eve. Stafford Bingley Hall. It's raining. The ten members of the support band were introduced as Rico, (he of Specials fame). Their set was not outstanding; a mixture of ska and reggae as expected, but just a little out of its depth. They did their bit and (none too quickly) made way for Messrs. Sting, Copeland and Summers.

The Police were excellent. No, even more than that. They sped through a sequence of their recent stuff, starting with their biggest success to date; "Don't stand so close to me", with clean cut and sharp renditionings of "Man in a Suitcase" and "Fallout" following. "De Do Do Do De Da Da Da" turned their set into a singalong with around 5,000 voices helping out. "So Lonely" "Next to You" and "Message in a Bottle" were all done so perfectly you couldn't help but be impressed. (And can't Andy Summers jump high for such an old man!!!?) Great stuff!

82 hours later I was off again and again I was bound for the Midlands. This time it was for Elvis Costello's Christmas Party at the National Exhibition Centre in Birmingham.

At this gathering of six bands and around eleven thousand people, I came to two not terribly outstanding conclusions; Music produced by such bands as The Selecter and Madness, labelled two-tone, is basically dead, and hard plastic seats which slope forward just a couple of degrees from the horizontal are bloody uncomfortable.

Squeeze were first and they tried very hard to make their classy singles sound at least average. Fortunately, they just succeeded which pleased me at least. They left wishing everyone a Merry Christmas, and I thought "Doesn't Chris Difford look just like Paul Brylov!? (Please excuse the private joke.

Rockpile were totally mediocre. Dave Edmunds and Nick Lowe took turns at bashing out numbers from their equally disappointing album. The highlight up to now had been the surprise guest appearance of John Cooper Clarke who, as he himself pointed out, was to act as compere. This consisted of introducing each band and the odd J.C.C. poem.

Next, Madness, The Nutty Boys, engulfed the stage. Their contribution to the evenings proceedings was, as ever, a mixture of over-loud sax.phone, 430 words-to-the-minute lyrics and a general melee of flailing limbs. The rest of the audience loved the singles, and so, to an extent did I, but every song was so predictable. Although this music is fun, it is on it's way out. (Sadly? - I don't think so!). The Selecter underlined this for me. They never were big, and if their latest stuff is their best, they never will be.

Then just to add a bit of spice to the Christmas Pudding (which was just about to go cold), Elvis Costello came on before his scheduled slot on the bill. It was just as well, as this was like putting the brandy on the pudding and lighting it. His set, featuring tracks from his new album, was short, It was also extremely good, precise and well executed containing just enough old hits to make a fine and rather nice sounding balance.

UB40, "Wid di fake Jamaican accent man" boogied onto the stage and boogied off again with an advertisement for the better class of ska/reggae music in between. They had the style which separated them from the likes of Madness and the Selecter.

All in all it was a very good (if very late) night with plenty of Christmas cheer but not quite any Christmas crackers.

'81 and the Manchester Apollo played host to the Irish in the shape of the Boomtown Rats and The Atrix. The latter are another in a long line of Undertones pop bands to emerge from across the water.. and that, just about sums them up. They were good.

Bob Geldof, in a black jacket and beret rattled through "Mood Mambo" before the large backdrop was pulled back to reveal the rest of The Rats. Their new material from Mondo Bongo sounded "crazy man" as did The Tonic For the Troops numbers with "I don't Like Mondays" and "Keep it Up" being the only worthwhile numbers from the embarrasingly awful Fine Art of Surfacing. I thought they were excellent and very entertaining despite the Sounds/N.M.E. reviews.

17/1/81 - "The Magical Mystery Tour is Coming to Take you Away"! - To Buxton!! That was the location of the best kept secret this side of Iran. Echo and the Bunnymen's film "They Shine So Hard" seemed a good excuse to bewilder thousands yet enlighten only the lucky 400 pass-holders. It was a hell of a fuss but worth it all the same. They walked onto the stage, seemingly straight from their Chieftan tanks, and whilst cameras A B C and D were hurtling madly around the tiny Buxton Pavillion, McCulloch and the Bunnymen zipped through Crocodile and a few more besides. Their set was a superb reconstruction of the album with several extended effects. "Going Up", "Villiers Terrace" and "All that Jazz" were highlights of an event which I'm sure was meant to be a lot more but never-the-less was good fun.

So as I madly try to get this written in time, Merry Christmas and a Happy New Year - 'cos, I seemed to miss them both!! Goodnight.

— Andy Stevens

SINGLES MELT-DOWN →
- absolute & flawless verdicts given gratis by Steve Brown & Nick Toczek

THEATRE OF HATE-'Original Sin' c/w 'Legion' (SS Label: SS3). Heavy on bass & drums with rasping vocals that are loud & powerfully appealing. Very mixed feelings about the use of sax. Both songs have real drive + exciting build-up of intensity. Not pop; but highly creative music that's fresh without stepping beyond the standard boundaries of rock. **BLURT**-'My mother was a friend of an enemy of the people' c/w 'Get' (Test Pressing: TP1). Monotonous drum-&-bass rhythm + shouted vocals interspersed with alternately melodic/freeform sax. B-side has catchier dm/bass + jazzy sax which gives way to shouted vocals. Raw & minimal. One man's music is another man's noise. Ted Milton & Co. taking eccentricity as an end in itself. **ACROBATS OF DESIRE**-'Parking Boys' + 'In Control' c/w 'African Sailors' + 'Scrapin' Tapioca' (Desire Records: DES 001). York-based novelty acoustic rockers, using cello, violins, dbl. bass, assorted perc., kazoo, whistle, female vocals, etc. African music meets folk & popular classical. Reminiscent of Bonzo Dog at the height of their musical lunacy. Lightweight but cheerful choons that are mildly infectious. Had us both smiling. **DAYSHIFT**-'Living in The UK' c/w 'Cedric Wazza, Superstar' + 'Yeah Eh Oh Yeah Oh!' (Wot Records: WOT 1). A-side features washboard, kazoo, acoustic guitar & perc. with sing-along vocals on this topical busker's blues. Bright, cheering & catchy... but is The UK ready for a street-music revival? (& where are you now, Don Partridge?) First on B-side is 60s-ish Dylan-influenced rock with that ubiquitous sax. 2nd is a more off-beat creature with constantly changing melody & tempo that makes it unnecessarily unpleasant. **THE MEMBRANES**-'Fashionable Junkies c/w 'Almost China' (Vinyl Drip: VD 005). A 30p flexi-disc from the band who also produce the fanzine Blackpool Rox. Simple new wave that's already dated. The interesting vocals thankfully overshadow the tedious backdrop of keys & bass. Harmless & unremarkable. **ARTERY**-'Unbalanced' c/w 'The Slide + free live EP ('Perhaps', Turtle, 'Toytown' & 'Heinz'). (Aardvark Records: Steel 3). Long-awaited single from Sheffield combo. 1st track: with so much happening here, it's not surprising that some things (wailing harmonica & sax, in this case) spoil the overall effect, though perc. & kbds. are good. Flip side: for their best live number which features perc. + vocals only. The slow beat lacks impact on disc, but the song'll still stand out on The Peel Show. Live EP conveys their real appeal as a distinctive & commercial 80's rock band. Buy this live EP & get a free studio single with it. **MANDY MORTON**-'Ghost of Xmas Past' c/w 'Black Nights' (Polydor: 2052 187). Totally bland folk-rock that's good of its kind but 10-15 years too late to do anything that plummet on the pop/rock scene... & with the folk market in rapid decline, it's got to be a non-starter. B-side's got more bite but Pentangle, Steeleye Span & Renaissance are among the many who've already plundered this territory. **LOUDER ANIMAL GROUP**-'Six Magnificent Cathedrals' c/w 'Pip Pop' (Ears Pop Products: POP 701). Jangling guitars & chopped rhythms to the usual monotonous drumbeat that haunts experimental post-punk music. Bleak, but mildly innovative & more accessible than you might expect - especially B-side with its Clash-like vocals on the fade-out. **VIC GODDARD & SUBWAY SECT**-'Stop That Girl' c/w Instrumentally Scared + 'Vertical Integration' (Rough Trade: RT068). Early Beatles in style with pleasant but watered-down melody & clichéd love song vocals. Hard to believe that this is the same Goddard/Sect that pumped out raw punk in '77-'79. B-side opens with an undistinguished drum-laden instrumental. 2nd track has Goddard's voice + acoustic guitar (with band in deep background) borrowing a lot from early Who - & from 'My Generation' in particular. Goddard's living up to his threat to go back to the 60's. He does it well, but needs stronger & less plagiarised material. (Bernie Rhodes produced). **THE VINCENT UNITS**-'Carnival Song' c/w 'Everything Is Going to be all Wrong (Y Records; Y8). Two pieces of white reggae dominated by strident sax & trebly guitar. As the title suggests, the B-side goes weird at the end. Good music, but it lacks any distinguishing feature to single the band out from a million others. **ED SIBBS**-'I think I think too much' c/w 'Santa Claus has died' (Oval Records: Oval 1014). 1979 song that predates much of the synthed rock that we now get in regular doses from the likes of Orch. Man, Visage, Numan & even Ultravox. Here the guitar adds another vital dimension. Fine single that should be re-released. **DELTA 5**-'Mind Your Own Business' c/w 'Now That You're Gone' (Rough Trade: RT03); 'Anticipation' c/w 'You' (RT 041); 'Try' c/w 'Colour' (RT 061). 3 singles to date from this Leeds band- all 3 are excellent in their own way. The negative side is that the songs are uniformly ace-paced & deliberately restrained. On the plus side, though, are A1 female vocals over hypnotic guitar riff built round highly infectious one-line tune. On the latest, a double A-side, they sound similar to Girls At Our Best, who also hail from Leeds. **THE TEENAGE FILMSTARS**-'I Helped Patrick McGoohan Escape' c/w 'We're Not Sorry' (Fab Listening: FL1). Hands up all those who remember 'The Prisoner'... here are your lyrics. Hands up all those who remember early Beatles songs... your music. B-side's more original & a drums/vocals duel at the end is fun. As catchy as it's forgettable. **NOISE ANNOYS**-'Tomorrow' c/w **BATTERY BOYS**-'Cheapazeal Talent' (Adult Entertainments: ADD1) Side 1: good song / bad mix / out-of-tune overload bass & guitar. Side 2: same awful unexist, perhaps whole band is the same. Both are punk but guitar doesn't cut through - an all-important flaw.

No Room for HORRIBLE NURDS OR DONKEYS - sorry!!

JAZZ VIOLENCE FROM SHEFFIELD - SHOCK REVELATIONS
by Andy Darlington

Clock DVA has ten legs. It is lost behind a storm of strobes. From where I'm sitting at the 'F Club' in Leeds, backed up against the amp. stack, I get fragmented repetitive impressions of green luminous digitals set into the high technology backdrop; a mangrove-bearded saxist shredding bits of Coltrane into spacio-temporal dislocations; a guitarist with white pointed toe boots (which I envy), and two broken strings; and a vocalist with a Tommy Steele quiff and bagged uniform pants rasping what remains of a tormented cow across a violin. Now in silhouette, now in stark white leprous light. Clock DVA is doing "Brigade", a nuclear love song, which was their contribution to a compilation E.P. of Sheffield bands, "1980 - The First Fifteen Minutes". It's an industrial romance.

When the nukes start to fall / and the evening (of civilisation) is nigh, we will celebrate like this.

It's a strange night. Earlier Genesis P. Orridge (in military fatigues) supervises setting up Monte Cazazza equipment, synching the tapes, sound check reverb careening across packed heads and poking holes in the smoke. This is a two-piece fifteen minutes of concrete white noise. A girl who is probably Cosi Fanny Tutti, in leather sits engrossed in evoking discord from a guitar, and a guy with a synthesiser howls incomprehensible lyrics through voice distortion. It's cut-ups of sound like Boulez and Stockhausen used to construct in Paris Arts Labs in the late Fifties, the kind of thing aimed at elitist modern classical audiences and reviewed in Ultra-serious arts magazines. A little more agressive now perhaps, and here in Leeds kids are bouncing up and down like it's Blondie or something. Spontaneous reactions striking intuitively at unprepared brain centres.

Lights around the stage event horizon drill upwards. As it gets hotter and the air gets more congested the lights get buried beneath discarded leather jackets. Internal combustion results in columns of smoke drifting hazily accoss the snaking wires and control boxes. People stand around, watching like it's 'Special F-X', Queen's Dry-Ice or something. I'm watching, lager in hand, but at fifty pence a pint I'm not offering to extinguish the immunent conflagration. Sound grates on. From the back of the stage Genesis watches plumes of smoke gather and dissolve, gesticulating like a refugee from Martha Graham's Modern Dance, and Roadies slam to the front hurtling smouldering leather jackets (button-badges of Throbbing Gristle / Police / Toyah) at odd trajectories into the crowd. A strange sight.

Let's take a CRUISE to oblivion / this time we'll REALLY get high.

Shift of location. Now Clock DVA is playing dates in Rotterdam, 'Jazz Violence' with label mates Vice Versa. A venue that is a converted shipping refinery where previously Joy Division played and William Burroughs read excerpts from his next novel. Vice Versa has six legs. It is a three-piece post-Modernist Rock band, which means they don't use guitars and have no drummer. What they do have is sharp intelligent songs fused through punk-fueled adrenalin-rush and processed by a daunting armoury of electronic noise. They have an E.P., 'Music Four', on their own Neutron label which includes the soundtrack sequence called 'Riot Squad' / 'Camille'. A chillingly tactile threat cannibalising spoken inserts which fade into focus before being submerged in multi-layered incandescent electronics. Vice Versa spout the regulation New Austerity speil, their 'product', their 'advertisers perception of truth'. Yet behind such cutesy relentless modernity they have the intellectual intensity to give it content, make it more than just a this-year's-model stance. This is Rock with the appliance of science. They make all the correct cultural connections and write a mean Manifesto that arch-Futurist Marinetti would smile on. When you buy Neutron you buy a conceptual package deal. You buy the full coporate image, the whole shrink wrapped, date stamped philosophy. The music is not necessarily the product. It is a vehicle, the weapon-strike delivery system through which the product is targetted, channelled, and communicated.

"Modern as in Mary Quant" is an as yet unrecorded song, their paen to consumerism. "Mary makes the most of your trash aesthetic / Mary is the messiah of the trash aesthetic". It is contagious, it irradiates the stage with lethal hooklines. I hear it once and I can't get it out of my head.

In the corner of a pub before the gig, Mark White talks in fast humerous epithets. He is around twentyone, intends staying there, has freshly shorn dark hair he keeps irrigating obsessively with the fingers of boths hands. He disclaims my tentative analogies with other synthesiser bands. "All the cliches are there now. It's all become so stereotyped. You're either Gary Numan or the Human League."

So what about chart bands like Cure or Orchestral Manoeuvres?

"No. We work against that to produce a reaction. We do everything conceivable to discount this. Anti-feeling. In a way it's negative, but it produces a positive thing." Martin Fry speaks more carefully, calculating effect. On stage he will later lead a between-numbers "Omm" chant that will perplex the nouveau trendy; and kindle odd memories of the Fugs and Allen Ginsberg in those who (like me) have been around too long. The most recent edition to Vice Versa, his effect on the band's direction has been considerable. "I was always interested in synthesisers. It was such a stylistic revelation. We were into that kind of feeling. But we feel we have exhausted that form of sythesis".

White puncuates and emphasises within infectous animation, a constant infusion of main line energy that he will excercise on stage in a ritual auto-destruction of his jacket. Each balletically induced tear captured by the voyeuristic swoop of a video camera freezing the event for future scrutiny. I suggest that the rigidity of a drum machine works counter to improvisation, straightjackets spontaneity.

'Yes it does in a way', but it's good because the improvisation comes out vocally. We don't stick religiously to it because then your just static. We are developing towards **a kind of Funk Vision."**

Speed - reading their biographical - data print out / **Manifesto.** "Our methods involve seduction by cheap sexual fantasy, lies, appealing to the consumers greed and the implications of romantic blackness and modernity. The effect is of shrink-wrap beef burgers". Vice Versa come from Sheffield and their motives are 'situationist or subversive, moral and Dada". Stephen Singleton, insistant propogandist and sometime sax player is being interviewed by Radio Hallam. Stage front man and vocalist White sits on the edge of his chair, leaning forward to establish conversational territory. Percussionist and synth player Fry slouches back in the well worn leather upholstery, a slurr of blonde hair infiltrating his forehead, voice sometimes dropping beneath the level of background pub inanities.

From them I piece together geneologies. The band coalescing around '77, drawing inspiration from punk, but resisting the cliché of falling into the three - chord thrash, channeling it rather, into more unorthodox forms. I list other possible influences for reaction.

Bowie? "He's offered a lot of blueprints".

Pistols? "There wouldn't be a massive underground now if it wasn't for the Pistols, the climate wouldn't have existed where a whole underground could spring up." A calculated pause. "Alright, it's gone a bit sour but a lot of things have come up which wouldn't have

happened otherwise, which EMI would not have supported, which CBS would have let die."

Dada? "The thing about Dada is that, whether they call it Dada or not, it's a permanent force, a perpetual revolution. It's a substitute word for punk I suppose. The original Cabaret Voltaire connection. Hugo Ball. Tristan Tzara."

Chic, Moroeder? "Disco is an excellent vehicle."

Acid Punk? "The Standells. Thirteenth Floor Elevators. 'I had too much to dream last night'. I bought Lenny Kaye's "Nuggetts" Album' cos I was desperate to get hold of first statements."

Early experiments dispensed with the bulky human drummer in favour of rhythm generator and they took improvisation into the realm of formless aural mosaic. This direction was curtailed as an incestuous self indulgence. Masturbation limited in appeal to both listener and musician. The further disposal of guitars in favour of synthesisers and a variety of prepared tape segments was seen as a miniaturisation policy in preparation for becoming the first attaché case computer band.

Martin Fry originally came round to interview the band for his "Modern drugs" fanzine and he never left.

So there's still a chance for me?

"We're sizing you up."

Fry redirects conversation to Neutrons current preoccupations." What interests us is the speed of operation. Shelf - life for everything. Everything is marked 'Sell by.' Records should have a sticker on, 'This will be out of fashion in three and a half minutes'

White concurs. "On the way things are burning themselves up. We did a song, "Artists at War", exposing the cyclical fashions. Mods coming back, you didn't think it had gone away, but it's back. Gradually speeded up. A snowball effect. You can't even see them they're going so fast. Now you get one-hit Disco wonders which is a true Warhol fifteen minutes.

Fry admits to 'walking in a dead man's shoes' through his first months with Vice Versa. They toured with Cowboys International, treading the line between energy and experimentation, meeting and subducing/deflecting skinhead opposition at the Middlesborough Rock Gardens. They recorded "Genetic Warfare" for the "1980 - The First Fifteen Minutes" compilation. Organisation of the records was along democratic lines, each of four local bands allotted four minutes vinyl time and thirty-six square inches of art area in the six sided fold-out sleeve. Netron pressed it up in successive batches of 1,000. It was voted 'Best Package of the Week' by "Melody Maker", and scored heavily on various alternative charts. Vice Versa supported the best at Sheffield's Top Rank; played a series of half hour sets in the local Virgin shop interspersed with customer-relations chat; and played the Leeds Futurama Festival.

But now it is 1980 - the next fifteen minutes.

"The next thirty minutes" asserts Fry.

The material that has become manifest since Fry joined provides evidence of a remarkable evolution. Two numbers in particular stand out, "Mary Quant", and "Jazz Drugs, Jazz Violence", the latter available in cassette form on their Neutron C60 "Eight Aspects of April '80".

"On the earlier recorded material the lyrics were mine" offers Mark White. "Since then they've been a combination of the band. We did "Body Scuplture", "Jazz Drugs", and it was quite different. The sound is much denser. More dark, less erratic. We've pooled together more on these song".
Will this product be placed on vinyl?

"At the moment we're a bit disillusioned with the independant market. It's just saturated with rubbish. We appreciate the punk ethic, do what you want, anybody can do it. But it's got no commitment. It's manifesting itself in Rough Trade's attitude. They are becoming more and more selective. With the independants you're reaching a certain market. A certain ideology. We don't want that, we want populism. You've probably heard this line before from bands. It's a dangerous line between populism and crass commercialism You tend to sacrifice one for the other".

Shift of location. After the Continental tour they play home turf. At Sheffield City Hall Vice Versa ride that dangerous line, and acquit themselves magnificently. And Clock DVA is a nihilistic Captain Beefheart with a black, black light show of repetitive verticals and pure monochrome Bridget Riley grids. A full frontal pandamonium shadow show with the deranged vocalist and the mangrove-bearded saxist as components in a tightly controlled visual / audial spectacle. A full relief cerebral massage. They figure in all the right mythologies. Vocalist and tape-coaxer Adi Newton was involved with two founder members of the non-human league in an enterprise called the Future. Their contribution to the North-Eastern "Hicks from the Sticks" compilation L.P. "You're without Sound", was produced by Cabaret Voltaire at their Sheffield Western Works studios.

Adi compounds the bands mystique, contending that "your dislike is our wanted reaction". With "events too perverse to perform openly, too decadent for Sheffield by far".

Clock DVA-tions? "From the very beginning our aim was to provoke, to gain adverse response, to create the perfect, pornographic, electronic violence. A wall sound that sweeps". It is a devastating multipurpose concept that they are capable of translating into an all-encompassing sensory event, encapsulating on vinyl, or placing on film. Their movie, "Genitals and Genosis", features 'pornographic surrealism'. It splices film of the Myra Hindly and Ian Brady trial with domestic scenes of Genesis P. Orridge at home.

In performance the voice is treated as just another instrument, a device for producing sound and atmosphere rather than a conveyance for lyrics. It is melded well down into the aural wash and is distorted into incomprehensibility. Even the two poems read at the City Hall, with their cold-war allusions, are treated as a sound (rather than a literal) exercise. An 'aural wallpaper' using unconventional music on conventional instruments, form and formless".

It is the demarcation line between the two bands. For Vice Versa there is no such deliberate obscurantism. Their lyrics are well-structured, and their importance to the band is not to be underestimated.

To misquote Chuck Berry, I looked at Clock DVA, it was three-quarters-way past 1980, and THIS is the next fifteen minutes! Next year when Vice Versa are scoring sharp perceptive Top Thirty hits (like"Jazz Drugs" and"Modern as in Mary Quant"), and Clock DVA are making ponderous hypnotically intense chart albums (like their "Clock DVA-tions" cassette), I will remember this fistful of nights.

FURTHER INFORMATION AND ART WORK ABOUT 'NEUTRON RECORDS', VICE VERSA, and CLOCK DVA CAN BE OBTAINED FROM :-

Stephen Singleton,
44, Bowood Road,
Sheffield.
S11 8YG
Telephone Sheffield (0742) 665605

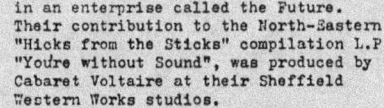

VICE VERSA
Line-up
Mark White - synthesizer
Stephen Singleton - rhythm generator
Martin Fry - synthesizer

DISCOGRAFIA
'Music Four' E.P.
(include 'New girls', 'Neutrons', 'Science Fact', 'Riot', 'Squad', 'Camille' Neutron 791
'Genetic warfare'
(da '1980: the first 15 minutes' E.P. Neutron)
'8 Aspects of Vice Versa' (cassette)
(include: Democratic dancebeat', 'Stylarg', 'Eyes of Christ', 'Body sculpture', 'Trapped', 'Artists of war' e 'Idol' cassette celluloid, 'Artists of war' e 'Idol' cassette aprile 1980 . Neutron.

CLOCK DVA
Line-up
Charlie Collins - sassofoni, clarinetto
Steve Jameson - basso, tapes
Adi Newton - voce, violino, tapes
Roger Quayle - batteria
David Tyme - chitarra

DISCOGRAFIA
'Brigade'
(da '1980: the first 15 minutes' E.P. Neutron)
'You're without sound'
(da 'Hicks from the sticks' L.P.)
Brigade'/'Blue tone'
(45 giri/1980 - Neutron)
'White Souls In Suits (cassette Industrial Records
'Them Fingrs (cassette Neutron)

DURY

The 3-piece on-stage at St. George's are Blurt. Drums and guitar set up regular discoid rhythms (detractors would call them blandly repetitive) over which Ted Milton crazes with his sometimes orthodox/most times freeform/sometimes anarcho-anti-musical sax playing; this interspersed with hoarsely screamed poetry that he chants into the shape of vocals. Aurally, it's a blend of innovation and masochism-for-the-masses. As theatre, it's fun. As unleashed eccentricity, it's delicious.

Basement 5 are 3 black guys and one white drummer. Kris Needs of Zigzag rockmag manages, so I expected more than silly outfits and punkish reggae/reggaeish punk. The only 'more' that I got was more and more bored. A big disappointment.

Dury & Blockheads - were a pre-Xmas treat. About half of "New Boots" plus a whole bunch off the new album. The band are as tight and exciting as they are ugly and OLD. Drury's clever and often X-cert lyrics plus his showman persona turn him into an F-1 hybrid of Max Miller and Gene Vincent. The unforgettable subtlety of the opening line of 'Plaistow Patricia' ("Arseholes, bastards, fucking cunts and pricks..."); the despair of "Manic Depression", the compassion of "Sweet Gene Vincent" and the cheeky humour of "Clever Trevor" and "Billericay Dicky" - all lay bare Drury's vulnerably mercurial personality. A cynic might step back and ask who (audience or performer) was patronising whom. Me, I couldn't care less. Drury is an extraordinary performer who blends the traditions of rock'n'roll and music hall to produce an unparalleled species of entertainment. Coupled with one of the best rock bands in the country, he's his own hero.

— Nick Toczek.

VENEWS...

AMNESIA is a new Leeds venue that's next door to the station. Certainly novel in decor & design, offering 70's U.S. superhero murals, small video displays on the walls, lamppost lighting, split-level drinking arena & a stage perched half-way up the wall & way above the heads of the punters. From this lofty position, D.J. & (several nights a week) bands pump out a wide spectrum of music that covers all but H.M. & punk. Ian Dewhurst (D.J. & live bands organiser):- "H.M. we leave to Fforde Grene & punk to the Fan Club." Bands may not like the weird effect of being levitated out of reach of the punters & (at the moment) all gear has to be humped up a metal ladder that awkwardly placed behind the bar. The other side of the coin is that it's good to play a new and fairly well attended (central, cheap in, pub price beers) venue + they are paying all the bands + the publicity's excellent with a lot of plugging (press, posters, leaflets) for featured bands.

TIFFANY'S (who put the 'FAN' in...) is being launched (again this is in Leeds) as a regular large venue featuring major bands. The man at the wheel this time (as often before) is the Fan Club/Futurama magician, John Keenan. Bad Manners + The Boys (15th Feb) & Judge Dread (22nd) are the first of a string of dates that he's lining up.

With THE ODEON in The Merrion Centre rumoured to be on the verge of opening to bands, it looks like Leeds is at last getting the number of venues that its size merits.

FORGE INN (York Rd, Tadcaster) has changed management since advertising in issue 10. They're not currently putting on live rock & have cancelled all bands booked by previous manager. SCAMPS in Bradford has closed down. PALM COVE's future looks a bit uncertain if their late licence doesn't come through soon. GATSBY's has a heavy rock disco once a week & may even put on bands if the disco takes off & pulls a good crowd of headbangers & guitar fantasists. And finally, still with Bradford, Tiffany's on Manningham Lane is trying out hard-core punk - weird place for it, but they've big name bands (Upstarts/Infa-Riot/etc).

— Nick T.

MUSIC BAR
CITY SQ., LEEDS 1.
LEEDS: 34945

MON. TO SUN. : 5.30 P.M. — 10.30 P.M.

DO YOU LIKE?

DAVID BOWIE ● BRUCE SPRINGSTEEN ● ULTRAVOX ● U.B.40 ● THE HUMAN LEAGUE
ADAM AND THE ANTS ● FUNK ● JOY DIVISION ● SPANDAU BALLET ● STEELY DAN
ORCHESTRAL MANOEUVRES ● B 52's ● ELVIS COSTELLO ● PETER GABRIEL ● VISAGE
JOHN FOXX ● THE PRETENDERS ● REGGAE ● DEVO ● AND *ALTERNATIVE* MUSIC

IF YOU DO, LOOK NO FURTHER —
MUSIC EVERY NIGHT PLUS :

LIVE ACTS 3/4 NIGHTS WEEKLY - WATCH POSTERS AND PRESS & LISTEN
TO LOCAL RADIO FOR DETAILS EACH WEEK.

"AMNESIA - AN ALTERNATIVE TO THE ORDINARY!"

THE CHEATERS at Foggy's, Halifax

"Foggy's" (21, Silver Street, Halifax - off George's Square) began putting on bands just before Christmas and so far is a success. The Wednesday night gigs have proved a success. The aim is to provide a wide range of music, from Reggae to Heavy Metal. The mood on Wednesday night was good, and Manager, Kevin Quill, stated that up to press there had been no hassles. Bands that have played there (e.g. Rough Justice, Private Dicks, Ramma Jamma) rate it as a venue. A door at the back of the stage provides easy access for gear and the size and shape of the room makes it easy to establish rapport with the audience. Decor is tasteful (if baths, loos and coffins suspended from the ceiling appeal to you). All in all, this Christmas pressie is just what Halifax needed. (contact Kevin on Halifax 53668).

Now for the band. Well, "Keep music live" read the stickers and if more bands were up to the standard of Manchester's "The Cheaters" there'd be no problem. On Wednesday night at "Foggy's" we were witness to a bunch of guys laying out music that defied the punters not to dance. Their brand of rhythm and blues is exciting, powerful, tight, energetic and one hell of a lot of fun. The freshness of the performance was impressive, considering they've played over 300 gigs in two years (from John o' Groats to Penzance.) But that experience obviously accounts for their professional edge. From the start of the set to the encore the band exuded an energy that was contagious. Vocalist Mick bounding around the stage (and off) like a maniacal Zebedee cajoled the audience into movement. John and Stuart on bass and drums respectively provided a solid driving beat while the guitar breaks from Neil were everything you'd demand from rhythm and blues - no self indulgent over long solos. Mick's voice had that slightly gritty quality that gave force to the lyrics and his excellent harmonica playing had shades of "War" (not another little Walter clone). Older elements in the audience muttered the volume was too loud but it sounded just fine to us, and the mix was well balanced by the sound engineer Yvonne Ellis.

From a consistently good set of songs its hard to pick faves, but memorable for us were the two from their first single (Ind. Label Pre-Fab) "I Wanna be a Policeman" and "From the Hip" (a cheeky little number); also "On the Under:round", "Gonna get myself a Car" (nifty lyrics here) and from their latest single "Nothing ever Happens on a Saturday" (EMI Parlophone). The Cheaters are currently signed to EMI and have material ready for an album, whenever that mega-company deigns to let them record it (two target dates have already been and gone without the vinyl being blemished by even so much as a count in). But on the plus side they've been advanced enough cash to buy a good van and the best sound equipment available. They feel this was a wise investment as it frees them from the hassle of hiring, and ensures them a good live sound and makes for reliability in getting to gigs. So, 'nuff said. Give yourself a treat, go see them (they should be back in West Yorkshire around March.) For bookings contact: Manager Pete Hawkins - 01-240-1605, or band members at 061 - 2263439 - Flat 4,7 or 11.

Ann and Anne.

THE WAREHOUSE
19-21 SOMERS ST.   LEEDS 1.   tel. 468287.

- Su. 1st - Best Friends (lunch)
- Mo. 2nd - DEPECHE MODE
- Tu. 3rd - MO-DETTES + support
- Su. 8th - Best Friends (lunch)
- Mo. 9th - Naked Lunch + Blancmange
- Tu. 10th - MOONDOGS
- We. 11th - SPLIT RIVITS + Lucky Strike
- Th. 12th - DARTS
- Su. 15th - Whamm [formerly 7-Year Itch] (lunch)
- Mo. 16th - MONOCHROME SET + Fast Set
- Tu. 17th - JOHN COGAR
- We. 18th - SWITCH (3piece white reggae)
- Th. 19th - Baracudas
- Su. 22nd - Best Friends (lunch)
- Mo. 23rd - Illustration
- Tu. 24th - LUU Music Soc (ring for details)
- We. 25th - Roy Wood's Helicopters
- Th. 26th - FATAL CHARM

FORTHCOMING: 4th March - Wilko Johnson's Solid Senders.

PRINT-STINT First issue of SHINEY CALIPERS (ed. Hitch, 128 Otley Rd., Guiseley, W.Yorks) covers Jan/Feb '81. Reviews, interviews, photos, graphics, features on bands local and national, fox hunting & CND. Small format, 24pp for 30p. It's a good & readable mag. Layout's fine too.// Issue 17 of NMX (New Musical Excess) is Sheffield's long-standing fanzine. This is the October '80 issue (latest that I've seen – have been told Martin Russian (ed) is now in U.S of A). Features 'I'm So Hollow', 'Fatales' & 'Brian Brain' + reviews, info, photos. Cheap production makes it on the expensive side at 35p esp. as large typeface make for a brief read. Disappointing, considering its reputation.// Good issue of BEATEN TO THE PUNCH. Why no address for this mag (or NMX)? From York, by Geoff Holden, Nov '80 issue, 10pp for 20p. Well printed with good photos. 'Piranhas interview, York bands family tree, 'Looze Covers', 'Ansell Collins', local bands and reviews, etc. Good readable 'zine.// Andy Darlinton's being producing the excellent LUDD'S MILL for a while now (previously was done by Steve Sneyd). Issue 16/17 has 44 large pages crammed with poetry, graphics, stories, articles, etc. Cooper Clarke, Devo, ex-hippie Tuli Kupferberg. Features on Kerouac and Burroughs-influenced writing. Extensive disc/tape/mag. reviews. Lotsa sci-fi. Try it from 44 Spa Croft Rd, Teall St, Ossett, W. Yorks. WF5 0HE.// Issue 8 of one of the country's best-selling & best fanzines - VAGUE. 28pp piled high with good reading for a mere 30p. - Ants/Bunnymen/Bauhaus/Futurama II/Tribalism/Skids/Specials/local bands & news/fanzine round-up/feature on WCR (!!)/ much, much else. Send for it from Tom, Vague Mansions, 45 Walpole Rd., Boscombe, Bournemouth, BH1 4HB. On-the-road-with-the-Ants-entourage feature is a good piece.// Another mag that's impressed me is No.17 of Coventry's ALTERNATIVE SOUNDS. Sadly, it's the final issue for a while – but worth all thirty of the pence it'll rush you. God's Toys/Fall/Wild Boys/Abstracts/fanzine feature/Civil Servants/cassettes/info/The Silence. All & more from Martin, 143 Moat Ave, Coventry, CV3 6BW.// Also out of Coventry is DED YAMPY (ded = dead, as in dead good, etc.; yampy = crazy/a good laugh). It's all about beer drinking + some lunacy & a Jerry Dammers interview. It lives up to its name! Cartoons/photo collages/nonsense. A laugh indeed. 20p from Pete Polanyk, 12 Welgarth Ave., Coundon, Coventry. This is the 1st issue.
AUTOPSIA- 'an art or antiart/gang' are an anti-social, anti-commercialism, anti-state Yugoslav group who sent me a printed package (mags/sheets/posters/leaflets/stickers/photos) that visually and verbally exciting/violent/political – opposed mainly to state control of freedom of expression. Mostly in English, it's good hard commitment. Creative and powerful. From:- Rade Milinković, Iriska 42, 22400 Ruma, Yugoslavia. He's promised me a demo of his group. Send him a package of your own or your local art/rock output & ask him for his package. You'll like it. I'll feature some in next WCR.

AH-HA! Well, you see, Huddersfield Poly. pulled out their advert at the last minute giving me all this EXTRA SPACE to fill. On the cover it says SIOUX from Ilkley – but, having changed their name to MYSTERONS two months ago, they only told me today – so I've had to drop their feature. If they hold that name for another month, then they'll be in next issue. I think I'll review a couple more albums here.... how about picking 2 that I've been sent that are totally contrasting? THE MEKONS (Leeds band) on Red Rhino (York label) have long been a passion of mine & this album's no disappointment. They've come via Fast Records (excellent Edinburgh label that also 'discovered' The Scars', 'Human League', 'Gang of Four', etc.) and Virgin Records (for whom this album was originally cut but never released). Always uncompromising, they are a blend of raw amateurism, pioneering innovation and risky experimenting - a combination that, in their case, succeeds almost every time. Imagine a low-budget Talking Heads doing it without Eno and you've got them. If you like pop music then skip this album, but if you're keen to catch a band who're doing something positive in the bland eighties then this one's yours. Production's O.K., but not great. The raw edge gives a good view of what they're trying to do. Based around drums/bass/keyboards/vocals, they use only the bare essentials for each song (violin, saxes, guitars added when needed). There are no obvious influences - just a band producing new music out of themselves. The lyrics are always interesting and the whole thing's refreshingly unpredictable. The second album's been out for a while but is well worth chasing up. HONKY TONK DEMOS is on Charlie Gillett's Oval label. It's a collection of demos 'sent to him (1975-78) for his Honky Tonk programme on Radio London. All the bands here are trying hard-as-hell to be commercially pop/rock. Pre-fame, then, you get Dire Straits (early version of 'Sultans of Swing'), Darts, Chas + Dave, Charlie Dore (country rock), Graham Parker (minus Rumour - a semi-acoustic number), the polished excellence of Live Wire, Geraint Watkins (who's played in numerous semi-successful outfits) and a bunch of others. Good sleeve notes (there are none on the Mekons album). The whole album's a great mixture of look-where-they've-got-to-since and how-come-they-never-made-it-big... why didn't ABC's 'Rhythm on the Radio' or Night Shift's 'Dance in the Moonlight' become hits? A great party album and an interesting one to play to friends - "Guess who this is"

Finally, a mention for Tom Robinson's 'Sector 27' (well, he gave Ulterior Motives' single a good review in NME !!). The band's first album is out on Fontana and includes their current single 'Total Recall'. It's a fine album. I got sent it a few weeks ago and it's been in the shops since then. He's moved on since the mixed output of TRB (weak 2nd album in TRB2) & this is a fine band/good debut album.

LEEDS UNIVERSITY'S
UNION RECORDS
→ SPRING SALE NOW ON

1,000's of bargains from 50p + numerous 1980 releases at half price !!!

Stranglers tickets on sale from Mon. 2nd Feb.

We now sell tickets for all Leeds University & Leeds Polytechnic concerts & for Leeds Playhouse & The Grand Theatre, Leeds.

Shop phone: 444972

SHOP IN BASEMENT OF UNION BUILDING   OPEN: MON-FRI   9.30a.m.-5.00p.m.

CHEVY
PRINCEVILLE, Bradford.

Chevy played americanised hard rock with precise four part harmonies and a water tight, note perfect sound. Supported by a mix of rare depth and clarity, they immediately struck as a very professional band indeed, comprising five extremely accomplished and versatile musicians.

Fronted by vocalist Martin Cure, who, despite suffering from a dodgy throat condition, still sang with great power and feeling, bringing Rogers, Coverdale and Springsteen to mind, Chevy opened in fine style with their name-sake gaining audience respect and participation from the start.

Every song had a memorable hook line, though not exactly lacking their quota of standard rock cliches as the titles "Rock City", "Rock On", and "Shine On" suggest. Chevy tend to stick to a particular formula when writing songs cramming as many ideas and intricacies as possible into each number, which, in my opinion, their only real problem lies. Despite their outstanding high musical standards, Chevy sometimes lack the essential gripping excitement as their delivery becomes cold and clinical. Their tightness is almost like a barrier making them distant, deliberative and slightly tedious. However, over the last half of the set this problem was completely overcome and the finale of "Johnny B Goode" could not have contrasted more. Even the audience were invited on stage.

Chevy produced a strong set, free of self indulgence which they save for the epic "Rock On" when numerous magnesium flares were introduced to enliven a, by now, riotous show.

Having recently supported Alvin Lee of Ten Years After fame, on his British tour, Chevy are currently promoting their debut album "The Taker", the title track of which was particularly prominent in the live set.

Chevy are bound for better things, an observation they themselves believe as their song "Chevy" states ; "Come on Chevy we can make it, Come on Chevy we can make it". They will and they can.

Steve Brown.

ADVERTISING

NERVE CENTRE require good tight rock drummer for gigs and studio work. Ring Garry on Leeds 620238 or the other Garry on York 797999.

25 C.W.T. VAN HIRE. Bands, gear, light removals. Cheap rates. Ring Dennis on Cleckheaton 878626.

Echo unit for sale (with footswitch and leads). Ring Nick on Bradford 21867. (£45 o.n.o.)

Belated Happy Birthday to Simon
Tony says 'hello' to everyone in the Ferrets
Looby - you can't go to Paris with a five-man tent and three suitcases - love Ian

...of course, he's not a patch on his dad... he were a proper gaffer... never passed an employee without spitting or striking him...

LIVE MUSIC
at The Queen's Hall
LIVE BLACK MUSIC Every Friday Night.

AND THE VAULTS BAR
Heavy Rock + New Wave and Jazz Bands every : SUN. MON. WED.

Bradford College Students' Union
Queens Hall
Morley Street
Bradford BD7 1BW
Tel: (0274) 392712/3/4

..."KEN'S PAGE" INCLUDING THE ROCKWORD AND REVIEW OF GIG AT BINGLEY ARTS CENTRE 3/1/81...

New Year's Resolution — to make all the clues even more obscure? Ken Turner. (or in other words - Wool City Rockword No 10)

Partial grid fill-in: **TO BAR OW**

Clues Across.

1. Don't step on them! (4,5,5)
8. Found each side of ape as on the collar. (5)
9. Grins with three orientals makes power consumers. (8)
11. Ran about in wing at the red light! (7)
12. Foes music papers? (7)
13. Has the endings - hurry! (5)
15. Sting into what you'd do with a stool? (7,2)
17. Gosh! Teens make what you can 14-to! (4-5)
20. Blow a party drink. (5)
21. What's lost is lost. (7)
23. Cast lie in confusion. It comes back! (7)
25. Toss beer about to the least affected? (8)
27. Audiences moved — or the reverse. (8,6)

Clues Down.

1. Undersea Steeleye Span album, perhaps. (5,3,4)
2. Above the top. (5)
3. Idiocy. (9)
4. Oriental joined to come out. (7)
5. Always relax a mountain. (7)
6. Whisky drunk in Holland? (5)
7. What to do when not having a night out? (7,2)
10. Possibly shown in the Tarot? (2,2,3,5)
14. What to do with Max! (4,5)
16. Bust, broken and mended? (2,7)
18. Part of Keighley band. (7)
19. Tear Ted brushed away for changed result. (7)
22. Tear Les initially brushed away — more aware. (5)

Solution to Rockword No 9:
CHRISTMASDAY / CHEERUP / SOUNDED / LINETHECOFFERS / PARTY / BRANDYSIR / APPLE / ICE / STRIP / THESPIS / THEMAGI / REELOFF / REUNION / STEELTESTSET

(Hope you all had a good Christmas and New Year!)

Angry Young Men In Bingley. And I Get Vexed!

A totally strange gathering in the Arts Centre for CND in which the first to appear was Gaius. Sat in his armchair, with a standard lamp his only illumination, he looked incongruous, but with tales of machines and men, brains, sci-fi, and realism, brought to the ears by a caustic solution he was possibly the most vehement creature of the evening. Funny how tame he looked — and with his equipment against him, he worked better than most. Then Faculty and The Shamanists were sax + percussion + flute + guitar = rubbish. Too disturbing to be nice — but definitely dangerous. It was sonic theatre and troubled minds at work. How creative? How noisy. How lost.

Seething Wells is a nervous, fast, but local poet, supported by pissheads à la audience. With tributes to Bikermen, Cadillacs in Bradford and Teddy Boys (who when all's said and done are named after loveable bears) ripped to shreds in nasty but poignant prose, he was hasty, and amateurish — and impressive! Jon followed by disco — mainly good reggae — then Eaten Alive By Insects. Not so much a fate, more an adventure. They were memorable only for the setting — except that scandal was rife — Margaret is madly in love with Looby, the bassist — and the voluminous slide backing did the band a favour. As one bloke in the audience put it — "they're bloody wierd! But I'm watching. I must be mad!" Enough said. Bob Cryer (M.P.) added the genuine touch to the proceedings with tales of nuclear holocausts and accompanying noises from Vex's synthesiser!! Then Gaius and Seething Wells again, tossing the ball into each others' court and both hitting the net. But only just! Good poems, and well liked. And now VEX. Jon, Rick, Dave and Andy gave of their best with a heartfelt performance. And not wishing to sound sycophantic — they were absolutely great! They deserved the good reception though they got. I confess, it's the first time I'd seen them, and I'd been told that VEX were crap. Well I don't agree with that at all. I really enjoyed their set, and when they played the encore, "Switch me on" I got the impression that most folks in the audience were wondering why Saturday night couldn't be extended by a few hours into Sunday. In short, I think we could have lived through the whole thing once again quite happily. And thankfully CND are arranging more gigs. Jolly Dee!! Kay

A NEW 8-TRACK STUDIO

WOODLANDS

RECORDING STUDIO

£50 per 10-hour day

Garden St, Normanton, West Yorks
Phone Neil on Altofts (0924-81) 293

A NEW 8-TRACK STUDIO

OK

ROCK 'n' ROLL RARITIES
PUNK and NEW WAVE
HEAVY and PROGRESSIVE
GOLDEN OLDIES
IMPORTS and COLLECTORS' ITEMS
BLUES, POP, REGGAE etc.

COLLECTIONS BOUGHT
PART EXCHANGE

GEROL'S RECORDS

AIRVIEW STUDIOS

WILLERBY — HULL

INCREASING THEIR RECORDING FACILITIES FROM 8 TRACK TO:—

24 TRACK

OPENING RATE WILL BE £12.50 PER HOUR

FULL DETAILS OF ALL OUR FACILITIES CONTACT:
(HULL) 0482-653116

Yorkshire gig guide for February 1981

SU 1
Top Rank, Sheffield = THE BLUES BAND. Royal Park, Leeds = 156
Groucho's, Hull = LONDON BOYS. Haddon Hall, Leeds = HERESY.
Fforde Green, Leeds = MONEY.
Warehouse, Leeds = BEST FRIENDS (L).
Princeville, Bradford = MASK (L)
Vaults Bar, Bradford = VEX.
Blackamore Head, Pontefract = STREETFIGHTER.
Staging Post, Leeds = BREAKER.
White Lion, Huddersfield = SIMON LE GEYT ALL-STARS (L) // MIDDLE 8 (E)

MO 2
Theatre Club, Wakefield = GEORGE HAMILTON IV.
Warehouse, Leeds = DEPECHE MODE.
White Lion, Huddersfield = Yamaha Jazz Concert.
Funhouse Bar, Keighley = CHRONIC + LIVING DEAD.
Vaults Bar, Bradford = HEADHUNTER.
Marquis of Granby, Leeds = RHABSTALLION.
Fforde Grene, Leeds = JOHNNY & THE ROCCOS.
Royal Park, Leeds = ART, BART & FARGO.
Haddon Hall, Leeds = EIGA.

TU 3
Warehouse, Leeds = MO-DETTES.
University, Hull = BAD MANNERS.
Fleece, Lindley, Huddersfield = PHONETIC SCHEME.
Amnesia, Leeds = SHAKE APPEAL.
Marquis of Granby, Leeds = NERVE CENTRE.
Kings Head, Keighley = RHINO.
Limit Club, Sheffield = DEPECHE MODE

WE 4
White Lion, Huddersfield = CATCH.
Foggy's, Halifax = HERESY.
University, Bradford = THE BLUES BAND.
University, York = LINDISFARNE.
Amnesia, Leeds = TWISTED NERVE.
Marquis of Granby, Leeds = SICK BENEFIT + LITTLE BROTHER + BIG IF & THE QUESTIONAIRES.
Royal Park, Leeds = NEW OPERA.

TH 5
Fan Club, Leeds = PASSIONS + REALLY!
Wellington Club, Hull = THE CRACK.
Royal Park, Leeds = HERESY.
Amnesia, Leeds = DALE HARGREAVES' FLAMINGOS.
Penguin Club, Sheffield = CONFESSOR
Royal Park, Leeds = HERESY.
Haddon Hall, Leeds = REMEMBER THIS.

FR 6
University, Leeds = BODICEAN + STILETTO + DALE HARGREAVES' FLAMINGOS
Penthouse, Scarborough = MORE.
Princeville, Bradford = DEDRINGER.
Royal Park, Leeds = WHITE EAGLES.
Polytechnic, Sheffield = DR. FEELGOOD.
University, York = NO SWASTIKAS.

SA 7
Bircotts Leisure Centre, Doncaster = DEDRINGER.
Thirsk & Sowerby Institute, Thirsk = ROCKABILLY REBS.
White Lion, Huddersfield = LEGAL AID (ex-Gordon Giltrap).
Endyke, Hull = RED EYE.
Royal Park, Leeds = TALISMAN.
University, Sheffield = GORDON GILTRAP.
Haddon Hall, Leeds = DODGY TACTICS.

SU 8
Opera House, Leeds = LINDISFARNE. Royal Park, Leeds = 156.
Unity Hall, Wakefield = MATCHBOX. Haddon Hall, Leeds = KNIFE EDGE.
Warehouse, Leeds = BEST FRIENDS (L).
Groucho's, Hull = DEDRINGER.
Princeville, Bradford = TAROT (L).
White Lion, Huddersfield = SUPERSTITION (L) // WAMM (E).
Vaults Bar, Bradford = BABY TUCKOO.
Blackamore Head, Pontefract = STILL EARTH
Staging Post, Leeds = ROUGH JUSTICE.

MO 9
Speakeasy, Wakefield = RHABSTALLION. Haddon Hall, Leeds = MUNROES.
Warehouse, Leeds = NAKED LUNCH + BLANCMANGE.
Vaults Bar, Bradford = Poetry in Motion (local poets).
Funhouse, Keighley = MYSTERIOUS FOOTSTEPS + supp.
Amnesia, Leeds = SECOND THOUGHTS.
Marquis of Granby, Leeds = ENNAUS.
Penguin Club, Sheffield = CRAFTY AVENUE.
Royal Park, Leeds = THE MESS.

TU 10
Civic Hall, Halifax = SUPREMES.
Marquis of Granby, Leeds = NOSFERATU V.
Kings Head, Keighley = THE SHAKES.
Warehouse, Leeds = MOONDOGS.
Amnesia, Leeds = THE NOISE.
Limit Club, Sheffield = NAKED LUNCH + BLANCMANGE.

WE 11
Royal Park, Leeds = NOSFERATU V. Marquis of Granby, Leeds = AUTOMATIC TOYS.
Speakeasy, Wakefield = RHABSTALLION.
Warehouse, Leeds = SPLIT RIVITT + LUCKY STRIKE.
University, Bradford = ANY TROUBLE. University, Leeds = HERESY.
White Lion, Huddersfield = TOM & THE QUADS.
Foggy's, Halifax = WANDA & THE DENTISTS.
Queens Hall, Bradford = MYSTERIOUS FOOTSTEPS + REFLEX.
Polytechnic, Sheffield = LINDISFARNE.
Amnesia, Leeds = NEW KING SNAKE. Royal Park, Leeds = (T.B.A)

TH 12
Princeville, Bradford = DIAMOND HEAD.
Polytechnic, Leeds = HARRY CHAPIN.
Warehouse, Leeds = DARTS.
Wellington Club, Hull = NO SWASTIKAS + SONS OF THE POPE.
Fan Club, Leeds = THE SOUND + HOBBIES OF TODAY.
Penguin Club, Sheffield = ALIX.
Royal Park, Leeds = GIMMICKS.
Haddon Hall, Leeds = ROUGH JUSTICE.

FR 13
University, York = HARRY CHAPIN.
Polytechnic, Sheffield = THOMPSON TWINS.
Royal Park, Leeds = WHITE EAGLES.
Penthouse, Scarborough = CLASSIX NOUVEAU.
Fforde Green, Leeds = DIAMOND HEAD.

SA 14
Adelphi, Leeds = TALISMAN + NOSFERATU V.
University, Leeds = BURNING SPEAR.
North Bierley Labour Club, Bradford = ROCKABILLY REBS.
Polytechnic, Leeds = THOMPSON TWINS.
White Lion, Huddersfield = TWISTED NERVE.
Royal Park, Leeds = DODGY TACTICS.
Haddon Hall, Leeds = LUIGI ANA DA BOYS.

SU 15
Tiffany's, Leeds = BAD MANNERS + THE BOYS. Royal Park, Leeds = 156.
Fforde Grene, Leeds = DEDRINGER. Haddon Hall, Leeds = SURFACE TENSION.
Warehouse, Leeds = WAMM (L).
Textile Club, Dewsbury = ROCKABILLY REBS.
Princeville, Bradford = SPIDER (L).
White Lion, Huddersfield = ORAL SAX (L) // TALISMAN (E).
Vaults Bar, Bradford = BACKSLIDER.
Blackamore Head, Pontefract = CHINATOWN.
Staging Post, Leeds = THE MUNROES.

MO 16
Rotters, Doncaster = BAD MANNERS. University, York = THOMPSON TWINS.
Annabella's, Hull = LONDON BOYS.
Warehouse, Leeds = MONOCHROME SET + FAST SET.
Funhouse, Keighley = DMEN + supp. Haddon Hall, Leeds = AOIA.
Vaults Bar, Bradford = SHAKES.
Marquis of Granby, Leeds = CHAINSAW.
Amnesia, Leeds = TALISMAN.
Royal Park, Leeds = (T.B.A).

TU 17
Warehouse, Leeds = JOHN COUGAR.
Amnesia, Leeds = THE WHIPPS.
Marquis of Granby, Leeds = SLIDER.
Kings Head, Keighley = GOFF JACKSON & THE HUNS.
Limit Club, Sheffield = MONOCHROME SET + FAST SET.

WE 18
Polytechnic, Sheffield = THE STRANGLERS.
City Hall, Hull = GEORGE HAMILTON IV.
Warehouse, Leeds = SWITCH.
University, Bradford = ROY WOOD'S HELICOPTER.
White Lion, Huddersfield = NEW MODEL ARMY.
Foggy's, Halifax = THE SHAKES.
Marquis of Granby, Leeds = ANOTHER COLOUR + HOUSEHOLD NAME.
Amnesia, Leeds = SHARP PRACTICE.
Royal Park, Leeds = (T.B.A).

TH 19
Warehouse, Leeds = BARRACUDAS.
Limit Club, Sheffield = DARTS.
Princeville, Bradford = SILVER WING.
Fan Club, Leeds = UK DECAY + THE NOISE.
Penguin Club, Sheffield = FIXER
Royal Park, Leeds = TREATMENT.
Haddon Hall, Leeds = 52 AMERICANS.

FR 20
City Hall, Sheffield = CAMEL.
Polytechnic, Huddersfield = MISTY IN ROOTS.
Polytechnic, Sheffield = (T.B.C.).
Community Hall, Grimsby = BAULK MOSAIC + NORMAL BIAS.
Royal Park, Leeds = WHITE EAGLES.
Penthouse, Scarborough = THE LOOK.

SA 21
Brighton St. W.M.S., Heckmondwike = ROCKABILLY REBS.
University, Bradford = JUDIE TZUKE.
White Lion, Huddersfield = CONFESSOR.
Queens Hall, Bradford = THOMPSON TWINS + MYSTERIOUS FOOTSTEPS + REFLEX
Royal Park, Leeds = WAMM.
Haddon Hall, Leeds = DALE HARGREAVES' FLAMINGOS.

SU 22
Warehouse, Leeds = BEST FRIENDS (L).
Princeville, Bradford = BABY TUCKOO (L).
White Lion, Huddersfield = PUZZLER (L) // LEON BLANK BAND (E)
Vaults Bar, Bradford = ALTERNATIVE DANCE.
Blackamore Head, Pontefract = DIAMOND HEAD.
Staging Post, Leeds = SHAKE APPEAL
Royal Park, Leeds = 156
Haddon Hall, Leeds = SHARP PRACTICE.

MO 23
Pestle & Mortar, Grimsby = LONDON BOYS, Tiffany's, Leeds = DREAD + supp
Warehouse, Leeds = ILLUSTRATION.
Vaults Bar, Bradford = XENON PIRATES. Royal Park, Leeds = CONFESSOR.
Tiffany's, Hull = DEDRINGER. Haddon Hall, Leeds = PROPELLORS
University, Bradford = DARTS.
Funhouse, Keighley = SHAKES + supp
Marquis of Granby, Leeds = XANOS.
Amnesia, Leeds = (TBA).

TU 24
Kings Head, Keighley = NOSFERATU V.
Warehouse, Leeds = local bands (TBA).
Marquis of Granby, Leeds = ROUGH JUSTICE.
Amnesia, Leeds = (TBA).
Limit Club, Sheffield = ILLUSTRATION.

WE 25
University, Leeds = SIOUXIE & THE BANSHEES.
Foggy's, Halifax = WHIPPS.
Warehouse, Leeds = ROY WOOD'S HELICOPTERS.
White Lion, Huddersfield = THE MUNROES.
Polytechnic, Sheffield = WEAPON OF PEACE.
Amnesia, Leeds = HEAVEN 17.
Marquis of Granby, Leeds = AMOEBAS.
Royal Park, Leeds = (T.B.A.).

TH 26
Warehouse, Leeds = FATAL CHARM.
Princeville, Bradford = BLITZ.
Fan Club, Leeds = THE CRAMPS.
Penguin Club, Sheffield = ALIBI.
Rotters, Doncaster = ODESSEY.
Royal Park, Leeds = ROUGH JUSTICE.
Haddon Hall, Leeds = GANAMAR.

FR 27
Penthouse, Scarborough = LONDON BOYS.
Polytechnic, Sheffield = GEORGE MELLY.
Bingley Arts Centre = SHAKES + PYRAMID.
Royal Park, Leeds = WHITE EAGLES.

SA 28
Fforde Grene, Leeds = ALKATRAZZ.
University, Leeds = THE STRANGLERS + MODERN EON.
City Hall, Sheffield = KROKUS.
Polytechnic, Huddersfield = ROY WOOD'S HELICOPTER.
White Lion, Huddersfield = KNIFE EDGE.
Penguin Club, Sheffield = PRISONER.
Royal Park, Leeds = TALISMAN.
Haddon Hall, Leeds = LUCKY STRIKE.

Other Clothes

The County Shopping Hall,
County Arcade, Leeds.

Leathers, tartans
best American recycled,
etc. ... etc. ...

The name says it all!!!

Ram Recording Studios — Ram Records
64 Armley Road Leeds LS12 2DR
Tel.(0532)445044

STILL ONLY £65 (+VAT) PER 10-HOUR DAY or £7.50 (+VAT) PER HOUR

THE YEAR OF THE RAM

"The days of sweating blood in Ram Studios during July, September and December 1980 have paid dividends for Susan Fassbender and Kay Russell. On the strength of the Ram tape, Bradford-based Fassbender-Russell signed publishing and recording contracts that have culminated in their first single ('Twilight Cafe' on CBS Records) soaring into the charts and have also lead to national TV and radio exposure, including Top of the Pops. Congratulations to the band and a pat on the back to Ram".
With The Beans, The Motivators and Paraskos all working in Ram and each on the verge of signing major deals, 1981 looks like being the year of The Ram.

LEEDS UNIVENTS PRESENT

Sat. Jan. 31 = THE BLUES BAND (£2-50) + Sat. Feb. 14 = BURNING SPEAR (ticket price TBA) + Wed. Feb. 25 = Siouxie & The Banshees (£3-50) + Sat. Feb. 28 = The Stranglers + Modern Eon (£3-50)
...ch. 7 = BEANO featuring: the fab FRANTIC ELEVATORS, Diagram Brothers, Famous Names, sword swallowers, fire eater, juggler, Dancing Bear. * HEADLINE ACT TO BE ADDED
+ Sat. March. 14 = Stray Cats

...Union Records Leeds 444972) & ...door on the ... EVERYBODY WELCOME.

FEBRUARY

BRADFORD	4th	THE BLUES BAND
UNIVERSITY	11th	ANY TROUBLE
BRADFORD	18th	ROY WOOD
UNIVERSITY	21st	JUDIE TZUKE
BRADFORD	23rd	DARTS
UNIVERSITY		
BRADFORD		MARCH
UNIVERSITY	7th	SLADE
BRADFORD	11th	NINE BELOW ZERO
UNIVERSITY	14th	PAULINE MURRAY Bursting through the COSMOS
BRADFORD		
UNIVERSITY		
BRADFORD		
UNIVERSITY		

Marvel Music

BRADFORD UNIVERSITY

TICKETS FROM H.M.V. RECORDS AND UNION SHOP. ENQUIRIES TO BD. 34135 EX. 42... MARION FOUNTAYNE.
PLUS.......DISCOS EVERY FRIDAY IN THE COMMUNAL BUILDING, BAR TILL MIDNIGHT. ONLY 50P
JAZZ EVERY THURSDAY IN THE COMMUNAL BUILDING...20p

BACK ISSUES
...PUNTERS ...ERE WILL BE ...D TO BITS TO ...THAT DUE TO ...POPULAR ...COPIES OF ALL ...ARE STILL AVAILABLE AT THE THING ...H (+20p POSTAGE) FROM THE THING ...TOCZEK at 5 BEECH TERRACE, UNDERCLIFFE, ...RD, BD3 0PY, WEST YORKS. (tel. 0274-21867).

FRONT ISSUES
MASOCHISM IN THE FORM OF A 10-ISSUE SUBSCRIPTION IS AVAILABLE AT £4.50 FROM THE ABOVE ADDRESS. COPIES'LL THEN PLAGUE YOUR LETTER BOX AT REGULAR INTERVALS. HOWZAT GRAB YER?.

CURRENT PRINT RUN = 3½ thousand. Average of 5 humans glance at each copy so total readership is around 18 thousand. And at an average height of 5' 10" that's 20 miles of readership laid end to end. Now wash behind your ears.

⇒ THIS GIG GUIDE WAS FREE WITH ISSUE No 12 OF
Nick Toczek's
WOOL CITY ROCKER
IT'S THE NORTHERN ROCKSCENE MAGAZINE
Still only 30p ~ do you read it?

NEW ADVERTISING RATES

size of advert	1st advert placed	2nd ad. & thereafter
square box (c. 3")	£25-00	£12-00
2 boxes (c. 3" × 6")	£35-00	£20-00
½ p. in mag* (c. 6" × 4½")	£50-00	£30-00
full page* (c. 6" × 9")	£75-00	£50-00

TYPESETTING, LAYOUT and DESIGN by arrangement.
* exact page dimensions may vary according to packaging and design.
2 COLOURS — EXTRA COLOURS £25 EACH
CLASSIFIED ADVERTS STILL ONLY 10p PER WORD.
COPY DATE:- 10 days before end of previous month. RING NICK ON (0274) 21867. Copy & payment to NICK TOCZEK, 5 Beech Terrace, Undercliffe, Bradford, BD3 0PY, West Yorkshire.

THE CHEATERS

BOW WOW WOW at The Warehouse, Leeds
Photo: John Tempest

HOLIDAY SNAPS & PORNOGRAPHIC PHOTOS

Mistress

LONDON BOYS
Photo: Geoff Grimack

Wilko Johnson being a Blockhead at St George's Hall, Bradford

DONKEYS

FUNHOUSE BAR
131 North St., Keighley. Tel. 603796

LIVE ROCK EVERY MON.
8-11 p.m.

February bookings:-
- 2nd — CHRONIC + LIVING DEAD
- 9th — MYSTERIOUS FOOTSTEPS + support
- 16th — OMEN + support
- 23rd — THE SNAKES + support

Licenced bars.   Bar snacks.
Normal admission price only 50p.

HMV HMV HMV
HMV HMV HMV
SALE! 21/2/81

RIC-RAC Sound Studio

THE FIRST 24-TRACK
RECORDING STUDIO
IN YORKSHIRE

8-, 16- & 24-track recording
in extended studio area

For all studio enquiries ring Mick on Leeds 633717

Break the circuit and maybe win yourself some singles:

All albums £2.50 inc. p+p.

Local Heroes SW9   Don't be ■, buy Oval

JUNIOR MAILORDER — 13, BURNEDGE LANE, GRASSCROFT, OLDHAM OL4 4EA

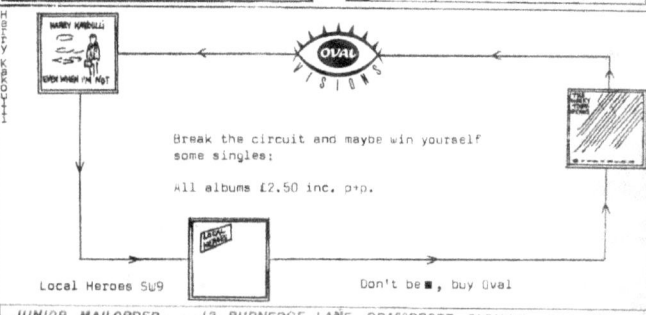

JSG Music
YORKSHIRE'S LARGEST GROUP SHOP

108B Main Street, Bingley.   Tel: 0274-568843
(Open till 9 pm every Monday and Thursday; Friday and Saturday till 5.30 pm)

FOR THE BIGGEST SELECTION OF GROUP GEAR AT THE LOWEST POSSIBLE PRICES

In the Guitar and Amp shop choose from:

Gibson, Fender, Washburn, Guild, Ovation, Rickerbacker, WAL, Lincoln, Peavey, full HH Concert Rigs, HH Performer, HH VS, Marshall, MM, Custom Sound, Carlsboro, Laney, Vox, Roland, Hill and RSD. 1,000 watt Rigs ready to go. Mics by: AKG, Shure and Beyer. Accessories by: Electroharmonix, Boss, Dod, Vox, etc.

In the Keyboard Department:
Wurlitzer, Moog, Roland, Rhodes, Korg, Hohner, Crumar, etc.

ALL THIS **PLUS** HIRE SERVICE, REPAIRS, HUGE SELECTION OF USED GEAR AND WE BUY FOR CASH

JSG STUDIOS

8 TRACK   **JSG RECORDS**

ECHO, REVERB, NOISE GATES, COMPRESSORS/LIMITERS, ALLEN/HEATH, TASCAM, REVOX QUAD TANNOYS, AURATONES.

KEYBOARDS AVAILABLE INCLUDE:-
POLYMOOG, MINIMOOG, OBERHEIM OBX, ARP SOLINA, FENDER RHODES,
MOOG TAURUS

ALSO **FREE** USE OF DRUMS, BASSES

£7 p.h. or £50 per day (8 hours)

ENQUIRIES phone Paul or John on:
Bradford 568843/832187

ISSUE #13

March 1981, 2,000 copies printed, 10 A4 pages + A4 sheet of cartoon cards + A2 2-sided Yorkshire/Lancashire gig guides

Financially and physically exhausted, I produced this inadequate issue printed on as many loose-leaf sheets as my meagre funds could muster. I knew I was under-performing and had to take a lot of flak from disappointed regular readers. It was a tough time. My editorial sums it up. That said, there was good content, and the spirit of WCR was still clearly in evidence. Also, the list of Lancashire venues and phone numbers on page 2 again proved very useful to bands. Including this sort of info was a prequel to one of my post-WCR projects, Twisted Pleasures & Drastic Measures. *(TPDM was a non-profit venture through which I worked in various ways to help over 4,000 bands during the mid-1980s, notably via a vast collection of constantly updated and extended A4 photocopied info sheets, The Independence File, which came in a plastic bag. It listed venues and recording studios, gave reams of advice on how to organise a band, etc. I bunged everything applicable to indie bands into those pages. There were no mobile phones and no internet in those days, so my file contained much of stuff that twenty-first-century indie bands can simply Google).*

Notes on people featured in this issue.

Lovely to have put the almost forgotten eccentric, Ted Milton, frontman of Blurt, on the front cover. Tim Charge, the keyboard player with Modes for Mutants, played a notable role in the Bradford music scene. He'd previously drummed (albeit briefly) in The Hustler Street Band (who became New Model Army), and he'd go on to play keyboards in Radio 5. I know all this because I recently interviewed him for the biography of Steven Wells (a.k.a. Seething Wells), which I'm currently co-writing with James Collingwood.

Another interesting character in this issue is Bill Byford (who wrote the live reviews of Alex Harvey Band and The Thompson Twins). He once played (again briefly) in The Pink Faries. Having written for WCR, he went on to front the local band, Ik, and then to manage and play in The Rhythm Sisters. After that, he pursued a solo career under the name Heath Common, releasing a series of excellent albums before sadly passing away in 2025.

If you won't come quietly I'll have to ask you to soundproof your bedroom...

EDITORIAL – All you young thugs and villains who listen to rock music and sit around in pubs have got to stop taking drugs and stealing things. If I catch any of you sniffing Domestos or nicking Barry Manilow albums I'll be left with no option but to ~~beat the living daylights~~ arrest you.

Sorry there's no flexidisc this time. I'm lining up several others, so keep your Dansettes plugged in. Meanwhile, I hope this package makes March more zappy for ya! I've made the lettering a bit bigger because so many of you moaned about the mini-print of past issues. Like to welcome Lancs. readers on board even though they live on the wrong side of the Pennines and wear clogs and cotton frocks.

> **STOP PRESS:** Since writing the above, I've taken time out to rethink future plans. I'm now lining up a bunch new projects - some journalistic, some to do with releasing vinyl, some to do with performing. Wool City has been taking up as much as twenty hours a day (it's 4.15 a.m. as I write this) &, given the inescapable choice between turning the mag. into a full-time business with employed staff or folding it, I've opted for the latter. I launched the mag. as a fun venture, but it's gradually turned itself into a full-time job... not what I want. If anyone out there wants to take over, I'm open to offers. Failing that, this is the last regular issue - although I'll do a special "W.C.R.-The Final Statement" in May/June - should be a goody! And I'll explain myself more fully then. Meanwhile thanks to everyone - readers, helpers, reviewers, advertisers, steeplejacks, creditors, etc. for your support.
>
> So this is the penultimate goodbye ('sniff, sniff')
> ah, well - life stumble on towards the abyss,
> love & order, Nick-Nick

So, where to now...

Who did what to whom...

Nick Toczek did most of this to no avail.

Ken Turner did the X-word to ▢▢▢▢▢▢ (2 words)

Stan Engel did the cartoonz to sublimate aggression.

Steve Brown, Andy Stevens & Bill Byford reviewed to get their names here

5 Beech Terrace
Undercliffe
Bradford BD3 0PY
West Yorkshire
Telephone 0274 21867

Some other 'zines you might like to pick up to help you keep pace with the frantic scene...
SUBVERT is a new one that's based in Keighley. No.1 kicks off well with a mixture of local & national bands + an extensive A-Z of fanzines. Editors Richard Jevons & Andy Plews are lining up a good 2nd edition. It looks like this mag. will be covering much of the West Yorks. scene - so look out for it. Richard Jevons is at 7 Laurel Crescent, Keighley, W. Yorks. (K'lly 605825). **MOLOTOV COMICS** is a collection of poems by the (f)Airies Ents. mob - Little Brother, Wild Willy Beckett, Seething Wells, Gaius, Julz + J.Cooper Clarke interview. Layout is fun but print quality makes bits illegible. Good crazy performance pieces included in here. **BEATEN TO THE PUNCH** looks like becoming the latest edition to the bunch of good regular fanzines to come out of York. Layout's very formal & bland but coverage of things-in-York is interesting & looks fairly comprehensive. **CHICKEN FEED** is produced by the Dole-Q Club who also run a fortnightly Wednesday gig at The Marquis of Granby. Issue 1 has more Airies Ents. poetry + reviews + articles on employment (the lack of it) + a competition X-word. Finally, don't forget the other Yorkshire fanzines - a list of which appeared in the competition/quiz answers in WCR 12. Record shops & alternative bookshops are the most likely places to find fanzines on sale, though they also crop up in some clothes shops, at venues, etc.

/// All the money that I would've spent on future issues will go into a fund to buy my own nuclear strike force - just as a defense tactic, of course. The people in the next street look aggressive!

FOR YORKSHIRE VENUES SEE ISSUE Nº 12... some that I missed include: Doncaster's New Outlook Club (0302-64434), York University (0904-412328 wrong no. given in issue 12), Hull Tiffany's (0482-28250), Royal Hall, Harrogate (0423-66631), plus Adelphi, Leeds & Entertainer, Dewsbury.

LANCS. VENUES

This list of venues has been compiled with the stance of Steve Hindle who runs Junior Records, manages Lancs. band 'Localeroes' and distributes records. Thanks to him for the time & work that gave me over half of the venues phone nos. He's at 13 Burnedge Lane, Grasscroft, Oldham, OL4 4EA. Incomplete, but better than a mouthful of raw fish, here's the list:-

MANCHESTER (061-)
Apollo = 273-1112
Free Trade Hall
University = 273-5111
U.M.I.S.T. = 236-9114
Polytechnic (halls) = 273-1162
Rafters = 236-9788
Mayflower = 223-4416 (Pauleth)/ 223-1013
Cyprus Tavern = 236-3786
Portland Bars = 236-8414
Beach Club = 236-9849 (New Hormones)
Band on The Wall = 832-6625 (Jazz venue only)
Carousel Club = 225-1308 (Clive)
Millstone = 225-2441
Bulls Head = 790-2441
Pips = 834-7155
Rotters = 236-4934
Swan Hotel
Devonshire
Golden Garter
Ardri
Kim Philby Club (at Devilles) - closed at Xmas but they're lining up a new venue soon... perhaps.

LIVERPOOL (051-)
Bradys = 236-7881/3959
Masonic = 355-5805
Warehouse
University = 709-4744
Rotter's = 709-0771
Empire = 709-1555
Moonstone = 489-1305
Royal Court
Lincolns Inn
Philharmonic Halls

BIRKENHEAD (051-)
Gallery Club
Sir James Entertainments = 647-8282

BOLTON (0204-)
Swan Hotel = 27021
Tippings Arms = 32349
Technical College = 31411
The Gaiety
Aquarius Club

PRESTON (0772-)
Warehouse = 59926 (Gary)
Moonraker = 59907 (Walter)
Polytechnic = 58382

DARWEN (0254-)
Craven Heifer = 72618
Duke of York = 42197

BURNLEY (0282-)
Bank or Miners = 26695 (Peter Holding)

BLACKPOOL (0253-)
Jenks Bar = 293203
Norbeck Castle = 52341

BLACKBURN (0254-)
King Georges Hall
Bay Horse (New Inns) = 48443

CHORLEY (02572-)
Joiners Arms = 70661 (Rock Formula)

ROCHDALE (0706-)
Lamplighter Club = 54747
Rawstons Arms = Whitworth 2570
Roches Bar
Wheatsheaf = 84 9425

LANCASTER (0524-)
University = 65201

OLDHAM (061-)
Tower Club = 624-5491
Moorend = 624-4454
Pennine Lounge = 624-0257
Lancashire Hotel = 624-9782
R.A.F. Station (Forces gigs - agency booked)

TAMESIDE (061-)
Ashton Hotel = 330-1445
Spread Eagle = 330-5732
Commercial Hotel = 338-2875
George Lawton Hall - Mossley 2223

SALFORD (061-)
Moonrakers = 872-5644
De La Salle College = 643-6012
Electric Club

BURY (061-)
Derby Hall = 761-7107
Platform Club
Bridge Inn

ALTRICHAM (061-)
Unicorn

SADDLEWORTH (045-77-)
Civic Hall = 3689

WIGAN (0942-)
Trucks (A1163)

CLASSIFIED ADVERTS.

only 10p per word

ring Nick on B'f'd 21867.

DRUMMER urgently wanted by Radio 5 for recording & gigs. New Peel session, record co. + publicity/managing co. both interested. Ring Jock on B'f'd 632553.

BASS/VOCALS, also plays rhythm/lead - wants to join/form rock band. Ring Mick on B'f'd 581707.

VAN HIRE - bands, gear, light removals. Good rates. Efficient service. New LT40 van. Ring Malc. on B'f'd 44428.

AND SO SOME PEOPLE GET THEIR FACES INTO W.C.R.13 THANKS TO THE CAMERA OF JOHN TEMPEST

HYPERSON Glenn Simpson — POZ of THE NOISE — A SQUARE named Brian Hogan — A SHAKE — LITTLE BROTHER — A START — AN AUTOMATIC TOY

SINGLES - reviewed by Nick Toczek & Steve Brown.

ROBERT WYATT - 'Stalin Wasn't Stalling' c/w PETER BLACKMAN - 'Stalingrad' (Rough Trade: RT046). Common theme to both sides is the Germano-Russian conflict during WWII. Wyatt's side is sung/chanted gospel-style vocals with minimal percussion & multitracked gospel backing vocal. Over-simple but it grows on you. He's always, since the days of Soft Machine, persued his own musical tack, & this is off-beat enough to draw interest. B-side's a contemporary poem recorded straight, by the author, in a very BBC accent.

ESSENTIAL LOGIC - 'Music is a Better Noise' c/w 'Moontown' (Rough Trade: RT053). 2nd of 3 projected singles from the band, it comes out just as the band's split up. Both sides are more commercial than the previous output from Laura Logic (ex-X-Ray Spex) & her Essentials. Bass & sax are complimented by light vocals. Despite choppy rhythms, the songs make pleasing listening, but lack impact. Funk guitar adds to the accessibility on side 2.

MOONDOGS - 'Talking In The Canteen' c/w 'Make Her Love Me' & 'You Said' (Real Records: ARE14). Undertones gtr./attractive pop-punk vocals/heavy-handed drumming. A highly commercial (over)production job on a trio of strong pop songs. B-side leans towards heavier rock on the first track. Another Irish band with chart potential.

TELEVISION PERSONALITIES - 'I know Where Syd Barrett Lives' c/w 'Arthur The Gardener'. A-side has acoustic gtr. & birdsongs to back up silly vocals that neatly piss-take the soppy I'm-at-one-with-nature early Floyd. B-side has a go at Keith West's Teenage Opera outtake, 'Grocer Jack', in the same way. T.V. Pers. are great. Their stuff's so silly!

METHODISHCA TUNE - 'Orchestra' c/w 'LFD' (Eustone Records: TO3). Their 2nd single. Tinny gtr./stop-start rhythm/high vocals/piano play-out make for an O.K. but slightly disappointing B-side that's totally forgettable. Characterless musak. B-side is made more interesting by instrumental variety but still suffers from being built entirely out of a one-line tune. Incidental music.

DEPECHE MODE - 'Dreaming of Me' c/w 'Ice Machine' (Mute Records: Mute 013). Robert 'The Normal' Wenn's label gives out vinyl debut of this 'New Romantics' band. Post-Numan synth-pop with good use of piano & predictable dm. machine. Good B-side too, with a full, rich sound. Top marks for the producer. Should put the band up there alongside S.Ballet/Visage.

PERE UBU - 'Not Happy' c/w 'Lonesome Cowboy Dave'. A-side features Goon Show voices over music that's more throw-away/less inventive than this band usually produce. B-side tries harder musically, but the result is more chaotic than it is constructive. The Spike Milligan voice begins to grate. Are the band losing their sense of direction? Or are these tracks just studio out-takes.

THE FATAL CHARM - 'Western Language' c/w 'Dark Eyes' (Double D Records - a freebie flexi originally issued for the band's '80 tour). Haunting melody lines with excellent Blondie-ish vocals. A tight, well-produced & exciting band with lots to offer. Both of us are very impressed.

L.P.'s - same reviewers.

PYLON - 'Gyrate' (Armageddon Records: ARM5). Much-acclaimed U.S. band, side-kicks of the B-52's, who were over here touring a couple of months ago. J.J. Burnel bass. Weak Patti Smith/Runaways vocals. Whole rhythm section's very basic. Stripped-down, semi-strange Yankie new wave. Mildly interesting amateurism, but the ideas need developing. Parallels with pre-Eno Talking Heads. A potentially good band in desperate need of a sympathetic producer/arranger.

CLASS OF 81 - 'Music For Upper Class People to Do Something To' (Upper Class Records: CHIN1). Bram Tchaikovsky produces & his influence is obvious from the first few notes that're straight out of The Motors' 'Airport'. Strange that no musicians are credited - so how many ex-Motors are there here!! Bass sounds very Nick Garvey. Melodic rock with a clean production & some consistently interesting instrumental interplay. Good songs, but they lack that spirited directness that we've come to associate with BramT.

THE SOFT BOYS - Underwater Moonlight' (Armageddon Records: ARM1). First song's a rip-off of Rolling Stones' 'We Love You' - but impressive for all that. The whole L.P. has lifted a fat bunch of ideas from commercial mid-sixties rock classics & successfully revamped them in a nearer-to-the-eighties package. You can play spot-the-influence on virtually every number (Lou Reid/Bowie/Dylan/Floyd) but the band put their own stamp heavily on it all, and there's an impressive variety of styles with each successive song in marked contrast to those that've gone before. Covering the whole spectrum of rock styles of the decade '65-'75, S.B.'s come over as the rock musician's antidote to The Barron Knights. A recommended album!

LOCAL TAPES - us again!

RHABSTALLION - 'Steel It'/'Hard Luck Man'/'Chain Reaction' Steve: "Fast, run-of-the-mill H.M. I wasn't particularly impressed when I saw them live late last year. Here, they seem to have improved musically but are no closer to an original style. The music's still heavily cliched which is a shame as the musicianship's obvious." Nick: "Vocals are their most impressive side"

EQUIVALENT VIII - 'Blurred'/'Accept The Day'/'Threshold'. Light appealing pop tunes given synthed rock treatment with sparse gtr/bs/dms. rhythm section + spoken vocals with an edge of echo. Uninspired, tho', with little that's novel.

TWO WORDS - 'Stranger'/'No Room For Love'. Recorded J.S.G. Studios. Same instruments as E.VIII, but an altogether harder sound. Overloud strident vocs. Songs are less melodic than E.VIII's. Rhythm is more fragmented. Arrangements are more adventurous. Less commercial, but by far the more interesting.

PRIVATE DICKS - 'Roxette' + a bunch of others. A roots R'n'B band from Hudds. They feature some immaculate harmonica + good vocals. A tight outfit working in a field that offers little room for innovation. Vocalist sounds very similar to Lee Brilleaux of The Feelgoods.

THE SQUARES - 'Oh, Buddy Holly'. Demo of forthcoming single on new Leeds label, Hype. A blatantly commercial slice of mid-sixties pop strong on melody & harmonies. Will be played to extinction on Radio One & should chart.

MODES FOR MUTANTS - 'Violence'/'Jealousy & Me'/'Repetition'/'Rise with The Plan'/'Slant Chant R'n'R'/'Subculture'/'25th Hour'. Recorded Ric-Rac & Cargo. If 2 Words were a step up from Equiv. VIII, then M.F.M. are at least 3 or 4 further steps. A driving, exciting sound with strong songs, insistent rhythms. Good work on Reys in particular. The band produce a dense & consistent web of music. There's a rare sense of unity & direction here. Easily this month's best tape.

BLURT

57
(squeal of tyres)
What?!
No!!!
— Ted Milton.

SO THERE
My Neo-Brutal love will grow
vaster than skyscrapers
down below,
& when you
RISE!
UP!
ABOVE!
AHOY!
HELP!
— TED MILTON

STROUD POEM: The groiniest day of my life/Whole Green Forelocks!/(supported by the Grace of God/ and visitors from Outer Space)/ Close Ranks! Close Ranks!! — TED MILTON

KEEP DRY
Little Paratrooper
What struts on Sunday morn
I'll pick my nose in my own backyard
That way only my nostril will get worn.
— POEM by TED MILTON

A BOOKLET OF TED'S POEMS — 'Milton: The Works. Vol. One. Poems & Letters' — IS AVAILABLE FROM THE MAN HIMSELF AT 84 HORNS RD STROUD, GLOS. FOR A MERE 65p INCLUDING P. & P.

EPITAPH
There's only room for one of us in this world a thousand million
Wiloni pressed
— TED MILTON.

Blurt 'In Berlin' (Armageddon: ARM6) is a live recording from a Rock Against Junk concert in Krautland last December. Solid one-riff-throughout-each-song rhythm section backs up Ted Milton's screamed vocals & demented sax. This 3-piece (T.M. on voc./sax. + brother Jake on dms./bit of voc. + Pete Creese on gtr./occasional trombone) create a bassless musical world of their own. Their noise comes over with charmless masochistic appeal. Percussive train rhythms meet Milton's Zappa-like over-the-top style(!) that makes no concessions to anything you'd recognise. Strangely, they went down well when I saw them at Futurama II & again on the recent Dury tour. Against all odds, they pull out a primitive appeal. I like them myself, but wouldn't dare to suggest you bought this album... so why not go out & buy this album? —pre-release L.P. reviewed by Nick Toczek.

Letter from: RADE MILINKOVIC/Mr., IRISKA 42, 22400 RUMA, YUGOSLAVIA   10 JAN 81

Dear Nick Toczek, Here are some Autopsia products. I hope you make good use of them. Autopsia is art/or antiart/gang. With increasing uneasiness we are experiencing an absence of enthusiastic activities which could & should free us from the lethargic state in which we have found ourselves/ for a long time now we have been deceiving ourselves claiming that the void which has arisen is the result of saturation/ as if we've already done everything we possibly can/ we feel a dismal void & lack of human & artistic activity/ to be sure, anaemic & depressing surroundings do not serve as much encouragement/ we ask ourselves is that the only reason for surrendering to a passive existence? shouldn't we look to ourselves for the causes of recession? The sphere of our activity can be very broad/ I wonder should we reconcile ourselves to the combination of elitist commercialism/ to the flood of provincial small-town taste/ to senseless trite profit-making actions? This is a proposal for an artistic/ not only artistic!/ offensive which in its own specific way should reduce to dust & ashes international cretinism and castrated culture/ yours Rade

P.S. Autopsia will soon be working on a demo tape.

"(OUR MUSIC) IS TERRIBLE BUT IT IS THE ONLY REAL MUSIC/OUR SONGS ARE NOT BEAUTIFUL, BUT THEY ARE TRUE" — Autopsia.

WE DON'T KNOW HOW TO PLAY/ WE DON'T KNOW HOW TO SING/ WE'RE MUSICAL PRIMITIVES/ NO COMPARISON MIGHT BE MADE BETWEEN OUR SONGS AND ROCK MUSIC/ THE DIFFERENCE BETWEEN THESE TWO IS SO GREAT AS IS THE DIFFERENCE BETWEEN DIRTY WORDS WRITTEN ON THE WALLS OF A CLOSET AND BELLETRISTIC LITERATURE/ WE DON'T PLAY ROCK MUSIC BECAUSE WE HATE IT/ WE WOULD BE VERY HAPPY IF WE WERE ABLE TO DESTROY IT/ ROCK 'N' ROLL DOESN'T EXIST AT ALL/ ROCK BUSINESS EXISTS ONLY/ THE WORST OF ALL IS THAT THERE ARE SOME BASTARDS WHO KEEP ON TALKING: "WE ARE GENIUS, WE CREATING ART, NOBODY CAN PLAY WHAT WE CAN"/ IN FACT THE THINGS THAT THEY ARE MAKING ARE THE ACCUMULATION OF SHITS/ WE HATE ROCK MUSICIANS BECAUSE THEY AMASS MONEY AND ARE NOT ABLE TO ADMIT THAT ROCK MUSIC MAY BE PLAYED BY EVERYBODY/ HARD ROCK, POP, DISCO... ARE MODELS CREATED BY BUSINESSMEN/ MODELS FOR MASS PRODUCTION AND SALE/ WE HAVE REJECTED THESE MODELS AND RULES...

BANDS

MODES FOR MUTANTS (Keighley).
John Hanby (bass); Tim Charge (synth); Michael McGrath (dms); Simeon Warburton (gtr./voc.).

Mick & Simeon were in a '77 punk band called Sulphate, kept in touch, formed Neutral Zone with John in early '80, added Tim in July, became M.F.M.

Simeon: "All the bands I have ever met refuse to categorise their music. We, as might be expected, are the same. If anything, we like to be thought of as a crossover between punk & electronic music. At first I used to write all the songs but as we've progressed it's become the whole group's domain. I've got to admit that in general the material's become a lot stronger since we've started doing this. We are all very enthusiastic about the way things are going, it's brilliant when playing and something just clicks and for a short time you're not an individual anymore but part of something much bigger just pumping out sound."

The band's excellent tape is reviewed elsewhere in this issue. To contact them, ring Simeon on B'f'd 306064 (day) or Haworth 42055 (evenings).

XENON PIRATES (W.Yorks - K'ly/B'f'd/Leeds)
JOHN CANN (DMS.); GRAHAM BROADBENT (VOC.); MARK LUPTON (GTR. & VOC.); ANDREW EATCH (BASS).

FORMED EARLY IN NOV. '80, THEY'VE BEEN REHEARSING A SET OF EARLY 60'S & LATE 50'S ROCK 'N' ROLL STANDARDS ('SHAKIN' ALL OVER', 'SWEET LITTLE 16', 'BONEY MORONEY', ETC.) + SOME MORE RECENT NOS. IN A SIMILAR STYLE (PISTOLS' 'STEPPIN' STONE' & 'LONELY BOY', CLASH'S 'ENGLISH CIVIL WAR', ETC). THE RESULT IS ALSO A RUB OFF FROM PREVIOUS BANDS (MARK WAS WITH PUNX 'TOTAL CONFUSION', WHILE JOHN PLAYED IN H.M. COMBOS 'WICCA' & 'HARD RAIN'). THE BASIC AIM NOW IS TO PLAY A SET OF FUN MATERIAL THAT EVERYONE KNOWS - WITH THE 'POST-KIDD PIRATES' AS A PRIME INFLUENCE.

THEY'VE BEEN PRACTICING AT CODA IN BRADFORD, BUT ARE AFTER THEIR OWN REHEARSAL ROOMS & THEIR OWN P.A.

AROUND XMAS THEY DID 3 GIGS AS 'OSIRIS', WHICH WENT WELL EXCEPT FOR MOB VIOLENCE AT ST. FRANCIS YOUTH CLUB! GRAHAM JOINED IN JANUARY &, DURING FEB., THEY DID BRADFORD GIGS AT VAULTS BAR & PALM COVE. MORE ARE BEING LINED UP INCLUDING ONE WITH OTHER BANDS AT BINGLEY ARTS CENTRE.

CONTACT: JOHN (K'L'Y 605927) OR MARK (PUDSEY 566832)

VENGEANCE (Bradford).
Dave Malt (voc); Jeff Ryan (gtr.); Mitch Wilson (gtr. & b.voc); Mark Stothars (bass); Roy Hannan (dms).

Formed in Dec. '80, they've had a few line-up changes before settling on the current one. After Mick Mitchell (ex-Ulterior Motives (gtr.) & Jeremy Peet (dms.) left, the band split briefly, but soon reformed with Mitch & Roy coming in.

They now have their own 600 watt P.A. (which is available for hire), are building a lighting rig, and will be lining up late spring or early summer gigs.

They play heavy rock (Dave: "I don't like the term heavy metal!"), and do all their own material except for Gillan's 'Vengeance' & 'Smoke on the Water' for an encore number.

With plans to also invest in their own van, they view the band as much more of a commitment than just a casual gigging unit.

CONTACT: Mark on B'f'd 497067/Dave on 636809.

EQUIVALENT VIII!
MARTIN FELLOWS (KEYS); JONATHAN WOLSTENHOLME (RHYTMS); ROBERT WALKER (FOUR STRINGS); CHRIS PEARSON (SIX STRINGS); PETER MILLS (VOICE).

"We formed 12 months ago, time spent consolidating ideas into a distinctive, modern, sound-intelligent, dance music."

"We try to avoid playing the traditional rock venues, preferring to concentrate on more modern, alternative clubs. West Yorkshire is not overblessed with venues, but those who cry "no gigs" are not trying hard enough; the venues are there to be played if you want them. We are playing several clubs in the area in the next two months."

"Our sound is not cold & doomy, but warm yet challenging modern music. We have already turned down one record deal, are currently considering another one, and plan to record a single shortly."

"Our public performances so far have met with a good response. We are looking to play throughout & beyond W. Yorks. & would like to hear from forward-looking venues in the area.

CONTACTABLE: Leeds 657699, 655007, 658896.

MUSIC BAR
CITY SQ., LEEDS 1.
LEEDS: 34945

MON. TO SUN. : 5.30 P.M. — 10.30 P.M.

DO YOU LIKE?

DAVID BOWIE • BRUCE SPRINGSTEEN • ULTRAVOX • U.B.40 • THE HUMAN LEAGUE
ADAM AND THE ANTS • FUNK • JOY DIVISION • SPANDAU BALLET • STEELY DAN
ORCHESTRAL MANOEUVRES • B 52's • ELVIS COSTELLO • PETER GABRIEL • VISAGE
JOHN FOXX • THE PRETENDERS • REGGAE • DEVO • AND *ALTERNATIVE* MUSIC

IF YOU DO, LOOK NO FURTHER —
MUSIC EVERY NIGHT PLUS :

LIVE ACTS 3/4 NIGHTS WEEKLY - WATCH POSTERS AND PRESS & LISTEN
TO LOCAL RADIO FOR DETAILS EACH WEEK.

"AMNESIA - AN ALTERNATIVE TO THE ORDINARY!"

J S G STUDIOS

8 TRACK   **JSG RECORDS**

ECHO, REVERB, NOISE GATES, COMPRESSORS/LIMITERS, ALLEN/HEATH, TASCAM, REVOX QUAD TANNOYS, AURATONES.

KEYBOARDS AVAILABLE INCLUDE:-
POLYMOOG, MINIMOOG, OBERHEIM OBX, ARP SOLINA, FENDER RHODES, MOOG TAURUS

ALSO **FREE** USE OF DRUMS, BASSES

£7 p.h. or £50 per day (8 hours)

ENQUIRIES phone Paul or John on:
Bradford 568843/832187

JSG Music

YORKSHIRE'S LARGEST GROUP SHOP

108B Main Street, Bingley.   Tel: 0274-568843

(Open till 9 pm every Monday and Thursday; Friday and Saturday till 5.30 pm)

FOR THE BIGGEST SELECTION OF GROUP GEAR AT THE LOWEST POSSIBLE PRICES

In the Guitar and Amp shop choose from:

Gibson, Fender, Washburn, Guild, Ovation, Rickerbacker, WAL, Lincoln, Peavey, full HH Concert Rigs, HH Performer, HH VS, Marshall, MM, Custom Sound, Carlsboro, Laney, Vox, Roland, Hill and RSD. 1,000 watt Rigs ready to go. Mics by: AKG, Shure and Beyer. Accessories by: Electroharmonix, Boss, Dod, Vox, etc.

In the Keyboard Department:

Wurlitzer, Moog, Roland, Rhodes, Korg, Hohner, Crumar, etc.

ALL THIS **PLUS** HIRE SERVICE, REPAIRS, HUGE SELECTION OF USED GEAR AND WE BUY FOR CASH

COMPTON ARMS in LEEDS.

TETLEY/E.M.I. SUPERGROUP

The Tetley's/E.M.I. Supergroup Contest had been a mounting concern in the minds of hundreds by the time I pick up the story. Unfortunately, I start at the end, with the final, which is a shame as I cannot do full justice to the many people who made the competition such a success.

The competition was one of quite staggering facts and figures. In all, 17 bands from all over the North East of England entered and, nearly ten months later we arrive at the 26th of January together with just three bands for the Grand Final.

Noise, heat, trodden on toes and claustrophobia were all the rage as around threehundred people crammed into the Compton Arms.

And so, to a cocophony of horns whistles and cheers, Smart Ass took the stage. They presented themselves as a typical club act, complete with white satin shirts open to the waist, baloons and crap jokes. As bands go, they were average - mistake number one. Tonight was no time to be just average.

Next up were Leeds' own Knife Edge. They're brill. anyway but tonight they pushed themselves just that extra little bit. Charly got a new red leather jacket for the occasion and Mark has his favourite coat on. What more could you ask for? "I Go Wild", "Me And My Girl", and the new but already famous "Bombing Pearl Harbour". - Great Stuff. They put in a great set but there was obviously something missing in the audience reaction.

Anyway, they went off to be interviewed by B.B.C. about what it's like to be a punk band, to spit and jump in the air. Not that they do!).

The Gents who I suppose could be described as a mod band came on just this side of midnight. They were a sad cross between the Beatles, The Chords and Madness. However, they didn't half burn it on. On an off night this band could quite easily be utterly ordinary. Tonight, they were excellent, but just slightly annoying in their total mimicry of Madness.

And so, to the decision. The tension was quite extraordinary. Smart Ass came third and picked up £300. in doing so. This was expected, but no-one dared separate the totally different acts of Knife Edge and The Gents. The biggest hush of the night descended as the second place envelope was opened. Second place was read out and the cheers which completely drowned out the winners' names resounded around Leeds. Contrary to my review, Knife Edge are not considered a Supergroup. - The Gents are Congratulations. Andy Stevens.

FORDE GREENE, LEEDS (8/2/81)

ALEX HARVEY BAND

Few performers have survived the long arduous trail from the birth of white rock and roll in the fifties to the present day and of those who have made it through, few have placed their talent and reputation on the line so many times as Alex Harvey. Five years ago, in the halcyon days of The Sensational Alex Harvey Band, I saw the man deliver a performance at New York's Radio City Music Hall which resulted in the majority of the audience refusing to leave the theatre until the band played a third encore. Great times - and at nearly fifty years of age one would have assumed that Harvey would have recognised such scenes as the pinnacle of his career and hung up his boots..... but not so.

Last Sunday I saw the seasoned campaigner again, returning to the type of pub which must have supported him during the era of his Big Soul Band in the early sixties. The Club room was packed with an audience eagerly awaiting yet another Alex Harvey Band lineup and when the sound system pumped out "Faith Healer" riff immediately prior to the band's appearance, expectations were high. Unfortunately these hopes were dashed when Harvey chose the number to open his set and the pianist's attempts to capture the same haunting sound resulted in something not dissimilar to the sound of Sooty's piano. Many of the assembled were obviously disturbed by the shaky start but forever the survivor, Harvey was able to pull it all back together with a blistering version of "Midnight Moses" and from there the set never looked back. "Framed", "The Maffia Stole My Guitar" and other vintage wares were executed with a precision comparable with the old band and the night climaxed with a version of a song which must be close to Harvey's heart, "Last of the Teenage Idols" - as the audience rushed the stage to embrace the man, who would have disputed his claim? They banged anything they could lay their hands on to summon his return and did it really matter whether they were applauding the man's music or his myth? Bill Byford.

LEEDS UNIVERSITY 14 Feb 81

THE THOMPSON TWINS

Cynics might suggest that, aside from living out the aesthic lifestyle perpetuated by the Spandau Ballet brotherhood, THE movement to be in on at the moment is the Anti-Nukes brigade - simply everyone's joining don't you know. It's an unfair criticism of course but it's one many may be tempted to aim at The Thompson Twins as they traverse the country on the first ever "No Nukes Music Tour". You know the old line of attack - bunch of novices looking for quick break jump on back of popular cult. Well for all such doubters The Thompson Twins have the perfect answer - with a five figure debt around your neck and a road crew of fourteen you don't hit the road with a guarantee of no wages unless you believe passionately in what you are doing, The Thompson Twins do. They pick up the pieces The Grateful Dead dropped in the sixties and The Clash somehow manage to dispense with in the late seventies and put their money where their mouth is, playing music wherever they discover a cause worth supporting in return for a fee to keep the wolf from the door.

One Saturday the band performed for seventy people in a hall whose capacity is probably ten times that number. They immediately captured the attention of a potentially apathetic audience with one of the most powerful opening numbers I've ever heard a band perform. It later transpires the song is called 'P+Q' and is taken from the Band's debut album soon to be released on the Hansa label. There is no denying their charismatic presence and in bassist Tom Bailey they obviously have a unique front man. Dressed in white 'lab coat', his dead pan, pedantic vocal delivery provides a perfect foil to twin guitarists John Roog and Pete Dodd whose guitars soar all over the hall, finally meeting up somewhere near the end of each song. The set is perfectly constructed and one killer number follows another so that by the end the audience is tightly packed around the front of the stage eating out of the Twin's hands. The encores are inevitable and it is rather pitiful listening to seventy+ hoarse throats echoing round an empty hall when the band have worked so hard.

It's nearly two months since I last saw The Thompson Twins playing a New Year's Eve Gig at the ICA in London and speaking to them later in the dressing room I am struck by their new found confidence and determination. It's become obvious to them, if not to everyone else, that their going to make it and now it is just a matter of time. Bill Byford.

MOONDOGS/TV21/SPLIT RIVITT/DARTS all at Warehouse LEEDS

TV21 and The Moondogs,(they're Irish y'know!) were in attendance on my first visit to The Warehouse. This was quite a big night for The Moondogs as, after two successful tours as thoroughly good support to The Pretenders and The Undertones, this was the first night of their very own U.K. Tour.

TV21 rattled through a catchy set but sadly were generally ignored and forced to address their feelings to an embarassingly empty space. The Warehouse audience seems to have developed a rather neat habit of listening to a band whilst appearing to be totally preoccupied with boredom.

TV21 left to mingle and circulate amongst the audience. What followed was quite amazing...... It was three lads called The Moondogs. They are a very modest trio and, like their teachers The Undertones, they overflow with the image of being real Ol Likely Lads. (They're Irish y'know)!

I saw them on both the previously mentioned tours and my most vivid memory was this young bass guitarist whose introduction to songs consisted of a deluge of unrecognisable sounds, supposedly drawn from the English language, over-dubbed with a completely incomprehenisble accent (They're Irish y'know)......but, tonight..... at times, the sound was dreadful and they spasmodically lapsed into periods when they were about as tight as The Titanic on it's way down but, The Moondogs were probably the best band I've seen in the last six months or so.

Songs with catchy choruses, more "1,2,3,4's" than S.L.F., Harrington jackets and training shoes, "Whose Gonna Tell Mary", Irish charm, Irish wit, run across the stage and back again, we are The Moondogs, goodnight, God-bless =Magic!

My second visit to The Warehouse was brought about by yours truly being hurled into the upper echelons of self imposed stardom when Phonogram Records asked me to go and review Split Rivitt on their 1981 "Spell it RightTour".

What they did I am sure they did very well, but not being a strong R and B man I can't really say more than that!

One interesting little note, Mark Hughes, who plays harmonica, has a case with over 200 of the things in it. They're all set at different keys, all with a different feel.

Finally, a band who beat Clock DVA by eight legs (see issue number 12) Darts came to The Warehouse. A not overlarge crowd was there, but Darts were excellent. They included many numbers from their new album and also a fair smattering of their now famous hits; "Daddy Cool", "Reet Petite" and "Duke Duke Duke, Duke of Earl, Duke Duke...."etc., Sporting a couple of new faces, they are still that potential hit machine of a couple of years back.

Just a word about the venue. It's a great place for bands run by a great set of people who worked very hard to make three great nights; Darts were good, Split Rivitt didn't do much for me, but The Moondogs - they summed it up themselves with one chorus line, "Yeah, This is Power Pop". Andy Stevens

THE WAREHOUSE
19-21 SOMERS ST. LEEDS 1. tel. 468287.

— MARCH GIGS —

- MON 2nd = THE dBs plus THE RAYBEATS "Yankee Doodle Dandies"
- WED 4th = WILKO JOHNSON'S SOLID SENDERS + SIGNS
- MON 9th = NASH THE SLASH "oh, Bandage - Up Yours"
- TUE 10th = RELUCTANT STEREOTYPES + KEEPING DARK
- WED 11th = PRIVATE DICKS + WHIPPS
- MON 16th = NEW MUSIK plus SNIPS
- TUE 17th = THE VAPORS
- WED 18th = PHOTOS +++ JOOL$ HOLLAND & HI$ MILLIONAIRE$ ← SQUASH & SQUEEZE
- THU 19th = ORANGE JUICE
- TUE 24th = TAURUS
- WED 25th = the polecats
- TUE 31st = THE GAS

LIVE MUSIC at The Queen's Hall
LIVE BLACK MUSIC Every Friday Night

AND THE VAULTS BAR
Heavy Rock + New Wave and Jazz Bands every: SUN. MON. WED.
Bradford College Students' Union
Queens Hall
Morley Street
Bradford BD7 1BW
Tel: (0274) 392712/3/4

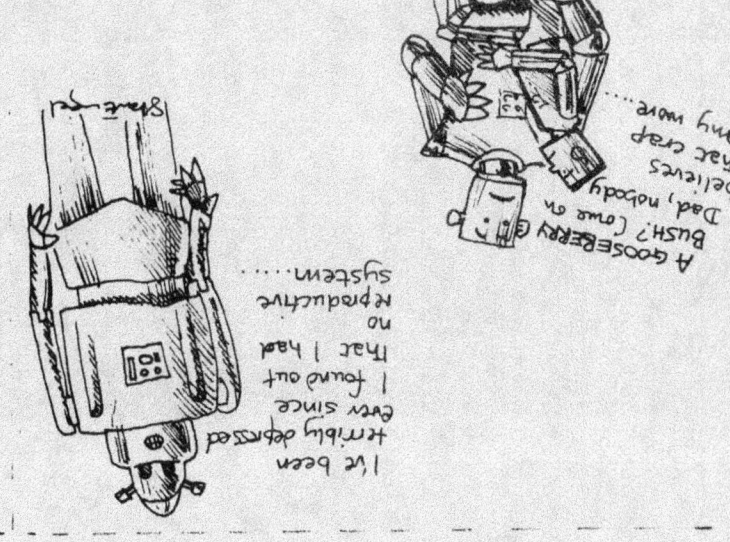

Wool City Rocker Bootleg Bookmark

© WOOL CITY ROCKER/STAN ENGEL 1981

Whatever you're celebrating around now, here's a card to prove that I'm tuned in to your happy vibes ooo

...D IN ALONG THIS LINE OR I'LL THROW UP INTO YOUR HANDBAG - O.K.!

© Wool City Rocker/Stan Engel 1981

The Message is this...

© Wool City Rocker/Stan Engel 1981

Advertising in Wool City Rocker is cheap & effective ... ring Nick on Bradford 21867 for details.

POST CARD

— © WOOL CITY ROCKER/STAN ENGEL 1981 —

THIS SPACE FOR COMMUNICATION

ADDRESS TO BE WRITTEN HERE

POST CARD

— © WOOL CITY ROCKER/STAN ENGEL 1981 —

THIS SPACE FOR COMMUNICATION

ADDRESS TO BE WRITTEN HERE

THE SQUARES are a commercial pop band from Leeds. Brian & Paddy Hogan (brothers) on gtr./voc. & bass/voc., respectively, formed the group in '78 & released 'No Fear' c/w 'Nobody's Fool' on their own Airebeat Label (with drummer/vocalist Kevin Bates completing the trio). Peel gave it a couple of spins, one of which was heard by Seymour Stein (who owns Sire Records). He phoned Brian from New York(!) & as a result, they signed to his label. In mid-'78 they re-recorded 'No Fear' at Air Studios, London, with Tommy Erdelyi (a.k.a. Tommy Ramone) producing & the thing came out on Sire in Sept. '78. They gigged a bit, including 2 supports to The Rezillos. A second track from the Air session, 'Magic Love', went onto the Sire compilation, 'The Sire Machine Turns You Up', which came out in Dec. '78. 'This Is Airebeat' c/w 'Stop Being A Boy' (double A-side) were recorded in Feb. '79 at Rockfield Studios with Hugh Jones (Adam & The Ants prod.) overseeing. This single came out in May '79. They toured with The Undertones & then did a short tour with The Straits. Sire don't do much promotion & the singles did ok, but not great. More gigs during '79 & then, in 1980, they put down 4 tracks: 'Buddy Holly', 'I May Be Better', 'You're A Square' & 'Carry Me Home', at Good Earth Studios, London. Brian: "Then it all started falling apart with Sire - they kept setting release dates but they were having a lot of internal troubles & eventually ceased operating as a record co. when Warners took them over, a couple of months ago. N.T.: "By that time you'd left them...?" Brian: "Yes, we'd fulfilled our contractual obligation to them but found ourselves in limbo for a few months, still tied to them legally, but with them not even prepared to talk to us on the phone - a terrible situation to be in." Drummer at that time, Andy Caves (ex-Jerks), left to join Roy Sundholm. It was Glenn Simpson of Hype Records (just setting up in Leeds) who got Brian & Paddy to reform the band with Ray Richards (aka Roy Romance) and Tim Mills (aka Tim Slim, Mit Lims & other semi-anagrams), both formerly with The Neat. Glenn took on management, picked up the 4 tracks from the last Sire session, signed them to Hype & is releasing their forthcoming single 'Oh, Buddy Holly' (out this month). Local gigs and wider touring are being lined up at the moment. CONTACT: Brian/Paddy on Leeds 620593 or Glenn at Hype on Leeds 445102.

RHABSTALLION
Mark Crowther (dms.); Stuart Toddington (ld.gtr.); Dave Thompson (ld.gtr.); Graham Hooper (bass); John Anderton (voc.).
The band (previously under the names Rogue and Stallion) has been in existence for 2½ years & has undergone seven line-up changes, leaving Dave as the only original member. They play hard, fast, loud rock - The Halifax Currier (with 3 chappatis -oops, 'Courier') described it as their "aggressive brand of wild & exciting rock." They've extensively played the pub, club & hall circuit around West Yorks. Graham: "We now like to play medium-to-large venues like sports centres & so on, that being where we're able to use our p.a. to the full & are at our best. We've a 1KW p.a. & a lighting rig." I asked about the 'New Electric Warriors' album... Graham: "On my debut gig at The White Lion, Huddersfield we got a 'phone call from Des Moines asking for a demo. He liked it & so we went into Cargo in May to record the master of 'Chain Reaction' which went onto the sampler album that came out at the end of 1980 on Logo Records." When the New Electric Warriors Tour was called off after one badly-publicised gig in Lowestoft, Dawnwatcher set up a gig at St George's Hall, Bradford (the 2 of them + Turbo & Jedediah Strutt) that pulled 600. A similar repeat gig is now planned & there's a single lined up - 'Day by Day' c/w (probably) 'Breadline' which they're recording at Steve Walker's 8-track Airedales Studios in Cleckheaton & releasing in May on the band's own label. As are most bands, they're looking for gigs and can be contacted on Bfd'A 96999 (Graham).

Sorry to muscle in on your mouth but here's the Wool City Rockword No 11 to make your grey matter groan and cause you to curse a compiler! K.T.

Clues Across.
5. Don't do it to ants or certain shoes. (4,2)
6. Snake makes noises for audience reaction. (6)
9. Dan Dare's enemies on record? (6)
10. Band makes lax tour to Vienna initially — odd! (8)
11. Opening in records, literally, for one of the band. (4)
12. Winning fruit for absolute lunatic, perhaps. (5,5)
13. Mike sacks 'em — that's roughly how I feel! (5,2,4)
18. Rats run round the middle where we can play. (4,5)
21. Bill & Ben's pal into dope? (4)
22. A band, a periodical, and part of a gun. (8)
23. Record cover on my arm. (6)
24. Clocked between gigs? (6)
25. Where the Hull "Boys" come from? (6)

Clues Down.
1. Note meal eaten. It's refreshing! (5,3)
2. To d-drink? Spin a coin (4,2)
3. Lost hair for madam! Some woman. (8)
4. One step and sounds like a dancer. (1,5)
5. Dan, the heavy musician? (6)
7. Stir 1 with them, or play them, perhaps. (6)
14. Setting levels every day before dark? (8)
15. Leaders in cattle-markets. (8)
16. So Marg. comes to climax! (6)
17. Above all, band who had to have this number. (6)
19. Delays those in front of stage. (6)
20. No turning back after blended teas, Sheena! (6)

Solution to Rockword No 10

B	L	U	E	S	U	E	D	E	S	H	O	E	S
E	P	I		M		V		A		A		Y	
L	A	P	E	L		E	N	E	R	G	I	E	S
O		E		L		R		R	U	N		I	
W	A	R	N	I	N	G		E	N	E	M	I	E	S
		T		N		E		S				I	
H	A	S	T	E		S	I	T	T	I	N	G	O	N
E			I		S							N		I
S	O	N	G	S	H	E	E	T		P	U	N	C	H
A		G			L		R		L					E
L	E	A	K	A	G	E		E	L	A	S	T	I	C
T		L			M		A		S		O			A
S	O	B	E	R	E	S	T		T	O	B	A		G
		N		R		N		E			E			O
A	G	I	T	A	T	E	D	C	R	O	W	D	S	

Well, here's anutha mutha for ya! Have yourselves a real good time.

---

the FAN CLUB AT Brannigans, CALL LANE, LOWER BRIGGATE, LEEDS 1. phone: 446905
OPEN EVERY THURSDAY
Start 8.30pm   Close 1.00am
further enquiries phone 663252
SUPPORT YOUR LOCAL GROUPS! EACH WEDNESDAY LISTEN TO RADIO LEEDS' 'METROGNOME' 6.30pm OR READ 'POP POST' 7.00pm IN THE Y.E.P.

THURSDAY 26th FEB. - Blah! Blah! Blah! plus THE LOVED ONE members 1.00 non 1.25
THURSDAY 5th MARCH - the POISON GIRLS AND THE CRAVATS members 1.25 non 1.50
THURSDAY 12th MARCH: ARTHUR 2 STROKE AND THE CHART COMMANDOES + the ANTI-POP PACKAGE members 1.00 non 1.25
THURSDAY 19th MARCH - ALTERED IMAGES plus 'SISTERS OF MERCY'
THURSDAY 26th MARCH: BASEMENT 5 AND EQUIVALENT 8 members 1.25 non 1.50
THURSDAY 2nd APRIL - BLURT! plus BRIAN BRAIN members 1.50
THURSDAY 9th APRIL - A SHEFFIELD PACKAGE DETAILS SOON
THURSDAY 16th APRIL - 'T.V. SMITH'S EXPLORERS' + SUPPORT

Now it's DEFINITE! A REGULAR ROCK VENUE EVERY SUNDAY 7.30pm - 11pm
TIFFANY'S MERRION CENTRE LEEDS Leeds (0532) 665252 or 31440/9
ADVANCE TICKETS FROM VIRGIN, JUMBO, TIFFANY'S AND THE UNI RECORD SHOP. NORMALLY 50p CHEAPER THAN ON THE DOOR!

SUNDAY 15th MARCH GANG of 4 * PERE UBU * DELTA 5 TICKETS £2.50 ADVANCE FROM VIRGIN, JUMBO, UNI.
SUNDAY 22nd MARCH LEEDS ROCKAROUND ALL DAY CONCERT 12 OF THE BEST KNOWN LOCAL GROUPS FROM 2pm to 11pm IN AID OF THE YEAR OF THE DISABLED PERSON TICKETS £2.00
SUNDAY 29th MARCH "2002 REVIEW" WITH 'CLASSIX NOUVEAUX' 'THEATRE OF HATE' 'SHOCK' 'NAKED LUNCH' 'EYELESS IN GAZA'. STARTS AT 6.00pm FINISHES AT 11.00pm TICKETS £2.50 ADVANCE
SUNDAY 5th APRIL 'KEN HENSLEY' OF URIAH HEEP AND FRIENDS plus EXTRA HEAVY SUPPORT.

TRY US OUT!!! ADVANCE TICKETS £2.00 (£2.50 on DOOR.)
* NO DRESS RESTRICTIONS! SEPERATE BAR! AGE 15 AND UPWARDS. *
GARY NUMAN TICKETS STILL AVAILABLE FROM :- 19, SOUTHSIDE, CARLETON RD LONDON N7 0QH SEND £16 BY P.O. MADE OUT TO ARAGORN PROMOTIONS (ENCLOSE SAE) THIS INCLUDES FULL TRANSPORT.

LEEDS UNIVERSITY'S UNION RECORDS

HUGE REDUCTIONS ON 1000's OF ALBUMS

come and see for yourself — the shop is in the basement of the Union Building

We also sell tickets for all Leeds Univ. & Polytech. concerts, & for Leeds Playhouse & The Grand Theatre.

SHOP HOURS: MON.-FRI. 9.30 a.m.-5 p.m.

Ram Recording Studios

64 Armley Road, Leeds LS12 2DR. Tel. (0532) 445044

STILL ONLY £65 (+VAT) PER 10-HOUR DAY or £7.50 (+VAT) PER HOUR

THE YEAR OF THE RAM

"The days of sweating blood in Ram Studios during July, September and December 1980 have paid dividends for Susan Fassbender and Kay Russell. On the strength of the Ram tape, Bradford-based Fassbender-Russell signed publishing and recording contracts that have culminated in their first single ('Twilight Cafe' on CBS Records) soaring into the charts and have also lead to

---

March 1981 Yorkshire Pudding (Hull)

Su.1 Unity Hall, Wakefield = AFTER THE FIRE. City Hall, Hull = DR. FEELGOOD. Blackburne Head, Pontefract = TAURUS. Florde Grene, Leeds = HONEY + SPIDER. Royal Park, Leeds = 156 BAND. Staging Post, Leeds = LIMELIGHT. Vaults Bar, Bradford = MIDDLE 8. Princeville, Bradford = ROUGH JUSTICE (1). White Lion, Huddersfield = (1) BUCK MOSEY & THE AUSTRALIANS. (2) NEW KING SNAKES.

Mo.2 Victoria, Huddersfield = PRIVATE DICKS. Warehouse, Leeds = THE DB'S + THE RAYBENTS. Limit Club, Sheffield = ORANGE JUICE. Funhouse, Keighley = CONFESSOR + SWAKARA. Marquis of Granby, Leeds = STAGE B. Marples Club, Sheffield = WARLORD.

Tu.3 Vaults Bar, Bradford = WARLORD. Haddon Hall, Leeds = THIN RED LINE.

We.4 St. George's Hall, Bradford = JOHNSON. Warehouse, Leeds = WILKO JOHNSON + SIGNS + TRUST. Limit Club, Sheffield = BREAKER. Foggy's, Halifax = PRIVATE DICKS. Marquis of Granby, Leeds = THE VOLUNTEERS. Royal Park, Leeds = IRONMAIDEN + NOSWEAT. Vaults Bar, Bradford = ORAL SAX. Fan Club, Leeds = POISON GIRLS + MAYHEM. Ocean Club, Hornsea = BLITZKREIG PATROL. Wellington Club, Leeds = STORMY MONDAYS. Carriage College, Leeds = THE PACKHORSE. White Lion, Huddersfield = LUIGI ANI 7A BOYS. Kings Head, Keighley = SLIDER. Princeville, Bradford = LIMELIGHT. Haddon Hall, Leeds = HERESY.

Th.5 Limit Club, Sheffield = ALEX HARVEY. Royal Park, Leeds = PRIVATE DICKS.

Fr.6 University, York = WILKO JOHNSON. Yorkshireman, Skipton = PRIVATE DICKS. Polytechnic, Sheffield = THE VAPOURS. Taboo, Scarborough

Sa.7 St. George's Hall, Bradford = ELVIS COSTELLO & THE ATTRACTIONS. University, Sheffield = PRIVATE ELEVATORS + DIAGRAM BROTHERS. University, Leeds = ONLY ONES + FAMOUS NAMES. Polytechnic, Huddersfield = SHADER. Boudicean's, Leeds = KNIFE EDGE. Backhorse, Leeds = SPECIAL GUESTS (advertised). White Lion, Huddersfield = BLITZKREIG PATROL. Haddon Hall, Leeds = RED EYE.

Su.8 Florde Grene, Leeds = DIY + BLITZKREIG (3pm). Top Rank, Sheffield = DURAN DURAN. Esshalt & Airedown Sports Club, Airedale = 156 BAND. Staging Post, Leeds = RED EYE. Vaults Bar, Bradford = BELLADONNA RIGHT. Princeville, Bradford = SATANIC RIGHTS (?). White Lion, Huddersfield = BODY LANGUAGE(?). Haddon Hall, Leeds = DODGY TACTICS.

Mo.9 Warehouse, Leeds = NASH THE SLASH. Marples, Sheffield = ARTERY. Funhouse, Keighley = SPEED + SUPPORT. Marquis of Granby, Leeds = YOU & THE NIGHT & THE MUSIC. Royal Park, Leeds = VOLUNTEERS. Roster, Doncaster = JAZ INDEX. Marples Club, Sheffield = B TROOP + SAX + PYRAMID. Vaults Bar, Bradford = ANKH.

Tu.10 City Hall, Sheffield = IRON MAIDEN + TRUST. Warehouse, Leeds = NASH THE SLASH. St. George's Hall, Bradford = GILLAN + DEDRINGER. Rotters, Doncaster = FRANKIE VAUGH & THE FOUR SEASONS. Marquis of Granby, Leeds = TALISMAN (T.B.C). Kings Head, Keighley = OMEN.

We.11 Unity Hall, Wakefield = SWEET. Polytechnic, Sheffield = EQUIVALENT VIII. Marquis of Granby, Leeds = ARTERY. Warehouse, Leeds = KROKUS + MORE. Vaults Bar, Bradford = PRIVATE DICKS + WHIPPS. White Lion, Bradford = ORAL SAX. Haddon Hall, Leeds = FOGGY'S HALLABALOO SHADER.

Th.12 University, Bradford = DR. FEELGOOD. Princeville, Bradford = SHADER. Entertainer, Dewsbury = STROKE + SMP. Fan Club, Leeds = MACHINE + NEW EFFECT APPEAL. Tiffany, Bradford = SHAKE APPEAL. Princeville, Bradford = BTROOP + SAX + DELTAS + THE ODDS. Haddon Hall, Leeds = ANKH.

Fr.13 Penthouse, Scarborough = STEPPIN' WOLF. City Hall, Sheffield = DIAMOND HEAD + HERESY. Florde Grene, Leeds = SLIDE TIME FRESHIES. Polytechnic, Bradford = ROYAL COMET COMMANDOES. University, Sheffield = SAN, York = LIMIT. University, Leeds = SHAKIN' STEVENS. Polytechnic, Bradford = ROUGH JUSTICE + ABONY COLUMN. College of Ripon & YC, Ripon = MUSIK + SMP.

Sa.14 Polytechnic, Huddersfield = ANT PEOPLE. University, Leeds = STRAY CATS + MARAUDERS. Warehouse, Leeds = SHARP BLUES BAND (local band). New Theatre, Hull = MIKE HARDING. Marquis of Granby, Leeds = THE PHOTOS + WIRES. Kings Head, Keighley = THE 65 MILLIPPS. Limit Club, Sheffield = NEW MUSIK + SNIPS.

Mo.16 Warehouse, Leeds = NEW MUSIK + SNIPS. City Hall, Sheffield = ELVIS COSTELLO & THE ATTRACTIONS. Funhouse, Keighley = WHAM + BON NOW NOW. Marquis of Granby, Leeds = ANT PEOPLE. Vaults Bar, Sheffield = QUEVAGONTI. Haddon Hall, Leeds = AVENGERS = FAT ELSIE + NEW MUSIK + SNIPS (with Jenny Ham).

Tu.17 Amnesia, St. George's Hall, Bradford = EQUIVALENT VIII. Polytechnic, Sheffield = HOTGOSSIP, University, Bradford = STORY + BARRACUDAS. Tiffany, Leeds = GANG OF 4 + PERE UBU + DELTAS. Staging Post, Leeds = RHIAD. Vaults Bar, Bradford = SHAPER. Princeville, Bradford = AVENGER (with JENNY HAM). White Lion, Huddersfield = PRIVATE DICKS (t.p.c.) Vaults Bar, Leeds = WHIPPS.

We.18 University, Sheffield = HOTGOSSIP. Marquis of Granby, Leeds = DOLE 9 CLUB (local band). Warehouse, Leeds = PHOTOS + 30oz HOLLAND & HIS MILLIONAIRES. Vaults Bar, Bradford = ORAL SAX. Ocean Club, Hornsea = COOL TO SMOG. White Lion, Huddersfield = SLIDER.

Th.19 Royal Park, Leeds = KNIFE EDGE. Fan Club, Leeds = ALTERED IMAGES + SISTERS OF MERCY. Warehouse, Leeds = ORANGE JUICE. Tiffany, Bradford = COCKNEY REJECTS. Princeville, Bradford = (T.B.A.)

Sa.21 Royal Park, Leeds = DODGY TACTICS. Polytechnic, Huddersfield = Q-TIPS + SUPPORT. University, Leeds = MERCURY (Swaland). Palm Cove, Bradford = MERCURY + RED EYE. White Lion, Huddersfield = HACKSAW'S FLAMINGOS.

OK GEROL'S RECORDS

ROCK 'N' ROLL RARITIES, PUNK and NEW WAVE, HEAVY and PROGRESSIVE, GOLDEN OLDIES, IMPORTS and COLLECTORS ITEMS, BLUES, POP, REGGAE etc.

PART EXCHANGE — COLLECTIONS BOUGHT

MERRION STREET, LEEDS
(Tel Leeds 452705 or at home 075284 - 669)

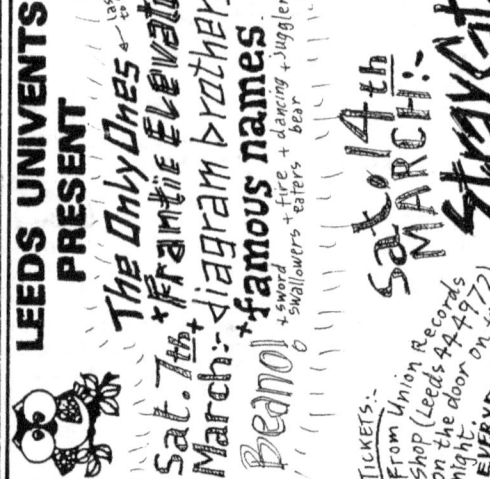

LEEDS UNIVENTS PRESENT

Sat. 7th March:- The Only Ones + Frantic Elevators + Diagram Brothers

Sat. 14th March:- Stray Cats + Support

Beano! + famous names + sword swallowers + fire eaters + dancing bear + juggler

TICKETS:- From Union Records Shop (Leeds 44-4972) or on the door on the night. EVERYBODY WELCOME.

FUNHOUSE

131 North St., Keighley. Tel. 603796

EVERY MON. 8-11 p.m. LIVE ROCK

2nd. March = CONFESSOR + SWAKARA
9th. March = SPEED + SUPPORT
16th. March = WHAM formerly "Year Itch"

Theatre of Hate

→ L.P. — "Live at The Warehouse, Leeds"
OUT NOW ON S.S. LABEL at only £2.49

→ New Single — "Rebel Without a Brain" c/w "My Own Invention"
OUT SOON

See the band on the ZOOZ Review at TIFFANYS, LEEDS 29th March.

University of Bradford Union

RICHMOND ROAD, BRADFORD, WEST YORKSHIRE BD7 1DP
Tel. Bradford 34135/8

ADVANCES

MARCH
- 12th — DR. FEELGOOD. Plus Radio I's Richard Skinner LIVE!! CB.
- 18th — WEAPON OF PEACE. Reggae at it's finest. £1.25 in advance. CB

MAY
- 2nd — ECHO AND THE BUNNYMEN. £2.50. CB Tickets available from March 7.

JUNE
- 6th — PAULINE MURRAY CB. £1.75 in adv.
- 6th — TEARDROP EXPLODES.
- 13th — JOHN COOPER CLARKE CB.
- 27th — MAGAZINE CB.

CB = Communal Bldg.
GH = Great Hall.

Tickets from Union Shop & H.M.V. Records

"Richard Skinner...huh!...for out. Marten, far out!!" (N.T.)

OPEN TO THE PUBLIC

L.P.U. Ents Presents...
THE Q-TIPS
+ SUPPORT

at The Riley Smith Hall, Leeds Univ. Students' Union
SAT. 21st MARCH
7.30 p.m.

Tickets: £2.50 from Leeds Poly. Union Information Point (Leeds 30171) & Leeds Univ. Union Record Shop (Leeds 44972) & on the door on the night.

LPUSU ADULT ONLY – Normal door price = 3.50

Civic Theatre...
Polytechnic...
Staging Post, Leeds = ROSE
Palm Cove, Bradford = REFLEX.
Princeville, Bradford = BRICK MARINE (L)
Staging Post, Leeds = WAMM (L+P)
White Lion, Huddersfield = (Gregory Isaac's backing band) (T.B.A.)
Haddon Hall, Leeds = DALE HARGREAVES. Haddon Hall, Leeds = LUCKY STRIKE.

Fr.20 Alhambra, Bradford = MIKE HARDING — THE FREEBIES. Penthouse, Scarborough = THE FREEBIES.

Mo.23 Funhouse Bar, Keighley = MIKE HARDING. Marquis of Granby, Leeds = GREMLINS + WHIP. Vaults Bar, Bradford = OPP TADCON + HINE. Royal Park, Leeds = FIERCE VOLLEY. Marples Club, Sheffield = ROACH STURGEON. Haddon Hall, Leeds = DIVINE COMEDY.

Tu.24 Retters, Doncaster = NOSFERATU + THEATRE OF HATE + EYELESS. Marquis of Granby, Leeds = TAURUS. Vaults Bar, Bradford = KEEPING DARK. Warehouse, Leeds = MIXED LUNCH.

Th.26 Princeville, Bradford = CHINATOWN. Royal Park, Leeds = ANT. Alhambra, Bradford = MIKE HARDING + SEMENT III. Fan Club, Sheffield = THE PAGEANTS. Lime Club, Leeds = TREATMENT. Princeville, Bradford = AVENGER'S. White Lion, Huddersfield = (with Sonny Hazard) Haddon Hall, Leeds = NEW KING SNAKES.

Fr.27 Alhambra, Bradford = MIKE HARDING. Tiffany's, Leeds = ZOOZ REVIEW + featuring CLASSIX NOUVEAUX + THEATRE OF HATE + SHOCK + NAKED LUNCH + EYELESS + GAZA. Unity Hall, Wakefield = BOW WOW WOW. Staging Post, Leeds = (T.B.A.) Vaults Bar, Bradford = MODES FOR MUTANTS. Princeville, Bradford = DR. ROGER. White Lion, Huddersfield = PUZZLER. Haddon Hall, Leeds = TROUBLE IN THE SHADE.

Sa.29 Theatre Royal, York = MIKE HARDING. Kings Head, Keighley = SPEED. Warehouse, Leeds = THE GAS.

Mo.30 City Hall, Sheffield = MIKE HARDING. Vaults Bar, Bradford = BASE EQUIPM. Royal Park, Leeds = TREATMENT. Marples Club, Sheffield = CHINTOWN. Haddon Hall, Leeds = ROADSPICE ROCK BAND.

Tu.31 City Hall, Sheffield = MIKE HARDING.

Huddersfield Polytechnic
Great Hall, Queensgate

- SAT. 14th March = Climax Blues Band + Legal Aid
- SAT. 21st March = New Musik + Snips
- SAT. 28th March = Limelight + Still Earth (FUTURE EARTH RECORDS PACKAGE)
- FRI. 3rd April = Mo-dettes

Tickets from Woods + Brapleys + Union Travel Office or on door on night - doors open 8.30 p.m.
Ring Huddersfield 38156 for info. on prices, etc.

→ THIS GIG GUIDE WAS FREE WITH ISSUE No. 13 OF

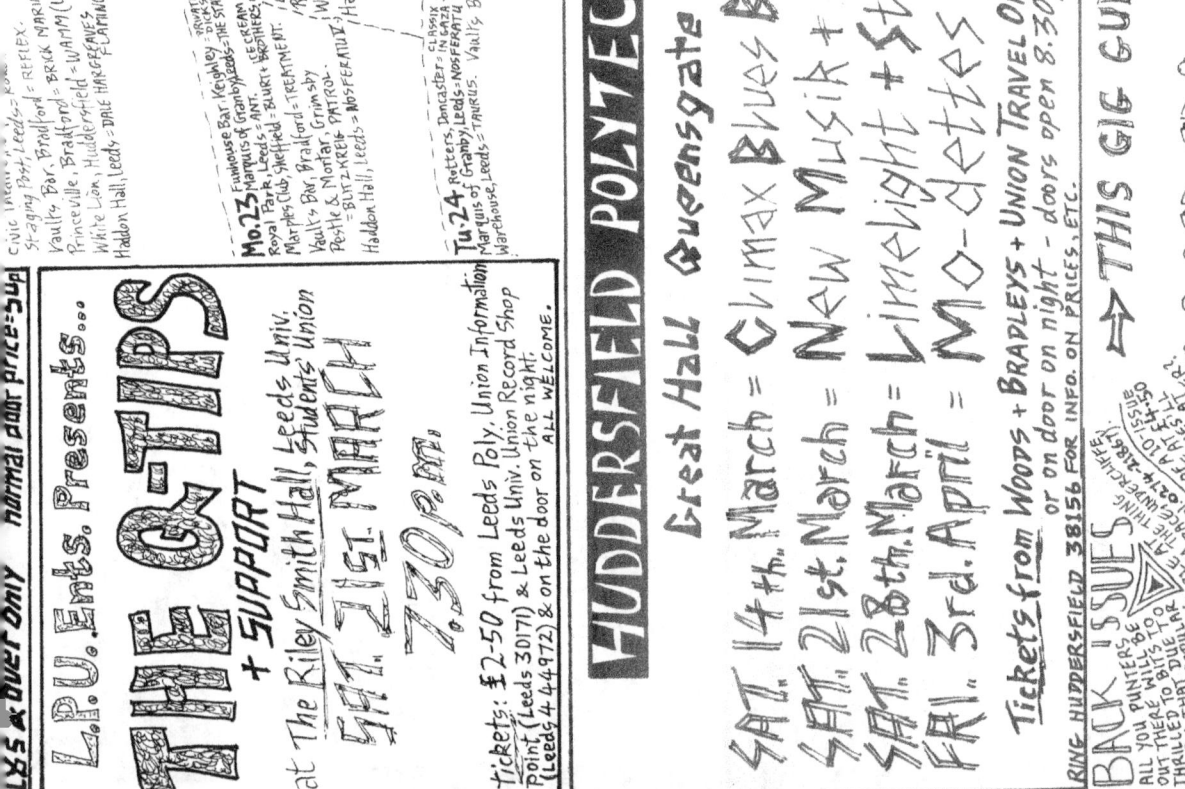

Nick Toczek's WOOL CITY ROCKER

IT'S THE NORTHERN ROCKSCENE MAGAZINE
Still only 30p ~ do you read it?

BACK ISSUES

ALL PUNTERS WILL BE THRILLED TO DISCOVER THAT POPULAR DEMAND HAS KEPT ALL PREVIOUS ISSUES AVAILABLE FROM US. (+20p postage per issue). 30p EACH. ISSUE 9 CALLED TO C-ZEK OX, BRADFORD BD3 OPY. MASOCHISM ROCKS FROM THE REGULARS. SUBSCRIBE NOW! 20 MINUTES AROUND LEEDS AFTER DINE THE UNDERCLIFFE, IN GAZA + ROCK + MIXED LUNCH. STILL AVAILABLE AT £1 (inc. POSTAGE) & 1st ISSUE AT £4.50. FRONT PRINT RUN = 3½ thousand (at a glance at around ½ of read and now binners).

CURRENT: ISSUE 13 = FREE TEARDROP

NEW ADVERTISING RATES

size of advert	1st advert placed	2nd & thereafter
square box (c. 3")	£25.00	£12.00
2 boxes (c. 3"×6")	£35.00	£20.00
¼p in mag. (c. 6"×4½")	£50.00	£30.00
½p each (c. 6"×9")	£75.00	£50.00

FULL PAGE: exact price/ad. dimensions may vary according to packaging and design. RING NICK ON (0274) 21.1867. Copy & payment to NICK TOCZEK, 5 Beech Terrace, Undercliffe, Bradford BD3 OPY, West Yorkshire.

TYPESETTING, LAYOUT and DESIGN by arrangement.

COPY DATE: 10 days before end of previous month. 2 COLOURS - EXTRA COSTS £25 EACH. CLASSIFIED ADVERTS – 25p PER WORD.

RIC-RAC Sound Studio

THE FIRST 24-TRACK RECORDING STUDIO IN YORKSHIRE

RECORD WITH RIC-RAC AND MIX WITH THE RIGHT PEOPLE!

For all studio enquiries ring Mick on Leeds 633717

A NEW 8-TRACK STUDIO

WOODLANDS
RECORDING STUDIO

£50 per 10-hour day

FAIRVIEW STUDIOS
WILLERBY – HULL

ARE INCREASING THEIR RECORDING FACILITIES FROM 8 TRACK TO:—

24 TRACK

OPENING RATE WILL BE **£12.50 PER HOUR**

FOR FULL DETAILS OF ALL OUR FACILITIES CONTACT:
(HULL) 0482-653116

March 1981 Lancashire & Merseyside Hot-Pot March 1981

Mo.2 Apollo, Manchester = WHO + RUTS D.C. Rafters, Manchester = ORANGE JUICE.
Brady's, Liverpool = DURAN DURAN.
Kingsgeorge, Blackburn = SIOUXSIE & BANSHEES + COMSAT ANGELS.

Su.1 Royal Court, Liverpool = SIOUXSIE & BANSHEES + COMSAT ANGELS.

Tu.3 Golden Garter, Manchester = ODYSSEY.
University, Salford = JUDIE TZUKE.
Polytechnic, Manchester = STRAY CATS + PARAMIND.
Empire, Liverpool = CAMEL.
King Georges Hall, Blackburn = GILLAN+DERINGER.
Lamplight, Rochdale = WANDA & THE DENTISTS.

We.4 Brady's, Liverpool = THE DOG'S + THE RAYBEATS.

Th.5 Apollo, Manchester = SIOUXSIE + SLADE + EXPORT.
Polytechnic, Manchester = MASH THE SLASH.
Warehouse, Preston = U.K. DECAY.

Fr.6 Free Trade Hall, Manchester = GAMMA + PRAYING MANTIS.
Royal Court, Liverpool = STRAY CATS + PARAMIND.
Mayflower, Manchester = STRAY CATS + PARAMIND.
Warehouse, Liverpool = DISCHARGE. College, Tipstoll.
Bradys, Liverpool = DIAMOND HEAD+CHINATOWN.
Graves Hotel, Lancaster = THE CHIRONS.
Moonrakers, Salford = WANDA & THE DENTISTS.
University, Lancaster = SLADE + IDENTITY PARADE.
Millstone, Lancaster = MARILYN + WORD OF MOUTH.

Sa.7 University, Manchester = STRAY CATS+WARRIORS.
Polytechnic, Preston = JEFF BECK+CLIMAX BLUES BAND.
Apollo, Manchester = U.K. DECAY.
Red Lion, Warrington = HEAD HUNTER.
Polytechnic, Preston = STRINGZ.
Moonrakers, Salford = RAPID FIRE.
Millstone, Manchester =

Su.8 Apollo, Manchester = ELVIS COSTELLO & THE ATTRACTIONS.
University, Lancaster = STRAY CATS + BARRACUDAS.

Mo.9 Mayflower, Liverpool = SHIDER.
Polytechnic, Preston = PERFORMING FERRETS.

Tu.10 Moonrakers, Preston = SHAPER.
Polytechnic, Manchester = THE VAPORS.
UMIST, Manchester = AFTER THE FIRE.

We.11 Apollo, Manchester = GILLAN + DERINGER. SKYX, Lancaster = WANDA & THE DENTISTS.

Th.12 Golden Garter, Manchester = CHAS & DAVE.
Royal Court, Liverpool = SWEET.
UMIST, Manchester = STEPPENWOLF.
Polytechnic, Manchester = NINE BELOW ZERO.

Fr.13 University, Lancaster = ELVIS COSTELLO & THE ATTRACTIONS.
Golden Garter, Manchester = THE SELECTER.
Royal Court, Liverpool = LOCALEROES.
Moonrakers, Salford = CIMARONS.
Mossside Community Centre, Manchester = WANDA & THE DENTISTS.
Millstone, Manchester = CINEMA.

Sa.14 Polytechnic, Preston = THE SELECTER.
Golden Garden, Manchester = GANG OF 4 + PEREUBU + DELTA 5.
University, Manchester = CHAS & DAVE.
Brady's, Liverpool = BOW WOW WOW/HOTGOSSIP.
Moonrakers, Salford = THE FEELHEARTBEATS.
Millstone, Manchester = ILLUMINAIRE.

Su.15 Empire, Liverpool = ELVIS COSTELLO & THE ATTRACTIONS.
Royal Court, Liverpool = BOW WOW WOW.
Apollo, Manchester = STATUS QUO.
Unicorn, Altrincham = SURGICAL SUPPORTS.

Mo.16 Apollo, Manchester = STATUS QUO.
Aquarius Club, Bolton = SHADER.

Tu.17

We.18 University, Manchester = GANG OF 4 + PERE UBU + DELTA 5.
University, Lancaster = SWEET.
Sports Centre, Bolton = THE SELECTER.

Th.19 Polytechnic, Manchester = THE SELECTER.
Apollo, Manchester = ROSE ROYCE.
Queen Elizabeth Hall, Oldham = MIKE HARDING.
UMIST, Manchester = NEW MUSIK + SHYS.

Fr.20 Theatre, Southport = ROSE ROYCE.
Mayflower, Liverpool = LOCALEROES.
Moonrakers, Salford = BLUE WHEELS.
Millstone, Manchester = MAD VICARS.

Sa.21 Polytechnic, Manchester = THE PHOTOS + SOULS.
HOLLAND & HIS MILLIONAIRES.
Vaults, Oldham = FAT ELSIE.
Moonrakers, Salford = HOLLOW MOUNTAIN.

Su.22 Empire, Liverpool = MIKE HARDING.

PRIESTLEY'S T-SHIRTS

36, BOOTHAM YORK
TEL 0904-23114

ADULT T's £4.00
KIDS T's £3.00
SEND S.A.E.
U.S. SWEATS £7.50
FOR CATALOGUE

HMV HMV HMV
we sell
rok reggae pnuk
jazz disco folks
blues 12 inchers

INDEPENDENT CASSETTES & 'ZINES

SMART DISTRIBUTION CO., 104 Sandford Road, Moseley, Birmingham 13.

CASSETTES: The Stuff:'Stuff'.Interesting and meaningfull noises from the South.Sound quality-v.good - 80p only. Bron Area:'One Year'.A classic in its own time,one of the best cassettes yet.Sound quality-v.good - £1.25p. Stick Insects:'Puritan Ethic'.Interesting and fun,from famous Nuneaton persons.Sound quality-v.good - £1.00. "Waiting for Bardot".Synth/Tape noises with content.Sound quality-v.good - £1.25p.

'ZINES: '0533':cassettes,graphics,Ronnie Slicker and the Banditz... 20p. * 'Bizarre Angel' No3.art,poetry,reviews,writing at 80p. * 'Stereotype' No2. 20p. * 'Smart Verbal' No5-Close Rivals,Au Pairs,Fast Relief,cassettes,poetry how to...25p. * 'Damn Latin' No7-local band reviews, eyeless in gaza,cassette 'zine reveiws 25p......
PLEASE ADD 20p P&P or SEND 20p STAMPS,make cheques/p.o.'s payable to M.White

FOR FULL CATALOGUE AND FURTHER INFO SEND S.A.E. to SMART DISTRIBUTION CO.

tape it tape it tape it tape it tape it tape it tape

ULTERIOR MOTIVES

FORMER MEMBERS OF THIS BAND ARE NOW IN VEX,SUSAN FASSBENDER, REFLEX AND 'AYE, HE SAID' — RECORD ON A RADIO SHOW — LIFETIMES — ANOTHER GHOST — YOU GOTTA KNOW — LOOKS LIKE LOVE — SANSKY GANDHI'S PLANE — BREADLINE — COMMODITY — ROCK+POP — HEAD GAME — KICKS

THE NEW LINE-UP IS BACK IN A FEW WEEKS – LIVE,ON VINYL AND ON CASSETTE – BAD TASTE IS BACK!

Gig listings
- **Th.26** Apollo,Manchester = TOM WAITS. Warehouse,Liverpool = NEW MODEL + SNIPS.
- **Fr.27** Brady's,Liverpool = THE POLECATS. Moonrakers,Salford = THE NAUGHTY BOYS. Moonstone,Manchester = KICKS.
- **Sa.28** Philharmonic,Liverpool = STEELEYE SPAN. Moonrakers,Salford = SLY MOVE. Moon+Forte,Manchester = FINS.
- **Su.29** Polytechnic,Preston = BLACK SLATE.
- **Mo.30** Rotters,Liverpool = CLASSIX NOUVEAUX + THEATRE OF HATE + EYELESS IN GAZA + SHOCK + NAKED LUNCH.
- **Tu.31** Polytechnic,Manchester = MUSIC FOR PLEASURE.

CHEERERS MUSIC STORE

(WHY TRAVEL? WE'RE HERE IN LEEDS CENTRE...)

AMP. DEPT. H/H MAIN DEALER.. MARSHALL, VOX, PEAVEY, M.M., RAVEN, McGREGOR. WE ARE NOW TEAC MAIN DEALERS. WEM, & VHS....

GUITAR DEPT. FENDER, GIBSON, IBANEZ MAIN DEALER, HONDO II, KRAMER, PEAVEY, GORDON SMITH + VARIOUS SECOND HAND.

DRUM DEPT. PREMIER MAIN AGENTS, TAMA, SONOR, PAISTE etc. PART EXCHANGE and PERSONAL LOANS AVAILABLE.

TEL: 449692

8, THE MERRION CENTRE, LEEDS 2.   9.00 to 5.30

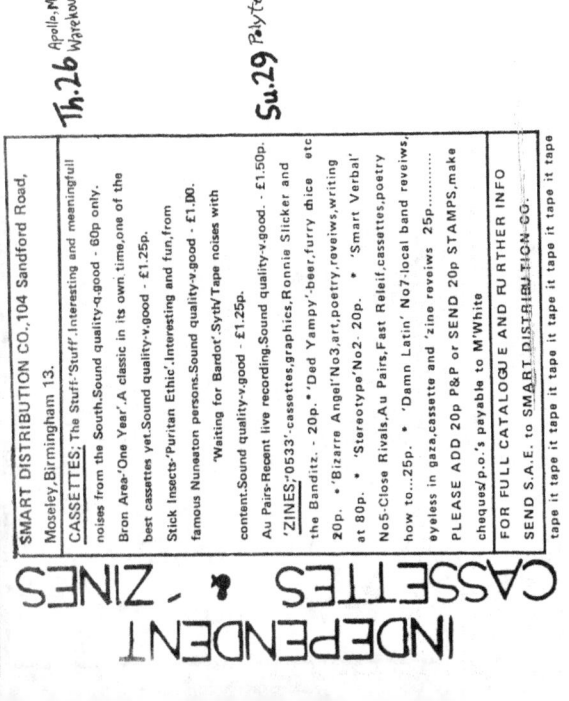

The ROCKY ROCK DEMOS

Break the circuit and maybe win yourself some singles:

All albums £2.50 inc. p+p.

Local Heroes SW9

Don't be ■, buy Oval

JUNIOR MAILORDER — 13, BURNEDGE LANE, GRASSCROFT, OLDHAM   OL4 4EA

WOOL CITY ROCKER

→ THIS GIG GUIDE WAS FREE WITH ISSUE No 13 OF NICK TOCZEK'S WOOL CITY ROCKER — IT'S THE NORTHERN ROCKSCENE MAGAZINE — still only 30p ~ do you read it?

ADVERTISING RATES
NEW ADVERT. 1st advert placed / 2nd ad. & thereafter
- size of advert.
- square box (c.3") — £25.00 / £12.00
- 2 boxes (c.3"x6") — £35.00 / £20.00
- ½ page (in mag)(c.6"x4½) — £50.00 / £30.00
- ½ page (c.6"x9") — £75.00 / £50.00
- TYPESETTING and DESIGN by arrangement

Extra pages & mirrors may vary according to exact packaging and design. EXTRA COLOURS £25 EACH
Copy & payment to NICK TOCZEK, 5 Beech Terrace, Undercliffe, Bradford, BD3 0PY, West Yorkshire. (0274) 21862.

BACK ISSUES
ALL YOU PUNTERS OUT THERE WILL BE THRILLED THAT DUE TO POPULAR DEMAND COPIES OF ALL ISSUES ARE STILL AVAILABLE — 30p EACH (inc. P&P). ISSUES 1-4 ARE NOW CALLED 'OLDIES' AND ISSUE 5 ONWARDS ARE 'MASOCHIST ISSUES' — PRINT RUN 3 THOU. COPY 20p each.

FRONT ISSUES
REGULAR SUBSCRIPTION £4.50 FROM N.TOCZEK. SUBSCRIPTIONS = 18 mags for a fiver. BACK ISSUE £1 + SAE.
CURRENT RUN = 3 thousand.
PRINT: Glance 7, 4 Sand St, Bradford.

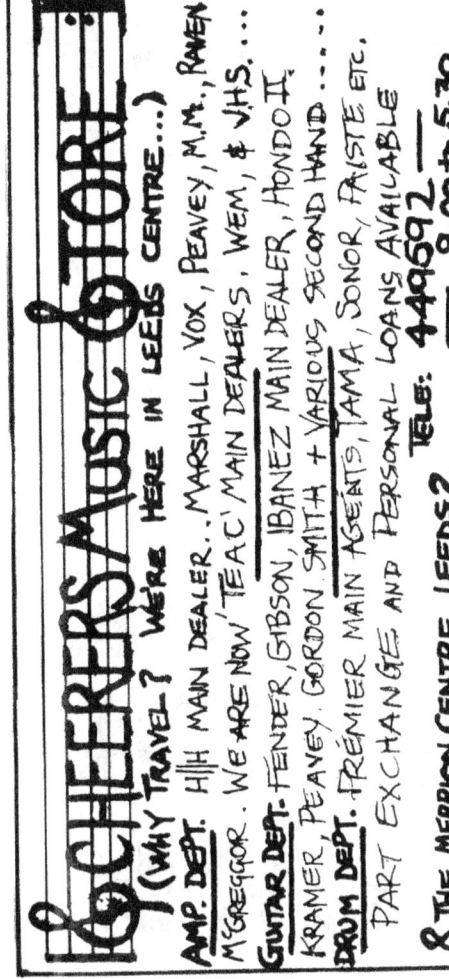

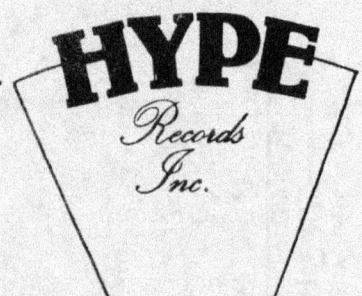 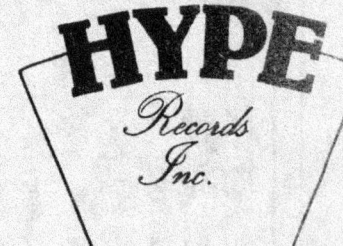 

32 SOVEREIGN ST   LEEDS LS1 4BJ   Tel: (0532) 445102/445108   Telex: 557061 (Link Up G)

WEST YORKSHIRE'S FIRST NATIONAL RECORD LABEL WELCOMES

THE SQUARES

WITH THEIR DEBUT SINGLE

"BUDDY HOLLY"

IN THE SHOPS MARCH 20th

WATCH OUT FOR OUR COMPILATION L.P. "UP THE M.1."

ISSUE #14

Summer 1981, 2,000 copies printed, 20 A4 pages + 5-track flexidisc of Hull bands + A2 single-sided poster featuring the 5 bands on the flexidisc

In every way, this—the final published issue—was the best one yet. The cover price had risen from 30p to 40p, but it was an awe-inspiring package. The plastic bag contained a full-sized magazine, plus the flexidisc and poster. Quirkily, the whole 20-page magazine read from the back to the front (i.e. front page on page 20, editorial on page 18, etc., with the back cover on page 1). I had a brilliant student on placement with me from Trinity and All Saints College (now Leeds Trinity University). He was Duncan McCarroll whose tireless work earned him the post of WCR's Assistant Editor.

Notes on bands featured in this issue.

In 1981, Hull had some bands with deliberately provocative names. Sons of the Pope (with a track on the flexidisc) took the immorality of the Catholic priesthood to the very top. There was also a fairly successful Hull indie band called Nyam Nyam, the members of which were also active under the name Lord Mountbatten's Bits and Pieces. Lord Mountbatten was a cousin of Elizabeth II who was particularly close to the young Charles, our present king. His 'bits and pieces' were his personal papers, later sold to Southampton University. However, on 27 August 1979, he was assassinated by the IRA when they blew up his boat off the coast of Ireland. Adopted so soon after his brutal killing, that choice of band name took on a totally different meaning to most people.

Order form in plastic bag containing each copy

OK

ROCK 'n' ROLL RARITIES
PUNK and NEW WAVE
HEAVY and PROGRESSIVE
GOLDEN OLDIES
IMPORTS and COLLECTORS ITEMS
BLUES, POP, REGGAE etc.

COLLECTIONS BOUGHT — PART EXCHANGE

GEROL'S RECORDS
MERRION SUPERSTORE LEEDS
(Tel: Leeds 457765 or at home 075784 - 669)

A NEW DEAL FROM CARGO

8 TRACK RECORDINGS
(10 hour bookings day or night)
COULD COST JUST

£40 *

RING US NOW
And ask for the Special Deal Details.

CARGO RECORDING STUDIOS
KENION ST., ROCHDALE, LANCS.
(0706) 524420
(* Tape + VAT extra)

RED RHINO RECORDS
9 GILLYGATE, YORK, YO3 7EA
0904-36499

Record Shop
~ INDIES, REGGAE & ANYTHING ELSE POSEY

Wholesalers
~ ALL INDIES + WIDE SELECTION OF AVANT GARDE IMPORTS & PRE-RELEASE REGGAE L.P.'s

Record Label
~ DO YOU REMEMBER THE NORMIL HAWAIIANS?

NOW OPEN AGAIN!

16 LUMB LANE, BRADFORD 8.

ROOTS RECORD SHOP

TEL. Bradford 32721.

BRADFORD'S REGGAE SHOP

FUNHOUSE BAR
131 North St., Keighley.   tel. 603796

ROCK CONCERTS
EVERY MONDAY 8-11 pm   50p admission
STAR BANDS + SUPPORTS
NEW WAVE · PUNK · HEAVY METAL

with:- The Elements · Shake Appeal · Speed · Knife Edge · The Whippos · New Model Army · Little Brother · Bovver & The Wombats · Private Dicks · The Shakes · Confessor · Still Earth · Modes For Mutants & MANY OTHERS

LEEDS UNIVERSITY...

Elvis Costello & The Attractions + REALLY GO
TUES. 23rd JUNE... tickets = £4.00

Iggy Pop
THURS. 2nd JULY... tickets = £3.00

Doors Open At 8.30

Tickets on sale as usual at Union Records in the basement of the union building.

THIS MAGAZINE ISSUE IS DEDICATED TO BOB MARLEY...

EDITORIAL

Hi-di-hi, pop-pickers, here's another dreary bloody issue of this atrocious rockist rip-off. Duncan McCarroll, on a 6-week student placement from Trinity & All Saints College, guests as editorial assistant & religious adviser. So, with his help, this is the biggest issue yet.

Last issue I announced that this one would be the final issue. I've since modified my thinking and shall be doing more issues after all - sorry if that news distresses you. However, it's no longer going to be monthly. No.15 will come out around September (probably) & No.16 around December (probably).

News from the home front: I've just (today) had £700 stolen from me by a mad computer in Middlesborough. Are financial hassles the sum total of life on planet Earth? This issue's flexidisc is of trax from a forthcoming sampler album of Hull bands called 'Mrs. Wilson's Children' which is coming out on Vital Records. Thanks to Kari Brown & the rest of the population of Hull for the part they've played in injecting the flexi & poster into this issue.

Looks like the gigs featuring punk bands at Gatsby's (see advert on p.23) are blown out -as we go to press, Rab (the promoter) is chasing another venue but no-one seems to like their premises saturated with eau-de-bostick glue perfume.

Kapitalist korner: on the market soon are the following goodies (a) 'Unlucky For Some' -a package of the first 13 Wool City Rockers; (b) 'Rock'n'Roll Terrorism' - a book of my own prose, lyrics & poems (published by Aquila Press); (c) likelyhood of a cassette album from my band 'Ulterior Motives'; (d) possibility of a solo album of my writings & performance pieces.

Scraps, one of my 2 dogs, is now recovering from his recent castration. Gaynor's working hard for her A-levels & I've just got some new curtains for the front room & a new speaker for the stereo. What with all this plus all the famous people getting shot & the notorious ones going on self-imposed crash diets, I get to feel that this journal plays a less-than-vital role in the making of 20th century socio-political reality. But maybe if I were to get the whole of this paragraph printed on a badge...

Everybody here at Wool City Rocker is chuffed as warm shit about Charlie & Di's wedding. Both of them are regular readers of the mag. & familiar figures in many northern rock venues. A revue of the whole St. Paul's gig + their first night together will doubtless feature (with fotos) in the colour supplement of WCR 15.

Wool City Rocker's ½-yearly accounts will be out soon after this issue. It is anticipated that profits will be slightly down on the anticipated figure of 45 billion (sterling) - this due to increased overheads (cigs costing more).

Get summerised - we'll be returning autumnatically, over & out, *Nick Toczek*

5 Beech Terrace
Undercliffe
Bradford BD3 0PY
West Yorkshire
Telephone 0274 21867

THE CRAP IN THIS issue INCLUDES (with bands' towns of origin in brackets)

- 4. X-PORT (Leeds) / DEFECTORS (Hull) / TV 21 (Edinburgh).
- 5. Record reviews (including Rondolet feature).
- 6. DELTA 5 (Leeds).
- 7. WHAMMER JAMMER (Doncaster) / REALLY (Leeds).   STREETLIGHT BLUES BAND
- 8. ALTERED IMAGES (Edinburgh) / SISTERS OF MERCY (Leeds) / ORANGE JUICE (Edinburgh) / (Bradford)
- 9. FLOCK OF SEAGULLS (Liverpool) / XANTHOS (Harrogate) / ASWAD (London) / ISRAELITES (London).
- 11. PLASTICS (Tokyo, Japan).
- 12. PAULINE MURRAY (Newcastle) with INVISIBLE GIRLS (Manchester).
- 13. BILL NELSON (Wakefield).
- 14. Tape reviews.
- 15. SHEDS (Bradford) / GANG OF FOUR (Leeds) / PERE UBU (Cleveland, Ohio, USA) / DELTA 5 (Leeds).
- 16. SPIZZLES (Birmingham) / TYGERS OF PANTANG (Newcastle) / MAGNUM (Birmingham).
- 17. CRASS (London) / BONE IDLE (Bradford).
- 19. EQUIVALENT VIII (Leeds) / WEAPON OF PEACE (Birmingham).
- 20. Record Reviews.
- 21. PATRICK MOORE & THE ALL-STARS (Bradford) / FURTHER EXPERIMENTS (Barnsley).
- 22. THE MESS (Leeds) / GILLAN (London) / DEDRINGER (Bradford/Leeds).

WOOL CITY ROCKER
ISSUE 14.   SUMMER '81.

Editor:
NICK TOCZEK

Assistant Editor:
DUNCAN McCARROLL

Contributors:
JULZ (of Delta 5)
STAN ENGEL
HARRY MARSDEN
MARY SAMUEL
JOHN TEMPEST
STEVE BROWN
TINO PALMER

TERMS OF SALE: 40p each direct to public or 60p each by mail. Bulk orders of 15 or more copies at ⅓ discount.

ADVERTISING RATES: First time advertisers pay the higher rate (given in brackets). Thereafter they are on the lower rate. Typesetting, special position & extra colours by arrangement + extra for reduction & origination.
Full page=(£75) £50.
Half page=(£50) £30.
Third page=(£35) £20.
Sixth page=(£25) £12.
Smalls=10p per word.
READERSHIP=20,000+

235 Pennine Radio

BOB PREEDY PRESENTS

PENNINE ROCK
TWO HOURS OF THE BEST ROCK MUSIC
7.00 P.M. WEDNESDAYS
Pennine Radio 235m MW & 96.0 VHF Stereo
THE SOUND IS ALL AROUND.

BETTER BADGES

100 BADGES
1½" black and white

£13.50
inc. p.&p.

sae for production price list and other details.

286 PORTOBELLO ROAD
LONDON W10 960 5513

X-PORT (formerly 'The Runners')

Humans: Paul Harper/dms, Tim Pickard/basso, Roddy Hall/ld.gtr, Chris Bray/kbds, (last 3 also do bkg vocs), Lobby Robinson/gtr'n'voc.

Minus Lobby, they formed 2 years back as The Numbers with Chris on voc/rm. gtr. They were then York-based with 2 members at college there. It was when they moved back home to Leeds that they recruited Lobby (from HM outfit Elwing) & underwent major surgery to achieve the name-change to The Runners (patience, readers, we're getting there slowly). Under this name, they won their heat of the Tetley/EMI Rock contest. This got them a track on the EMI "Rock On" LP. 'Bad In My Head' was recorded in 4 hours at September Sound with John Goodison producing: "The mix is very rough - he told us he'd be remixing it before putting it on the album, but he didn't."

Enter Lindsay Frost (the producer who was interviewed in WCR 9) to take the helm on a 26th March recording session at JSG Studios, Bradford (the review of this is elsewhere in this issue). The band feel that the past eight months they've been fairly apathetic after their initial band-enthusiasm. Lindsay's arrival has put the energy back and he's now trying out as their manager.

They have just embarked on their latest voyage as X-port, a name Lobby's they adopted after a band member's mum saw a clairvoyant who came up with enough convincing facts to amaze mum, among which was:"A relation close to you is in a band which should change its name to one beginning with 'E' then they'll succeed." (But X-port begins with 'X'...?!). This has been a true story.

They describe their music as pop-rock moving towards a smooth, not trashy, disco/funk feel. Chris, Lobby (the one with a birth mark on his thigh the size of a 10p piece, so he tells us) and Roddy all songwrite. Right now, they want no more from the whole disgusting rockscene than to gig & to entertain. Debut as X-port is at The Meanwood Arms in Leeds on 27th May. Contact: Lindsay on Leeds 623306.

Post script: Lobby Robinson gets sick of being told he looks like Art Garfunkel... what can we say except (all together, now): "So here's to you, Mrs. Robinson..."

THE DEFECTORS

They crop up on the flexi with this issue (& so are A. from Hull & B. on the album 'Mrs Wilson's Children'). Self-description: a funky-post-moderne band, a four-piece. They've also got a cassette album 'Winter At The Rehearsal Rooms' coming out on their own Louder Records (from which came their debut single moons ago). Forthcoming from that label are 'a sirenen whistle' and a cassette album by The Luddites, a Hull-based 'experimental' band. Label address: 2 Adderbury Grove, Beverley Rd, Hull, HU5 1AS (tel. 0482-41788 ask for Maureen - band bookings same no.).

TV21

LINE-UP: Norman Rodger/voc+gtr: Dave Hampton/tpt+perc+bkg.voc: Neil Baldwin/bass+bkg.voc: Ali Patterson/dms: Ally Palmer/gtr+bkg.voc.

DISCOGRAPHY: 1st single: 'Playing With Fire' c/w 'Shattered By It All' (on their own Powbeat Records label, April '80). 2nd single (actually a triple a-side EP): 'Ambition'/'Ticking Away'/'This Is Zero' (Powbeat Records, Sept '80). 3rd single: 'On The Run' c/w 'End Of A Dream' (Demon Records, Feb '81). 4th single: 'Snakes & Ladders' c/w 'Artistic Licence' (+ a freebie of their first 2 a-sides) (Deram, May '81). The Deram deal is a 5-year one giving the company an option on 3 singles & an album per year. Next single may be "I Deal With Life'.

SESSIONS: Peel Show (Nov '80), Richard Skinner (Jan '81), In Concert (April '81).

TOUR SUPPORTS: Another Pretty Face (Oct '80), Moondogs (Feb '81), Undertones (May '81).

* Not bad for a year's work!

Palmerama
in which cool'n'suave Tino Palmer reviews some discs...

Echo & The Bunnymen. 'Shine So Hard' 12" E.P. (Korva).
4 tracks for a quid is good value from anyone. Never listened to Echo before but enjoyed this - for a live recording very good sound quality indeed. First up, 'Crocodiles'. Bit ordinary, but enjoyable. 'Zimbo' could've done with the vocals beefing up a bit. Turn over & skip 'All That Jazz' completely! 'Over The Wall' from soon-come LP 'Heaven Up Here' takes the prize of best track - interesting textures & great drumming. (By the way, does ferrying the fans to Buxton make their film a rockist epic? Answers on a postcard to Sounds + ENEMY!).

Fad Gadget. 'Make Room'/'Lady Shave' 7" 45 (Mute).
'Lady Shave' - too one level-ish. Vocals sound just like Barry Andrews' 'Rossmore Road'. 'Make Room', however, starts promisingly & stays there - proper drums, good bassline (not overly funky but could be if it tried) + fine backing vocals. Rob Gotobed (ex-Wire) guest on drums.

The Mess. 'Tried & Trusted'/'I'm Falling' 7" 45 (Reasonable Records).
Stars of Bradford T&A's Rock On column - isn't Celia Barlow the world's most wonderful human being? This record is a mess - b-side's not bad but I wouldn't spend my ackers on it.

B.Troop. 'Emotional Assassin'/'Computer Logic'. 7" 45 (Hotshot).
Not bad, but not good. Nothing to distinguish it from most other dull indies - not even the vomit-coloured vinyl. A miss, David.

Second Layer. 'World Of Rubber'. LP (Cherry Red).
How to review an LP in 5 minutes. The world stinks, rubber stinks & this LP stinks! Even the cat threw up!

Original Mirrors. 'Dancing With The Rebels'/'Sure, Yeah' 7" 45 (Mercury).
Already been a minor hit - sounds better on the objet d'art than it does on the radio. Good handclaps can really make a record - it's worked on this. Love it - great!

Stranger Than Fiction. 'Losing You'/'You Don't Turn Me On Anymore' 7" 45 (Ambergris Records). Produced by Bill Nelson - did a good job too. Another of the millions of discs (groovy, huh?) recorded at Cargo. I like this - everyone else did too. I can stand 'Losing You'! B-side's good too - nice beat, proving that even electronic bands sound better with real drums.

Medium Medium. 'Hungry, So Angry'/'Nadsat Dream' 7" 45 (Cherry Red).
Good radio record - strong bassline & disco-ish guitar, make for da beat, & it's got a highly rememberable(?) chorus line. Pity about the duff b-side.

Five Or Six. 'Another Reason'/'The Trial' 7" 45 (Cherry Red).
Crap. B-side is too, and that's produced by Kevin Coyne! Good for about 30 secs - not good actually but...

The Undertones. 'It's Going To Happen'/'Fairly In The Money Now'. 7" 45 (Ardeck)
B-side is sort of semi-autobiographical I think - a jolly little ditty about a band that makes it big. Not a patch on the A-side which, even as you read this, is winging its way up the dirty thirty. A great summery sound, nice fade in - a rare t'ing - fine brass section (taking a tip from Teardrop Explodes?) & a deserved hit. Great fab triffic, Aunty Kath, pass the pay cheque etc. Goodnight & goodbye!

ROCKABILITY
THE COMPLETE RONDOLET RECORDS CATALOGUE...

Rondolet, a Mansfield record shop turned label, signed 3 bands - each of them specialists in a particular style of rock: H.M., punk & melodic. In addition, they've recently signed a licensing deal with Ron Weiser's U.S. rockabilly label, Rollin' Rock. What follows is a rundown of their entire catalogue as of now (Spring 1981). Reviews by Nick Toczek & Duncan McCarroll.

SINGLES

Witchfynde - "Give 'em Hell" c/w "Gettin' Heavy" (Round 1)
Good debut single (for band and label) of basic H.M. Plenty of power, with the band sounding much better on disc than they do live (rare for H.M.) Good b-side too.

Anti Pasti - "4 Sore Points" E.P. (Round 2)
4 songs: "No Government", "1980", "Two Years too Late", "Something New". Classic Punk - complete with droning sustained guitar, simple drumming and tuneless singalong chants. Identical rhythm on all trax - each lasting just over a minute. The guitar is perfect with b-side having the best 2 trax.

Brooklyn - "I Wanna be a Detective" c/w "Two Wheels" (Round 3)
Melodic rock aimed at the Sad Café/10cc/Supertramp market. A-side is a passable album track but fails dismally as a single. The over-the-top, fragmented, arrangement lacks polish or class. B-side is a better but more clichéd no. - very Boston. Powerful, and features some neat lead guitar: by far the better track.

Witchfynde - "In the Stars" c/w "Wake up Screaming" (Round 4)
A-side is well balanced and commercial no. Opens just like the b-side of the first single. Flip opens with distinctive drumming. All else is predictable, though well produced stuff. Lotta class to this band so it's a real shame that they repeatedly blow it in live performance.

Anti Pasti - "Let Them Free" c/w "Another Dead Soldier" + "Hell" (version) (Round 5) [on Red Vinyl]
Marginally more sophisticated/melodic with improved mix. 2 fine tracks + live 'Hell' which is great except for atrocious guitar break and messy ending, which is also great except if you're a musician, which is great......

Brooklyn - "Hollywood" c/w "Late Again" (Round 6)
More boring mid-Atlantic, mid-road, mid-snooze, mid-iocrity. Fine if you're a boring musician; boring if you're a fine musician. Hell's Teeth! there's an album of this stuff to fossilize thru' yet. B-side features castrated vocals and... zzzzzzzzzzz

ALBUMS

Witchfynde - "Give 'em Hell" (About 1) + "Stagefright" (About 2)
2 fine albums - first includes both sides of first single, second has both of second single. Excellent guitar work from Montalo throughout. Andro Coulton (bs) replaced by Pete Surgey for second album. Strong material on both albums that is fresh even though the musical style is dated.

Brooklyn - "You'll Never Know What You'll Find" (About 3)
Yes you will. We'll tell you. You'll find both sides of both singles + 6 other equally (insert your own adjectives) songs. Actually this band would do well on U.S. radio stations - so how about a collection to get rid of send them over there?

ROCKABILLY SINGLES

Ray Campi and His Rockabilly Rebels - "The Newest Wave" c/w "Once is Enough" (Round 1000)
Odd voice, great guitar, short song, like it. Flip: this guy's voice gets weirder - camp as in Campi. This stuff's blues/R'n'R crossover with novelty appeal.

Ravenna and the Magnetics - "Mean, Mean Man" c/w "Mean Little Mama" (Round 1001)
Good standard R'n'R with female vocalist who's something special: she's got balls, if you know what we mean. B-side has male vocals and he's great too. Classy guitar work on a stompin' rocker. Very impressed with this band.

Johnny Legend and His Skullcaps - "The South's Gonna Rise Again" c/w "Rockabilly Rumble" (Round 1002).
A-side features Benny Hill show sax over pro-Confederate lyrics (with 'Yeee-hah' whooping even!). Hot diggedy dawg - it's obnoxiously cheerful war mongering. B-side is pure rockabilly at full tilt. South-side story ballad of streetfighting. Credibility if you're into red neck rockabilly.

Ray Boy and Lil Jimmy Lee (I don't believe this) - "I Need Love" c/w "Love Me" (Round 1003)
Rough recording (sounds ancient!) with sax, kids and fast alternating vocals. Atmosphere, amateurish and enthusiastic. Flip has a neat slice of close harmony singing to a catchy rockabilly tune.

Jimmy Lee Maslon - "Turn me all Around" c/w "Your Wildcat Ways" (Round 1004)
A good A-side with great voice - sounds like Buddy Holly in the top range. Flip's formula fast Rockabilly with more neat vocal work and some tasty guitar picking over hectic double bass. Another very appealing single.

ROCKABILLY ALBUMS

Ray Campi and his Rockabilly Rebels - "The Newest Wave" (About 1001)
This guy's a killer - he's got to be piss taking the genre - but he does it so well. The vocal overdone on one track, then one instrument out of tune on the next, then a straight track, then a falsetto/fem. vocal with crazy solos and plonking piano, etc. Playing it straight he's great, but his winning skill is self-parody. The Gary Glitter of Rocabilly. Good Album.

Ravenna and the Magnetics - "Rockabilly Fools" (About 1002)
This is an immensely commercial album. They've got everything going for them - vocals/guitar/rhythm section/songs/arrangements - all are shit hot. They ooze originality in a field that is singularly lacking in it. If you think you don't like Rockabilly, try this. If you do like Rockabilly then you must get this. Half the tracks are originals, rest are covers that include "Rock Around with Ollie Vee", by Sonny Curtis (one of the Crickets) and Buddy Holly's "Changing all those changes".

Jimmy Lee Maslon and His Crazy Sounds - "Your Wildcat Ways" (About 1003)
This guy's voice is great - high like Buddy Holly to low like Elvis, + all points in between. He runs round his Telecaster like it's as easy as eating cornflakes. 12 tracks include Percy Sledge's slow ballad "Warm and Tender Love" and Gene Vincent's "She She Little Sheila" plus 4 or 5 originals.

Johnny Legend and his Skullcaps - "Rockabilly Rumble" (About 1004)
Album of standard rockabilly that's O.K. but unremarkable, especially when set alongside the rest of these.

A LETTER FROM DELTA 5

Fotofit L→R
KELVIN (dms)
ROS (fretlessbass/voc)
BETHAN (bass/voc)
JIM (roadie)
ALAN (gtr./voc)
JULZ (gtr./voc)

Dear Nick, it is 4am on the morning of Saturday 11th of April & this is being written by Julz of Delta 5. A few hours ago I returned from a gig we just played in St Albans (incidentally the first one we have ever done there) & as I was not sleepy I started to reply to some 'fan mail' not all of which was complimentary. One letter was a (may I add justified) complaint about a gig we played recently in London, the problem being it was a seated venue & some drunken people got rather inconsiderate about the space they were taking up. Anyway, I remember that when I met you at Leeds I said we would get something together that you might be able to use in your excellent paper. Well as I'm the only one still awake & trying to organise the whole band can be quite a task & as I'm in the mood to write, here we are. Also I should tell you that I am going to Belgium tomorrow to see The Scars - now our labelmates - & the prospect of the trip is exciting me out of sleep. I hope you like their album, I think it is rather good as pop albums go.

What has happened to us recently is after deciding not to put out any more records with Rough Trade (I presume you are aware of the set up with them - one doesn't actually sign as such; the cost of recording is split 50/50 as are the profits from the records). We had 3 singles on RT: Business/Nowhere, Anticipation/You & Colour/Try. The last one was actually released in USA rather than being available on import & reached No.20 in the Billboard charts. We remixed that single in San Francisco when we were on tour in The States in Sept/Oct last year. I don't know if you have any information about it but we did 23 (I think) dates over there: East Coast - N.Y., Washington, Philadelphia, Boston, flew to L.A. wow man, played there San Fran, Seattle & Vancouver. We were there for about 6 weeks. Went over having only 2 singles out on import, stayed in hotels 3 nights, the rest of the time spent on people's floors etc. We played 9 gigs in the first 8 days. Before that we had only ever done 4 consecutive dates. We came back with a tour profit of $15, had a great time & learned an awful lot. Many of the places we played weren't usual venues. The East Coast gigs were set up by Ruth Polski from Hurrahs (NY cult venue - ed.) & the West Coast by Sue (now our manager) from the newly-opened Rough Trade San Fran. On that occasion we were given gigs for other RT bands - Young Marble Giants & Cabaret Voltaire toured soon after us using the RT set up. Anyway we decided in Dec not to record our album with RT for various reasons many of which are too boring & too past history to go into. For several months we continued to live as we had done since June, when Ros finally finished her degree, on money earned from gigs + a little from publishing & record sales - in fact £20 a week, this after much swapping of contracts & solicitors making a packet in the process no doubt. The day after budget day we signed to Pre. The only other existing (Manicured Noise are no longer together) British band on this label are our friends The Scars so it isn't like being just another band on a major record label even though Pre is part of Charisma. Then we did the tour with Gang of 4 & Pere Ubu, which was great fun plus invaluable experience for us. That finished last Monday. We are going into a studio on 15/16 April to demo with producers etc. Hopefully the album will be out in June or July. Hey, as we are having great difficulty in deciding what to call this product do you

.... continued page 7 →

LETTER FROM DELTA 5 (cont.)...

fancy doing a Blue Peter type thing & asking your readers to send in suggested names for it? They can send them to us at 32 Seymour Place, London W1.

At the moment we are all pretty happy. Ros & Bethan have just found a flat - before one was squatting, the other living with her mother. We get enough money to live on, more than dole for a change. We are doing what we all want to do. We travel - in May we are probably going back to America. It's things like that which keep us going spiritually (wow man, that's a bit heavy!). The idea of going on tour in places that we've never been to or wouldn't have the chance if we were in a 9-5 job etc. Anyway, hope this has been of some use to you. Do write back if there's anything you specifically want to know, even if it's getting someone's opinion other than mine. There aren't any recent photos at the mo but when I get hold of some I'll send them. Thanks a lot JWZ

WHAMMER JAMMER

Tight, exciting r'n'b from Doncaster - that's how Whammer Jammer sell themselves. Nick Wraith (voc/harm/gtr) formed the band in late '79. Lead gtr/songwriter Fiery Jack also doubles on some neat slide-playing. They're the blues section, to which are added Graham Bee (dms) & Sue Straight (bs).

Together, they've built a reputation as one of the best pub/club blues outfits in the north.

Contact: Tony on Donc.65062 or 64331.

REALLY! Live at The Royal Park, Leeds.

Really are: Marion Lux (formerly Sheeny of '& The Goys' fame) on voc, David Bowie (his real name!) on bass, Ansell Roderick on dms, Grant Spencer on organ & Mark Cresswell on gtr. Together, they're one of the finest & most thoroughly entertaining bands that I've come across on the local circuit.

Their set opened with 'Intro', a funky instrumental. Then came a slightly-reggae popsong '9 to 5' (not that one, I said Sheeny, not Sheena!) which set the tone for the evening. Dms & bass really (sic) make this band; an immaculate rhythm section being the keynote of professionalism. 'Change' is pop funk. "Red Alert" has rm gtr to the fore in a slow popsong that showcases Marion's vocal power. It gathers pace. "Something' ("You are really something; really, really something" - a clue to their name) is a clicky blend of reggae/carib/pop. "Q & A' is off-beat reggae with an insistent one-bottom-note bassline on the verses. Simplicity & pure pop appeal underline the band's formula. Already I'm convinced that I'm seeing a band who're in line for enormous success. 'Absurd' is a punctuated rock song that relies on timing & a spoken/pause/spoken lyric. 'Last Men' (brief titles, these - as brief as are the pauses between songs). Again, that tight confidence with each musician exactly in place - cool, back seat & polished. They make it seem so easy. 'Trouble', a slower ballad based around the kbds, is atypical but wins through - Sheeny's vocal talent carrying it. 'No Comfort' jumps from rhythm to rhythm &, if 'Red Alert' or 'Something' is to be the first single, then this will be your favourite track on their first album. Ringing gtr & military dms open 'Tommy' which feeds us more reggaed pop. But the band has a sound & style that are genuinely their own. Another funky-pop ballad in 'Innocent', with vocals belted out. And there's that constant near-reggae reference point which is the band's anchor, but not their identity. They're much more than the sum of their reggae/pop/funk content. 'Narcissus', a driving rhythmic winner, is another potential single. 'Outro' is a fast rework of 'Intro'. Encores: '9 to 5' & 'Red Alert'.

~ Nick Toczek.

IMPRESSIONS OF CRASS & CO.

Gear everywhere. Anti-nuke slogans across the back of the stage. Lots of teenage punx already queuing out front. Soundchecks.

Half-hour chat with Steve (Crass vox & youngest member at about 20). He's a Londoner. The band have a house in a village near Epping where they all live. From here they run band, record label, related ventures. The firmly independent/anti-mass-media stance of the band/organisation is one they're determined to maintain. Actually, it isn't that difficult. The rock press (Sounds, NME et al) still try to get copy on them occasionally - even offering them the chance to do their own pieces, but they decided against even that. He expresses his disappointment with Honey Bane (who was originally a Crass label artist & now does commercial trash - my words, not Stevo's - for a major). None of Crass claim SS. Despite the fact that Crass discs sell well below the price of most records, the band get an income:"We lost on the early stuff, but 'Stations of The Crass' continues to sell well & so do the current LP's & singles." The rest of their income is mainly from gigging.

Anxiety Annie opens the show. A 5/10 minute set of emotional chanted poetry/theatrics/screams over a taped backing track. A luke warm reaction.

Before & after her set are films - these made specially for/with the Crass set-up by Mick Duffield... some original film, other bits pirated from newsreel/adverts/etc. The sequences change every few seconds: a foetus, a wedding ring, a kitchen furnishing advert, robots, street scenes, bomb explosions - all to distorted sound effex/snippets of political speeches, lectures & interviews, patriotic poetry, etc. The film after her set is better quality (production-wise). Called 'Total Product', it features music by Poison Girls.

A 15-minute chat with P.Girls' drummer. He describes his band's lyrics as more personal than directly political. The band came together in Brighton - ran a venue called Vault (from which came the popular Brighton sampler albums 'Vaultage'79' etc). The link with Crass came after a London gig that they did. P.Girls got themselves a house in Epping near to where Crass live. The first two P.G. singles were on Small Wonder. Since then they've been with Crass label.

Live, Poison Girls are good. Funk/punk intensity. A naked charm. Percussive rhythms/chanted & infectious choruses - they're a 4-piece, 3 of them on vocals, ages averaging out around 35, I guess. A good tight basic band.

Anxiety Annie returns for a longer set. Broken black rhythmic tape music to her breathless spoken vocal performance. TV screens either side of the stage show a face (hers) mouthing out of synch. But she goes on too long & everyone's impatient for Crass.

Here they are at last. Crass plus friends (Anxiety Annie among them) guesting on vocals. All in black. Good sound, clean. They're motionless. Come over as raw punk. The audience love it. Video on the TV screens flickers on & off. Film overhead projected onto a suspended screen. Hammering drums, ringing rhythm gtr. A hard anarchic formula of 77 punk. The vocals lose their meaning towards the back of the mix. They make the odd departure from punk into a kind of stripped down pop-funk, but these are brief expeditions with a swift return to pure-punk-base. A narrow spectrum of music to stick with, but they excel at it. Where to from here - or can they perpetuate '77 through the '80's?

BONE IDLE LIVE AT PALM COVE BRADFORD

With Dave Ellis on dms, Graham Cooke on gtr/voc & Beezer Bob on bs/ld.voc + occasional poems, Bone Idle dive into 3-piece action at this their debut gig. 'Ivan', the opener, is the first of what turns out to be a set of predominantly powerful & appealing songs. Their material, self-written, is a clever blend of standard rock & new wave freshness. Weakest is when they stray over the border in HM territory. Strong points are the Stranglers bass sound coming from BB's Marshall amp & the pacing (though their obvious nervousness tended to slow down the numbers - no hassle, that'll go over the next few gigs). Several memorable songs in the set including: 'Black Man/White Man' which reminded me of The Fall's 'Elastic Man', 'Welfare State' with its poppy Jam-like arrangement, 'Cliff Richard' that's all rhythm & punch, & the excellent 'Fireball' - their strongest song.

~Nick Toczek

FLOCK OF SEAGULLS
LIVE IN LEEDS at STAGING POST

Dapper in their black suits, bow-ties & white shirts, Flock of Seagulls come on tight, hard & loud with their opening number - "Modern Love Is Automatic". They're a 4-piece: Mike Score (voc/gtr/synths), Paul Reynolds (ld.gtr), Frank Maudsley (bs/voc) & Ali Score (dms). 'Pick Me Up' and 'Telecommunication' both impress - particularly the latter with cowbell & solid gtr/bs riff that produced an edgy & echoing rhythm. All four are from Liverpool, have been together in Flock for 3 years & in various other local outfits before that. The p.a. is giving them a crystal-clear sound & this is an excellent start.

'Intro' is an instrumental with tidy rhythm changes & a simple but instant melody line. The band oozes power & also scores for precision. The last two numbers are, respectively, the a- & b-sides of their second single. The first, released May '81, is '(It's not me) Talking' c/w "Factory Music' on Bill Nelson's Cocteau Records label. Nelson produced all 4 sides.

Over the next few numbers, which included the brand new 'DNA', 'Standing In The Doorway', 'Need A Girl Like You','Committed' & 'The Day She Goes', they veered first towards the Echo/Teardrop L'pool sound & then (disappointingly) slid into thinly disguised heavy rock. At the end, I felt that my initial enthusiasm had been deflated - like reading a good who-dun-it & then guessing who two chapters from the end. They were good but what looked like originality faded before they left the stage. They need more fresh & inventive/up-to-date material. That apart, they've a lot going for them. And, live, the singles sound like they'll do things for to band. ~reviewed by Nick Toczek.

XANTHOS IN PROFILE

A Harrogate band playing what they call good quality rock, they've been in existence a while, but have just finished extensive remodelling with Tim Brierley (bs) as the only founder member remaining. Mark Rowan (gtr) joined last August, with Nigel Harrison (dms) & Tim Barret (gtr) as the latest newcomers. Vocalist J.C. Leva, who completes the line-up, has been in the band for a while. 3-month rehearsing took them to the start of live work at the end of Feb. & they are now setting up gigs throughout the north of England. With about 5 grand's-worth of gear between them, a single & a German tour in the pipeline, they're in with a better chance than their namesake (a city which twice sustained major seiges that terminated in the self-destruction of the inhabitants & all their property: against the Persians under Harpagus in 546BC & the Romans under Brutus in 43BC, both bad gigs!)

aswad + israelites
LIVE AT BRADFORD UNIVERSITY

Over the Top Reviews Inc. present a Grove Muzic night out at Bradford Uni with ASWAD and King Sounds Israelites. First ASWAD. What can I say? An incredibly good performance from a marvellous band (somewhat loud mix at times & some feedback). Brinsley Ford seemed to have a frog in his throat at first, but he got over it giving a good performance and introducing Vin Gordon with genuine reverence. The brass section could not be faulted - brought on for 'Rainbow Culture','Babylon', and an absolutely epic 'Warrior Charge', they certainly did nice up the dance. Great Sax work from Michael 'Bami'Rose, and nice blowing from Eddie Chan. Vinnie Gordon though was wonderful - a true master of his instrument. Credit must go to the dread at the controls who mixed a good sound, using the echo unit very well and leaving the brass section blowing up a storm after everyone had left the stage and making Drummies contribution sound like a runaway train on speed! Drummie was, by the way, absolutely terrific - taking an echoed drum break, he stopped half-way through to look at his drums in amazement as they carried on, then crashed back in; timbales echoed, cymbals crashed and locks flew! Loved every minute. Most of the better known numbers came out - 'Three Babylon', 'It's not our wish' (with Drummie on vocals), and the three previously mentioned. For the encore, introducing the members of the band, Brinsley dragged on the Stepping Master who proceede to liven-up things with some great dance work. That ended with a hilarious sequence where Brinsley couldn't get his bike (?) to work, and with some great synth work from Clifton on keyboards (made a sound just like my bike!) started it up, rode round the stage (shades of the Hair Bear Bunch!) then off, leaving the band to finish the set. Superb!

Support, the Israelites, came on to a coolish reception, but had the crowd warmed up by the third number 'Natty Go To Jail After a few more numbers they introduced their leader, King Sounds, and on he strolled - a militant stepping natty dread in military gear and praising Jah, 'Iry Collie (one of the songs) and chanting down Babylon ('Muzzle Us'). I love to see/hear good reggae singers who enjoy singing about something they truly believe in, and King Sounds was passionate to the extreme - shaking his locks and smiling as he sang. One of the songs had a line - 'You can be a baldhead and like reggae music'. Seen brother seen! ~reviewed by TINO PALMER.

PLASTICS · PLASTICS · PLASTICS · PLASTICS · PLASTICS · PLASTICS · PLASTICS · PLASTICS

The Plastics, a Japanese new wave pop 5-piece, have their first Western-released album 'Welcome Back Plastics' out on Island (with free picture flexi). They are Hajime Tachibana (gtr/harm/b.voc), Toshi Nakanichi (perc/voc/gtr), Chica Sato - female (voc/perc), Takemi Shima (rm.mach/gtr), Ma-Chan Sakuma (bs/gtr/kbds).

A large & enthusiastic audience feasted on their energetic set at The Warehouse, Leeds in which they virtually took us on a guided tour of the album. Western sixties-influenced new wave with crisp freshness to it. There are Japanese musical undertones & oriental theatrics. Musicianship shines through - Hajime's gtr & Toshi's work on percussion being the linchpins.

An after-gig talk with Hajime... They've been together 5 yrs, though Takemi & Ma-Chan only came in 2 yrs back, around the time that the band went pro. They've had 3 LP's in Japan in the last year or so which have established the band out there. The UK album's a compilation from those. Hajime lived 8 months in London &, back in Japan, sent a copy of their single 'Copy' over to a friend who hawked it round town. The result was that Rough Trade released it. Then came the UK deal with Island & a US deal with Warners. A US tour last year, but this is their first time in Europe, taking in Holland, Germany, France & UK; 6 weeks in USA then follow before they head back to J.

The scene out there... Very small & very large venues abound, but there's little in between. Big US/UK/Euro influences since the war - but since '77 & punk, Jap music's been coming into its own, esp. in Tokyo. He's not too keen on Yellow Magic Orch. but mentions Spoil (a sax/bs/gtr/rm.mach. 3-piece) & Hikashu as ones to watch. Major labels still hold sway & indies are few.

Their music... he writes it all, lyrics from Toshi & Chica. Says his early influences were Beatles/Stones/1910 Fruitgum Co./Monkees & he still goes for pure & immediate pop. They started out "inorganic" (ie motionless on stage & very mechanical) but get increasingly "organic" - with theatre, humour, dance & (in Japan) much use of lighting & effects.

He was (& still is) a graphic design artist. He did the posters for The Talking Heads' first Jap. tour & went on to design an album sleeve for them. This contact lead to a management deal (they share man. co. with T.Heads, B52's & Ramones) & so to last year's US tour.

Next album will be of new material - "easy listening avant garde - that's what it should turn out to be". -N.T./D.M.

PAULINE MURRAY & The Invisible Girls
Live In Oslo
reviewed by John Tempest

Half the band arrive - the others missed the ferry from Felixstowe and have to travel through Copenhagen at a great rate of knots.

Not much money - their manager hasn't arrived yet - the press conference held in the hotel bar seems to have gone well. Met some of the band and crew - very genuine and likeable and wondering what I'm doing here. They'd be very happy for me to photo them; which mag was it again?

Met Pauline for the first time (I was in a suit and it didn't impress) - I was later told that nott much impresses our little star. "Would I be writing as well as taking pix?" "If you want, though I must know beforehand." We left it that I would contact her manager when he arrived. Left a message in his pigeon-hole and left it at that. Receptionist: "Yes, he's definitely arrived and I gave him your message.

Eventually tracked him down to the ABC Theatre where he wasn't over enthusiastic - "Pauline isn't too keen..." he tailed off, "....with this being the first date of the tour and a new band, and, quite frankly we didn't expect anybody from England to be here." Ah, so now we get to the nitty gritty - what's good enough for dear old Oslo isn't OK for U.K. Could the image be slipping, are the rough edges beginning to show? Read on. We agreed that he should have another word with Pauline to see how she felt.

Got the impression that I was being given the bum's rush... Tenacious to the end I decided to hang on in there and keep pitching - more to see how far he'd go than anything else - "How about if I take the pix, give you the films (what?) and if they're great keep them; if they're not, sling them." "Well, if you give me them tonight then that'll be OK, but I'll just check with Pauline to make sure....."

Ah well! Didn't fancy the idea of giving my films up anyway, (a bit like being told what to write.)

The guys in the band and crew seemed surprised that I'd no camera with me. I explained the problem, they nodded as if they'd expected it; still, I was going to the gig and they seemed quite happy at that. Out of the van, towards the stage door and we're surrounded (well approached) by four Norwegian teenage punk females who proceeded to shout and scream abuse at us - with one accord we turned round and did passable imitations of Muppet Swedichefs at them.

Backstage they all went, side of stage I stayed. The support band were very energetic and deserved an encore - afterwards the drummer had to have his arms pulled (to get them back into their sockets perhaps?)

Rear of stage the floor is like spaghetti junction - "God knows what we'll do if something goes wrong. We'll never find out which wire goes where."

Norwegian TV are there to record the happy event though the pictures aren't too good - they were smoking at the front. Dozens of locals are there with everything ranging from Nikons to Instamatics - also to record the happy scene.

"How do you know that they won't send pix to England? After all, it's very easy to put a picture on the wire these days."

"Ah well, I don't know you do I ?"- a good old manager's cliche. Then the moment we've been waiting for, Pauline enters, wearing a suit....(I'm impressed).

"There's no atmosphere. Where are they all ?" - I could've told her that they were all in the disco downstairs but I didn't think she could handle it. They go on, their audience come back in dribs and drabs then the disco stops and they're all there. The front row is made up of punks, one of whom is intent on spitting at our heroine - the others try without much sucess to prevent this.

Keyboards monitor is fucked, it's the lead - Pete can't hear a thing. Pauline turns round "Can you turn the keyboards down ? I can't hear a thing!" And so the set soldiers on - the PA isn't too good, the better one that they could've hired was three times as expensive - they make do.

Robert's lead comes out - he kicks a junction box across the stage at the backline man. All is not well; and still the fans at the front mouth the words as our diminutive one utters them.

They storm off stage, everyone is unhappy; Pete on keyboards is pissed off - and no one can really blame him. The crew don't venture backstage until they have to; "Horrific" - from their very competent sound-man Gary.

No encore for Oslo, and so 450 fans make their way home through the drizzle, and so do I. (I half expected that, had I stayed, I would have been asked to take the blame.) There's a lot of mileage between Oslo and England, which is just as well in this case.

Maybe she's practising at being a big star who doesn't want to be photographed - like maybe Howard Hughes. Could be true - she certainly looked half-dead when I picced her from my hotel room window as they left for Stockholm on Saturday. And to think that Manfred Mann was appearing in Drammen only 40km away. Oh well, there's always the Who on the box tonight.

Poor Lean Murray.

NICK TOCZEK & DUNCAN McCARROLL SPOKE WITH BILL NELSON FOR AN HOUR IN RIC-RAC STUDIOS, LEEDS (28/4/81)

BEBOP DELETE THE NEW BILL NELSON

Bebop Deluxe: That band was really finished two years before he wound it up. The last major statement was 'Sunburst Finish'. The band members were good technicians but more rooted in 70's rock than forward-looking. It got progressively harder for him to express his ideas through the band. The band was stretched on the next album 'Modern Music'; a factor that became all too apparent on their last 'Drastic Plastic'. All the Bebop material has been deleted by EMI, though they've a compilation album of the singles (a- & b-sides) ready for release if his brand new album takes off. He says he no longer listens to any of this material - it tends to depress him. He feels, though, that it should be available if only for its validity in terms of mid-70's rock or as a retrospective reference source for anyone interested in his work & development. He views his recorded work as a diary - with the first few episodes now missing.

Red Noise: They put out one album 'Sound on Sound' which met with a lot of resistance within the industry. Everyone told him it was far too experimental/inaccessable, whereas he felt then & still feels that it is one of his most accessible works. The live work by the band was well-received & sales of the album then & since have proved the record co. & management critics wrong - even on a purely financial assessment. However, opposition was so strong that his US label dropped him & relationships with his UK label (still EMI) & with his management (who simply took a back seat) progressively worsened.

Solo: Lack of record co. interest meant that by the end of '79 he found himself with about 60 pieces - many of them instrumentals recorded as demos in his home 4-track studio. Everyone said they were good but not commercial enough. With his management co. about to go out of business owing him 1,000's of quid (that he never saw), he put the last of his money into forming Cocteau Records & releasing 'Do You Dream In Colour' (solo, except for brother Ian on sax). The flip was at 33⅓rpm with 3 tracks: 'Instantly Yours' (a Red Noise track recorded at Rack in early '79) + 'Ideal Homes' (also RN from same session) + 'Atom Man Loves Radio Girl (with Ian, summer '79 at Rockfield). With no real promotion or distribution the record got into the top 50 & would have gone higher if the MU strike hadn't stopped a TOTP appearance. Going back to the record co's who'd rejected the single, he now got: "Great single, what have you got that's like it?" Churning out formula songs wasn't what he wanted, so still no deal. Eventually, after he'd done some work in Belgium, a label out there, Crepescule, asked to hear demos. He sent some of the home 4-tracks & they were so keen that they released them as they were. (Mortgaged up to the hilt & with a minimal income at this time, he couldn't anyway afford to use a large studio). 'Rooms With Brittle Views' was coupled with an instrumental 'Dada Guitar'.

Nelson is now signed to Mercury (a subsid. of Phonogram). His first single for them was 'Banal' which he recorded near his home in Selby, Yorks. on the Rolling Stones mobile studio. The flip had 3 tracks: 'Turn To Fiction' & 'Hers Is A Lush Situation' (both home 4-tracks) plus 'Mr Magnetism' (from the Rockfield sessions with Ian). The title 'Banal' comes from some "advise' he got from his old management co. who told him that it wasn't even enough to write commercial songs - they had to be banal to be hits! His new album is 'Quit Dreaming And Get On The Beam'- material written in '78 & recorded in '79. With the first 10,000 comes a second album 'Sounding The Ritual Echo' which is a selection from 5 hrs of home recorded instrumentals that he describes as "ambient music'. See review elsewhere.

He has just finished the music to a play by The Yorkshire Actors' Co. - 'The Cabinet Of Dr Caligari' (based on the classic early horror film). He's also very busy producing in the studios for other bands including The Skids, Nash The Slash and a whole bunch of lesser-known northern outfits - several of them with singles coming out on his own label, Cocteau.

STOP PRESS: Bill Nelson is currently rehearsing a new band & will be gigging with them from end of May onwards. He has a few solo gigs lined up as well. Also, there are plans in the air for him to work on a joint project with Andy Partridge (XTC) & David Byrne (Talking Heads) - though this, if it came off, would be some time in the future when all three can clear a mutual space in their various hectic schedules. Nelson is also getting involved in photography & has taken the photos on his new album cover(s). He hopes to sometime soon bring out a book of his camera work.

CELLAR-TAPE: the demos...

Van-Deller and Hope Evans (London) 4-tracks
2 guys, ex-Danceband, gtr/bs/voc + jaw harp/processed horn/voc + rhy. machine. "Zero Zero" is very catchy with a nice bass hook. "Truth and Logic" is electro pop with bouncy rhythms. A clean mix and processed instrumental sounds. Spoken power politics for lyrics. Stylish combination of commercial appeal and modernist originality. Band to get a major deal out of this.

Bone Idle (Bradford) 3-tracks
3-piece of drums + bs/voc + gtr/voc. Very catchy material, average musicianship, thrash vocals. Boogie-rock — Stranglers/new wave. Overall a fine debut demo from a new band.

X-Port (Leeds) 2-tracks
"Take me to the Dolphin" has a catchy bass hook with high guitar rhythm and keyboard melody. Reminiscent of Fassbender-Russell with nursery rhyme kids. American bubblegum teen-rock feel. "Telephone" is much weaker. Monkees trying to be raunchy. Good production for Lindsay Frost.

Pre-mental Tension (Baildon) 5-tracks
Poor quality home-recording, so difficult to get a decent impression. Young 5-piece who write all their own material. Promising debut although a lot of work needs to be done especially on the band arrangements.

Surfin' Dave and The Absent Legends (Leeds) 2-tracks
Two tongue-in-cheek Rockabilly epics. Usual American teen themes (Snow storm in Bournemouth etc). Lotsa fun. Gets the foot a-tappin'.

English Assassin (Bradford) 3-tracks
Excellent musicians playing middle-of-the-road pop ballads. Wasting time trying local pub circuit — should go for major support to Judie Tzuke or similar. Immediate mass appeal. Not very appropriate name as leads one to expect a rougher sound. Compare with Sad Café.

SELLER-TAPE: released cassettes...

Autopsia - "Balkan SFRJ", cassette album (own label)
Yugoslavian band - anti-rock, perverse minimalism with political (anti-state) overtones. This really is weird release. "Darts" sounds like the Muppets on planet Kuzbane. We derived a lot of juvenile fun from this music (!) Translation of lyrics reveals the only serious note. Recommended.

Eaten Alive By Insects - "E.A.B.I" album (Tapir Products TAP4)
Mixture of live and studio trax covering the past two years of sporadic activity and line-up changes for this Bfd. band. Wide-spectrum; musical eccentricity. Live trax are heavily percussive and rhythmic while others are intensely atmospheric. An adventurous and anti-commercial, ad hoc unit. E.A.B.I are this man's meat but another man's poison.

NME/Rough Trade "C81" compilation cassette album (Rough Tapes 001) Available thru NME.
This really is a suprisingly excellent and varied sampler, more due to the pioneering influence of R.T. than the playsafe stance of N.M.E. (and the London press in general). A good balance of commercial new music and modernist avant-garde covering the post '77 era. A must for any discerning punter. Features Scritti Politti, Furious Pig, Wah Heat, Pere Ubu, Raincoats, Ian Dury, Specials and more.

Cameras in Cars - "C. in Cars" E.P. (Tapir Products TAP 5)
3 trax: "What Can I do", "Germania", and "Perfect Day". A Bfd band who are not easy to classify, sitting somewhere between pop, electronic and straight rock.

Policeman with A Loaf of Bread - "AWKOB" album (TAP 6)
Live cassette album (recorded at Bibi's, Bfd) by the city's most eccentric band, professing a Dadaist identity. Atrocious (non-)musicians and deliberately so. They laugh at themselves and the audience but work hard at what they do. The audience laughs or gets angry but stays to the end of the set. He who laughs last....... Without bands like this life would be boring; with them it's still boring. Ah philosophy!

S-T-R-E-T-C-H album (TAP 7)
Also known as "You've Been Dreaming in Class Again Ski-bop Di-bop." Fusion free-faith jazz-funk that suffers from poor quality live recording (again at Bibi's) and untogetherness. That said, this is potentially one of the more promising Bfd bands, in that they are breaking free from the standard pub-rock formulae.

Pyramid - "Crash Landing" E.P. (own label)
3 trax entitled: "Crash landing", "Airway", and "I wish you Wouldn't". From this Bingley band. Range from heavy-metal sound to Byrds-like melodic rock. Doesn't quite come off due to arrangements and musicianship — annoyingly out of tune and time. Unfortunately this sort of music relies heavily on good musicianship - they are merely competent. Poor arrangements leaves them bland and ordinary.

THE SEMI-VINYLS: tapes of pre-release discs....

Donkers 7" - "Let's Float" c/w "Strike Talks" (MCA)
Commercial pop tune with good harmonies. Never quite gets going; keep expecting the drums to let go but they never do. Flip sounds like the Jam - can't be bad. Very strong commercial sound - short but sweet. Grows on you! Altogether a nice package. Could be a hit given air-play and with 3 strong singles behind them they deserve a break.

Nik Townend - "Gunslinger" (Vital Records)
Reggae feel to this one with unusual full organ sound in the background. Lilts along with a carefree air. Vocals sound lazy and half-hearted.

Jets Go To War - "Messerschmitt" and "Too Many Faces" (Vital Records)
Rough and ready post-punk sound on the former track. Very amateurish with a singer that doesn't. However, it generally chugs along quite pleasantly. Doesn't set the world on fire but at least I kept my food down. The latter track once again has tuneless vocals but over hum-drum guitar and video-game kids. Disappointingly boring.

Knife Edge - "Bombing Pearl Harbour" c/w "Me and My Girl" (No Hassle Records)
Forthcoming second single from Leeds band. Doesn't exactly grab one by the throat. Tends to drag with the constant repetition of "I saw them Bombing Pearl Harbour". Tempo change in the middle didn't quite work for me. Air-raid siren at the beginning and explosion at the end courtesy of Cliché's Record Library. T'other side starts a lot zappier, but again is nothing to write home to mum about. O.K. but nothing more.

Rockabilly Rebs - "Rockabilly Romeo" (EMI)
A-side of forth coming single. A remix of the album track (written and produced by John Goodison). Good but too mono-paced/laid back to be a chart success. Shame; live they're much better than this.

Various - "Mrs. Wilson's Children" (Vital)
Most commercial track: "Special Stuff" by Johnny Solo and "Vital Seconds" by Human Zoo. You've got bits of five others on the flexi. The Ashtrays have a catchy track in "Justify it", and the London Boys are over-poppy on "You Know". The rest is made up of an interesting mix of mostly keyboard-based contemporary rock - with Cool to Trog's "Satisfaction Week" proving more than satisfactory.

~ reviews: TOCZEK/McCARROLL

Back Issues: complete your fab. collection of this trendy 'zine. Only 30p each (+ 20p P.&P) from 5 Beech Terrace, Undercliffe, Bradford, BD3 0PY, W.Y.

GANG OF 4 / PERE UBU / DELTA 5

Live at Tiffany's in Leeds reviewed by Nick Toczek

Unmistakable. That's the sound of Delta 5 as, under a hard rain of drums, they swing their high female vocals & sharp knives of edgy guitar into the firing line.

Three alternative chart hits behind them, they hustle a winning hand of fast, tangy, modernist pop with loose confidence.

We get the excellent 'Anticipation' plus a selection from the other singles & the forthcoming album.

Julz spins & bounces round the stage. Kelvin drops his towel on a lamp & it bursts into flames, smoke everywhere. John Lee (of former local fanzine Damaged Goods) tells me not to use the phrase "twin bass attack". The return of D5 to their home town could have been hard work, but they make it easy for themselves & the punters.

Energetic, unpretentious & chatty: next time they'll headline.

Strange situation for Pere Ubu - to be a cult band on the strength of a bunch of 4-year-old songs. Still fronted by the certainly strange persona of David Thomas, they've since made the notable addition of Mayo Thompson of Red Crayola fame. His influence has underlined their uncompromising musical eccentricity.

Live, Pere Ubu's a noisy farmyard blend of human & animal conversation - an elusive grin underlaying every move. Orthodox rock rhythm section is the only fixed point in a jungle of keyboard, vocal & guitar interplay that is semi-improvised.

An initial atmosphere of audience/performer uncertainty restrains their spontaneity & the band doesn't quite take off. Do we English take our music too seriously?

Eventually, current single 'Not Happy' paradoxically breaks the ice. They win through. By the encore, we all want to be in on their adventure.

A tight knot of rhythm that thunders out from paced, up-front bass. Gang Of Four, like D5, are a Leeds band with big things (?!) to prove here: their most prestigious tour to date. The band, alternately in silhouette, yellow light, red light, dress less like rocksters - more like officeboys.

A blown amp shoots down their opening pace in flames. Tough. A minute's silence, then guitar hammering back like a train over iron drum rails. Their music is a relentless percussive tide; almost too formal to be fun.

'Paralysed' is their bleakest & barest number, with its freeze-pauses & spoken interjections. The tension persists.

Take a hard clean beat. Fill the spaces with a constant variety of novelty & cliche. This is a serious game!

I'm watching a machine as it welds each wrought rhythm & steel pace change into place, driving it home. Hollow ring of echo brought into play on the vocals.

I hear the whole Gang chant in unison the chill chorus: 'If-I-could-keep-it-for-my-self/If-I-could-keep-it-for-my-self...'

The vocals weren't clear enough to really pick up on their politics, so they are no part of this review. The gig, less of a performance, more a demonstration of how they work: their creative process. They function well. I was impressed by what they did, but didn't <u>enjoy</u> it. We English, you know we take our music too seriously.

THE SHEDS

Live review by Mary Samuel...

When I was told about this gig at Robert Town Community Centre, my <u>1st</u> reaction was - oh no, not another antiseptic waiting room type gig with embarrassed pauses & dreadful or non-existent organisation, & with more than a fair share of grannies & screaming uncontrolled kids.

Not a bit of it! This was a really good 'do'; well but unobtrusively organised with excellent grub & ale & best of all, very fine entertainment.

The live sounds came from that elusive group of chaps (grannies/grub/chaps-is this the new rock jargon? - ed.) known collectively as <u>The Sheds</u>. In two sets, they provided a mixture of r'n'b, West Coast, r'n'r & pop (a revamp of 'Then He Kissed Me').

The music was well-executed & tight with Roger (gtr/voc) showing some neat solos that actually sounded original. His vocals sometimes verged on the Bob Dylan grind but, along with original numbers sung by himself & Dave Thomas, some very neat vocal & guitar harmonies came out.

The rhythm from Geoff Coghill (dms) & some luvly driving bass from Pete Southwood brought the whole evening really out. After the first couple of numbers the dance floor was packed to capacity & at one point, when the disco tried to resume, the audience shouted them off in favour of more live music.

So, Sheds, how about getting off your arses & gigging around a bit more, eh?!

ATHLETICO SPIZZLES ENERGI OIL '77

Spizz started off solo at a Barbarella's Punk Festival on 29th August 1977, improvising material on a borrowed guitar.

October '77 saw several appearances by Spizz and former schoolfriend Pete Petrol at London's Vortex Club, whose promoter Dave Woods agreed to act as their manager. Billed as Spizz '77, the duo played short and spontaneous one-off improvisations of old Bowie songs and an audience participation number called 'I've been switched off' written after a club manager turned off the power during one of their earliest performances.

By 1978 the name Spizz Oil was coined, inspired by extensive coverage of North Sea oil in the media. The duo played a series of odd gigs culminating at the Roundhouse in July, when they played with Siouxsie and the Banshees. The consequences of this gig were an invitation to do a BBC Radio session for John Peel, and a deal with the newly formed Rough Trade label which resulted in the release of: '6000 Crazy' and the EP 'Cold City:4'.

Spizz Oil stopped gigging at the end of a long U.K. tour with the Banshees and The Human League, and months of deliberation resulted in the emergence of a four man line-up in March '79 playing under the new name Spizz Energi, featuring Jim Solar on bass and Mark Coalfield (kbds). As a drummerless quartet they performed another John Peel session and joined a nationwide tour organised by RT with Kleenex and the Raincoats.

Their first venture into the recording studio was with guest drummer Brian B. Benzine, and a day's work without any rehearsal produced three songs; 'Soldier Soldier', 'Virginia Plain', and 'Where's Captain Kirk' which were subsequently released by RT. Benzine never played live with the band, and Pete Petrol left to form his own group 'Repetition' whilst Spizz Energi gigged with an assortment of guitarists and drummers for the rest of the year.

'Where's Captain Kirk' sat at the top of the Alternative charts for seven weeks and during this period the first stable line-up emerged with the introduction of C.P. Snare on drums and Dave Scott on guitar. This warranted yet another new name and Athletico Spizz 80 commenced extensive live work throughout the U.K. in early '80, as well as venturing into Europe for the first time in March with fellow RTers The Mo-Dettes.

A new single, 'Spock's Missing/ No Room', was released on their return and went straight to the top of the indie charts. The time had come to record the repertoire that had taken shape over the previous 12 months and the album 'Do a Runner' was recorded over the Bank Holiday weekend in May 1980.

Within weeks A & M Records had signed up Athletico Spizz 80 and immediately released the album which went straight into the top 20. They performed a lengthy tour of Britain and in September performed at the Lyceum Theatre, part of which was filmed for inclusion in the forthcoming movie 'Urgh! - A Music War'.

A short period of inactivity was followed by the departure of Mark and Dave to pursue solo projects. A new line-up embarked on a long U.S. tour with Lu, formerley of the Damned and the Edge, taking Dave's place and discarding a permanent keyboards player. This outfit toured as The Spizzles and released an album entitled 'Spikey Dream Flowers' which included stage faves 'Scared', 'Brainwashing Time', and 'Central Park' as well as a new version of 'Soldier Soldier' and the single 'Dangers of Living'.

TYGERS OF PANTANG + MAGNUM LIVE at EROS, HUDDERSFIELD.

The Tygers of Pan Tang supported by Birmingham-based Magnum was the impressive double bill presented by local promoter John Keenan at Huddersfield's Eros Club.

Magnum have been around for a few years now and have achieved limited success without actually 'making it'. With two albums, various singles and E.P.'s, as well as an appearance at last years Reading Festival and numerous tours, they have still not headlined. Despite this frustration, Magnum still perform their own brand of heavy rock with verve and vitality.

The line-up of Tony Clarkin (gtr), Bob Catley (voc), Colin Lowe (bs), Richard Bailey (kbds), and Kex Gorin (dms) is certainly a very strong unit but their material is perhaps a little too inconsistent, ranging from the mediocre 'Changes' to the powerful 'All of My Life'.

The Tygers are at the 'make or break' stage of their career with the recent release of their second album 'Spellbound'. With the addition of vocalist Jon Deverill, who replaced Jess Cox, they have gained a new dimension as Deverill is much more forceful (and in tune).

After an exellent start, the Tygers lost their way somewhat with guitarists Robb Weir and John James Sykes trying to play too quickly and so losing the sustained chord power of early-set numbers like 'Rock 'N' Roll Man'. The dual guitar sound really grabbed you by the throat but unfortunately that hold was too soon relinquished.

The rhythm section with Rocky (bs) and Brian Dick (dms) was competent and shone through on 'Wildcat', the title track of the first album, due to Dick's dynamic drumming.

The gig was highly enjoyable but could so easily have been outstanding if the potential shown by both bands had been maintained throughout. ~ reviewed by DUNCAN MCCARROLL

ALTERED IMAGES / SISTERS OF MERCY
LIVE AT FAN CLUB, LEEDS.

+ ORANGE JUICE
LIVE AT WAREHOUSE, LEEDS.

A busy night on the Leeds band circuit; Wasted Youth at Amnesia, Altered Images at the Fan Club, and Orange Juice at the Warehouse: two of Scotland's finest and one from London. Decisions decisions! But first the F Club. Sisters of Mercy, Altered Images & a cellarful of punks & Banshees clones. Leeds' own Sisters of Mercy came on and filled the air with throbbing bass, feedback, fuzzed guitar, and a taught controlled void somewhere near a less bored John Lydon. Underneath, a straight rhythm on the drum machine fought to appear through the music along with a tape of droning slabs of sound compounding into a formless block of noise. 'Songs' started and finished with random disregard for structure, rendered one-dimensional by the appalling music. The singer looked pretty intense but the significance was lost. Personally I wasn't too keen, but on a good night......

Altered Images made one smile for all their serious faces and vague blankness. Barely concealing their admiration for the Banshees, the Images gave the punks what they wanted with style and a promise for the future. With a pint-size girl singer sounding like Noosha Fox, and a musical leaning propelled by pounding drum patterns and nagging sparse guitar, they knocked out short pop songs with mounting confidence. The audience lapped it up and the set got better and better; I only wish I could have seen the whole set but......

On to the Warehouse, that rarity among rarities, a music club where you can enjoy yourself and a place suited to every band I have seen there; Orange Juice being no exception. Due to an administrative cock-up I missed half of their set as well and arrived to find the atmosphere full of pop songs purveyed in a Scottish brogue with child-like enthusiasm.

Looking like a bunch of Nashville hicks, they coasted through a set of neo-Country & Western/60's pop songs, firmly standing in the 80's and dominated by two, jangly, semi-acoustic guitars and brittle, strident vocals. Their amateur simplicity and naivety of stage performance gave the set a rare sense of humour which justly earned them two encores. ~HARRY MARSDEN

STREETLIGHT BLUES BAND

The Streetlight Blues Band are: Andy Fielding (rm.gtr), Steve Jones (bs), Rob Widdicombe (ld.gtr,voc,harp), Talib Yaseen (dms), Chris Gardner (pno). They started as an offshoot of Streetlight Robbery, of whom Rob and Andy were members. Steve was recruited through the Bradford Uni Guitar Club while Talib was introduced by a mutual friend. Chris lives and works in Preston and so is only an occasional member of the band.

They play mainly electrified Chicago-type blues and list influences as varied as Chuck Berry, Wilko Johnson, Muddy Waters, and Dave Brubeck. Based in Bradford, they can be regularly seen on the local pub circuit. CONTACT TALIB ON B'F'D 20047.

DO YOUR OWN THING ON A FLEXIDISC...

RESALE... GIG BOOKING... FAN CLUB... PROMOTION...

BLACK, GOLD OR COLOUR VINYL

LET US KNOW HOW MANY YOU WANT (MINIMUM 1000) AND WE WILL QUOTE......

SOUND FOR INDUSTRY

MANUFACTURERS OF "FLEXI-DISCS" SINCE 1965

Telephone: 01-403 0044
Telex: 883177 Albums G

Registered Office:
175 Bermondsey Street,
London, SE1 3UW

Cheerers Music Store

(Why travel? We're here in Leeds centre...)

AMP. DEPT. H|H MAIN DEALER.. MARSHALL, VOX, PEAVEY, M.M., RAVEN. M'GREGGOR. WE ARE NOW 'TEAC' MAIN DEALERS, WEM, & J.H.S. ...

GUITAR DEPT. FENDER, GIBSON, IBANEZ MAIN DEALER, HONDO II, KRAMER, PEAVEY. GORDON SMITH + VARIOUS SECOND HAND......

DRUM DEPT. PREMIER MAIN AGENTS, TAMA, SONOR, PAISTE ETC.

PART EXCHANGE AND PERSONAL LOANS AVAILABLE

8, THE MERRION CENTRE, LEEDS 2. TELE: 449592 — 9.00 to 5.30

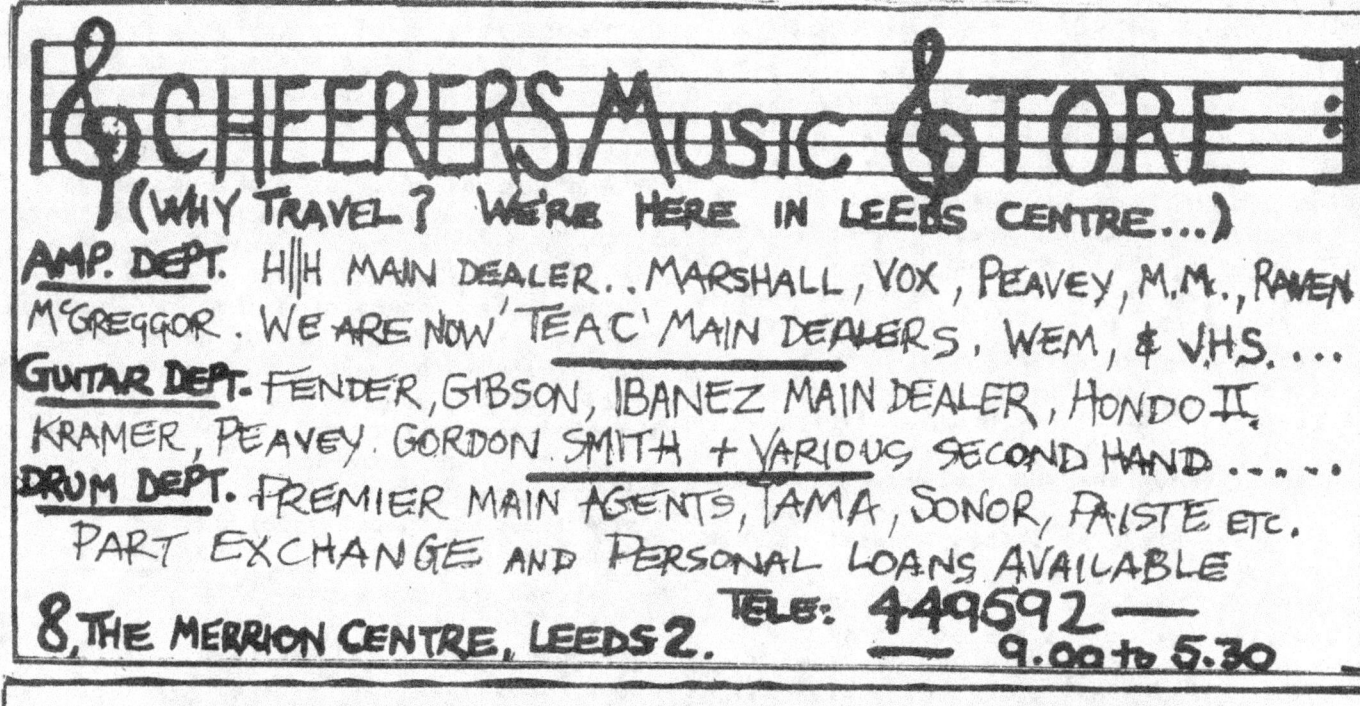

hmv hmv hmv hmv hmv h

WHERE ELSE

trinity st   cheapside
leeds   bradford

UNIVERSITY OF BRADFORD UNION

RICHMOND ROAD, BRADFORD, WEST YORKSHIRE BD7 1DP

Tel. Bradford 34135/8

BRADFORD UNIVERSITY BRADFORD UNIVERSITY BRADFORD UNIVERSITY BRADFORD UNIVERSITY BRADFORD UNIVERSITY BRADFORD UNIVERSITY BRADFORD UNIVERSITY BRADFORD UNIVERSITY BRADFORD UNIVERSITY

WED. 20 MAY
CABARET FUTURA
CB....£2.00

WED. 27 MAY
HONEYDRIPPERS &
ROBERT PLANT
CB....£1.50

SAT. 30 MAY
NINE BELOW ZERO
GH...£1.75

SAT. 13 JUNE
FASSBENDER-RUSSELL
GH....£1.50

TICKETS FROM HMV
RECORDS AND UNION SHOP
AND ON ZE DOOR!

WED. 17 JUNE
JUDIE TZUKE (AGAIN!)
CB.......

WED. 3 JUNE
ORIGINAL MIRRORS
CB....£1.25

FRI. 5 JUNE
TEARDROP EXPLODES
CB....£2.75

CB = Communal Building
GH = Great Hall

EQUIVALENT VIII / AUTOMATIC TOYS / THE SQUARES at The Warehouse Leeds

Equivalent VIII took the stage at about 9.30 & proceeded with a studious air of confidence & a hint of impending excitement which never actually appeared. With a sound underpinned by solid, sparse drum rhythms & heavy bass keyboards & scratchy guitar shouting over the top, the vocalist intoned in a mournful manner which inevitably suggested comparisons with Curtis, Morrison et al. Halfway through the set came a version of Lipps Inc 'Funky Town', note perfect, stripped down but without the excitement & bounce of the original. With a stage presence akin to their namesake (a pile of bricks), the initial atmosphere & tension lapsed, interest waned & rather than ending in a climax the set ran its course & no more. The band finished with their new single 'Blood' & drifted off into its own world of.....?

With the departure of Equivalent VIII the evening was relieved of all pretence of anything more than goodtime entertainment. The Automatic Toys bounced into our hearts with a set of skin dup (eh? - ed.) pop songs about girls, girls & situations with girls in them, or so went their theory. Using a 5-piece line-up they fashioned a style of light breezy pop in the 60's mould with a 70's attack & a penchant for using 3 chords when one would do resulting in a blunting of the cutting edge of simplicity present in the best pop songs. Pop songs without hooks? Sometimes it worked, sometimes it didn't, mainly depending on the performance of the lead singer though throughout the band provided a glossy slick performance which projected far past the speakers. Statistics prove this sort of thing is quite popular (nay very popular). Personally I'd prefer something a little more challenging.

And finally The Squares for whom tonight was promotion night for their new single. Basically The Squares are a traditional 60's pop band who dress like the 60's, act like it, play like it & are even of the age to make one suspect that they were actually there. Like all copyists they steal the most superficial elements of the original & ignore the rest, in this case creating a tacky cabaret image rather than a thrusting, exciting pop band. Short sharp pop songs with harmonies & mini guitar solos; verse, chorus, verse, chorus, middle 8, verse chorus, performed with a sluggishness that hinted that while the band were clearly in love with the period they were still a step away from totally believing in it. Time will tell. As yet we have no statistics about this band but I can't see them or any like them in the charts. Haven't we had a 60's revival? Anyone for a 60's revival revival?
~ Harry Marsden.

Arvon Foundation at Lumb Bank

poetry • *prose*
playwriting • *performance*

We offer the unique opportunity to live and work alongside established writers and other artists for five days at Lumb Bank in the heart of the Pennines.

For further details send S.A.E. to:
Arvon Foundation at Lumb Bank, Hebden Bridge, West Yorkshire, HX7 6DF.

WEAPON OF PEACE at Bradford University

Weapon of Peace generate reggae riffs & strut'n'dance about the stage party-fashion. A dance band &, for purists, a sell-out: doing an Eddie Grant. Bend you at the knees on every heavy beat. The formula's irresistable - boom-cha boom-chata-chata-cha (& repeat & repeat) & all of the punters are dancing. A lesson in how to go down well on the university circuit. A punk passes me joint. The overlay of jazzy sax. "All you students should know this word - the song's called 'Suss'..." Everyone jives away the message (is lost). Long slow notes on the keys. Punctuation of clicky wooden stix rim-shots on drums. A police siren over the end of the song wails out.

'If', a-side of the soon-come single, is as catchy as the rest. And a long dancer gives each one in turn a solo stint - showcase for their classy musicianship. So don't get me wrong, W.O.P. are a great band. Shameless crowd pleasers. Tight. Send the public homeward, hot & happy.

Like former stablemates & fellow Brummies UB40, they're at the Abba end of reggae's broadening spectrum.
~ Nick Toczek.

RECORD REV. HUGHES

45's • 45's • 45's

Theatre of Hate - "Rebel Without A Brain" c/w "My Own Invention" (Burning Rome Records)
A-side features some great up-front stereo drumming. Vocals grate but mix is excellent. Distinctive neo-punk style of their own. Semi-improvised sax is prominent addition on flipside.

Spiderking - "Do you want to die for England" c/w "Animals" (Test Pressings)
A-side is early Clash (Strummer vocals and sing-along chorus chant). Commercial though slightly dated. B-side is more original with overlay of modernistic keyboard but prominent bassline and militaristic drumming are too one dimensional.

Eyeless in Gaza - "Invisibility" c/w "3 Kittens" + "Plague Years" (Cherry Red)
A duo with a sparse and highly original style built round synths. Excellent vocals (like Jake Burns of SLF) on the impressive "Invisibility" but B-side is a waste of time.

Teardrop Explodes - "Treason" (12" remixed version) c/w "Traison" + "Use Me" (Mercury)
In the charts already, this is a classic example of the T.E.'s blatant commercialism. It's a good song if you go for ringing repetition. Excellent production; synth and acoustic guitar double well. Flip .... et, sacre bleu, c'est la même chanson en français .... et après ...... a long solo strummed on acoustic guitar and vocals and vocals. Folk-rock. Interesting only as a diversion from the band's norm.

The Fall - "Slates" (6 track 10") (Rough Trade)
Mark Smith, self appointed poet of the working-classes, and Co. are current John Peel faves. Semi-tuneless and idiosyncratic. Amateurism versus creativity. Definitely not for musicians. Post punk cult weirdness from the R.T. stable (where else?). Not easy listening - you either love or hate this band.

Pig Bag - "Papa's Got a Brand New Pig Bag" c/w "The Backside" (Y Records)
Funk instrumental featuring sax over heavy Afro-percussion rhythms. Flip has sax and ethereal vocals for openers then moves back into bass and build-up of percussion - great conga playing. Add a touch of keyboards and wailing vocals. Then stop dead. Strange stuff - will either be a big hit or a complete miss. Music is moving in this direction but they may have jumped the gun. Popular Afro-jazz is a year or so away yet.

Resistance - "Survival kit" c/w "Big Flame" (Fontana)
Pure formula pop that rips off Joe Jackson/Costello/60's etc. Only trace of originality is in good lyrics. Might get some air play before everyone realises how ordinary it really is.

Plastics - "Diamond Head" c/w "Peace" (Island)
Gold coloured flexi at 33⅓. 2 trax off the album - presumably as promo material. They're jerky abrasive pop that's a sort of XTC with rhythm machine + Eastern promise. Two tracks that are straighter and less remarkable than the rest of the album.

33⅓ • 33⅓ • 33⅓

A Certain Ratio - "To Each" (Factory)
S.B. + D.Mc. The album is dominated by a sharp rhythm section of bass and drums with synth/vocals left to create a mysterious atmosphere. Strong jazz/funk feel presented 80's style. Incidental vocals mixed way down with bass lines prominent. Afro-Carib flavour especially on 'Choir' and 'Back to the Start'. Variation is limited, but a solid album with obvious appeal. N.T. Manchester band and label. Funk rhythm section + very free instrumental/vocal overlay — the sort of music that will be huge a year from now. For me, the best L.P. so far this year.

Bill Nelson - "Quit Dreaming and Get on the Beam" (Mercury)
As musician/vocalist/songwriter, Nelson is still as sharp as ever. A winning album that shows him full of new and exciting ideas. It is a sort of futurist pop/rock with heavy guitar and synth elements. Only a couple of weak tracks ('False Alarms' + 'Youth of Nations on Fire') on an album that includes the excellent singles "Do You Dream in Colour" and "Banal". Another high point is the wonderfully atmospheric 'Life Runs Out Like Sand' which has an Oriental keyboard feel and Nelson's voice haunting over the top of the melody. Obvious comparisons are with early XTC material, and it is perhaps no coincidence that the producer of their material John Leckie, has a hand in this album. (SB + DMc)

"Sounding the Ritual Echo"
Simplistic electronic doodles on synth and guitar (?) Melody lines based mainly on British sacred and pastoral music (folk song, hymns and carols) + Oriental influences. Low key, restful, and hardly minimalist. (N.T.)

'Juke Box at Eric's' (Eric's Records)
Eric's is the recently-closed Liverpool club. These 16 trax, purporting to be rare Rockabilly, are in fact late 50's R'n'R & chasing a cash-in on current Rockabilly megahype. Obscure trax by obscure artists..... and in most of these cases it is easy to see why. A couple of really good numbers aren't enough to make this anything more than an item for archivists.

Theatre of Hate - "He Who Dares Wins (Live at The Warehouse, Leeds)" [SS Records]
Abysmal production destroys any chance of this being a decent album. It sounds like it was recorded at the back of The Warehouse with a portable and then pressed without any re-mixing. It retails at £2.49 and so is very cheap, unfortunately it is quite nasty as well. With no track listing or any other information it is a bit of a surprise package. Vocals are the worst aspect (Theatre of Grate?) but the drumming is very strong. Everything sounds the same - totally uninspiring. For a band so good in the studio this is a disappointment. "He who dares wins?" Not this time! Sorry! (D.Mc)

Plastics - "Welcome Back Plastics" (Island)
10 track album with free freeixidisc that features an early song 'Paté' and an off-beat cover of The Monkees' 'Last Train to Clarksville'. Their highly distinctive style blends 60's pop, new wave, and Oriental and is distinguished by dominant percussion and high speed vocals except on a couple of slower ballads. Lyrics very similar to Lou Reed. Deceptive child-like simplicity to this music. Very appealing. The balance between jerky and staccato (like Pere Ubu) and the commercial pop is spot on. Fine debut from a band who're going to be immensely popular. (N.T.+D.Mc)

Original Mirrors - "Heart-twango & Raw beat" (Phonogram)
They've been around a while. A good commercial band in danger of getting trapped in the Fischer Z/Q-Tips "3/4 - there - but - not - quite - making - it" syndrome. Arrangements, musicianship and production are great, but songs lack anything to make them distinctive enough. When pop is going through one of its occasional creative slumps this sort of stuff sells well - but not this year, I fear, Archibald. (N.T.+D.Mc)

The 101ers - "Elgin Avenue Breakdown" (Andalucia Records)
12 trax by the band Joe Strummer served his apprenticeship with before moving on to form The Clash. The production quality is not in any way big budget, but it does not deter an album of varied content. The first couple of trax sound as though they belong on the Eric's R'n'R compilation both in style and merit. However, 'Monkey Business', 'Shake Your Hips', and 'Junco Partner' all have a Clash feel about them i.e. neat changes and powerful distinctive backing. The album was recorded live apparently to show the band's forte. Whether you like this album or not is rather immaterial; if Joe Strummer had not made it big it would never have existed. (S.B. + D.Mc)
Nick note - Shame this isn't a studio album, if the band's first and only single ('Keys to Your Heart' on Chiswick) is anything to go by. This could've been an outstanding album rather than an interesting collectable.

Eyeless in Gaza - "Photographs as Memories" (Cherry Red)
Another new band experimenting with electronics for both rhythm and melody. Orch. Man. comparison with 'Eyeless' being a duo of Martyn Bates and Pete Becker. Not as commercial or appealing as 'Manoeuvres' though. Vocals are strong but indecipherable concentrating on sound rather than pronunciation: he puts feeling into it anyway, which Modern Music so often lacks. Not easy listening but may appeal to futurists and 'weirder' Orch. Man fans. (D.Mc)
Nick note - This band packs a lot of originality, both musically and lyrically, and come up with a tasty debut album that promises more and better for the future. One half of the duo is ex-Desperate Bicycles who were among the bands who pioneered D.I.Y. discs.

"What I say is.. If that's a rock musician, what does a total bloody idiot look like?"
...like Stan Engel.

SMALL AD. Dynamic female vocalist urgently required by Burnley-based WHAMM (formerly 7-Year Itch). Aged about 20. No ties. Dutch tour in July plus recording sessions. Ring Pat on 0254 - 886727.

PATRICK MOORE & THE ALL-STARS...

Kev Morris (gtr/voc) was out cycling when he had a crash with a car. The result was a badly severed finger & the need to rework his guitar-playing style completely... not a good start for the band.

Kev & Colin Hingston (bs) were both in Jed's Blues Band (& Colin also served time with club band Cruisin' '56 and disco/reggae outfit Splash.

Together since Sept '80, the other two members are Gary Whitfield (voc) & Sean Randle (dms). The band play r'n'b + bits of reggae & soul, all with the emphasis on rhythm - they aim to be danceable & entertaining.

Upwards of 60% of their live material is original (songs by Kev) with the rest made up of standards like "Superstitious", 'Shakin' All Over' & a reggae medley of 'Hang On Sloopy' & 'Wild Thing' (!).

They feel that they achieve a fairly full sound (& a versatile one) on the 3 instruments, but may add kbds some time in the future.

Contact Gary on B'f'd 394118 or Colin on B'f'd 44541 (before 7pm weekdays).

JIM   CARL GREG MARTIN

FURTHER EXPERIMENTS

Martin Steele (gtrs/voc), Greg Firth (gtr), Carl Firth (bs), Jim Baker (dms) have been together since the new year & are just getting underway as a gigging unit. The describe their music as 'Open Sound', with Red Noise & Cure as influences. Lyrics are by Martin, music by the whole group.
Contact: Steve on Barnsley 758024 or Martin on 755474.

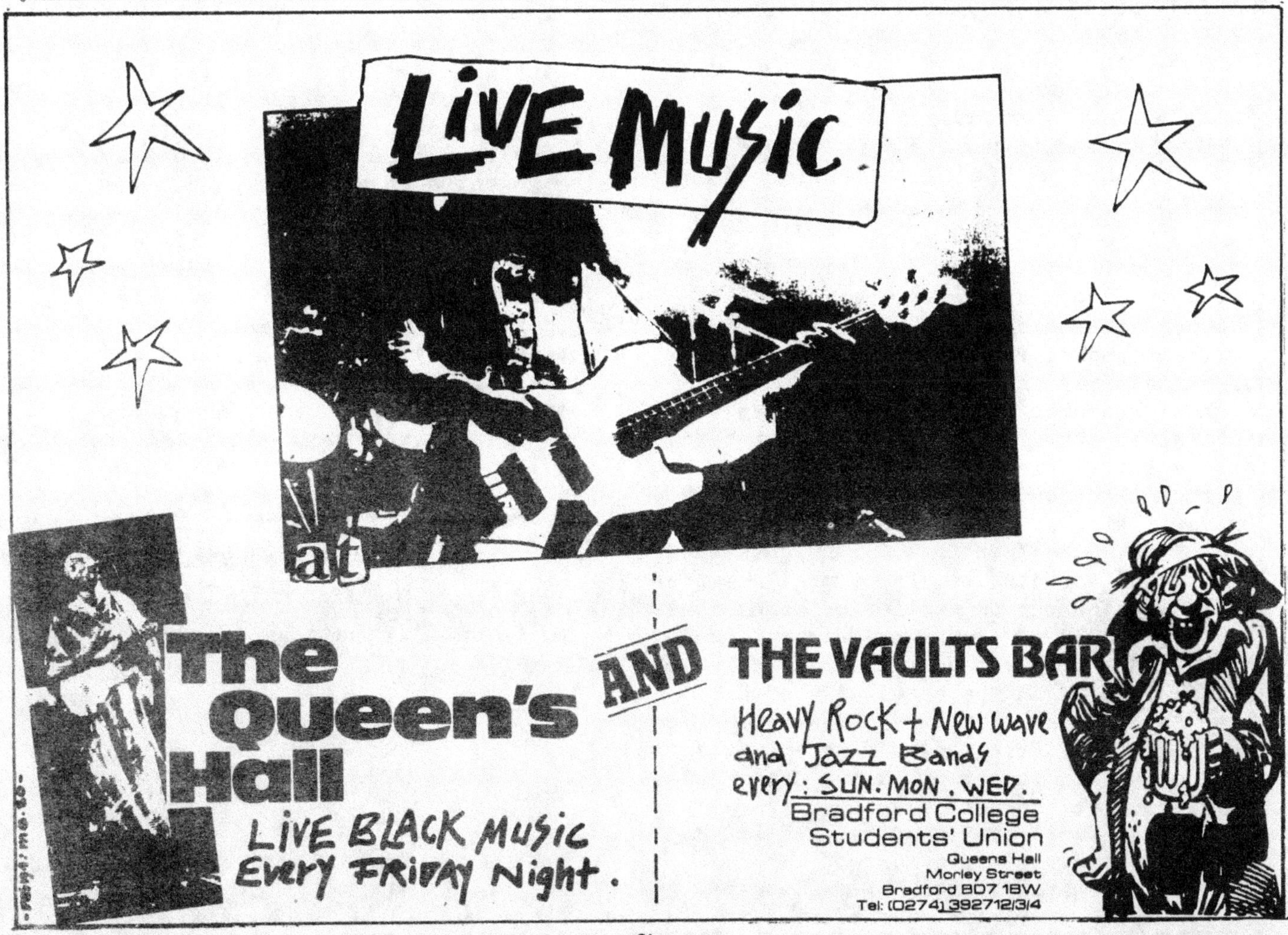

LiVE MuSiC at The Queen's Hall AND THE VAULTS BAR

LIVE BLACK MUSIC EVERY FRIDAY Night.

Heavy Rock + New Wave and Jazz Bands every: SUN. MON. WED.

Bradford College Students' Union
Queens Hall
Morley Street
Bradford BD7 1BW
Tel: (0274) 392712/3/4

THE MESS

At the end of March '81 Leeds band The Mess released their debut single 'Tried & Trusted' c/w 'I'm Falling' on their own Reasonable Records. The line-up on the record was Phil Mayne on gtr., Choc on bass & Mat Higgins on dms. Mat only spent a short time in the band & has since been replaced by Carl Rosamond. Originally formed in '77 as a joke punk band, they began to take the music a bit more seriously when Phil joined. They're now a pop band playing all their own material. Unlike many bands, they've been none too keen to gig for fear of getting caught up in the rut of doing the round off local venues. Carl likes live work, so they are taking some bookings - though the main plan is still to concentrate on recording & the prospect of more singles. A gig at The Royal Park in Feb. was their first in a year. They've since done others and describe their set as mixed pop - accessible rhythmic music with sparse guitar, Phil joking that he can't be bothered to play. Carl: "There's a lot of movement music in the set." The single which was recorded last Sept. is much fuller than their current sound. As Phil says: "We try to take advantage of studio facilities so it's not like our live sound." He put down 2 gtr. tracks on 'Falling' & an acoustic on 'T & T' ("For all folkies!"), but they've avoided overuse of effects. Contact: Reasonable Records Unltd. (Choc:"Un-everything, actually!") on Leeds 786671 - ask for Carl.

GILLAN + DEDRINGER at St George's Hall, Bradford

This tour for Leeds band Dedringer is their latest step on the road towards commercial success after slogging their way round the northern rock circuit for the past couple of years. They have already toured with Michael Schenker and Triumph and have a lucrative recording contract with Dindisc who recently released their debut album 'Direct Line' as follow up to the 'Sunday Drivers' single. However, are Dedringer worthy of such attention? On tonights showing I tend to think so. Particularly impressive was the rhythm section of Kenny Jones (not that one) on drums, and bassist Lee Flaxington. They not only provide the powerful drive in the band but also hold them together as tightly as possible. Dedringer's material is sufficiently strong and commercial to give them the chance of survival over the next couple of years. However, I can't ever see them headlining their own tour at this sort of level as the band do have a number of weaknesses. For example, Dedringer possess one excellent manic guitarist who could grace many a top band, while the other guitarist is, quite honestly, useless. In the long run this is bound to retard the bands' progress. Another weakness is the fact that they don't have one really outstanding feature to get them noticed. Criticisms apart though, I wish them well on their present success and hope they don't disappear into obscurity.

Gillan have no such worries. With the new album, 'Future Shock', crashing straight into the charts at No.2, the bands popularity is higher than ever before. A full house at St. George's Hall, Bradford saw a rather disappointing show due to the fact that Mr. Gillan himself was not on top form, breaking down mid-song on more than one occasion. At one point I expected to see a premature end to the evenings events, but to Ian's credit he threw aside his ailments and sang more like his old self over the last 20 minutes or so. The rest of the band were as solid and exciting as ever with Bernie Torme's distinctive and original guitar style the main attraction. His antics justify his status as a guitar hero, and, as far as I am concerned, his arrival in the band has guaranteed their success. Colin Towns provides the true class of the band with his haunting keyboards and melodious flute. His influence was particularly apparent in 'On the Rocks', where his skills were shown to be of the highest quality.

The band's set is so strong at the moment resulting in many brilliant numbers being left out. The ones that remained, such as 'Vengeance', 'Are you sure?', 'No Easy Way', and the timeless 'Smoke on the Water', went down a storm, as did their new material from 'Future Shock'.

Gillan will always be favourites with the crowds, simply because of their extensive touring and regular recorded material. They certainly have no plans for six nights at Hammy Odeon with only a couple of provincial dates besides. With a long tour of Britain planned for November - December, another studio album and then a live album, we're going to be hearing quite a lot of Gillan in the near future (shock).

~ STEVE BROWN.

SMALLS

2 in/6 out HMD racked P.A. AMP (MM), with 3-way electronic crossover & volume controls - 30x30 treble/60x60 mid/100x100 bs. Also, 3 Kai 100w monitors (1 with vol.control) plus 2 4x100 column speakers (Carlsboro). 200 quid the lot. Ring Eric (evenings) on Bradford 447092.

Intermusic 50 watt combo (with built-in phaser + flight case). As new. £125 o.n.o. Ring Nick on Bfd 21867.

Meatloaf - 'Bat Out Of Hell' c/w 'Heaven Can Wait' (12" red vinyl). Collector's rarity. £10.00. Ring Dave on Bfd 490871 (evenings).

LEEDS UNIVERSITY'S UNION RECORDS

HUGE REDUCTIONS ON 1000's OF ALBUMS

COME AND SEE FOR YOURSELF THE SHOP IS IN THE BASEMENT OF THE STUDENTS UNION.

We also sell tickets for all Leeds Univ. & Polytech. concerts, & for Leeds Playhouse & The Grand Theatre.

Shop Hours: Monday - Friday 9.30 a.m. - 5.00 p.m.

HUDDERSFIELD POLYTECHNIC
at GREAT HALL, QUEENSGATE

PSYCHEDELIC FURS
THE TALK·TALK·TALK·TOUR

Single: DUMB WAITERS / L.P: TALK TALK TALK

Friday 29th May
(doors open 8.30pm)

tickets: £2·00 from Woods or Bradleys Record Shops or on the door.

PUBLIC GIG..... ALL ARE WELCOME

THEATRE of HATE
NEW SINGLE (out end of May)
'CONQUISTADOR'
c/w 'PROPAGANDA'

on BURNING ROME RECORDS
32 Alexander St., London, W2 5NU.
(tel. 01-229-8236).

Theatre of Hate: June tour includes MANCHESTER POLY (2nd), LEEDS WAREHOUSE (3rd), BRADFORD SWEATBOX II (10th), plus dates being fixed in YORK & SCARBOROUGH.

SPACE INVADERS SWEAT SHIRTS

available in light blue, red or black
small, medium or large sizes

only £5·50 (inc. p.&p.)

cheques / P.O.'s payable to:-
BAD CAT TRADING (Dept. W),
7 Glenlee Road,
Lidget Green,
Bradford 7,
West Yorkshire.

Limited quantities per order only.
Please allow 21 days for delivery.

FAIRVIEW STUDIOS
WILLERBY — HULL

Fully equipped 24 track studio, catering for all types of professional recording.

Also high speed — high quality cassette duplication.

For details of all our services:-
Contact: Hull 653116.

New Punk Venue.. Top Up-&-Coming Bands
SWEATBOX II

THURSDAYS at GATSBY'S (off Manningham Lane, B'f'd)

May 14th = **DISCHARGE** + chronic
May 21st = **ANTI PASTI** + support
May 28th = **MARTIAN DANCE** + supp
June 4th = **EXPLOITED** + supp.
June 10th = **THEATRE OF HATE** + supp

& others to follow each Thursday.
entrance = £1·50 at door.

THE LONE GROOVER'S LITTLE READ BOOK By Tony Benyon.
A brand new, book-length adventure, in which Th' Groover sets out in quest of th' meaning of life... encountering en route hairdressers and hippies (with passing comments on th' state of th' art. £1.95

MODS! Compiled by Richard Barnes.
The definitive document on the '60s Mods, with over 150 photographs. £4.95

THE CLASH – BEFORE AND AFTER Photographs by Pennie Smith.
Pennie Smith's superb photos, with captions by The Clash themselves. "...the best book of rock photography that is ever likely to hit the shelves." – Zigzag. £4.95

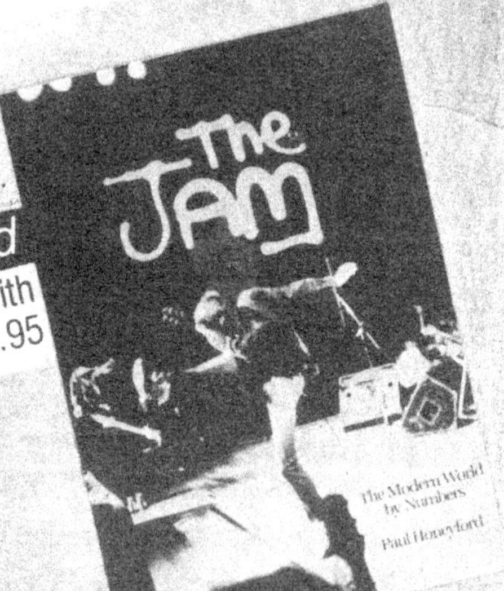

THE JAM By Paul Honeyford
A biography of one of Britain's premier rock bands, with photos by top rock photographers. £4.95

Available from all good bookshops and Virgin record shops, or send a cheque for £4.95 plus 75p p&p (for THE CLASH, THE JAM or MODS!) or £1.95 plus 30p p&p (for THE LONE GROOVER) to:

Eel Pie WCR, Bookpoint, 78, Milton Trading Estate, Abingdon, Oxon OX14 4TD
PLEASE MAKE CHEQUES PAYABLE TO BOOKPOINT.

EEL PIE PUBLISHING

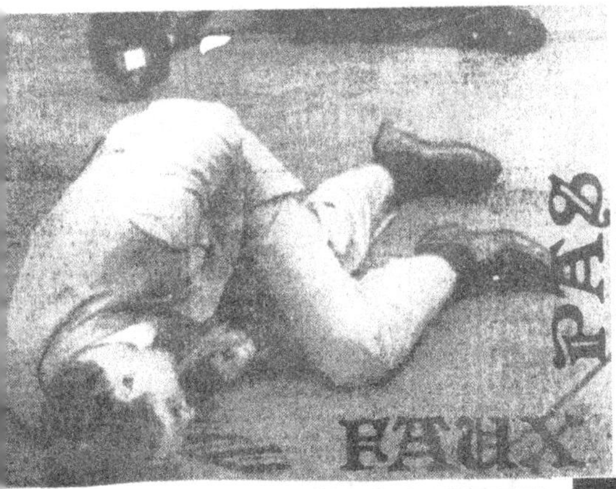

"The main thing is to remain on the same level as the audience and not be above them," Sons of the Pope 22.3.81

"Pope music is chaotic and has a catastrophic effect on the audience, it's not easy on the ear, it's music for disturbed people," Alan Burgess, Hull Daily Mail 11.8.80

"Mrs. Wilson is OK in my book. She can do no wrong as far as I'm concerned. She one lent me a quid, she was also very lenient with me when I spewed up on the landing when I couldnt make it to the bog in time." Christopher St. Pope 22.3.81

"The heretical SONS OF THE POPE were first on. Their best song "We're all Mrs. Wilsons children" a paean to the belle matron of the Wellington, implies strange behaviour in the Vatican. Most recent in a long list of Hull bands the Sons of the Pope play simple tunes reminiscent of the "Curse" and appear to enjoy themselves as much as the audience.
This group is obviously heading for the big time. Entering the stage to the "March of the Valkyries", the band made constant a plea a to be "bathed in" green light. Maybe you should welcome the new "Bath time Music" vision," Andy Wood Hulfire 13.10.80

"The song 'Mrs.Wilson's Children' epitomises the spirit of the Wellington Club, a relatively safe haven for the unemployed and other so-called eccentrics of society. In the final analysis we are all Mrs.Wilson's children!!" Sons of the Pope 22.3.81

"a dance sound based on a 12 – bar rythm and blues structure with modern influences" SOUNDS

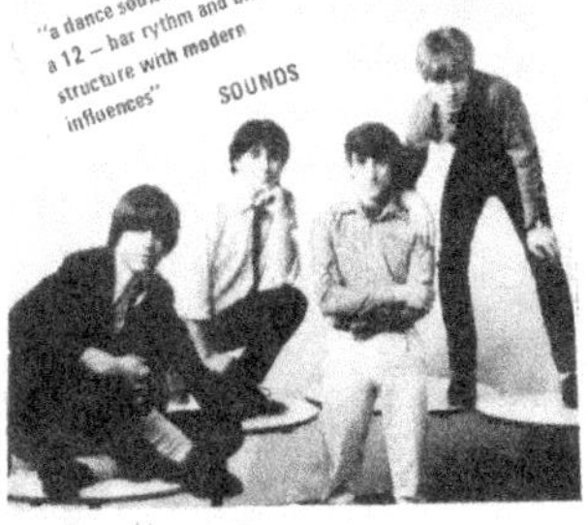

Human Zoo

Human Zoo have existed in their present form sine Sept '80. There have been two changes in line up. the addition of a Second Guitarist and a change in vocalist. The members of the band are:
JOCK LURIE : DRUMS
IAN ASHBRIDGE : BASS
PETE DUNHAM : LEAD GUITAR
KATE CAMERON : VOCALS
JOHN COULSON : RTHYM GUITAR
Highlights in their career have been supporting the Revillos, radio broadcasts, a 'private' gig for Des Moines, soon to be review in 'Sounds'. An independent single is planned. The band play mostly in Hull although they have played out of town on occassions.
Contact Ian Ashbridge Hull (0482) 848302.

London Boys

The London Boys are a Hull band who, to quote from their press release, play the music that people dance to – the speed of rock with the staccato reggae that eats your tapping feet, all bound in R+B.
A short promotional video of the band is to be shot by local enterprise Off Balance Films in the Spring.
Andy + Rory write the bands material and share vocals + guitar-work with Sarge on drums and Jon on bass.
They've a single 'Bleeding in my heart' lined up for soon-come release on their own One Way Rec. label and are also recording two tracks for inclusion on a Hull Compilation album that's to be released on Koala records in April.
You can contact the band through their manager Malcolm Williamson, on Hull (0482) ~~842445~~ 881308 (Nick Toczek Wool City Rocker Feb '81)

"Live, they are Hull's most talented and imaginative pop group, with a distinctive sound and professional ability" DAILY MAIL

JOHNNY SOLO

You've had a varied music career, how did you start and what have you done?
I was in an acoustic band with Chris Brown and Tom Cotton (3 Tiles East) and I was spotted by Mike Bradwell of Hull Truck and so became a boy, musician, stage manager, roadie etc with them for a year. Then I did a series of strange music, thats amplified kite strings through amps, also milk bottles, plastic bottles and things. Paul Cowhill came up and jammed with us for a while. I was then in a band called Johnny Cool and the Brazilian Sequinned Glitter Brothers. Then I formed the Moneymen, Hull's first punk band using Wreckless Eric's old musicians. I then went busking in Paris with Chris Brown and came back and formed the Johnny Solo band and six months later we won the NME competition.
But you're no longer called Johnny Solo and the Snapshots?
No, just plain Johnny Solo.
Have you gained anything from the competition?
Yeah, I mean that I learned a lot about music production arrangements, what makes a hit, writing techniques, that sort of thing.
But no record contract?
No I didnt really get any joy from the competition in that field so I've started my own record label. I hope to sign other bands if the single comes off which will be out at the begining of May.
It must be frustrating not being able to break through out of Hull when you're so popular here?
Yeah it seems strange that people cant get us gigs when we're so popular. Mike Hancock, the Beat's manager tried to get us a deal and he couldnt do anything either. So we plan to just keep on at it till something does happen.

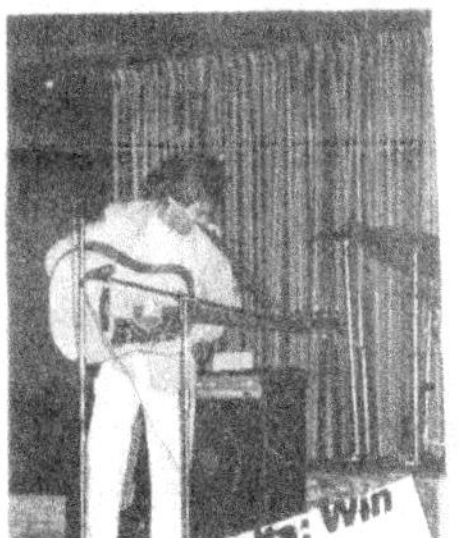

Comp Results: Win studio time with Nick Lowe — The Winners!

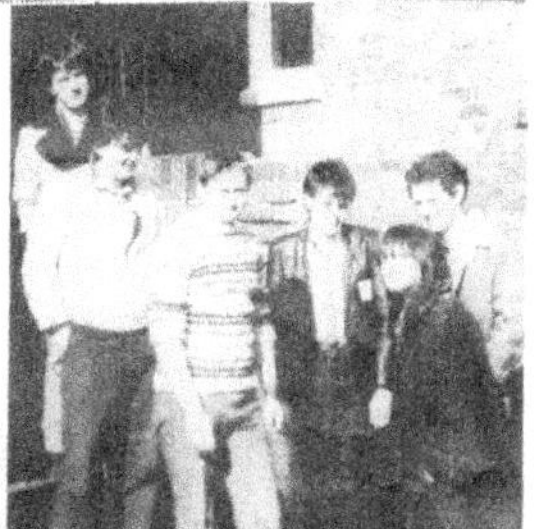

Sons of the Pope photo by Tim
Chris St. Pope – voice
Ian M. Barrass – voice
M – drums
Gordon Chelsea Babbage – bass
Romeo Smith Violence – guitar
Miss Sharren Abercrombie – Piano

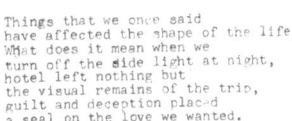

VITAL RECORDS
57 PARK AVENUE
HULL
NORTH HUMBERSIDE

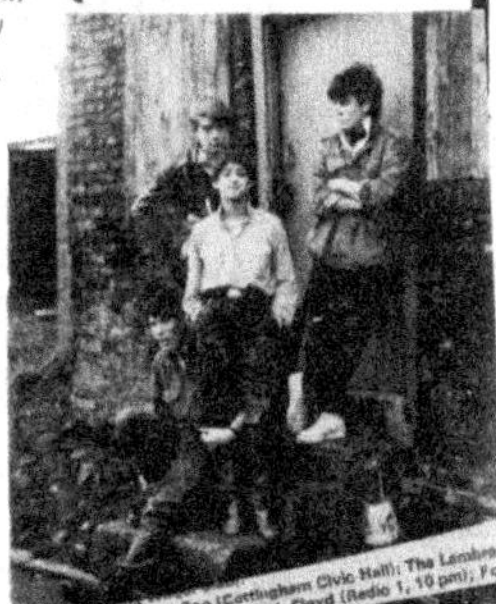

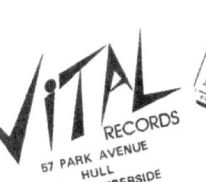

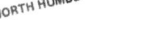

— Human Zoo (Cottingham Civic Hall); The Lambrettas (... Pavilion); Pink Floyd (Radio 1, 10 pm); Ful...

Thanx to the Byron Squad

VETS

SOLID Entertainments presents THE VETS
ISSUE 3
+ ELEVATORS
+ PUNK SOUNDS
AT WINTER GARDENS
Kingsway CLEETHORPES
Thursday 31st July 1980
8 – 12 MIDNIGHT
Advance Tickets £1.50
On The Day £1.75
No

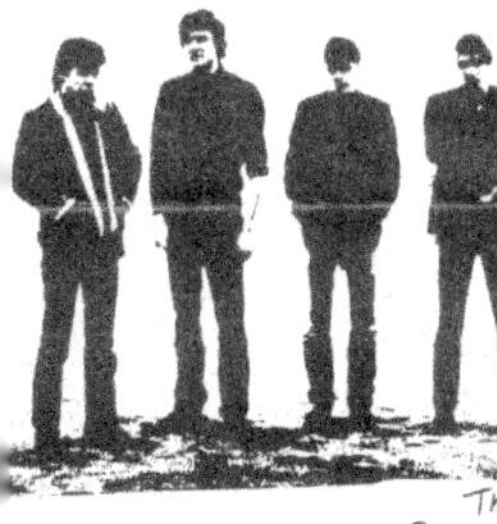

NOTHING REMAINS

Things that we once said
have affected the shape of the life,
What does it mean when we
turn off the side light at night,
hotel left nothing but
the visual remains of the trip,
guilt and deception placed
a seal on the love we wanted.

Nothing remains but a message on paper,
Nothing to gain from the words written there
Nothing remains but a message on paper,
Nothing remains.

Straight out of nowhere
to sour the virginal cloth,
a friend on a weekend
made sure that the bedclothes were soft,
to this that was missing
to the lover determines the link,
dinner and roses are long ago memories.

We must say now
what we'd want to say later
Nothing remains.

Roy Bickenson Voice
Richard Crossland Bass guitar
Ashley Smith Drums
Neil Scott Synthesisers and guitar

PSYCHOLOGIC

Q. Can you tell me what the name means?
A. ~~Common Vision~~ Psycho logic is the seeing of reality and dreams mixed. From my point of view it is a label for the use of imagination, mixing the reality of consciousness and dreams and sleep.
Q. Is this what the song is about?
A. The songs are about self realisation of the individual through experience. This particular song is a communication of the questioning of reality and it's a love song and it's a nonsense song and was written when hearing an ice cream van go past where I used to live.
Q. Is there a certain atmosphere you like to get across?
A. I like to try and communicate emotion through the use of my voice and imagination through the content of the lyrics.
Q. Yours is the only home recorded track on the album. In what way is it different?
A. It was recorded in a cellar with the use of a single borrowed stereo cassette deck. The vocals were done by direct injection into one of the channels of the cassette deck. The back line including drums and bass and rythym guitar were picked up by a single mike in the second channel of the deck. The vocals were again present in the back line by use of a second vocal mike.
Q. Is that an unusual way of recording?
A. It's a very effective and inexpensive way.
Q. Do you plan to stick to home recording in the future?
A. A record company would solve problems of distribution and reaching a larger audience. Everyone has access to a tape recorder but not everyone has access to large numbers of tapes.
Q. What are you into?
A. Meditation and vitamin B.

Nick Cooper – Bass
Billy Klingon – Vocals and guitar
Grant Ardis – Drums

KHCT

Nyam

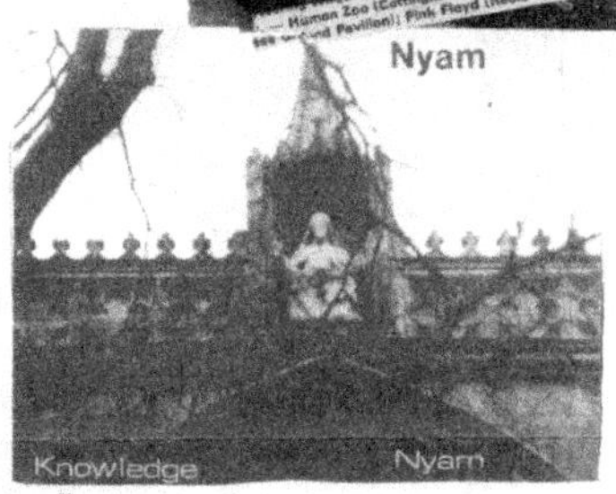

You say you have the right to command
You say you have the answers to hand
I know you dont
You tell me that you really care
That together we'll be going somewhere
I know we wont
The time you're most convinced you're in the right
is when you'll confirm your failure
And the time you think your problems are all solved
is the moment when they nail you
When you use a good man's knowledge without conscience
There's a lot it can do for you
But when ambition comes to be revealed
Knowledge will destroy you
cos I've seen your soul
And I know you dont
There's just a black hole
And I know you dont.

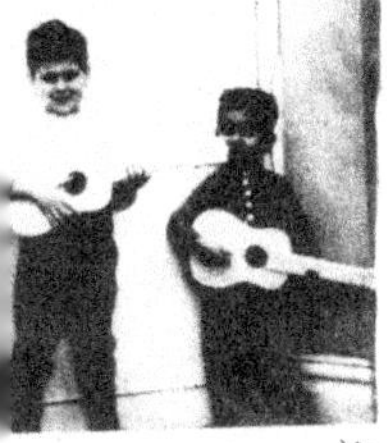

The Ashtrays

Dominic Robinson + Jim Band were the only two people left alive in Ferriby, or so it seemed. Dominic bought a Sax + Andy Pea was interested in a roadcrew. An old colleague from Colditz sprang into Dominic's mind, and Andy, a mechano fiend, built a bass guitar from the spare parts. Geoff "what I'm trying to say" Seger discovered that Beat was not to be found in Rock + made the pilgrimage to Ferriby which at least shared a first letter with Funk.
Then Maurice Glasman, underprivileged student met Dominic in a public lavatory. They both agreed about some kind of Rhythm method and out of the order, chaos was gradually emerging. Joe gave up smoking to join the band and Mikey brought with him a trumpet and 'borrowed' percussion.
Then the band discovered rhythm. All-day-long-rhythm, dance, pulse, gaps, holes, spaces, craters, sex and it emerged as Funk. Rhythm Salvation was the ends, Funk was the means. And the Ferriby Funk found its way to Hull.
Hull is closed to rhythm, we are looking for the gaps (holes + craters)

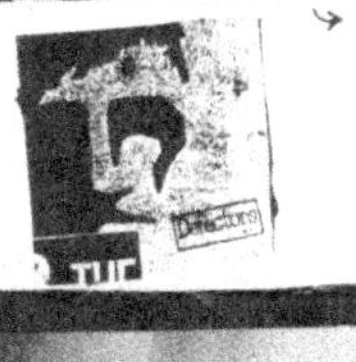

Photo by Charlie

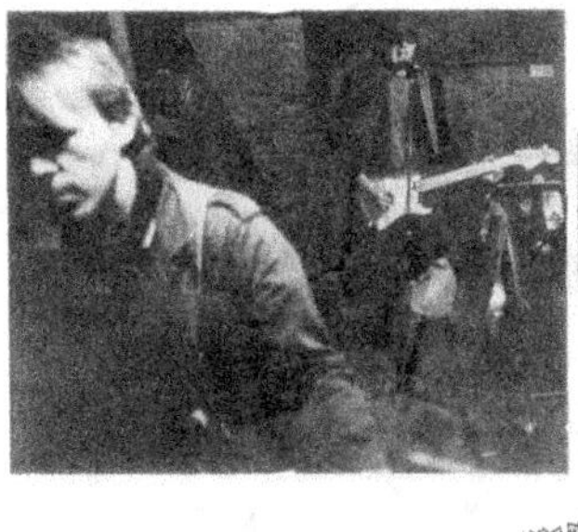

BLITZKRIEG PATROL

Ring 445701 (Kari)

A street play – about survivors in a nuclear fall-out shelter – and a pop group entertained the crowd before the march ... continued to Wawne

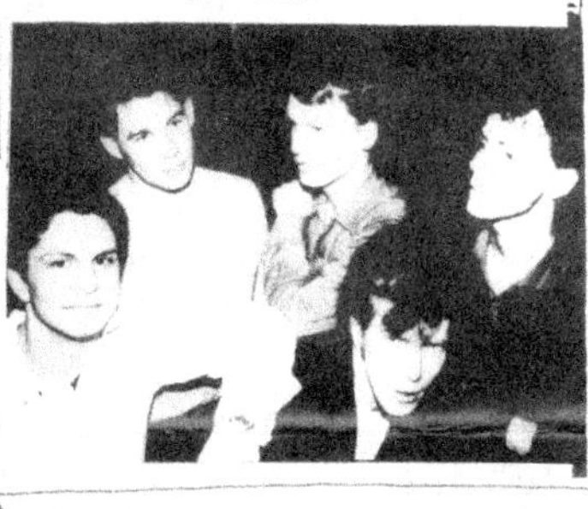

f Photo by me!

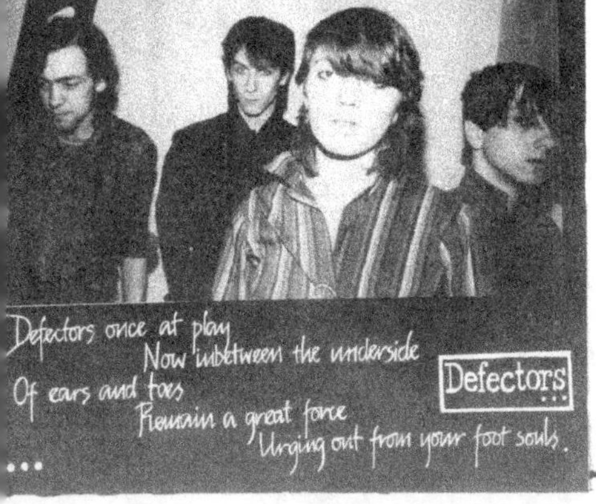

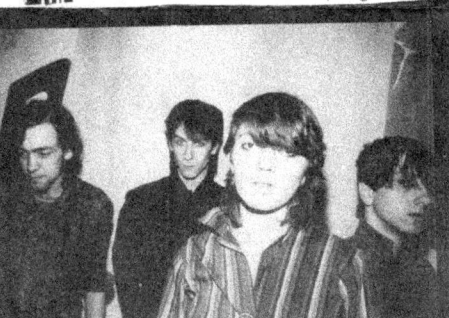

Defectors once at play
Now wedged between the underside
Of ears and toes
Remain a great force
Urging out from your foot souls
...
Defectors

This group's so cool!

COOL-TO-SNOG don't like Sheena Easton.

While she is content to watch her man catch the early morning train, work from nine till five, and catch one home again, the Hull four-piece lament the plight of the housewife.

One of their numbers, "The House Wife Song," hits out at the frustrations a women has to endure in the home, trapped in a man's world — the complete antithesis of the Sheena Easton syndrome.

"There is far too much sex discrimination in the music world," claims blonde guitarist Kari Kool. "There is just no equality."

Kari, well-known in Hull as the Wellington Club promoter, was inspired to become a female musician when she saw Suzi Quatro in the mid-Seventies and "all that leather and aggression."

Cool-to-Snog (the name is a social comment on people's inhibitions about showing affection) came together in March last year.

Since then they have been through four bassists and four singers, before settling for the enigmatic Irene Blood (Sharon), lead vocals and chief songwriter.

"The Housewife Song" is typical of the band's material, and is due for inclusion of Kari's forthcoming Humberside compilation album.

Says Kari: "Our prime concern is having fun. It is more important to enjoy ourselves on stage than be note perfect."

The other half of the band is male, Capt Scarlett on bass and Airfix (ex-Defectors) on drums. Both, however, are in their own bands, guitarists by nature, and eventually plan to leave Cool-to-Snog.

"There is a sort of innocence and naivety about this band that makes for a really good formula," says Airfix. "Kari and Sharon work well together on stage and will need a new rhythm section to keep the spirit of the band alive."

Kari would prefer an all-female line-up. Not just, she claims, because she is a feminist, but because girl bands are all too rare in the music world.

"Sharon and I are just more forward than most girls. All these local bands are followed around by a string of girlfriends who gloat about their blokes in the band — but it never occurs to them to pick up a guitar and have a go themselves." Cool-to-Snog are set to play Groucho's on February 22.

ALAN BURGESS

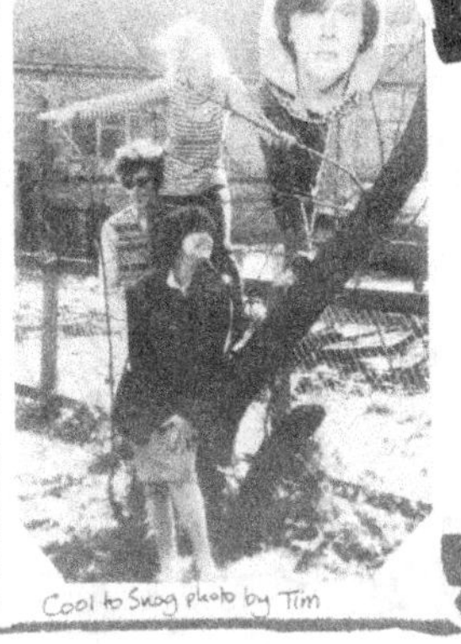

Cool to Snog photo by Tim

ONCE UPON A TIME in a strange land miles & miles away from the Kings castle lived four minstrels and a fool, who wooed maidens and played a unique blend of dance orientated musics. This band of merry gentlemen heard great tales of a wonderful quest to a place full of enchanting spells and a fortune of wonders beyond description – the dreams of reality. Energetically and full of enthusiasm they embarked on this, their mysterious crusade.

Joshua Zero · voice,
Airfix · guitar, Dean Stones · bass,
Samir Khan · keyboards, Marc Appleton · drums

To describe the music of BLITZKRIEG PATROL is not to categorise. It is both conscious and subconscious, an extension of the personalities involved. To date the experiment has established an amalgamation of power and delicacy which weaves and plots which threatens and caresses, and accumulates in a tender bombardment – almost uncomfortable pleasure. Hence the name. The Chemistry of Character and the personal politics are evident in the formulae used to create atmospheres, which act as their trademark. Nothing else can be said now, which has not already been said, or that will not be said in the future.

Today is only yesterdays Tommorow.

Thanx to the Byron Squad

Nyam

London Boys

London Boys are a Hull band who, to quote their press release, play the music that people dance to - the speed of rock with the staccato reggae that was your tapping feet.

The London Boys are a Hull band who to quote from their press release, play the music that people dance to - the speed of rock with the staccato reggae that was your tapping feet. The band is to shortly be shooting a promotional video of the bands material and all being well in the Spring write the bands material and be shot by local enterprise Off Balance Films in the Spring. Andy + Rory write the bands material and Andy + Rory vocals + guitar - work with Sarge on drums and Jon on bass. "Bleeding in my heart" singles and Jon "Bleeding in my heart" theyre a single - come - release on Cone. They're up for soon - Come release and are also lined up for One Way Rec. label and are also on a Hull compilation album in April through their own One Way Rec. label. Hul's to be released on Hawk records in April through Hull (you can contact the band through Hull manager Malcolm Williamson on Hull (0482) 847475 (NIGEL TOCZEK BOOG1) 881308 (0482) City Rocker F.18/1)

"Live, they are Hull's most talented and imaginative pop group with a distinctive sound and professional ability." DAILY MAIL

"a dance sound based on a 12 - bar rythm and blues structure with modern influences." SOUNDS

Human Zoo

Human Zoo have existed in their present form since Sept '80. There have been two changes in line up, the addition of a second guitarist and a change in vocalist. The members of the band are:

JOUL LURIE : DRUMS
IAN ASHBRIDGE : BASS
PETE DUNHAM : LEAD GUITAR
KATE CAMERON : VOCALS
JOHN COWSON : RHYM GUITAR

Highlights in their career have been supporting the Revillos on radio broadcasts, a private gig for Des Moines soon to be reviewed in 'Sounds'. An independent single is planned. The band play mostly in Hull although they have played out of town on occasions.

Contact: Ian Ashbridge: Hull (0482) 848302

VITAL RECORDS
57 PARK AVENUE
HULL
NORTH HUMBERSIDE

PSYCHOLOGIC

Q. Can you tell me what the name means?
A. Psychologic is the seeing of reality and dream-reality. My point of view is a label for the use of imagination, mixing the reality of consciousness and dreams and sleep.
Q. Is this what the song is about?
A. The songs are about self realisation of me...

SONS OF THE POPE

"The main thing is to remain on the same sound level as the audience and not be above them." Sons of the Pope 22.3.81

"Pope music is chaotic and has a catastrophic effect on the audience, it's not easy on the ear. It's music for disturbed people." Alan Burgess, Hull Daily Mail 11.8.80

"Mrs.Wilson is OK in my book. She can do no wrong as far as I'm concerned. She one moment is stupid and was also very lenient with me when I spewed up on the landing when I couldn't make it to the bog in time." Christopher St. Pope 22.3.81

"The heretical SONS OF THE POPE were first on. Their best song "We're all Mrs. Wilsons children" a paean to the belle matron of the Wellington, implies strange behaviour in the Vatican. Most recent in a long list of Hull bands the Pope play simple tunes reminiscent of the new 'Beat' time audience to bathed in" green light. Maybe you should welcome the new 'Beat' time Music/Vision." Andy Wood Hulfire 13.10.80

"The song 'Mrs.Wilson's Children' epitomises the spirit of the Wellington Club, a relatively safe haven for the unemployed and other so-called eccentrics of society, in the final analysis we are all "Mrs Wilson's Children" Sons of the Pope 22.3.81

Sons of the Pope photo by Tim
Chris St.Pope - voice
Ian R.Barrass - drums
Gordon Chelsea Boothage - bass
Romeo Smith Violence - guitar
Miss Sharren Abercrombie - piano

NOTHING REMAINS

Things that we once said
have affected the shape of the life,
What does it mean when we
turn off the side light at night,
hotel left nothing but
the visual remains of the trip,
guilt and deception placed
a seal on the love we wanted.

Nothing remains to gain from the words written there

JOHNNY SOLO

Q. You've had a varied music career, how did you start and what have you done?
A. I was in an acoustic band with Chris Brown and Yom Cotton (3 Tiles East) and I was spotted by Mike Brickwell of Hull Truck and so became teaboy, musician, stage manager, roadie etc with them for a year. Then I did a series of kite music, thats amplified kite strings through a PA, also Tilk bottles, elastic bottles and things. Lol Coxhill came up and jammed with us for a week. I was then in a band called Johnny Solo and the Brazilian Sequinned Glitter Brothers. Then I formed the Moneymen, an old musicians band based in Paris with Chris Brown and then back and Rod the Johnny Solo bandband two months later we won the NVK competition.
Q. But you're no longer called Johnny Solo and the Snapshots?
A. No, just plain Johnny Solo.
Q. Have you gained anything from the competition?
A. Yeah, I mean that I learned a lot about music production arrangements, what makes a hit, writing techniques, that sort of thing.
Q. But no record contract?
A. No I didnt really get any joy from the the competition in that field so I've started my own record label. I hope to sign other bands it the single comes off with the beginning of May.
Q. The music of Hull when you're so popular through the musicans that people cant get us Yeah it seems strange that people cant get us gigs when we're so popular. Mike Hancock the Beat ex manager tried to get us a deal and he couldnt do anything either. So we plan to just keep on at it till something does happen.

Comp Results: Win studio time with Nick Lowe - The Winners!

SOLID PRESENTS
THE VETS
ISSUE 3

The Ashtrays

Dominic Robinson, Tim Bead were the only two people left alive in Ferriby, or so it seemed. Dominic bought a sax + Andy Lee was interested in a road crew. An old Colleague from Colletts sprang into Dominic's mind, and Andy, a mechanic fund, built a bass guitar from the spare parts. Geoff "What I'm trying to say" Seger discovered that Brat was not to be found in Kent but made the pilgrimage to Ferriby which at least stood just little bit Funk.

Then Maurice Glasman, underprivileged student met Dominic in a public lavatory. They both agreed about some kind of Rhythm method and out of this order, chaos was gradually emerging. Joe gave up smoking to join the band and Mike brought with him a trumpet and 'borrowed' percussion.

Then the band discovered rhythm. All-day-long rhythm, dance, pulse, gaps, holes, spaces, crackers six and it emerged as Funk. Rhythm Salvation was the end. Funk was the means. And the Ferriby Funk pundits way to Hull, Hull is closed to rhythm, we are looking for the Gaps (holes & craters)

Boy Bickenson Voice
Richard Crossland Bass guitar
Ashley Smith Drums
Neil Scott Synthesisers and guitar

Defectors once at play
Now indetween the underside
Of ears and ears
Remain a great force
Urging out from your foot soul.

photo by Charlie

Defectors

---

a single borrowed stereo cassette deck. The vocals were done by direct injection into one of the channels of the cassette deck. The back line including drums and bass and rythym guitar were picked up by a single mike in the second channel of the deck. The vocals were again present in the backline by use of a second vocal mike.

Q. Is that an unusually way of recording?
A. It is very effective and incoming way.
Q. Do you plan to stick to home recording in the future?
A. A record company would solve problems of distribution and reaching a larger audience. Everyone has access to a tape recorder but not everyone has access to large numbers of tapes.
Q. What are you into?
A. Meditation and vitamin B.

Nick Cooper - Bass
Billy Klinton - Vocals and guitar
Grant Ardis - Drums

BLITZKRIEG PATROL

Ring 445701 (Kari)

A street play — about a protester in a major fall-out shelter — and the crowd before the march continued.

---

dinner and roses are long ago memories.

We must say now
what we'd want to say later
Nothing remains.

You say you have the answers to hand
I know you dont
You tell me that you really care
That together we'll be going somewhere
I know we wont
The time you're most convinced you're in the right
is when you'll confirm your failure
And the time you think your problems are all solved
is the moment when they nail you
When you use a good man's knowledge without conscience
There's a lot it can do for you
But when ambition comes to be revealed
Knowledge will destroy your soul
cos I've seen your soul
And I know you dont
There's just a black hole
And I know you dont.

↓ Photo by me!

ONCE UPON A TIME in a strange land ruled by minstrels and a fool, who wooed maidens and played a unique blend of dance orientated musics. This band of many gentlemen heard great tales of a wonderful quest to a place full of enchanting spells and a fortune of wonders beyond description, the dreams of reality. Enigmatically and full of enthusiasm they embarked on this, their mysterious crusade.

Joshua Zero: voice,
Arfix: guitar, Dean Stones: bass,
Sumer Khan: keyboards, Marc Appleton: drums.

To describe the music of BLITZKRIEG PATROL is not to categorise. It is both conscious and subconscious, an extension of the personalities involved. To date the experiment has obtained an amalgamation of power and delicacy which weaves and plots within theatres and caresses, and accumulates in a tender bombardment almost uncomfortable pleasure. Hence the name. The chemistry, character and pleasure of the personal politics are evident in the formulae used to create atmospheres which stir as their trademark. Nothing else can be said now, which has not already been said, of that will not may be said in the future.

Today is only yesterdays tomorrow.

This group's so cool!

COOL-TO-SNOG don't like Sheena Easton.

While she is content to watch her man catch the early morning train, work from nine till five, and catch one home again, the Hull four-piece lament the plight of the housewife.

One of their numbers, "The House Wife Song," hits out at the frustrations a woman has to endure in the home, trapped in a man's world — the complete antithesis of the Sheena Easton syndrome.

"There is far too much sex discrimination in the music world," claims blonde guitarist Kari Kool. "There is just no equality."

Kari, well-known in Hull as the Wellington Club promoter, was inspired to become a female musician when she saw Suzi Quatro in the mid-Seventies and "all that leather and aggression."

Cool-to-Snog are a name, a social comment on people's inhibitions about showing affection, came together in March last year.

Since then they have been through four bassists and four singers, before settling for the enigmatic Irene Blood (Sharon), lead vocals and chief songwriter. "The Housewife Song" is typical of the band's material and is due for inclusion of Kari's forthcoming Humberside compilation album.

Says Kari: "Our prime concern is having fun. It is more important to enjoy ourselves on stage than be note perfect."

The other half of the band is made up of Capt Scarlett on bass and Arfix (ex-Defectors) on drums. Both, however, are in their own bands, guitarists by nature, and eventually plan to leave Cool-to-Snog.

"There is a sort of innocence and naivety about this band that makes for a really good formula," says Arfix. Kari and Sharon work well together on stage and will need a new female back-up to keep the spirit of the band alive.

Kari would prefer an all-female line-up. Not just, she claims, because she is a feminist, but because girl bands are all too rare in the music world.

"Sharon and I are just more forward than most girls. All these local bands are followed around by a string of girlfriends who gloat about their blokes in the band — but it never occurs to them to pick up a guitar and have a go themselves. Cool-to-Snog are set to play Groucho's on February 22.

ALAN BURGESS

Cool to Snog photo by Tim

ISSUE #15

Autumn 1981, part-prepared pages of the never-published A4 issue

It's such a shame that I ran out of both the money and the energy required to finish and publish this issue. Not only was it set to be a rebellious and fiery issue, but it would have also broken fresh ground. Adverts were now coming in thick and fast. They were the mag's main source of income. Collecting the small payments due from countless outlets had become an exhausting and often thankless task. I'd therefore wisely decided to do away with all of that draining hassle by simply making the magazine free. Perhaps, if I'd had some reserves of courage and determination, I could have turned the whole venture into something refreshed and dynamic. It wasn't to be. I felt trapped and burnt out. I thought about selling the magazine on to a new and enthusiastic editor/publisher, but even that prospect seemed daunting.

Anyway, many new magazines were emerging, several of them inspired—at least in part—by WCR. These included two new Leeds-based fanzines - *Rouska* (run by Richard Paddison a.k.a. Richard Rouska) and *Roar* (run by the redoubtable Len Liggins), and the Otley-based fanzine *Tongue In Cheek* (run by Ian Cheek). Nowadays, I'm a resident columnist, reviewer, and occasional features writer for Sean McGhee's bimonthly UK music mag *R'n'R*. It's a job I've been doing for the past fifteen years. What I didn't know when I started writing for it (it was then called *Rock'n'Reel*) was that Sean, as a young teenager, had been inspired to start the mag after having bought a copy of WCR in a Blackpool music shop while he was there as a pupil on a school trip. I like to think that I bowed out at the right time for both me and WCR. We'd both done what we'd needed to do.

Notes on bands featured in this issue.

The key bands featured in this unpublished issue were ABC and Heaven 17 (both from Sheffield), Soft Cell (from Leeds), and Bradford's New Model Army. All four were on the verge of becoming major players on the UK music scene. Indie music was taking off, and the north was suddenly getting the attention it so richly deserved. Venues were multiplying, live gigs were rammed, music festivals were taking off, and it seemed like everyone between the ages of thirteen and thirty was involved in an emerging band. I was thirty-one. It was time for me to step aside, but not from music, performance, or publishing. I'm now seventy-five, and I'm still fully active in all three arenas. Only death will put a stop to that.

Nick Toczek's WoolCityRocker

Northern Musak

ISSUE No. 15

FREE!

so give the money to CND

Soft Cell
Heaven 17
ABC
Afraid of Mice

READ THIS ZINE THEN GIVE IT AWAY TO THE NEXT HUMAN!

Blowing the gaff on chart return shops

COVER BY NICK TOCZEK

I originally wrote this article for the now-defunct national rock weekly 'Musicians Only' — in which it appeared 22 Nov '80. I reprint it here because I reckon the info in it is basic stuff that every band should know. Hope you agree. — Nick Toczek...

HYPING YOUR BAND on the public and the mass media

CHOICE of publicity material depends on how much money you have and what you're prepared to do. Managers or self-managing bands either sit home with a phone, a typewriter and a stack of envelopes or else zoom round in the van with posters and a bucket of flour-and-water paste. Best bet is to do both. Here's a list of useful methods.

Badges (for the group to wear and to sell or give away). Cheapest are cardboard discs with a safety pin taped on the back. Blank tin badges in a range of colours cost only a few pence each from a good stationer, then all you need are a couple of tins of Humbrol model paint, a very fine brush and some Humbrol clear enamel to give a final protective layer. For larger quantities and a really professional job, there are plenty of badge manufacturers. Prices vary according to size and number of colours (eg Better Badges do 100 1 inch black and white buttons for £13.50).

Photos (preferably live ones) should be black and white with good clear contrast so that they'll print well in a newspaper.

Headed notepaper makes the all-important good first impression. If you appear professional, then you're half way to getting treated that way in return. Cheapest is to do your own design and take it to a cheap local printer to get litho copies run off. Always do original artwork in black on white paper. For a little extra you can have the printing done in coloured ink on coloured paper.

Band info sheets (line-up, gear, availability, contact phone number, brief history, achievements, press quotes). Be confident but not too immodest in what you say. Keep it readable, relevant and concise — organisers, agents and press reporters don't have all day to read about you!

Posters. From chalking or spraying on walls, sticking up hand-written posters (using waterproof ink paint!), doing your own silkscreen printing (easy to learn and fun to do) or getting them printed professionally — however you do it, make it eye-catching and large — posters are the essential items. Reckon on putting up one poster for every person you want at the gig. N.B. Most places you'll find the law will caution and then prosecute if they catch you at it.

Demo tapes. No more than half a dozen songs, well recorded (a bad demo being worse than no demo). If you do it yourself, borrow or hire a 4-track rather than recording direct onto a cassette recorder (unless it's exceptionally good). Best bet, though, is to record in a studio and get cassette copies run off. You can always recoup some of the cost by selling copies to friends and at gigs.

Regular press releases listing gigs and giving news about the band. Mail these (in good time to catch copy dates!) to the national music press, local papers, local radio, your favourite fanzines, agents and venues that you want to seduce and anywhere else that might get results.

Stickers. These are done by specialist printers. Do your own design. They're good for shops and venues, for easy flyposting and make for popular freebies at gigs — as well as on the band's gear, van, clothing, etc.

Leaflets listing future gigs and giving some info on the band can be handed out at your own gigs, at other bands' gigs, in pubs and venues, left on counters in shops or even handed out in the street. Lyric sheets are also a nice idea for fans at gigs.

So that's it. You might think of other material or gimmicks — balloons, pens, T-shirts, etc. Prices vary enormously, so shop around. Use the Yellow Pages and Exchange & Mart as well as the music press to find printing and other services.

Now to the second part — how to do the job or hyping. The first rule of publicity is persistence — keep pushing, it pays off in the end. To publicise gigs, in addition to posters, word-of-mouth, etc use the free listing of the gig guides in the national music weeklies. Send info on tours to the news editors. Let them know if you're opening at a new venue or doing any special gigs.

Write to and/or ring the reviews editor if you're chasing a review (but try to be sure that you're inviting them to a *good* gig!). They may not show any immediate enthusiasm — it's up to you to persuade them that you're more interesting than the thousands of other bands gigging around the country. Make sure they know what sort of music you play — the wrong reviewer will probably pan you even if you're the best mod/HM/punk/jazz-rock combo in your street!

Push your local radio stations — they'll publicise gigs, maybe do an interview or even play your demo. Call in and talk to them. Likewise the local press and fanzines. Have a go at regional TV producers and reporters. Remember, though they're often inundated with hopefuls and can consequently seem blasé, it's their job to cover what's interesting and newsworthy. You might even find that while your boundless musical talent draws a blank, your drummer's wooden leg earns you a double-page spread.

Hard-pressed journalists will be more ready to use you if you make their job easier. A package (demo tape, photos, info on the band, a full list of gigs, a contact number giving the best time to ring, etc) is better than a scribbled letter with an address on it. Don't underestimate fanzines. A write-up in a small mag will probably be read by several journalists on the nationals and by a few DJs.

Finally, then, how to find out exactly who does what and where. You can get the names of reviewers/editors and the relevant addresses/phone numbers for the national music press from the masthead inside each paper. Address letters or make phone calls to specific staffers by name. For fanzines you should use Rough Trade, Better Badges and Compendium Books (all in London) who stock extensive selections from around the country. For local and national radio and TV go to your library and ask for The BBC Handbook (a BBC publication) and Television and Radio (published by IBA).

DIY hyping . . . it's as easy as that. Try it.

Attention All Bands!

* Do you want to see yourself on T.V.?
* Do you want a top quality video demo tape to promote your act?
* DO YOU WANT TO LATCH ONTO A GOOD DEAL?

Then read on......

Cargo Recording Studios in association with Cedar Video Promotions are making a very special offer which will not be repeated or matched.

You can now have a full colour sound and vision live recordings of your band filmed by professionals at the once only price of £99.

This is an offer you cannot afford to miss!

For more details phone either:-

John Brierley at Cargo } 0706-524420

or: Ian Ogden at Cedar } 0706-74298

HEAVEN 17 steering well clear of the whole rockstar syndrome to strike a casual pose in their dayclothes →→→

PIC: ALAN BALLARD.

A 3-piece band called The Future was at work in Sheffield a few years ago. One member of that line-up was Addy Newton (now with Clock DVA). The other 2 were Martin Webb & Ian Craig Marsh, a pair of composer-musicians using synths.

'Golden Hour of The Future', an album

/continues top of column two (cos I fucked up the pasting up)...

/continued from foot of column two...

instruments - 4 songs: 'The Banana Boat Song' (!) sung without music, 'Fascist Groove Thang', 'Soul Warfare'(off the album) + 'Play To Win' - last three with 3-part live vocals & taped backing trax. They go down well with the capacity audience but the brevity leaves some feeling cheated - free badges, posters, etc. keep most happy.

Ian: "We want to steer well clear of the whole rockstar syndrome. B.E.F. gives us all the freedom we want to work on various projects that interest us... there's so much flexibility in it... We've no fixed plans or ambitions apart from continuing to do what we enjoy doing doing. We're toying with the idea of doing a video magazine, but at the moment the whole video market is in such a mess. That'll have to wait.

of what Ian describes as "fairly rough early recordings intended for people who want to hear how we started out", will be available soon.

Martin & Ian went on to form Human League & then split off from this to form B.E.F./Heaven 17.

Ian: "Sheffield band 2.3 had a single on Fast. They put us in touch with Bob Last & he put out 'Being Boiled' c/w 'Circus of Death' on Fast as the debut single from Human League." This single - seminal electronic pop on a Fast-becoming-cult label - still sells steadily 3 or 4 years on. Yuri Gagarin in full uniform walks on a long carpet down a Russian street lined with crowds on the cover 'Dignity of Labour' - the 12" EP that followed. A couple of singles (one as The Men) & an album followed on Virgin Records before M & I ducked out. Human League went on to their own brand of commercial success.

Ian: "The 3 of us, Martin, myself & Bob Last, formed B.E.F. (British Electric Foundation) as our own management/production company to provide a base from which we could work in various units. The first of these was Heaven 17. Glenn Gregory is signed to B.E.F. as H17 vocalist."

The B.E.F. output is released through Virgin. First up was H17's debut single 'We Don't Need That Fascist Groove Thang'. A complete change from Human League, it was electronic disco funk. A top thirty hit, it was followed by 'I'm Your Money' & then 'Play To Win', both similar in style. From anticipating electronic music, the duo had gone on to anticipate pop funk.

B.E.F. work hard. In the shops now or soon are five albums. There's The Future's LP, B.E.F.'s cassette-only 'Music For Stowaways', H17's 'Penthouse & Pavement', a 2nd B.E.F. album of favourite songs ('Perfect Day', 'Hang On Sloopy' & 'Wichita Lineman' among them) with a different guest vocalist on each (including Gary Glitter, Sandie Shaw & Sugs from Madness). Finally, they've done the music for the new Hot Gossip LP (ie they play/the dancers sing) & most of the songs are theirs - H17 & old Human League numbers plus one written by Sting & Talking Heads' "Houses In Motion'.

There've been no H17 or B.E.F. live gigs - nearest 'thang' was a low-key H17 promo tour in October. Saw & interviewed them when this brought the bunch of them to The Warehouse, Leeds. Dumping any pretence of mega-star pose they came onto bare stage in straight dayclothes proffering acapello dental decay & Brylcremed anti-chic. What we got was a less-than-half-hour set sans

HEAVEN ON PAGE SEVEN.   /continues in column one...

an intellectual thing."

Large-label distribution was identified as target. Martin. "From before Xmas to mid-June seems we spent a lot of time on the train going to London, speaking to various people. London is just the centre of the music industry."
They took with them a complete album-full of potential danceable hits. "We set about writing a catalogue of songs basically. There was no immediate desire to play live gigs. It is the most important thing for us to do now, 'cos the actual song is like the..."

"Statement," appendages Martin.

The package of songs/band/manifestoes/spiel was swallowed whole by Phonogram, complete with a series of buffer devices in the contract to ensure artistic freedom, and own-label independence. Why Phonogram? "Because when you speak to them they do hear. The people who work at Phonogram impressed us as music fanatics rather than businessmen."

PIC: JILL FURMANOVSKY.

Martin fills in blanks. "We'd bump into them in the megastore on Saturdays searching for Dionne Warwicke albums!"

"We've both got the same aim which is to make hit records. It is a good relationship. We've got good enough ideas. We know where we want to go. What we want to do. So it's a lot easier for Phonogram to deal with us. We presented them with the complete package and they said, 'yes, that's what we're interested in.'"

"It's not as though we want to go in there and spend a lot of money for the hell of it - or that they want to drag us through a treadmill."

Phonogram is actually a distribution organisation for labels like Decca and Mercury. They distribute Kraftwerk. What ABC have is all the freedoms of an Indie, plus all the advantages of a major. "A lot of good records on independent labels just disappear because people are not made aware of them. We don't want that to happen with ABC. We think it is a special thing, a special music, and we want everybody to hear it," contends Steve.

The major problem with Indies is distribution, I suggest. "And commitment, and finance," adds Martin. "I don't mean a mass of money to spend, but just the time you consume doing everything yourself, from sticking every stamp on every letter to listening to a record being mastered. Neutron is now like the Independent philosophy but in the '80's; it's more grown up. It's more realistic." He comments that the industry is like the rule of law. "You've got the Police, the Monarchy, and the Judges. All interrelated, a monopoly. In the music business you've got the acts, the record companies and the press. People talk of 'selling out', or a compromise having to be made....."

["Northern Soul was the REAL 'Industrial Music'"]

Steve contends, "a lot of people use the record companies as a whipping post - for credibility. Like 'I'm an artist and the Company doesn't understand me m-a-a-a-a-n!"

"The Company love that. It means the artists sell more records!"

"But we found that Companies realise they've made mistakes in the past and they are looking for new radical intelligent ideas - and people who can carry them out." So ABC deliver their tapes to Phonogram? "No. It's not a deal set up like that. They foot the bill and they just let us do what we intend." But recording ABC tracks at the London Phonogram studios must constitute a step up from the home-technology of the Vice Versa product? Not so. To Singleton "the actual tools are the same, just larger and more advanced. You have to sing and play the same things. It's just more comfortable. Easier because there are more tracks. Easier technically but there wasn't a big change. What we do intend to do is to set up our own studios in this area, just as a songwriting tool."

Images and Information. Revolutions at 45 rpm and digging it yeah!!! I've seen their videos. Heard their tapes. The device works - devastatingly. The Funk mutation wins whatever games you can envisage, rhythmic or cerebral. Late '81. Me and Martin Fry back on a Sheffield street. My C60 bubbling over with words. "We should meet again this time next year and make another tape," he says. "Check out the success ratio. Make a further progress report."

Progress should be vast. Perhaps I'll get a C90 for '82.

Hanging out in singles bars...

Northern mag, so we'll take Northern bands first:-

- VOLUNTEERS - 'Action Man' c/w 'Francis' (Volunteers: VOL 001)
- LEGAL AID - 'That's Life' c/w 'Limbo' (Earshot: ERA1)
- FLOCK OF SEAGULLS - 'Telecommunication' c/w 'Intro' (Jive: JIVE 4)
- AFRAID OF MICE - 'I'm On Fire' c/w 'Down In The Dark' (Charisma: CB 383)
- AFRAID OF MICE - 'Intercontinental' c/w 'What Shall We Do?' (Charisma: CB 389)
- AFRAID OF MICE - 'Popstar' c/w 'What I Want' (Charisma: CB 395)
- JAB JAB - 'Loneliness Is Not Happiness' c/w 'Sweet Socca Music' (Shades: SH 3)
- ABC - 'Tears Are Not Enough' c/w 'Alphabet Soup' (Neutron: NT 101)
- DISEASE - 'No Future' c/w 'I Know How' (Disease Discs: DD1)
- SOFT CELL - 'Mutant Moments E.P.' (A Big Frock Records: ABF1)
- SOFT CELL - 'A Man Can Get Lost' c/w 'Memorabilia' (Some Bizzare: Hard 1)
- SOFT CELL - 'Tainted Love' c/w 'Where Did Our Love Go' (Some Bizzare/Phonogram: BZS 2)
- WAH! - 'Forget The Down' c/w 'The Checkmate Syndrome' (Eternal: SLATE 1)
- THORNS OF AFFLICTION - 'Panic Stricken' c/w 'Eyes of the Dead' (Cargo: CRS 011)
- SOME ARE NOW - 'Aftermath' c/w 'A to B' (Cargo: CRS 012)
- NIGEL STONIER BAND - 'Still Not Over You' c/w 'In The Paperbacks' (Cargo: CRS 013)
- THE OUT - 'Better The Devil' c/w 'It's Not Enough' (Cargo: CRS 014)
- XPOZEZ - 'Systems Kill E.P.' (Retaliation Records: Fight 1)
- TURBO - '3 Track E.P.' (Cargo: CRS 004)

19 singles, 15 different bands, and at least a dozen of these stomp round well-mapped areas of music - albeit that the majority do so convincingly. So you get a lot of good musicians & some fine musics - but too many re-hashed formulae and a scarcity of innovation. Let's go then...

VOLUNTEERS from Leeds and LEGAL AID from Barnsley are both polished pub-rock bands with jazzlines threading their hyper-classy arrangement. These are two excellent own-label debut singles. The catchy 'Action Man' coupled with the more subtle and expressive 'Francis' lacks only a little of the raunchy bite of 'That's Life' & 'Limbo'. LEGAL AID could collar a major deal. They're sailing dangerously close to mainstream but are distinctive enough to cut a niche entirely their own. LEGAL AID - first name to remember.

Two Liverpool bands now - FLOCK OF SEAGULLS & AFRAID OF MICE. The former are a standard rock band trying to jump the post-disco edge-of-Futurism bandwagon. Saw them live & was initially impressed but finally bored. Bill Nelson produces the A-side & gives them more than they'd otherwise be heir to. It's an OK song with also-ran appeal. Flip is instantly forgettable. AFRAID OF MICE deserve more thought. The songs are simple pop with complex arrangements. These 3 singles, released in quick succession, are followed by a free flexi & then an album that includes the 3 A-sides. Lotsa ads in the music press too. 'Intercontinental' (clever, sexist lyric) should've scored in the charts. The L.P. probably will. Varied songs and a flash live act add mileage to this outfit. Listen out for them... second name to remember.

A pair of bands - JAB JAB & ABC (Huddersfield & Sheffield, respectively) who draw their music directly from black roots. JAB JAB have taken far too long to come up with this debut single. Their only previous release was one track (an excellent one) on the Huddersfield compilation cassette album 'Only A Northern Song'. They're one of the best and most distinctive reggae bands in Britain & this single does them justice. Catch them live if you get the chance... third name to remember. Formerly ABC will probably have charted by the time you read this. They're now into guitar semi-experimental synth-pop combo VICA VERSA as commercial gold by Eno funk. Territory opened up for all white men as commercial gold by English Talking Heads Co. Ltd. ABC do pop-funk better than any other English band outside London... fourth name to file for future reference. They're the closest yet to real originality - they don't just ride the genre, they add to its vocabulary.

DISEASE share ABC's Sheffield hometown - far-&-away the most adventurous and creative city for rock, provincial-style. Their urgent rythmic pop debut doubles two hypnotically entrancing songs. Good recording job (Fairview Studio's, Hull, with Kevin 'Comsat' Bacon on production). Vast improvement on their track on 'Bouquet of Steel', the Sheffield compilation album. One of the few bands here to show some real originality/individuality. Consequently they'll probably sink without trace - no justice in this tacky crapola biz.

Ah, SOFT CELL. Ironic to look back at their 1980 E.P. with Marc singing "We have got potential" among a 4-song bunch of pretentious and punchless laid-back ditties. Oh, they're OK, but without the timely intervention of Some Bizzare/Daniel Miller, they'd pretty surely have faded - not with a bang, but with a wimp. 'Memorabilia', had it been the A-side, would've given them a hit one single sooner. 'Tainted Love' is one of the best singles of '81. From acorns to mega-oaks...

Methinks that when Liverpool's Wah Heat became WAH! they lost heat in more senses than one. This single tries hard, but melodrama is too thin a veil to hide ordinariness. If they've nothing more to offer than this, then they might as well drop the rest of the name & go home.

Four now from Cargo - all recent releases by Lancs. bands most of whom probably used to work in cotton mills on the outskirts of Manchester. 'Panic Stricken' by THORNS OF AFFLICTION would be good if they took the strong hookline & built round it instead of settling for the soft option of repetition. Flip side is a pop-punky thrash. Not a hopeless case, but nor is it a debut they can be too proud of. Next time might be more interesting. Wait & see. So to SOME ARE NOW whose minimalist mood-music builds well until the vocalist steps in with spoken extract from his unpublishable first novel (I dare say). The overall result is another semi-finished piece hitting vinyl prematurely. Same goes for similar B-side. These two sound like they were written in the studio. THE NIGEL STONIER BAND aren't quite as straight as their name implies - but very nearly. A-side is sixties Beatles-pop with synth added. Good arrangement breaks up the verse-chorus pattern, but 1981 isn't a year for pretty pop songs. B-side is even better of its kind. 16 years ago they'd have been putting out hit singles on Decca every nine weeks & doing regular spots on 6-5-Special and touring with Dusty Springfield, Dave Clark 5, Freddie & The Dreamers and The Fourmost. In the eighties, they'll go down well in pubs & clubs. Full-stop. 'Better The Devil You Know' shows THE OUT to be a curious blend of hard guitar rock-pop, eighties synth-work and pure-pop songwriting. A band with enough to them to get up there if given a couple of lucky breaks. I'd have thought this single could've got them support slots on a major tour or two. They've been around a while without really making waves, but I'd still give them points. What are they like live? Aha! "Murder! Slaughter! Execution!" with guitar thrash and pummelled drums. Punks Not Dead... at least, not in Huddersfield. THE XPOZEZ are another band from the impressive 'Only A Northern Song' compilation. I love good/bad '77 punk & this is totally it! Almost as tasteless delightful as The Exploited. Fuck musical ability, this is fun! And lastly TURBO. Another crowded field here - heavy rock. The titles tell it all: 'Stallion', 'Running', 'Take My Life' → clichéd lyrics. They trot out all the predictable guitar/drums/vocals bits, but do it better than most. Post from Burnley must be slow - this came out a year ago & topped Sounds HM chart. Line-up changes and a new set of songs see this band on form & back in action around the north. They're better than the general run of HM macho-strutters. Try one of their gigs - you don't have to be a cardboard guitar moron - there's more to them than that.

Southwards for some indies & minor majors...

- VITAL DISORDERS - 'Prams E.P.' (Vital Disorders: vd 1)
- THOMPSON TWINS - 'Animal Laugh' c/w 'A Dub Product' + 'Anything Is Good Enough' (T Records: TEE 2)
- ELECTRIC GUITARS - 'Health' c/w 'Continental Shelf' (Fried Egg Records: EGG 012)
- NORMIL HAWAIIANS - 'Gala Failed' (12" EP) (Red Rhino Records: RED 8)
- DIAMOND HEAD - 'Diamond Lights' (12" EP) (DHM Records: DHM 005)
- WASTED YOUTH - 'Rebecca's Room' (Bridgehouse/Fresh Records: BHS 12/FRESH 30)
- LESTER & THE BREW - 'A Bad Day at the City' (Lester Records: PL EP1)
- DEPECHE MODE - 'New Life' c/w 'Shout!' (Mute Records: MUTE 014)
- VIVIEN GOLDMAN - 'Launderette' c/w 'Private Armies' (Window: WIN 1)
- VIRGIN PRUNES - (No title) (Baby: baby 001)
- ZOUNDZ - 'Demystification' c/w 'Great White Hunter' (Rough Trade: RT 069)
- VIRGIN PRUNES - 'In The Greylight' 'War' c/w 'Moments & Mine' (Rough Trade: RT 072)
- ESSENTIAL LOGIC - 'Fanfare in the Garden' c/w 'The Captain' (Rough Trade: RT 074)
- TAN TAN - 'Theme from A Summer Place' c/w 'Princess' (Rough Trade: RT 076)
- WIRE - 'Our Swimmer' c/w 'Midnight Bahnhoff Cafe' (Rough Trade: RT 079)
- ROBERT WYATT - 'Grass' c/w DISHARHI - 'Trade Union' (Rough Trade: RT 081)
- LAURA LOGIC - 'Wonderful Offer' c/w 'Stereo' (Rough Trade: RT 087)
- VIRGIN PRUNES - 'A new form of beauty 1' (Rough Trade: RT 089)
- VIRGIN PRUNES - 'A new form of beauty 2' (Rough Trade: RT 090) (10" 45)
- THE MISUNDERSTOOD - 3 track single (Cherry Red: Cherry 22)
- DEAD KENNEDYS - 'Too Drunk to Fuck' c/w 'The Prey' (Cherry Red: Cherry 24)
- BEN WATT - 'Can't' c/w 'Tower of Silence' + 'Aubade' (Cherry Red: Cherry 25)
- FELT - 'Something Sends me To Sleep' + 'Red Indians' f/w same (Cherry Red: Cherry 26)
- THOMAS LEER - '4 Movements' (Cherry Red: Cherry 28) (12" 45)

Two of my favourite live bands for starters. VITAL DISORDERS followed me 'Tough Times' is fast, bright soulish pop - keys, brass and 3 girls up front onstage at this year's Rougham Fair. This EP is the Norfolk band's debut. Vocally. Instant fun. 'Prams' is a clever feminist song of tamed ambitions. Slow, gentle start then - 'pow!' - "Let's talk about prams & washing machines/ Let's talk about the end of childhood dreams". Chaotic, grating, marvellous Flip is 'Snatcher' (anti-Thatcher reggae). Lazy, easy reggae. The band are simply one of the best bands in the country. A stunning debut. Get it VITAL DISORDERS. use of studio has been A1. Rougham Fair were STEEL 'n SKIN - an Afro-rock band - watch for them too! Tremendous on stage. THOMPSON TWINS' debut offering

GOOD GOD, IT'S PAGE TEN, EDGAR!

Chart Return Shops

..With alternative/independent/HM/disco/reggae/etc charts now being published in the national music press, the power of the national weekly charts has diminished slightly. However, local radio airplay, Top of The Pops, much of Radio One's airplay and - as a consequence - much of what the public buys is still determined by the returns on sales made by selected UK shops. This system wrecks the chances of most independent & small label singles while preserving the monopoly of the majors who have the power, money and backup to hard sell (hype) their wares in these shops....

[Long handwritten list of record shops across the UK, including: Barnards, London EC4 / Virgin, Marble Arch, London W1 / City Sounds, London WC2 / A1 Stores, London SE17 / Diamond Records, West Croydon, Surrey / Bonaparte Records, Bromley, Kent / W.M. Payne, Hayes, Kent / Alders, Croydon, Surrey / Addiscombe Music Centre, Croydon, Surrey / T.W. Records, London SE18 / Reg W. Reed (Music) Ltd., London SE15 / Bonaparte Records, Croydon, Surrey / Treble Clef, London SE26 / Music Shop, London SE18 / Grants, Croydon, Surrey / Record Rendezvous, London SW16 / E. Whiting, London W4 / Spinning Disc, Orpington, Kent / Welling Record Centre, Welling, Kent / T.W. Records, Bexleyheath, Kent / other Bonapart, Croydon, Surrey / Harum Records, London / Dancy's, London N8 / Paul for Music, London E1 / P.&J. Records, London E8 / Derek's Records, London N8 / Roy's Records, London N4 / Les Aldrich, London N10 / Stores, London N17 / Phase 3, Enfield / David's, London NW1 / Derek's, London E1 / Hi-Way, Enfield / Keatings & Rumens, London N14 / Derek's, London N9 / Phase 3, London N16 / Tudor Records, London N10 / Arcade Music, London N12 / Carnival Records, Dagenham, Essex / Gilbert's, London E7 / Roach's Records, London E11 / Melodyman ... (continues with hundreds of shops across UK regions) ... Card & Pop Inn, Kilmarnock / J. Menzies, Airdrie / Taylor's, Helensburgh.]

...the above list is a couple of years out of date but it's the best I could get. As far as I know, no-one has previously published what is supposed to be a secret but is common knowledge among the reps working for major labels. The list makes interesting reading in that the vast majority of the shops are mainstream stockists who are unlikely to push or even sell much of the small label output. So, even if a minor label record sells well nationally, it's highly unlikely that it'll chart. Without a chart placing, it loses media coverage and so fails to gain further sales. Catch 22! This list is taken from a bunch of sheets each headed with a rep. number - i.e. they were handed out to major label reps as the list of shops where each had to really push the records (singles & albums) that the business wanted in the charts. Stinks, doesn't it!

MUSICIANS AND ROADIES
DO YOU KNOW IT ALL?

We are running a 6-week course on P.A. systems and equipment to help you to understand how you can get better results from your P.A./sound equipment. Send a cheque or postal order made payable to Bradford Metropolitan Council for £7.20 to reserve a place. First meeting February 2nd Tuesday, 7.30-9.30 p.m. at Ilkley College, Wells Road, Ilkley. Tel. 609010 for further information. Tutor Steve Jones.

Ilkley College

The NORTHERN ROCK ROADSHOWS

Touchstone Promotions will present the best of emergent local rock talent live in concert with Mega-disco & lights. Superb p.a. provided. Auditions at popular live music pubs, colleges and club venues with disco continuity - live - to select bands for extended tour.

Interested Bands GET IN TOUCH!

TOUCHSTONE

Back in May 1980 W.C.R. 6 carried a review...

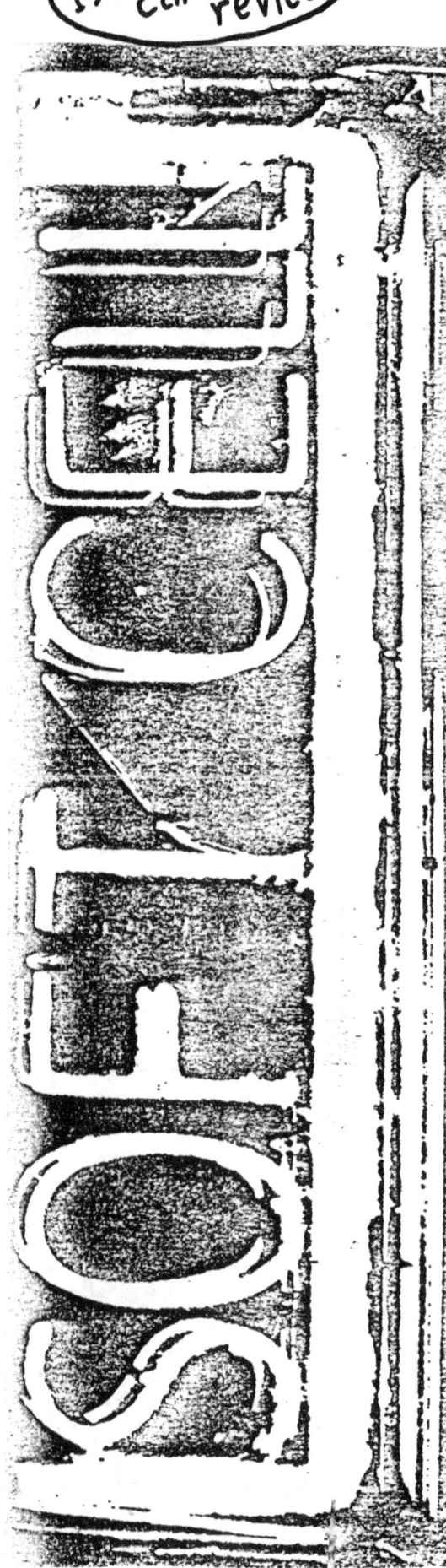

of a 5-song demo of electronic pop that was rather badly recorded. It was passable but unexceptional. The band was new Leeds duo Soft Cell. They played Splash 1 here in Bradford on 6th May to a small and unimpressed audience. In September they played Futurama II (which I reviewed in the now-defunct Musicians Only). Physically & acoustically dwarfed by the venue, they didn't make much of an impression on me, though a fair proportion of the audience did seem keen. Mark, all movement and gestures, held the spotlight centre-stage while Dave worked motionless & in near darkness far left of him. They only recently gave me their debut EP but I heard and liked their track on the Some Bizarre album that launched New Romanticism. In May '81 came their excellent first single & I saw them live at Amnesia in Leeds two weeks later - a stunningly good performance in which new pa, tight performance and a well-rehearsed high-power set coupled with sell-out audience won the day for them. On 30/6/81, self & Dave Glennon interviewed them over lunch-time drinks in Amnesia. 'Tainted Love' came out a few weeks later and made No.1 in the charts. Now read on...

Q What about the early days - the demo & EP? DB We were both students of Art & Design at Leeds Poly - that's where we met. Mark's from Southport, I'm from Blackpool. MA The demo & EP were recorded around the same time in the Poly's Art Dept sound studio which has just a pair of two-track machines.

Q And then the Some Bizarre deal...? MA Stevo liked our EP & was compiling the Futurist chart for Sounds. He put it at No.1 & then asked us to put in a track for his album. At that time we were doing minimal-sounding electronic pop. The track cost us only £20 to record yet it was one of the best-received on the LP. When we gigged over in France all the kids knew the words! We then signed a 5-year deal with Some Bizarre who have a licencing & distribution deal with Phonogram.

Q Tell me about working with Daniel Miller... MA We knew we'd be out of our depth in a large studio & would need a producer for guidance. We asked for Daniel because of his varied experience - from a pop approach with (say) Silicon Teens to less accessible music like that of DAF & Non.

Q So how did it go? MA It got to the stage where all 4 of us - Pete Maben the engineer included - were over the mixing desk at the same time.

TWELF YOURSELF.

Q So the single's really a 4-man effort...? MA Yes, very much so. We described what we were aiming at & Daniel & Pete were able to give us it.

Q What's your feeling about the first single & why wasn't 'Memorabilia' on the A-side? MA It was on the A-side of the 12-inch version, but the record company felt it wasn't 'housewifey' enough for radio play, more dancefloor orientated. When I first heard 'A Man Could Get Lost' I took it off the turntable and said: 'That'll make a nice ashtray'! The mix is really bad – 'Memorabilia' & 'Persuasion' (both on 12-inch, all three done in the one recording session) come over much closer to what we wanted.

Q And the second single – why's it to be cover versions? MA We've a lot of material of our own (the album'll be all original material) but we're both fans of Northern Soul & Tamla & we wanted to do these two songs. DB We had Mike Thorne in as producer for this session. He was interesting to work with musically because his approach to synthesisers is sequencer-biased, whereas Daniel's is digital.

Q Do you have a title for the album yet? MA No, we're still playing with ideas... 'Die By Day, Live By Night' is a possible one – it reflects our lifestyle.

Q What about live gigs? MA When we started out, we were using poor quality 2- or 3-t DB The technology to do in live per our finances. MA depressed at doin that were always current thinking. the necessary equ facilities was ho by the time the S along things had for us. DB The la Glamour Club in E know why they cal was with Depeche we were terrible. ever. After that things so we stop got better gear a we like doing dis Close contact wit important – I lik down among the au to get up on stag rock venues you'r faceless crowd. with the audience MA We use props – sign above us... large padded cell designed for on stage with neon bars in it. DB Mar very active & showy in performance whereas I come over as straight, conservative and quiet. I'm more involved in producing the music ar haven't got much stage presence – the sharp contrast between us that seems to work in a live context. Actually, I don't really enjoy a g until after the show's over. When first started working together it Mark who went on stage and did his own theatrical performance while did the music backstage.

Q What do you feel about being a DB We're not an electronic band – just two people working together. MA ...a cabaret twosome. With Dave a musician & me as a singer we d get the usual hassles that come w a larger line-up. Because we work separate and distinct areas there no conflict & we're both free to follow our own ideas within the u

Q What about the others onstage w you at the Amnesia gig? DB Josie some vocals and Brian (her boyfri played percussion. They're just friends of ours, though I'm invol with them in a separate project. doing tapes for them to work with under the group name of Vicious P Phenomena. Mark's also working on some solo stuff of his own. In th future we'd like to do some sort 'Soft Cell Soiree' with these oth projects featured along with Soft

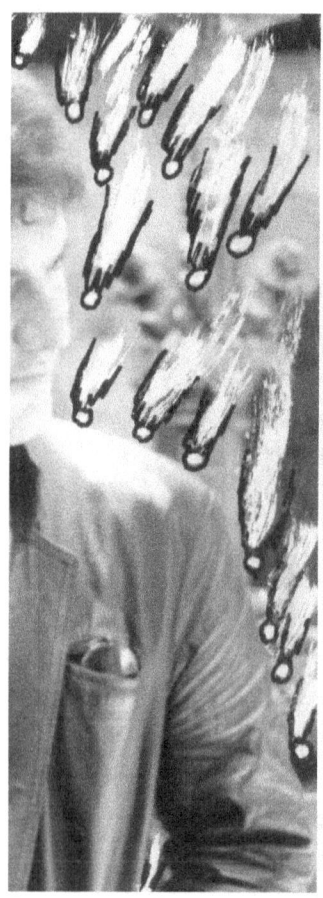

quality 2- or 3-track backing tapes. DB The technology for what we wanted to do in live performance was beyond our finances. MA We were getting depressed at doing dates with tapes that were always months behind our current thinking. Lack of money for the necessary equipment and recording facilities was holding us up. In fact by the time the Some Bizarre deal came along things had just about stagnated for us. DB The last straw was at The Glamour Club in Essex - though I don't know why they call it that. Anyway, it was with Depeche Mode supporting us & we were terrible... MA ...our worst gig ever. After that we had to improve things so we stopped gigging until we got better gear and tapes. Nowadays we like doing discos, clubs and so on. Close contact with audiences is important - I like to be able to get down among the audience & we like them to get up on stage. At traditional rock venues you're just playing to a faceless crowd. DB We want intimacy with the audience - we're not elitists. MA We use props - the neon Soft Cell sign above us... & now we've had a large padded cell designed for on stage with neon bars in it. DB Mark's very active & showy in performance whereas I come over as straight, conservative and quiet. I'm more involved in producing the music and haven't got much stage presence - it's the sharp contrast between us that seems to work in a live context. Actually, I don't really enjoy a gig until after the show's over. When we first started working together it was Mark who went on stage and did his own theatrical performance while I did the music backstage.

Q What do you feel about being a duo? DB We're not an electronic band - just two people working together... MA ...a cabaret twosome. With Dave as a musician & me as a singer we don't get the usual hassles that come with a larger line-up. Because we work in separate and distinct areas there's no conflict & we're both free to follow our own ideas within the unit.

Q What about the others onstage with you at the Amnesia gig? DB Josie did some vocals and Brian (her boyfriend) played percussion. They're just friends of ours, though I'm involved with them in a separate project. I'm doing tapes for them to work with under the group name of Vicious Pink Phenomena. Mark's also working on some solo stuff of his own. In the future we'd like to do some sort of 'Soft Cell Soiree' with these other projects featured along with Soft Cell and a DJ playing music that we have selected. MA Our aim is & always has been to create a party atmosphere rather than just to do a gig.

Le fin, mes amis.

ATTRITION

So, you want something zappy huh? Zappy! I'll give you bloody zappy! This'll be so zappy you won't even know you've been zapped. "Give me something zappy on Attrition," he says. He sits there dishevelled and coughing and tells me to be zappy. Well, I mean it isn't as if I'm boring; well some people have said I am slightly boring (although someone did once say that I was better than Horlicks but that's another story!) and no one has said I am downright boring but I told him that I didn't know a thing about oral sex - but that's another story!

Anyway, there's this really KAZAMPOW band called Attrition doesn't exactly kick you in the genitals does it? and it's from that FLABOOM city of Coventry. They've been really together now babe (neat huh?) since late 1980 and have blitzed Coventry and its surrounds with their own brand of 'Sounds'). ZAP ZAP ZAP. Cor baby this is really megagigs (I learnt that from 'Sounds'). ZAP ZAP ZAP. Cor baby this is really being media conscious, they put together (man) an information sheet every month and have made a barrage of tapes, one of which I have before me (presses button marked 'Play'). I'm sure they're gonna get you yeah! It's different. Beware of Attrition cos they played at Brum's Star Club. It is quite and a 'live' (bzz bzz) tape of a gig they've got two - bassists that is - namely Julia and bassic, as is the band, 'cos they vibrating their vocal cords (or is it chords?). Martin who also make sound waves by synth and drums respec. I mean, it isn't as if Attrition Ash and Robbo complete the line-up on 'Stiletto', (not that you can hear 'em). Their I don't know why he said I had to be zappy, wake up, I've been talking are a zappy band. I think they're quite monotonous and dreary actually, although some of the lyrics are fairly good, especially the least bit zappy. Aw come on chaps, wake up, I've been talking music's a sort of rhythmic mumble - not in the 'Stiletto', (not that you can hear 'em). Their journalistic wizardry eh chaps? Chaps.....? Aw come on chaps, especially to you......

New Model Army. Probably the three best-known words in the West Yorkshire music world. They are emblazoned over thousands of billboards, fire hydrants, call boxes, as well as people. They refer to a three-piece band based in the Leeds-Bradford area who are notable in that they have one of the most ardent followings in the area and a reputation in the industry of being very difficult to get on with.

In accordance with their 'reputation' they nearly walked out on us before we had even started. However, diplomacy gets the better of them and we finally sit down together over a drink. Justin, tall, thin and dark, is an enigmatic character; one who has travelled the world, slept under bushes in Mexico and such like, and one who is tense. He explains the tension is bad. "Just a hatred of interviews. It transpires that this hatred, from past experiences of misinterpretation and philosophy which seems to be anti-press 'biz as well. Rob, the drummer in the band, is strong, quiet and imposing. He doesn't say much but when he does, it is emphatic. "If their hatred of interviews; "you wanting to talk to us makes us out to be New Model Army are anti-rock 'biz and we don't think we are. Anyone could get up on stage and something special, and probably better. We're no different from anyone else!" The band consciously try to break down any barriers between them and the audience; "If do what we do, and we don't think we are. Anyone could get up on stage and see someone in the audience at three or four of our gigs we feel we owe it to them to try and get to know them.... buy them a drink, my judgement deferred. But a number of

I leave the interview a little confused. They are anti-press but hot on publicity; they are anti-rock 'biz but confess I am certain of is that they are one of the tightest bands in the area, paradoxes seem to emerge. One thing I am certain of is that they are one of the tightest bands in the area, a tape they gave us for review shows this. Their music is a sort of Jam/Tom Robinson band crossover which on a couple of the tracks sounds dated, and yet on others, such as 'Betcha which was recorded 'live' at Keighley's Funhouse, it is exciting and invigorating.

DUNCAN McCARROLL wrote this page - lovely, innit..?

WHY WEREN'T YOU RIOTING WITH THE REST OF US?

COULDN'T, MATE, I'M ON THE SICK..

NEW MODEL ARMY

& unexpected. Poet's Afro pop chant, sub-titled Oumma Aularesso. It's shit-hot for what it is, but at least 2 years ahead of UK tastes. Dusted off & re-released in '83, it'll be a hit. By then, TJ's'll either be stars or disbanded. Flip-side tracks are ½-formed & disappointing. 2nd track title is wrong. ELECTRIC GUITARS offer slithering guitar runs, soaring keys & militaristic rhythm with the deep echoey vocals typical of Bill Nelson & some Zoo & Factory label bands. Second track is the stronger of the two. Yeah, I like this single. Major label cash-power could've got it lotsa airplay. ❚ Neither Normal nor Hawaiian, NORMIL HAWAIIANS's 5-track 12" for York's Red Rhino label features coarse rhythm guitar over weird bass/drum/percussion action. Spoken/chanted vocals. A sort of semi-experimental celebration with neat touches (high echoing piano on track three + choral backing vocs). OK, so they've got my interest, but where do they take their music from here? They need some solid ground to build on. I don't see land on their horizon, just a photo of a 1920s freakshow half-man on the flipside label. ❚ And so to the darlings of Midlands HM, via the info that NORMIL's home is around Kent... DIAMOND HEAD serve up a 4-track meal of hard melodics. Bit bassy on the mix leaving it thinnish up top (not unlike me!) - but for Led Zep copyists they're good enough - anyway, Bonham's drumming's not what it used to be (sicko joke!). Me, I can take 'em or leave 'em. Think I'll leave 'em now. ❚ Saw WASTED YOUTH twice in summer 1981 (P. Furs tour & C. Nouveaux tour). Good live band → good single with distinction of (a) being on two labels & (b) having a b-side called: "Things never seem the same as they did even before they've happened" she added as an afterthought...' which, needless to say, is an instrumental. ❚ Brum's LESTER & THE BREW feature PAUL LESTER (poet) & an old friend of mine, experimental/freeform muso DAVE FANTON. Worst quality recording & spoilt by being a vehicle for merely spoken poems. With a good producer, this might've had more of a chance. Dave's crazy percussion'n'brass has the lunacy of which new style is born - but not here. Lester's poetry is too twee & school-magish. ❚ 'New Life' came & went in the charts. It's in my top ten of this year's releases. B-side makes good use of electro-percussion. From any other band, this could've been a good A-side in it's own right. DEPECHE MODE have panache, individuality and know what they're about. Next? Daniel Miller owns a huge slice of today's (PRODUCER/LABEL OWNER) star's mega-stars. He's shown 'em all how it ought to be done & has broken the guitar monopoly of the past 25 years of rock. ❚ VIVIEN GOLDMAN, one of the best-known of UK rock journalists, might have been an embarrassment on disc - not so. Musicians here include John Lydon & Keith Levene (P.I.L., Christ, where've you been since '76?!), George Oban (ex-Aswad), Robert Wyatt, a Slit & a Raincoat. Result is an odd bridge between pure strangeness & pop. No idea how much is her talent, but there's plenty in evidence here. Creative music is better than formula pop - albeit less easy listening. Shit, what I'm trying to say is that it's no bad thing at all to come up with songs that make the listener do a bit of work. Pop'n'rock are too often just switch-off-&-tap-your-feet escapism. ❚ Debut from an interesting band (see their 'A new form of beauty' reviewed 8/9 singles on from here). This is a 7"er that (VIRGIN PRUNES) plays at 33⅓ r.p.m. A Dublin band. Bits play backwards. They're a discordant, dramatic/theatrical outfit. Artistically naive & not doing anything for those who know just what sort of music they like. Approach them with an open mind. They produce out of human physical & mental suffering. Why bother, you'll probably think they're crap - which they are here - but they've a germ here that offers something new & radically separate from Radio One or any of the other commercial dross on the kitchen table. ❚ ZOUNDS had a 3-track on Crass. This, their 2nd release, precedes the album 'The Curse of Zounds'. Raw rock band with a song that reminds me of a rough Wreckless Eric - & that's to say they're good. Touches of sixties pop guitar c/w punky vocals. Listening to this much music, I really begin to wonder if there's any point at all in just being one more good band. ZOUNDS are fun & their music's got that primitive edge that makes it sound like it's from a real band rather than some studio-processed glossy package - but all this reviewing becomes not unlike train-spotting, & it's hard to get excited about numbers and wheel arrangements and timetables and engine modifications. I think I'll go for a wank before I play the next disc. Maybe that'll improve matters. I somehow doubt it. ❚ 2nd of 4 from the perverse VIRGIN PRUNES - they extend the exploration of new sounds. Clock-tick + backwards vocals - (fairly) straight rock song. 2 nos. on flip. Echo-drums/vocal scream. Heavy bass guitar on 2nd track. Jungle Warfare. Almost gentle towards the end. Next issue of WCR I'll run a feature on this band. ❚ ESSENTIAL LOGIC's final R.T release

is an early recording from summer '79 - soon after she left X-Ray Spex. More melodic & poppy, more accessible than their later work. Choppy, tuneful. Flip has a rhino taking a bath in the studio while they're recording. Some elephants pass by. Yeah, this is a fun single. Give the band an ear some time. They were an interesting sideline. ❚ TAN TAN is a Jamaican trumpeter. THE Jamaican trumpeter. In UK he's done sessions for just about every major performer you care to name in pop - Stones & Beatles included. Here's a reggae'd version of the hit tune of two years ago. Flip is fairly straight small band/big band stuff. An oddity for Rough Trade in that it's not odd! Class easy listening. ❚ The now-defunct WIRE offer a '79 recording - days when big things were being predicted from all sides for this band. Never happened. 2 'Live at The Roxy' trax, 2 fine albums ('Pink Flag' + 'Chairs Missing' if memory serves right). These 2 tracks are interesting enuf to merit posthumous release. A distinctive minimalist band producing strong atmospheric popsongs. ❚ The tuneless vocals of ROBERT wheelchair hippy soft Machine WYATT couple with his percussion & Indian tabla/sitar/harmonium band for this love'n'peace, inoffensive ramble. Flip for DISHARI's own trade union recruitment song - only Bangladeshi (or any Asian) music by a UK (London) band that I've ever heard of on a white-owned UK label. A poor reflection on our supposedly multi-racial society! This is an appealing rarity. More, please! ❚ LAURA LOGIC's 'Wonderful Offer' is close to living up to it's name. Little bit too much of a pop compromise for my tastes. Disco beat, high vocals, tasty bass, squeaky soprano sax + trimmings. 'Stereo' is odder & consequently more distinctive - she should succumb to these Afro-jazz influences & give up on lame-duck, dead-from-the-neck-down popshit. This flip is novel & truely wonderous. And so... back to THE VIRGIN PRUNES. Their 7-part 2-month project 'A New Form of Beauty' includes 7", 10" & 12" discs + cassette + video + book + live gig & also involves song-writing, theatre, sculpture, artwork, photos, etc. A first-ever attempt by a band to use simultaneous multimedia to such an extent. Here are the first two parts. The target of 'new beauty' is one they may actually be reaching - reserve judgement till the rest of the project comes out. These are both novel & attractive slabs of vinyl. Particularly like the reworked/transformed Irish folksong style of 'Sweet Home...' Throughout, there's creative use of instruments/tapes/vocals. The new is always initially ugly & alienating. Are you prepared to make the effort to get into this? They ARE pioneering a possible route out of rock music's cliche-ridden & blinkered self-imposed narrowness. ❚ Wow! Only 5 to go in this bunch - then THE MAJOR LABEL SHIT! ❚ All 5 are from Cherry Red. THE MISUNDERSTOOD are Yankies in London ('66) playing Yardbirds post-R'n'B/pre-hippy rock. They were the first wave of psychedelia & their 'Who Do You Love' became a standard number for many bands. All three tracks are excellent & I can't understand why The Misunderstood were misunderstood/ignored 15 years ago. If the new (81/82) psychedelia has more sense, then maybe we'll get an album of their stuff. Anyone wanna buy early Yardbirds singles? ❚ DEAD KENNEDY's get no review here because I've never heard 'Too Drunk To Fuck' or the flip. My dogs bit the record in half when it came through the door. Must be that they censor my mail - it's the only time they've ever done that to a record! ❚ BEN WATT offers 2 slices of folk-rock. Good pieces but somewhat outta step with current tastes. Piano piece to finish. This guy's good. Nice ideas, clean & pure sound. What a shame that 99% of you cretins out there can't see beyond your half-dozen favourite bands & a music that's of the same predictable flavour every day of the week. Cherry Red's a special label (as is Rough Trade to a slightly lesser extent) because of the catholicity of its output. That alone's enough to deter most punters - such is life with a bow-legged wife! ❚ Felt like FELT so put them on the dansette. Twangy guitars & sleepy vocals / sleepy guitars & twangy vocals. Raunchier versions of the same on the flip. Toss a record - heads you tails, lose you win. I drink rat soup, eat pig eggs. Omadoodle - oloop. Prefer side two. ❚ THOMAS LEER's 'Private Plane' was an electronic single long before Gary Numan started out on the road to nowhere. This 12"er's much more melodic - not yet straight, but straightening. Funky feel. Drum machine, gtr./synth. Chunky stomp. I was waiting for a guy called John Row in Norwich bus station when I read an intelligent interview with this boy in NME. So he must be good. Bit of a Spanish feel to this stuff too. Oh, go out & buy the fucking record for yourself. It's great. Fab. Don't you just love it? Course you do... twat! (Actually, I think it's pretty nifty too.

Now, major label stuff... Not much room (heh!heh!) 12"er from HAIRCUT ONE HUNDRED 'Favourite Shirts' c/w 'Boat Party' is nifty enough. Fab hunks of funk. SPLODGENESSABOUNDS Cowpunk EP + free flexi is the finest one. TEARS FOR FEARS are wimps but this single's OK - 'Suffer the Children' c/w 'Wino' - file under Orch. Man. copyists. ❚ THE CREATURES double single pack inc. 'Mad Eyed Screamer' is GREAT!! MONKEES ❚ TROY TATE ❚ KIKI DEE ❚ ORIGINAL MIRRORS ❚ DIESEL ❚ RUSH ❚ SABBATH lotsa others trotted past. I slept through them all.

NICK TOCZEK WAS HERE 10/11/81

NINETEEN AND CRAZY!

JUMBO RECORDS

102 MERRION CENTRE
LEEDS LS2 8PJ **TEL: 455570**

THIS IS A SAMPLE OF OUR PRICES...

- Joy Division - 'Still' — 4.75
- Bauhaus - 'Mask' — 2.99
- Human League - 'Dare' — 3.99
- Bow Wow Wow - 'See Jungle' — 3.49
- STOP PRESS!! Adam & The Ants (NEW LP - WHEN RELEASED) — 3.79

...SO WHY NOT GIVE US A TRY?

WE SPECIALISE IN SINGLES

NICK'S WORK ALONGSIDE WCR
OR HOW TO KEEP GOING WHILE RUNNING A NON-PROFIT ZINE
Fanzines, magazines and collections 1979 - 1981

Throughout the time I spent writing, editing, publishing, and distributing *Wool City Rocker*, I was also writing, recording, and gigging throughout Britain. In 1979, the year we launched the zine, I worked as an unpaid freelance journalist for various magazines and published the last two editions (Nos. 10 & 11) of my long-running poetry magazine, *The Little Word Machine*.

That same year, Xenias Press published a beautiful booklet of my poem *Complete Strangers Tell You Nothing*, Rivelin Press published my poetry collection *Lies*, Kawabata Press published *The Credible Adventures of Nick Toczek*, a selection of my short stories, and Wayzgoose Press published *Acts of Violence* another set of short stories... and my band, Ulterior Motives, released their debut single. Busy times indeed! Then, in 1981, Aquila Press published *Rock 'n 'Roll Terrorism*, a collection of my poems, lyrics, and stories.

From June 1980, while still editing *Wool City Rocke*r, I secured paid freelance work as a regular reviewer and features writer for *Musicians Only*, a short-lived weekly music paper which was an offshoot of *Melody Maker*.

From October 1980, while still editing *Wool City Rocker*, I secured additional paid freelance work as a columnist and occasional features writer for *The Month in Yorkshire,* a monthly newspaper produced by the Yorkshire Arts Association. My column, *Another Stick of Yorkshire Rock,* provided a second outlet for my regional rock journalism. My monthly rock column continued after the newspaper changed its name to *Arts Yorkshir*e in October 1981. A few months later, however, the focus of my column shifted when it became *The Outer Limits of The Arts*.

ABOUT THE AUTHOR

Photo by John Bolloten

Nick Toczek is a British Writer and performer who lives in his hometown of Bradford in Yorkshire. He has published more than 50 books, released numerous albums (of music and of spoken word) and has visited dozens of countries as a writer in schools. He's also a professional magician, puppeteer, metal detectorist and music journalist. He's currently a columnist, reviewer, and features writer for two national magazines, the bi-monthly music mag, *R'n'R*, and the leading monthly metal detecting mag, *Treasure Hunting*.

For more information visit: www.nicktoczek.com

Most Recent Books

The Columbus Memoirs and Other Tales (with Matt Webster) (Mutiny 2000 Publications, 2022)

Corona Diary (Mutiny 2000 Publications, 2022)

Voices In My Head (Caboodle Books, 2020)

Dragons Are Back! (Caboodle Books, 2016)

Haters, Baiters and Would-Be Dictators (Routledge, 2016)

Selected Recent Discography

The Columbus Memoirs (with Signia Alpha) (Mutiny 2000 Records, 2022)

Walking The Tightrope (with Signia Alpha) (Mutiny 2000 Records, 2021)

Death & Other Destinations: The Second Bavariations Album (with Thies Marsen) (Not-A-Rioty, 2021)

Motormouth Volumes 1 & 2 (Not-A-Rioty, 2017)

Totally In Toczekated (Mutiny 2000 Records, 2007)

www.ingramcontent.com/pod-product-compliance
Lightning Source LLC
Chambersburg PA
CBHW081100070526
44583CB00018B/2505